D0916970

The Causes
and Prevention
of War

The Causes
and Prevention
of War

Seyom Brown
Brandeis University

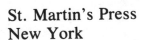

St. Martin's Press
New York

Cover design: Ben Santora

ISBN 0-312-00473-7
ISBN 0-312-12532-1 (pbk.)

Library of Congress Cataloging-in-Publication Data

Brown, Seyom.
  The causes and prevention of war.

  Includes index.
  1. War.   2. Violence.   I. Title.
  U21.2.B75   1987   303.6'6   86-26208
  ISBN 0-312-00473-7
  ISBN 0-312-12532-1 (pbk.)

For Jeremiah, Matthew, Benjamin, Nell, Eliot, Steven, and Lisa

Preface

This book addresses the central survival question facing our species: How can we reduce the role of large-scale violence in world society? To explore this question, the book builds on the best thought of scholars and statesmen concerning the determinants of war and the conditions of peace. But mostly it results from my own studies and observations of world politics, both as a foreign policy analyst in Washington, D.C., and as an academic in the field of international relations.

Experience convinces me that no segment of the political spectrum has a monopoly on the desire for peace, nor is any profession the principal repository of wisdom about the causes and prevention of war. My net for seeking insights is therefore cast widely across ideological orientations and fields of knowledge. My approach is primarily inclusive, but it is neither a survey of views nor neutral with respect to the merits of the views analyzed. The objective is synthesis: an integrated strategy for the prevention and control of large-scale human violence, especially—and most urgently—the prevention of nuclear holocaust.

The writing is directed toward concerned laypeople as well as academic and official specialists involved in national security and war-and-peace issues. The analysis does not assume sophistication in any particular discipline or technical field; accordingly, the book is appropriate for introductory courses in world politics or peace studies. Yet the fundamental nature of the questions posed and the theoretical implications of the recommended policies also make it appropriate for graduate-level courses in political science, sociology, and international relations.

Although my principal arguments have theoretical and methodological implications for the academic discipline of international relations, these implications are not the book's subject matter. I am informed by and respect much of the theoretical and methodological work of my fellow academics, and the notes frequently make this explicit; but the following exposition is driven and controlled primarily by the "real world" predicament of having to deal urgently with life-and-death policy choices before all the knowledge is in. Even so, my formulation of the crucial policy choices now facing governments and human society at large is more "academic" (in the sense of being rooted in philosophical and systematic inquiry) than either the usual official definitions of war-peace issues or the alternatives championed by various factions of the peace movement.

The analysis and policy prescriptions put forward in this book are in large part the product of many oral and written dialogs I have been engaged in over the years that do not lend themselves to citation in the notes. These exchanges—with both policymakers and scholars—are too numerous to catalog here, but I would like to mention a few that have been particularly helpful to me during the final writing stages.

Colleagues in the Peace Studies Program at Brandeis University who commented on sections of the manuscript and shared their wisdom with me include Jack S. Goldstein, professor of physics, with whom I cotaught the Brandeis senior seminar in peace studies; David Hackett Fischer, professor of history, with whom I cotaught the introductory course in peace studies; Susan Moller Okin, professor of politics, with whom I cotaught a seminar on justice and international relations; Henry Linchitz, professor of chemistry; Leslie McArthur, professor of psychology; Sissela Bok, professor of philosophy; Gordon Fellman, professor of sociology; and Robert J. Art, professor of politics.

Other colleagues offering important comments on parts of the manuscript were J. David Singer of the Mental Health Research Institute, University of Michigan; Paul M. Kattenburg, professor of public affairs, University of South Carolina; and Martha Morelock, of the Department of Child Study, Tufts University. Among the reviewers who read the manuscript and made helpful suggestions at various stages of its development are John Armitage, University of Virginia; David Meyers, University of North Carolina-Greensboro; Herbert Tillema, University of Missouri-Columbia; and Stephen Walker, Arizona State University.

In recording my debts to these various scholars for their insights, I by no means wish to suggest that they endorse what I have written.

My writing has also been immeasurably stimulated and informed by my participation in the Faculty Seminar of the Avoiding Nuclear War Project of the John F. Kennedy School of Government, Harvard University. But it should be noted that no part of this book has been sponsored by the project or formally included in its deliberations.

Working with St. Martin's Press has been a creative experience all along the way. The sensitive editorial therapy of Robert Weber, Joan Emma, and Anne McCoy was always empathetic with my purposes.

My two youngest sons, Matthew and Jeremiah, deserve special thanks for their help with the index. But most important, their unique and compelling presence during this period in my life has been my most powerful reminder of how much is now in jeopardy if we do not improve our understanding of the causes and prevention of war.

S.B.

Contents

PART I

Violence in Human Affairs

The principal concern of this book is violence between countries—international war. This is the kind of violence that now threatens to destroy the world. Why is the human species, having been so inventive in developing the instruments of world destruction, so remiss in learning how to organize itself for peace?

Chapter 1 considers the most elemental questions: Is the human animal "naturally" violent? And is peace therefore a condition that has to be imposed by devices to deter violent behavior through penalties and punishments? Or are humans naturally peaceable, with violence an aberration caused by conditions of abnormal deprivation, pain, or frustration? Most of the evidence and studies reflected in the chapter support neither of these extreme explanations for human violence. They do suggest, however, that all humans have the capacity to act violently and destructively as well as peacefully and constructively.

To determine, when, where, and under what circumstances violent behavior is most likely to appear, and how it can be prevented and controlled, we need to be sensitive to the interplay of a complex range of factors: the individual psychologies of the involved actors, the basic social and cultural conditions that may be inducing violent behavior, and the characteristics of triggering events.

Useful insights into the factors conducive to violent or nonviolent

1

behavior are gleaned from various fields of study, including biology, psychology, anthropology, sociology, and political science.

Chapter 2 focuses on political violence and civic peace within countries. The historical record reveals that force is used domestically by those in charge of the prevailing order as much as by those who would challenge it. Governments are shown to be intimately linked with coercive force, as monopolizers of society's lethal capabilities, and as enforcers of society's laws. Governments are humankind's ubiquitous invention for controlling the violence produced by interpersonal and intergroup conflict. Yet because they are in such a strategic position to determine the distribution of privileges and amenities, in many countries the contests over who should control the government often turn violent.

Revolutions and rebellions are for the most part struggles over who should govern and by what rules. The chapter summarizes the prevailing understanding on the part of sociologists and political scientists about the conditions conducive to revolution, rebellion, and intercommunal violence, and the extent to which differences among countries in the frequency and intensity of domestic violence are attributable to variances in culture and socioeconomic conditions or to their political systems and governing structures.

The purpose of the first two chapters is to see what can be learned about the general phenomenon of violence, of which international war is only a part, and what insights about the causes and prevention of intergroup violence are transferable to the international system.

Chapter 3 provides a transition to the analysis of the determinants of war in Part II. It describes the reasons national leaders and publics typically give for incurring the often terrible costs and risks of war against foreign countries or political groups. It shows that the "reasons of state" for which countries go to war have much in common with the motivations of smaller collectivities and of individuals who resort to violence: security of persons; maintenance of or enlargement of material holdings; protection or propagation of a way of life; rectification of perceived injustice; honor; revenge; emotional catharsis.

For countries, no less than for domestic groups and individuals fighting one another, some combination of these motives usually must be present to spur them on to incur the costs and risks of combat. But the national leaders who decide whether to take their countries into war are burdened with the awesome responsibility of assessing the costs, prospects for success, and risks of failure for the whole nation. As shown in Part II, these decisions on war and peace are therefore heavily influenced not only by notions about the national interest, but also by assessments of the geopolitical situation, including the capabilities and intentions of hostile and friendly countries.

You are interested, I know, in the prevention of war,
not in our theories. . . .
Yet I would like to dwell a little . . .
on this destructive instinct. . . .
We are led to conclude that this instinct
functions in every living being,
striving to work its ruin and to reduce life
to its primal state of inert matter.

—*Sigmund Freud*
letter to Albert Einstein

The Semai are not great warriors.
As long as they have been known to the outside world,
they have consistently fled rather than fight. . . .
They had never participated in a war or raid
until the Communist insurgency of the early 1950s,
when the British raised troops among the Semai. . . .
Initially, most of the troops were probably lured
by wages, pretty clothes, shotguns, and so forth.
Many did not realize that soldiers kill people.
When I suggested to one Semai recruit that killing
was a soldier's job, he laughed at my ignorance
and explained, "No, we don't kill people, brother,
we just tend weeds and cut grass."

—*Robert Knox Dentan*
The Semai: A Nonviolent
People of Malaysia

War alone brings up to their highest tension
all human energies and puts a stamp of nobility
upon the people who have the courage to meet it.
All other trials are substitutes,
which never really put a man in front of himself
in the alternative of life and death.
A doctrine, therefore, which begins with
a prejudice in favor of peace
is foreign to Fascism.

—*Benito Mussolini*
Doctrine of Fascism

CHAPTER 1

Why People Fight

When humans try to kill or physically injure other humans—or threaten such violence—what is going on? Is the violence socially approved, even taught? Or does it contradict prevailing notions of right and wrong? Is the violent behavior largely a spontaneous reaction to a particular provocation or stimulus? Or is it something that has to be induced through appeals to courage, duty, or patriotism, or even by threats to punish those who refuse to fight?

At times human violence appears to be primarily an intense expression of emotions: anger, hate, fear, rivalry, revenge; at times it seems to be the product of irrational impulses to dominate, hurt, or destroy. But at other times the violence appears to be mainly premeditated and instrumental, consciously chosen as a means to prevent or compel acts by others.

In most cases of interpersonal and intergroup violence there is likely to be a considerable admixture of raw emotion and calculation, compounded with a good deal of social conditioning. And it is difficult to separate these out, even for purposes of analysis.

Yet when it comes to preventing or controlling particular acts of violence it is important to discover as much as possible about the extent to which the behavior of the belligerents is motivated by passion or by strategic design. Efforts to induce antagonists to lay down their weapons, reconcile their differences, or divert their conflict into nonviolent channels are unlikely to succeed if they are premised on basically inaccurate assessments of what is driving the violence on each side. For example, those obsessed by a desire to inflict terrible pain on their enemies in retribution for past humiliations (say, the pillaging and raping of one's townspeople) are likely to resist, and even resent, efforts to get them to negotiate rather than fight. By contrast, where violence has emerged as a last-resort "bargaining" tactic in a dispute over some tangible interest (say, access to common fishing areas) marginal concessions by one or both of the warring parties may be all that is needed to avert or stop bloodshed.

To be sure, protagonists who are largely driven by emotion are usually also affected by considerations of the costs and gains they will incur by their violent behavior (although the costs may need to appear awesomely large for them to decide to terminate the violence); and those whose resort to violence is initially part of a calculated carrots-and-sticks effort to pressure an adversary to come to terms may well find that once the exchange of blows starts, new feelings of rage and hate well up, and a determination to smash the opponent overwhelms the original motive to use force only as a prod to serious negotiations.

It is precisely because most violence probably does result from an amalgam of motives, immediate stimuli, and social conditioning that practical efforts to resolve or control conflict require careful analysis—situation by situation—of what influences are at work and how they are interacting with one another.

Various scholarly disciplines have contributions to make to this effort. Some important investigations and theories about human violence emphasize the emotional and irrational factors. Some emphasize human "nature." Some emphasize "culture," or basic economic and political conditions. Others emphasize the conscious calculations or strategies in the minds of antagonists who come to blows. There are important insights to be gained from these different emphases.

THE EMOTIONAL AND IRRATIONAL ASPECTS OF VIOLENT CONFLICT

Even among those emphasizing violence characterized by predominantly impulsive, emotional, and seemingly irrational behavior, there are divergent explanations of the primary causes of such destructive outbursts. One school of thought attributes the violent behavior largely to human instincts. Another gives more weight to environmental circumstances. But again, most serious students of human violence recognize some mixture of innate predisposition (which may vary with individuals) and situational conditions.

The search for the causes of intense human urges to maim and kill has engaged some of the best minds in the fields of biology, anthropology, psychoanalysis, social psychology, sociology, and political science. It is not the intention here to arbitrate among the various explanations, some of which may seem to contradict one another, but rather to cull from the wide body of research and speculation on violence between individuals and groups those factors that may have a bearing on the phenomenon of war between countries—its outbreak, prevention, and control.

Are Humans Biologically Programmed for Violence?

The proposition that violence is part of human nature has been advanced by some biologists in the fields of ethology (the study of animal behavior) and sociobiology—most prominently by Konrad Lorenz and Edward O. Wilson. The empirical scientific observations by these biologists have been of nonhuman species; and the inferences they make from their studies of insect and lower-animal behavior to human behavior are highly speculative (indeed they admit this).

In his book *On Aggression*, Konrad Lorenz speculates that the human animal contains a store of aggressive energy that seeks release and can be rather easily triggered in situations of rivalry and perceived threat. In this respect, the human being would be like many other species in the animal kingdom whose survival has been aided by such instincts. By a process of "natural selection" (the most aggressive would be most likely to survive, to mate, and to pass on their aggressive traits to their offspring), the evolutionary process may well have favored the development of human beings with high intelligence and a propensity to fight.[1]

This hypothesis of the survival of the most aggressive is echoed in Edward O. Wilson's contention that human beings are disposed to react with "unreasoning hatred" to perceived threats to their safety or possessions. There is a "profound human tendency to learn violence," says Wilson. "Our brains appear to be programmed . . . to partition people into friends and aliens. . . . We tend to fear deeply the actions of strangers and to solve conflict by aggression." He speculates that these "learning rules are most likely to have evolved during the past hundreds of thousands of years . . . and, thus, to have conferred a biological advantage on those who conformed to them with the greatest fidelity.''[2]

Not all ethologists agree with Lorenz and Wilson. Many fault them for their rather freewheeling extrapolation from the behavior of lower animals to animals higher on the phylogenetic scale. Some also challenge their conclusions about aggression among lower animals, pointing out significant variations in intraspecies aggression observed among different populations of the same species, and arguing that the Lorenzians overemphasize the genetic inheritance of instincts and give insufficient weight to environmental factors such as natural habitat and ecology and social conditions of rearing the young.[3] Indeed, Lorenz and Wilson themselves, in the parts of their work that have occasioned less public controversy, have discovered variations among species and even within species in the counterviolent traits of bonding and altruism.[4]

It would be unfair to attribute to Lorenz and Wilson the kind of Social Darwinism that endorses the survival of the most aggressive. The implications of their theories are stark; but they hardly view them as positive. Lorenz himself states:

> An unprejudiced observer from another planet, looking down on man as he is today, in his hand the atom bomb, the product of his intelligence, in his heart the aggressive drive inherited from his anthropoid ancestors, which this same intelligence cannot control, would not prophesy long life for the species.[5]

The genetic determinism and cross-species generalizations of these pessimistic ethologists perhaps make it too easy to dispose of some of their important insights—namely, that the course of human evolution up to now does seem to have conferred privilege and power on those who are not very strongly inhibited from killing their fellow human beings; that in the age of mass-destruction technologies, the continued favoring of this characteristic works against rather than for the survival of the species; and that therefore major new acts of deliberate social construction, utilizing the unique human capacities to learn from experience and to exercise foresight, are required to avoid species extinction in the future.

The Freudian Concept of a "Death Instinct"

Sigmund Freud, the founder of the psychoanalytic movement, was centrally concerned in his theory and in his clinical practice with extreme forms of human aggression—violence directed against others in homicide and against the self in suicide. The implications of his observations for efforts to prevent war were drawn in his famous exchange of letters with the great physicist Albert Einstein.

Einstein wrote to Freud in 1932 for help in understanding, and he hoped correcting, what seemed to him to be an irrational refusal of humans to dispense with the international war system and national military establishments. The physicist could find only one explanation for such stubborn adherence to these presumably obsolete human institutions:

> Because man has within him a lust for hatred and destruction. In normal times this passion exists in a latent state, it emerges only in unusual circumstances; but it is a comparatively easy task to call it into play and raise it to the power of a collective psychosis. Here lies, perhaps, the crux of all the complex factors we are considering, an enigma that only the expert in the lore of human instincts can resolve.[6]

"I entirely agree with you," replied Freud. "I believe in the existence of this instinct and have recently been at pains to study its manifestations." He thereupon summarized for Einstein his theoretical work on how a postulated death instinct "that . . . functions in every living being" comes into conflict with the life instinct (Eros).[7]

Both of these instincts, claimed Freud, are expressions of an even more basic drive, "the pleasure principle," which motivates humans toward the elimination of all pain and the absence of all desire. Expressed through the death instinct, the pleasure principle leads to suicide; but fortunately for most individuals, Eros puts up an effective fight, the result being a displacement of the death instinct onto others in the form of interpersonal or intergroup aggression.

Freud also theorized that for humans to live peacefully with one another, for "civilization" to prevail, this natural interplay of the basic instincts has to be suppressed; or, put another way, Eros has to be relieved of its combative role against the death instinct and freed to express itself in human creativity and love. The necessary repression of destructive instincts and aggressive behavior, however, requires intervention—restrictions and discipline by parents over children, by institutions over individuals, by the state over society, and internationally by a world government over the otherwise anarchic international system. Civilization thus requires a lot of repression. But repression itself causes unhappiness, neurosis (we are all neurotic according to the Freudians), irrational behavior, and sometimes violent aggression. This is where psychotherapy steps in to help sustain civilization's basic regime of control and deflection of violent emotions: The psychoanalyst aids individuals to understand, work through, and find constructive outlets for their inevitable discontent.[8]

Erich Fromm's Location of Violence in Alienation

Freud's instinctivist explanations for violence have been cogently disputed by one of his most influential disciples, Erich Fromm. In *The Anatomy of Human Destructiveness*, Fromm distinguishes "malignant aggression" from "defensive aggression," which in some circumstances may be rational and adaptive. He argues that a humane civilization, indeed the survival of the human species, requires first and foremost the prevention and control of the malign kind of aggression, in which the perpetrators of violent acts are passionately driven to injure others (sadism) or themselves (masochism). But Fromm attributes even these malign forms of aggression more to social conditions than to innate predispositions.

Fromm finds such malignant aggressive traits present in "alienated" individuals and groups—those who are profoundly separated, in a psychological sense, from their fellow human beings, and who are irrationally driven to avenge their terrible loneliness and feelings of impotence through "godlike" acts of destruction. The alienated are also ready candidates for recruitment into violent communal and nationalist organizations where individuals can compensate for their lack of human connectedness by "losing themselves" in a group bound together by its hatred of the outsiders.[9]

Fromm's work provides a bridge to the efforts of social psychologists, sociologists, and anthropologists to discover which social conditions are most likely to provoke the intense negative emotions that drive humans to acts of violence, and which social conditions are most conducive to more rational and peaceable means of dealing with conflict.

The Frustration-Aggression Hypothesis

An entry point into the exploration of the societal causes of violence is the influential frustration-aggression hypothesis, originally advanced by the psychologists John Dollard and Leonard Doob in the late 1930s, and subsequently refined and modified by other behavioral scientists. The key to much aggressive, and especially violent, behavior, according to these behavioral scientists, is "frustration"— that is, substantial interference with or blocking of goal-directed activity. Frequently the result is intense anger, expressed in attempts to hurt or destroy the object or person perceived to be preventing one from attaining the goal.

In its sophisticated versions the hypothesis does not state that all frustration leads to aggression, for it is obvious that humans, especially adults, have a wide variety of adaptations to frustration, some of them constructive and creative. What it does state is that where violent and destructive behavior is present there usually is a discoverable basic cause for that behavior, and more often than not this will be an intensely experienced frustration of activity directed toward the satisfaction of a strongly desired objective.[10] (Variations on the frustration-aggression hypothesis figure prominently in the recent scholarly literature on revolution and rebellion, and will be reviewed in Chapter 2.)

The focus on frustration as the primary cause of violence reflects a strong emphasis in contemporary social analysis on the so-called environmental factors in human behavior, the social and material situations of individuals as distinct from their inherited biological equipment. When it comes to efforts to reduce the role of violence in human affairs, it is particularly useful to be able to isolate such environmental determinants, since they often are more readily observable and tangible than the causes that may lie within human beings, and—on both practical and ethical grounds—are more subject to restructuring.[11]

Some Evidence from Anthropology

Important corroboration for the thesis that human violence is determined more by social structure and cultural norms than by instincts is found in anthropological investigations of peaceful societies. The existence of even very few societies in which physical violence (actual or threatened) is virtually absent would call into question the theory of a strong innate predisposition to violence in the human species. Tribal societies exhibiting remarkably little violence are the Zuni Indians of the American Southwest, the Kung Bushmen of the Kalahari Desert in southern Africa, the Arapesh of New Guinea, and the Semai of Malaya, among others.[12]

The Kung Bushmen, for example, are reported to disparage physical combat as a means of settling differences. In their folklore the most admired are those who survive adversity by trickery and deception, not force. The violation of social norms seems to be handled by public ostracism rather than physical punishment, and individuals who violate the norms against interpersonal violence are condemned.[13]

Comparative studies of these internally peaceful societies cast doubt not only on the sufficiency and usefulness of instinctivist explanations for violence, but also on a number of conventional environmental hypotheses.[14]

One conventional hypothesis is that population density is the crucial determinant of interpersonal and intergroup violence; but the anthropological evidence shows no significant correlation between spatial dispersal and peace. What does seem to coincide with violence is scarcity of necessary subsistence resources; this is probably one reason why most of the peaceful societies discovered tend to fulfill their subsistence needs by hunting and gathering rather than by subsistence agriculture (although hunter-gatherers also can come into violent conflict when, temporarily, some of them converge on areas where the game and vegetation or water is scarce).

Another environmental explanation is that internal social peace is a function of external threat—domestic cooperation and community spirit being necessary to defeat the aggressor. But some of the most internally peaceful tribes observed by anthropologists were not under external threat, nor did their legends emphasize warrior virtues (which would be a clue to memories of, and expectations of, the need to be prepared for intertribal conflict).

A related proposition attributes internal social peace to hierarchy of authority and/or governmental centralization—these institutional arrangements presumably being crucial for adequate dispute resolution (and their absence, internationally, being a principal reason for the prevalence of war). But again, the anthropological evidence shows no necessary correlation. Some of the most peaceful societies are highly decentralized, with dispute resolution being performed on a peer-group basis.[15] And we certainly have ample contemporary evidence that centralization of authority and power often are as closely associated with brutal enforcement of laws (and violent reactions to such brutality) as with the gentler arts of dispute resolution.

It should be noted, however, that none of the internally peaceful societies studied by anthropologists seems to operate on the premise that its members would automatically refrain from violence, that there is a strong "instinct for peace," as it were, that operates without social inducement. Tribal cosmology, rituals, legends, and institutions for airing and resolving disputes (including ostracism for violating group norms) all assume a propensity by some members of society to resort to violence; everywhere there are socializing devices to constrain and deflect such violent inclinations.

Violence as Learned Behavior

The fact that some human societies exhibit markedly more violence than others, even when their material conditions are not basically different, strongly suggests that humans can be taught to be more or less violent or peaceful. The "teaching" can be direct, through behavioral punishments and rewards to train fighting capabilities and to remove inhibitions (the "basic training" of raw recruits into the military is of this sort). It can be indirect—through myths and legends defining heroism and courage as the willingness to risk one's life in physical combat against the enemies of one's group, through ideologies and propaganda engendering hatred toward members of enemy groups and dehumanizing them, and through religious and ethical concepts and social mores that justify killing under certain circumstances.

Explicitly or implicitly, groups (from families to gangs to nations) convey to their members what kind of conflictual or cooperative behavior is admired or disparaged; and such group norms can work to reinforce, channel, or deflect aggressive desires to dominate others or to strike out at those believed to be responsible for one's deprivations and frustrations.

There is a body of investigation by social psychologists such as Albert Bandura, on the social learning of aggression, that demonstrates the mediating and highly determinative effects of belief systems and learned cognitive processes and routines on the way different individuals react to the same external stimuli.[16] An understanding of these learned and cognitively mediated responses by different individuals (even within the same national culture) to conflict situations may aid in efforts to reduce the kinds of misperception and miscalculation by high policy officials that can lead to unwanted war and uncontrollable escalation.[17]

CALCULATED AND INSTRUMENTAL USES OF VIOLENCE

While social scientists and theorists investigate and debate the extent to which all or some humans are genetically or socially programmed to behave aggressively or peacefully, deliberate acts of violence continue—as a matter of conscious choice—between individuals, between groups, and between countries. Those who want to find ways of reducing the role of war in the world therefore must also study the calculated, instrumental resort to violence, even where the violence seems to emanate at base from emotional or subconscious causes. (As we will observe more directly in Part II, wars usually are threatened and fought as a matter of policy—that is, the final decision to use military force is typically surrounded by an elaborate process of deliberation among high officials, involving assessments of the advantages and disadvantages of alternative courses of action.)

It is a fact of life that in many human circumstances violence is an option, sometimes an attractive option. Violence is one of the means available, frequently regarded as legitimate, for bringing pressure against another human being or group to get one's way when opposed, or to prevent being inflicted with pain or humiliation. And it is a fact, however distressing, that it can and often does "work."

The situations in which humans tend to choose violence as a means of protection or getting their way can be grouped into two types: (1) when there appears to be no tolerable alternative; and (2) when violence seems the most efficient of available means.

When There Is No Alternative

The laws of most societies, and most social philosophers, grant that violence can be legitimate when it is necessary for self-defense—

that is, when one's own survival or protection against extreme violence requires the violent disabling of an attacker. The definition of legitimate self-defense ordinarily extends at least to the protection of one's immediate family. Organized societies provide community resources, including police forces, to help protect people against violent attacks, and these official law-enforcement agencies are provisioned with superior weapons and with generally wide writs of authority to use violence sufficient to overwhelm individuals or groups engaging in illegal activity. But the police are not always close enough to offer timely protection, and in such circumstances violent acts of self-defense may well be rational.

Of course, the definition of the precise circumstances in which violent acts of self-defense may be necessary is controversial, and usually left to the courts to decide on a case-by-case basis. (Is it justifiable, for example, to shoot someone who has threatened harm to your family when that person enters your immediate residential neighborhood on an obvious mission to carry out that threat—or must the would-be attacker have entered your home?) It is not my intention here to resolve such practical and philosophical issues, but only to observe that there are categories of violence, whether engaged in by organized society on behalf of citizens or by individuals on their own behalf, that some societies consider both rational and morally justifiable. (However, see Chapter 7 for the views of pacifists such as Mohandas Gandhi and Martin Luther King, Jr., on the immorality of all violence.)

Calculated, deliberate acts of violence or threats of violence also are resorted to for purposes other than defending against physical attacks upon persons. Conscious premeditated violence often is used as a last resort to protect property against vandals, thieves, and trespassers when nonviolent prohibitions are disregarded. In most communities, the resort to such violence in the defense of property normally is supposed to be undertaken by the community's police force; but, again, where timely protection by community law enforcers is unavailable, self-help, even including the use of deadly force, is widely regarded as permissible. In the nation-state system, self-defense to protect the "territorial integrity" of the country is a standard reason for going to war, and is regarded as legitimate by most international legal authorities.

The claim of last resort is often a mobilizing device of leaders of revolutionary movements: "When a long train of abuses and usurpations . . . evinces a design to reduce [a people] under absolute despotism, it is their right, it is their duty, to throw off such government" (American Declaration of Independence).[18] "The proletarians have nothing to lose but their chains. . . . Workingmen of all countries, unite!" (Marx and Engels).[19] And then: "Only the violent overthrow of the bourgeoisie, the confiscation of its property, the destruction of the whole of the bourgeois state apparatus . . . can ensure the real subordination of the whole class of exploiters" (Lenin).[20]

A variant of such instrumental encouragement of violent emotions is the championing of "liberationist" violence by the black revolutionary leader Frantz Fanon:

> The practice of violence binds them [the colonized peoples of the Third World] together . . . as a part of the great organism of violence which has surged upwards in reaction to the settler's violence in the beginning. . . . [This] violence is a cleansing force. It frees the native from his inferiority complex and from his despair and inaction; it makes him fearless and restores his self respect.[21]

Communities also generally assert the legitimacy of using violence when necessary to protect important religious, cultural, or political values—"ways of life"—against those who would desecrate them. Although people who believe themselves to be fighting for a way of life characteristically exhibit the emotional intensity associated with violence produced by elemental subconscious drives, the resort to violence in such situations (the threats and then the actual fighting) often results from a calculated strategy fashioned by political leaders. President Woodrow Wilson's claim in 1917 that the United States was entering World War I because "the world must be made safe for democracy" is an example of an instrumental stimulation of popular emotions in order to obtain sufficient public support for governmental decisions made largely on geopolitical grounds.

The deliberate whipping up of popular emotions on behalf of a way of life is also evident in the violent tactics of the Catholic Irish Republican Army in predominantly Protestant Northern Ireland, and in the street violence by the followers of the Ayatollah Khomeini in Iran before the overthrow of the shah. In many such cases, an impartial observer could conclude that the stimulation of the group's emotions to a level of intensity where it was ready and willing to fight is understandable, indeed highly rational, granting that the basic values of the group are at stake.

The prevention of the violence of last resort is especially difficult once the antagonists begin to mobilize themselves for physical combat. Appeals for reasonableness in such situations are likely to fall on deaf ears, not so much because emotions have taken over as because a calculated decision has been made that violence is the only feasible alternative to an intolerable sacrifice of one's basic values ("Give me liberty or give me death!"). To avoid violence, the conditions which the side preparing to attack deems intolerable must first be substantially ameliorated, or at a minimum the aggrieved side must be promised immediate negotiations to achieve such amelioration.

When "Sticks" Seem More Efficient Than "Carrots"

Between individuals, groups, or states, violence at times is resorted to with conscious calculation even though other means of protecting or asserting one's values are available. Those who initiate the violence calculate that the ratio of gains to costs will be better if they use (or convincingly threaten to use) force than if they do not.

Many "bullying" situations between children are the product of this kind of simple calculation: Two groups of children converge on an unreserved athletic field. An argument ensues, but neither will give way. The members of one group, clearly older and stronger, start pushing and shoving their rival claimants, who then concede the field rather than accept the challenge to a fight they are sure to lose. The older and stronger group has other options—inviting the younger group to play with them, suggesting a time limit on the use of the field by each group, flipping a coin, and so on—but a quick calculation of the "balance of power" convinces them that they can easily scare off the younger group and have the field entirely to themselves as they planned.

The history of American frontier settlements in areas not yet under established civil authority is replete with such violent encounters,[22] the plot for many a Wild West movie or TV drama: Neighboring ranchers are grazing their herds in the same grassland, and the area is becoming overgrazed. The owners of the Circle X ranch erect a fence around roughly half of the grazing area and put "No

Trespassing" signs along the fence. The owners of the Bar Y ranch are outraged at this unilateral act and, since their herd is 50 percent larger than the Circle X herd, demand that the fence be moved back closer to the Circle X corral. When their demand is refused, the Bar Y ranchers—in the first act of "violence"—chop down parts of the fence to allow their cattle again to wander the whole grassland. The Circle Xers drive the Bar Y cattle back and repair the fence, while warning the Bar Y ranchers that any of their cattle found again within Circle X territory will be shot on sight. The possible next steps in this escalating conflict need not be drawn here. The point of the illustration is only the calculated rationality of the steps taken by each side up the conflict-escalation ladder.

In many such situations alternative moves of a less provocative nature are available but are not taken. Why? Lacking generally established procedures for mediating or arbitrating conflicts of this sort, and lacking enforceable rules prohibiting unilateral aggressive behavior, and further lacking a sense of community among those sharing a particular resource, aggressive moves are highly tempting. The analogies to the arena of international relations, populated as it is by sovereign nation-states, are obvious; but the lack of central community procedures and norms does not provide a sufficient explanation of why some encounters in anarchic situations result in violence and others do not.

Both the playground and the cattle-grazing illustrations also show how threats of violence may be rational "bargaining" ploys when the resources for positive-payoff exchanges are scarce—a condition, as we will see in Part II, also frequently encountered in international conflict situations.

Bargaining between adversaries typically involves both "carrots" and "sticks." It is when the available sticks appear to one or another of the adversaries to be considerably more efficient than the available carrots that the likelihood of bargaining by blows is highest. This is one of the reasons why the calculated resort to violence (or threats of violence) between individuals or groups even of essentially equal power is generally more prevalent between children than between adults, between relatively poor people than between the comfortably affluent, and between the politically disenfranchised than between those with easy access to the central institutions of society.[23]

It is precisely with respect to the phenomenon of violence as negative bargaining that deterrence—the dissuasion of an action through the threat of imposing costs on the potential aggressor in excess of his anticipated gains, even though not necessarily prevailing over the aggressor—may appear to be the most efficacious means of controlling violence. In basically anarchic situations (unsupervised playgrounds, unpoliced neighborhoods with high crime rates, countries pervaded by civil conflict, the international system), the deterrence of violent behavior often requires that the individuals or groups trying to protect themselves display a credible capability and will to inflict unacceptable damage on their would-be attackers.

Of course, the more a society is centrally organized and is expected to function as a community, the more the responsibility not only for preventing simple thuggery and bullying, but also for assuring that intense feelings of injustice and alienation do not give rise to violence, is lodged in the organs of the whole community. Thus, the problem of violence, including war between countries, is closely tied to the problem of effective and just government—a relationship we begin to explore in the next chapter.

NOTES

1. Konrad Lorenz, *On Aggression* (New York: Harcourt Brace & World, 1966). Instinctivist hypotheses are also advanced by Irenaus Eibl-Eibesfelt, *The Biology of Peace and War* (New York: Viking, 1979).

2. Edwin O. Wilson, *On Human Nature* (Cambridge, Mass.: Harvard University Press, 1978), p. 119.

3. J. P. Scott, "Biological Basis of Human Warfare: An Interdisciplinary Problem," in M. Sherif and C. W. Sherif, eds., *Interdisciplinary Relationships in the Social Sciences* (Chicago: Aldine, 1969) pp. 121–136; and Ashley Montagu, ed., *Man and Aggression* (New York: Oxford University Press, 1973). For a summary of ethological literature contesting Lorenz on aggression, see Samuel S. Kim, "The Lorenzian Theory of Aggression and Peace Research: A Critique," in Richard A. Falk and Samuel S. Kim, eds., *The War System: An Interdisciplinary Approach* (Boulder, Colo.: Westview, 1980), pp. 82–115. For defenses of Wilsonian sociobiology see James H. Fetzer, ed., *Sociobiology and Epistemology* (Boston: D. Reidel, 1985).

4. For work in the Lorenzian-Wilsonian tradition that gives major attention to the counterviolent propensities in various species, see Irenaus Eibl-Eibesfelt, *Love and Hate: The Natural History of Behavior Patterns* (New York: Holt, Rinehart and Winston, 1972).

5. Lorenz, p. 48.

6. Letter of Albert Einstein to Sigmund Freud, 30 July 1932 (Geneva: League of Nations: International Institute of Intellectual Cooperation, 1933); reprinted in William Ebenstein, *Great Political Thinkers: Plato to the Present* (New York: Rinehart, 1951), pp. 802–804.

7. Sigmund Freud, Letter to Albert Einstein, September 1932, included in the above League of Nations publication and reprinted in Ebenstein, pp. 804–810.

8. Sigmund Freud, *Beyond the Pleasure Principle* (New York: Liveright, 1950); *Civilization and Its Discontents* (New York: Norton, 1962); and *An Outline of Psychoanalysis* (New York: Norton, 1959).

9. Erich Fromm, *The Anatomy of Human Destructiveness* (New York: Holt, Rinehart and Winston, 1973); and *Escape from Freedom* (New York: Holt, Rinehart and Winston, 1941).

10. The original version of the frustration-aggression hypothesis is in John Dollard, Leonard W. Doob, Neal E. Miller, et al., *Frustration and Aggression* (New Haven, Conn.: Yale University Press, 1939). Subsequent refinements are well reflected in Leonard Berkowitz, *Aggression: A Social Psychological Analysis* (New York: McGraw-Hill, 1962).

11. See B. F. Skinner, *Beyond Freedom and Dignity* (New York: Knopf, 1971), for a disquisition on how the analytical techniques of the behavioralist can be transmuted into instruments of social control and reform.

12. Some of the pioneering anthropological investigations of these peaceful societies—notably Margaret Mead's account of the Arapesh in her *Growing Up in New Guinea* (New York: New American Library, 1930), and Ruth Benedict's account of the Zunis in her *Patterns of Culture* (New York: Houghton Mifflin, 1934)—have been shown by subsequent research to have inadvertently underplayed the presence of overt or suppressed violence in these societies; but their original findings that some societies are markedly more peaceful than others have been amply confirmed.

13. Elizabeth M. Thomas, *The Harmless People* (New York: Knopf, 1959).

14. David Fabbro, "Peaceful Societies," in Richard A. Falk and Samuel S. Kim, *The War System: An Interdisciplinary Approach* (Boulder, Colo.: Westview, 1980) compares evidence gained by anthropologists on eight peaceful societies along fourteen socioeconomic, cultural, and political dimensions. My rendering of the anthropological evidence draws heavily on his analysis.

15. For accounts of how dispute resolution is performed in societies with minimal government see Lucy Mair, *Primitive Government: A Study of Traditional Political Systems in Eastern Africa* (Bloomington: Indiana University Press, 1977), especially Chapter 2.

16. Albert Bandura, *Aggression: A Social Learning Analysis* (Englewood Cliffs, N.J.: Prentice-Hall, 1973).

17. See Robert Jervis, *Perception and Misperception in International Relations* (Princeton, N.J.: Princeton University Press, 1976). John G. Stoessinger in his *Why Nations Go to War* (New York: St. Martin's, 1985) emphasizes the personalities of leaders, and finds "misperception" to be "perhaps the most important single precipitating factor in the outbreak of war." See also Chapters 5 and 6 in Richard Ned Lebow, *Between Peace and War: The Nature of International Crisis* (Baltimore, Md.: Johns Hopkins University Press, 1981), for an analysis of the role of "cognitive closure" and "misperception" in intense international conflicts.

18. Carl L. Becker, *The Declaration of Independence: A Study in the History of Political Ideas* (New York: Harcourt, Brace, 1922).

19. Karl Marx and Friedrich Engels, *The Communist Manifesto* (New York: Appleton-Century-Crofts, 1955).

20. V. I. Lenin, "Theses on the Fundamental Tasks of the Second Congress of the Communist International," July 4, 1920, *Selected Works* (New York: International Publishers, 1935), Vol X, pp. 162–179.

21. Frantz Fanon, *The Wretched of the Earth*, translated from the French by Constance Farrington (New York: Grove Press, 1963), p. 73.

22. See N. Eugene Hollon, *Frontier Violence: Another Look* (New York: Oxford University Press, 1974).

23. For data on how a scarcity of resources for exchange correlates with violence see Robert Bensing and Oliver Schroeder, *Homicide in an Urban Community* (Springfield, Ill.: Charles C. Thomas, 1960). For exposition of the logic of this relationship see H. L. Nieburg, *Political Violence: The Behavioral Process* (New York: St. Martin's, 1965).

CHAPTER 2

Violence and Governance

Who should govern is often a fighting issue, for those in control of the government have a lot to say about who gets what, when, and how. Many governments rely heavily on force to maintain themselves in power and to assure that general community rules are obeyed within their jurisdictions: in performing self-protective and law-enforcement functions, governments normally are expected to apprehend, disarm, or even destroy the perpetrators of illegal violence. In most states, in fact, the only legal violence, other than necessary acts of self-defense by citizens, is undertaken by the government or specifically authorized by it. And since control of the government tends to give political legitimacy with the right to use force to some groups but to deprive others of this power, it is hardly surprising that human history has been marked by so many civil wars and violent changes of government.

Countries in the modern nation-state system are especially susceptible to internal political violence, given the popularity of the nationalist principle that there should be an identity between *nation* (a people which considers itself to be a distinct culture and community) and *state* (the source and enforcer of law), and—in its more democratic variants—that the government of a nation-state should function according to the consent of the governed. Many nation-states are bloodied in crises over the legitimacy of the government—over whether the state does broadly represent the nation or nations in its jurisdiction—over appropriate means of obtaining the consent of the governed, and over what in fact the governed have consented to. Often the belligerents in such civil wars seek and receive military help from foreign countries or nongovernmental groups outside their borders, sometimes in the form of direct foreign intervention in the fighting.

Understanding the pattern of political violence inside countries is pertinent to the study of the causes and prevention of war between countries for two reasons: First, as mentioned, domestic violence can precipitate military intervention across national boundaries (a subject to be explored further in later chapters). Second, the analysis of violence within countries can provide insight into the relationship between the way a society is organized and the prevalence of the use of force within it, as well as into the relative efficacy of deterrence or accommodation in dealing with threats to peace.[1] This analysis generates a good deal of the discussion in this chapter.

To be sure, there is a fundamental difference in structure between countries and world society: in most countries a central government operates under a mandate with the capability of enforcing the rules of society, whereas there is no central government to speak of for world society. Caution is therefore in order in transferring insights about the causes and prevention of violence from the national to the international realm. But, granting the perils of direct analogies, studies of the conditions of domestic peace and violence can provide useful clues to what will and will not be effective in preventing and controlling international war. They cast doubt on the "reformist" notion that the problem of war in world society could be largely solved by giving a central authority sufficient military power to enforce world law. But they also cast doubt on the "realist" premise that international peace is best maintained by military deterrence.

VIOLENCE BY THE GOVERNMENT

Governments are mandated to use their official monopoly, or near monopoly, of capabilities for violence in their jurisdictions to secure the safety and other values of the community. Sometimes this involves resorting to violence against other states; but often it involves using governmental force against domestic crime, disorder, civic violence, and insurrection. Governmental resort to force against the citizens of the country is most often called "police action," but is properly regarded as civil war or internal war when large numbers of nongovernmental forces continue to fight over a long period.

Governments may sometimes be the real initiators of civic

violence even when the first violent attack is by an antigovernment group. In such instances the government sets the stage for violence and is the immediate provocateur. Governments of relatively democratic societies may resort to this ploy when they believe that the official use of force against nongovernmental or antisocial groups is likely to gain more support if it can be shown to be in response to violence. More autocratic regimes that want to demonstrate their legitimacy, national or international, also find it useful.

In a study prepared for the Presidential Commission on the Causes and Prevention of Violence, appointed by President Johnson, the sociologist Charles Tilley offered these conclusions about civic violence in modern Europe:

> [T]he authorities have far greater control over the short-run extent and timing of collective violence . . . than their challengers do. . . . The authorities usually have the technological and organizational advantage in the effective use of force, which gives them a fairly great choice among the tactics of prevention, containment, and retaliation. . . .

> The authorities also have some choice of whether, and with how much muscle, to answer political challenges and illegal actions that are not intrinsically violent: banned assemblies, threats of vengeance, wildcat strikes. A large proportion of the European disturbances we have been surveying turned violent at exactly the moment when the authorities intervened to stop an illegal but nonviolent action. This is typical of violent strikes and demonstrations. Furthermore, the great bulk of killing and wounding in those same disturbances was done by troops or police rather than by insurgents or demonstrators. . . .

> All this means that over the short run the extent, location, and timing of collective violence depend heavily on the way the authorities and their agents handle the challenges offered them. Over a longer run, however, the kinds of challenges they face and the strength of those challenges depend rather little on their tactics of crowd control and a great deal on the way the entire political system apportions power and responds to grievances.[2]

The degree to which a particular state relies on using force to assure public order and adherence to the society's rules cannot be determined by statistics on civic violence. Some countries that may seem to be characterized by domestic peace, such as the Soviet Union, deal with any substantial individual or group deviation from the promulgated social norms by swift and overwhelming official coercion; others, including contemporary Britain and the United States, though constrained not to apply governmental force against citizens, exhibit a higher frequency of domestic violence, including more recorded incidents of resorting to force to re-establish order. Surely, however, this does not mean that the governments of the Soviet Union, China, and Chile treat their citizens less violently than do the governments of the United States, Britain, and Japan. In most cases they simply have convincingly threatened their citizenry with the prospect of swift punishment for deviant behavior.[3]

In addition, indoctrination, social ostracism, and other group-conformity pressures are used extensively in totalitarian countries; and the pervasiveness of such psychological instruments of control surely is one reason for the surface impression of law and order in these countries. The conformity resulting from indoctrination is reinforced by the awareness of citizens that the state will not hesitate to use force against them whenever the nonphysical means of control appear not to be succeeding. Indeed, some governments that rely heavily on psychological instruments of control make it a policy to periodically engage in the selective use of force to demonstrate the consequences of not abiding by officially sanctioned norms.

No governing regime will admit that it maintains itself in power primarily by controlling the instruments of coercion. Even autocracies and totalitarian dictatorships claim that their power is based on popularity with the general citizenry, and that they use force only against criminal elements and subversive minorities, especially those aided by the state's foreign enemies that want to overthrow the legitimate order.

Governments do always have justifications—credible at least to themselves and their loyal supporters—for resorting to force inside their own countries. (Usually they claim to have exhausted their nonviolent options.) Leading the list is the need to suppress illegal violence. Next is the need to counteract even nonviolent acts of subversion that could prevent the government from performing its essential functions or that could weaken the country's ability to resist its foreign enemies. Finally, there is the residual justification of the need to "uphold the law" when crowds will not obey official orders to disperse, when lawbreakers resist arrest, and so on.

It is not necessary to pronounce on the validity of justifications for governmental violence in particular cases to demonstrate that government per se cannot be relied on to eliminate the recourse to force in human society. The existence of government may not even reduce the role of violence in determining winners and losers in contests over resources and privilege, though it obviously affects who will be most able to use violence. This realization that there is no necessary correlation between domestic peace and the centralization of legitimate capabilities for violence has significant implications for the international realm, for it goes far to invalidate the notion that international anarchy is the principal cause of war, and that only by establishing a centralized world government can we achieve peace. Chapter 7 will further explore the inadequacy of this prescription.

One of the reasons governments are tempted to escalate domestic conflicts to a level of threatened or actual violence is the pervasive belief that in tests of strength the government will win. Its role is to act decisively and call out the troops. The demonstrators will disperse, and those that stay to resist can be swiftly overwhelmed.

But does experience validate the supposition that governmental resort to force usually succeeds? The answer depends in part on what is meant by the "success" of an action; but even allowing for subjectivity in evaluating outcomes, case studies of the use of force by governments to counter domestic political opposition do not support confidence in its efficacy. From their review of the historical record for the Presidential Commission on the Causes and Prevention of Violence, the directors of the Task Force on Historical and Comparative Perspectives draw these conclusions:

> Not surprisingly, the list of successful governmental uses of force against opponents is much longer than the list of dissident successes against government, because most governments have much greater capacities for force, provided they keep the loyalty of their generals and soldiers. . . .

> But the historical evidence also suggests that governmental violence only succeeds in the short run. . . .

Primary reliance on force has indeterminate outcomes at best. If popularly supported, public force will contain specific outbreaks of private violence, but is unlikely to prevent their recurrence. At worst, public force will so alienate a people that terrorist and revolutionary movements will arise to challenge and ultimately overthrow the regime.[4]

To better understand the conditions under which governments are more or less likely to use the powerful instruments of violence at their disposal in domestic conflict, we must look closely at the arrangement of satisfied and dissatisfied social forces in each country, as well as at the norms and institutions each society relies on to manage its inevitable intergroup conflicts. It can be expected that governments will rely more intensively on violent means of social control to the extent that the societies under their jurisdiction are infused with economic jealousies, resentments, ethnic rivalries, and alienation of the citizens from the legal institutions of governance. But, paradoxically, these are the characteristics of societies in which governmental resort to force is most likely to exacerbate the conditions prompting violence in the first place.

VIOLENCE AGAINST THE GOVERNMENT

World history is largely a record of rebellion and revolution. Major changes in societywide distributions of material goods, social privilege, or political power more often than not have been accompanied by violent movements against existing governments.

What can be distilled from the record, initially discouraging to those who hope to achieve both justice and peace, can help us define the conditions of war and peace among countries.

From the literature on domestic rebellion and revolution a number of general propositions can be gleaned about the basic conditions that predispose groups to engage in political violence against the government.[5] We can call these *preconditions*; and the situations that turn these preconditions into actual violence can be considered *precipitating conditions*. Not all of the conditions discussed here will be present in every outbreak of civil violence, but some combination of preconditions and precipitating conditions almost invariably is present in domestic conflicts that turn violent.

Precondition I: Relative deprivation perceived to be unjust. Groups are susceptible of being mobilized for revolutionary action against the established political regime to the extent that they perceive themselves to be unjustly deprived by the regime of valued amenities of life—amenities enjoyed by other groups.[6] The objective condition of having less than other groups is not the crucial determinant of intense resentment: a group must believe itself to be unjustly deprived, whether or not this belief conforms to the "reality" of presumably objective observers. Note that the determinant of revolution need not be the perception of having less than other groups. Some groups turn to violence when their favored status is diminished in relation to upwardly mobile groups, even though the upwardly mobile in no way threaten to surpass them. Some middle-class taxpayers' revolts, for example, have resulted from the sacrifice of income required to help finance marginal improvements in the lot of the very poor. To recapitulate, the most important variable is the group's perception of justice or injustice in the social distribution of amenities. Groups wedded to the ideology of a market economy may therefore take their lumps without intense reaction when the distribution of amenities results from the interplay of market forces; but groups adhering to social justice doctrines of government-induced equalization may become violently antagonistic to upholders of the market economy when the economic system appears to them to have caused persisting or widening gaps between the rich and the poor.

Precondition II: Homogeneity of socioeconomic traits among the aggrieved. An aggrieved group is more likely to resort to violent means of pressing its demands when its members feel they have more in common with each other than with groups represented by the government. When those who consider themselves unjustly deprived as a result of government action or inaction belong not only to a particular economic class but also the same ethnic and religious group and, in addition, happen to live in a definable location within the larger jurisdiction, and when it appears to them that those governing the larger jurisdiction come for the most part from other economic, ethnic, and religious groups, the potential is high for intense intergroup alienation and antigovernmental violence.

Conversely, it is more difficult to mobilize group members for violent action against outsiders, either rival aggrieved groups or governing elites, with whom they share important cultural or class characteristics. The relationship between the bases on which social groups are organized and the potential for intergroup grievances to be expressed violently has been a theme of important works in political sociology and is often discussed in treatises on the essential characteristics of pluralist democracies.[7] The basic structural characteristics of a well-functioning, peaceable democratic society are posited by William Kornhauser:

> Where individuals belong to several groups, no one group is inclusive of its members' lives. Associations have members with a variety of social characteristics (e.g., class and ethnic identities) and group affiliations (e.g., trade unions may possess members who go to various churches). . . .
>
> Such extensive cross-cutting solidarities favor a high level of freedom and consensus; these solidarities help prevent one line of social cleavage from becoming dominant, and they constrain associations to respect the various affiliations of their members lest they alienate them.[8]

Respecting the "various affiliations of their members" makes it unlikely that members will be willing to take up arms against their brothers and sisters in other groups. This leads to the proposition that the more a society is infused with crosscutting group memberships, the less its intergroup conflicts will tend to polarize it and become violent—a highly suggestive explanation of the prevalence of interstate war in world society and an argument for devising structural reforms to reduce the role of war in international affairs. (See Chapters 4 and 10 for the development of these related ideas.)[9]

Precipitating condition I: Government nonreaction or negative reaction to legal and nonviolent pressures.   When groups that consider themselves unjustly deprived have their peacefully asserted demands for rectification repeatedly ignored or rebuffed, and especially when their defeats are processed through a political system they believe is stacked against them, their willingness to resort to violent pressure grows. The more undemocratic a political system is, the more it is prone to engender such violent inclinations in aggrieved groups—which are in turn likely to stimulate repressive policies by the fearful government.

But democratic systems also may develop this precipitating condition, since the full, legitimate working of the democratic process, based on a one-person, one-vote electoral system, can severely offend minorities. Even groups constituting numerical majorities in democratic systems sometimes conclude that the normal political process works against them, when more affluent minorities appear able to control governmental policy through expensive media advertising and other means of "buying" votes in decision-making bodies and electoral contests.

Precipitating condition II: Militant leadership. Even if all the preconditions for intense hostility toward the government in power are present, violence against the government may still be unlikely unless a militant leadership for the aggrieved group is also present to show that the situation requires violence and to organize action. Militant leadership, in fact, usually is needed even for the emergence of the preconditions, which mature only when they are defined and recognized as intolerable by a sufficient mass of the aggrieved group. This requires articulate and gifted leadership: Lenin to form an intellectual revolutionary "vanguard" of the Russian proletariat in 1917; Pierre Poujade in the late 1950s to mobilize elements of the French middle class (hard hit by the taxation system) into the Union for the Defense of Shopkeepers and Artisans; Yasir Arafat and the PLO to organize the West Bank Palestinians against the state of Israel after 1967.

Militant leaders similarly are essential to precipitating violent conflict between countries. States do not go to war automatically, even when such threatening and provocative preconditions materialize as an enemy invasion of a country's important alliance partner. Supposedly firm commitments of alliance must be invoked by leaders who define ongoing events as requiring the nation to place itself at total risk. The construction national leaders put on threatening events is crucial to the outbreak of war, as is the way they array and evaluate the country's options during crises.

LARGE-SCALE VIOLENCE NOT INITIALLY INVOLVING THE GOVERNMENT

Much of the intergroup violence within countries does not initially involve the government, as either a target or an employer of force, though in modern societies the government almost inevitably eventually becomes involved to maintain law and order. In the social science literature, such violence variously comes under the headings of "primitive," "communal," or "primordial"—suggesting that highly emotional kinship and tribal bonds are at work.[10] Some of this type of violence, however, may be between economic classes or occupational groups and have nothing to do with racial or religious rivalries. (Of course, when ethnic or religious divisions do coincide with economic divisions, the conflicts are likely to be more intense.)

The distinguishing characteristic of this kind of intergroup violence is that the warring groups believe themselves to be operating in a largely anarchic arena for determining winners and losers: no overarching norms determine who is right and wrong, no legitimate and effective superordinate institutions or processes resolve the territorial claims, allocate the material goods, or define the societal roles over which conflict has developed. When the belligerents are essentially on their own (though some may believe God to be on their side), it is their might that makes right.[11] The analogies with interstate conflicts are striking, and some scholars of international relations have made forays into the corpus of anthropological literature on the evolution of primitive societies for clues as to whether and how world society might evolve into a more orderly political system.[12]

Sometimes initially anarchic violence is conducive to the creation of new overarching social norms and institutions; indeed, such institutional development may be the objective of the perpetrators of the violence. An outstanding example is modern labor-management legislation, including state-adjudicated and enforced collective bargaining in "free market" societies, which evolved from the society-disrupting labor-management violence of the nineteenth and early twentieth centuries. Other examples of anarchic violence prefiguring the development of orderly governance occurred in pioneer societies on the geographic frontiers of established communities and in remote colonies where vigilantes took law and order into their own hands to establish civic peace and stability in newly settled areas.[13] In some respects violent strikes are analogous to international acts of terrorism: they disrupt the normal functioning of civil society to compel the established powers to intervene and establish what the strikers consider justice on their behalf. Frontier vigilantism provides a partial analogy to the attempts of great powers to act as "world policemen" to enforce "international law" in their spheres of influence.

TERRORISM AS A SPECIAL KIND
OF POLITICAL VIOLENCE

All the political violence so far considered can involve terrorism—in the sense that acts of violence or threats of violence can be taken against individuals or groups who are not themselves in direct violent opposition to those acting violently. Official armed forces can engage in terrorism—in attacks against noncombatants—domestically or internationally. Insurgent or revolutionary groups engage in terrorism when they attack or threaten to attack unarmed government officials or supporters of the government. And communal antagonists become terrorists when they violently disrupt the civic life in their rivals' places of commerce, culture, or religion.

In recent years particular forms of terrorism have received the most media attention—namely, taking civilian hostages who have nothing directly to do with the terrorists' grievances and threatening to do them harm unless the enemies of the terrorists accede to their demands; and clandestine kill-and-run attacks on individuals associated with those the terrorists blame for their plight.

Some degree of terrorism in one form or another has always been an element of acts of political violence. Today, however, it may indeed be increasing because of the widespread accessibility to terrorist attack of those who might be able to influence government policies. Representatives and ordinary constituents of governments travel a lot, using highly exposed transportation systems—tempting hijackings, airport bombings, and the like. When those threatened are constituents of advanced democratic systems, fears of citizens and governments that they may not be able to conduct their normal everyday activities can be exploited by the terrorists to force concessions to their demands.[14]

INTERSTATE WAR AS A SPECIES
OF HUMAN VIOLENCE

The brief exploration in this and the preceding chapter of the general phenomenon of violence, especially political violence, is based on the logic, in accord with historical evidence, that interstate war has much in common with domestic violence.

Traditional international-relations theory holds that domestic violence is fundamentally different from war among states because domestic societies have centralized systems of governance, whereas the interstate system is essentially anarchic. But the traditional approach exaggerates this difference; it describes only a subset of the historical record of political conflict and focuses on a very narrow dimension of the dynamics of violence.

In the most explosive domestic situations, those that have turned into revolutions and civil wars, there has been no clearly definable single locus of authority and power. Tests of strength between groups that were, in effect, sovereign to themselves were the very essence of the struggle. And the fact that in domestic war, in contrast to interstate war, the victors are expected to establish or re-establish an authoritative central government can also be made too much of, considering that international victors may well set up imperial systems of dominance over defeated rivals. There are, in short, potentially useful insights to be gleaned about the causes of war—and how it can be prevented and controlled—from exploring the common dynamics, in both domestic and international domains, of intergroup conflict—the effects of balances of lethal capabilities among warring groups, the effects of varying group structures, and the role of the psychologies, ideologies, and grand strategies of group leaders.

NOTES

1. For an excellent general analysis of political violence see H. L. Nieburg, *Political Violence: The Behavioral Process* (New York: St. Martin's, 1969).

2. Charles Tilley, "Collective Violence in European Perspective," in Hugh Davis Graham and Ted Robert Gurr, eds., *Violence in America: Historical and Comparative Perspectives* (New York: Signet, 1969), pp. 39–40.

3. Tilley reports that in modern France under the most repressive regimes (Louis Napoleon's in the 1850s and the Vichy government in the 1940s, following the Nazi occupation), there was almost no open large-scale violence. The same pattern holds true for Spain, Germany, and Italy. "In the heydays of the . . . Fascists, virtually the only violence to occur was at the hands of Government employees." *Violence in America*, pp. 28, 39.

4. Conclusion by the editors (Hugh David Graham and Ted Robert Gurr) to the Report of the Task Force on Historical and Comparative Perspectives on Violence in America, *Violence in America*, pp. 784–789.

5. In addition to works cited as specific references in this section, efforts by social scientists to develop a general understanding of revolution, rebellion, and civil war are well represented by Harry Eckstein, *Internal War: Problems and Approaches* (New York: Free Press, 1964); Chalmers Johnson, *Revolutionary Change* (Boston: Little, Brown, 1966); Jacques Ellul, *Autopsy of Revolution* (New York: Knopf, 1971); Mark N. Hagopian, *The Phenomenon of Revolution* (New York: Dodd, Mead, 1974); Lewis A. Coser, *Continuities in the Study of Social Conflict* (New York: Free Press, 1967), especially Chapters 3–5; and James C. Davies, "Toward a Theory of Revolution," *American Sociological Review*, XXVII (February 1962), 5–19.

6. This emphasis on perceived unjust deprivation is a variant of the relative deprivation hypothesis as formulated by Ted Robert Gurr, in *Why Men Rebel* (Princeton, N.J.: Princeton University Press, 1970). It also incorporates some of the refinements and elaborations introduced by Samuel P. Huntington in his "Civil Violence and the Process of Development," *Adelphi Papers*, No. 83 (London: International Institute for Strategic Studies), Dec. 1971, 1–15.

7. See Lewis A. Coser, *The Functions of Social Conflict* (New York: Free Press, 1956); Seymour Martin Lipset, *Political Man: The Social Bases of Politics* (Garden City, N.Y.: Doubleday-Anchor, 1963); Ralf Dahrendorf, "Toward a Theory of Social Conflict," *Journal of Conflict Resolution*, II (June 1958), 170–183; and the works cited in notes 8, 9, 10, and 12, below.

8. William Kornhauser, *The Politics of Mass Society* (Glencoe, Ill.: Free Press, 1959), pp. 80–81. Kornhauser draws particularly on an important earlier work by the German sociologist Georg Simmel, *Conflict and the Web of Group Affiliations* (translated by Kurt H. Wolff and republished by Free Press, 1955).

9. The important role of crosscutting group memberships is also pointed to by the social psychologist Morton Deutsch, who observes that

in a cross-cutting social structure, members of the conflicting ethnic groups are likely to be members of common work groups, common neighborhood groups, and so on. Their common memberships will make it difficult to polarize individual attitudes about ethnic conflict. Doing so would place the individual in the dilemma of choosing between loyalty to this ethnic group and loyalty to other groups that cut across ethnic lines. Thus cross-cutting memberships and loyalties tend to function as a moderating influence in resolving any particular intergroup conflict within a society. (*The Resolution of Conflict: Constructive and Destructive Processes* [New Haven, Conn.: Yale University Press, 1973], pp. 83–84, 99–100.)

Anthropological studies that confirm this insight are presented in R. A. Levine and D. T. Campbell, *Ethnocentrism: Theories of Conflict, Ethnic Attitudes, and Group Behavior* (New York: Wiley, 1972).

10. Samuel P. Huntington, *Political Order in Changing Societies* (New Haven, Conn.: Yale University Press, 1968); and Charles Tilley, *From Mobilization to Revolution* (Reading, Pa.: Addison-Wesley, 1978).

11. For analysis of the dynamics of such communal violence, see Tilley, "Collective Violence in European Perspective," in *Violence in America*, pp. 13–15; for data on the post–World War II period, see Fred R. Von Der Mehden, *Comparative Political Violence* (Englewood Cliffs, N.J.: Prentice-Hall, 1973).

12. See Roger Masters, "World Politics as a Primitive Political System," *World Politics*, XVI (July 1964), 595–619.

13. See the following essays in *Violence in America*: Ben C. Roberts, "On the Origins and Resolution of English Working-Class Protest," pp. 238–269; Philip Taft and Philip Ross, "American Labor Violence: Its Causes, Characteristics, and Outcome," pp. 270–376; Richard Maxwell Brown, "The American Vigilante Tradition," pp. 144–218.

14. The growing scholarship on contemporary terrorism is well represented in Michael Stohl, ed., *The Politics of Terrorism* (New York: Marcel Dekker, 1983) and Yonah Alexander, David Carlton, and Paul Wilkinson, eds., *Terrorism: Theory and Practice* (Boulder, Colo.: Westview, 1979). On the special vulnerabilities of democracies to terrorist attacks, see Paul Wilkinson, *Terrorism and the Liberal State* (New York: New York University Press, 1986).

CHAPTER 3

War and Reasons of State

Countries usually convince themselves that their wars are fought for "reasons of state"—to secure or advance important national interests. Even though war is considered "normal" in international relations, in the sense of being an available option, it is generally recognized to be an extreme action that in most countries requires both practical and moral justification.

When fought by industrialized nation-states, war risks involvement of the whole population: not only as provisioners of the massive war machines but also as targets of attack. Consequently, for most economically developed countries the national interests that justify going to war almost invariably are presented by the advocates of war as interests of the whole nation, not merely as the special interests of a segment of the society. Conversely, opponents of going to war usually insist that the prowar party has not demonstrated that vital national interests really are at stake. If a particular war risks confrontation with an enemy armed with nuclear weapons or with other weapons of mass destruction, the burden on the prowar groups is all the heavier to show both that the alternative to war is an inevitable loss of vital national interests and that the war can be fought to a successful conclusion without subjecting the country to massive destruction or terrible economic dislocation.

What are the presumably vital interests that nations are likely to invoke to justify going to war?

Some are physical, tangible interests, such as territory and economic assets that supposedly need to be defended or acquired for the nation to sustain itself in an acceptable material or economic condition.

Some are ideational interests, such as a religion, an ethnic-linguistic culture, or a particular kind of political system, without which life itself is believed to have drastically diminished value.

Other interests that may be deemed worth a war are derived, by strategic reasoning or psychologically, from the basic material and ideational interests of a nation-state. Foreign military interventions on behalf of allies and friends often are justified by such strategic or psychological extensions of basic national interests.

When modern countries enter into major wars, especially wars likely to require protracted fighting beyond their home territory as part of an international coalition, all or most of these kinds of national interests nearly always are asserted to be in jeopardy.

MATERIAL INTERESTS

Once constituted as an independent nation-state, a country tends to act like a biological organism in response to attacks. No part of the country's territory can be violated (intruded upon without permission, invaded, physically struck) without the country's treating the action as an attack on the whole. It does not matter that the violated part may be of little strategic or economic value, or that no one lives there; the fact that it is organically a part of the nation is normally sufficient to evoke a violent response. The "territorial integrity" of a country is, by definition and a priori, a vital national interest.

Still, though violations of a country's territorial integrity are universally regarded as acts of war, aggressors can sometimes get away with such violations without having to engage their victims in combat. This can occur when the violated country knows it will be beaten badly if it puts up a fight, as when Hitler invaded Czechoslovakia's Sudetenland in 1938 "without firing a shot" because, despite the good training and fortifications of the Czech military, President Beneš knew that his country could not stand up to Hitler's *Wehrmacht* unless Czechoslovakia's Western friends were willing to come to its assistance—which, as they had made clear in their appeasement of the dictator at Munich, they were not.[1]

It is also true that, although countries claim a vital interest in protecting their citizens and material assets from harm even when these are located outside the national territorial jurisdiction, attacks on extraterritorial deployments do not necessarily provoke a violent response. Whether or not an attack against extraterritorial assets is defined as an act of war in any particular case depends on many considerations, not the least of which is the calculation of a country's ability to defend its assets or to retaliate for an attack without great cost or risk—in contrast to the claim that no cost is too great to pay to defend the nation's territorial integrity. Another consideration is how central the extraterritorial assets are to other important interests. Are they a dispensable luxury? Of high political value as symbols of one's international power? Essential components of global military capability, like the U.S. fleet docked at Pearl Harbor in December 1941? Or are they important but marginal assets, like the military communications facility at Kagnew, Ethiopia, that the United States did not value sufficiently to justify any kind of military action to prevent the change of regime that took Ethiopia into the Soviet camp in the 1970s?

Traditionally, countries have regarded their ships at sea (navies or major commercial vessels owned by their nationals) as if they were organic extensions of the nation; but, again, the translation of this sentiment into a definition of an attack on the ships as an act of war is likelier for the maritime powers than for countries with relatively small navies. The norms with respect to aircraft are a bit fuzzier, in large part because of the ease with which aircraft can violate sovereign airspace, and also because of the right governments claim—and exercise rather often—of shooting at trespassing planes. The norms for orbiting space satellites, though not yet fully elaborated, can be deduced from the proposition, iterated in numerous United Nations resolutions, that all of outer space is an international realm, like the high seas: surely, another country's direct attack on a nation's orbiting spacecraft must be regarded as an act of war.

Apart from territorial integrity, the national interest of highest priority for most countries is maintaining military capability, their own or in combination with reliable allies, sufficient to deter attacks on their territory and other interests and to successfully defend these when attackers are not deterred. Countries, accordingly, may decide to resort to war simply to avoid a disadvantageous balance of military capability when they perceive war to be the most feasible way of maintaining the balance they believe they need. This potential cause of war is the subject of Chapter 6.

An additional national interest often thought worth a war to advance or sustain is the basic economic well-being of the country. During the centuries of great-power imperial expansion, this motive was as important as any other in initiating major wars, many of which started in remote overseas areas as empire builders got in each other's way. The U.S.-Japanese war of 1941–1945 had its origins in Japan's burst of imperialist effort in Asia to establish what the Japanese called their "co-prosperity" sphere; and the Japanese attack on Pearl Harbor was precipitated by the U.S. government's decision, in reaction to Japan's invasion of Indochina, to freeze Japanese economic assets held by American financial institutions while embargoing the shipment of oil to Japan.

In the post–World War II period, with the breakup and delegitimation of colonial empires, economic aggrandizement has become a less obvious motive for war, but countries still claim the right to go to war "defensively" to prevent others from hobbling their economies. Secretary of State Henry Kissinger, for example, would not rule out war against the oil-producing countries of the Middle East if their restrictions of supplies or pricing policies should threaten to produce a "strangulation of the industrialized world."[2]

IDEATIONAL/POLITICAL INTERESTS

Nearly as sacrosanct as the territorial integrity of a nation-state, and often closely bound up with it, is the country's claim to exercise of sovereign authority in running its own affairs, free of outside interference. Each country insists on making its own rules to regulate interpersonal relationships and the management of its society, and each further insists that other countries must respect its domestic jurisdiction.

An active policy by one country to subvert another's domestic regime—through material and organizational aid to groups that reject the legitimacy of the existing system of governance, especially groups attempting to disrupt the society's activities by general strikes or terrorism—can provoke a decision to initiate open warfare against the sponsor of the subversion. Austria's stated reason for going to war against Serbia in the summer of 1914, thus starting World War I, was not simply to retaliate for the assassination of the Archduke Francis Ferdinand by a Serbian terrorist but to prevent Serbia from further organizing national-separatist revolutionary movements among Serbs and other Slavic peoples within Austria-Hungary.[3]

The claim of national sovereignty is a two-sided sword in the international system. Though it cuts at foreign sponsors of "subnational" separatism and can be used to justify making war against them, the claim also cuts at a state that forcibly denies "self-determination" to the nationalities within its jurisdiction, and it can be used to justify making war against such a repressive state. If all nations have the right to be sovereign, then no government has the right to lord it over my nation: my nation will wage war, if need be, to establish its autonomy. Further, if my war for national independence is a just war, surely other countries have a right to intervene on my behalf to help ensure my success.[4] Such logic, invoked many times to justify foreign interventions in civil conflicts, was Napoleon Bonaparte's justification for his imperialistic wars to help "nations" in other countries obtain their "liberty" in the late eighteenth and early nineteenth centuries. In recent times, preventing Pakistan from putting down the Bangladesh independence movement was India's justification for going to war against Pakistan in 1971. Arab nations have attempted to justify their protracted warring against Israel by claiming the goal of statehood for the Palestinians. And a bloody war of "national liberation" could yet engulf southern Africa as countries neighboring the Republic of South Africa come to the assistance of the black majority in that country who are fighting for rights equal to those of the white minority.

Another ideational interest over which terrible wars have been fought is religion. Though religious conflict appears to be flaring up again during the last quarter of the twentieth century, governments are not nearly so inclined to fight religious wars as they were during the sixteenth century and the first half of the seventeenth century, when countries engaged in military action against each other to spread a particular religious faith or to protect members of a faith from persecution at the hands of a government of a different faith. In 1648 the Treaty of Westphalia ending the devastating Thirty Years' War between Catholics and Protestants in Europe established the principle that each country's religious regime—whether secular or theocratic—is its own business and not the concern of any other country.

Most governments since then have respected the Westphalian principle. Yet in the modern state system religious differences some-times still feed intense hostility among the peoples of countries in dispute over other issues, and religion often is an important part of the mix of motives that bring these countries to blows. Examples are conflicts between the mostly Muslim Turks and the mostly Eastern

Orthodox Greeks in Cyprus; between the mostly Hindu Indians and the Muslim Pakistanis over Kashmir; between the Jewish Israelis and the Muslim Arabs over the size and shape of the state of Israel; and between the Shiite Muslim Iranians and the Sunni Muslim Iraqis in their border war. But for the most part—the Iran-Iraq war is a significant exception—religious rivalry does not drive belligerents to attempt to impose a particular religious regime on their enemy.[5]

The contemporary functional equivalent of the wars of religion of past centuries has been the wars of ideology between countries professing adherence to some variant of Marxist state-run socialism and countries professing adherence to a "free" capitalist political economy. Often such wars of ideology start as indigenous revolutionary wars, caused by any number of the factors described in Chapter 2, with local participants who may or may not initially define their conflict as part of the global struggle between Marxists and capitalists. But if one or more of the local warring parties obtains help from either the Marxist superpower, the Soviet Union, or the capitalist superpower, the United States, the war becomes to many of its participants an expression of the universal ideological conflict.

This does not mean that all superpower interventions into civil wars that become parts of the global ideological conflict are motivated entirely, or even predominantly, by ideological as opposed to material or geostrategic considerations on the part of the superpowers' top decision makers. It means that whatever the "hard"-interest calculations determining involvement, the justifications offered by the responsible decision makers to gain public support for the war tend to emphasize ideational or "way of life" interests presumably at stake. And once the ideological definition of the conflict is invoked as an essential part of the official reason for a country's military involvement, ideology does become one of the motivating forces for waging the good fight.

The Truman Doctrine provides a clear example of the way ideology can create a strong incitement to war. In order to gain congressional and popular support for an emergency economic and military aid package for Greece and Turkey in 1947, President Truman defined the Soviet-American rivalry as a global struggle between freedom and communist totalitarianism. This definition of the situation made it highly likely thereafter that the United States would go to war anywhere in the world where it seemed that American military force was a feasible means of preventing communists from dominating a country. George Kennan, then head of the Policy Planning Staff of the State Department, argued in vain to get Truman to tone down his rhetoric, fearing that it would give nations around the world a blank check on American assistance, one they could cash by simply defining their internal opponents as communists. Kennan also worried that the doctrine's failure to make distinctions between geopolitically significant threats and lesser provocations would give rise to indiscriminate public pressures for military intervention where vital interests of the United States were not really in jeopardy.[6]

Kennan's apprehensions about allowing ideology to define American interests seem to have been borne out, as successive administrations—in order to "contain communism"—involved U.S. forces in combat, or came very close to doing so, without compelling national security or economic reasons.

Ideologically driven military moves show up in the Eisenhower administration's brink-of-war policies against China in the Formosa Straits in 1954 and 1958; in its covert military operation against the Arbenz regime in Guatemala in 1954; in its close-call decision of 1954 not to become militarily involved in Indochina on the side of the French; and in its deployment of U.S. marines to Lebanon in 1958.[7]

Examples of ideological determinism at work during the Kennedy-Johnson years include the Bay of Pigs invasion of Cuba by CIA-organized Cuban exiles in 1961, when sending in significant military forces of the United States was narrowly avoided by a courageous moment-of-truth decision by President Kennedy; President Johnson's dispatch of American marines to the Dominican Republic in 1965; and, most prominently and disastrously, the U.S. military intervention in Vietnam.[8]

American policy seemed to be turning away from an ideological anticommunist definition of vital interests during the Nixon-Ford administrations under the tutelage of Henry Kissinger's *realpolitik*, in which the containment of Soviet power, not necessarily of communism, was the principal objective. Obviously, global balance-of-power considerations and not ideology dictated the rapprochement with the People's Republic of China. And the first two years of Jimmy Carter's presidency included an attempt to move even further beyond cold war preoccupations.[9]

With the election of Ronald Reagan in 1980, however, the good-versus-bad definition of America's worldwide struggle with the

Soviet Union was revived. The president of the United States championed a renewed global "crusade for freedom" against Marxist-Leninists generally, publicly charging the Kremlin leaders with being liars, cheats, atheists, and the "focus of evil" in the world. Under this restored self-righteousness, the United States invaded Grenada—ostensibly to prevent a Marxist dictatorship from consolidating its power—openly aided an insurrectionary movement against the Marxist regime in Nicaragua, and prepared a range of contingency plans, not excluding the direct employment of U.S. military forces, to counteract an alleged Soviet grand design to establish a satellite empire in Central America.[10]

The Soviet Union's use of force beyond its borders surely has been affected by its ideological definition of the world struggle, but only partly so. Although the good life is defined according to Marxist-Leninist precepts, and ideological conformity is an essential instrument for Communist Party control over society in the Soviet Union and its Eastern European satellites, the Kremlin has not dispatched military forces into combat primarily for ideological reasons. Soviet troops and tanks have put down changes of regime in Eastern Europe that would have brought into power elements diverging significantly from the Kremlin's ideological line, as in Hungary in 1956 and Czechoslovakia in 1968; but the overwhelming consideration impelling Soviet military interventions has been geopolitical— the Kremlin's fear of losing control over the Soviet security belt in Eastern Europe.[11] And on the southern flank of the Soviet Union, it was primarily the fear of losing control over a strategically significant border region, not an ideologically prompted desire to communize another nation, that led the Soviets to invade Afghanistan in 1979.[12]

Ideological motives, in addition to military and economic self-interest, do seem to have been among the determining reasons for the Soviet Union's occasionally generous transfer of economic and military resources to particular countries and revolutionary movements in the Third World. From their vantage point in the world's most powerful Marxist country, the leaders of the Communist Party of the Soviet Union have felt compelled to give the "historical dialectic" (the economically determined, inevitable collapse of capitalism and victory of socialism) a push from time to time.

Ideology is part of the explanation of the Soviet Union's relations with Fidel Castro's Cuba, whose sugar the Soviets have purchased beyond their needs and whose economy they have had to bankroll.

An ally in Cuba does provide the Soviets with forward military and communications facilities in the American hemisphere, but these are not essential to the security of the Soviet Union. Moreover, providing military protection to Cuba has proved to be expensive and at times, as in the Cuban missile crisis, risky to the Soviet Union itself. Premier Nikita Khrushchev's deployment of the missiles in Cuba in 1962 was dictated by Soviet intercontinental strategic deficiencies, but these were rectified by the late 1960s. Thus the Kremlin's continuing support of Castro is motivated to some extent by the "softer" obligation felt in Moscow to help other Marxist regimes secure themselves against the principal capitalist enemy. Soviet support for Marxist Nicaragua is an even clearer case of ideology potentially putting the Soviets in harm's way. The considerable expense of playing Big Brother to the Sandinistas and the resulting risk of a direct confrontation with the United States do not seem warranted, given the fact that the Soviets already have a military outpost in Cuba, unless the ideological factor—the fraternal obligations among Marxist-Leninist parties—is heavily weighted. Similar considerations undoubtedly are part of the mix of motives behind the growing Soviet presence in Africa.

DERIVED INTERESTS

Many of the interests for which countries fight, or have said they are prepared to fight, do not appear to have the characteristics of either highly valued material assets or sacrosanct ways of life. Among the numerous cases in point are Germany's support of Austria's invasion of Serbia in 1914; the Soviet Union's threat to launch missiles at Britain, France, and Israel in 1956 if they did not pull their forces out of Egypt; the Kennedy administration's 1961 threat to use force to maintain access to the city of West Berlin; the American involvement in the Vietnam War from 1963 to 1973; and Britain's military action against Argentina in 1982 to regain possession of the Falkland Islands.

For such cases, the answer to the question, Is the immediately threatened interest worth a war?, would usually be no. But the question does not encompass all the calculations of national interest. The definition of the stake a country has in the outcome of any particular conflict is shaped in part by estimates of indirect effects of alternative outcomes—such as the future geopolitical situation of one's country (what the Soviets call the "correlation of forces") and the resulting attitudes of friends, enemies, neutrals, and domestic political forces.

Geopolitical Concepts

Decisions about whether a country can afford to lose any particular place on the globe to potential enemies or, conversely, whether it can afford to pass up an opportunity to gain access to or control of a place from which it has been excluded are affected profoundly by the geopolitical theories its decision makers carry around in their heads. These are notions—sometimes arrived at through systematic analysis, sometimes only intuitively developed impressions—about the significance of a country's geographic situation for its ability to fight wars successfully. Such geopolitical theories include an amalgam of assumptions about the current and future lineup of the country's probable allies and adversaries around the globe, assumptions derived from assessments of their material and ideational interests.

Each country responds to its unique geography by arriving at a unique set of geopolitical perceptions and preoccupations. Countries with long coastlines usually formulate very different defense and security requirements from those of landlocked countries. Countries separated from their neighbors by rugged mountain ranges are less likely to be intensely and continuously watchful of political developments across their borders than countries that share the same open plain.

The differing geographies of the United States and the Soviet Union, accordingly, might be expected to produce very different geopolitical imperatives in Washington and Moscow. Remarkably, however, the dominant geopolitical concepts shaping the grand strategies of the superpowers are quite similar, because both are largely mirror-images of the other's situation. This similarity in geopolitical concepts reflects more than the fact that the superpowers are locked in a nuclear balance of terror, and indeed it predates the emergence of mutual strategic deterrence.

Contemporary American geopolitical views, which have had a determining impact on national security policy from World War II to the present, are still strongly influenced by the classical Anglo-

American geopolitical theories developed at the turn of the century by Sir Halford Mackinder and Captain Alfred Thayer Mahan, as they were refined in the 1940s by Nicolas J. Spykman. This theoretical legacy infused the military containment and alliance-building policies with which the United States has confronted Soviet expansionary inclinations since 1947.

The classical geopolitical theories postulate a natural, or geographically determined, rivalry for great-power dominance of the vast rimland of the Eurasian landmass. The great powers largely dependent upon the sea, the "insular" powers, need secure dominions on the rimland, or at least spheres of influence, for naval bases, servicing facilities for their commercial fleets, lines of communication, and raw materials. And since the power or powers dominating the central expanse of Eurasia, the heartland, need, as a minimum, to secure access to the rimland and freedom of movement through it to assure their commerce with the rest of the world, they regard the insular powers' dominance of the rimland as a constricting encirclement. Moreover, in case of war, control of the rimland is crucial to both. For the insular powers, the rimland can be a staging ground for attacks into the heartland; for heartland powers, in addition to providing a necessary buffering area against such attacks, the rimland can provide a staging ground for disrupting strategic lines of communication and navigation between the insular powers and their allies. Consequently, the understandable efforts of the insular powers on the one hand and of the hegemonic heartland powers on the other to cultivate rimland allies and clients are regarded by each side as hostile acts threatening to its security, and perhaps even as a bid by the rivals to achieve global dominance.[13]

The Kremlin, looking at the world from a different geographic vantage point but through very similar geopolitical lenses, calls the rimland activities of the United States and its coalition partners—that is, their military provisioning and economic buildup of allies and clients—"capitalist encirclement." Soviet strategists justify their country's drive to counter these activities on the rimland and to achieve warm-water ports and servicing facilities for their expanding naval and commercial fleets by quotations from Mahan and Mackinder.[14]

In fact, the geopolitical concepts prevalent among strategists in both Washington and Moscow, combined with understanding that the other side is acting in accord with similar concepts, provide justification for the globally extensive definitions of vital interests that increase the potential for superpower clashes and confrontations virtually anywhere on earth.

Credibility, Honor, and
Other Psychological Preoccupations

Once a nation publicly articulates the material interests and social values it considers important at home and in the world, striking postures simultaneously to reassure friends and warn adversaries that it will fight for them militarily if necessary, it creates an additional "vital" interest—which is to have these promises and threats believed. It is possible that the value calculations that produced the national commitment initially may change to the extent that reassessment would indicate that a particular interest is no longer worth fighting for; but the original, now objectively obsolete commitment may still be adhered to, even if war results, because of the perceived need of the country to sustain a reputation for honoring its commitments. Similarly, circumstances may tempt an adversary to challenge vaguely formulated or very general commitments, only to be confronted with more belligerence than is warranted on a relatively minor issue.

The fashionable catchall term for the considerations that enter into such thinking and actions is *credibility*—maintaining the credibility of a nation's commitments or, more grandly, maintaining its own credibility.

The United States fought the first big war of the post–World War II period, the Korean War of 1950–1953, precisely because of a concern for the credibility of its new security commitments to the NATO countries and Japan rather than because of the military-strategic judgment that the possession of South Korea as well as North Korea by a Soviet ally would adversely change the balance of power in Asia. Indeed, the Joint Chiefs of Staff in 1947 had considered the Korean peninsula to be of minor strategic importance in another war and had advised against deployments and commitments that could lock the United States into defending South Korea. But President Truman and his top national security advisers defined the North Atlantic Treaty in particular as publicly and unequivocally "drawing the line" against further communist expansion after the Soviet takeover of Czechoslovakia in 1948. Although the line was not drawn that clearly in Asia—General Douglas MacArthur and Secretary of State Dean Acheson had publicly implied that Korea, legally under the jurisdiction of the United Nations, was outside the U.S. "defense perimeter"—the credibility of all U.S. commitments to resist military aggression by the communists was instantly seen to be at stake once the North moved against the South. For this reason, and no other, the United States went to war again in Asia, albeit under the United Nations' flag, after just five years of peace; the "police action" it undertook resulted in the deaths of over 34,000 American soldiers, more than 800,000 South Koreans, at least 500,000 North Koreans, and perhaps as many as 2,000,000 Chinese.

When President Dwight D. Eisenhower prepared the American public for a possible U.S. military intervention in Vietnam to save the French from defeat in 1954 by comparing Indochina to the first of a row of dominoes—one that could topple the whole row by being knocked over—he was concerned not with the strategic value of Indochina itself, which he was prepared to write off, but rather with how a failure to help the French in their hour of peril might embolden enemies of the United States and demoralize its friends.

Once again it was primarily the credibility factor, accorded the heightened emotional definition of national honor, that first prompted the direct entry of the United States into the Vietnam War in 1965 during the administration of Lyndon Johnson and then prevented the Nixon administration from finally terminating U.S. participation in the war until 1973—on what turned out, after all, to be "humiliating" terms: 50,000 young American men had lost their lives in the futile effort to prevent communist control. "The commitment of 500,000 Americans [troops deployed to Vietnam] has settled the issue of the importance of Vietnam," explained Henry Kissinger. "For what is involved is confidence in American promises. However fashionable it is to ridicule the terms 'credibility' or 'prestige,' they are not empty phrases; other nations can gear their actions to ours only if they can count on our steadiness."[15] For President Nixon, the worst fate to be avoided in Vietnam was "humiliation." His most aggressive moves, including the 1970 invasion of Cambodia that enlarged the war, were rationalized by this anxiety. "If and when the chips are down," said Nixon,

> the world's most powerful nation, the United States of
> America, acts like a pitiful, helpless giant, the forces of

totalitarianism and anarchy will threaten free nations and free institutions throughout the world. It is not our power but our will and character that is being tested.[16]

A similar invocation of national character and resolve, this time in the guise of an opportunity to revive lost glory, was operative in Prime Minister Margaret Thatcher's dispatch of the British Royal Navy to take back the Falkland Islands from Argentina, in response to General Galtieri's April 1982 occupation of the British-controlled islands off the Argentine coast.

A felt need to demonstrate an unsqueamish willingness to use force to defend the national honor can drive national leaders to relatively easy-win power plays against largely defenseless opponents. Such a compulsion appears to have been at work in the Ford-Kissinger dispatch of U.S. marines to rescue the crew of the freighter *Mayaguez* from communist Cambodia in May 1975: Accomplishing this act of bravado required overlooking the fact that the Cambodians had already decided to release the crew. A similar psychology appears to have been present in President Reagan's successful but probably unnecessary marine invasion of the tiny Caribbean island of Grenada in 1983. His stated justifications were, first, to prevent American medical students from being taken hostage by the island's new Marxist regime and, second, to depose a regime that, with Cuban and Soviet aid, was planning to subvert its neighbor governments. The timing was especially welcome in the White House, coming in the wake of the terrorist car-bombing attack on a U.S. marine barracks in Lebanon—for which the United States had been unable to find an effective reprisal. Grenada allowed the administration to give its frustrated constituents the catharsis they had been denied in Lebanon.

Pride, honor, and the desire for a national catharsis were also part of the compound of considerations that led President Reagan to order U.S. aircraft to attack terrorist headquarters in Tripoli, Libya, in April 1986, in reprisal for a terrorist attack on a West Berlin discotheque that killed an American serviceman and wounded more than fifty other Americans. The administration's principal publicly stated rationale for its air raid on Libya was deterrence—to dissuade Libyan dictator Muammar al-Qaddafi, who was alleged to have been behind the discotheque bombing, from instigating additional acts of terrorism. "We are successfully sending the message," said Secretary of State Shultz, "that terrorism is going to pay a cost." There was also the objective of undermining Qaddafi's support in the Arab world and among his own people. "If a coup takes place," said Shultz, "that's all to the good."[17] But, clearly, the reprisal raid was undertaken despite considerable uncertainty in the administration as to whether it would accomplish these objectives, or do just the opposite: stimulate Qaddafi to more extreme acts of violence and rally even moderate Arabs to his side.[18] There was an additional objective, however, that was attainable existentially through the action itself; and that was the feeling, expressed openly by citizens in media interviews and evident in the tone and demeanor of high officials of the administration, of at last doing something, after years of just "taking it," to get back at the terrorists.

This chapter has focused on the standard national justifications and pretexts for resorting to force. Virtually every country, at some point in time, is likely to find itself in one or another of the variety of international conflicts that can lead to military confrontation. Is it any wonder, then, given the paucity of authoritative and enforceable dispute-resolution processes in the international system, that wars have been fought so frequently?

But we can just as well turn the question around. Why aren't there more wars than there are? Why are there regional enclaves of peace and substantial periods of peace among countries with substantial conflicts of interest? Put differently, some countries seem to be in a chronic condition of war, or impending war, with each other; but others seem to manage their conflicts of interest—even intense ones—without coming to blows. What accounts for these differences? The following chapters attempt to answer this question.

NOTES

1. For a vivid description of Czechoslovakia's decision not to fight Hitler's invading armies, see Leonard Mosley, *On Borrowed Time: How World War II Began* (New York: Random House, 1969), pp. 75–88.

2. Interview with Secretary of State Henry Kissinger, *Business Week*, January 13, 1975.

3. Austria's reason for war was contained in her government's notorious 48-hour ultimatum to Serbia on July 23, 1914, in which the Austrian

government asserted its "duty of putting an end to the intrigues which form a perpetual menace to the Monarchy." Among the "intrigues" that Vienna demanded the Serbs stop immediately were: anti-Austrian publications, anti-Austrian instruction in Serbian public schools, and allowing the existence of anti-Austrian societies. See Laurence Lafore, *The Long Fuse: An Interpretation of the Origins of World War I* (New York: J. P. Lippincott, 1971), pp. 225–226 and John G. Stoessinger, *Why Nations Go to War* (New York: St. Martin's, 1985), Chapter 1.

4. Michael Walzer, *Just and Unjust Wars: A Moral Argument with Historical Illustrations* (New York: Basic Books, 1977).

5. In the Iran-Iraq war that began in 1980, the Iraqis initiated military hostilities to regain control of the Shatt-al-Arab waterway, taken over by Iran in a previous conflict. The Iranian government, a theocracy of fundamentalist Shiite Muslims, defined its purposes in the war to extend beyond the defense of its territory, including deposing the mostly Sunni regime of Saddam Hussein in Baghdad and installing a regime representative of the majority of Iraqis who are Shiite.

6. George F. Kennan, *Memoirs: 1925–1950* (Boston: Little, Brown, 1967), pp. 314–315, 319–320.

7. Seyom Brown, *The Faces of Power: Constancy and Change in United States Foreign Policy from Truman to Reagan* (New York: Columbia University Press, 1983), pp. 65–145.

8. *Ibid.*, pp. 149–307.

9. *Ibid.*, pp. 321–561.

10. For an analysis of the revival of an ideological foreign policy under Reagan, see Brown, pp. 567–628.

11. On the Soviet use of military force in Hungary in 1956, see Adam Ulam, *The Rivals: America and Russia Since World War II* (New York: Viking, 1971), pp. 262–266. On the 1968 intervention in Czechoslovakia, see Jiri Valenta, *Soviet Intervention in Czechoslovakia, 1968: Anatomy of a Decision* (Baltimore, Md.: Johns Hopkins University Press, 1979).

12. Raymond L. Garthoff, "Detente and Afghanistan," in Erik P. Hoffmann and Frederick J. Fleron, Jr., eds., *The Conduct of Soviet Foreign Policy* (New York: Aldine, 1980), pp. 756–761.

13. The Anglo-American geopolitical "classics" are Halford J. Mackinder, "The Geographical Pivot of History," *Geographical Journal*, 23 (1904), 421–441; Alfred T. Mahan, *The Problem of Asia and Its Effects upon International Relations* (Boston: Little, Brown, 1900); and Nicholas Spykman, *The Geography of the Peace* (New York: Harcourt Brace, 1944). For the incorporation of these classics into cold-war geopolitics, see Stephen B. Jones, "Global Strategic Views," *Geopolitical Review*, 45 (1955), 492–508.

14. For the influence of Anglo-American geopolitical views on Soviet

thinking, see Michael McGuire, ed., *Soviet Naval Developments: Capability and Context* (New York: Praeger, 1973).

15. Henry Kissinger, "The Vietnam Negotiations," *Foreign Affairs* (January 1969), 47(2):218–219.

16. Richard Nixon, radio-TV address to the nation, April 30, 1970, *Department of State Bulletin*, No. 1612 (May 18, 1970), 62:620.

17. Secretary of State George Shultz, Press Conference of April 17, 1986. Text of key portions in *New York Times*, April 18, 1986.

18. A revealing account of the uncertainties and disagreements within the administration surrounding the raid on Libya is provided by Bernard Gwertzman, "U.S. Officials Appear Uncertain on Further Raids to Fight Terror," *New York Times*, April 14, 1986.

PART II

The Determinants
of War

There has hardly been a moment in history when there has not been some international war or brink-of-war crisis somewhere in the world. The international system seems to be prone to violence. No country lacks a military establishment. Indeed, war appears to be a "normal" feature of world society.

Yet many countries do not go to war against each other when their important interests clash.

Some regions of the globe have a lower frequency of war than others.

Some periods in history have fewer wars than others.

Some wars are fought in highly constrained ways—localized and limited in their destructive intensity. Some even stop before either side has won.

What explains these variations?

Is it possible to distinguish conditions under which war cannot be avoided from conditions of peace?

Chapter 4 examines the impact of domestic, regional, and global political structures on the propensity of antagonistic countries to go to war or to prosecute their conflicts of interest peacefully.

Chapter 5 shows how diplomacy—particularly when the international bargaining relies heavily on coercive threats—can sometimes be part of the problem rather than part of the solution.

Chapter 6 analyzes the role of armaments in either deterring or provoking war. It examines the features of military balances between antagonists that can induce one side to launch the first or preemptive military blow.

The objective of the analysis in these chapters is to arrive at insights on the determinants of war that can be translated into strategies for its prevention and control, the subject of Part III.

A prince . . . should have no other aim or thought,
nor take up any other thing for his study,
but war and its organization and discipline. . . .
The chief cause of the loss of states
is the contempt of this art, and
the way to acquire them is to be
well versed in the same.
                              —Niccolo Machiavelli

Political power grows out of the barrel of a gun. . . .
As advocates of the abolition of war,
we do not desire war;
but war can only be abolished through war—
in order to get rid of the gun,
we must first grasp it in hand.
                              —Mao Tse-tung

Modern history offers no example
of the cultivation by rival powers
of armed force on a huge scale
that did not in the end lead to an outbreak of hostilities.
And there is no reason to believe
that we are greater, or wiser, than our ancestors.
                              —George F. Kennan

CHAPTER 4

Structural Factors

The conflicts of interest over which countries are willing to fight usually are symptoms of underlying political and socioeconomic relationships. Who goes to war against whom cannot be understood apart from the basic affinities and antagonisms among national, ethnic, religious, and ideological groups. Frequently the antagonisms that lead to war are rooted in, or at least reinforced by, economic rivalries or hegemony/dependence relationships that some countries find intolerable. Internationally, these various conflicts are prosecuted through a virtually anarchic interstate system that often is itself one of the determinants of war. These foundational, or structural, conditions need to be taken into account and perhaps transformed in any serious strategy for reducing the role of war in world society.

Questions about the structural causes of war can be posed on three levels: Is the popular notion valid that certain kinds of domestic political and economic systems are more likely to initiate war than others? Are some basic configurations in international relations more conducive to war than others? Or is the structure of the interstate system as a whole so war prone that nothing short of its replacement by an entirely different kind of world polity can have a substantial effect on the inclination of nations to settle their disputes by force?

DOMESTIC STRUCTURE

Advocates of particular forms of socioeconomic and political organization often see warlike tendencies in countries with the "wrong" structure. Marxists find capitalist countries inherently imperialistic. Capitalists believe that communist states, because of their

59

ideology of class conflict and their inability to generate adequate economic growth, are structured to subvert and engage in violent aggression against the noncommunist world. Democrats see autocratic states as the least inhibited from going to war, and autocrats regard democracies as driven by fickle popular passions that undermine the prospects for coolheaded diplomatic bargaining.

It is easy to dismiss such gross judgments about which systems are most warlike as not proven or simply unprovable.[1] But if we move beyond the ideological debates over who is most warlike, there are useful insights to be gained into the determinants of war and the conditions of peace by examining the ways particular kinds of domestic polities operate in the international threat-bargaining system.

Many countries today do tend to view others as basically friendly or hostile depending on their location along the socialist-capitalist spectrum. These ideological definitions of who's on whose side often manifest themselves in military commitments and interventions, sometimes violent, to prevent defections of allies or neutrals to the adversary's camp or to engender favorable changes in the international balance of power.

The fact that the leadership group governing the Soviet Union claims to be Marxist-Leninist profoundly affects the international behavior of the Soviets and the reaction of other countries to their behavior. Two elements, especially, in the belief system of the Soviet ruling group are crucial for international relations: (1) the Marxist historical prophecy that socialism, eventually communism, must supersede capitalism as the next stage in the development of human society, and (2) the Leninist premise that capitalists will initiate wars to arrest the world's progress toward socialism unless socialists, under the leadership of the Soviet Union, are sufficiently armed and ready to fight to prevent counterrevolutionary aggression.

To the extent that the leaders of the Soviet Union and of regimes and movements in other countries adhere to these tenets of Marxism-Leninism, they will attempt to form interstate and transnational alliances with Marxist-Leninists wherever they can be found. Members of such international coalitions intervene on the side of the "progressive" forces in "wars of national liberation" (for example, in Angola in the mid-1970s), and in civil wars deemed to express the global class conflict between capitalists and workers (El Salvador in the 1980s); sometimes they take sides in a civil or international conflict with no intrinsic ideological content simply to weaken the capitalist camp (as in the continuing conflict between Ethiopia and Somalia over the Ogaden).

Accordingly, the Soviet-led coalition has looked aggressive and expansionist to countries in the capitalist camp. Led by the United States, the capitalists have constructed anticommunist alliances on every continent and have engaged in counter or preemptive intervention to contain Soviet expansion. This anticommunist coalition-building, from the Soviet perspective, validates the Marxist-Leninist prediction of a worldwide capitalist conspiracy to smash the socialists.

The simple fact of having either a Marxist-socialist or a capitalist domestic structure is not always decisive as a determinant of international military alignment, though it does dispose a country to treat members of the rival ideological group as potential if not immediate enemies—and therefore to arm and to frequently resort to coercive diplomacy against them. Communist China's antagonism toward the Soviet Union and, after 1972, its increasing alignment with the United States, illustrate the operation of factors other than domestic structure and ideology on the determination of international enmities and friendships. Yet where the Soviet Union, against which the Chinese have special and intense grievances, has not already preempted the role of coalition leader, China more often than not comes forward as a leader of the anticapitalist forces. Indeed, part of China's rivalry with the Soviet Union is over which of them can most ably lead the Marxist-socialist camp in the Third World.

Marxists point to the military arsenals of capitalist countries and the instances of their resorting to war as "evidence" that capitalist political economies need war in order to function. According to Marxist theory, the domestic contradictions of capitalism inevitably produce rivalries for foreign markets that can become so intense as to generate "imperialist wars" among the capitalist states.[2] Twentieth-century Marxists also claim that capitalist regimes use armament buildups artificially to stimulate their economies when they appear to be heading for depression—and that the capitalists then provoke international crises and wars to justify the buildups.[3]

No valid empirical evidence sustains these Marxist theories. Although lobbying in favor of particular arms programs by corporations and labor unions that benefit from weapons contracts is widespread within the capitalist world, there is always counterlobbying by corporations and interest groups in competition for budgetary out-lays. The largest corporations are multiproduct firms, often heavily involved in international trade and investment and usually opposed to the disruption of normal domestic and international commerce that accompany intense international crises and war. In recent years the most vocal and potent American lobbies for détente with the Soviet Union and unpoliticized commerce with the communist countries have been the National Association of Manufacturers and the U.S. Chamber of Commerce.

To be sure, some of the fluctuations between periods of bitter U.S.-Soviet tensions and periods of détente have reflected changes in domestic conditions and leadership styles in the two countries, but since the end of World War II neither has undergone a fundamental change in political-economic structure. We also find that countries have sometimes gone to war after long periods of peace or nonviolent conflict between them—the Japanese-American war of 1941–1945 is a case in point—when the shift to belligerency bears no discernible relation to basic domestic structural change.

INTERNATIONAL STRUCTURE

Part of the explanation of the degree of belligerence between countries must be sought in the structure of their external relations, or more generally in the system of international relationships within which they interact. Four structural dimensions of relations among countries appear to be influential in determining whether conflict among them can be kept on a nonviolent plane or is likely to express itself in war—and then, if war does break out, what its intensity and scope will be. These interrelated structural variables are (1) the *balance of power*, (2) the *pattern of interdependence*, (3) the *alliance structure*, and (4) the cumulative expression of these three elements in the international *pattern of polarization*.

The "Balance of Power"

Quotation marks appear around *balance of power* to indicate the special meaning given here to an otherwise ambiguous concept. As used here, this term refers to the relative capabilities countries have for coercing one another. Balances of power may be global or local, and their components will vary with different issues. When we examine the role of military balances of power as a determinant of war in the discussion of armaments in Chapter 6, we shall see that military components usually constitute the heaviest weights in a coercive balance. But the balance of power also includes nonmilitary pressures that countries in conflict can bring to bear on each other.

The components of a particular balance may be almost entirely economic, as in the balance of power between Japan and her oil suppliers in the Middle East. In such cases, the balance of power is virtually indistinguishable from the pattern of interdependence.

Weights in the scales of the balance sometimes may be in the form of votes in international forums. This kind of power is often important to countries that are relatively weak militarily or economically. For example, the developing countries in the United Nations Law of the Sea Conference from 1974 to 1982 were able to withhold approval of certain provisions of a treaty desired by the advanced maritime countries—especially navigational rights through international water-ways—until the maritime powers acquiesced in provisions desired by the developing countries for a UN authority to manage the mining of deep-sea minerals.

When there are economic and political goods and privileges that the parties can provide or withhold from each other in a given negotiation or conflict, these assets constitute the balance of power for the issue at hand, and altercations over the issue have a good chance of being resolved without the invocation of the military balance between the participants.

However, if the overall balance of power between the countries in an altercation is lopsided in favor of one of them when the nonmilitary weights are counted, but lopsided in favor of the other when the military balance is calculated, the militarily superior country will be tempted to invoke the military balance to compensate for its nonmilitary inferiority. Thus in bargaining over oil supply issues and the Arab-Israeli conflict, threats by the Arab oil producers to embargo oil shipments to the United States and some of its NATO partners typically produce counterthreats, often in the form of public speculation by Western military experts about appropriate action to secure the oil supplies.

Generally, countries engaged in a rich range of transactions across a number of issue areas can invoke many bargaining counters—opportunities to withhold or proffer items of value to each other, that is—without resorting to military threats. The converse also generally holds: countries not normally engaged in substantial nonviolent interaction with one another may jump quickly to the military balance as the only balance of power relevant when conflicts arise.

It follows that in both of the cold war camps the proponents of "détente" (a relaxation of tensions, and peaceful coexistence) usually also are champions of expanding East-West commerce, scientific and technological cooperation, and institutional mechanisms for consultation and bargaining on such political issues as the Arab-Israeli conflict, and even the sensitive issue of human rights. Their assumption is that the more nonmilitary pressure points there are between countries, the less likely it is that conflict between them will escalate to the level of military confrontation. The opponents of détente also recognize the buffering effects that may be produced by expanding the opportunities for peaceful intercourse, but they assess the overall implications differently. Suspecting the rival camp of using East-West transactions to subvert their side's militancy in resisting the rival's expansion of power, those who oppose détente are generally opposed to enlarging opportunities for East-West interaction. They are more comfortable with continued primary reliance on the military balance of power to deter aggressive moves by the other side. At issue is whether a more elaborate structure of interdependence is likely to weaken or strengthen a country's bargaining power in conflicts with major opponents.

The Pattern of Interdependence

Interdependent relationships clearly are not necessarily peaceful. The nature of the dependencies and the context of the overall relationships among the parties will determine whether interdependence is likely to produce conflict and violence or cooperation and peace. Indeed, the presence of crucial dependencies—in which one country is highly dependent on others for military security or for its basic economic well-being—can also provide opportunities for intolerable provocations that seem to be "worth a war" to terminate.

Energy-dependent relationships, because they often involve exchanges crucial to the security and well-being of the energy consumers, are tempting for the suppliers to use as a trump card in tough bargaining, but for this very reason are dangerous to use in this way.

In the 1970s, threats by petroleum-producing countries of the Persian Gulf to embargo shipments to particular consuming countries provoked counterthreats of military intervention. In 1941, the American denial, along with the Dutch, of the petroleum imports Japan required to fuel its industries and its navy convinced the Japanese government that it would have to go to war against the United States.

Navigation-route dependencies also provide tempting opportunities for highly provocative power plays. Thus when Egyptian President Gamal Abdel Nasser announced in 1956 that he would prohibit Israel's ships from using the Suez Canal and other waterways essential to Israeli commerce with East Africa and Asia, the Israelis colluded with the British and the French to invade Egypt to restore international control over the canal.

Superpowers are often dependent on the cooperation of lesser powers, and sometimes will act brutally to assure themselves of such cooperation. Since World War II the Kremlin has been convinced that the security of the Soviet Union depends on the existence of a protective belt of loyal allies between Germany and the western borders of the USSR. Accordingly, the Soviet leaders found the impending shift toward neutralism by Hungary in 1956 and by Czechoslovakia in 1968 so intolerable that they intervened with Red Army tanks and troops to discipline these nations and keep them in line; and in the early 1980s the Soviets threatened a military invasion of Poland to counteract the nationalist challenge of the Solidarity movement to the authority of the ruling Polish Communist Party.

In short, it is often the fact of mutual dependency that can turn even presumably close friends into mortal enemies. If a pattern of heavy cooperation between countries fails to produce what either or both had been led to expect would be the result, there may be greater bitterness and much less room for compromise than in disputes among countries whose interactions have concerned only secondary or peripheral interests. Where there are the highest incentives to cooperate, because vital interests are involved, noncooperation becomes all the more intolerable and the sanction of war looms, implicitly or explicitly, in the background.

Alliances

A prominent structural feature of international relations is the pattern of alliances. Usually formed against a common opponent or set of opponents, alliances typically involve mutual pledges of military help in case one or more of the members is attacked. An important determinant of who is likely to fight whom—when, where, and how—alliances themselves reflect balance-of-power needs and material dependency relationships. They also can reflect ideological or cultural affinities and enmities, sometimes even those that contradict material needs. On the basis of the historical record, whether alliances tend more often to cause or to deter wars remains an open question.[4]

Sometimes alliances deter war by presenting a would-be aggressor with an adverse balance of power. But, on the other hand, when they increase the aggressor's power, they can make the outbreak of war likelier. Sometimes merely the formation of an alliance is regarded as a serious provocation by the country or countries it is targeted against—stimulating them to threaten one or another of the member countries to "test" and possibly break the alliance by exposing the fact that the commitment of some members is not firm or credible.

The range of possible responses to alliances and our inability to specify the effect they generally have on the tendency of countries to resort to war does not mean that alliances play a trivial determinative role. The existence of an alliance always importantly shapes the calculations of potential war outcomes, costs, and risks. By affecting the amount of armed forces available, the existence, membership, and terms of any alliance help determine the deterrent or provocative effects of coercive threats, including the decision to go to war, and they contribute importantly to the dimensions of wars that are fought.

The important role played by alliances and the fact that the role varies greatly in differing international circumstances is starkly revealed in the diplomatic maneuvering that preceded both World War I and World War II.

The decade leading up to World War I began in 1904 with the negotiation of an *entente cordiale* between Britain and France.[5] Explicitly defined as an agreement to bury their rivalry and facilitate their cooperation, the entente was implicitly a combination against the new imperialistic thrust of Kaiser Wilhelm's Germany. The two countries preemptively excluded Germany from the competition for colonies in northern Africa by dividing the region into two spheres of influence, France endorsing the British occupation of Egypt and Britain recognizing French dominance in Morocco. They further agreed to support one another should other countries oppose their assigned spheres of influence.

Incensed, the Germans decided to test the *entente cordiale*, believing that the British would not really support France if it meant having to go to war on behalf of their former rival. In March 1905— while the French were still in the process of consolidating their control over Morocco—the Kaiser ostentatiously sailed into Tangier harbor on a German warship and made a fiery speech demanding Moroccan independence and, calculating that the British would accept a diplomatic formulation to provide them a legitimate escape from their commitment to France, called for an international conference to deal with the issue. But at the ensuing Algeciras Conference, the assembled great powers, including the United States, supported the French position; Austria alone sided with Germany. Not only was Germany rebuffed, but in response to Kaiser Wilhelm's Moroccan power play, Britain and France began talks to transform their entente into a military alliance.

France also redoubled her efforts to build a broad international coalition against Germany, hoping in particular to effect a reconciliation between England and Russia, who were rivals for influence in the disintegrating Ottoman Empire. Having been humiliated by Japan in the Russo-Japanese war and now fearing Austrian and German collusion to reduce Russian influence in the Balkans, Russia was ready to be relieved of the need to confront Britain in the Near East. The result was the Anglo-Russian convention of 1907, in which Britain recognized a Russian sphere of influence in northern Persia in return for Russia's recognizing a British sphere of influence in southern Persia. France achieved her long-sought Triple Entente boxing in Germany from all directions.

In response, Germany attempted to revive its Triple Alliance with Austria-Hungary and Italy, originally negotiated in 1882. Italy proved to be an unreliable ally throughout this period, attempting always to see whether she could gain more by association with the French or the German coalition or by remaining neutral. But the Austrians and Germans found common cause in their opposition to Russian hegemony in Eastern Europe.

The German-Austrian alliance faced its pre–World War I test in the Bosnian crisis of 1908. To counter the national independence fever rising among ethnic-linguistic groups in provinces Austria had taken from the Turks, Austria decided to formally annex the two

Serbian provinces of Bosnia and Herzogovina. Russia, on grounds of slavic fraternalism and anxious to extend her own sphere of influence, struck a posture of unequivocal support for Serbian independence. This gave Germany's Kaiser Wilhelm just the opportunity he had been waiting for to act tough. Doubting that Russia really intended military intervention so soon after being exhausted by the Russo-Japanese war, and confident that Britain and France would not feel bound to back the czar in a Balkan adventure bringing Russian forces to the shores of the Mediterranean, the Kaiser called the czar's bluff by publicly pledging Germany's firm support for Austria's annexation move, and threatening counterintervention against any nation that might step in against Austria. Emboldened, Austria persisted in formally absorbing Bosnia and Herzogovina, while a humiliated Russia stood back and the Kaiser felt vindicated. Berlin's swift invocation of its alliance with Vienna both allowed Austria to defy Russia and overnight gave Germany the status it had been seeking of an awesome power.

However, in the nation-state system a successful power play by one alliance tends to stimulate compensatory solidification of opposing alliances. Thus, when the Austrian archduke was assassinated on June 28, 1914, in the Bosnian city of Sarajevo, Germany's attempt to once again deter Russia from intervening against Austrian suppression of the Serbian nationalists provoked a counterthreat by France. Each alliance partner believed its opponents were bluffing; but no nation was willing to have its bluff called, and each believed there was a high premium on striking first if war were to come. Consequently, Austria's bombing of Belgrade, the Serbian capital, on July 29 was followed on July 30 by Russia's general mobilization of its armed forces, which in turn was followed, between August 1 and August 3, by countermobilizations and declarations of war by Germany on one side and France on the other. World War I had begun—catalyzed by the alliances and balances of power that were supposed to deter war. By the time the bloodied and exhausted belligerents were ready to lay down their arms four years later, more than 8.4 million soldiers and 1.4 million civilians had been killed.

In the decade leading to World War I, then, the major alliances encouraged the confrontational diplomacy that brought on the war and determined its scope. But in the decade leading up to World War II the absence of weighty opposing alliances encouraged Adolf Hitler,

Benito Mussolini, and the Japanese military to launch aggressions that finally provoked another global war.[6] The previous system of alliances had been deliberately scuttled by the "winners" of World War I—consonant with President Woodrow Wilson's convictions, supported by broad strands of public opinion on both sides of the Atlantic, that the balance-of-power/alliance system is the principal cause of war.

The Germans, Italians, and Japanese were contemptuous of both the "collective security" system embodied in the League of Nations and the grand peace pacts of the day, the Locarno Pact of 1925 and the Kellogg-Briand Pact of 1928, that were supposed to substitute for the discredited balance-of-power system as the means of preventing war. Their contempt was to a large extent warranted. The logic of the League presumed the existence of a common world interest against war that normally would override all other national interests: all that was needed was a world institution in place to give expression to the common interest. As it turned out, national desires to avoid fighting other nations' wars overrode the collective obligations of the League; and, ironically, the very existence of the League made it easy for countries to pass the buck to the world institution to oppose aggression, providing each nation with a rationale for noninvolvement in the absence of concerted action organized by the League. The "spirit of Locarno" also had become part of the problem, for the pacts against war, by catering to the popular wishful thinking that coercive statecraft had become obsolete, only strengthened opposition in the Western democracies to the kinds of war-risking confrontations that might have restrained the Machiavellian dictators of the 1930s.

By the time the democracies were ready to reinstitute an alliance to oppose the expansionist powers, it required overt belligerency to give credibility to the intention of its members to resist aggression. And by the time the new alliance could put together enough military power to balance that of the aggressors, the Germans had brutally overrun the European continent and much of North Africa, and the Japanese had conquered almost a third of China and all Southeast Asia.

Even Hitler's bullying and absorption of Austria in 1938 and his demands that Czechoslovakia give up the German-speaking Sudetenland were not enough to make France and Britain respond positively to Stalin's plea for a firm stand by the former allies against further German expansion. Instead, when Prime Minister Neville Chamberlain and French Premier Edouard Daladier met with Hitler and Mussolini in Munich they agreed to let Hitler occupy the Sudeten Czech areas as long as he guaranteed to respect the territorial integrity of the rest of Czechoslovakia. It was not until Hitler violated this promise by seizing Slovakia and Bohemia in March 1939 that the British and French were ready to reinstitute the triangular alliance and explicitly threaten Hitler with war if he attacked Poland. But now Stalin was the holdout: he insisted on a degree of Soviet hegemony in Eastern Europe that Britain and France were not ready to grant him. Then, interpreting the Anglo-French rejection of his conditions as evidence that the Western capitalist countries were secretly conniving to allow Germany to destroy the Marxist-socialist state in Russia, he turned the tables and signed his notorious pact with Hitler giving the Soviets control over eastern Poland and adjacent areas in exchange for Stalin's acquiescence in Germany's occupation of western Poland. With the Soviet Union now neutralized and Britain and France in no position to physically prevent his action, Hitler's *Wehrmacht* thundered across the German-Polish border on September 1, 1939. On September 3, Great Britain and France finally declared war on Germany.

Only the invasion of the USSR itself by Hitler in June 1941 brought the Soviet Union into the war against Germany; and the United States finally was roused into sloughing off its formal stance of neutrality by the Japanese bombing of Pearl Harbor. The Western powers and the Soviets at last reconstituted the alliance that had fought against the Kaiser in World War I, with British Prime Minister Winston Churchill rationalizing the new crossideological collaboration on the grounds that he would be willing to make an "alliance with the Devil" if that was what it would take to defeat Hitler. Defeat Hitler the West did, and Tojo too—but only after more than 50 million human beings had died in the most destructive war in history.

The lesson seems to be that, just as generals can lead their forces to defeat by trying to fight the last war, diplomats can help generate the very wars they are trying to avoid by managing the last prewar crisis. On the eve of World War I, the crisis in the Balkans was mismanaged because of overcommitments by the great powers to their smaller allies. What policymakers thought they learned from the fiasco of 1914 was that alliances are pernicious and more often than not will cause unwanted wars. But partly because the policymakers disparaged and discouraged alliances during the interwar period, Hitler was able to roll over his weaker neighbors with ease until the cumulative and diplomatically irreversible effects on the balance of power made another world war virtually inevitable.

What, then, can be said in general about alliances as a determinant of war? Not any more than can be said, really, about the role of armaments and coercive diplomacy: Like weapons and threatening postures, alliances may either deter or provoke an opponent. The existence of an alliance does mean that if a war comes, it will probably involve more parties. This is what happened in World War I, as an alliance commitment from Germany brought an otherwise timid Austria to the brink of war under the mistaken assumption that her immediate opponents, Serbia and Russia, would be intimidated by the coalition they would face, as well as inhibited by the conflicting interests within their own coalition.

Polarization

The calculations of antagonists about the array of armed enemies they will face if they go to war are affected not only by formal alliances but also by the extent to which alliance members and other prospective parties to the action are bound to one another and for what reasons.[7] If most of the international system is polarized into only two camps, and if the bonding between countries in each camp is known to be tight across a range of issues, almost any war within the system has the strong potential for becoming a world war.

In such a tightly polarized system, however, miscalculations of the balance of power because of false assumptions about which countries will fight on each side are less likely, and therefore war should be less likely, than in more loosely structured international systems.

Abstracted from other complicating factors, the effects of various degrees and types of polarization on the war-proneness of an international system—and on the extent of geographic expansion if war does break out—can be represented as shown in the accompanying chart.

Polarity and the Likelihood of War
and Its Geographic Expansion[8]

Higher roman numerals indicate greater likelihood of war; *higher arabic numerals* indicate greater likelihood that war will turn into a world war.

	Tight Coalitions	*Loose Coalitions*
Bipolarity	I (5)	III (4)
Multipolarity	II (2)	IV (3)
Polyarchy (no dominant coalition pattern)		V (1)

This model, admittedly simplifying reality, highlights the effects of two structural dimensions of world society on the chances and shape of war.

The first dimension is the number of dominant power centers, or poles of attractions: *two are called bipolarity*; a few, say three to ten, are referred to as *multipolarity*; and many, more than ten, perhaps even hundreds, are termed *polyarchy*.

The second dimension is the degree of coalescence of groupings of states, nongovernmental associations, political movements, and other entities around the polar centers. In a refined model, this could be plotted on a continuum; but for our purposes it is sufficient to establish two categories: *tight coalitions* and *loose coalitions*.

Summarizing the implications of each structural alternative for the likelihood of war and its geographic expansion, the chart represents the following four hypotheses:

The most dangerous international systems tend to be those characterized by either loose bipolarity or loose multipolarity. They are dangerous in two respects: the likelihood of war and the likelihood that war anywhere in the system will draw in the major powers. War is likelier because the ambiguity of mutual security commitments in the loose coalitions leads to opportunities for miscalculation and bluffing. These characteristics also provide temptations for great-power intervention in local conflicts and the need for smaller powers to invoke coalition ties, however loose, to deter their adversaries from ganging up.

These dangerous instabilities are present in the current loose and still largely bipolar configuration of international alignments and antagonisms. They are both the product of and exacerbated by a set of mutually reinforcing conditions: (1) each superpower can devastate the other in a nuclear war, no matter which one strikes first; (2) each superpower exhibits a substantial but not total inhibition from going to war against the other in defense of its allies or clients; (3) there is tremendous disparity between the military power of the United States or the Soviet Union, on the one hand, and the military power of any other country, on the other; and (4) national values and interests diverge greatly among the coalition partners within both the U.S.-led and the Soviet-led coalitions.

These conditions of today's ambiguous pattern of polarization can create terrible temptations on the part of either superpower to use force against lesser powers—even against allies of the rival super-power—in confidence that the rival superpower will be inhibited from countermoves that carry a high risk of direct military engagement between them. Either the Soviet Union or the United States might well try such a power play, placing on its principal rival the choice of accepting the new status quo or attempting to reverse it at the risk of igniting World War III.

The most ominous prospect is that the move to establish such a fait accompli by one of the superpowers will be vigorously met by the other, embroiling them in a fateful nuclear confrontation from which neither can back off without great humiliation. (See the discussion of the "game of chicken" in Chapter 5). This seemingly insane scenario is even "rational" within the structure of the loose bipolar system. And though humanity has been lucky that such a mutually suicidal superpower confrontation has not yet materialized, only a naive optimism would rest content that this luck will continue to hold.

The safest international system presented in the model is tight multipolarity. In the multipolar configuration, the world is divided into a number of international subsystems, each a largely self-con-tained commercial and security community. Conflict is managed within these communities, with little likelihood of outside intervention in their affairs.

While in theory tight multipolarity should reduce the chances of a world war, this optimistic result is derived simply by defining the subsystems as self-contained. The optimism seems unrealistic, if only because of the progressive global interdependence of nations across all traditional regional lines, along with the increasing economic and strategic importance to all major countries of the "commons" areas (the oceans, the biospheric environment, and outer space) where countries can get in one another's way. Why should new regional subsystems, any more than the regional empires of the past, be expected to be sufficiently content with what they have and refrain from balance-of-power games against each other?

Even the formation of such intended self-contained regional subsystems appears entirely theoretical, for there no longer are universally acceptable definitions of which peoples constitute what regions. Are not some countries in the "Middle East," for example, part of Africa or Southwest Asia or Southeast Europe? Who is to decide disputes over such regional definitions, and by what criteria? In most continents, there is profound jealousy and suspicion that would-be regional hegemons, like Brazil, or Japan, would lord it over other members of a self-contained regional community. Moreover, if multipolar regional subsystems do temporarily emerge, the ever-present prospect of their disintegration will present outside powers with temptations to cultivate local clients and, in the event of actual disintegration, to intervene competitively.

War is least likely in the tight bipolar system, but is most difficult to contain. Tight bipolarity seemed the direction in which world society was moving during the first two decades after World War II, and many leaders and theorists in the United States and the Soviet Union looked favorably upon this configuration as one likely to reduce the prospect of war. This was because of the expectation that as the coalitions became internally more integrated, between them encompassing most of the countries of the world, two constraints would more strongly operate on them. First, members of each coalition would have little opportunity for significant international action not authorized by the entire coalition. Second, since an attack on any part of the rival coalition would be on the the whole coalition, the attacker could not hope to control his risks by attacking a small or weak opponent under the assumption that the target country's allies would not want to become involved. The temptation to "nibble" at or "salami slice" the rival coalition that characterizes loosely polarized configurations would be minimized in the tightly polarized system.

The principal deficiency of tight global bipolarity is that it is an all-or-nothing deterrence system. If, despite the built-in inhibitions against war, a conflict between two tightly polarized coalitions should escalate to major open hostilities in some corner of the globe, the war—unless terminated at once—would almost certainly expand into a world war with few if any sanctuaries and with high prospects of rapid escalation to nuclear holocaust.

A world in the configuration of polyarchy (which may well be the way ours is evolving)[9] *would be more warprone than others, but more likely than others to keep wars localized.*   A polyarchical world society would feature many sources and patterns of rule, authority, and power, not all of them congruent with the nation-state basis of the existing international system. Such varied identities, loyalties, and associations—based on nationality, domicile, ethnicity, religion, economic role, social class, occupation, and ideology— would determine who is on whose side and who is likely to fight against whom or to attempt to make peace with other units in the polyarchy. Many groups would transcend the borders of particular nation-states, and institutions representing various identities and interests would often come into conflict over their respective juris- dictions and over which of them has the primary or ultimate authority in particular fields.

With so many crosscutting loyalties and associations, credible multinational alliances would be difficult to sustain. Every country would have to be prepared to fend for itself. War might therefore be less deterred than in the polarized systems, unless most countries developed their own nuclear arsenals or other mass-destruction capabilities—a distinct possibility; on the other hand, the thickening and spread of diverse interdependencies across national and ideolog- ical lines might inhibit the degree of nation-to-nation hostility that must be generated to fight large wars. In general, the prognosis would be for more wars than in the bipolar or multipolar models; but wars which did break out might be more easily isolated or dissipated locally before engulfing the whole system.[10]

The opportunities for a statecraft designed to affect the degree of polarization of world society are discussed in Chapter 10.

IS THE NATION-STATE SYSTEM
THE PRINCIPAL CAUSE OF WAR?

Most of this chapter's analysis has focused on the determinants of war found in the nation-state system as it usually functions. We have seen, left to its own devices, the system is not sufficiently self-equilibrating, in the sense of automatically thrusting forward war-opposing forces and mechanisms to counter war-provoking threats and forces. Does this apparent deficiency lead to the conclusion that the nation-state system is essentially a "war system?" This indeed is the premise of much of the standard international-relations literature—conservative as well as reformist. The standard view is capsulized by Kenneth Waltz: "With many sovereign states, with no system of law enforceable among them, with each state judging its grievances and ambitions according to the dictates of its own reason or desire—conflict, sometimes leading to war, is bound to occur."[11]

War, sadly, is part of the essence of international relations. Force is the *ultima ratio* of who gets what, when, and how. And to "realists" like Hans Morgenthau it is hardly surprising that "All history shows that nations active in international politics are continuously preparing for, actively involved in, or recovering from organized violence in the form of war."[12]

In the nation-state system individual countries cannot rely on the community of states to enforce interstate agreements or even to protect their most basic right, sovereignty itself. Enforcement of international agreements and the defense of a nation's vital interests, including national survival itself, ultimately depend on a country's own ability, sometimes in conjunction with allies, to impose enough costs on aggressors to outweigh any gains they might hope to achieve.

Accordingly, countries normally maintain large arsenals and permanent military establishments to enable them to hold their own in conflicts that may turn violent. Even countries with populations of basically peaceful disposition are compelled, by "the system," to be prepared to use force to avoid being pushed around and humiliated by opponents more disposed to use military power. It is also true that, unlike what happens in domestic society, where the outbreak of intergroup violence often places the whole system in jeopardy, wars and threats to resort to war have traditionally been regarded as "normal" attributes of the world of nation-states.

It is easy to conclude that the very structure of the nation-state system impels statesmen to threaten to employ military force if another country does not respect their interests. This means maintaining credible war-fighting capabilities and, from time to time, engaging in shooting war.

But the technological developments of the twentieth century have rendered the "normalcy" of war unacceptable. The survival of the human species—it is now agreed by communists and capitalists, nationalists and cosmopolitans, idealists and realists—requires that war be made abnormal, at least to the extent of being eliminated as a means of direct conflict between the great powers.

After we look more closely in Chapters 5 and 6 at patterns of diplomacy and armament that often lead to war in the existing international system, we will try to determine, in the book's last two parts, whether the imperative of preventing global holocaust demands a wholesale restructuring of world society or some combination of less drastic remedies.

NOTES

1. For a trenchant criticism of attempts to locate the cause of war in domestic structures, see Kenneth Waltz, *Man, the State, and War* (New York: Columbia University Press, 1959), Chapters IV and V.

2. V. I. Lenin, *Imperialism: The Highest Stage of Capitalism* (New York: International Publishers, 1939).

3. Paul A. Baran and Paul M. Sweezy, *Monopoly Capital* (New York: Monthly Review Press, 1969).

4. The Correlates of War Project at the University of Michigan treated alliances as a central variable, but was unable to determine a statistically significant positive or negative relationship between the presence of alliances and the onset of war. As might be expected, the project's studies did show a correlation between the scope of war, measured in numbers of countries involved, and alliances. See J. David Singer and Melvin Small, "Alliance Aggregation and the Onset of War," in J. David Singer, ed., *The Correlates of War: I. Research Origins and Rationale* (New York: Free Press, 1979), pp. 225–264.

5. For the basic story leading to the outbreak of World War I, see

Laurence Lafore, *The Long Fuse: An Interpretation of the Origins of World War I* (New York: Lippincott, 1971).

6. A succinct, yet sufficiently detailed, rendering of the period between World War I and World War II is given by William R. Keylor, *The Twentieth Century World* (New York: Oxford University Press, 1984), pp. 95–184.

7. See Morton A. Kaplan, *System and Process in International Relations* (New York: Wiley, 1957), for a pioneering attempt to assess the effects of polarization on system stability.

8. The "polarity" model represents relationships similar to those hypothesized by Richard Rosecrance in his *International Relations: Peace and War* (New York: McGraw-Hill, 1973), as well as to those suggested by the historical-statistical investigations of Michael Haas, *International Conflict* (Indianapolis: Bobbs-Merrill, 1974). These studies, however, do not resolve the scholarly controversy over whether bipolar or multipolar systems are more war prone. In a recent review of the statistical studies, Francis A. Beer found that

> the research results on either side are not sufficiently strong for us to conclude that there is a valid, reliable, direct relationship between characteristics of peace and war, on the one hand, and international differentiation, on the other. Each theoretical school has some evidence supporting the influence of bipolarity or multipolarity. This evidence, however, is still incomplete and contradictory. (*Peace Against War: The Ecology of International Violence* [San Francisco: Freeman, 1981], p. 165)

9. I have developed the thesis that the world is evolving toward a polyarchic configuration in my article "The World Polity and the Nation-State System: An Updated Analysis," *International Journal*, (Summer 1984), 39(3):509–528.

10. The war-inhibiting effects of multiple and crosscutting coalitions are analyzed in Karl W. Deutch and J. David Singer, "Multipolar Power Systems and International Stability," *World Politics*, 16(3):390–406; and in Seyom Brown, *New Forces in World Politics* (Washington: Brookings Institution, 1974), pp. 109–119.

11. Waltz, p. 159.

12. Hans J. Morgenthau, *Politics Among Nations: The Struggle for Power and Peace* (New York: Knopf, 1978), p. 42.

CHAPTER 5

Coercive Diplomacy

Lacking a powerful central arbiter of conflicts among them, countries in the nation-state system characteristically prosecute their international conflicts by bargaining: offering or withholding positive inducements and threatening or easing threats to persuade each other to accept particular outcomes. *Diplomacy*, the officially conducted bargaining process among national governments, is normally an admixture of the positive and the coercive. How such diplomatic bargaining is conducted can determine whether threats and counterthreats cause adversaries to arrive at deals or physical blows.

That war itself can be considered a kind of coercive diplomacy is one of the meanings of the much quoted observation by the military theorist Karl von Clausewitz that war is "a continuation of political commerce . . . by other means."[1] Military strategists often talk of "upping the ante" (which in the game of poker means that a player increases the stakes by increasing his or her bid) to describe escalating threats of force to higher levels or enlarging the dimensions of a war in progress.

But despite the prevalence of war as a means of dealing with international disputes, and despite the persistence of political bargaining during war, the threshold between the threat of violence and its actual use is one of the most significant boundary lines in human behavior: its crossing constitutes a dramatic change in a prevailing relationship. Because of the great pain and sacrifices nations suffer in war, statesmen and diplomats, however readily they may invoke coercive threats, usually try to keep the bargaining process from spilling over the peace-war threshold.

The resort to international violence, in fact, is conventionally regarded as a failure of diplomacy, rather than simply its continuation

79

by other means. Though we will give some attention to diplomatic power plays designed specifically to provoke war, and (in Part III) to the role of diplomacy in controlling and terminating wars, the focus of this chapter reflects the conventional view that the purpose of diplomacy is to avert or stop wars.

WHEN DOES COERCIVE DIPLOMACY FAIL?

In international bargaining, just as in bazaar haggling, asking prices usually are higher than real settling prices; but the conduct of the bargaining differs significantly. In the bazaar, when buyer and seller fail to agree on a settling price, the interaction normally is terminated and both parties go their own ways; whereas in international relations, if coercive threats of injury are injected into the bargaining (as is not unusual), the failure to rescind or ameliorate unrealistic demands can mean violence. Under the threat of violence, the incentives to settle are high, but so are the opportunities for miscalculation that can prolong and intensify conflict.

Persisting with Nonnegotiable Demands

War may result from coercive bargaining when a country represents its demands as nonnegotiable and in need of urgent fulfillment but its opponent finds them unacceptable. The Arab-Israeli war of 1973 is a prime example of this dynamic. In the years following their defeat in the Arab-Israeli war of 1967, Israel's Arab neighbors had been demanding a complete return of the territories Israel captured from them in that war: they refused to engage in negotiations to establish rules of peaceful Arab-Israeli coexistence until Israel agreed to their demand. The Israelis were just as adamant in insisting that the willingness of the Arabs to negotiate a regional regime of coexistence was a precondition for the return of the conquered territories. The Arabs punctuated their demand by enlarging and modernizing their military forces, with major assistance from the Soviet Union, and Israel, predictably, engaged in a competitive arms buildup, helped mainly by the United States. With no compromise in the offing, it was only a question of time until war broke out again, as it did in October 1973 when Egypt and Syria, feeling at last sufficiently strong, launched a surprise attack against Israel on the day of Yom Kippur.[2]

Calling Bluffs When Threats Are Real

War is also a likely outcome of coercive situations in which the demanding country incorrectly believes that an opponent, although calling the demands unacceptable, is only engaging in a bargaining ploy, and that when push comes to shove it will not really fight. With the threatened country's posture of defiance seen as a bluff, the demanding country may move to implement its coercive threat—but the threatened country in fact will resist. A well-known case of defiance thought to be mere bluff resulted in Germany's invasion of Belgium in 1914, despite the British reiteration of their guarantee of Belgian neutrality. The larger result was Britain's entry into World War I against Germany. Students of misperception and cognitive failures in international crises continue to puzzle over how the Germans could have made such a gross miscalculation of British intentions;[3] but the fact is that countries are often quite ignorant of their adversaries' real motives and intentions, and this conceptual myopia is what makes coercive diplomacy so dangerous.

One of the most notorious failures of coercive diplomacy since World War I occurred during the Korean War in 1950. (Actually the failure resulted from a military commander's defiance of the political directives of leaders who sought a more prudent course.) When the Chinese threatened to enter the Korean War in the the fall of that year, as General Douglas MacArthur's advancing forces approached the North Korean border with China, MacArthur insisted that the Chinese were bluffing and that the Truman administration should call their bluff by threatening to bomb China itself if Chinese forces invaded Korea. President Truman and his advisers, however, did not want to draw the United States into a war with China, and feared that bombing China might activate the Sino-Soviet alliance, which would mean the start of World War III. Accordingly, as MacArthur advanced northward the U.S. government tried, through diplomatic intermediaries, to reassure the Chinese leaders that the United States had no desire to threaten the security of China, and the Joint Chiefs of Staff directed MacArthur to halt his advance considerably short of the Yalu River, which separates North Korea from China. MacArthur nevertheless drove close enough to the Yalu to cause the Chinese to intervene, as they had threatened they would, and to overwhelm MacArthur's forces. In effect, the Chinese called the implicit American bluff of retaliating against China proper. Truman dismissed

MacArthur for insubordination and made sure that U.S. military action would be limited to fighting the Chinese on the Korean peninsula. But now a bloody and expensive Sino-American war, albeit limited to Korea itself, was going full blast, and continued for another two years, until terminated in a truce at the original dividing line between North and South Korea.[4]

Getting into a "Game of Chicken"

If avoiding war is a country's objective in resorting to coercive diplomacy, then the most imprudent diplomatic gambit it can engage in is to publicly define the situation in "zero-sum" terms: your gain is my loss, and vice versa. This definition is likely to generate a brink-of-war confrontation that closes off all rational opportunities for striking a compromise; and in the most dangerous versions of the resulting game, the rival sides visibly begin wartime deployments of military forces that will be very costly (militarily, economically, and psychologically) to reverse unless the opponent backs down. Both sides thus become locked into a "game of chicken" in which neither can withdraw from the impending war without suffering great humiliation.

Germany and Russia were locked into such a game in July 1914 by their threats and counterthreats of intervention on behalf of their respective allies, Austria and Serbia, and by their competitive mobilization of armed forces. Historians are still debating whether the kaiser and the czar really wanted a war at that time; as it turned out, their underlying intentions did not finally matter. So assiduously did German and Russian officials play the game of chicken that when Austria invaded Serbia in a two-country war which might otherwise have been quarantined to the Balkan area, neither the kaiser nor the czar felt he had any alternative but to attack the other.[5]

A way to play the game of chicken "successfully" has been prescribed by the American strategist Herman Kahn. Invoking the source of the analogy—the sport played by two teenage drivers in stripped-down automobiles who drive toward each other down the center stripe of a highway, knowing that whoever swerves out of the way first is a "chicken," or coward—Kahn advises: "Get in the car drunk, wear dark glasses, and throw the steering wheel out of the window as soon as the car has gotten up to speed. If the other side is watching, one is almost certain to win.[6]

The macho player is not supposed to ask what happens if the opponent fails to swerve out of the way, for the question could weaken his resolve, or appear to weaken it, thus encouraging the opponent to persist in the confrontation. The macho player must have unswerving (the pun is deliberate) confidence that his opponent is bluffing and must not be afraid to call his opponent's bluff. But if there are *two* macho players . . .

WHEN DOES COERCIVE DIPLOMACY SUCCEED?

Coercive diplomacy is most likely to achieve the aims of the country making demands without bringing on a war when the country is recognized by its opponent as being at least its military equal and when the demander can credibly claim that the fulfillment of its demands is an absolutely vital interest, but the opponent cannot credibly claim so high an interest in resisting. Without these minimally propitious political factors, coercive diplomacy can easily provoke an escalation of conflict into war. But even with them, there is no guarantee of avoiding dangerous escalation of conflict.

Success or failure also depends on the nature of the prevailing global and local balances of military power and on such unpredictable contingent factors as the existence of other international or domestic crises that can affect the behavior of the parties to the conflict. But perhaps the most important element is the quality of statecraft on each side.

The Cuban missile crisis, in which President John Kennedy compelled the Soviets to withdraw the nuclear missiles they had started to install in Cuba, is the most dramatic recent example of successful coercive diplomacy. Kennedy's success was in part due to his ability to believably take a public stance of being totally convinced the Soviet missiles in Cuba would create so adverse a change in the balance of power that the United States could not possibly accept their presence—thereby making it credible that the United States would use any means necessary, including war with the Soviet Union if it came to that, to assure the removal of the missiles. As Kennedy put it, in his October 22, 1962 address on radio and television:

This secret, swift and extraordinary build-up of Communist missiles, in an area well known to have a special and historical

relationship to the United States and the nations of the
Western Hemisphere, in violation of Soviet assurances, and in
defiance of American hemispheric policy—this sudden,
clandestine decision to station strategic weapons for the first
time outside of Soviet soil, is a deliberately provocative and
unjustified change in the status quo which cannot be accepted
by this country, if our courage and our commitments are ever
to be trusted again by either friend or foe. . . .

Our unswerving objective . . . must be . . . to secure their
withdrawal or elimination from the Western Hemisphere.[7]

Moreover, the Kennedy administration was able convincingly to
convey to the Kremlin the urgency of the missiles being removed by
a specific date, just prior to the time when, according to U.S.
intelligence analysts, the weapons would be sufficiently installed to be
usable. The ultimatum was that if the missiles were not removed by
the specified date, the United States would have to remove them—the
clear implication being by an air strike.

Premier Khrushchev, facing this entirely credible stance by
Kennedy—punctuated by a U.S. naval blockade around Cuba and
menacing movements of U.S. forces all over the world—and having
no credible vital security rationale of his own to justify keeping Soviet
missiles in Cuba, was inhibited from taking up the challenge to war by
the overwhelming U.S. military superiority in the Carribbean and the
still-impressive U.S. strategic superiority. He had no rational course
but to yield.

Even the managers of the American success in the Cuban missile
crisis, however, worried, up to the moment they received unmistak-
able evidence that the Soviet missiles were being dismantled, that the
American coercive diplomatic strategy might provoke a desperate
Khrushchev into additional coercive countermoves—say, around the
city of Berlin, where the Soviets had military superiority. To help
prevent this dangerous possibility, Kennedy threw some American
concessions into the negotiations to help Khrushchev save face—
namely, pledges not to invade Cuba and to dismantle the obsolete
U.S. medium-range missiles deployed in Turkey. A few advisers,
including former Secretary of State Dean Acheson and then Harvard
professor Henry Kissinger, criticized these concessionary moves not
only as unnnecessary, but also as weakening Kennedy's basic stance

that Soviet missiles in Cuba were absolutely intolerable and that the United States would go to war to remove them, if necessary.[8]

As a model of successful coercive diplomacy, the missile crisis illustrates the wide range of factors likely to come into play. Managing their often subtle interaction is an art form more than a management science with operational rules that can be codified. A sampling of recent scholarship on international crises shows that at least the following variables are likely to be present to substantially affect the outcome where one side or the other tries to get its way with coercive diplomacy:[9]

- the legacy of international instruments (treaties, international charters, and the like) with historical precedent affecting the assertion, and conviction, of legitimacy by the parties to the conflict;
- alliance obligations on each side;
- calculations by both sides of the net gains or costs (to both of them) of having to fight a war;
- opportunities and resources available for attempting to alter the adversary's net gain/cost calculations of giving in or compromising instead of fighting;
- risk-taking propensities on each side;
- knowledge, or misperception, of the rival country's intentions and capabilities; and
- diplomatic and crisis-management skills in manipulating these variables.

Being wrong in assessing or clumsy in manipulating any of the variables can easily tip a diplomatic success into a failure. Coercive diplomacy requires an ability to sustain the credibility of a country's threats while retaining the option of modifying them. To avoid provoking an unwanted war, the threatening country must be willing, in case of unanticipated stubbornness by its opponent, to hold back on implementing its threat of violence, and even to moderate earlier unequivocal demands.

Like war itself, the arena of military threats, once entered into, is a realm of vast unknowns, where being wrong can spell irretrievable disaster. Inevitably a part of the international political game, coercive diplomacy is quite often responsible for provoking war rather than avoiding it.

COERCIVE DIPLOMACY AS A
DELIBERATE PRELUDE TO WAR

One type of coercive diplomacy, indeed, is designed to lay the groundwork for a war that a government has decided is worth fighting. This is the other side of the war-peace continuum that prompted Clausewitz to define war as a continuation of political diplomacy by other means; here diplomacy is an anticipation, by other means, of war. The diplomatic encounters, called "justification of hostility crises" by Professor Richard Ned Lebow, are really power plays to weaken the target country's will to resist an oncoming attack and/or to whip support in the aggressor country for military action and to engender international acceptance of the forthcoming use of force. Lebow explains that

> justification of hostility crises are unique in that leaders of the initiating nation make a decision for war *before* the crisis commences. The purpose of the crisis is not to force an accommodation but to provide a *casus belli* for war.[10]

Austria's ultimatum to Serbia on July 23, 1914, is one of history's most notorious examples of this kind of diplomacy. The terms of the ultimatum required Serbia to take the blame for the assassination of the Archduke Francis Ferdinand and to assume a posture of complete contrition for having given aid and comfort to anti-Austrian subversive movements within the Austro-Hungarian Empire. They also required Serbia immediately to outlaw and punish all anti-Austrian nationalist activists as well as to allow Austrian officials free rein to conduct the investigation of the assassination within Serbia. These demands were to be accepted unconditionally by Serbia within 48 hours, with the clear implication that otherwise Austria would take military action against Serbia. The Serbs did reply just before the expiration of the time limit, virtually capitulating to all of the Austrian demands. But though Kaiser Wilhelm of Germany, Austria's ally, called it a great moral victory for Austria, the Austrians found details indicating a lack of sincerity in Serbia's reply and pointed to the fact that the Serbians were mobilizing their armed forces—an understandable defensive move under the circumstances—as evidence of Serbia's lack of penitence. Without allowing any further negotiations to take place, Austria mobilized her armed forces, declared war on

Serbia, and on July 29 began the artillery bombardment of Belgrade that was the opening fusillade of World War I.[11]

Adolf Hitler's demands on Czechoslovakia in 1938 and on Poland in 1939 to allow the German ethnic populations in these countries to excerise their right of "self-determination" by uniting with Germany were also exercises in this type of coercive diplomacy. Knowing that he was demanding the intolerable, Hitler looked forward to the refusal of his demands as giving him justification for military invasion.

Usually countries threatening to use military force assume that those who are the targets of the threat would not expect to win in an actual exchange of blows. It follows that the military balance of power—or, more precisely, the assumptions held by governments about their own military capabilities relative to the military capabilities of their adversaries—will have much to do with where and when coercive diplomatic gambits are tried.

The determining effects of the distribution of military power among countries on decisions to threaten or engage in war are analyzed in the next chapter.

NOTES

1. Karl von Clausewitz, *On War*. Translation by Michael Howard and Peter Paret (Princeton, N.J.: Princeton University Press, 1976), p. 147.

2. Congressional Quarterly, *The Middle East: Fifth Edition* (Washington, D.C.: Congressional Quarterly, 1981), p. 20.

3. See Richard Ned Lebow, *Between Peace and War: The Nature of International Crisis* (Baltimore, Md.: Johns Hopkins University Press, 1981), pp. 119–147, for an analysis of German decision making leading to their miscalculation of Britain's willingness to fight for Belgian neutrality. See also all of Robert Jervis, *Perception and Misperception in International Politics* (Princeton, N.J.: Princeton University Press, 1976), but especially pages 193–195 for insight into how countries mistake serious threats for bluffs.

4. Alan S. Whiting, *China Crosses the Yalu: The Decision to Enter the Korean War*. (New York: Macmillan, 1960).

5. See Lebow, pp. 67–69, 232–259.

6. Herman Kahn, *Thinking About the Unthinkable* (New York: Horizon Press, 1962), p. 188.

7. John F. Kennedy, Radio-TV address of October 22, 1962, *Public

Papers of the Presidents: John F. Kennedy, 1962, (Washington, D.C.: U.S. Government Printing Office, 1963), pp. 806–809.

8. On the rationale and method of proffering quid pro quos to the Soviets in the Cuban missile crisis, see Robert Kennedy, *Thirteen Days: A Memoir of the Cuban Missile Crisis* (New York: Norton, 1969).

9. Useful scholarly sources in addition to Lebow's work (cited in note 3) are Thomas C. Schelling, *Arms and Influence* (New Haven, Ct.: Yale University Press, 1966); Glenn H. Snyder and Paul Diesing, *Conflict Among Nations: Bargaining, Decision Making, and System Structure in International Crises* (Princeton, N.J.: Princeton University Press, 1977); Barry M. Blechman and Stephen S. Kaplan, *Force Without War: U.S. Armed Forces as a Political Instrument* (Washington, D.C.: Brookings Institution, 1978); and Alexander L. George and Richard Smoke, *Deterrence in American Foreign Policy: Theory and Practice* (New York: Columbia University Press, 1974).

10. Lebow, p. 25.

11. Laurence Lafore, *The Long Fuse: An Interpretation of the Origins of World War I* (New York: Lippincott, 1971), pp. 225–275. See also John G. Stoessinger, *Why Nations Go to War* (New York: St. Martin's, 1985), Chapter 1.

CHAPTER 6

Military Arsenals and Balances

"Guns Don't Kill People, People Kill People" asserts the automobile bumper sticker of the National Rifle Association. An analogous view of international relations is that national military arsenals are not the cause of war, but rather the symptom of the intense conflicts among countries that cause war.

This partial truth omits consideration of some essential relationships between military forces and war. Armaments are never merely a symptom of an underlying conflict. Their very presence in a conflict situation, along with the specific characteristics of the arsenals of the antagonists, are among the crucial determinants of whether a conflict will express itself in war and, if it does, what kind of war will be fought.[1]

Nor are the size and characteristics of a country's military arsenal directly deducible by objective scientific analysis from the country's international political relations. As shown in Chapter 3, the highly subjective factors of ideology, prestige, credibility, and honor often are parts of a country's definition of its national interests and affect its assessments of the international threats it faces and the characteristics of the military forces needed to counter them. (Most countries also maintain some of their armed forces to deal with domestic conflicts.)

Even when a country's grand strategists can simplify reality sufficiently to give their military experts a set of carefully defined and prioritized national security objectives, the experts, more often than not, will strongly disagree among themselves about the kinds of military capabilities needed to service these objectives.

However, to recognize these complexities does not preclude our making some general observations about how the size and other characteristics of military forces around the world can affect the likelihood and shape of war and the prospects for peace.

WHY COUNTRIES ARM

The national armaments countries maintain for possible use against each other result from two basic features of the nation-state system. The first is that every country has some adversaries that it suspects would injure it if they could do so with relatively little risk of being injured in return. The second is that the virtually anarchic structure of the nation-state system compels each country to rely on its own means of self-defense, sometimes combined with help from allies. Even without considering any of the aggressive motives for using force discussed in previous chapters, no nation could hope to remain an independent state able to preserve public order within its jurisdiction, facilitate peaceful domestic commerce, operate a regime of social justice, and maintain its cultural values—if it could not defend itself against destructive attack by external opponents.

While the levels and kinds of armaments that any country maintains must depend on varied, sometimes changing factors—its unique set of foreign adversary and alliance relationships, its internal security needs and domestic political economy, its style of diplomacy, and its national-security doctrines—no country allows itself to be completely without military forces for external defense.

The Uncertainty of How Much Is Enough

When countries arm against each other—as do the United States and the Soviet Union, NATO and the Warsaw Pact, Greece and Turkey, Israel and her Arab neighbors, Iran and Iraq, Ethiopia and Somalia, India and Pakistan—what determines the size and power of their arsenals?

A popular view holds that the world is overarmed: If current trends continue, by 1990 military expenditures will surpass $1 trillion a year. Is all the lethal power that these funds buy really necessary? Aren't there much better uses for the resources? If only half of this amount each year could be transferred as purchasing power to the 800 million human beings suffering below rudimentary levels of subsistence, none of them would have to live in abject poverty. Wouldn't such a transfer of resources get at some of the sources of war—the domestic instability and revolutions generated by poverty and despair? Do the approximately 10,000 strategic nuclear warheads now deployed by each of the superpowers (almost every one of them packing more destructive power than 50 Hiroshima-type bombs) relate to any sane human purpose?[2]

Marxists attribute the apparent overarming to the profit motive of private corporations that manufacture and market arms; but socialist as well as capitalist countries maintain bloated arsenals. The analysis here locates a large part of the problem in the way national governments, whatever their ideological persuasion, typically do their military planning.

To being with, military planners find it difficult to estimate just which of the many possible combinations of their country's allies and adversaries are likely to be directly or indirectly involved in future belligerencies. Some typical uncertainties follow:

- Should Pakistan attempt to match India's manpower or can the Pakistanis lessen their requirements by counting on China's help in pinning down Indian troops on the Sino-Indian border in the event of war?
- Can the Indians count on the Russians to pin down China's troops on the Sino-Soviet border?
- Given the Israeli-Egyptian peace treaty of 1979, can the Israelis, in establishing their military requirements, subtract the Egyptian armed forces from the combined Arab front they would have to counter in a war? Should they add the forces of Libya? Of Algeria?
- If Angola should attack Zaire across its northern border, would the Republic of South Africa attack Angola from the south? Would Mozambique stand idly by?
- Even the countries belonging to the stable and well-organized alliance systems of NATO and the Warsaw Pact cannot be sure which of their supposedly loyal alliance partners will actually fight beside them in the crunch, or to what degree they will commit resources. Thus, in calculating the East-West military balance in Europe, analysts and military planners on both sides come to widely divergent conclusions about national military requirements—depending, for example, on whether they count France or Greece in or out of potential conflicts and on whether

they assume that the Poles and Czechs would support the Soviets with high dedication or would instead subvert the Warsaw Pact's military operations.[3]

To such political uncertainties must be added the wide range of technical uncertainties caused by inadequate intelligence about the quantity and quality of even a single opponent's armaments. Military technology is, in fact, so volatile that today's estimates of what would happen if Country X fought Country Y tomorrow can be made obsolete literally overnight. Assume that Country X has a vast superiority over Country Y in battlefield tanks; Country Y's successful test of a precision guidance system for its antitank artillery could portend a neutralization of this superiority in ways that would be too expensive for Country X to counter.

Rapid changes in existing military balances can also be brought about by transfers of military technologies through sales or military assistance agreements among countries. Thus the Israelis are made very jittery by new purchases of sophisticated air defense systems by any of the Arab countries: it has been primarily through air superiority that Israel has compensated for the overwhelming manpower advantage of its hostile neighbors.

Since a nuclear arsenal can give a country decisive superiority over an opponent lacking such weapons, the possibility that a rival may develop or otherwise acquire its own nuclear weapons engenders special fears and suspicions. It is widely believed that in addition to the five countries now openly deploying them, at least twenty-five other countries could produce nuclear weapons within ten years. Among the twenty-five are many pairs of intensely antagonistic countries: India and Pakistan, Israel and Iraq, Egypt and Libya, South Africa and Nigeria.[4] Some countries, specifically India, Israel, and South Africa, may already have nuclear arsenals that they choose not to reveal for fear of the reaction of other countries. If any one of them were to admit that it has the bomb, its rivals would not be far behind in deploying their own—if not home-produced, then either bought or stolen.

Given the rapidity with which balances of military power can change, military planners for most governments, including basically peaceful countries that maintain arms only for defensive purposes, usually want to hedge against uncertainty by overarming. The worst the hedger fears is that he will be charged with having asked for more than is really needed. Yet he probably will be praised if the result is either military superiority over the enemy or the enemy's reactive military buildup—which the hedger then can point to as justifying his original recommendations! By contrast, the military planner who asks for too little runs the risk of being blamed for endangering the country's security. In sum, the psychological dynamics combined with bureaucratic and technological factors tend to push governments in the direction of too much arming rather than too little.

The Role of Military Doctrine

Decisions countries make about the size and qualitative characteristics of their military arsenals are also affected by the military doctrines that gain favor in their governments. In the United States, the strategic nuclear arsenal in particular has been shaped by prevailing doctrinal predilections.

Assured Destruction and MAD.   In the 1960s Pentagon strategists developed a crude formula for determining the minimum strategic capability the United States would have to maintain to deter a strategic attack on the United States by the Soviet Union. This formula (which persists to this day) defines the minimally necessary arsenal as including strategic forces that, after absorbing the most devastating first strike the Soviets could mount against the United States, could still inflict a retaliatory blow to destroy at least a quarter of the population of the Soviet Union and one-third of its industry. The Soviet Union seems to have a similar crude basis for determining the minimum strategic capability it would need to deter a U.S. attack, but the Russians have not publicly revealed the details of their concept.

Secretary of Defense Robert McNamara in the mid-1960s turned this minimum criterion for deterrence based on an assured level of retaliatory destruction into a maximum as well: "This much and no more." The rationale for imposing such a limit on the strategic arsenal was that the United States should forget about "winning" a thermonuclear war, or even limiting damage to this country if deterrence failed, for there could be no winners and the horrors of survival in the aftermath of nuclear holocaust would be worse than death. Moreover, if both sides would adopt this restrictive criterion for determining their strategic force requirements—if, in other words, the strategic

balance was simply one of mutual assured destruction, or MAD—
then there would be stable mutual deterrence.

During the early and mid-1970s, both superpowers appeared to be
ready to adopt MAD as a sufficient criterion for strategic force
planning. The Strategic Arms Limitation Talks (SALT), the SALT-I
Treaty and Agreement of 1972, and the follow-on negotiations for
SALT-II were expressions of movement toward a deterrence-only
definition of the role of strategic forces: Most strategic
"counterforce" weapons (those with the function of destroying the
opponent's strategic weapons) were to be prohibited. Both sides
agreed that it was legitimate for each to maintain levels of forces
sufficient to destroy the other's key cities and industries, but that
anything more was unnecessary for deterrence and therefore either
should not be deployed or, if already deployed, should be negotiated
away.

Credible deterrence and beyond.   Despite the SALT accords,
new weapons developments accompanied by second thoughts of
strategists on both sides about the validity of a MAD-only regime for
strategic deterrence had generated a brand new arms race by the
mid-1970s.

The anticipation of greater accuracy in Soviet intercontinental
ballistic missiles (ICBMs), which some U.S. planners estimated could
by the middle or late 1980s give the Soviets an ability to destroy
perhaps as many as 95 percent of America's ICBMs, stimulated
research and development efforts to close this "window of vulnerability," as it was called. The vulnerability-reducing options included
efforts to make the U.S. ICBMs mobile, to hide them, to put them
under deeper and harder ground cover, to protect them with antiballistic missiles (ABMs), or to program the ICBMs to be launched on
warning that an enemy attack was on its way. Anticipation of the
increasing vulnerability of the land-based strategic forces also accelerated programs for enhancing the striking power of American
strategic weapons carried by submarines and airplanes.

Missile guidance improvements and other developments making
for high accuracy in targeting, in conjunction with the maturing of
capabilities for launching many warheads on a single missile—
multiple independently targeted reentry vehicles, or MIRVs—made it
impossible to distinguish "counterforce" strategic missiles from
those threatening cities. The MIRV technology allowed either side to

multiply the number of its deployed warheads virtually overnight, perhaps without immediate detection by the opponent. Accordingly, even the deterrence-only posture seemed to require considerable redundancy, perhaps double or even triple the lethal megatonnage demanded for the assured-destruction mission, simply as insurance against technological breakthroughs or surprise deployments by the other superpower. In the absence of such redundancy, the opponent might be tempted to believe that by a well-executed first strike he could preclude intolerable retaliation.

The rethinking by strategic analysts of the implications of a MAD-only regime centered on two possibilities. The first was the increased temptations for limited-war power plays under the canopy of absolute mutual deterrence of all-out strategic nuclear war. The second was the terrible "what if" problem: What if for some reason—miscalculation, accident, irrationality, for example—a strategic nuclear attack by one superpower against the other should occur? Would the next step inevitably be a preprogrammed massive nuclear retaliation, which certainly would provoke a massive nuclear attack in reply? If so, wasn't MAD truly insane?

The implications of absolute superpower inhibitions against nuclear escalation were potentially shattering to NATO. A central premise of the alliance was that if a Soviet attack on Western Europe could not be contained and thrown back by the NATO forces deployed in Europe, the United States would be willing to employ its strategic arsenal against the Soviet Union to reverse the tide. But under a MAD regime, this NATO strategy would lack credibility, and the Soviets therefore might be more inclined to start a conventional war under the assumption that the risks were controllable.

Furthermore, some American strategists argued that even the credibility of strategic retaliation in response to the enemy's strategic first strike against the U.S. homeland might be questioned if U.S. forces were designed only for assured destruction of the enemy's cities and industries.[5]

In addition, evidence that Soviet strategists and force planners had never really bought the MAD concept anyway and, despite the SALT agreements, were proceeding to deploy a war-fighting (as distinct from war-deterring) strategic arsenal finally compelled even those U.S. policymakers who had initially championed the MAD concept to favor giving U.S. forces greater clout against Soviet military installations and forces.

These reassessments and alterations of the MAD concept were codified in Jimmy Carter's Presidential Directive No. 59 of August 1980. Labeled "The Countervailing Strategy," the revised criteria for determining what kind of strategic arsenal to deploy provided a nonpartisan rationale for the incoming Reagan administration's plans to substantially enhance the U.S. strategic arsenal. As outlined in the January 1981 report to Congress of Carter's secretary of defense, Harold Brown, the countervailing strategy responded to the "unquestioned Soviet attainment of strategic parity," which "put the final nail in the coffin of what we long knew was dead—the notion that we could adequately deter the Soviets solely by threatening massive retaliation against their cities." It also addressed what had been learned of the Soviets' strategic doctrine: their contemplation of a relatively prolonged nuclear war; the "evidence that they regard military forces as the obvious first targets in a nuclear exchange, not general industrial and economic capacity"; and the fact that "certain elements of the Soviet leadership seem to consider Soviet victory in a nuclear war to be at least a theoretical possibility."

Our national military deployments, said Brown, are designed to tell the world that the United States has the capability and will to deter aggression, whatever the level of conflict contemplated.

> To the Soviet Union, our strategy makes clear that no course of aggression by them that led to the use of nuclear weapons, on any scale of attack and at any stage of conflict, could lead to victory, however they might define victory. Besides our nuclear power to devastate the full target system of the USSR, the United States would have the option for more selective, lesser retaliatory attacks. . . .

> Our planning must provide a continuum of options, ranging from the use of small numbers of strategic and/or theater nuclear weapons aimed at narrowly defined targets, to employment of large portions of our nuclear forces against a broad spectrum of targets. . . .

> At any early stage in the conflict, we must convince the enemy that further escalation will not result in achievement of his objectives, that it will not mean "success," but rather additional costs. To do this, we must leave the enemy with sufficient highly valued military, economic, and political

resources still surviving but still clearly at risk, so that he has a strong incentive to seek an end to the conflict.[6]

Secretary of Defense Brown's advocacy of limited and flexible strategic options was a sign of the times. He had been one of McNamara's protégés, flirting with the idea of controlled counterforce in 1961 and 1962, but rejecting damage-limiting strategies and forces as futile in the mid-1960s, and criticizing the Pentagon for departing from the assured-destruction-only criterion during the Nixon and Ford administrations. At his 1977 confirmation hearings, the secretary-designate gave every indication of wanting to reinstitute the mutual-deterrence-through-MAD regime that Secretaries Melvin Laird and James Schlesinger had begun to dismantle. Now here he was, leading the fight from the Pentagon against the force-planning assumptions he had earlier championed.

At the end of the Carter administration, both superpowers were ordering new strategic forces designed to fight a nuclear war effectively—albeit justified on grounds of credible deterrence. Both sides henceforth would be competitively augmenting their forces considerably beyond what they needed to destroy each other's cities. Many laypersons saw this as "overkill," while many, but by no means all, national security planners regarded the increased counterforce deployments as strategically essential.[7]

The case for increasing U.S. counterforce capabilities was strongly asserted in 1983 by President Reagan's Commission on Strategic Forces, chaired by Brent Scowcroft. "Deterrence is not, and cannot be, bluff," said the commission's report. "In order for deterrence to be effective we must not merely have weapons, we must be perceived to be able, and prepared, if necessary, to use them effectively against the key elements of Soviet power."[8]

The Scowcroft Commission pointed to Soviet deployments of SS-18 and SS-19 ICBMs as reflecting evidence of Soviet plans to attack the main U.S. strategic forces in the event of a nuclear war. Its principal justification of various U.S. strategic force modernization measures, including the controversial MX (the new highly accurate ten-warhead missile), was to avoid "a one-sided strategic condition in which the Soviet Union could effectively destroy the whole range of strategic targets in the United States, but we could not effectively destroy a similar range of targets in the Soviet Union." Such a one-sided condition, argued the commission, would be "extremely unstable . . . and would clearly not serve the cause of peace.'' It even "could tempt the Soviets, in a crisis, to feel they could successfully threaten or even undertake conventional or limited nuclear aggression in the hope that the United States would lack a fully effective response.''[9]

Notably, the Scowcroft Commission frontally rejected the notion that the only purpose of the U.S. strategic arsenal was to deter a Soviet strategic attack on the United States:

> The Soviets must continue to believe what has been NATO's doctrine for three decades: that if we or our allies should be attacked—by massive conventional means or otherwise—the United States has the will and the means to defend with the full range of American power. . . . [E]ffective deterrence requires that early in any Soviet consideration of attack, or threat of attack, with conventional forces or chemical or biological weapons, Soviet leaders must understand that they risk an American nuclear response. . . .

> Similarly, effective deterrence requires that the Soviets be convinced that they could not credibly threaten us or our allies with a limited use of nuclear weapons against military targets, in one country or many. . . .

> In order to deter such Soviet threats *we must be able to put at risk those types of Soviet targets—including hardened ones such as military command bunkers and facilities, missile silos, nuclear weapons and other storage, and the rest* [my emphasis]—which the Soviet leaders have given every indication by their actions they value most.[10]

Internal Pentagon guidance for force planners during the early 1980s went even beyond these criteria for effective and credible deterrence to set forth the requirement that the United States must be able to "prevail" over the Soviet Union in a "protracted" nuclear war.[11] Secretary of Defense Caspar Weinberger publicly denied any intention of operating under a "war-winning" strategy, insisting that the planning objective was only to "acquire the capability to respond appropriately to any potential level of aggression against us," including the "prolonged" nuclear strike strategy he attributed to the

Soviets. But he refused to disassociate himself from the concept of "prevailing."[12] If, indeed, both the Soviets and the Americans were modernizing their strategic arsenals with the objective of winning a nuclear war, there would be no foreseeable limit to the ever-spiraling arms race.

Strategic defense of the population—and SDI. A military doctrine that includes the imperative of protecting the population during a strategic nuclear war substantially changes the design requirements for the strategic arsenal from those needed to provide assured destruction or credible deterrence. When added to the deterrence objectives, this objective calls for vastly augmented strategic capabilities.

In the 1960s Secretary of Defense McNamara dropped this objective, which then went under the name of "damage limitation," because of its highly uncertain technical feasibility, the great cost of even attempting to achieve such a capability, the relative ease with which an opponent could overcome it, and its inconsistency with arms limitation agreements based on the premise that neither side should need any more nuclear weapons than would provide it with an assured-destruction deterrent. McNamara turned down proposals for a nationwide shield of antiballistic missiles, and convinced his Soviet counterparts that it would be to the advantage of both superpowers not to attempt to negate the vulnerability of their societies to the other's strategic weapons, since this could only provoke new and awesomely expensive offensive arms buildups to preserve the levels of assured destruction on which deterrence rests. It was this McNamara logic, adopted temporarily by Richard Nixon and Henry Kissinger, that produced the ABM treaty of 1972 curtailing ballistic missile defenses, as well as the accompanying accord putting a ceiling on new offensive strategic forces.

The surprise announcement by President Reagan in March 1983 that the United States was now going to make a determined effort to achieve a population defense produced shock waves in the military planning communities of both the United States and the Soviet Union, for it suggested that the force-design and arms-control doctrines of the previous two decades were being thrown overboard. As the excerpts below show, Reagan challenged the prevailing doctrines on both moral and strategic grounds:

> [We must] break out of a future that relies solely on offensive retaliation for our security. . . . I've become . . . deeply convinced that the human spirit must be capable of rising above dealing with other nations and human beings by threatening their existence. . . .
>
> Wouldn't it be better to save lives than to avenge them? . . .
>
> I believe there is a way. Let me share with you a vision of the future which offers hope. It is that we embark on a program to counter the awesome Soviet missile threat with measures that are defensive. . . .
>
> What if free people could live secure in the knowledge that their security did not rest upon the threat of instant U.S. retaliation to deter a Soviet attack, that we could intercept and destroy strategic ballistic missiles before they reached our own soil or that of our allies? . . .
>
> I clearly recognize that defensive systems have limitations and raise certain problems and ambiguities. If paired with offensive systems, they can be viewed as fostering an aggressive policy; and no one wants that. But with these considerations firmly in mind, I call upon the scientific community in our country, those who gave us nuclear weapons, to turn their great talents now to the cause of mankind and world peace, to give us the means of rendering these nuclear weapons impotent and obsolete.[13]

Background briefings to the press indicated that the president was particularly intrigued with the possibility of accomplishing this goal through the development of a space-based ABM system that, with lasers or other exotic technologies, could efficiently destroy enemy ICBMs just after launch in their "boost phase" before they let loose their multiple warheads. Dubbed "Star Wars" by journalists, the orbiting interceptor idea was soon revealed to be just one element of a mammoth research and development project for a multilayered shield against ICBMs: the Strategic Defense Initiative (SDI). The overarching concept of the SDI is that the ABM system would attack ICBMs at various stages along their trajectories—including liftoff, inertial flight through space, reentry into the atmosphere, and terminal homing in on their targets. Since enemy ICBMS that were missed at the first stage could be attacked at the second stage, and so on, the assumption is that very few would finally get through to their targets.

Proponents of the SDI argued that the feasibility and desirability of a population-defense ABM looked very different in the light of new technological developments: new and improved means for sensing and discriminating targets, for directing interceptors to targets, and for destroying targets demanded at least an agnostic view toward whether ABMs would prove to be cost effective.[14]

Opponents of the SDI argued that all of the projections of technical feasibility were highly conjectural, being based on still largely untested technologies and unsupported assertions about a new ability to overcome what has been the stark nuclear-age reality that aids to offensive penetration are cheaper than defensive screens. They also pointed out that the SDI, in its current concept, was directed only at the threat from ICBMs. Even if a perfect defense were someday designed against ICBMs, the population would still be vulnerable to nuclear attacks delivered by nearby submarines, by aircraft, and by clandestine means. In addition, a large-scale commitment to develop the ABM by either superpower would surely challenge the other side's assured destruction capability, stimulating a new and enormously expensive round of competition in offensive weapons, which then would pose an even larger threat for the ABM system to counter.[15]

Some proponents of the SDI, under the barrage of criticism from respected strategic experts and weapons technologists, have retreated to a more limited rationale for justifying the new ABM effort: that the technologies spawned in the quest for the ambitious, and possibly elusive, goal of population defense meanwhile can be applied to good effect in reducing the ICBM threat to the deterrent forces and other military targets, thereby further reducing any incentive the enemy might have to initiate strategic nuclear war.[16]

Whoever is right about the SDI—its proponents, opponents, or agnostic skeptics—the research and development genie for ballistic missile defense efforts is out of the bottle. Unless there is a decisive reversion back to the MAD orthodoxy, constituting a major reversal in both the Pentagon and the Soviet Ministry of Defense, or unless there is a surprising breakthrough in the Soviet-American arms-control negotiations, a new and very expensive round in the strategic arms race—focused on ABMs and efforts to counteract them—appears unavoidable.

DO ARMS RACES CAUSE WAR?

Apart from the drain on resources that otherwise might be used for more constructive purposes, are high levels of armaments and arms races necessarily bad? As a means of assuring that adversaries don't dare attack, perhaps arms buildups are preferable to efforts to augment national power by imperialistic expansion, or to attempts to subvert an opponent's government, or to direct military blows to disable an opponent. When there is mutual suspicion of a temptation or an inclination to attack, intensive arming by both sides may be the only way to discourage war—by denying the prospect of easy victory to either.

The historical record shows that wars were most frequent between the major powers of Europe in the era characterized by relatively low levels of armament: that is, when military establishments were organized for fighting limited wars of minimum destruction and short duration during the period of the Classical Balance of Power (from the Treaty of Westphalia, 1648, to the French Revolution, 1789). In modern times, as war has become more destructive, the major powers have been more constrained from going to war than previously because of the prospects of large-scale suffering even for those who may emerge victorious.

But just as competitive arming can sometimes help prevent war, it can also contribute to bringing on a war.[17] If much depends on the political circumstances surrounding any particular military balance, this does not mean that we should concentrate only on nonmilitary variables and forget that armaments can play a crucial role in precipitating war.

There probably are optimal levels of armament to discourage war between adversaries. If the armament of one or both of the parties is either above or below this optimum, while their political hostility remains intense, war is more likely than if both countries remain at this optimum, even with the same degree of political hostility. The difficulty, of course, is in knowing just where the optimal armament levels are in any adversarial relationship, as well as in inducing both sides to stabilize their arsenals at these levels. At the center of the difficulty is the problem we have already identified: what is perceived by one country or alliance to be the optimum for deterring its opponents may be perceived by the opponents to be intolerably threatening.

Stable and Unstable Military Balances

Certain kinds of military balances (or imbalances) are inherently more threatening than others, and some of them may provide more incentives to one or both sides to launch an attack. Frequently what is most provocative is an impending dramatic augmentation in an opponent's force levels that seems to threaten an imbalance.

Gross imbalances. If there exists between intensely antagonistic countries a large imbalance of military power favoring the country dissatisfied with the prevailing political or economic relationship, the imbalance will tempt the dissatisfied but militarily superior country to escalate conflict to the brink of war and, if this does not induce concessions by the adversary, to launch an attack. Japan's military operations against China in the 1930s were this type of aggression. So were Hitler's attacks on Germany's neighbors before World War II, the North Korean invasion of South Korea in 1950, and India's attack on Pakistan in 1971 to prevent Pakistan's suppression of the Bangladesh independence movement. In other words, the military aggressor usually needs a clear prospect of victory in order to attack. A substantial imbalance in military capability usually is a crucial and necessary determinant, though not in itself a sufficient cause, of war. The defending country, on the other hand, does not need a clear prospect of victory to be motivated to fight. All it needs is some likelihood of making the war painful enough to the aggressor country to compel it to modify the expectation that violence can obtain what is desired without great cost; sometimes the victim of attack will fight even without the hope of changing the aggressor's calculations simply because surrender is an intolerable alternative.

Where gross imbalances favor the satisfied power, there usually is "peace" in the sense of a lack of overt warfare. But if peace is an imposed or imperialistic peace over peoples who believe their values are being intolerably suppressed, and if the suppressed peoples begin to agitate against being dominated, the imperial power, with overwhelming military force at its disposal, may forcibly intervene to put down the challenges to its dominance. The British military intervention against restless North American colonies in 1776 was of this sort, as were the French wars against the Vietnamese and Algerian independence movements after World War II. Similarly, it was the overwhelming military power of the Soviet Union in Eastern Europe that allowed the Kremlin to order its tanks and troops into Hungary to shoot down those revolting against Soviet dominance in 1956 and then to inflict the same kind of brutal punishment on the Czechoslovakian reformist movement in 1968. The Soviet invasion of Afghanistan in 1979 was a still more recent instance of the attempt to reinforce dominance by military might. In each case, the superpower acted according to its calculation that the victim was a military pushover and lacked allies that might redress the imbalance of power.

As these typical examples of aggression reveal, the initial calculation by an aggressor that it possesses sufficient military superiority to overpower its opponent may easily turn out to be mistaken. Sometimes, as in an imperial power's wars to hold on to its dominions, because the aggressor is fighting in only one of several places of tension that may need the commitment of military resources, the stronger country may be unwilling to expend human life and material resources beyond a certain point—while its nationalist opponents, fighting for what they regard as the integrity and life of their nations, place no limit on the sacrifices they will make. This was the essential dynamic in both the unsuccessful attempt by Britain to put down the American independence movement and the more recent failure of the French to hold on to Algeria; and a related example of a superpower that could not overwhelm a small power because of the small power's greater will to fight is, of course, seen in the U.S. failure in Vietnam from 1964 to 1973.

It is also true that the military superiority an aggressor counts on can be negated by the entry of additional countries into the war. Hitler's attempts in the late 1930s to pick off his European neighbors one by one provoked the formation of the worldwide military coalition that eventually defeated him. The North Korean invasion of South Korea in 1950 appears to have been based on the mistaken assumption that the United States would not intervene in a Korean war.

Despite the many lessons history provides of aggressors' miscalculations of the pertinent balances of power, however, the existence of an apparently large imbalance of military power between adversary countries tends to stimulate the war hawks in the militarily superior country, and the imbalance can be the most significant factor in pushing decision makers into acts that precipitate war.

Challenges to a prevailing balance. Another type of situation in which armament levels can themselves increase the likelihood of wars between political antagonists occurs when it appears virtually certain that the prevailing balance is about to be significantly altered by new deployments. If the prevailing equilibrium of force is challenged by the arms program of side A, and side B, for reasons of domestic economics or other constraints, finds it highly undesirable to initiate compensatory arms programs of its own, side B may be tempted to consider a preventive war while the balance is not yet unfavorable. Serious discussion of a preventive war against the Soviet Union, for example, resulted from the anticipation in policy circles in the United States and the United Kingdom, in the 1947–1949 period, that the Soviets would soon attain a nuclear-weapons capability likely to unbalance the post–World War II equilibrium of Russian conventional military superiority in Europe on the one side and America's possession of the atomic bomb on the other.

Sometimes a challenge to a prevailing imbalance also is provocative. The outbreak of hostilities between Israel and the Arabs has on a number of occasions been triggered by new Arab arms buildups (sometimes including arms infusions from the Soviet Union) that portended an elimination of Israeli military superiority. In the 1967 war Israel decided to strike first, in a war it regarded as inevitable, while it was still militarily stronger than its enemies. And Japan's bombing of the American fleet stationed at Pearl Harbor, Hawaii, on December 7, 1941, was motivated at least in part by its desire to hobble American naval capabilities in the Pacific before they could be built up in the two-ocean naval program authorized by the U.S. government in 1939.[18]

Inherently destabilizing deployments. Even when they are part of an essentially equalized balance, certain types of military deployments can provide an adversary or both adversaries with high incentives to strike first in a war-threat situation. There are enemy weapons or troop concentrations that are major elements of the enemy's military capability but that are highly vulnerable if attacked in their present locations or condition of readiness. As a political conflict escalates to the brink of war, the existence of such exposed time-urgent and lucrative targets can provide an almost irresistible temptation to strike first. If the enemy is assumed to perceive a similar advantage in striking first at one's own vulnerable deployments, the temptations are multiplied and reinforce each other, particularly if the forces that the enemy would use first are themselves immediately vulnerable.

The fact that America's ships deployed at Pearl Harbor in 1941 were not only the core of the military capability the United States could use against Japan in a war (that the Japanese apparently believed was inevitable anyway), but were also clearly sitting ducks for a surprise air attack, undoubtedly provided the clinching arguments when Japanese decision makers weighed the risks of their action.

An earlier classic case of military deployments inducing attack resulted from the mobilization of the Russian army against Austria on the eve of World War I. As Austria prepared to humble Serbia militarily in retaliation for the assassination of Archduke Francis Ferdinand by a Serbian nationalist, the Russians, to deter the impending invasion of their client's country, mobilized their own military forces. Because the Russians feared provoking Germany to join with Austria in fulfillment of the terms of the existing German-Austrian alliance, the czar announced that his mobilization was directed only against the Austrian threat to Serbia. However, the Russian armies were so organized that it was impossible for them to engage in a partial mobilization. That the whole army had to get ready to fight unavoidably threatened Germany as well as Austria. Moreover, given the prevailing techniques of warfare in 1914, the country that first completed the mobilization of its forces might well be able to win the decisive early battles of the war. The consequence was an immediate mobilization of forces by Germany and its declaration of war against Russia.

The contemporary strategic-arms competition between the United States and the Soviet Union contains a destabilizing feature of fearsome dimensions: the efforts on each side to maintain capabilities that could hobble the other side's strategic-offensive forces in a war. The mere possession of these counterforce capabilities increases the likelihood that a nonnuclear war or other extreme crisis between the superpowers would escalate to a strategic nuclear war: the more effective such capabilities are, the higher the incentive to get in the first strike in an exchange of strategic blows. The most dangerous situation exists when both sides possess substantial strategic counterforce capabilities vulnerable to the other side's counterforce attack. In an escalating war or crisis, each antagonist therefore may feel that it must use or lose its counterforce weapons. Neither would want to wait to retaliate until it had absorbed the opponent's first strike. (Disabling counterforce strikes could be aimed at either the weapons themselves or the command and control centers from which they are operated, or both. ABMs, if then part of the first-striker's arsenal, would be used to blunt retaliation by any of the victim's ICBMs that survive the attack or are launched preemptively.) And since each side would probably program its vulnerable strategic forces to be launched on warning of strategic attack by the enemy, the opportunities for terrible miscalculation would be intense. The nightmare is that in an escalating crisis each side rushes to put its forces on high alert and prelaunch readiness—moves interpreted by the other side's intelligence analysts as preparations to launch a preemptive counterforce blow—leading to irresistible pressures on both sides to strike first to preempt the other side's preemption!

Efforts to reduce these dangerous instabilities in the U.S.-Soviet balance of terror are discussed in Chapter 9 and part of Chapter 10. It is enough now to emphasize that particular configurations of arms races are more war prone or escalation prone than others. The notion that only political conflict causes wars and that arms races are only the symptoms of political conflict is a vast—and dangerous—simplification of the complicated relationships between possessing weapons and resorting to violence.

NOTES

1. For a more formal theoretical analysis of many of the relationships looked at in this chapter see Bruce Bueno de Mesquita, *The War Trap* (New Haven, Ct.: Yale University Press, 1981).

2. For yearly updates on global military expenditures and aggregate armament estimates, see Stockholm International Peace Research Institute, *World Armaments and Disarmament: SIPRI Yearbook* (London: Taylor & Francis). Comparisons with nonmilitary expenditures are published annually by Ruth Leger Sivard, *World Military and Social Expenditures* (Leesburg, Va.: World Priorities). Vivid graphic representations of the data are in Michael Kidron and Dan Smith, *The War Atlas* (New York: Simon & Schuster, 1983).

3. The latest quantitative expressions of these uncertain military

estimates are displayed in the annual publication of the International Institute for Strategic Studies, *The Military Balance* (London: IISS, each autumn) containing a compilation of forces deployed in various theaters and special analysis of the East-West balance in Europe.

4. Leonard S. Spector, *Nuclear Proliferation Today* (New York: Vintage, 1984).

5. Fred Charles Iklé, "Can Deterrence Last Out the Century?" *Foreign Affairs* (January 1973), 51(2):267–285, and Paul Nitze, "Deterring Our Deterrent," *Foreign Policy*, 25 (Winter 1976–1977), 195–210.

6. Harold Brown, *Department of Defense Annual Report, Fiscal Year 1982* (Washington, D.C.: U.S. Department of Defense, January 16, 1981), pp. 38–44.

7. For the development of strategic force-planning concepts through the 1970s, see Lawrence Freedman, *The Evolution of Nuclear Strategy* (New York: St. Martin's, 1983). A lively account of the debates among the strategists is provided by Fred Kaplan, *The Wizards of Armageddon* (New York: Simon & Schuster, 1983).

8. *Report of the President's Commission on Strategic Forces* (Washington, D.C.: Office of the President, April 6, 1983), pp. 2–3.

9. *Ibid.*, p. 6.

10. *Ibid.*, pp. 5–6.

11. Richard Halloran, "Pentagon Draws Up First Strategy for Fighting a Long Nuclear War," *New York Times*, May 30, 1982.

12. Leslie Gelb, "Weinberger Calls His 'Basic Outlook' Unchanged," *New York Times*, June 15, 1982. See also Secretary Weinberger's letter to the *Boston Globe*, June 23, 1982.

13. President Ronald Reagan, Address to the Nation, Washington, D.C., March 23, 1983, full text in Department of State, *Current Policy*, no. 472.

14. Office of Technology Assessment, Ballistic Missile Defense Technologies (Washington, D.C.: U.S. Government Printing Office, 1985), pp. 55–64.

15. *Ibid.*

16. Fred S. Hoffmann, "Ballistic Missile Defenses and U.S. National Security," excerpts from a 1983 report prepared for the Undersecretary of Defense for Policy, in Harold Brown, Fred S. Hoffmann, Paul Nitze, and Ronald Reagan, *Essays on Strategy and Diplomacy: The Strategic Defense Initiative* (Claremont, Calif.: Keck Center for International Strategic Studies, 1985), pp. 5–15.

17. Statistical studies of the incidence of war have not succeeded in establishing any significant correlation between arms races and the onset of war, other than the obvious fact that countries that fight one another must to some extent have armed against one another. Lewis Richardson, in *Arms and Security* (Pittsburgh, Pa.: Boxwood Press, 1960), p. 740, concludes that "the evidence, as far as it goes, is that only a minority of wars have been preceded

by arms races." More recent quantitative studies have not contradicted Richardson's findings. See J. David Singer and Melvin Small, *The Wages of War, 1816–1965: A Statistical Handbook* (New York: Wiley, 1972).

18. See two articles by Samuel P. Huntington: "Arms Races: Prerequisites and Results," *Public Policy* (1958), 41–83; and "To Choose Peace or War," *United States Naval Institute Proceedings*, 83 (April 1957), 360–366.

PART III

The Prevention and Control of War

The continuing reliance on threats of force and the resort to war as "normal" instruments of international relations no longer can be viewed as a sane prospect for human society. With increasingly powerful weapons of mass destruction available to more and more countries and political movements, it has become evident that another world war could jeopardize the survival of the human species and that even an initially small war could ignite a global holocaust. Yet, as shown in Part II, the factors reinforcing the war system are as strong as ever.

Attempts to deal with this most serious and unprecedented human predicament operate at three levels of ambitiousness:

1. Efforts to purge war from the world by radically transforming either the structure of world society or human propensities to resort to violence are analyzed in Chapter 7. Most of the radical structural reforms envision a world law-and-order system, analogous to domestic systems of governance, with centralized rule-making and enforcement. The precondition for the realization of such a legal-political transformation of the world system, however, is the forging of a sense of community among the diverse peoples of the planet that does not seem likely in the decades ahead. Gandhian and similar approaches that depend upon groups and countries forswearing violent means of protecting and asserting their interests would seem to require a

globally extensive moral revolution in order to substantially eliminate the prospect of a third world war. A synthesis of the structural and Gandhian approaches is suggested by Johan Galtung, but it too would require a long-term and far-reaching process of social transformation.

2. For the present, hopes for avoiding the earth-destroying holocaust that human beings are now capable of unleashing reside largely in skillful diplomacy and the enhancement and utilization of existing institutions and processes for international conflict control. These means for reducing the role of war in world politics without having to await a radical transformation of world society are analyzed in Chapter 8.

3. As shown in Part II, however, the instruments of warfare themselves, if dangerously designed and deployed, can provoke unwanted wars, despite the efforts of statesmen on behalf of peace. Attention to and correction of such provocative weapons systems and military deployments to reduce their war-prone characteristics is the special province of arms control, as are measures to assure that once wars start there will be opportunities to limit and terminate them short of total holocaust. Chapter 9 is devoted to this increasingly crucial field of war prevention and control.

Frequently, advocates of the more ambitious efforts to purge war from the world are at odds with those who emphasize relatively modest measures to control the escalation of conflict. The former worry that any impression that wars, once started, can be controlled reduces the inhibitions on going to war. The latter are concerned that an emphasis on currently infeasible radical solutions will divert attention and support from urgently needed controls. Part IV will suggest an integrated strategy for war prevention and control designed to synthesize these contending approaches.

It may well be that we shall, by a process of sublime irony,
have reached a stage in the story
where safety will be the sturdy child of terror
and survival the twin brother of annihilation.
                                                        —Winston Churchill

In view of the fact that in any future war
nuclear weapons will certainly by employed,
and that such weapons
threaten the continued existence of mankind,
we urge the governments of the world to realize . . .
that their purposes cannot be furthered by a world war,
and we urge them consequently, to find peaceful means
for settlement of all matters of dispute between them.
                                        —Bertrand Russell and Albert Einstein

The moral to be legitimately drawn
from the supreme tragedy of the atomic bomb
is that it will not be destroyed by counter bombs,
even as violence cannot be destroyed by violence.
Mankind has to go out of violence only through nonviolence.
Hatred can be overcome only through love.
Counter hatred only increases the surface as well
as the depth of hatred.
                                                —Mohandas K. Gandhi

CHAPTER 7

Efforts To Purge War from the World

The recognition that a world war fought with today's weapons could threaten the survival of the human species has convinced many government officials, social scientists, theologians, political activists, and other concerned citizens that there is no more urgent or important task than the banishment of the institution of war itself. Partial measures, from this perspective, not only are inadequate but are likely to be counterproductive. Especially dangerous are the notions of "limited war" and "firebreaks" between different levels of warfare, for these can encourage the delusion that modern war is manageable, with risks that can be controlled—and that therefore crossing the threshold from peace to war need not be regarded as the awesome step it is.

The condemnation of war as a social institution, and the search for alternative means to deal with intense international conflicts, though never before so widespread a popular concern, antedates the nuclear age. There is a long history of prominent thinkers and political leaders who have come to the conclusion that war is never, or hardly ever, sane or morally justified, and who have attempted to translate their convictions into workable proposals for eliminating war as an instrument of statecraft.

These efforts have been of two kinds: (1) the political-constitutional restructuring of world society, usually based on the assumption that the primary cause of war is the anarchic nation-state system itself; and (2) the reeducation and moral-psychological reform of human beings, based on the assumption that wars are started by people who have distorted values, perhaps not adequately sensitized to the horrors of violence or aware of viable alternatives to war. Sometimes the two approaches have been fused, but most proposals have given primacy to one or the other as the essential precondition for eliminating war.

RADICAL TRANSFORMATION OF THE WORLD'S POLITICAL STRUCTURE

If a single government could be established over all of the world society, exercising a sufficient monopoly over the tools of violence to overwhelm attempts by subordinate groups to use violence, then war could be eliminated—or, failing that, rapidly suppressed by the central world government. The logic of this idea has appealed less to practicing statesmen than to philosophers, some of whom have attempted to give political flesh and bones to their visions. We need not give attention here to proposals for merging or federating states under the aegis of an imperial power—for example, the poet Dante Alighieri's plan in *De Monarchia*, and the "Grand Design" of King Henry IV of France. Rather the focus of this section is on the voluntary restructuring of the world polity for the express purpose of eliminating interstate war.

Crucé's Proposal

In 1623 a French monk, Emeric Crucé, formulated an early proposal, called *Le Nouveau Cynée*, to give the fragmented world society a central governing structure. Membership in the proposed community of states would be universal, encompassing not only the European states, but also Turkey, Persia, India, China, and kingdoms in Africa, as well as the pope and representatives of the Jews. All of the important entities would send delegates to a permanent Council of Ambassadors, whose decisions, arrived at by majority vote and enforced, if need be, by the pooled armed might of the majority, would be binding on all members. Crucé's *Cynée* also provided for an elaborate structure of voluntary negotiation and arbitration and for a world court to resolve disputes, prior to action by the Council; the plan was that the world body's military enforcement would be an ultimate sanction that rarely would have to be used.[1] Predictably, because no monarch of the time was willing to subordinate his sovereign realm to a higher authority, the ideal scheme remained only a paper exercise for want of a powerful sponsor.

Penn's Plan

Seventy years later, in 1693, the prominent colonizer and Quaker missionary William Penn published a similar plan in his *Essay Toward the Present and Future Peace of Europe*. As the title suggests, Penn confined his call for political union to the monarchs of Europe, and like Crucé he insisted that they subordinate their sovereignties to the rules and decisions of a general parliament representing all of them. Decisions would require a three-fourths vote, with the wealthier states having more votes than others in the parliament. And also like Crucé, Penn, compromising his Quaker pacifism, provided that member states would combine their military strength when necessary to compel reluctant states to submit to the procedures and decisions of the all-European government:

> If any of the sovereignties that constitute the imperial State shall refuse to submit their claims or pretentions to them, or abide and perform the judgement thereof, and seek their remedy by arms, or delay their compliance beyond the time prefixed in their resolutions, all other sovereignties, united as one strength, shall compel the submission and performance of the sentence.[2]

Bellers's Plan

A plan resembling Penn's was published by John Bellers in 1710 in his essay *Some Reasons for a European State*. Bellers advanced the dialogue on the potential merger of states by dealing with the problem of unequal power of states expected to become constituent parts of the new Federation. He proposed that all Europe be divided into one hundred equal provinces, each of which would have one representative in the Central Senate and contribute equal military units to a common force. The military contingents, Bellers believed, would "prevent the rash from such dismal adventures as are the consequences of war, while they know that every man in the Senate hath one or two or three thousand men to back what he concludes there."[3]

Saint-Pierre's Project

A more elaborate scheme for a powerful supranational state to prevent war was submitted to the French monarchy, soon afterward, in 1712, by the Abbé de Saint-Pierre in his *Project of Perpetual Peace*. Saint-Pierre conceived of an all-European Union whose central authority would be a Senate of Peace. Composed of two representatives from each of the twenty-four states of Europe, the Senate would sit permanently at the Dutch city of Utrecht, presided over by a president called the "Prince of Peace" chosen weekly by rotation among the members. The only treaties and territorial changes permitted among the member states would be approved by a three-fourths vote of the Senate. If disputes arose among members, the Senate would first appoint mediating commissioners to try to achieve a compromise; if the mediations failed, the Senate would arbitrate the dispute, with the understanding that its awards would be binding on the members.

States entering into treaties on their own, refusing to abide by decisions of the Senate, or making preparations for war would be brought to submission by the combined forces of the Union. And the defeated offending states would be made to pay the financial costs of the war, with their principal ministers subject to punishment by death or life imprisonment as disturbers of the peace.

The enforcement process provided for in the *Project* would depend on the Union's commanding a military force superior to the forces of its members. Each member state was to provide an equal number of troops; smaller states unable to finance their recruitment would be subsidized from funds contributed to the Union treasury by the wealthier states. The Generalissimo of the Union Forces, appointed by and responsible to the Senate of Peace, would have supreme command over the generals of the members states.[4]

The French minister André Fleury did not reject the desirability in the abstract of such a radical transformation of the world polity but exhibited the sophisticated statesman's typical reaction to such schemes: "You have forgotten an essential article," he told the abbé, "that of dispatching missionaries to touch the hearts of princes and to persuade them to enter into your views."[5]

Rousseau's Criticism of Saint-Pierre's Project

The philosopher Jean-Jacques Rousseau admired Saint-Pierre's work, but in embracing it gave it a kiss of death. In his 1761 publication explaining the abbé's logic, *Extrait du projet du paix perpetuelle de Monsieur l'Abbé de Saint-Pierre* and in his 1762 publication assessing its feasibility, *Jugement sur la paix perpetuelle*, Rousseau convincingly demonstrated the utopian nature of the contemplated centralization of power.

Saint-Pierre was correct, wrote Rousseau, that the only way to bring peace to Europe would be to set up a commonwealth

with powers to pass laws and ordinances binding upon all its members; it must have a coercive force capable of compelling every state to obey its common resolves. . . . ; finally, it must be strong and firm enough to make it impossible for any member to withdraw at his own pleasure the moment he conceives his private interest to clash with that of the whole body.

But despite the necessity of such a union to achieve peace, it could never be brought into existence: it was "an absurd dream" requiring sovereigns to perceive that the comon interest in peace outweighed their particular interests. This could not be, since peace was not an end in itself for most statesmen but, like war, a condition or means for the realization of other interests. Moreover, Rousseau argued, the separate sovereigns would oppose giving whatever commonwealth could be formed the powers it would require to enforce laws throughout the realm: "Is there a single sovereign in the world who . . . would bear without indignation the mere idea of seeing himself forced to be just, not only to foreigners, but even to his own subjects?"[6]

In these and related essays, especially his *L'Etat de guerre*, Rousseau advanced the elemental idea that sovereign national governments are mankind's historic response to the anarchic "state of war" within domestic society and that their merger in a federation requiring substantial diminution of the power of the separate governments would be feared, by those states that had achieved substantial security within the existing order, as a retrogression toward either a state of war or a forced subjugation by an imperial sovereign. Such a federation could be brought into being, he concluded, only by violence on such a scale as would stagger humanity.[7] In other words, international anarchy, the correlate to national sovereignty, is paradoxically the necesary condition for domestic. peace.

Thinking About World Order in the Nineteenth and Early Twentieth Centuries

Rousseau's criticisms of the feasibility of establishing a world government to eliminate war provided philosophical support for the dominant view among political and legal thinkers and statesmen for the next century and a half: the society of states would have to rely principally on diplomacy and the balance of power to prevent war. If there were to be any institutionalized arrangement among nations to moderate their conflicts and encourage cooperation, it could be no more than a confederal organization of still-sovereign states to facilitate mediation and other voluntary conflict-resolution procedures and—most ambitiously—to mobilize concerted action against states that were overaggressive, or immoderately expansionist, or otherwise contemptuous of the norms of the moderate state system. (Efforts to seek peace without a fundamental transformation of the system of sovereign states, such as Immanuel Kant's in the realm of philosophy and those of the League of Nations and the United Nations in the realm of practice, will be treated in the next chapter.)

A revival of interest in truly supranational government was sparked by organizations such as the United World Federalists following the failure of the League of Nations to keep the peace after World War I. Chapter VII of the United Nations Charter, containing the basic international security provisions of the UN, in some respects reflects the efforts to give the new organization enforcement teeth that the League of Nations had lacked; but, as will be shown in Chapter 8, the charter provides only a framework on which supranational enforcement machinery can be constructed if the major member states choose, which they have not—for essentially the same basic reasons Rousseau pointed to earlier.

Clark and Sohn's Proposal for World Law

A detailed proposal for transforming the United Nations into a peace-enforcing world state was developed in the late 1950s by two distinguished international legal experts, Grenville Clark and Louis B. Sohn of the Harvard Law School, who published it in their volume *World Peace Through World Law*.[8] To accomplish the goal of the title, say the authors, "nothing less will suffice than a comprehensive plan whereby there would be established on a world scale institutions corresponding to those which have been found essential for the maintenance of law and order in local communities and nations."[9] Since police forces are necessary to maintain law and order even within a mature community or nation, "similar forces will be required to guarantee the carrying out and maintenance of complete disarmament by each and every nation and to deter or suppress *any* attempted international violence."[10]

Accordingly, Clark and Sohn propose a "World Peace Force" composed of 200,000 to 600,000 full-time professional volunteers, to act as an enforcement arm of the controlling bodies of a revised United Nations organization. The force would be provisioned with "the most modern weapons and equipment," initially to come from the transfer of weapons and equipment discarded by national military forces during the disarmament process. Subsequently, the arsenal of the World Peace Force would be produced by a United Nations Supply and Research Agency. The World Peace Force would not have nuclear weapons as part of its normal operating equipment, but it could obtain them from a reserve held by a UN Nuclear Energy Authority, should they be needed to deter the use of nuclear weapons by a country that had clandestinely retained some in violation of the disarmament agreement.

Overall direction of the World Peace Force would be completely and continuously the responsibility of the deliberative political organs of the revised United Nations. Its military commanders, appointed by the Executive Council of the UN, could be removed at any time by the council, and the commanders would have no discretionary authority in advance of any contingency.

Clark and Sohn's revised United Nations would make the Executive Council responsible to the General Assembly, much as the British cabinet is responsible to the House of Commons. The General Assembly would have a weighted system of voting based primarily on the population of member nations. Decisions of the assembly and council would have the status of world law, enforceable directly upon individuals and member nations through a strengthened UN court system serviced by a 10,000-man civil police force in addition to the World Peace Force.

In essence, Clark and Sohn have proposed a representative world federal government with enforcement powers superior to the powers of any of its constituent units. If sufficient consensus existed among the powerful constituent units to found such a system by disarming themselves and transferring their weapons to the world government, the prospect of such a world government able to make enforceable decisions might have some plausibility. But the authors do not attempt to outline the political and economic conditons required to bring about the required consensus. *World Peace Through World Law* therefore remains an exercise in abstract constitution-building, leaving it to political scientists and statesmen to stipulate and construct the political conditions that might make the scheme a realistic proposal.

Falk's Strategies for Radical Change

Another promiment American professor of international law, Richard Falk, has attempted to construct a set of "transitional strategies" to provide a realistic base for just such radical transformation of the world's political system.

Falk's own "Preferred World Polity," as he calls it, is designed to serve four basic values: the minimization of large-scale collective violence; the maximization of social and economic well-being; the realization of fundamental human rights and conditions of social justice; and the maintenance and rehabilitation of ecological quality. A World Polity Association would be built on a "central guidance system" having all the attributes of a world supranational state (although Falk shies away from the terms "world government" or "world state"). Its central deliberative body would be a three-chamber General Assembly, with different bases of representation in each chamber and checks-and-balances voting arrangements among the chambers to assure that world laws are based as much as possible on the consent of the governed.[11]

Like Clark and Sohn, Falk envisions a World Security System with armed forces of its own "to maintain international peace under all possible circumstances," assuring that the legislative and judicial decisions of the World Polity Association are adhered to and enforcing the disarmament agreement that must precede establishment of the new system. Falk hopes that most of the "enforcement" will be by nonviolent techniques, but does not rule out the use by the World Security Forces of violent weapons, and even nuclear forces, to counter groups that retain or build weapons of mass destruction in violation of the disarmament agreement.[12]

Falk is a realist, however, in recognizing that "No world order solution which presupposes the substantial modification of the state system can be achieved unless the advocates of the new system are aligned with important social and political forces within the existing structures." Accordingly, he outlines a transition process with associated strategies and tactics to create and enlarge constituencies for his preferred polity that, by virtue of their size and political power, would compel officials with formal authority in the state system to negotiate the required institutional transformations. The transition process comprises three stages:

1. an era devoted to raising the consciousness of the general population and of specific interest groups to realize that they cannot adequately maintain their security and other values in the existing world order system and therefore a drastic change along the lines of the Preferred World Polity is necessary;

2. an era of political mobilization converting the new consciousness into active interest-group lobbying and electoral politics to bring pressure on existing elites and put forward new political elites in countries throughout the world, resulting in committing national governments to the required institution-building at the global level;

3. an era of transformation during which disarmament of the nation-states and the simultaneous buildup of world institutions and power are undertaken and completed.

Falk and contemporaries of similar outlook recognize that their current efforts to raise consciousness must contend against the multitude of tangible incentives, sanctions, and doctrines reinforcing continued majority acceptance of the status quo. In their pessimistic moments they grant that it may take a catastrophe—that is, a worldwide economic collapse, an immediately looming breakdown of life-sustaining ecologies, or World War III—to shake loose the prevailing attachments to the nation-state system. They also are aware that a consensus against perpetuating the existing world system is hardly the same as a consensus on the structure of its successor, for the latter will require a worldwide convergence of values to implement institutional designs that is nowhere is evidence now. Undaunted by these difficulties, they continue their writing and speaking to persuade as many as they can that, because the existing system is sufficiently irrational and bound ultimately to destroy itself, a new system is necessary and can be made feasible.

Whether or not such schemes for wholesale restructuring of the world polity will one day be feasible, they provide contemporary statesmen with no practical means for dealing with immediate threats of war. This is a principal reason that the schemes are largely ignored by government officials.

UNIVERSAL ADOPTION OF A PACIFIST MORALITY

In contrast with champions of global structural reform, pacifists locate both the cause of war and the ability to prevent war within individuals. To have peace depend on eventual changes in the structure of the world polity not only is insufficient, they say, but provides justification for resorting to war until the restructuring is finished. The pacifist regards war as unjustified whatever the structure of the polity—even anarchy or brutal empire. These and all other political structures, as well as the role of violence within them, result from the ways humans behave toward each other. To change the political structure without changing the individual moralities of most human beings will only deflect immoral behavior (violence being the grossest immorality) and rearrange its manifestations in society. A world society that establishes a world government without first universally educating humans on the immorality of all violence will still experience war: it will simply be called "civil war."

Pacifists believe that the only way to finally purge war from the world is to convince people that all violence is wrong, whether it is committed by states against individuals, by individuals against states, by states against states, or by private individuals against each other. Though they acknowledge other injustices in world society, pacifists insist that war must be regarded as the greatest injustice; otherwise people will be provided a rationalization for supporting "just wars." The concept of just wars allows each side to convince itself of the legitimacy of using violence to defend the nation's sovereign independence or its way of life, as well as to protect allies from more powerful enemies.

Pre-Christian and Early-Christian Pacifism

Contemporary pacifists trace the roots of their moral philosophy to the pre-Christian period, citing both the wisdom of Asian sages such as Lao-tse and Buddha and portions of the Hebrew scriptures, especially *Isaiah*, whose prophet would have nations "beat their swords into plowshares, and their spears into pruning hooks." But the principal early source of their inspiration is the moral imperatives enunciated by Jesus Christ in his Sermon on the Mount, as recounted in the New Testament:

> You have heard that they were told, "An eye for an eye and a tooth for a tooth." But I tell you not to resist injury, but if anyone strikes you on your right cheek, turn the other to him too; and if anyone wants to sue you for your shirt, let him have your coat too. And if anyone forces you to go one mile, go two miles with him. . . .

> You have heard that they were told, "You must love your neighbor and hate your enemy." But I tell you, love your enemies and pray for your persecutors, so that you may show yourselves true sons of your Father in heaven, for he makes the sun rise on the bad and good alike, and makes the rain fall on the upright and the wrongdoers.
>
> (*Matthew* 5:38–46)[13]

Until the fourth century many Christian church fathers invoked these passages to protest any use of war by the state. But after the conversion of the emperor Constantine, establishing the union of church and state in Rome, Christian theology retreated to the more pragmatic doctrine advanced by Augustine of dividing wars into two categories, the just and unjust, with the just wars those waged on behalf of the empire of Christendom against the barbarians. In later centuries, pacifism was advocated by small and politically ineffectual sects of Christians, while the dominant churches gave their blessings first to the Crusades to regain the Holy Lands from the Muslim infidels, and then to the wars of religion between Protestant and

Catholic states that devastated Europe for a hundred years before the Peace of Westphalia in 1648.

The Reassertion of Pacifism by Erasmus

In the early sixteenth century Erasmus of Rotterdam took exception to the Church's departures from Christ's teachings on nonviolence. Claiming that violence was contrary to the essential nature of man, in 1514 he published an eloquent but futile plea to the "Christian" statesmen and politicized churchmen of his time to renounce war:

> Ye say ye make war for the safeguard of the commonwealth; yea, but noway sooner nor more unthriftily may the commonwealth perish than by war. . . . Ye waste the citizens' goods, ye fill the houses with lamentations, ye fill all the country with thieves, robbers and ravishers. For these are the relics of war. . . . If ye love your own subjects truly, why resolve you not in mind these words: Why shall I put so many, in their lusty flourishing youth, in all mischiefs and perils? Why shall I depart so many honest wives and their husbands and make so many fatherless children?[14]

Contributions of Thoreau and Tolstoy

Most Renaissance and modern social and political philosophers, even while deploring the killing and disruption of civic life caused by war, have regarded war as they have the state's use of violence against its domestic enemies: as a necessary evil, a means often justified by the ends of state security, order, and justice. It was not until the nineteenth century, in the wake of the devastating nationalistic wars of the Napoleonic period, that an influential counterculture of pacifism emerged again. The most prominent of the new pacifists were literary intellectuals: the American poet and essayist Henry David Thoreau (1817–1862)[15] and the Russian nobleman and novelist Leo Tolstoy (1828–1910)[16] blended a back-to-the-simple-life philosophical anarchism with the basic Christian ethic of nonviolence, and both urged individuals to refuse to cooperate with governments that would make them go to war against the dictates of reason and conscience.

The Nonviolent Resistance
of Gandhi and His Followers

The pacifist leader from whom contemporary devotees of nonviolence draw most inspiration, Mohandas K. Gandhi (1869–1948), was himself a close student of the pacifist philosophers of Thoreau, Tolstoy, the Quakers, and Christ. Fusing this Western pacifist tradition with the Buddhist, Jain, and Vedic Hindu philosophies of nonviolence, and inventing new techniques of exerting political pressure, Gandhi developed nonviolent resistance into a political force that often could substitute for violent coercion.

Gandhi championed the philosophy and practice of nonviolence not only as a way of life for individuals but also as an instrument of politics for groups and nations. The central and animating concept was *ahimsa*, the brotherhood, common dignity, and moral interdependence of all human beings, which when deeply felt would render a man or woman incapable of deliberately inflicting harm on others. Its essential method was *satyagraha*, or "soul force," the active resistance to evil and cultivation of the good, first in oneself and then in others—good being the truth and nonviolence of ahimsa, and evil being falsehood and violence. British colonial rule over India violated the dignity of Indians and falsified the truth that they were brothers of the English, not their subjects; Indian independence, therefore, was a necessary condition of ahimsa. But independence had first to be achieved through nonviolent resistance to British overlordship, and by peaceful techniques of noncooperation: work stoppages, boycotts of British goods, sit-ins and lie-ins against attempts by British officials to use their power—never with hate against the individual British official, and always with a reasoned and communicated explanation for the resistance to the evil act. Gandhi persuaded millions of Indians to join him in the satyagraha method of agitating for national independence, in contrast with millions recruited by rival Indian nationalist movements that relied on violent subversion of British rule. For a complex of reasons, the British finally granted full independence to India after World War II; undoubtedly one reason was the sympathy and respect for the Indian cause that Gandhi had evoked in many Britons.

When asked whether an independent India would adopt satyagraha as an instrument of state policy, internally and externally, Gandhi was candidly pessimistic; his realization that the independent government set up by Jawaharlal Nehru in 1947 would rely on armed police to enforce domestic order and on a well-equipped military establishment to protect India's borders was a principal reason Gandhi declined to join the government. However, he remained distressed to the end of his life—he was, ironically, killed by an assassin's bullet—that an independent India would not try the noble experiment satyagraha. The following dialogue, which took place with an American questioner in 1940, reveals his feeling about extending nonviolence to the nation-state system:

> *Questioner*: Suppose a free India adopts Satyagraha as an instrument of state policy, how would she defend herself against probable aggression by another sovereign state?
>
> *Gandhi*: I fear that the chances of nonviolence being accepted as a principle of state policy are very slight. . . .
>
> But I may state my own individual view of the potency of nonviolence. I believe that a State can be administered on a nonviolent basis if the vast majority of the people are nonviolent. . . . Supposing, therefore, that India attained independence through pure nonviolence, India could retain it too by the same means. A nonviolent man or society does not anticipate or provide for attacks from without. . . . If the worst happens, there are two ways open to nonviolence. To yield possession but non-cooperate with the aggressor. Thus, supposing that a modern edition of Nero descended upon India, the representatives of the state will let him in but tell him he will get no assistance from the people. They will prefer death to submission. The second way would be nonviolent resistance by the people who have been trained in the nonviolent way. They would offer themselves unarmed as fodder for the aggressor's cannon. The underlying belief in either case is that even a Nero is not devoid of a heart. The unexpected spectacle of endless rows upon rows of men and women simply dying rather than surrender to the will of an aggressor must ultimately melt him and his soldiery. Practically speaking there will be probably no greater loss in men than if forcible resistance was offered. There will be no expenditure in armaments and fortifications.[17]

By so explaining the essential characteristics of a country's nonviolent defense against an aggressor, Gandhi stipulates conditions that, according even to his own speculations, make it very unlikely that it could become the dominant regime of international relations. Most of the people in a state practicing nonviolence must themselves be dedicated to the philosophy and trained in nonviolent action. They must be willing to yield physical possession of their country to an aggressor rather than engage in violence to prevent its being taken over. They must not submit to the aggressor's regime, however, even if he takes over the country, and they must be willing to be killed rather than submit. Ultimate success, or the eventual relinquishing of control of the country by the aggressor, follows from the assumption that the moral superiority, or soul force, of such absolutely dedicated and pervasive resistance changes the aggressor's desire to subdue the country.

Since almost all the people of the world would have to be devotees of nonviolence for war to be purged from world society, and since the required moral conversion of humankind would take a long time (decades? centuries?), during the process of conversion those who did not believe in the philosophy still would run most of the world. The few countries with war machines dismantled or paralyzed by the activities of domestic believers in nonviolence would be open to military occupation or domination by adversaries with war machines still operating.

Gandhi and his disciples might be willing to accept this as a temporary result, in the belief that matters indeed might have to get "worse" before they got better. Gandhian absolutists, in any event, would define success as being morally right rather than merely physically preserving themselves.

Statesmen, however, normally put political objectives ahead of morality—even though the best statesmen are constrained by moral considerations—and would act on the assumption that their highest political objective, as mandated by the constituents of the polity for which they are responsible, is to maintain the physical survival of the people of the country. To be sure, this objective may sometimes require surrender to a militarily more powerful opponent (as Japan was forced to surrender in August 1945, but only as a last resort) when it becomes clear beyond doubt that the alternative to surrender is ultimate defeat with an even greater loss of life.

The renewed appeal of Gandhi's ideas in the post–World War II period is a product of the growing fear that going to war with the massive lethal power now available to belligerents will unavoidably negate the objective of national survival. The Gandhian prescription of choosing instead to live under conditions imposed by the opponent, while working to subvert his regime, may be the more practical, let alone moral, alternative even for nations that have not yet been militarily defeated in war. Indeed, there is a growing body of historical research on Danish and Norwegian nonviolent subversion of the regimes Hitler imposed on those countries during World War II that supports the argument that the techniques developed by Gandhi may be more effective means of preserving the dignity and eventual liberation of a militarily occupied country than violent resistance, which is likely to provoke greater retaliatory violence with more destructive weapons.[18]

Some of Gandhi's disciples have been attempting to elaborate and apply his concepts and techniques of nonviolent resistance to the contemporary problems of deterrence and defense under the threat of nuclear holocaust. Gene Sharp, the director of the Program on Nonviolent Sanctions in Conflict and Defense at Harvard University's Center for International Affairs, has even taken on the task of showing that countries could better protect themselves against potential Soviet aggression if they were to organize themselves for determined nonmilitary resistance instead of continuing to rely on the increasingly incredible threat of nuclear escalation. In his cogently reasoned treatise *Making Europe Unconquerable: The Potential of Civilian-based Deterrence and Defence*, Sharp argues that NATO countries have mindlessly reacted to their predicament by digging themselves into a deeper hole where "the capacity to defend in order to deter has been replaced by the capability to destroy massively without the ability to defend."[19] Under Sharp's proposed alternative grand strategy,

> Deterrence and defense are to be accomplished by civilian
> forms of struggle—social, economic, political and
> psychological. Many kinds of political noncooperation, strikes,
> economic boycotts, symbolic protests, civil disobedience,
> social boycotts, and more extreme methods of disruption and
> intervention are among the weapons of this policy. . . . The
> aims are to deny the attackers their objectives and to make
> [the] society politically indigestible and ungovernable by the

attackers. Consolidation of foreign rule, a puppet government, or a government of usurpers becomes impossible. In addition, the civilian defenders aim to subvert the loyalty of the aggressor's troops and functionaries, to make them unreliable in carrying out orders and repression, and even to induce them to mutiny.

. . . Potential attackers are deterred when they see that their objectives will be denied them, political consolidation prevented, and that as a consequence of these struggles unacceptable costs will be imposed on them politically, economically, and internationally.[20]

Sharp builds the case for the policy of nonviolent resistance on strategic rather than moral grounds, distinguishing his approach from the traditional pacifism that rejects all violence a priori and puts peace ahead of all other social objectives. He insists that nonviolent resistance, like the strategies it proposes to supplant, be evaluated on grounds of cost-effectiveness for assuring the survival of the country and its values. On these grounds, he concludes, it is much superior to the strategies for securing the integrity of the NATO countries through the threat of nuclear retaliation in response to intolerable provocations. For if nuclear deterrence fails, the consequence is likely to be holocaust and national annihilation; but "the failure of civilian-based defense preparations to deter invasion of Western Europe does not bring likelihood of annihilation, but instead application for the first time of the real [nonviolent] defense capacity."[21]

THE GALTUNGIAN SYNTHESIS

Like many pacifists, Johan Galtung, the influential contemporary Norwegian social scientist, sees the solution to the problem of large-scale violence in the reform of basic interpersonal and intergroup relationships. But Galtung regards violence as a much broader phenomenon than physical attack and destruction. In his definition it includes "anything avoidable that impedes personal growth."[22]

Like the advocates of world government, Galtung maintains that a wholesale transformation of the structure of the existing world political/institutional system is a necessary condition for the ascendancy of nonviolent human relationships; but he differs from many world federalists in his insistence that the structural reforms need to reach down into the basic organization of social, economic, and political relationships within and between local communities. Galtung's nonviolent world would consist of

> many small societies, more of them and smaller than the countries in today's world. . . . I strongly hold that only in smaller societies can the distance between the ruler and ruled be small enough to permit self-expression to everybody, and only with smaller societies can large-scale hegemonial tendencies be avoided [In Galtung's lexicon "hegemonial" relationships are closely associated with violence].[23]

These small, territorially based societies would be crisscrossed and tied together by a "strong web of nonterritorial organizations . . . putting everybody in community with local neighbors as well as with distant neighbors."

Cheap means of mobility would be available to everyone, and there would be no visa or passport restrictions. Citizenship would become "more like membership in an association, to be discarded when there is no longer any commitment" to a particular society. But,

> Could there also be multiple citizenship or no citizenship at all? Why not? Some persons might opt for multiple membership at both the community and the social levels, and they might refuse citizenship in anything corresponding to today's nation-states. The world would not go under for that reason.[24]

Galtung is not content to leave all regulation of interpersonal and intergroup relations entirely to voluntary cooperative processes, however. He recognizes that

> there must somewhere be some central authority that can make and enact plans for such matters as world food distribution, world employment, world ecological balance, world water and oxygen budgets and that can administer the riches that belong to all, such as the seabed and oceans, the bio-atmosphere, the cosmos, subterranean desposits.[25]

Though he admits that "the reconciliation of this need with the need for decentralization would continue to be problematic," Galtung outlines one possible design for a world authority to preserve maximum decentralization consistent with imperatives for world order and justice, a design quite similar to Falk's "preferred world polity." It provides for direct election of representatives to a House of States (representing the territorial units), a House of Minorities (representing emerging states), a House of Transnational Associations ("like a parliament or congress"), and a House of Supranational Organizations (representing functional groups). All four houses would articulate the concerns of their constituencies, some of which obviously would overlap, and would pass resolutions. When it comes to making binding decisions, however, Galtung places most authority, initially at least, in the House of States.[26]

Galtung envisions that the basic means of obtaining compliance with the decisions of the world central authority would be the authority's "remunerative power," not coercive force:

> I see a world central authority as having enormous resources for constructive use at its disposal, which means capital, goods and know-how. The authority should be able to disburse all three where they are needed . . . , but there could also be above-normal remuneration to those who comply particularly well with the international norms. In short, I am thinking of a system of positive sanctions much more than negative sanctions, for the simple reasons that the latter do not seem to work as an instrument of compliance and the former are at the same time vehicles of global development.[27]

The Galtungians, like the Gandhians and the advocates of a supranational federal world government, quite consciously are dealing with the long term. When it comes to dealing with the threat of nuclear holocaust, they must join their contemporaries in choosing among the relatively limited means of controlling conflict available within the still-prevailing nation-state system.

GENERAL AND COMPLETE DISARMAMENT

There is an attractive simplicity to the notion that war can be eliminated as an instrument of international relations if states will give up their military arsenals. Its attraction lies in its apolitical neatness: it requires no precondition that adversaries first solve their political conflicts or agree on a new world constitutional system, and it expresses no need to affect a moral revolution turning all human beings into Christians or Gandhian saints who love their enemies. All it requires is a mutual recognition that the costs and risks of war in the modern world outweigh any gains a state might hope to achieve by going to war, that no statesmen or nations really want war, and that the only reason nations prepare for war is to deter others from resorting to force of arms against them and their allies. Disarmament would be tangible confirmation of the universal recognition that war is no longer a cost-effective means of advancing state interests, and it would remove the self-defense rationale that most states invoke to justify their arsenals and war-fighting strategies. Any government that began to build an arsenal in an otherwise disarmed world would be admitting to the world, including its own people, that it had aggressive designs; other states would isolate it economically and politically, and its own citizens would organize against it.

Periodically, the attractiveness of the idea of general and complete disarmament generates popular support from war-weary or frightened populations, and statesmen have occasionally become its champions. (Most official diplomatic efforts at "disarmament" have been limited to specific weapons and have attempted to set tolerable ceilings on retained arms. We will look at some of these specific arms-limitation efforts in detail in Chapter 9.)

Woodrow Wilson's Fourth Point

President Woodrow Wilson, in the fourth of his Fourteen Points defining the peace that would follow World War I, came close to embracing general and complete disarmament by insisting that "national armaments will be reduced to the lowest point consistent with domestic safety."[28] This formula surely would have been difficult to negotiate among sovereign states of vastly different size and domestic systems of law and order; but assuming that some agreement could have been reached on different levels of "domestic" police forces, it would have constituted as much of an approximation as could be expected, short of world government or moral-pacifist revolution, of a blueprint for a disarmed world. When it came to incorporation of Wilson's peace proposal in the Treaty of Versailles, however, his fellow statesmen found Wilson's fourth point too radical; the American delegation was compelled to explain that "domestic safety" implied not only internal policing "but the protection of territory against invasion." Article 8 of the completed treaty finally contained the totally noncontroversial statement that "the maintenance of peace requires the reduction of national armaments to the lowest point consistent with national safety."[29] The rationale for standing armies and awesome national arsenals was once again legitimized.

The Superpower Disarmament Charade

The idea of general and complete disarmament was revived by the Soviets in September of 1959. Addressing the United Nations General Assembly, Premier Nikita Khrushchev said that

> the Soviet Government, after examining from all angles the situation which has arisen, has reached the firm conclusion that the way out of the impasse must be sought through general and complete disarmament. This approach completely eliminates the possibility of any state gaining military advantages of any kind. General and complete disarmament will remove all the obstacles that have arisen during the discussions of the questions involved by partial disarmament, and will clear the way for the institution of universal and complete control.[30]

Then, anticipating that the United States and its allies would not find this a workable proposal and would brand it mere propaganda, the Soviet leader reiterated some of the Soviet Union's standing proposals for "partial disarmament," on which it was still "prepared to come to terms."[31]

The U.S. government's counterproposals, presented in February 1960, predictably focused on feasible measures "to create a more stable military environment" as the urgent first step—feasible meaning verifiable through reliable national means of inspection. Once such measures could be successfully implemented, reducing the risk of war, the world could move on to a "second stage of general disarmament." As explained by Secretary of State Christian Herter,

> Our objective in this second stage should be two-fold: *First*, to create universally accepted rules of law, which if followed

would prevent all nations from attacking other nations. Such rules of law should be backed by a World Court and by effective means of enforcement—that is, by international armed force. *Second*, to reduce national armed forces, under safeguarded and verified agreements to the point where no single nation or group of nations could effectively oppose this enforcement of international law by international machinery.[32]

This Soviet-American dialogue, or rather, debate, over general and complete disarmament was transparently an elaborate stage play, cynically concocted by leaders on each side to pander to the hopes of the presumably unsophisticated general population. The Soviets were proposing that all nations should destroy all their weapons, without any reliable procedures to assure that some parties to the agreement would not retain theirs while the others disarmed: controls would follow disarmament. The Americans were proposing that world government should be set up prior to general disarmament. Neither presented its grandiose proposals with the idea that the other could possibly accept them. Indeed, neither side would have been willing to implement its own proposals!

The superpowers continued this charade during the early 1960s, until the Cuban missile crisis focused the minds of statesmen on the need to get down to serious negotiations. The high point, or perhaps low point, in the general and complete disarmament game was the presentation by both governments of elaborate draft treaties to the Eighteen Nation Disarmament Committee in the spring of 1962. The Soviet draft treaty provided for a four-year disarmament process, to be carried out in three consecutive stages, at the end of which the states would retain "only strictly limited contingents of police (militia) equipped with light firearms, and intended for the maintenance of internal order and for the discharge of their obligations under the United Nations Charter."[33] The Kennedy administration's counter-proposal was for general and complete disarmament in a decade-long process, also to be implemented in three stages. At the completion of the process, "states would have at their disposal only those non-nuclear armaments, forces, facilities, and establishments as are agreed to be necessary to maintain internal order and protect the personal security of citizens." In the American plan, a United Nations Peace Force would be built up simultaneously with the phased reductions in national armament to assure, at each step, that somewhere in the international system there was sufficient military power to deter or suppress aggressive threats or use of arms.[34]

On the surface, the superpowers had converged on the goal of general and complete disarmament to be accomplished by a phased approach, and even on many of the types of substantive reductions within each stage. Most encouraging was the Soviet acceptance, in principle, of an International Disarmament Organization with the function of overseeing the process from the start and the authority to assure verification of all agreed reductions at each stage. But in their detailed provisions for such a supervisory body, the key to the practicality of even the first stages of limited arms reduction, the superpowers were as far apart as ever. The Soviets insisted that the International Disarmament Organization should be under the direct control of the UN Security Council, where they could veto any verification or control measures they disliked.[35] By contrast, the American plan provided that the "International Disarmament Organization and its inspectors would have access without veto to all places necessary for the purpose of verification."[36]

The Gorbachev-Reagan Debate on General Nuclear Disarmament

From the late 1960s on, during the period of serious Soviet-American negotiations to limit strategic forces, both Moscow and Washington abandoned their competitive catering to popular hopes for general and complete disarmament. In early 1986, however, the Soviet leader, Mikhail Gorbachev, reopened the propaganda contest by proposing a program for "ridding the earth of nuclear weapons, to be implemented and completed within the next 15 years, before the end of this century."[37] Like the general disarmament schemes of the early 1960s, the Gorbachev proposal also included a phased process, starting with agreements that were not entirely unrealistic. Stage one, for example, would reduce by one-half the nuclear arms that could reach the other superpower's territory. But the Soviet leader made clear that even stage one would be impossible to negotiate unless the Reagan administration first abandoned its Strategic Defense Initiative. The consensus in the U.S. government was that Gorbachev was playing to the public galleries and had not really offered a serious proposal for negotiation.

Nevertheless, President Reagan and his advisers were apparently taken by surprise at the October 1986 meeting between Reagan and Gorbachev in Reykjavik, Iceland—in what was supposed to be a down-to-business preparatory session for a forthcoming full-dress summit meeting—when the Soviets proposed that both countries cut their respective strategic arsenals in half over the next five years. Not to be outdone, the Americans promptly offered the counterproposal of eliminating *all ballistic missiles* in ten years, which the Soviets were not about to accept, given U.S. superiority in nonballistic strategic weapons (bombers and cruise missiles). Gorbachev thereupon revived the essence of his early 1986 proposal, an elimination of *all nuclear arms* by the end of the coming decade. Reagan, misinterpreting the advice of his arms control experts, conveyed the impression to Gorbachev that he would be willing to agree to the complete nuclear disarmament proposal. If the two leaders had agreed to complete nuclear disarmament, their October 1986 Iceland meeting truly would have been a momentous event in world history. But Gorbachev again made it clear that the comprehensive agreement as well as other more specific arms control measures being discussed were still linked to Reagan's willingness to forgo his Strategic Defense Initiative. The meeting broke up at this point, with both leaders blaming the other for their failure to reach agreement.[38]

Even if Reagan and Gorbachev had been able to agree on the principle of general nuclear disarmament, it is doubtful that their two governments really were ready to move in this direction. Strategic experts in the United States and most NATO countries, upon hearing that the president was ready to agree to the Gorbachev proposal, were quick to raise the objection that the elimination of nuclear weapons would leave the Soviet Union and the Warsaw Pact in a dominant position, on the basis of their superiority in nonnuclear forces. And would the superpowers really be willing to dismantle their nuclear arsenals unless they could at the same time be assured that China and France and all prospective nuclear-weapons countries would also renounce nuclear arsenals?

Unfortunately, such worldwide nuclear disarmament requires either the establishment of a powerful supranational authority to enforce it or a degree of trust among previously armed rivals that would allow each to accept on faith claims by the others about the content of their arsenals. In short, the massive political and/or moral changes that need to be instituted in the world-transforming approaches to peace—world government, universal nonviolence, or the Galtungian synthesis—are also the preconditions for total nuclear disarmament or general disarmament. Any such grand disarmament scheme that fails to provide for political and moral transformation can be no more than an exercise in wishful thinking or propaganda.

NOTES

1. On Crucé's proposal see F. H. Hinsley, *Power and the Pursuit of Peace* (London: Cambridge University Press, 1963), pp. 20–28; also Edith Wynner and Georgia Lloyd, *Searchlight on Peace Plans* (New York: Dutton, 1949), p. 33.

2. William Penn, *An Essay Toward the Present and Future Peace of Europe by the Establishment of an European Dyet, Parliament or Estates* (London: Society of Friends, 1936).

3. Quotations from the Bellers plan taken from Hinsley, pp. 38–39. See also Wynner and Lloyd, pp. 36–37.

4. Abbé de Saint-Pierre's *Project of Perpetual Peace* is outlined by Wynner and Lloyd, pp. 37–38.

5. Minister Fleury's reaction to the abbé's *Project* is quoted by Frederick Schuman, in *International Politics: The Western State System and the World Community* (New York: McGraw-Hill, 1958), p. 205.

6. Hinsley presents Rousseau's reaction to the abbé's *Project*, pp. 48–49.

7. See Stanley Hoffmann's essay, "Rousseau on War and Peace," in his *The State of War: Essays on the Theory and Practice of International Politics* (New York: Praeger, 1965), pp. 54–87.

8. Grenville Clark and Louis B. Sohn, *World Peace Through World Law* (Cambridge, Mass.: Harvard University Press, 1960).

9. *Ibid.* p. xi.

10. *Ibid.*, p. xxix.

11. Richard A. Falk, *A Study of Future Worlds* (New York: Free Press, 1975), pp. 224–275.

12. *Ibid.*, pp. 242–248.

13. *The New Testament. An American Translation* by Edgar J. Goodspeed (Chicago: University of Chicago Press, 1948).

14. Lewis Einstein, ed., *Erasmus Against War* (Boston: Merrymount Press, 1907).

15. See Henry David Thoreau, *On the Duty of Civil Disobedience* (Boston: Fellowship Press, 1853).

16. See Leo Tolstoy, *The Kingdom of God Is Within You* (New York: Crowell, 1899) and *The Law of Love and the Law of Violence* (New York: R. Field, 1948).

17. M. K. Gandhi, *Non-Violent Resistance* (Ahmedabad, India: Navejivan Trust, n.d.), pp. 383–387.

18. See Gene Sharp, *The Politics of Nonviolent Action* (Boston: Porter Sargent, 1973) and Adam Roberts, ed., *The Strategy of Civilian Defense* (Harrisburg, Pa.: Stackpole Books, 1968).

19. Gene Sharp, *Making Europe Unconquerable: The Potential of Civilian-based Deterrence and Defence* (Cambridge, Mass: Ballinger, 1985), p. 31.

20. *Ibid.*, p. 50.

21. *Ibid., pp. 107–108.*

22. Johan Galtung, *The True Worlds: A Transnational Perspective* (New York: Free Press, 1980), p. 67.

23. *Ibid.*, p. 92.

24. *Ibid.*, p. 93.

25. *Ibid.*, p. 93.

26. *Ibid.*, p. 348.

27. *Ibid.*, p. 351.

28. *Supplement to the Messages and Papers of the Presidents: The Second Administration of Woodrow Wilson*, 8421.

29. U.S. Department of State, *Foreign Relations of the United States, 1918 Supplement* (Washington, D.C.: U.S. Government Printing Office), Vol. 1, p. 405.

30. Nikita S. Khrushchev, Address to the U.N. General Assembly, Fourteenth Session, Plenary, *Official Records*, 799th mtg. (United Nations: September 10, 1959), p. 36.

31. *Ibid.*, p. 37.

32. Christian A. Herter, "National Security with Arms Limitations," *Department of State Bulletin*, 42 (March 7, 1960), 355–356.

33. Soviet Draft Treaty of March 15, 1962, United States Arms Control and Disarmament Agency, *Documents on Disarmament 1962*, Vol. I (Washington, D.C.: U.S. Government Printing Office, 1963), 103–127.

34. United States Treaty Outline of April 18, 1962, *Documents on Disarmament 1962,* Vol. I, pp. 351–382.

35. Soviet Draft Treaty, *ibid.*, pp. 123–126.

36. U.S. Treaty Outline, *ibid.*, p. 352.

37. Excerpts from Mikhail Gorbachev's comprehensive arms control proposal of January 1986, *New York Times*, January 17, 1986.

38. There is no single official record of the discussions of October 11–12, 1986, at Reykjavik. Both governments issued contradictory versions. I have relied primarily on the following reports: Leslie H. Gelb, "The Summit: New Issues," *New York Times*, October 25, 1986; Gerald M. Boyd, "U.S. Says 2 Leaders Discussed Ending All Nuclear Arms," *New York Times*, October 24, 1986; Fred Kaplan, "Reagan Can Thank His Lucky 'Star Wars,'" *Boston Globe*, November 2, 1986.

CHAPTER 8

Efforts To Reduce the Role of War in the International System

The apparent infeasibility of attempts to purge war from the world in the foreseeable future has compelled those determined to improve the odds for human survival to search for ways to at least reduce the role of war in the existing system.

Some of the approaches to reducing the role of war emphasize legal and institutional mechanisms, some diplomatic strategies and tactics, and still others limits on the deployment and use of military force. Having more modest goals than the complete elimination of war, these near-term approaches assume, for the time being, both the continued existence of the nation-state system and the reliance of statesmen, at least in part, on military balances of power and alliances designed to secure the interests of their countries.

This chapter analyzes four principal kinds of war-reduction efforts: international law, diplomatic accommodation and restraint, collective security institutions, and special measures to settle disputes and resolve conflicts. All are attempts to control the most dangerous tendencies in international relations rather than to overhaul the structure of world politics. Clearly, arms-control measures are a part of this approach, but their special requirements and implications warrant treatment in a separate chapter.

INTERNATIONAL LAW

Practitioners and theorists working on peace and security issues in the field of international law tend to share the conviction that statesmen can and must agree to certain limits on the permissible behavior of countries, without which the system of sovereign states would degenerate into brutish anarchy.

This elementary premise was given its classical philosophical statement in 1625 by the great Dutch jurist, Hugo Grotius, in his treatise *On the Law of War and Peace*. Grotius reiterated a secular version of the medieval church doctrine that there is a law above nations—"natural law"—which follows from the assumption that humankind is at base, and ultimately, one community. The substantive content of natural law can be determined for particular relationships among states by "right reason." From the "nature of man" right reason can deduce the laws that should govern the interaction of individuals in civil society, and similarly it can deduce from the "nature of states" the laws that should govern the interaction among states in international society.

On the assumption that human nature is characterized essentially by "sociability," the desire for a peaceful life that has led men and women the world over to establish communities of law and order, Grotius reasoned that the highest laws of these communities, or states, are those necessary to maintain a peaceful social life. And because the nature of states, derived from the nature of human beings, is defined primarily by this function of maintaining domestic communities of law and order, the governments of the separate states must be sovereign within their own realms.

Grotius argued therefore that the laws governing relations among nations must first and foremost protect the sovereignty of the states themselves, through rules designed to prevent interference in one another's jurisdictions. The other principles of international law, Grotius taught, can be gleaned from the durable arrangements sovereign states have made among themselves—including peace treaties, boundary agreements, and allocations of fishing and navigation privileges in commonly used waters. These "customary" international laws result for the most part from negotiations undertaken to prevent war or to terminate ongoing wars; peace requires that these customary laws be given presumptive validity. Defending the international legal order may even justify resorting to war to prevent the retrogression of world society into anarchy.[1]

Still operating largely in the Grotian tradition, contemporary jurists in defining international law draw on concepts invoked by the International Court of Justice, on the dominant principles and language of treaties and of the charters of international institutions, and on legalistic rationalizations governments offer to justify their international acts. This dominant tradition of international law is essentially conservative, in the sense of respecting and guarding the basic state-sovereignty structure of world society and the inherited corpus of specific agreements, or customary law, that has proved relatively durable.

The Marginal Influence of International Law on War and Peace

When wars result from acts that violate norms of the state system and widely accepted agreements, invoking international law can provide a framework for appeals by citizens who oppose the warlike actions of their own governments, as well as for appeals by international forums to restore the conditions of peace. But to the extent that wars are themselves the product of unresolved conflicts of sovereignty over territory or population or of new economic or political developments not adequately anticipated in past formal arrangements—in short, most of the determinants of war identified in Chapters 3 through 6—international law itself, other than providing some established procedures for settlement of disputes (see the discussion on pp. 163–170), affords few if any rules for avoiding wars.

The Role of International Law

By codifying the outcomes of disputes resolved through benign bargaining, coercive diplomacy, or war, international law does play a role in discouraging new confrontations that can lead to war. The treaties that define the boundaries of states or their rights of access to particular resources can prevent the kinds of misunderstandings and miscalculations, and tests of strength, that often result from leaving valued areas or assets up for grabs.

A growing area of creative international law is the formulation of agreed-on "rules of the road" for traffic in nonland areas—rivers, oceans, airspace, and outer space. As these "commons" areas are used more heavily, such rules have become crucial for avoiding accidents, misunderstandings, and confrontations of the sort that can easily engage the prestige of contending states, inflame popular passions, and lead to war.[2]

Environmental policy is another increasingly important field in which international law, by formulating new rules to be negotiated among countries, is crucial to avoiding bitter conflict; guidelines must be developed to deal with environmental pollution that crosses state boundaries or affects commonly used water or air. Without specific environmental impact treaties establishing permissible and impermissible activities, warning and accountability procedures, and liability obligations, countries may become intensely angry at injuries inflicted by other nations on the health and well-being of their peoples. This need was dramatically highlighted in 1986 by the explosion at the Chernobyl nuclear facility in the Soviet Union, which spewed radioactive clouds over many countries.

Particularly in the burgeoning fields of international transportation, communications, and transborder pollution control it has been the modest achievement of international law to remove ambiguities in the rights and mutual obligations of states, thus reducing the need to rely heavily on coercive bargaining with its attendant risks of conflict escalation.

A STATESMANSHIP OF RATIONAL RESTRAINT

Much international law tends to be an after-the-fact device for reducing the likelihood of war—a clarification of rights and obligations in situations that have already led to intense conflict, under the assumption that future war-threatening situations will be of the same type. But not all situations that can lead to dangerous conflict can be sufficiently anticipated in current legal arrangements. Because circumstances change, the laws codifying the old circumstances can become irreievant to new clashes of interests and new balances of power.

In international relations, peace more often than not has been the result of prudent statecraft in advance of the legal codification of rights and obligations, rather than the result of the implementation of existing law. The succession of the period of relative peace in nineteenth-century Europe, under the Concert of Europe, by the period of general war in the twentieth century shows this dominance of diplomacy over law.

The Concert of Europe

The elaborate set of territorial treaties of consultation that constituted the new law of nations after the defeat of Napoleon Bonaparte in 1815 were designed to prevent a revolutionary imperialist like Napoleon from launching a new rampage of expansion. Unfortunately, the elitist consultative Concert system that developed did not deeply reflect the underlying social, economic, technological, and political forces transforming the domestic character of states and their relations with one another. The result was the explosion of the two devastating world wars of the twentieth century.

Yet a moderate and relatively war-free international system did prevail for most of the post-Napoleonic nineteenth century. However, this was less due to the constraining force of the new international legal order than to the diplomatic brilliance of the leading statesmen of that era—especially Metternich, Castlereagh, and then Bismarck—who manipulated international relations within a self-imposed set of restraints against actions that could fundamentally challenge the security of any of the major states of Europe. It was the dismissal of Bismarck by Kaiser Wilhelm in 1890, in fact, that signaled the end of the period of restrained statesmanship: international relations quickly degenerated into the anarchical arms races and power plays that brought on World War I.[3]

The Legacy of Immanuel Kant

Important characteristics of the moderate statecraft of post-Napoleonic Europe were anticipated by the philosopher Immanuel Kant in his pamphlet *Perpetual Peace*, published in 1775 and widely read by eighteenth-century intellectuals.[4] In our time Henry Kissinger, a prominent intellectual-turned-statesman—whose major academic contribution was an admiring history of the diplomacy of Metternich, Castlereagh, and Bismarck—claims to be more a devotee of the works of Kant than of any other philosopher.[5]

Kant argued that no war is "just," and that wars cannot be cleansed of their inherent evil by the good purposes for which they may be fought. Rather war is the greatest evil in human civilization: more than any other social institution it violates the primary ethical imperative that humans must treat each other as ends, never mainly as means to other ends.

For Kant, the key question was how to move the world away from reliance on war as a normal instrument of statecraft and toward the ideal of a warless world. He recognized that war is so much a part of international relations that it cannot be simply legislated out of existence; the goal of perpetual peace therefore must be made a project for statesmen, with a set of realistic imperatives for, and limitations on, state action that would constitute progress toward the ideal world. The specific international legal instruments Kant proposed as steps in this project were a multistate treaty of permanent mutual nonaggression, and a confederation, or permanent congress of sovereign states, through which they could bargain to adjust their differences; but he considered the instruments less important than the commitment of governments to policies of mutual restraint based on respect for each other's domains, national values, and citizenry.

Countries must cultivate a sense of limits beyond which they cannot push each other without provoking war, according to Kant. Like individuals in peaceful domestic communities, nations must learn to treat each other as entities worthy of respect and therefore—most important—immune from physical violation. Republican countries, in contrast with monarchical or despotic ones, are likely to adhere to and strenghten such restraint, Kant argued, because of the natural inclination of the ordinary citizenry to tend to their domestic pursuits without the disruptions caused by war.

Kant also urged the abolition of standing armies, and eventually of all military force that might be used in external adventures; this would further limit the temptations of states to engage in war-provoking actions.

Between the two world wars of the twentieth century, these Kantian notions found expression in the Locarno Pact of 1925 and the Kellogg-Briand Pact of 1928—both reactions to the failure of the collective security mechanisms of the League of Nations to limit the traditional game of power politics.

The "Spirit of Locarno"

By the end of 1922, the new peace and security system installed after World War I appeared to be on the verge of collapse. When Germany defaulted on the war reparations payments imposed by the victorious Allies, France, in an effort to force the defeated nation to pay, sent troops to occupy the German industrial area of the Ruhr.

And because Germany also dragged its heels on implementing the disarmament provisions of the Versailles Treaty, the French in 1925, when the Allies were scheduled to implement the Versailles agreements to end their military occupation of the Rhineland, postponed evacuating their troops.

In an effort to counteract the reforging of an anti-German alliance, Gustav Stresemann, the German foreign minister, fashioned a major peace initiative: he proposed a set of nonaggression and arbitration treaties principally among France, Britain, Italy, and Germany. These countries, as well as Belgium, Czechoslovakia, and Poland, met in the Swiss town of Locarno in the fall of 1925 in an omnibus negotiation of a pact to remove the scourge of war from Europe. A treaty on the Rhineland provided for that region's full demilitarization, pledging France, Germany, and Belgium to refrain from resorting to war against each other, except for a flagrant breach of the Locarno Pact itself or as a part of a League of Nations action against an aggressor state. France also signed two special treaties of guarantee with Poland and Czechoslovakia providing for mutual assistance against Germany in case that country should violate her new obligations. Finally, Germany signed arbitration treaties with each of the other countries, agreeing to submit her disputes with them to a conciliation commission and then, if necessary, to the World Court and the Council of the League. As the icing on the cake of peace, Germany was admitted to the League of Nations.[6]

The Kellogg-Briand Pact

The official enthrallment with pacts of peace reached its apogee with the General Treaty for the Renunciation of War signed by fifteen countries in Paris in 1928 and joined by forty-six more over the next two years.

The new peace effort started with a modest proposal by the French foreign minister, Aristide Briand, to the U.S. secretary of state, Frank Kellogg, that the two countries celebrate the tenth anniversary of the American entry into World War I with a statement outlawing war between France and the United States. Briand's initiative was greeted with unexpected enthusiasm in the United States, where the Hoover administration was energized to expand it into a universally binding agreement among all countries to renounce war as an instrument of national policy.

The British and the French governments were not pleased with the American attempt to convert Briand's limited bilateral initiative into a global spectacular, for a universal prohibition against resorting to military force would conflict with such standing alliance commitments as French guarantees to Poland and Czechoslovakia, as well as with British and French colonial responsibilities. France insisted that the prohibition on resorting to force be interpreted as restricting only "wars of aggression"; and Britain agreed to join the pact provided that joining did not interfere with its freedom of action in "certain regions of the world, the welfare and integrity of which constitute a special and vital interest for our peace and safety." With these unilateral French and British "understandings," the General Treaty, as signed, stipulated that its adherents (1) "condemn recourse to war for the solution of international controversies and renounce it as an instrument of national policy in their relations with one another," and (2) "agree that the settlement or solution of all international disputes or conflicts . . . shall never be sought except by peaceful means."[7]

Kant would have been pleased with these provisions and the simple fact of their being solemnly affirmed on a universal basis, for even though unenforceable, they advanced international standards or "imperatives" of state behavior needed for lasting peace. He would not have been pleased, however, with the reservations exempting specific wars and collective security obligations, which like the "just war" notions of his time allowed a hole wide enough to march an army through any time a signatory country determined the action was in its national interest.

Morgenthau's Rules of Diplomacy

Kantian ideas of rational restraint also underlie the principal recommendations for avoiding a civilization-destroying third world war presented by the twentieth century's most influential "realist" philosopher of international relations, Hans J. Morgenthau. Morgenthau expressed a limited hope for avoiding cataclysmic war by utilizing and improving diplomacy to control conflicts among countries. He offered nine rules of diplomacy that countries—especially the superpowers—should follow to sustain their interests short of war:

1. Divest diplomacy of the crusading spirit. Universalistic crusades to wipe the forces of evil from the earth or, short of this, efforts

of a country to identify its own national interests with a universally valid morality—what Morgenthau called the vice of "nationalistic universalism"—are incompatible with the accommodation among nations necessary to avoid the total nation-to-nation hostility that results in society-destroying wars. (Henry Kissinger too, as shown below, advocated this kind of restrained *realpolitik* diplomacy in U.S.-Soviet relations).

2. Restrict the definition of vital national interests—those that cannot be compromised—to national security interests, namely, survival and maintenance of the essential economic well-being of the population. This is the most controversial and difficult to implement of Morgenthau's rules, for it implies abandoning any protection of allies and friends that is not warranted by concern for one's own national security. Before the nuclear age, Morgenthau explained, countries could afford to pursue less restrictively defined national interests; but today the prospect of total destruction of the nation in a nuclear war requires the narrower *security* definition of the interests a country should be willing to go to war to defend. (Morgenthau's text renders this rule as: "The objectives of foreign policy must be defined in terms of national interest and must be supported with adequate power." I have rephrased it to better reflect his explanation of its meaning.)

3. Look at the political scene from the point of view of other nations. It is important that a country truly understand its opponents' definitions of their national interests, for otherwise rivals are likely to miscalculate how much they can challenge each other short of intolerable provocation, and when the opponent's threat to use force is only a bluff or real.

4. Be willing to compromise on all interests that are not vital. Knowing how to bargain skillfully over secondary interests is an essential part of the diplomatic art. (In fact, Morgenthau's remaining five rules are all facets of this basic diplomacy of compromise.)

5. "Give up the shadow of worthless rights for the substance of real advantage." This is the practical bargaining guidance that follows from clearly distinguishing between vital and secondary interests. It implies that it is unwise for countries to engage their honor, prestige, credibility—"machismo," if you will—over anything beyond what is required for national security.

6. "Never put yourself in a position from which you cannot retreat without losing face and from which you cannot advance

without grave risks." This means not only having the ability to implement rule 5 but also having good intelligence on the prevailing balance of military power and the scale of values of your opponents, to avoid assuming positions that will be opposed by force of arms. (Khrushchev came perilously close to violating this rule in the 1962 Cuban missile crisis.)

7. "Never allow a weak ally to make decisions for you." This has been an important but difficult rule to follow in the post–World War II system of two vast opposing alliances, each led by a superpower. One of the causes of the Sino-Soviet split was the determination of the Soviet Union to adhere to this rule in the Quemoy-Matsu crisis of the 1950s when the Chinese, for reasons of their own over which the Soviets were not willing to risk nuclear war, engaged in a confrontation with the United States. The rule was violated, however, in the U.S.–South Vietnamese relationship that began in 1954, when the United States took over from France as South Vietnam's protector against North Vietnam, and ended only in 1973, when the United States finally negotiated its withdrawal from Vietnam despite strong objections from South Vietnam.

8. Keep the armed forces an instrument of diplomacy, not its master. The military mind, observed Morgenthau, is trained to think in the absolute—life or death, victory or defeat—and military instruments are designed to destroy an opponent or break his will to resist. The military mind "knows nothing of that patient, intricate, and subtle maneuvering of diplomacy, whose main purpose is to avoid the absolutes of victory and defeat and meet the other side in negotiated compromise."

9. In formulating and conducting foreign policy, the government must not become the slave of public opinion. To practice the often delicate and subtle art of compromise, a diplomat requires some degree of freedom from direct democratic control; the necessary bargaining must include conceding some of the other side's objectives and giving up some of one's own, even if the compromise and accommodation are unpopular in the short run. Further, the statesman, leading public opinion to understand how vital national interests can be served by concessions on secondary or tertiary interests, must "neither surrender to popular passions or disregard them" but "strike a prudent balance between adapting himself to them and marshaling them to support his policies."[8]

Morgenthau recognized that the implementation of these pre-

scriptions for a diplomacy to preserve peace depends on the possession of "extraordinary moral and intellectual qualities" by the
world's leading statesmen. "A mistake in the evaluation of one of the
elements of national power, made by one or the other of the leading
statesmen may spell the difference between peace and war. So may an
accident spoiling a plan or power calculation." Diplomacy is not
enough, but it is essential:

> It is only when nations have surrendered to a higher authority
> the means of destruction which modern technology has put in
> their hands—when they have given up their sovereignty—that
> international peace can be made as secure as domestic
> peace. . . . Yet as there can be no permanent peace without a
> world state, there can be no world state without the
> peace-preserving and community-building processes of
> diplomacy.[9]

Henry Kissinger and Détente

Like Morgenthau, Henry Kissinger has subordinated any ultimate vision of a peaceful world polity to here-and-now requirements
of preventing a nuclear holocaust. In his academic writings and his
stagecraft, Kissinger has emphasized two essential conditions for a
tolerably peaceful international order: (1) an equilibrium of power
(primarily military) among the most powerful countries, so that no
country can expect to beat any of the others decisively in war or to
dictate the conditions under which they must live; and (2) an
acceptance by the great powers of the legitimacy of the existing
distribution of power and of the territorial and other arrangements of
control and influence that are associated with it.

Kissinger's appointment to high office in 1969 came when
changes in the world situation and in American domestic politics led
him to try his hand at weaving such an equilibrium and legitimacy
system. His overriding aim was to reduce the likelihood of nuclear
holocaust without reducing American power vis-à-vis that of its
principal geopolitical adversary.

Kissinger was able to persuade President Richard Nixon that,
because of the Soviet Union's sluggish domestic economic performance, the Kremlin was hungry for trade with the West, and so might
now be willing to assume a "stake in the equilibrium." The United

States could make the Soviets pay a current price for expanded commerce in the coin of international moderation, meanwhile luring them into a long-term position of economic dependence. The United States could simultaneously gain additional leverage on the Kremlin by moving to establish cordial relations with the Soviet Union's archrival in Asia. A diplomacy of limited accommodation and mutual restraint, *détente*—or "negotiation rather than confrontation," in Nixon's formulation—might now be able to supplement the military balance of power as the essence of the new statesmanship for avoiding World War III.[10]

Drafted primarily by Henry Kissinger, the Declaration of Principles signed by President Nixon and General Secretary Brezhnev in 1972 gave a remarkably neo-Kantian expression to this strategy:

> The United States of America and the Union of Soviet Socialist Republics . . .
>
> HAVE AGREED as follows:
>
> *First*. They will proceed from the common determination that in the nuclear age there is no alternative to conducting their mutual relations on the basis of peaceful coexistence. Differences in ideology and in the social systems of the U.S.A. and the USSR are not obstacles to the bilateral development of normal relations based on the principles of sovereignty, equality, noninterference in internal affairs and mutual advantage.
>
> *Second*. The U.S.A. and the USSR attach major importance to preventing the development of situations capable of causing dangerous exacerbation of their relations. Therefore, they will do their utmost to avoid military confrontation and to prevent the outbreak of nuclear war. They will always exercise restraint in their mutual relations, and will be prepared to negotiate and settle differences by peaceful means. Discussions and negotiations of outstanding issues will be conducted in a spirit of reciprocity, and mutual accommodation and mutual benefit.
>
> Both sides recognize that efforts to obtain unilateral advantage at the expense of the other, directly or indirectly, are inconsistent with these objectives.

The prerequisites for maintaining and strengthening peaceful relations between the U.S.A. and the USSR are the recognition of the security interests of the parties based on the principle of equality and the renunciation of the use or threat of force.

[There are twelve principles in all.][11]

At the time of negotiating these accords, Kissinger was not totally convinced that the Soviets really intended to live up to pledges that would involve considerable constriction of their international revolutionary aims.[12] But given the terrible dangers of relying solely on military containment in the nuclear age, he felt it was worth giving the Soviets a chance to become enmeshed in the conservative international order. An adequate balance of military power could be maintained in the background to deter them from revolutionary adventurism, and other coercive pressures—a closer Chinese-American alignment and withdrawal of commercial privileges—could be threatened at any time to remind the Kremlin that peaceful coexistence was conditioned on adherence to the principles signed at the 1972 Moscow summit.

By the time Kissinger left office in 1977, he was disappointed in the results of détente and angry at the Soviets for attempting, especially in Africa, to exploit to their own advantage the unwillingness of the U.S. Congress, in the isolationist mood following the country's withdrawal from Vietnam, to support coercive countermeasures against Soviet power plays.

Kissinger's grand strategy was also frustrated by congressional refusal to to provide him with sufficient tools, in the form of trading and credit opportunities to be offered the Soviets, for conducting the carrot-and-stick diplomacy needed to make détente work. In the Jackson-Vanik and Stevenson amendments to trade and credit legislation, Congress denied the Soviets "most favored nation" trading privileges (meaning as good as any other nation's) and long-term government credits, both of which Nixon had promised Brezhnev in the 1972 détente package, unless the Kremlin first liberalized its restrictions on Jewish emigration.

Kissinger's experience with détente points up the central limitation of attempts to preserve peace largely through a diplomacy of mutual restraint and accommodation: the top foreign policy officials of the participant countries are required to have at their disposal sufficient resources—carrots and sticks—and negotiating leeway to make the kinds of international adjustments and deals necessary to avoid dangerous confrontations. But unlike conditions in the period of classical European diplomacy from which Kissinger derived many of his insights, contemporary domestic political systems, especially democracies, seldom provide their diplomats with such resources or negotiating flexibility.

INTERNATIONAL COLLECTIVE SECURITY

An alternative to enlarging the prospects for peace by prudent and flexible state-to-state diplomacy is a collective security system encompassing and supported by the major powers. A collective security system does not presume ideological consensus among its members, require their agreement on the just international society, or even depend on a commitment to preserve the existing territorial status quo or balance of power. It requires only that member countries renounce the use or threatened use of force as an instrument of foreign policy and make provision to restrain and/or punish, through cooperative or coordinated action, any country that attacks another with military force for any purpose other than to defend itself against military aggression or to help in a collective security action authorized by the system.

Collective security, so defined, is the basis of the two most significant international experiments of the twentieth century: the League of Nations and the United Nations.

The League of Nations

The widespread idea that World War I was caused by the balance of power/alliance system stimulated a flurry of proposals for a universal alliance against war itself—a league of nations to enforce the peace following the war. President Woodrow Wilson was a true believer in this idea, and it was because of his efforts that the Covenant of the League of Nations was incorporated into the Treaty of Versailles and each of the other major peace treaties of 1919.

The collective security provisions of the League of Nations were Articles 8 through 17 of the Covenant:

- Article 8 stated that "the maintenance of peace requires the reduction of national armaments to the lowest point consistent with national safety and the enforcement by common action of international obligations." The responsibility for formulating arms reduction plans was given to the Council of the League (its restricted-membership executive organ, as distinct from the Assembly). Although each member government was to adopt a plan according to its own constitutional processes, once adopted the armament limits were to be maintained, and could only be increased with the concurrence of the Council.

- Article 9 established a permanent commission to advise the Council of the League on the execution of the arms-reduction and other military provisions of the Covenant.

- Article 10 obligated members to "respect and preserve as against territorial aggression" one another's "territorial integrity and existing political independence."

- Article 11 provided that "any war or threat of war, whether immediately affecting any members of the League or not, is . . . a matter of concern to the whole League, and the League shall take any action that may be deemed wise and effective to safeguard the peace of nations."

- Articles 12 through 15 established procedures that member nations were obligated to follow "if there should arise between them any dispute likely to lead to a rupture." First, they were to submit such disputes either to the Council of the League, to the Permanent Court of International Justice, or to other certified international tribunals for resolution. Second, they were prohibited from waging war against members who complied with the awards or decisions of these League bodies. Third, the members of the League agreed "in no case to resort to war until three months after the award by the arbiters or the judicial decision or the report by the Council"—this was the so-called cooling-off period. But if the appropriate League bodies were unable to render an award or decision, "the members of the League reserve to themselves the right to take such action as they shall consider necessary for the maintenance of right and justice."

- The provisions of Article 16, often called the heart of the League's collective security system, included the following:

1. Should any member of the League resort to war in disregard of its covenants under Article 12, 13, or 15, it shall *ipso facto*,

be deemed to have committed an act of war against all other Members of the League, which hereby undertake immediately to subject it to the severance of all trade or financial relations, the prohibition of all intercourse between their nationals and the nationals of the Covenant-breaking State, and the prevention of all financial, commercial or personal intercourse between the nationals of the Covenant-breaking State and the nationals of any other State, whether a Member of the League or not.

2. It shall be the duty of the Council in such a case to recommend to the several Governments concerned what effective military, naval or air force the Members of the League shall severally contribute to the armed forces to be used to protect the covenants of the League.

3. The Members of the League agree, further, that they will mutually support one another in the financial and economic measures which are taken under this article. . . .

4. Any Member of the League which has violated any covenant of the League may be declared to be no longer a Member of the League by a vote of the Council. . . .[13]

Clearly, the Covenant of the League of Nations did not outlaw war itself. War was still legitimate if waged in behalf of the principles of the League—especially if in response to a call by appropriate League agencies for enforcement action, even unilateral military action by members, provided the warring action followed an unsuccessful attempt to utilize the League's conflict-resolution machinery. And, of course, members retained the right of self-defense in cases when military aggression started before League action was possible. In short, the League system did not alter the fundamental ambiguity of the international law against aggression, or basically change the decentralized nature of international law enforcement.

What the League of Nations did was legitimize and provide a framework for collective action against international aggression—to the extent that countries were willing to cooperate in such action. By providing specific mechanisms for determining when illegitimate military attacks had taken place and for facilitating coordinated counteraction against aggressors, the League was a serious attempt to reduce the need of countries to resort to war even in self-defense. Most idealistically, arms races, alliances, and provocative threats of war, such as those that brought on World War I, would no longer be necessary, since deterrence would now be provided by the prospect of concerted international response to any aggressor.

How did the League system of collective security work in practice?

In a number of instances, the League machinery acted as intended by preventing disputes from exploding into war—notably in the border disputes between Albania and Yugoslavia in 1921 and between Greece and Bulgaria in 1925. In these cases, no great power was providing significant assistance to either side, nor had any an important stake in the outcome.

But the League proved to be either irrelevant or impotent when a great power was engaged in aggression. When China brought Japan's 1931 attack on the Asian mainland before the League, charging Japan with blatantly violating the Covenant, the League appointed an investigatory body, the Lytton Commission, and on the basis of its report passed a resolution refusing to recognize the new Japanese-controlled government in Manchuria. Japan thereupon resigned from the League in anger, but remained in physical control of Manchuria without suffering any of the sanctions provided for in Article 16.

Again in 1933 when Italy, a permanent member of the Council of the League, bombarded the Greek island of Corfu in retaliation for the killing of Italian officers who had been demarcating the Greek-Albanian border, the League proved unable to assume effective jurisdiction of the matter. Under the organization's voting rules, Italy did not have a formal veto, but it was nonetheless in a position to discourage League action.

Two years later the League did formally brand Italy's invasion of Ethiopia an illegal aggression, and the Council invoked the Article 16 sanctions system. Fifty-two countries cooperated in instituting an embargo on the sale of arms and "strategic materials" to Italy. But the embargo proved to be porous, especially since oil was exempted from it. Moreover, France and Britain, the only two powers who could have challenged Italy militarily, were so preoccupied with domestic problems that neither was willing to assume the burden of organizing military sanctions in response to an action that did not put their own vital geopolitical interests in immediate jeopardy. Italy, like Japan, literally got away with murder, while the powers upon whom the world relied to make the collective security system work stood idly by. Adolf Hitler observed that no country of any weight was prepared to go to war to defend the status quo, let alone to defend a concept of world order; he fashioned his own aggressive plans accordingly.

Following the full-scale Japanese invasion of China in 1937–1938, with the failure of the League to do anything more than declare that members were entitled to apply Article 16 sanctions (which none chose to do), Hitler made his moves: the Anschluss with Austria, the ultimatum at Munich, the military occupation of the Sudetenland and then all of Czechoslovakia, and finally his attack on Poland in 1939, which discounted warnings from Paris and London that German military aggression against Poland would activate their alliances with Warsaw. As an indication of how irrelevant the League had become, when England and France finally declared war against Hitler in reaction to his invasion of Poland, they did not even bother with the formalities of attempting to invoke Article 16.

The United Nations

Trying to learn from the failures of the League, the victorious Allies in World War II once again tried to construct a world collective security system. They hoped to do a better job this time on two counts. All the victor powers would belong from the start (the United States had failed to ratify the Covenant and had never joined the League) and would be committed to making the system work. Second, the peace-enforcing machinery of the United Nations would be given "teeth" in the form of standby military capabilities earmarked for a UN force that could be fleshed out almost immediately to implement Security Council decisions.

The teeth of the UN collective security system are provided for in Chapter VII of the Charter, especially Articles 42 through 47:

- Article 42 stipulates that the "Security Council . . . may take such action by air, sea, or land forces as may be necessary to maintain or restore international peace and security."
- Article 43 obligates all members "to make available to the Security Council, on its call in accordance with a special agreement or agreements, armed forces, assistance, and facili-

ties, including rights of passage, necessary for maintaining international peace and security."

• Article 44 provides that member nations not represented on the Council whose forces are involved in a particular League military operation will participate in the military decision making of the Security Council.

• Article 45 obligates members to "hold immediately available national air-force contingents for combined international enforcement actions."

• Articles 46 and 47 outline the structure and functions of a Military Staff Committee to advise and assist the Security Council on all questions relating to the military requirements of international peace and security. The Military Staff Committee, to consist of the military Chiefs of Staff or their representatives from each of the five permanent members of the Security Council and the military representatives of any member nations whose participation is required, "shall be responsible under the Security Council for the strategic direction of any armed forces placed at the disposal of the Security Council. Questions relating to the command of such forces shall be worked out subsequently."

Because of the impasse between the Soviet Union and the United States which pervaded most UN agencies from the start, a permanent UN armed force or command, or even a standing framework for rapidly assembling such a force, has never materialized. Clearly an agency for planning UN enforcement operations would be the last place to expect Soviet-American cooperation. The impasse between the superpowers continues, and the Military Staff Committee, although it has met occasionally since 1947, has no forces to command on behalf of the United Nations.

The United Nations' police forces that have been formed for limited "peacekeeping" actions, as distinct from collective security actions, have been organized on an ad hoc basis and have been directly responsible to the Security Council and/or to the secretary general, bypassing the Military Staff Committee. Their function, conflict control rather than deterrence or punishment of aggression, will be discussed below along with other measures of this type.

Some of the basic UN collective security mechanisms of Articles

42 through 47 were ostensibly used in the "United Nations Peace Action" to repel the North Korean invasion of South Korea in 1950. In reality a U.S. response draped in the UN flag, the United Nations' role mandated by the Security Council was possible only because of the temporary absence from the Council of the Soviet Union, which otherwise would have vetoed the authorizing resolutions. The Soviet absence allowed the Security Council to designate the United States government and its Joint Chiefs of Staff to direct peace enforcement functions that normally, in the Charter's conception, would have been directed by the UN's Military Staff Committee.

The Security Council resolutions of July 7, 1950 recommended that member states "make . . . forces and other assistance available to a unified command under the United States" and requested "the United States to designate a commander of such forces."[14] The Unified Command established by the Truman administration was essentially identical to the U.S. Far East Command, under which General Douglas MacArthur had been directing battle operations from Tokyo for ten days before the UN vote. General MacArthur was to take his orders from the U.S. government, not from the United Nations, and the shape and pace of the military operations, including the momentous political decision to advance into North Korea, were determined by the Americans in accordance with their views of U.S. national interests. UN endorsements of these unilateral U.S. decisions were sought to give them international legitimacy, and General MacArthur was referred to in all official U.S. statements as "Commander of the UN Forces." But under the cover of universal collective security, the United States was transparently using the United Nations as an instrument for prosecuting its global rivalry with the Soviet Union.

To preserve the definition of the Korean action as a UN collective security operation even after the Soviets returned to the Security Council, the United States formulated a "Uniting for Peace" resolution that the General Assembly adopted in 1950 by a vote of 39 for, 5 against (the Soviet Union and its East European allies), and 11 abstentions. The resolution asserted the General Assembly's authority to act instead of the Security Council "if the Security Council, because of a lack of unanimity of the permanent members, fails to exercise its primary responsibility for the maintenance of international peace and security."[15]

Regional Security Arrangements

Recognizing that situations may arise when it is not possible to forge a worldwide consensus as to which are the aggressor countries and what sanctions should be applied against them, the founders of the United Nations included a series of clauses in Chapter VII of the Charter that allowed particular groupings of countries to organize themselves into regional security communities.

Article 51 allows for "individual or collective self-defense if an armed attack occurs against a Member of the United Nations, until the Security Council has taken the measures necessary to maintain international peace and security." And Articles 52 and 54, under the heading of "Regional Arrangements," encourage members that have formed into regional associations to "make every effort to achieve pacific settlements to local disputes through such regional arrangements . . . before referring them to the Security Council." The Security Council is authorized, where appropriate, to "utilize such regional arrangements or agencies for enforcement action under its authority."

The United States and its allies, when forming the North Atlantic Treaty Organization in 1949, cited Articles 51 through 54 to support their claim that NATO is consistent with the letter and spirit of the UN Charter; the Soviet Union and its allies made the same claim in forming the Warsaw Pact in 1955. Other regional groupings—such as the Organization of American States, the Organization of African Unity, the Arab League, and the Association of Southeast Asian Nations—also cite the UN Charter as authority for their existence.

Apart from NATO and the Warsaw Pact, each dominated by a superpower, regional associations have not proved very effective either in organizing collective external defense or in controlling intraregional conflict. One reason is that the recurring conditions that seem to justify violent conflicts between states (discussed in Chapter 3) most often inhere in neighboring countries, resulting in border conflicts, ethnic group rivalries and "liberation" movements, and in conflicts over commonly used water and other environmental resources (witness the chronic hostility between India and Pakistan, for example, and between Iran and Iraq). Another reason is that jealousies among countries and resentments at would-be hegemons (as, for example, toward Indonesia in Southeast Asia or Brazil in South America) tend to be more intense within regions and to frustrate collaboration, let alone integrative association of a sustained and deeply rooted nature.

The Basic Structural Problem of Collective Security

The weaknesses of both the League of Nations and the United Nations, and even of the smaller limited-membership collective security arrangements, are inherent in the basic structure of the world system of which all these organizations and groupings are subsystems. As long as the primary political units of world society are nation-states, determined to protect their independence above all other values except physical survival, run by leadership groups accountable to domestic interests ahead of world interests, no member nation of an international collective security association can be expected to participate in actions likely to put its independence and domestic interests at risk—unless such participation is clearly required to protect these interests.

This basic structural inhibition on international collective security action is reinforced by three features of contemporary world society: (1) the deepening and widening economic interdependence among countries; (2) the destructiveness of modern war; and (3) the domestic support required for sustained military operations.

1. Many a country is likely to enjoy a commercial relationship with a country that becomes the target of sanctions imposed by the collective security group to which it belongs. This means that some domestic groups are sure to be opposed to the disruption of normal commerce accompanying the application of sanctions. The more developed a country's economy is and the more it is involved in international commerce, the more this factor is likely to weigh against the country's participation in collective sanctions not clearly required for its immediate self-interests.

2. If collective security involves participating in military action against an aggressor country, those asked to participate are likely to assess carefully the aggressor's capabilities for military retaliation. Members within the range of highly destructive weapons of the aggressor will show reluctance to become one of the disciplining group. Increasingly, as countries deploy weapons of regional and intercontinental range, this factor is likely to inhibit all collective security actions except those directed against countries without sophisticated weapons.

3. To the extent that a contemplated collective application of sanctions involves going to war against aggressor countries, the economics of contemporary warfare works to inhibit the realization of any internationally organized sanctioning process. Because modern arsenals and armies must be fueled and replenished by many sectors of the domestic economy, domestic polities will weight their anticipated tangible sacrifices heavily against the vaguer world order values supposed to be served by active participation in a proposed international military action. Only when the consequences of nonparticipation are perceived as tangible, immediate, and more disrupting to the domestic society than war are countries likely to participate in a war to secure international peace and security. This means that decision makers, including legislative and popular support groups, would have to be convinced that the contemplated war could be so limited and controlled as to prevent costly disruptions of domestic life.

THE PACIFIC SETTLEMENT OF DISPUTES AND CONFLICT CONTROL

An alternative approach to reducing the role of war in the world is to develop and use nonviolent procedures and instruments to deal with the types of conflicts likely to give rise to military threats and actions, instead of threatening to smash or otherwise punish the aggressors. This approach, reflected in aspects of the League of Nations system, has carried over into the UN system, where it has been utilized more frequently than have the more dramatic collective security measures.

The standard procedures and instruments of pacific settlement are designed either to prevent conflicts from escalating to the level of violent encounters or to terminate ongoing violence—often through the intervention or good offices of an impartial "third party."

Mediation and Adjudication

Mediation depends on suggestions of a third party for compromise—suggestions that the adversaries are free to accept or reject. *Adjudication* usually involves a formal process, often called *arbitration*, of hearings, findings, and awards administered by a third party;

the adversaries agree beforehand that these will be binding on each of them.

In medieval Europe, the Church was the principal institution that offered mediation and arbitration services to warring princes. As the state system matured in the seventeenth, eighteenth, and nineteenth centuries, treaties between sovereigns frequently contained clauses in which the signatories agreed to submit their disputes henceforth to mediation or arbitration by a neutral statesman or international judicial tribunal.

In the contemporary world prominent statesmen are invited to become mediators—as President Jimmy Carter did in the 1978 Camp David meetings with Israeli Prime Minister Menachem Begin and Egyptian President Anwar al-Sadat that resulted in the Egypt-Israel Peace Treaty of 1979.

When adjudication or arbitration is desired, a dispute usually is submitted to the International Court of Justice (ICJ) or to a special judicial commission to determine the rights and obligations of the parties under international law. Members of the League of Nations were obligated by the Covenant to submit disputes to the ICJ for such adjudication if they could not settle them peacefully by diplomacy or mediation; but the obligation was usually bypassed.

The UN system more realistically leaves to the parties themselves the determination of whether or not to submit disputes to the World Court for adjudication, and some sets of countries have assumed advance obligations, in particular bilateral or multilateral treaties, to submit disputes to the ICJ. Even countries that have undertaken advance obligations with treaty partners to submit various classes of disputes to ICJ adjudication, however, can refuse to cooperate in particular proceedings that they fear might go against them by objecting to the Court's jurisdiction over the issue. This no-jurisdiction argument was the basis on which the Reagan administration refused to accept the legitimacy of the ICJ's 1986 rulings in the case brought before the Court by Nicaragua, charging the United States with illegal acts of force and violations of Nicaraguan sovereignty.

All in all, the international court system continues to play a meager role in the resolution of disputes, and more often than not is entirely bypassed in conflicts among major powers.

Cease-Fires and Cooling-off Periods

Sometimes what is sought immediately—before the resolution of the issues in dispute—is simply a cease-fire in an existing military conflict or a cooling-off period in a conflict on the brink of war.

Cease-fires are often possible, even though not always instituted at such times, when neither party to a dispute wants to continue bloodshed. All that it takes to terminate the fighting is a push for a cease-fire by a third party or international agency. Third-party initiatives are usually required because of the mistrust warring parties understandably have of each other's real intentions in proposing a cease-fire.[16]

The cease-fire may be "in place," meaning that neither side moves from the ground it has occupied in the last round of battle, but that both stop shooting at each other. It may be a pullback by one or both sides from the zone of immediate fighting, leaving a "no man's land" in between. It may be accompanied by promises not to augment fighting capabilities in the zone of confrontation; it may also involve the interposition of peace-observation or peacekeeping contingents from nonbelligerent countries or international institutions to assure that the cease-fire and/or pullback and capability limitations are adhered to. And it may be conditioned on good-faith participation by the adversaries in negotiations to resolve the dispute that precipitated the violence.

A cooling-off period may commence with a cease-fire or, as formerly provided for in Article 16 of the League Covenant, may be instituted to arrest the intensification of a dispute that appears to be heading toward a military confrontation. Typically, the adversaries in a cooling-off sequence agree to negotiate with each other directly or through the good offices of a third party to see if they can resolve their dispute short of war, meanwhile refraining from deploying or augmenting forces that would be used in a resumption of hostilities. The disputants may even withdraw forces already deployed in a threatening mode or remove them from alert status as in indication of their immediately pacific intentions. But as with cease-fires, proposals for such cooling-off arrangements usually stand a better chance of being accepted if they are initiated by impartial third parties or international institutions, thus reducing the chance that one of the adversaries will regard the plan as a trick to get it to lower its guard.

Peacekeeping Forces[17]

The most visible interposition of a neutral presence to control interstate conflict has been the multinational peace-observation groups and peacekeeping forces—the world's "soldiers without enemies."[18] Usually, but not always, organized under UN auspices, these multinational military units have been employed to monitor truces and cease-fires and/or to physically occupy space between belligerents to prevent the national armed forces from entering disputed areas or attacking one another.

The first established of these UN forces has been, strictly speaking, not a "force" at all, only a group of military officers assigned to accompany UN mediators in the Middle East to observe and report on compliance of the Arabs and Israelis with various UN-endorsed border arrangements, truces, and armistice agreements. Varying in size from 30 when it was created in 1948 to nearly 600 officers, this United Nations Truce Supervision Organization (UNTSO) has been staffed at different times by military personnel from some 100 countries. Similar UN corps of truce or cease-fire observers have been stationed in Kashmir, West Irian, the Yemen-Saudi Arabia border, and the Golan Heights between Syria and Israel.

A larger variety of UN military "presence," involving thousands of troops deployed between the belligerents, to separate them physically and make it necessary for them to crash through the UN glass window, as it were, to violate the truce, was first employed in 1956 on the Israel-Egypt border and at the entrance to the Gulf of Aqaba. This United Nations Emergency Force (UNEF) was mandated first to supervise the withdrawal of British, French, and Israeli troops that had invaded Egyptian territory in the Suez Canal crisis, then to monitor compliance with the armistice. Withdrawal of the force in 1967 at the demand of Egyptian President Gamal Abdel Nasser was one of the precipitating events leading to the 1967 Six-Day War between Israel and her Arab neighbors.

A second UNEF was deployed in the region in 1973 to patrol the new demilitarized zone in the Sinai and to verify the implementation of the Sinai disengagement agreements negotiated at the end of the Yom Kippur war. A parallel United Nations Disengagement Observer Force (UNDOF) was created in 1974 to supervise the small neutral zone created between Syria and Israel in their separately negotiated disengagement agreement.

The most ambitious and controversial of the UN peacekeeping forces was the intervention in the Congo in 1961, known by its French name, Opération des Nations Unies au Congo (ONUC). Directed by Secretary General Dag Hammarskjöld, the ONUC at full strength deployed 20,000 troops from twenty-five countries and a number of fighter aircraft: its authority was a rather loosely worded mandate from the Security Council to help the newly independent Congolese government keep the peace and stabilize control after the withdrawal the previous year of the colonial power, Belgium, and in the face of anticipated secession by the province of Katanga. Stretching the Security Council's mandate to allow for limited offensive military action, Hammarskjöld angered the Soviet Union; and after his death in 1961, the Soviets severely constricted the ability of the new secretary general, U Thant, to continue the ONUC. Though the force did not fully stabilize the Congo, the ONUC fulfilled one of its major assigned functions, to provide an external presence in the just-independent, still chaotic Congo to substitute for what otherwise might have been competitive military intervention by the Soviet Union and the United States.

Another major international military presence has been the UN force in Cyprus, created in 1964 and deployed at times in strengths up to 7,000. This force has tried to separate the Greek and Turkish communities to keep them from fighting, and has had the task of monitoring zonal and other intercommunal arrangements. But despite the presence of the UN force, a 1974 coup by militant Greeks seeking union with Greece itself ousted the Cypriot nationalist leader Archbishop Makarios; the accompanying intensification of communal strife brought on an invasion by Turkey, at which time the UN force—while keeping aloof from the fighting—helped to protect civilians. With the institution of a truce, the UN force returned to its principal peace-monitoring role.

The relative success of this instrumentality for peacekeeping, and the obvious logic of the concept, from time to time has led to proposals for creating a permanent UN peacekeeping force with an officer corps under the authority of the UN and permanently assigned troops—some of which the UN might directly recruit. This UN police force would be perpetually ready for dispatch to world trouble spots as needed. But so far the ad hoc approach of creating a special force tailored to the requirements and political idiosyncracies of each situation is the only one that has proved acceptable to both the Soviet

Union and the United States, as well as to other ideological rivals in the United Nations.

When a local crisis is too hot for the United Nations to handle, perhaps because the stakes are too high for either the United States or the Soviet Union or other powerful UN voting blocs, countries willing to participate in a peacekeeping operation can go outside the world organization to form a multinational force. A successful example of such a non-UN operation was the special Sinai peace-keeping force deployed at the Egyptian-Israeli border in 1982 after completion of the Israeli withdrawal provided for in the Egypt-Israel peace treaty. An unsuccessful effort was the multinational force deployed in Lebanon in 1982–1983, which had to withdraw under fire in 1984 as some of the warring elements in that conflict-torn country came to see the multinational force as a tool of a Lebanese government they regarded as illegitimate.

The virtue as well as the limitations of the peacekeeping system as it has evolved since the Second World War lie precisely in its consistency with the prevailing state-sovereignty norms of contemporary world society. The deployment of any international peace-keeping force must be with the consent of the country on whose territory it is to be stationed. Members voluntarily contribute personnel and equipment to be used by commanders responsible to a group of sovereign states, sustained by a consensus among those states—as long as that consensus lasts.

Creative Conflict Resolution

In recent decades, the catastrophic consequences of failing to resolve international conflict without war have drawn scholars from diverse disciplines, as well as experienced practitioners of negotiation from the private and public sectors, into the search for ways of inducing countries in conflict to back away from brink-of-war situations. Clinical psychologists and family counselors, labor-management negotiators, social psychology theorists, attorneys skilled in getting out-of-court settlements, game theorists—all have experience and wisdom that can be adapted to international conflict resolution.[19]

Diplomats are beginning to pay more attention to this field of inquiry. Some have attended seminars at the Nuclear Negotiation Project of the Harvard Law School and at similar projects to expand their repertoires of options that could be useful for avoiding or terminating dangerous international encounters. On occasion ideas for creative conflict resolution have found their way into high-level country-to-country negotiations with positive effects.

A simple, well-publicized, but probably underutilized idea is the technique of unilaterally making a concession—not with the intent of appeasing an adversary, but rather to bring pressure on him to make a reciprocal concession. This negotiating strategy has been elaborated by the social psychologist Charles E. Osgood in his papers on graduated reciprocation in tension reduction (GRIT). The key to the GRIT concept is the invitation explicit in a unilateral de-escalation for the adversary to follow suit, under the promise of further de-escalation if reciprocation materializes. The first unilateral move must not put the initiator at a disadvantage, and the promised further de-escalation should be even more attractive than the first but clearly indicated not to be forthcoming if the adversary fails to reciprocate.[20] Reportedly, President Kennedy deliberately applied Osgood's ideas in 1963 when he announced the unilateral ban on the atmospheric testing of nuclear weapons that preceded the successful Soviet-American negotiation of a partial test ban.[21]

One suggestive line of theoretical and experimental investigation in the field of conflict resolution deals with the vexing problem—typically present in efforts to achieve a cease-fire in wartime and also in many arms-control negotiations—of how to induce cooperation between parties where each side would benefit if both pursued cooperative strategies, as opposed to continuing hostile acts or deployments which would lead both to suffer great harm, but where there are opportunities available to each to cheat and thereby gain a substantial advantage over the opponent as long as the opponent does not simultaneously cheat. Researchers have devised experimental simulations that show some strategies are better than others for building cooperative, nonexploitative relationships even among rivals who are highly suspicious of each other's motives and propensity to cheat.[22]

Another creative approach to conflict resolution has been championed by Harvard Law School negotiating expert Roger Fisher, who calls it "fractionating conflict." Again the idea, simple to the point of being self-evident, is often ignored when countries are working themselves toward a major confrontation. It is perhaps best understood as the opposite of issue-linkage strategies in negotiation. The fractionating approach slices country-to-country disputes into small

but discrete issues, making it possible to deal with each "independently on its merits." Less resolvable disputes are not allowed to
stand in the way of ones that can be resolved.[23] Surprisingly, Henry
Kissinger, a champion of the opposed theory—issue linkage—showed
himself a deft fractionator in orchestrating step-by-step cease-fire and
disengagement agreements between Israel and Egypt and between
Israel and Syria at the end of the Yom Kippur war. President Carter
also used the fractionating approach to good effect in the Camp David
negotiations, though he used some linkage stratagems to compel
agreement as well. And it was quintessentially a fractionating approach by the Carter administration, advised by Roger Fisher, that
finally secured the release of the American hostages from Iran in
January 1981.

A hallmark of creative conflict-resolution approaches is that they
are *non*–zero-sum (to use the game theory term for outcomes of
benefit to both sides). As opposed to those of coercive strategies,
their objectives and their means are predominantly nonviolent; they
attempt to divert parties to a conflict from seeking victory (defeat for
the opponent) to looking for mutual rewards and satisfaction. They do
not presume that either side's values are illegitimate, but rather that
most intense conflict among large groups, which is what war is,
involves deep convictions on each side that its goals or grievances are
just. Creative international conflict resolution does not presume to
arbitrate at the level of determining which party is on the side of God
or "justice" and which is not. It tries to find a way around such
cosmic issues, putting priority instead on minimizing direct violence.

NOTES

1. The basic concepts of Grotius are well expounded in Walter Schiffer,
The Legal Community of Mankind (New York: Columbia University Press,
1954), pp. 30–48.

2. For detailed analysis of conflict in and rules of use of the non-land
areas, see Seyom Brown, Nina Cornell, Larry Fabian, and Edith Brown
Weiss, *Regimes for the Ocean, Outer Space, and Weather* (Washington,
D.C.: Brookings Institution, 1977).

3. See Henry A. Kissinger, *A World Restored: The Politics of Conser-
vatism in a Revolutionary Age* (New York: Grosset & Dunlop, 1964); see also

his essay, "The White Revolutionary: Reflections on Bismarck," *Daedalus* (Summer 1968), 97(3):888–924.

4. Immanuel Kant, *Perpetual Peace* (New York: Macmillan, 1917).

5. Kissinger's intellectual debt to Kant is analyzed in Peter Dickson, *Kissinger and the Meaning of History* (New York: Cambridge University Press, 1978).

6. Frank P. Chambers, Christina Phelps Harris, and Charles C. Bayley, *This Age of Conflict: 1914 to the Present* (New York: Harcourt, Brace, 1950), pp. 138–141.

7. *Ibid.*, pp. 141–142.

8. Hans J. Morgenthau, *Politics Among Nations: The Struggle for Power and Peace*, 5th ed. (New York: Knopf, 1978), pp. 550–560.

9. *Ibid.*

10. See Henry Kissinger, *The White House Years* (Boston: Little, Brown, 1979); and Seyom Brown, *The Crises of Power: An Interpretation of United States Foreign Policy During the Kissinger Years* (New York: Columbia University Press, 1979), pp. 19–48.

11. "Basic Principles of Relations Between the United States of America and the Union of Soviet Socialist Republics," *Department of State Bulletin* (June 29, 1972), 66 (1722):898–899.

12. In *A World Restored*, Kissinger warned against attempts to constrain the revolutionary power by agreements:

> Adjustments are possible, but they will be conceived as tactical maneuvers to consolidate positions for the inevitable showdown, or as tools to undermine the morale of the antagonist. To be sure, the motivation of the revolutionary power may well be defensive; it may well be sincere in its protestations of feeling threatened. But the distinguishing feature of a revolutionary power is not that it feels threatened—such feeling is inherent in the nature of international relations based on sovereign states—*but that nothing can reassure it.* Only absolute security—the neutralization of the opponent—is considered a sufficient guarantee, and thus the desire of one power for absolute security means absolute insecurity for all the others. (p. 2)

13. *Covenant of the League of Nations*, signed at Versailles 28 June 1919 (Geneva: League of Nations, 1920).

14. United Nations Document S/1587.

15. United Nations Document A/1481.

16. See Paul R. Pillar, *Negotiating Peace: War Termination as a Bargaining Process* (Princeton, N.J.: Princeton University Press, 1983).

17. For descriptive narratives of peacekeeping actions since World War II, see Henry Wiseman, ed., *Peacekeeping: Appraisals and Proposals* (New York: Pergamon, 1983).

18. Larry L. Fabian, *Soldiers Without Enemies* (Washington, D.C.: Brookings Institution, 1971).

19. For an inventory of diverse conflict-resolution ideas with applicability to international relations, see Richard Wendell Fogg, "Dealing with Conflict: A Repertoire of Creative, Peaceful Approaches," *Journal of Conflict Resolution* (June 1985), 29(2):330–358.

20. Charles E. Osgood, "Graduated Unilateral Initiatives for Peace," in Clagett G. Smith, ed., *Conflict Resolution: Contributions of the Behavioral Sciences* (Notre Dame, Ind.: University of Notre Dame Press, 1971), pp. 515–525.

21. Fogg, "Dealing with Conflict," p. 334.

22. See Robert Axelrod, *The Evolution of Cooperation* (New York: Basic Books, 1984), for a creative experimental approach to a version of this problem called "Prisoner's Dilemma" by some game theorists since it seems to fit a hypothetical situation in which two prisoners who have conspired with each other in a major crime are presented by the prosecutor with simultaneous but separate and secret offers to turn state's evidence on the other one: If both prisoners refuse to tell on each other, they will both have to stand trial and run the risk of being convicted or found not guilty; if one cheats on the other by confessing and giving the prosecutor information, the one that helped the prosecutor will ultimately receive a substantially more lenient sentence, and the other will receive maximum punishment for the crime; finally, if each confesses, both will be convicted and neither will get a break at time of sentencing. Clearly, the most tempting strategy to each is to confess and also tell on the other so as to get a substantially reduced punishment for oneself—but if each does this, both lose more than if each kept quiet. If the prisoners could communicate, it would do them well to agree that they should both keep quiet, but even if they did so agree, there would be great temptation to cheat. The theory itself contains no solution to the problem for either of the prisoners. However, in some computer-assisted simulations devised by Robert Axelrod and his colleagues, it was discovered that if the "prisoners" were provided with opportunities to play repeated rounds of such a game, they could learn the mutual advantages of cooperating with each other, and that there were certain strategies of retaliation in kind ("tit for tat") that reinforced such learning.

23. Roger Fisher and William Langer Ury, *Getting to Yes* (Boston: Houghton Mifflin, 1981).

CHAPTER 9

Arms Control

Arms control is a pragmatic adaptation to the difficulties encountered in each of the approaches to preventing and controlling war that are analyzed above. It starts from the assumption that military balances of power, for the time being at least, will continue to be weighty determinants of whether, where, and when wars break out and of how they are fought and terminated.

Arms-control efforts are directed primarily toward making military balances less likely to provoke war. Some efforts also have the objective of ensuring that if wars break out, their destructiveness will be kept to a minimum and they will be ended as quickly as possible. A third objective, making the arms race less expensive, also animates many arms-control efforts; but the effects of arms control on the incidence and shape of war are the main concern of this chapter.

Not all supporters of arms control have given up on efforts to purge war from the world by reforming the international system or by comprehensive disarmament; some remain hopeful of eventually attaining these more ambitious goals but see arms control as a here-and-now, politically feasible means of making progress toward world peace, and—given the prospects of an earth-destroying nuclear holocaust—the precondition for further progress. President Kennedy was of such a mind when in justifying the limited Nuclear Test Ban agreement of 1963 he quoted the Chinese proverb "A journey of a thousand miles must begin with a single step."[1]

EFFORTS TO MAKE MILITARY BALANCES LESS WAR PRONE

As shown in the discussion of coercive diplomacy (Chapter 5), countries tempted to use force against their adversaries will be more, or less, inhibited from doing so by their changing assessments of which side would prevail in the ensuing battle, as well as of the costs, risks, or advantages of waiting to fight at another time. Not only the existing "balance" of military capabilities (the quotation marks are put around *balance* to indicate that the term is applied to unequal or tipped balances as well as to essentially equal or level ones), but the changes a balance is undergoing, may need to be stabilized or controlled to avert a war.

An arms-control measure designed to affect a military balance need not always be negotiated or mutually instituted. It can be unilaterally adopted. What makes it arms control, as distinguished from normal defense or deterrence policy, is its purpose of relieving the other side of fears of being attacked.

Negotiated Balances

The naval limitations of the 1920s and 1930s. Antecedents of contemporary efforts to stabilize aspects of the East-West balance of military power were the naval agreements negotiated among the great powers between World War I and World War II, when naval capability was still the prime indicator of strategic clout.

The Washington Treaty of 1922 established a ceiling on capital ships (large battleships), and a ratio of capital ship tonnage among the naval powers of the day at 5:5:3:1.75:1.75, with Britain and the United States in the first rank, Japan in the second rank, and France and Italy in the third rank. The negotiated ratio reflected the shared desire of Britain and the United States, as friendly naval rivals, to avoid a costly arms race with each other and to keep the upstart Pacific power, Japan, in an inferior position. Japan reluctantly agreed under pressure from Britain, at that time its only great-power ally.

In the London Naval Conference of 1930, the United States, Britain, and Japan extended their tonnage-ratio agreement to encompass most of the main types of warships in their inventories, but with a new proviso, the so-called Escalator Clause, permitting construction above the limits if any signatory considered itself threatened by a nonsignatory power. When Japan withdrew from these obligations in 1933 in reaction to the British and American condemnation of its invasion of China, the other principals were no longer inclined to accept international limits on their naval buildups in the Pacific.

The Anglo-German Naval Agreement of 1935 was a bilateral

agreement between England and a remilitarizing Germany to keep their naval armaments programs somewhat restrained. Its principal effect was to legitimize the German buildup—which otherwise might have been in violation of the Treaty of Versailles—but under limits that would allow the British to maintain their traditional naval superiority without having to launch an expensive rearmament program. However, with the approach of war in the spring of 1939, Germany formally renounced the treaty's restraints. The ironic effect of the 1935 agreement, therefore, was to provide Germany with the wherewithal for a crash expansion of its navy while Britain drifted with its normal program.

The strategic arms limitations of the 1970s.   The Strategic Arms Limitation Talks (SALT) of the 1970s and the agreements they produced were designed to assure both superpowers that neither would attempt to gain superiority over the other and to reassure both sides that the strategic forces each deployed were entirely for purposes of deterring war—that is, that they were not for aggression or for victory in a war. These arms-control efforts were also based on the assumption that reinforcing and enlarging the constituencies for East-West cooperation provides the best hope over the long run for avoiding war. The negotiations and resulting agreements, in providing tangible evidence of pacific intent, would at least reduce the hostile rhetoric and posturing on each side.

The SALT I negotiation, starting in November 1969 and producing the 1972 Treaty on the Limitation of Anti-Ballistic Missile (ABM) Systems and the 1972 Interim Agreement on the Limitation of Strategic Offensive Arms, was clearly an effort at arms control rather than at disarmament. It reinforced the mutual assured destruction (MAD) basis of the deterrent balance of terror between the United States and the Soviet Union by virtually eliminating (in the ABM Treaty) the deployment on either side of defensive weapons that could substantially reduce the massive destruction likely in a strategic nuclear war, and by allowing (in the Interim Agreement) sufficient offensive power on both sides to guarantee that each would retain a capacity to inflict massive damage on the other in a retaliatory blow, no matter how large or well executed the first strike might be. Each side, in effect, was to hold the other's population "hostage" against any attempt to start a strategic nuclear war, and SALT I was a mutual suicide pact for deterring such a war.

The 1972 ABM Treaty, supposed to be of unlimited duration, permitted each side to have just two ABM deployment sites, with no more than 100 ABM missiles at each. The ABMs at one site were to be oriented to protect the country's capital; those at the other site were to guard an ICBM launching field. In 1974 the superpowers signed a protocol limiting each side to only one ABM site, giving each side freedom to choose to defend either its capital city or an ICBM complex.

Both sides also agreed to limit improvements in their ABM technology, to forego developing and testing multiple-missile ABM launchers and any sea-based, air-based, space-based, or mobile land-based ABM systems.

The 1972 Interim Agreement on the Limitation of Strategic Offensive Arms froze for five years the number of strategic ballistic missiles, land- and sea-based, deployed or under construction. It provided that the United States could deploy no more than 1054 ICBMs on land and 656 submarine-launched ballistic missiles (SLBMs) on 44 submarines, while the Soviet Union was allowed to deploy up to 1618 ICBMs and 740 SLBMs—though additional SLBMs could be deployed if they were substituted for older ICBMs. The agreement committed the United States and the Soviet Union to continue negotiating to produce an offensive arms treaty by 1977.[2]

The SALT II process, starting in 1972, was an attempt to tie up some of the loose ends left out of the SALT I accords—such as bombers, intermediate-range ballistic missiles, and cruise missiles— and to assure that "essential equivalence" was sustained into the 1980s as new weapons technologies changed the destructive capabilities of the weapons allowed under SALT I.

Two developments in particular threatened to undermine the basic deterrent balance agreed to in SALT I. One was the maturing of technologies for multiplying the number of nuclear warheads each ICBM could carry, resulting in multiple independently targeted reentry vehicles, or MIRVs; if one side installed MIRVs earlier than the other or if its ICBMs were equipped to carry more MIRVs than the other's the numerical ratios in SALT I could become unbalanced. The other complicating development was the improvement in the accuracy of missiles, reducing the ratio of the attacking warheads needed to destroy one missile in a ground silo to almost 1:1 (one attacking warhead to each missile silo to be destroyed). Married to MIRVs, the new accuracy would allow the attacker who struck first to use up only a fraction of his own force in destroying the bulk of his opponent's ICBMs. MIRVs and accuracy together revived the advantage of the strategic first strike, thereby negating a fundamental purpose of SALT: to reinforce the confidence on both sides that neither could contemplate "winning" a strategic nuclear war.

SALT II attempted to control the destabilizing effects of MIRVs and improved accuracy by establishing limits not only on the number of strategic delivery vehicles each side could deploy but also on the number of such weapons that could carry multiple warheads and on roughly the number of warheads each side could maintain in its strategic arsenal.

The SALT II Treaty—the complicated and detailed set of agreements signed in Vienna on June 18, 1979, by presidents Carter and Brezhnev—was never approved by the U.S. Senate. The unratified treaty limited each side to 2,250 strategic nuclear delivery vehicles, of which no more than 1,320 could be carriers of more than one weapon. Of the 1,320 multiple-weapon delivery vehicles, no more than 1,200 could be MIRVed ballistic missiles: the rest would be bombers carrying long-range cruise missiles; and of the 1,200 MIRVed ballistic missiles, no more than 820 could be ICBMs, with the rest SLBMs.

The SALT II Treaty also included special prohibitions on heavy-missile launchers; permission for each side to flight-test or deploy only one new type of light ICBM, not to carry more than ten warheads; a ban on increasing the number of warheads on existing types of ICBMs; a limit of fourteen warheads for each SLBM; and ceilings on the launch-weight and throw-weight of ballistic missiles, with a ban on converting light to heavy missiles.

Verification of adherence to the treaty provisions was to be accomplished, as in SALT I, by "national technical means"—meaning each side's reconnaissance satellites—and the sides agreed not to impede such verification. Since remote reconnaissance could not verify the number of warheads carried by each missile, however, SALT II stipulated a counting rule that once a missile of a particular type had been tested with MIRVs, all missiles of that type would be considered to be carrying the largest number of MIRVs observed in any flight-test of the type; similar counting rules were agreed to for cruise missiles and heavy bombers.[3]

The principal opponents of the SALT II treaty in the United States charged that the numerical limits gave a false sense of equivalence since the Soviets would be allowed to maintain more heavier missiles in their arsenal: the heavier Soviet weapons could carry on the average more MIRVs than the U.S. missiles and could deliver greater megatonnage against their targets. Some members of Congress, basically supportive of the treaty, worried that the verification procedures left too much uncertainty about Soviet compliance with its terms.

These and other issues were still being debated in the Congress at the end of 1979 when Soviet troops invaded Afghanistan—whereupon President Carter asked the Senate to defer its action on SALT II. The deferment became indefinite, and neither the U.S. government nor the Soviet government formally ratified the SALT II treaty. Yet both superpowers found it to their advantage to act as if the pact were binding on them. The Reagan administration, which had been expected to repudiate it, announced six weeks after taking office that "While we are reviewing our SALT policy, we will take no action that would undercut existing agreements so long as the Soviet Union exercises the same restraint." The statement reflected the judgment of the Joint Chiefs of Staff that for the time being the provisions of SALT II would require no elimination or retardation of ongoing U.S. weapons programs, but that without the treaty's limits the Soviets could increase their nuclear warheads at a faster rate than the United States.[4]

The START negotiations.   Early in 1981, the newly installed Reagan administration announced that it was thoroughly reviewing the past SALT approach. Most of Reagan's top arms-policy advisers had publicly condemned the SALT II treaty before the administration took office, and Reagan himself had called it "fatally flawed." The president said that the United States would not return to the negotiating table until the new American military buildup was sufficiently under way to allow the United States to "negotiate from strength."

When the Soviet-American strategic arms negotiations, renamed START for Strategic Arms Reduction Talks, resumed in 1982, the American side insisted that the objective of the negotiations should be to achieve real strategic equality through substantial reductions in heavy ICBMs, with specified ceilings for missile throw-weight and numbers of warheads. The Soviets saw in the U.S. proposals a design to reduce ICBMs asymmetrically in categories where the Soviets had greatest strength while allowing the United States to continue its own new strategic buildup and modernization programs. Accordingly, their opening position for the new round of negotiations was that SALT II had provided for essential parity in forces and that the current negotiations should re-endorse the SALT accords, using them as a base for whatever additional adjustments were needed to maintain parity. But when it appeared that the Americans with their emphasis on major reductions might be winning the propaganda battle, the Soviets apparently decided to compete for world approval by publicly announcing their own deep-cut proposals. Not surprisingly, the Soviet proposals, by emphasizing equality in launchers (as distinct from warheads), avoiding missile throw-weight limits, and insisting on stringent limits on air-launched cruise missiles, were full of asymmetries unfavorable to the United States.

By the time the Soviets walked out of the strategic arms negotiations at the end of 1983 in response to the American deployment of new intermediate-range missiles in Europe (see the discussion of the INF negotiations below), START was becoming little more than a public-relations arena. Indeed, what was supposed to be the central premise of strategic arms control—namely, that weapons with the purpose of destroying the other side's strategic deterrent force were destabilizing—was drastically undermined by President Reagan's endorsement of a major ABM program in his March 1983 Strategic Defense Initiative (the effects of which on mutual deterrence strategies and force postures are analyzed above in Chapter 4).

When the superpowers resumed their strategic arms control negotiations in 1985, they were more fundamentally at odds over the basic purposes of the negotiations than at any time since the start of the SALT era. The Soviets argued that the essential condition for further limits on strategic offensive forces, let alone deep cuts, was reaffirmation of the ban on ABMs and an explicit avowal to forego the kind of space-based, multilayered ABM defense of the country's population that the Reagan administration hoped to attain with its Strategic Defense Initiative. President Reagan, however, insisted that the United States would not bargain away SDI, for it was the best hope of rendering strategic nuclear war obsolete. The Soviets, he said, ought to want to cooperate in turning the world away from a security system dependent on maintaining capabilities for mutual annihilation. If there were to be negotiations on strategic defenses, they should be over how to phase them in, rather than how to preclude them. And to show that the SDI was not an attempt to gain strategic superiority, Reagan said that the United States, as it approached being able to deploy a comprehensive system for shielding its population from nuclear attack, would be willing to discuss ways of sharing the technology with the Soviets.[5]

The announced determination by the Reagan administration to develop a nationwide population defense was antithetical to the preexisting arms-control regime centered on the 1972 ABM Treaty. Not only did the SDI contemplate eventual deployment of the very weapons explicitly restricted by that treaty, but even the announced active pursuit of such a defensive capability, by either side or both, would generate major new compensatory buildups in each adversary's offensive strategic arsenal, which in turn—if the objective of population defense still animated policy—would require ever larger deployments of the defensive system, plus new offensive deployments just to maintain parity in offensive capabilities.

Following the October 1986 meeting between President Reagan and General Secretary Gorbachev at Reykjavik (see above p. 137), it was unclear whether their representatives at the follow-on arms talks were seriously negotiating or tabling proposals mainly to make the other side look obstructionist. At Reykjavik the two leaders came close to agreeing to cut their strategic arsenals in half over the next five years. The question after the Iceland meeting was what kinds of weapons would be permitted to remain in the strategic arsenals. The Americans were again pressing for stringent sublimits on land-based ICBMs, especially the heavy types in which the Soviets had an advantage. The Soviets were holding out for more flexibility for each side to retain whatever types it chose under a general ceiling. The Soviets were also insisting on continued adherence, for at least another ten years, to the ABM treaty, and were linking limits on offensive forces to an agreement by the Reagan administration to forgo all but laboratory tests of the SDI. The Reagan administration reportedly was divided over whether and how long the United States should agree to continue adhering to the ABM treaty, but in any event was still adamant about the necessity of proceeding with research and testing of components of the SDI.[6]

The intermediate nuclear forces (INF) negotiations. On November 30, 1981, the United States and the Soviet Union began a special round of negotiations focused on intermediate-range nuclear weapons based in western Russia that were capable of hitting Western Europe, and on European-based weapons in (or soon to be added to) the U.S. and NATO arsenals that could hit the Soviet Union.

The intermediate nuclear forces (INF) negotiations were undertaken mainly in reaction to Soviet deployments west of the Ural Mountains of new mobile, highly accurate missiles with ranges of approximately 3,000 miles, carrying three nuclear warheads each. Called SS-20s by Western intelligence analysts, these intermediate-range ballistic missiles (IRBMs) were largely a redundant addition to forces already in the Soviet ICBM arsenal. But since the IRBMs could have no other purpose than to hit targets in Western Europe, NATO analysts found them an awesome portent of the possibility that in a future East-West conflict the Soviets might try to intimidate the Western Europeans with the IRBM threat while holding off the U.S. deterrent with the Soviet ICBM threat.

The response of the United States and its European allies to the new Soviet deployments was the so-called Two Track decision of NATO's foreign and defense ministers on December 12, 1979. Track one provided for preparations to deploy new U.S. intermediate-range nuclear forces in Europe: 108 Pershing II IRBMs and 464 Tomahawk ground-launched cruise missiles. Track two was a U.S. effort to get the Soviets to agree to a mutual limitation on intermediate-range nuclear missiles in the European theater. If the Soviet-American negotiations showed no success by the end of 1983, the planned U.S. deployments would commence. But if there was success on the arms-control track, NATO would re-examine its decision to deploy the new Pershing and cruise missiles.[7]

The basic negotiating positions of the United States and the Soviet Union in the INF talks reflected their different geostrategic situations and perceptions. They also showed the extent to which each of the sides was rigidly locked into a political-military worldview that, however inaccurate it might be about the adversary's intentions to use military force to change the status quo in Europe, had achieved a life of its own.

The Soviets regarded their intermediate-range weapons targeted on Western Europe as counters to NATO weapons aimed at the Soviet Union and Eastern Europe. This basic Soviet perception has been aptly recorded by *Time* magazine's expert on military and arms-control policy, Strobe Talbott:

> The Soviets had persuaded themselves that the composition of NATO gave the U.S. unfair advantages and that the U.S.S.R.,

as a co-equal superpower, was entitled to various kinds of "compensation." NATO, in Soviet eyes, represented triple jeopardy: first, the U.S. was a threat in its own right, because of its strategic forces that Washington vowed to use in a European conflict; second, the U.S. had additional weapons for use against Soviet targets stationed on European territory; and third, France and Britain were not only covered by the American umbrella, but had their own nuclear weapons as well, weapons that could reach into the U.S.S.R.[8]

Accordingly, the Soviet negotiating stance was that the elements of any Euro-strategic nuclear force stabilization or reduction agreement must include all NATO forces in Europe capable of striking the Soviet Union. Essential parity existed between the United States and the Soviet Union in intercontinental nuclear forces, and in order to facilitate the SALT negotiations the Soviets had reluctantly agreed not to include NATO's forward-based nuclear strike forces (weapons in and around Europe capable of striking the Soviet Union) in the SALT limitations. But this left a strategic imbalance, from the Soviet point of view, in the continental-range forces: their SS-20 deployments were designed to redress it. If the United States was prepared to negotiate to achieve parity in the Euro-strategic forces, that was fine—but then they must be willing to count the French and British systems as well as the U.S. nuclear-capable aircraft on European bases and on U.S. aircraft carriers in the eastern Atlantic and the Mediterranean.

The U.S. government's perception of the Euro-strategic balance was consistent with its standing assessment that the overall NATO-Warsaw Pact military balance conferred a conventional-force advantage on the Soviets that the West needed to redress by relying on nuclear deterrence. Major increments on the Soviet side of the European nuclear equation, as represented by the SS-20s, were therefore profoundly destabilizing and required such compensatory augmentations in the West's Europe-oriented nuclear capability as the Pershing II IRBMs and Tomahawk cruise missiles.

The United States, accordingly, said it was willing to forego or reduce its planned Euro-strategic force augmentations in return for the Soviets' dismantling or substantial reduction of their new European-oriented missiles. But the United States would not negotiate away the British and French independent nuclear forces, which these countries maintained to deter Soviet attack or nuclear blackmail against themselves.

The fundamentally different assessments by the two superpowers of what should be accomplished by the INF negotiations have determined the gross as well as the highly detailed proposals each has put forward in this arena.

In the category of gross proposals is the Reagan administration's "zero-zero option," under which the Soviet Union would divest itself of the Europe-oriented SS-20 and the United States would forgo new nuclear missiles in Europe: but it would leave intact all the Soviet-oriented systems in and around the Continent as well as shorter-range nuclear forces the Soviets could target on Western Europe. Equally unrealistic is the Kremlin's proposal to make all of Europe a nuclear-free zone: unless accompanied by a heretofore unattainable equalization of NATO-Warsaw Pact conventional capabilities, it would leave the NATO countries severely disadvantaged in Europe.

Most of the more detailed, and presumably more serious, INF proposals have been exchanged between Soviet and American negotiators behind closed doors; those that have found their way into the press still suggest the impasse produced by profoundly antithetical geostrategic assessments. The most reported-on exchange, before the Americans proceeded with their new deployments and the Soviets walked out of the INF negotiations, is the famous Nitze-Kvitsinsky "walk in the woods"—a private discussion in July 1982 between Paul Nitze, the chief American negotiator, and Yuli Kvitsinsky, his Soviet counterpart, in which they informally agreed on an exploratory package for consideration by their respective governments: the Nitze-Kvitsinsky suggestion was that the Soviet Union limit its intermediate-range missiles in western Russia to 75 SS-20 launchers (requiring the elimination of about 168 SS-20 launchers already deployed and 380 SS-4s and SS-5s still in place) in exchange for the United States foregoing completely its planned deployment of 108 Pershing IIs and limiting its Tomahawk cruise launchers to 75 with 4 missiles per launcher. (The numerical advantage to be allowed the United States in warheads—300 cruises compared to the 225 MIRVs on the Soviet SS-20s—was compensation for the faster flight time and lesser vulnerability of the SS-20s.) Additionally, the Soviets would freeze their SS-20s deployed in Asia at the then-current level of 90 launchers. Each superpower would be allowed 150 medium-range nuclear-capable aircraft in the European theater, and for the time being at least nothing would be decided about the British and French forces.

The Nitze-Kvitsinsky "walk in the woods" came to naught because Moscow and Washington both rejected their negotiators' effort to break the impasse.

Kvitsinsky's superiors evidently balked at two implications of the informal agreement: (1) that they should concede to the West's claim that the SS-20s created a European imbalance that it was legitimate for NATO to try to redress, and (2) that the Soviets should assent to the U.S. refusal to count French and British nuclear forces in the Euro-strategic balance.

In the Reagan administration, the small group of strategy and arms-control advisers privy to the Nitze-Kvitsinsky intitiative was divided over its merits. The president ended by accepting the rationale of the secretary of defense and other hawks for opposing an INF agreement based on the walk-in-the-woods formula: namely, that it would take away the opportunity for deploying a state-of-the-art IRBM in Europe—Pershing II—which was needed to refurbish NATO's nuclear-deterrent posture whether or not the Soviets provided a political rationalization for it by deploying their SS-20s. Reagan was encouraged to reiterate his demand that the Soviets accept his zero-zero option of no intermediate-range nuclear missile deployments by either superpower; if their refusal left the United States no alternative but to proceed with the planned INF deployments, so much the better for the Americans from the public-relations viewpoint.[9]

Even though formally rejected, however, the Nitze-Kvitsinsky exploratory option showed the negotiators on each side that the other side's settling price might be considerably more moderate than its asking price. The Americans were stimulated to devise a wide variety of alternatives to test the waters, all of which allowed the United States to retain Tomahawks *and* Pershings to match the SS-20s the Soviets retained. The Soviets entered into the game of appearing flexible by also proposing alternatives; but in none of their variations did they grant even implicitly that the U.S. Euro-missiles scheduled for deployment were legitimate counters to their SS-20s. Rather, the Soviets' feelers that seemed to contemplate limits on their SS-20s were geared primarily to limiting the size of the British and French missile forces to be allowed.

As the negotiating stalemate continued and the end-of-1983 deadline for the United States to begin its deployments approached, the Soviets became more explicit in their threat to walk out of the INF and START negotiations if NATO went ahead with its "illegitimate" and provocative alteration in the balance of military power. The Kremlin also vaguely but ostentatiously threatened to "retaliate" by new deployments of its own, presumably stationed on the territory of its allies.

Neither side was able to bluff the other side into substantial concessions. The start of the American deployments was followed by the threatened Soviet walkout from both the INF talks and START. If the Soviets had hoped that an outraged world opinion would put the blame on the Reagan administration and Western governments that went along with Washington, 1984 was a disappointing year. The antimissile popular movements in Europe fizzled, and Ronald Reagan was returned to office for a second term with a huge electoral majority.

The INF negotiations resumed in the spring of 1985 as one of the forums in the "umbrella" negotiations between the superpowers on strategic weapons. Negotiators began to talk of merged limitations, perhaps establishing global and combined ceilings on warheads for intermediate and intercontinental systems.

In their proposals at Reykjavik in October 1986, the Soviets appeared ready to embrace the Reagan administration's earlier bid for a complete ban on superpower medium-range Euro-missile deployments. But the Kremlin was surely well aware that the NATO countries, having fully committed themselves to the new missile deployments, were now no longer seriously interested in Reagan's zero-zero proposal. Reagan's positive response to the 1986 Soviet proposals worried the West Europeans, particularly in light of new Soviet deployments of shorter-range nuclear missiles that would not be covered by the contemplated INF accord. The Soviets also appeared willing to allow France and Britain to keep their current forces, but with restrictions on their augmentation and modernization, restrictions the French and British clearly would not accept. The "theater" negotiations were in danger of becoming simply political theater.

Mutual and balanced force reductions (MBFR) in nonstrategic arms. The different geopolitical situations of the superpowers and their European alliances have also been reflected in East-West negotiations to reduce the nonstrategic, primarily nonnuclear, weapons and troops of NATO and the Warsaw Pact. While in formal structure the MBFR negotiations are multilateral, involving most members of the rival alliance systems, in practice the East-West bargaining is conducted almost entirely by the two superpowers.

At the outset of the European force-reduction talks in 1973, the Soviet Union established its basic position that the prevailing overall force balance in Europe was essentially equal and that therefore conventional-force reductions in the theater should be symmetrical. The United States represented the Western view that the existing conventional-force balance decidedly favored the Warsaw Pact and that therefore asymmetrical reductions down to "common ceilings" were required to achieve a balance. (The argument over the correct name for the negotiations reflects this difference: The Warsaw Pact countries say the subject of the talks is mutual force reductions, while the NATO countries insist on mutual and balanced force reductions, accounting for the B in MBFR.) Another difference at the start of the talks was the Soviet premise that reductions would be distributed across each of the alliances—the Soviets were particularly anxious to limit West German forces—as opposed to the U.S. emphasis on starting with Soviet and American reductions.

Not only these divergent notions of acceptable force-balance outcomes, but also the political functions the MBFR talks had for each of the superpowers, did not augur well for success. On the American side, the Nixon administration used the MBFR negotiations as a ploy to take the steam from mounting congressional pressures for substantial reductions in the approximately 300,000 American troops stationed in Germany. Henry Kissinger made it clear to the Soviets that their willingness to come to the MBFR negotiating table was a condition for U.S. participation in the Conference on Security and Cooperation in Europe that the Kremlin wanted to use to legitimize the territorial status quo on the Continent. For a long time the unspoken premise at the highest levels of both governments was that MBFR was a charade.

Yet if they could agree on a mutually acceptable formula, genuine conventional force reductions in central Europe might be of considerable geopolitical benefit to both superpowers. A more equal balance of conventional forces would enable NATO to reduce its dangerous and anachronistic reliance on the threat of nuclear escalation. (See the discussion below on the no-first-use policy and the discussion in Chapter 10 on means of achieving conventional-force equalization.) And if an overall lower level could be established for the European force balance, the Soviets would be less strained in having to allocate forces both to their western front against NATO and their eastern front against China.

Over the course of the protracted MBFR negotiations serious bargaining to explore the possibility of real reductions seems to have developed. Beginning in 1979, the Soviets have been willing to discuss asymmetrical reductions down to common numerical ceilings. More specifically, since the early 1980s the working assumption in the MBFR talks has been that the ceiling for numbers of military personnel deployed at the center of Europe should be limited to 700,000 for each alliance, with movement toward this ceiling initiated by reductions in Soviet and U.S. deployments, and with the Soviet reductions initially substantially larger.[10] The translation of this important agreement in principle into a detailed agreement for mutual reductions has been held up, however, by an East-West disagreement over how many troops the Warsaw Pact currently has deployed: the United States counts about 950,000 Pact troops, but the Soviets insist the number is no more than 805,000. Hope for further negotiating progress now seems to lie in compromises over what to count and how to count at different phases in the reduction process.

Problems with negotiated balance-stabilization. There is a compelling logic in efforts to reduce the likelihood of war by preventing both sides in an adversarial relationship from gaining sufficient advantage in military capability to contemplate victory. Balance-stabilization efforts start from the assumption that because neither side will voluntarily place itself in a militarily disadvantageous position, negotiations between adversaries that do not really want to push their conflicts into tests of military strength should produce agreement on mutually acceptable balances and on ways to stabilize them. But as shown especially by the recent experience of SALT, the Euro-strategic issues, and MBFR, it is one thing to state generally the criterion of a stable balance and quite another to agree on its precise characteristics.

The first problem is that of defining and calculating the elements of a military balance of power between any two adversaries with different geographic situations; varied industrial, economic, and technological capabilities; and sets of adversary and alliance relationships differently related to the two-way rivalry to which the military balance is supposed to apply. A country surrounded by land does not have strategic and tactical defense requirements like those of an island country. A country that must import oil and other strategic materials across thousands of miles of ocean has vulnerabilities and needs not at all symmetrical with those of a more strategically self-sufficient adversary. A country with an economic system capable of rapid mobilization of manpower and industrial output for military tasks gives up less security by accepting most arms-limitation agreements than a country with a peacetime economy that would require substantial restructuring to get ready for war. Finally, a country with more than one important military adversary finds it difficult to settle for military equality with an adversary that does not have to worry about others, just as a country with numerous smaller allies (to defend or rely on) has military requirements not really comparable with those of a country with few allies. Given the likelihood that between any pair of adversaries some of these essential differences are always present, arriving at the configuration of a mutually acceptable military balance of power is more of an art than a science.

The second problem is that of locking an agreed-on balance into a configuration that will not change so rapidly and/or clandestinely as to render the initial agreement meaningless almost before the ink is dry. The problem is not so much systematic cheating on an agreement as the inherent volatility of technologies that can change, literally overnight, the capabilities and vulnerabilities of weapons already deployed, to say nothing of weapons that may be deployed if and when an existing control agreement breaks down. Countries are not willing to shut down their research and development laboratories, yet it is in these laboratories, more than on the battlefields, that a given balance of power may be totally overturned. Accordingly, hedging against an adversary's technological "breakthroughs" has become imperative of national security; and research and development programs maintained for this purpose often involve more significant components of a military balance—such as the accuracy and other factors of effectiveness of weapons—than those "controlled" in the negotiated agreements.

Unilateral Measures To Make
Military Balances Less Dangerous

Some arms-control measures need not await negotiated agreements between adversaries. They can be instituted unilaterally without a loss in security to the side taking the initiative, sometimes even with a gain in military effectiveness.

Such unilateral arms control can serve various objectives: reduction of an adversary's temptations to attack or to escalate an ongoing military campaign; elimination of menacing forces or deployments that leave an adversary with no real choice other than attack or escalation; assurance of firm and continuing control by top political authorities over military operations.

Reducing the adversary's temptations. Unprotected military forces or those deployed in ways that make them seem vulnerable can tempt an adversary with the prospect of easy gain through attacking them. An arms-control orientation to military force planning includes recognizing such problems in a country's force posture and correcting them; this in some cases may require force modernization and augmentation. That arms control is not always antithetical to deterrence, or even to effective military performance, was recognized in the now-classic "primer" by Thomas Schelling and Morton Halperin, *Strategy and Arms Control*, first published in 1961:

> Whether the most promising areas of arms control involve
> reductions in certain kinds of military force, increases in
> certain kinds of military force, qualitative changes in
> weaponry, different modes of deployment, or arrangements
> superimposed on existing military systems, we prefer to treat
> as an open question.[11]

Concern that the conventional-force inferiority of NATO might tempt the Soviet-led Warsaw Pact to initiate military hostilities in some future crisis—say, over Berlin—has prompted some analysts and policymakers who consider themselves arms controllers to recommend a conventional force *buildup* by NATO.[12] The counterargument of strategists opposed to a conventional force buildup (see Chapter 10, pp. 248–250), is that augmenting conventional forces might reduce deterrence of a Soviet attack by conveying the impression that the West now had a tolerable alternative to nuclear escalation, and would therefore be completely inhibited from escalating a conflict to the nuclear level.

Measures to reduce enemy temptations to rapidly escalate a conventional war to nuclear levels also have been under discussion in NATO circles. They include pulling back nuclear land mines and battlefield nuclear weapons storage areas from the border between East and West Germany, and "hardening" the shelters for NATO attack aircraft and the new intermediate-range missiles.

Other measures to reduce temptations involve retiring weapons from deployment if they seem to be so vulnerable to destruction that they are "sitting ducks," leading an enemy to feel confident of an advantage in striking first. In 1961, for example, the United States decided to remove its medium-range Thor and Jupiter ballistic missiles from Italy and Turkey precisely because of their vulnerability to surprise attack. The American decision was a unilateral move that did not require reciprocation; and it was only a delay in implementing it that left the Juipters still in place in Turkey at the time of the Cuban missile crisis, allowing their removal to be part of the quid pro quo President Kennedy offered the Soviets for removing their missiles from Cuba.

In the late 1970s and in the 1980s, as both superpowers deployed highly accurate "counterforce" strategic weapons, the stationary land-based ICBMs on both sides became relatively easy targets—and therefore possible inducements to a first strike in an intense Soviet-American conflict. Accordingly, each superpower, on its own, initiated strategic force "modernizations" to retire the vulnerable ICBMs and rely more instead on strategic weapons to be fired from relatively invulnerable submarines or aircraft.

Animated by these concerns, some U.S. military analysts and members of Congress with excellent arms-control credentials have advocated the development of a mobile, single-warhead ICBM, the "Midgetman," as a substitute for the vulnerable MIRV-carrying ICBMs now prominent in the arsenal.[13]

Eliminating (or refraining from deploying) provocative military forces. From an arms-control perspective, certain kinds of military deployments that seem cost-effective to the military planner should be rejected unilaterally as too threatening to potential enemies. When viewed by an adversary, these deployments indicate (incorrectly) that the country plans to start a war or escalate an ongoing war. They are weapons that need not be in the inventory of military forces supposedly maintained only for deterrent or defense purposes.

Some forces are, of course, inherently ambiguous in their functions. Fighter aircraft can be used for air-defense, combat-support, deep-interdiction, and offensive-bombing missions. Army battle tanks can be used to defend a frontier or to launch a blitzkrieg raid across it. And in the age of intercontinental strategic warfare, weapons maintained to deter attack by assuring second-strike retaliation can also be used in a first strike against an adversary's home-based strategic weapons.

Some forces nonetheless carry a strong presumption of aggressive intent, especially if they are not essential for deterrent or purely defensive missions. The intermediate-range missiles the Soviets deployed to Cuba in 1962 were both offensive and unnecessary for defense or deterrence. So, too, are the IRBMs both sides are now deploying in Europe, the SS-20s and the Pershing IIs, with their high accuracy and short flight-times. Either side could dismantle or refrain from deploying these IRBMs, even if the other should go ahead with its deployments, without the other gaining any significant military advantage.

The multiple-megaton MIRVed ICBMs in the superpower arsenals, current and planned, are proper candidates for elimination as an element of unilateral arms control if mutual limitations cannot be negotiated. Monster ICBMs are tempting targets because of their vulnerability, and unnecessary because all their missions can be performed just as effectively by less vulnerable missiles and aircraft— except for the most provocative mission: a first strike to destroy the other side's ICBMs. Consequently, it is this first-strike capability that the adversaries attribute to one another as the motive for deploying huge multiple-warhead ICBMs. Even so—and this is when an arms-control orientation can lead to additional policy options—neither side needs to be able to threaten to destroy the other side's ICBMs in a retaliatory "counterforce" strike to maintain a credible deterrent against the adversary's attempting an attack. There are many important military targets other than ICBMs that could be destroyed in a retaliatory strike; threatening these should be sufficient for deterrence. Moreover, in the remote but plausible possibility that deterrence should not work, the first-striker, in the face of the enemy's having counterforce weapons left to retaliate with, would be sure to fire all his ICBMs in the first strike; but if the opponent had forsworn counterforce retaliation, the first-striker might have the incentive to withhold some destructive missiles. This could leave some chance to terminate the war short of total nuclear holocaust. (See Chapter 10, pp. 255–257.)

Assuring political control of military operations. Wars can start and get out of hand independent of decisions by a country's top decision makers, or even in violation of their policies, if military command and control arrangements are weak and not firmly subordinated to the highest national authority. This is an impetus for arms control that is most appropriate to deal with unilaterally, particularly as each country's procedures for assuring political control must be consistent with its political/constitutional system and therefore in some aspects unique.

Before the days of high-speed global communications, armies and navies had to operate under the most general of directives from their governments. Generals and admirals could make decisions with immense political implications: when to fight, where to engage in battle, when to terminate a war, and so on. But the technological revolution in communications has changed all this, making it feasible to exercise, continuously, detailed control from home headquarters. It is well that it has, for the contemporaneous revolution in weaponry has made it possible to execute enormous changes in the lethal and geographic dimensions of a conflict in a matter of minutes.

The incorporation of nuclear weapons into the arsenals of the superpowers has been the principal stimulus to command and control innovations that assure military responsiveness to political authority. One of the most important of the arms-control innovations has been the permissive action link (PAL); the weapons in a PAL system remain "unarmed"—that is, unable to deliver or detonate an explosive charge—until they receive a positive electronic signal that either arms them directly or allows them to be armed by human operatives. The PAL system permits the national command authority to retain a crucial inhibiting control over the pace of escalation of a conflict, without losing the capacity to flexibly decentralize control to local commanders when this is appropriate. Coupled with direct communications links from top authorities to battlefield commanders, the PAL system even allows a top political leadership that wants to exercise firm tactical direction of a military campaign to do so.

Working against the exercise of centralized, durable political control is the compression in the time that it now takes to inflict massive destruction. ICBMs take some thirty minutes from launch to impact. IRBMs of the kind deployed by both sides in the European theater take under ten minutes. Because it can prove impossible to contact and assemble the relevant political decision makers and expect them to make considered decisions in the narrow time frames between detection of an incoming attack and its impact, military planners have been pressuring their governments to predelegate authority to subordinate military commanders to make the appropriate military responses. Early alerting of forces in crises combined with devolution of authority to launch nuclear missiles and even, in certain circumstances, to launch on warning of attack are contemplated as necessary measures for the management of crises.

An arms-control orientation, on the other hand, generally regards early alerting of forces, especially strategic forces, and predelegation of launching authority as dangerous. Accordingly, arms controllers in recent years have been putting their minds to the command and control problem, directing their most urgent efforts toward ways of assuring the survival, under attack, of both retaliatory forces and the highest national command authorities. The more time a country can afford to take to respond militarily to an attack, the more opportunity there will be to retain political control of a war and to terminate it when necessary and appropriate.[14] (Chapter 10 offers some suggestions along these lines.)

CONFIDENCE-BUILDING MEASURES

Another form of arms control allows adversaries to communicate and exchange information in ways that reassure each other they are not about to begin a military attack or escalate an ongoing war to a higher level of conflict.

Such messages of reassurance have always been the province of diplomacy. Some of the recent and currently developing measures, however, are equally forms of arms control, for they require manipulations of military forces or communications describing the whereabouts and disposition of military forces.

The newer forms of confidence-building measures are the products of negotiations primarily in two arenas: the East-West follow-on negotiations after the Conference on Security and Cooperation in Europe that produced the Helsinki Final Act of 1975, and various bilateral Soviet-American forums dating from 1963. Confidence-building measures of this sort have also been instituted between Israel and Egypt to assure each other of adherence to their 1979 peace treaty.

In September 1986 a major confidence-building accord was reached in Stockholm by the thirty-five original signatories of the Helsinki Final Act of 1975 (thirty-two European countries in addition to the Soviet Union, the United States, and Canada). The Stockholm agreement obligates signatories to inform each other of any military exercises involving 13,000 troops or more or 300 battle tanks. If the activities involve more than 17,000 troops, or 5,000 troops in amphibious landing or parachute assaults, all signatories have the right to send observation teams to witness the maneuvers. Troop movements of 75,000 or more require two years advance notification, and those between 40,000 and 75,000 one year advance notification. Exercises engaged in exclusively by air forces or navies are not subject to the notification and observation requirements.

The most innovative provisions of the 1986 confidence-building accord (given the Soviet Union's traditional objections to on-site inspections) are those allowing signatories to carry out inspections on each other's territory if they suspect military activities are being conducted about which they should have been notified in advance. But the countries are hardly leaving themselves wide open to foreign inspection: Inspectors will be accompanied by representatives of the receiving state and can be kept from seeing "areas or sensitive points to which access is normally denied or restricted, military and other defense installations, as well as naval vessels, military vehicles and aircraft." The inspecting state can bring in its own observation equipment and cameras, but aerial inspections must be carried on from planes provided and flown by the host country. Moreover, no participating state is obliged to accept more than three inspections on its territory per calendar year or more than one each year from the same state.[15]

Clearly, countries planning to start a war can find ways—consistent with the letter of the new accord—to block on-site observation of their activities. The principal value of the confidence-building measures, however, is that they provide the means for countries to reassure each other against unwarranted suspicion that their military exercises are part of an on-coming attack; and they would seem to make it virtually impossible for any signatory to successfully pull off a major surprise invasion of another country, because the aggressor would first have to deny its cosignatories their rights of inspection.

The Soviet-American direct dialogue on confidence-building measures has been concerned primarily with avoiding accidents or miscalculations that might result in nuclear war. These discussions have produced a series of bilateral agreements:

- The 1963 agreement to establish a direct communications link (the "hot line");
- The 1971 Accidental Measures Agreement requiring each side to notify the other in advance of missile launches beyond its territory in the direction of the other's territory, as well as immediately to inform one another of any incident, such as the possible accidental or unauthorized detonation of a nuclear weapon, that could cause the outbreak of nuclear war;
- The 1971 agreement upgrading the hot line by providing for two satellite communications circuits;
- The 1972 Incidents at Sea Agreement enjoining the two sides to adhere strictly to international conventions for preventing collisions at sea and also to provide advance notice of actions on the high seas that might endanger their ships or aircraft;
- The 1985 agreement, also including Japan, to safety measures on air routes in the North Pacific.

In addition, Soviet-American technical working groups attached to various bilateral arms-limitation forums have been attempting to formulate new agreements on advance notification of missile launches, advance notification of major military exercises, exchanges of military data, and further hot line improvements.

Spurred by congressional resolutions and the endorsement of President Reagan and General Secretary Gorbachev at their 1985 summit meeting, negotiators also have worked on planning jointly staffed "nuclear risk reduction centers."[16] The concept of nuclear risk reduction centers remains controversial with military planners of a traditional orientation, for as envisioned by Senators Sam Nunn and John Warner, principal sponsors of the relevant congressional resolution, these centers, located in Washington and Moscow, would be in continuous direct communications with each other, and their staffs might include liaison officers from the opposite country. (Nunn and Warner also suggest that thought be given to the creation of a single center, staffed by military and civilian representatives of the two nations, at a neutral site.) The concept's sponsors see the potential functions of such nuclear risk reduction centers as including:

> First, to discuss and outline the procedures to be followed in the event of possible incidents involving the use of nuclear weapons. Among the contingencies that might be explored would be the unexpected explosion of a nuclear device, a terrorist threat to explode a nuclear weapon unless certain demands were met, the discovery that a nuclear weapon was missing, and similar possibilities. The discussion of these possibilities could provide a script which might be followed should the event actually occur. . . .
>
> Second, to maintain close contact during incidents precipitated by nuclear terrorists, thus facilitating cooperative actions to defuse the incident, and, specifically, to avoid the danger that the explosion of a nuclear device by a terrorist group might lead to a nuclear confrontation between the great powers.
>
> Third, to exchange information on a voluntary basis concerning events that might lead to nuclear proliferation or to the acquisition of nuclear weapons, or the materials and equipment necessary to build such weapons, by subnational groups. . . .
>
> Fourth, to exchange information about military activities which might be misunderstood by the other party during periods of mounting tensions. . . . [T]he existence of independent nuclear risk reduction centers might facilitate the exchange of information about military activities which might otherwise be misinterpreted and contribute to escalating suspicions and fears. . . .
>
> Fifth, to establish a dialogue about nuclear doctrines and activities. . . . Consideration also could be given to using this forum to maintain an agreed data base on the strategic forces of the two sides.[17]

Skeptics, particularly in the Pentagon, have doubted that such nuclear risk reduction centers, if they ever are established, would indeed be used by the highest levels of political and military authority in each country in time of extreme crisis. Secretary of Defense Caspar Weinberger, speaking for the military traditionalists, argued that "it is most likely that a center would be completely bypassed in national crisis decision making. If not, a center would create a cumbersome extra layer in the national and international decision processes, retarding action just when speed was most imperative." He also voiced worry that "the Soviets could transform it into a new source of sensitive intelligence data or attempt to exploit it for disinformation purposes."[18]

Traditionalist military objections notwithstanding, endorsement of the idea of centers to reduce nuclear risk in the joint Soviet-American statement at the end of the 1985 Reagan-Gorbachev summit gave impetus to further study by governmental and nongovernmental experts on how to facilitate their actual establishment in the near future.[19]

LIMITING THE DESTRUCTIVENESS OF WAR[20]

Throughout history, particular countries or groups of countries have sought to control the ways wars are fought by prohibiting the possession or use of certain kinds of weapons and by prohibiting certain classes of targets. This has commonly been prompted by moral revulsion against inflicting suffering indiscriminately on combatants and noncombatants alike. But just as often the rationale for the limitations, no less than for the arguments against the limitations, has been strategic in that the countries urging limitations would have their relative power enhanced or preserved if they were adopted.

Prohibiting "Cruel" and "Inhuman" Weapons

All weapons are, of course, "cruel" and "inhuman" insofar as they cause death, suffering, and destruction of highly valued possessions. But acts of war are perceived to be especially cruel and inhuman if they inflict more death, destruction, and suffering than is required to attain a defined political-military objective—in other words, if they are not dictated by military necessity. Often, however, it has been simply technological innovation in weaponry, giving one side an edge over the other, that has been characterized—by those on the inferior side—as morally impermissible.

Early Christian norms.   During medieval times the Church, rejecting the notion that all is fair in love and war, tended to oppose all military innovations as they came along, condemning their use in warfare among Christians, though not condemning their use against non-Christians. The Second Lateran Council in 1139, for example, condemned the crossbow (which could penetrate knightly armor) as "deadly and odious to God." Similar denunciations, often reflected in treaties between dynasties or states, were in turn directed at the first firearms, the bayonet, and devices on rifles and artillery that allowed rapid shooting instead of the previous shoot-reload-shoot techniques.

The Hague rules.   Before the two world wars of the twentieth century, the largest consensus among governments on the illegitimacy of particular weapons was forged at the Hague Peace Conferences of 1899 and 1907. The first Hague Conference was attended by twenty-six states, mostly European, the second by forty-four, representing nearly all the recognized national governments of the world.

The Hague conferences reaffirmed some traditional prohibitions and promulgated some new ones against "arms, projectiles, or material calculated to cause unnecessary suffering." The use of poisoned arms was prohibited, as was the use of dumdum bullets that flatten and expand on hitting the human body, causing large jagged wounds. Exploding bullets were not explicitly prohibited in the 1899 and 1907 conferences, though a wide consensus in subsequent interpretations by international lawyers was that the Hague rules implied their prohibition.

World Wars I and II, however, rendered the Hague distinctions between humane and inhumane weapons almost quaint as the belligerents developed and applied new technologies to warfare. Flamethrowers are an example: Early in World War I the French condemned the Germans as barbarian when they introduced the technique of projecting liquid fire against French troops. But by the end of the war the Allies were using flamethrowers against the Germans. Later, in their more improved napalm version, flamethrowers became an important element in U.S. battlefield tactics in the Second World War, Korea, and Vietnam. Once such weapons become commonplace, the initial psychological reactions against them tend to fade, and they are treated in military command manuals as if the suffering they produce were no less or more humane than suffering produced by the blast, fire, and direct body disintegration from more "conventional" weapons.

Prohibitions on biological and chemical weapons. The two principal legal instruments that prohibit resorting to biological and chemical weapons are the 1925 Geneva Protocol prohibiting both the wartime use of asphyxiating, poison, and other gases and bacteriological methods of warfare[21] and the 1972 Biological Weapons Convention prohibiting the development or possession of bacteriological and toxic weapons.[22] These standing conventions and current efforts to add to them are in part a reaction to fears of the novel and little-known effects on the human body of biological and chemical substances rather than to evidence that they cause more horrible suffering than other methods of warfare; they also result from assumptions that noncombatants could not be protected from their effects. However, the willingness of governments to forego their use (while still preserving the right of retaliation for first use by an enemy and, in the case of chemical weapons, of modernizing their arsenals) has been induced mainly by military judgments that they would be of little use on the battlefield and unpredictable in effect.

The special case of nuclear weapons. An important reason for the widespread revulsion against nuclear weapons is the lingering and delayed effects of radiation: As documented in numerous studies of the survivors of Hiroshima and Nagasaki, the suffering is never over, and it sometimes becomes an increasing torture during the remainder of a victim's life. The feeling against nuclear weapons, however, is equally a reaction to the wide circumference of the devastation—instant and lingering—carried in each warhead. Not only is it impossible to protect noncombatants, even those not in the immediate target area, from the effects of a strategic nuclear attack, but it has become generally recognized that massive strategic nuclear attacks of the kind contemplated in war plans of the superpowers threaten the survival of the whole human species. Still, the almost universal moral condemnation of nuclear war has not yet led to an agreement among the nuclear-armed powers to outlaw the first use of nuclear weapons.

(See the discussion on pp. 253–254 for an explanation of the unwillingness of some countries to be bound by a no-first-use pact.)

Protecting Civilian Lives and Property

Efforts to make attacks on noncombatants and their property an offense against basic civic and religious law are as old as the history of warfare itself. These efforts have been a reaction to strategies, that did not have to await the development of modern weapons, of besieging and bombing population centers, holding innocents hostage in order to break the will of the enemy to resist, and attacking civilian sources of military equipment, food, and other provisions to hobble enemy fighting capabilities.

The original Hague rules. The Hague Convention Respecting the Laws and Customs of War on Land, signed in 1907, and technically still the law today, includes the following provisions:

Article 25—The attack or bombardment, by whatever means, of towns, villages, dwellings, or buildings which are undefended is prohibited.

Article 26—The officer in command of an attacking force must, before commencing bombardment, except in cases of assault, do all in his power to warn the authorities.

Article 27—In sieges and bombardments all necessary steps must be taken to spare, as far as possible, buildings dedicated to religion, art, science, or charitable purposes, historic monuments, hospitals, and places where the sick and wounded are collected, *provided they are not being used at the time for military purposes* [emphasis added].[23]

What constitutes "military purposes" in the above proviso is left so vague that undefended places presumed to contain military factories and supplies, including fuel and even food and clothing for the military, can be attacked as military targets. Any civilian casualties or destruction to otherwise exempt buldings would, of course, be unintended collateral damage—an "unfortunate" side effect of the "necessary" military action.

Such loopholes were carefully crafted by the international lawyers who wrote the Hague conventions. In the Convention Concerning Bombardment by Naval Forces, the allowances for reasons of "military necessity" are unabashedly explicit. After Article 1 of the convention forbids bombardment of undefended ports, towns, and so on by naval forces, Article 2 provides that

> Military works, military or naval establishments, depots of arms or war *materiel*, workshops or plants which could be utilized for the needs of the hostile fleet or army, and the ships of war in the harbor, are not, however, included in this prohibition. The commander of a naval force may destroy them with artillery, after a summons followed by a reasonable time of waiting, if all other means are impossible, and when the local authorities have not themselves destroyed them within the time fixed.
>
> He incurs no responsibility for any unavoidable damage which may be caused by a bombardment under such circumstances.[24]

Post–World War I rules on aerial bombardment.   After World War I introduced bombing from airplanes to the world, the Hague rules prohibiting (permitting) naval bombardment were extended to cover this new form of warfare. The Hague Rules of Aerial Warfare, adopted in 1932, stipulate that aerial bombardment is "legitimate only when directed at a military objective, that is to say, an object of which the injury or destruction would constitute a distinct military advantage to the belligerent."[25] The Rules characterize these "legitimate" bombing targets as "military forces; military works, military establishments or depots, factories constituting important and well-known centers engaged in the manufacture of arms, ammunition or distinctively military supplies; lines of communications or transportation used for military purposes."[26]

The 1932 rules do prohibit aerial bombardment of civilian populations and structures "not in the immediate neighborhood of the operations of land forces";[27] but the rules explicitly allow for aerial attacks on some civilian centers:

> In the immediate neighborhood of the operations of land forces, the bombardment of cities, towns, villages, dwellings, or buildings is legitimate provided there exists some reasonable

presumption that the military concentration is sufficiently important to justify such bombardment having regard to the danger thus caused to the civilian population.[28]

Once again, a purported restriction becomes, through the overriding doctrine of "military necessity," a virtual license to kill and destroy everything "in the immediate neighborhood," provided the nonmilitary destruction is not "deliberate."

World War II and the erosion of constraints.   World War II totally washed away even the rules confining aerial bombardment of civilian targets to those within the immediate zone of land combat. Lawyers on both sides found legal justification in the Hague rules, as elaborated after the First World War, for attacking anything that was contributing to the war effort—including, of course, most factories; and the explicit allowance of attacks on "lines of communications and transportation used for military purposes" could justify bombing practically every modern city.

By the middle of World War II even the Hague's limiting criterion of "military necessity" was dropped as the belligerents engaged in terror bombing of each other's cities. The purpose, explained in various government directives, was to spread destruction over a large area to "destroy morale," and "to secure the heaviest possible moral and shock effect," thereby assuring that the enemy's "capacity for armed resistance is fatally weakened."[29]

The nuclear age: Obliteration of distinctions between combatants and noncombatants.   As the first nuclear bombs were readied to be dropped on the industrial cities of Hiroshima and Nagasaki in August 1945, most of the responsible decision makers had no qualms about killing tens of thousands of civilians in an aerial attack on an enemy city. The aftershock came with the realization of the massive destruction even single bombs could unleash. In a few years, after a brief and abortive—and probably not really sincere—attempt by statesmen to work out an international control and disarmament regime for nuclear weapons (the Baruch Plan and Soviet counterproposals), the United States began to incorporate the notion of a massive nuclear incineration of its new enemy into its deterrence and defense policies. And in 1954 the American secretary of state, John Foster Dulles, publicly declared that in order to deter the Soviet

Union from even local aggressions, the United States was maintaining a capacity to retaliate instantly and massively at times and places of its own choosing—meaning especially Soviet cities. By the late 1950s, the Soviets having followed suit, the two superpowers had come to understand, and largely accept, that each was holding the other's population hostage as assurance against being directly attacked—this was aptly called the "balance of terror."

Early in the Kennedy administration, Secretary of Defense Robert McNamara and some military strategists gave serious consideration to adopting a city-avoidance targeting strategy for nuclear war, along with associated "damage-limiting" measures to protect the American population, such as civil defense shelters and a nationwide antiballistic missile system. But McNamara's own studies led him to abandon the scheme as both strategically unrealistic and enormously expensive, especially in light of indications that the Soviets had no intention of fighting a limited strategic war if they ever came to blows with the United States and, moreover, that the Soviets could field offensive counters to the damage-limiting measures more cheaply than the United States could install them. McNamara also came to the conclusion that the increasingly expensive arms race could be arrested by mutual agreement if the mission of the strategic forces on each side could be limited to holding the adversary's cities hostage against a nuclear first strike—that is, by maintaining a survivable capacity to assure that the cities would be destroyed in a retaliatory blow. Thus by the end of the 1960s the world was presented with the supreme irony of its most dedicated arms controllers supporting the most destructive nuclear strategies—for purposes of deterrence and arms control. The arms controllers were partly vindicated during the 1970s as the morally questionable mutual assured destruction (MAD) relationship between the superpowers proved itself conducive to negotiation of mutual limits on strategic arms.

The reassertion of moral imperatives by the American Catholic bishops. The prospect of a nuclear holocaust, and the reliance on the mutual assured destruction relationship to prevent it, cut deeply across the grain of traditional Catholic strictures against killing noncombatants. A committee of American Catholic bishops took up the challenge in the early 1980s with a stringent program of self-education in strategic realities and doctrine. The result was the pastoral letter *The Challenge of Peace: God's Promise and Our Response*, approved by the National Conference of Catholic Bishops in 1983.[30]

The bishops' pastoral letter reaffirms the principle that "lives of innocent persons may never be taken directly, regardless of the purpose alleged for doing so. . . . Just response to aggression must be discriminate; it must be directed against aggressors, not against innocent people caught up in a war not of their own making" (Section 104).

The bishops, convinced by studies showing that once nuclear weapons have been introduced into a conflict the prospects for escalation to a war of total societal destruction are very high, concluded:

> We do not perceive any situation in which the deliberate initiation of nuclear warfare, on however restricted a scale, can be morally justified. Non-nuclear attacks by another state must be resisted by other than nuclear means. Therefore, a serious moral obligation exists to develop non-nuclear defensive strategies as rapidly as possible (Section 149).

And in perhaps their most controversial conclusion, they find even nuclear retaliation for a nuclear attack to be morally impermissible if it would kill many innocent people (Section 148).

The implications of these moral positions for a practical strategy of war prevention and control are explored in the following chapter. Here they simply offer evidence of a possibly popular and politically significant reassertion of the importance of moral limitations on warfare.

THE NUCLEAR NONPROLIFERATION REGIME

The Nuclear Non-Proliferation Treaty (NPT) of 1968 assumes an international consensus on the following propositions: (1) nuclear war is worse and (2) less controllable than conventional war, and (3) the fewer countries or nongovernmental groups capable of launching nuclear attacks, the better the world's chances of avoiding general nuclear war. If the treaty were strictly adhered to by all countries, it would freeze the number of countries with nuclear weapons at the current five: the United States, the Soviet Union, the United Kingdom, France, and China. But France and China have not signed the treaty, nor have some thirty-eight countries still without nuclear weapons.

The Nuclear Non-Proliferation Treaty is designed to be a bargain between the nuclear-weapon "haves" and "have-nots": that the latter will forego acquiring nuclear weapons in return for receiving substantial assistance from the nuclear-capable countries in developing their own peaceful nuclear programs.

- Article I of the NPT is a pledge by the signatory countries with nuclear weapons "not to transfer to any recipient whatsoever nuclear weapons or other nuclear explosive devices or control over such weapons or devices directly, or indirectly; and not in any way to assist, encourage, or induce any nonnuclear weapon state to manufacture or otherwise acquire nuclear explosive devices, or control over such weapons or devices."
- Article II pledges the signatory countries without nuclear weapons "not to receive . . . nuclear weapons or other nuclear explosive devices or . . . control over such weapons or devices directly, or indirectly; not to manufacture or otherwise acquire nuclear weapons or other nuclear explosive devices; and not to seek or receive any assistance in the manufacture of nuclear weapons or other nuclear explosive devices."
- Article III is a set of restrictions on the transfer, receipt, and use of peaceful nuclear materials, technologies, and facilities—safeguards provisions—necessary in fulfilling the bargain to help nonnuclear countries develop peaceful nuclear industries. The article obligates each nonweapon country signing the treaty to negotiate a specially tailored safeguards agreement with the International Atomic Energy Agency (IAEA) to assure, primarily through inspection by the IAEA, that there will be no diversion of nuclear energy or materials from peaceful uses to nuclear weapons or other nuclear explosive devices. The nuclear supplier countries also are obligated by Article III to subject their transferred nuclear material and equipment to IAEA safeguards.
- Articles IV and V round out the bargain by obligating the signatories to "the fullest possible exchange of equipment, materials and scientific and technological information for the

peaceful uses of nuclear energy . . . with due consideration for the needs of the developing areas of the world."
- Article VI reiterates the standing obligation of the nuclear powers to pursue negotiations leading toward the cessation of the nuclear arms race, toward nuclear disarmament, and toward eventual general and complete disarmament. This article was inserted primarily as a concession to the nuclear have-nots, who complained that the NPT consigns them to permanent second-class status and violates the norm of sovereign equality of nations unless the nuclear-armed nations eventually disband their own nuclear arsenals.[31]

One of the basic problems in fulfilling the double promise of the NPT—to prevent the spread of nuclear weapons while providing the abstaining countries with the fruits of nuclear technology—has been that the central mechanism for accomplishing these purposes, the IAEA safeguards system, would have to be made more supranational than the countries adhering to it find compatible with their national sovereignty. Indeed, even countries with "legitimate" nuclear weapons programs are not favorably disposed to granting the IAEA the degree of authority to penetrate national industries and research facilities required to verify that purportedly peaceful nuclear projects are not fronts for clandestine weapons programs. Important holdouts from the treaty, like India, Israel, Iraq, and South Africa, are unwilling to accept even the current superficial level of IAEA inspection, let alone what a foolproof system would demand. And many of the signatory countries are unhappy with the restrictive nuclear transfer policies adopted by some of the supplier countries as a hedge against ineffective IAEA controls. From the perspective of many nuclear have-not countries, the nuclear countries are failing to provide their part of the quid pro quo.

Another basic problem with the NPT, assuming that the provisions of Article VI on general nuclear disarmament remain unfulfilled, is that it reinforces rather than resolves the core security predicament of any country not in the nuclear-weapons "club" that finds itself in an intense, possibly war-provoking conflict with a country possessing nuclear weapons. The only recourse for the nonnuclear country is to ask another member of the nuclear club to protect it from humiliation at the hands of its adversary. Indeed, in anticipation of such predicaments, the United States, the Soviet Union, and the United Kingdom in 1968 submitted to the United Nations a tripartite resolution on "security assurances" requiring the UN Security Council to take note of the concerns of states party to the NPT and to recognize that nuclear aggression or its threat against such states would require "immediate action by the Security Council." Although the Security Council itself took no formal action on the proposed resolution, each of the three sponsoring nuclear powers issued a unilateral declaration pledging to seek Security Council action on behalf of any nonnuclear country victimized by a nuclear threat.

But security assurances for the nuclear have-nots in the form of pledges to seek Security Council action are all too obviously nuclear umbrellas with large holes, not the least of which is the fact that each of the current members of the nuclear-weapons club wields a veto in the Security Council, and thus if one of them were the nuclear aggressor it could block any Security Council action on behalf of the victimized country. Moreover, in the MAD world of nuclear deterrence between the superpowers, even such security assurances made unilaterally outside of the UN framework lack credibility—especially if they are offered to assure a nonaligned country that it does not need nuclear weapons of its own to feel protected.

Reflecting these concerns, a majority of the nonnuclear signatories to the NPT have, in effect, taken over the periodic treaty review conferences, demanding, above all, that the nuclear-armed members of the NPT regime adhere to their Article VI obligations to pursue negotiations leading to their own nuclear disarmament. The message from the majority is becoming loud and clear: their patience is wearing thin and they are not willing to put up with second-class status, including subjecting themselves to international inspection to ensure that they are not producing weapons, much longer. Meanwhile numerous nonsignatory countries pursue nuclear programs with a weapons potential—sometimes winked at, sometimes encouraged by nuclear-armed countries who are their allies—and the superpowers continue to vertically proliferate their own nuclear armaments even into outer space.

NOTES

1. President John F. Kennedy, Address to the American People on the Nuclear Test Ban Treaty, July 26, 1963, *Public Papers of the Presidents of the United States; John F. Kennedy, 1963*, pp. 459–464.

2. U.S. Arms Control and Disarmament Agency, *Arms Control and*

Disarmament Agreements: Texts and History of Negotiations (Washington, D.C.: ACDA, 1979), pp. 131–152.

3. U.S. Department of State, *SALT II Agreement: Vienna, June 18, 1979.* (Selected Documents, No. 12a).

4. Strobe Talbott, *Deadly Gambits: The Reagan Administration and the Stalemate in Nuclear Arms Control* (New York: Knopf, 1984), pp. 224–226.

5. Citation of President Reagan's statements on the SDI during the fall of 1985 from *Weekly Compilation of Presidential Documents.*

6. Michael Gordon, "U.S. Ideas on Arms Offered in Iceland Are Being Refined," *New York Times,* July 3, 1986.

7. Communiqué Issued at the Special Meeting of the NATO Foreign and Defense Ministers in Brussels, December 12, 1979.

8. Talbott, *Deadly Gambits*, p. 85.

9. Secretary of Defense Weinberger's opposition to the Nitze-Kvitsinsky compromise reflected the position of his assistant secretary, Richard Perle. On this see Talbott, pp. 135–144.

10. John G. Keliher, *The Negotiations on Mutual and Balanced Force Reductions: The Search for Arms Control in Central Europe* (New York: Pergamon Press, 1981).

11. Thomas C. Schelling and Morton H. Halperin, *Strategy and Arms Control* (New York: Twentieth Century Fund, 1961).

12. McGeorge Bundy, George F. Kennan, Robert S. McNamara, and Gerard Smith, "Nuclear Weapons and the Atlantic Alliance," *Foreign Affairs* (Spring 1982), 60(4):753–768, recommend a NATO conventional-force buildup as a necessary correlate to NATO's eliminating its reliance on the first use of nuclear weapons.

13. Alton Frye, "Strategic Builddown," *Foreign Affairs,* Winter 1983/84. Within the arms-control community, the advisability of the single-warhead "Midgetman" is the subject of an intense debate, with advocates emphasizing its virtue of reducing first-strike temptations and opponents contending that its mobility would make it difficult to count and therefore would undermine arms-limitation agreements.

14. Much of the work on the command and control problems is done within the Department of Defense or by its technical contractors at a high level of secrecy. The best recent authoritative reflection of this work in the open literature is Bruce G. Blair, *Strategic Command and Control: Redefining the Nuclear Threat* (Washington, D.C.: Brookings Institution, 1985). A journalistic account, but seemingly well informed, is Daniel Ford, *The Button: The Pentagon's Strategic Command and Control System* (New York: Simon and Schuster, 1985). An excellent study published earlier is Paul Bracken, *The Command and Control of Nuclear Forces* (New Haven, Ct.: Yale University Press, 1983). See also Bracken's more recent essay, "Acci-

dental Nuclear War," in Graham T. Allison, Albert Carnesale, and Joseph S. Nye, Jr., *Hawks, Doves, and Owls: An Agenda for Avoiding Nuclear War* (New York: Norton, 1985), pp. 25–53.

15. "Key Sections of Document at Stockholm Meeting on Security," *New York Times*, September 22, 1986.

16. On the function and value, and possible design, of Soviet-American confidence-building measures to reduce the risks of nuclear war, see William Langer Ury and Richard Smoke, *Beyond the Hotline: Controlling a Nuclear Crisis* (Cambridge, Mass.: Harvard University Law School, 1984). The Ury-Smoke report was the result of a study undertaken by the Harvard Nuclear Negotiation Project sponsored by the United States Arms Control and Disarmament Agency.

17. "A Nuclear Risk Reduction System" (Report of the Nunn/Warner Group on Nuclear Risk Reduction), *Congressional Record*, Vol. 130, No. 8 (February 1, 1984).

18. Secretary of Defense Caspar W. Weinberger, *Robert to the Congress on Direct Communications Links and Other Measures to Enhance Stability* (Washington, D.C.: U.S. Department of Defense, 11 April 1983).

19. Text of Joint U.S.-Soviet Statement: "Greater Understanding Achieved," *New York Times*, November 22, 1985.

20. My discussion in this section relies heavily on Myres S. McDougal and Florentino P. Feliciano, *Law and Minimum World Public Order: The Legal Regulation of International Coercion* (New Haven, Conn.: Yale University Press, 1961), pp. 520–731.

21. Protocol for the Prohibition of the Use in War of Asphyxiating, Poisonous, or Other Gases and of Bacteriological Methods of Warfare, *League of Nations Treaty Series*, Vol. 49 (Geneva: League of Nations, 1929).

22. Convention on the Prohibition of the Development, Production, and Stockpiling of Bacteriological (Biological) and Toxin Weapons and on Their Destruction. Text in U.S. Department of State, *Treaties and Other International Acts, Series 8062* (Washington, D.C.: U.S. Government Printing Office, 1975).

23. Convention (IV) Respecting the Laws and Customs of War on Land, signed at The Hague on 18 October 1907, in Josef Goldblat, *Agreements for Arms Control: A Critical Survey* (London: Taylor & Francis, 1982), pp. 122–124.

24. Convention (IX) Concerning Bombardment by Naval Forces in Time of War. Signed at The Hague on 18 October 1907. Text in Goldblat, *ibid.*, pp. 127–129.

25. Article 24(1), *Hague Rules of Aerial Warfare* (1932), quoted by McDougal and Feliciano, p. 643.

26. Article 24(2), *ibid.*, p. 644.

27. Article 24(3), *ibid.*, p. 645

28. Article 24(4), *ibid.*, pp. 645–646.

29. *U.S. Strategic Bombing Survey, Overall Report*, Vol. 2 (Washington, D.C.: U.S. Government Printing Office, 1945), p. 71; and the Bombing Survey's report on *The Effects of Strategic Bombing on the Japanese War Economy* (Washington, D.C.: U.S. Government Printing Office, 1946), pp. 37–38.

30. For both the text of the 1983 pastoral letter and a detailed account of debates over earlier drafts, see Jim Castelli, *The Bishops and the Bomb: Waging Peace in the Nuclear Age* (Garden City, N.Y.: Doubleday-Image Books, 1983).

31. *Treaty on the Non-Proliferation of Nuclear Weapons* (opened for signature 1 July 1968), in U.S. Arms Control and Disarmament Agency, *Arms Control and Disarmament Agreements* (Washington, D.C.: U.S. Government Printing Office, 1984), pp. 91–95.

PART IV

Conclusions

CHAPTER 10 Toward an Integrated Strategy of War Prevention and Control

No professional speciality or academic discipline can claim peace as its unique concern. The diverse causes of modern wars and their pervasive effects involve all elements of society: in this sense, there can be no "innocents." Strategies for the prevention, control, and termination of war are too important and complex to be left to the generals and national security officials.

The growing recognition that peace—and in particular the prevention of nuclear holocaust—is everyone's business has stimulated a proliferation of arms-control proposals and peace plans from a wide range of public interest groups, "think tanks," scholars, and theologians who, rightly, have assumed part of the responsibility for helping the human species to avoid its own extinction.

But this broadened participation in the search for ways to achieve peace has produced new problems. So many diverse and frequently contradictory peace and arms-control strategies are now being submitted for public consideration that the circuitry for policy-making is in danger of being overloaded. On the one hand, this situation has produced intense rivalry for media attention and access to the levers of political power among elements of the peace movement: the various factions sometimes seem more determined to discredit each other's proposals than to forge a coherent consensus. On the other, it has favored a return to elitism, where an insulated and unaccountable coterie of self-styled strategic specialists make godlike decisions in secret.

Chapter 10 is an effort to transcend the excessive pluralism and factionalism in the peace-policy arena. From the analysis in the previous chapters and from contemporary policy initiatives, it distills the basic elements for an integrated strategy of war prevention and control. This strategy incorporates the soundest proposals available in the realms of morality, the basic structure of international relationships, diplomatic practice, arms control, and military strategy.

The objective is not necessarily consensus—certainly not a consensus that obscures unresolved issues of importance or profound dilemmas. The objective is rather a synthesis of alternative strategies under a set of urgent imperatives (the highest being the avoidance of nuclear holocaust) and desiderata that will provide a basis for setting priorities and managing contradictions, while prudently leaving some of the important choices to be made as events unfold.

The political psychiatrist . . .
approaches the problem of war and revolution
as one detail of the whole task
of mastering the sources and mitigating the consequences
of human insecurity in an unstable world.
—Harold Lasswell

War is often thought of in terms of military conflict,
or even annihilation. But there is a growing awareness
that an equal danger might be chaos—
as a result of mass hunger, economic disaster,
environmental catastrophes, and terrorism.
So we should not think only of reducing
the traditional threats to peace.
But also of the need for change from chaos to order.
—Willy Brandt

Control over weapons of mass destruction
will not by itself create or maintain peace.
But it may well be the best place
to take hold of any attempt to build a durable peace.
And it can eliminate at least that aspect of the danger
that stems from . . . fear of surprise attack.
It serves as a sort of ground-clearing operation
for the numberless things that must follow
if the peace is to be real.
—Norman Cousins

CHAPTER 10

Toward an Integrated Strategy of War Prevention and Control

Just as there are many causes of the persistence and pervasiveness of war, so there are many imperatives in a basic strategy of peace. Single-cause and single-prescription approaches not only are wrong in an analytical sense; they can be counterproductive when it comes to reducing the role of violence in human society and preventing nuclear holocaust, for they tend to turn the advocates of particular approaches (say, moral pressure on governments to renounce the use of force) into opponents of other important measures (such as efforts to establish "firebreaks" between conventional war and nuclear war).

Some contradictions between the various approaches to war prevention and control are, of course, unavoidable at times, and leaders and publics may need to choose among them.

The best strategy is one that results in the least overall sacrifice in social value. Thus the best strategy for world peace would tend to the security and survival needs of existing communities without thereby reducing the survival chances of the human species; maintain peace and order without abandoning economic well-being, social justice, and cultural values; and further the welfare of the majority, without suppressing the rights of minorities.

More specifically, the central tasks of a strategy of war prevention and control must be to find ways of reducing the likelihood of war, without thereby reducing the capacity of adversaries to limit the damage from wars that do occur and to terminate them; and to devise measures for limiting the destructiveness of wars without seeming to reduce the risks involved in military conflict in ways that undermine inhibitions on likely aggressors.

An integrated strategy for peace will need to operate in at least five interlinked spheres: morality, social structure, diplomacy, military capability, and military strategy. Because changes in any sphere can affect what happens in any or all of the others, the integrated strategy must assess and reconcile the impacts of policy across spheres—though progress in some spheres need not wait on progress in others.

The moral sphere includes the convictions of leaders and publics about when it is right or wrong to use military force and about what the permissible and impermissible methods of warfare are.

The realm of social structure comprises the basic organization of society and underlying social, economic, and political conditions that affect the substance and intensity of conflicts, who is on whose side on various issues, and the institutions each side relies on to wage and resolve conflicts.

The sphere of diplomacy includes the offers countries make to one another, their demands on one another, and their styles of negotiation and confrontation.

Military capability refers to national arsenals, military personnel, and other tangible elements of military power, and their manifestation in global, regional, and bilateral military balances.

Military strategy, finally, directs and controls the way force is used or is planned to be used.

MORALITY

Prevailing beliefs about what is right and wrong and about the relationships between ends and means crucially affect both the willingness of societies to resort to war and their conduct of military operations. The substance of such moral beliefs (including the *realpolitik* notion that morality has virtually no role in the relations among nation-states) and the extent to which they are adhered to by public officials does much to determine the incidence and destructiveness of wars.

An effective statecraft of peace must therefore attend to the prevailing moral climate. And institutions and individuals concerned with the moral dimensions of war must attempt to sensitize officials and the wider public to the moral implications of alternative policies for national and international security.

Awareness of the enormous moral implications of events in the military sphere, especially the realization that "all of God's creation" has been put at risk by the weapons in the arsenals of the superpowers, prompted the American Catholic bishops in the early 1980s to break with their traditional reluctance to intervene in national debates over military policy by publishing a pastoral letter challenging current U.S. nuclear strategies.[1]

Recognizing the importance of moral considerations and moral pressures for a strategy of war prevention and control is only the first step. Once we take that step we enter a sea of ethical, philosophical, and theological controversy on the permissibility and impermissibility of various kinds of coercion and violence—a realm of its own with contending schools of thought and traditions—from which it might seem impossible to emerge with clear guidance for statesmen.

To be sure, moral discourse can reinforce disagreement, particularly when it comes to prescribing behavior. Yet the planet-destroying potential of military arsenals now in existence justifies the attempt to forge as broad a consensus as we can on the moral imperatives needed to constrain the violent actions of governments and political groups.[2]

Accordingly, the following premises are offered as candidates for inclusion in the moral consensus on permissible and impermissible acts of war:

1. *Acts that could destroy the biospheric conditions required for the survival of the human species are impermissible.* Major scientific studies have been undertaken in many countries and by international agencies—by physicists, meteorologists, astronomers, chemists, and biologists—to determine whether it is true, as popularly believed, that a major nuclear war could bring about the extinction of the human species.[3] Not surprisingly there is considerable disagreement among the scientists, for the contemplated events can only be artificially simulated with highly complex models of such phenomena as climatic patterns that are themselves dimly understood. Astronomer Carl Sagan and other supporters of the "nuclear winter" thesis contend that a nuclear war involving detonations of considerably less than half the strategic nuclear warheads currently in the arsenals of the United States and the Soviet Union would probably expose most, if not all, of the immediate survivors outside of the target areas to lethal radioactivity, pyrotoxins, cancer-producing ultraviolet light, and then to a cold dark winter lasting perhaps a year or more. As Sagan puts

it, "There is a real danger of the extinction of humanity. A threshold exists at which the climatic catastrophe could be triggered. . . . A major first strike may be an act of national suicide, even if no retaliation occurs."[4] The nuclear winter thesis has been challenged, however, in studies conducted by scientists at the National Center for Atmospheric Research (NCAR) in Boulder, Colorado. Claiming to have used more geographically realistic models than Sagan and his associates, the principal investigators at NCAR conclude that

> despite the continued potential for serious nuclear winter effects, there does not seem to be a real potential for human extinction. . . . The idea of automatic suicide is now unsupportable given that a scenario of weeks of continuous subfreezing temperatures on a continental scale is no longer plausible.[5]

Given this debate among reputable scientists over the ranges of plausible biospheric disruption from nuclear war and over the probabilities of different scenarios, what are the public policy implications of the stated moral imperative? One approach would defer any fundamental restriction on existing nuclear strategies, assuming they make sense on other grounds for deterrence and defense, as long as in the categories of nuclear force contemplated the threat to the human species has not been convincingly demonstrated. Another approach, which I advocate, would be to draw the threshold between permissible and impermissible military action at the level where reputable scientists, even if disputed by other reputable scientists, claim there is a nonnegligible risk of biospheric disruption threatening to the survival of humankind. (I favor this approach because the consequences of basing policy on what later may prove to have been overly alarmist assessments are surmountable, whereas the consequences of going ahead with nuclear attacks on the basis of overly optimistic assumptions may not be.) Any crossing of this threshold must be unequivocally condemned—and taken out of any country's wars plans—no matter what its presumed purpose, no matter who would be taking such action, whether as a "first strike" or in retaliation.[6]

I would go even farther and insist that if a country's national security policies or alliance commitments depend on threats to launch nuclear attacks of impermissible magnitude, even if only for purposes of deterrence, then such deterrent policies also should be changed. To be sure, there are circumstances among individuals and among nations when a morally questionable threat can be justified on the "consequentialist" grounds that the evil it deters would be worse than the consequences to oneself and to society of having to implement the threat; there are also circumstances when the high probability of the otherwise immoral threat working as a deterrent might justify bluffing—that is, making seemingly unequivocal promises to engage in actions that in the event of a failure of deterrence (in the "moment of truth") could still be reconsidered. But such consequentialist considerations are an inadequate guide to policy when the planned action could extinguish all human life, in which case all other consequences would be meaningless. The insistence on expunging from national security policy even threats to take action that could destroy the human species is based not only on the moral impermissibility of the destruction but also on the pragmatic consideration that its obvious monstrous immorality reduces the credibility of the threat, and that therefore reliance on such threats could tempt the very provocations they are supposed to deter.[7]

2. *Deliberate killing or maiming of unarmed innocent civilians is impermissible.* It is a part of the craziness induced by the advent of nuclear weapons that this proposition is particularly controversial among influential peace and disarmament groups, some of whom have embraced the mutual assured destruction concept as a basis for strategic arms control.

Once again, the American Catholic bishops in their pastoral letter of 1983 found it necessary to oppose what had been the prevailing strategic and arms-control orthodoxies, arguing that

> under no circumstances may nuclear weapons or other
> instruments of mass slaughter be used for the purpose of
> destroying population centers or other predominantly civilian
> targets. . . .

> Retaliatory action whether nuclear or conventional which
> would indiscriminately take many wholly innocent lives, lives
> of people who are in no way responsible for reckless actions of
> their government, must also be condemned. This
> condemnation, in our judgment, applies even to the retaliatory
> use of weapons striking enemy cities after our own have

already been struck. No Christian can rightfully carry out orders or policies deliberately aimed at killing non-combatants.[8]

I know that arms controllers and peace activists who oppose applying such moral criticism to mutual assured destruction do so with great anguish. Their justification is the belief that the assured destruction—only (meaning deterrence-only) strategy provides the only barrier to a no-holds-barred race to develop "war-fighting" strategic forces, and serves to arrest the growing fascination with nuclear war-fighting scenarios. That is, they defend MAD to inhibit developments that increase the likelihood of the otherwise "unthinkable" initiation of nuclear war becoming a real option for decision makers. The arms controllers and peace activists obviously are not arguing that mass destruction of civilians is moral. Their position rather is that any nuclear war is immoral because it will inevitably involve the wholesale destruction of civilian populations; therefore anything that undermines deterrence of nuclear war is immoral.[9]

Concern about making any nuclear war seem tolerable is warranted. Some strategists who have criticized the mutual assured destruction philosophy of deterrence indeed are advocates of usable nuclear options, and some are proponents of nuclear war-*winning* strategies and arsenals. And surely there is no ground for confidence that once the nuclear threshold is crossed, no matter how selective and limited the first use of nuclear weapons might be, the dimensions of the war can in fact be controlled.[10] It is a valid worry that seemingly tolerable military actions are likely, willy-nilly, to bring on the intolerable: not just mass killing of civilians but the destruction of human civilization. If at all possible, therefore, such seemingly tolerable first steps also ought to be prevented.

But the compelling moral reason for opposing even a first and limited use of nuclear weapons should not be lost sight of—namely, the unjustifiable evil of the result of escalation: massive destruction of populations, nuclear holocaust.

It is vital that we keep reminding ourselves of what we most want to avoid, for there are degrees of the horrible. All wars are bad, but some are worse than others. If the nuclear threshold is once crossed in a war and there is an exchange of nuclear blows, even strategic nuclear blows, will we not want to do all we can immediately to terminate the war as long any chance, however small, remains that it can be stopped short of the slaughter of tens of millions of people?

What was considered unthinkable will already have happened, but perhaps not yet the worst. If indeed there still has been little or no destruction of population centers, it would at that time be the height of moral criminality for those in control of the unused nuclear weapons to authorize their use against cities.

Will sensitizing ourselves to these awful possibilities, and to the moral distinctions it would be crucial to make if they ever materialize, increase the likelihood of their occurring? It is a central message of this concluding chapter that our increased moral awareness could have this consequence, but that there is no necessary reason why it will if we pursue the kind of integrated strategy presented here for preventing and controlling and terminating wars.

The moral basis for such an integrated strategy includes at least one more basic premise:

3. *The number of people killed or tortured as a result of individual or group action (or inaction) generally detemines the degree of moral evil of the action.* The easy availability of instruments for inflicting massive violence makes it both ethically and pragmatically imperative to include this proposition in the consensus constraining statesmen, despite the fact that it may be disputed by some moral philosophers. Without prejudging what should be done in particular cases, this moral principle provides a basis for mobilizing political pressures on governments to refrain from engaging in war in the first place, and at the least to limit the destructiveness of wars that are not prevented. It moves less in the direction of absolute pacifism and more in the direction of encouraging active nonviolent resistance to evil, including the evil of violence itself.

It is not an endorsement of absolute pacifism, since it allows for killing in self-defense when the only way to avoid being (or having one's people) killed or tortured is to kill. To say that self-defensive killing is "allowed," however, does not mean that it is devoid of evil, but only that it may in certain circumstances be a necessary evil, less evil than the acts it prevents.[11] Nor does an ethic looking to the minimization of violence constitute an endorsement of the "Better Red than Dead" position (or "Better Blue than Dead" if viewed from Moscow) or an argument on behalf of "surrendering" to those less conscientious about using violence. The basic principle is simply that it is morally superior to fight nonviolently against injustice, and even against those who have resorted to violence; it may become necessary to choose violent resistance when other means of resistance have not worked and the loss of ethical value in allowing the aggressor to get his way is deemed to be greater than the loss of value incurred by violent resistance—but the acts of violence reluctantly chosen must be constrained by the understanding that each act of killing compounds the evil.

All is not fair in war. It is necessary to assert an imperative to keep wartime violence as limited as possible and to terminate it as soon as possible.

Absolute pacifists and self-styled realists alike, pointing to the temptation to engage in large-scale violence on grounds of "necessity," may be inclined to dismiss the principle as having no practical effect. Indeed, this premise recalls the Hague conventions on permissible and impermissible kinds of warfare, which could not restrain the slaughter of millions in World War I and World War II.[12] The fact that the spirit, if not always the letter, of the Hague conventions was grossly violated and that the statesmen who authorized various acts of mass destruction were aware that this was the implication of their actions, has been largely responsible for the general cynicism since World War II with respect to virtually all moral/legal restraints on warfare.[13]

It is precisely this cynicism that now must be overcome. The third imperative calls for a public ethos of minimizing violence to direct the actions of leaders. Such an ethos needs constant reiteration by the shapers of opinion in society if it is to be an effective constraint on those in possession of the tools of destruction.

I am under no illusions that moral principles themselves can markedly reduce the role of war in international relations and substantially limit the scale of destruction in war. The moral imperatives must reinforce, and be reinforced by, calculations of self-interest by the holders of great material power.

Such considerations of rational self-interest are outlined below as integral parts of a strategy of war prevention and control.

SOCIAL STRUCTURE

The ways society is organized obviously affect the pattern of conflict and the extent to which conflicts are likely to turn violent. Leaders who have aspired to be international peacemakers—like Castlereagh, Metternich, Bismarck, Wilson, Franklin Roosevelt,

Churchill, De Gaulle, Hammarskjöld, Nehru, and Kissinger—have accordingly concerned themselves directly with the basic structure of world society, not merely with the military balance of power and the requirements of effective diplomacy within the existing system.

Given the fact that the basic structure of world society has evolved over many centuries, attempts at structural reform might seem too long-range and uncertain of attainment to be realistic elements of a peace strategy. Yet modern history has been marked by a number of deliberate structural changes in international relations. The Treaty of Westphalia ended the wars of religion in 1648 and established the principles of state sovereignty and noninterference in the domestic affairs of other states; these still constitute the fundamental norms of modern international law. The peace settlements of 1815 following the defeat of Napoleon instituted the so-called Concert of Europe wherein the leaders of the five most powerful countries pledged to engage in mutual consultation on matters that would affect the vital interests of any of them. The post–World War I creation of the League of Nations and the post–World War II establishment of the United Nations system were accompanied by decolonization of the vast empires of the European powers.

It is distressing to realize that virtually all the historically significant transformations of international relations have taken place in the wake of—in fact, in direct reaction to—cataclysmic wars. But since another world cataclysm could negate the possibility of reconstructing any type of human society, structural reforms will have to be achieved before the next world war—to assure that the war never occurs. In so urgent a process, other reformist objectives—such as a more equitable distribution of wealth and increased political democratization—may need to be subordinated to reform of the world order. It is not that neglected social disparities and grievances cannot lead eventually to major wars, which in turn could bring on the global cataclysm: because they can and because of their intrinsic importance they must be tended to in a peace strategy. But the highest priority now must be given to those reforms more immediately conducive to avoiding nuclear holocaust.

Since any war between the nuclear-armed superpowers is fraught with the danger of escalating to a planet-destroying war, the first order of business in the structural sphere is to change or modify the features of the world system most likely to draw the United States and the Soviet Union into military combat.

Fortunately, we can start from the fact that neither superpower needs to take territory away from the other to secure its own national integrity or material well-being. Each has a high interest in commercial and military access to virtually all regions of the globe; but there is nothing inherently incompatible with the security and well-being of each if the other also maintains such access. (If the Soviet Union should attempt to get preclusive access or control over the energy resources of the Middle East, for example, the United States might feel vitally threatened.[14] But there is no reason that the Soviets should need such preclusive access to supplement their own energy resources.) It is also true that the boundaries of neither state are overlapped by national or ethnic groups that the other feels compelled to "liberate" and incorporate into its own territory. Both superpowers could become embroiled, offensively or defensively, in "wars of national liberation," but they would initially be with third parties.

Our primary attention therefore should be directed to the structural features of the contemporary international system that could indirectly precipitate a Soviet-American clash by drawing the superpowers into local wars. These features are of two kinds: (1) the lack of adequate conflict-resolution processes and institutions for managing the often bitter disputes and rivalries among the smaller countries; and (2) the alliances and coalitions that make the United States and the Soviet Union rival protectors of warring countries or groups.

The sources of the first structural feature—inadequate controls over local conflicts—lie at the very foundation of the nation-state system, making substantial reform in the foreseeable future highly problematical, yet nonetheless very important to work toward. The nation-state system is embedded in a deep substratum of beliefs about the value for each national community of having its own autonomous territorial state. Each nation-state is supposed to be sovereign: no other state and no transnational or supranational organization can dictate its behavior. But because the definition of nationhood is highly subjective, this makes for a most unstable system. Any particular group of people who come to feel that their common traits make them a unique community may consider themselves a nation, with the result that at any particular time not all nations will be states and not all states will be nations. War can result from the push by dissatisfied nations or dissatisfied states to establish an identity between the nation and the state.[15] The pervasive nationalistic rivalries among small states—especially those created from former European empires, with boundaries often drawn without respect for the location of indigenous ethnic groups—are further stimulated by conflicts over vital economic resources: river waters, ocean fishing grounds, mining areas, hunting and agricultural lands.

All it takes for one of these local conflicts to become globalized is for either the United States or the Soviet Union to offer help to one side. Once the other superpower, fearing enlargement of its principal rival's sphere of influence, feels compelled to counterintervene, the ensuing intensification of competitive involvement can be difficult to reverse. (Risks of such escalation have accompanied the 1971 India-Pakistan war over Bangladesh, the continuing border war between Ethiopia and Somalia, and various phases of the Arab-Israeli conflict.)

Local conflicts are particularly susceptible to competitive intervention by the superpowers and to escalation when the indigenous belligerents base their antagonisms not only on ethnic differences or conflicts over scarce resources, but also on different sides of the capitalist-communist ideological rivalry championed by the superpowers.

The ideological impetus to superpower involvement is heightened by the polarized coalition structure that has dominated international relations since World War II. The fact that each superpower has coalition partners (political movements if not states) on every one of the world's continents (even Australia) means that virtually any interstate or major civil war anywhere on earth could catalyze World War III. The more polarized into the cold-war coalitions any region is, the likelier it is that any local conflict could spark a global conflagration.

For such precipitants of a potential third world war to be adequately controlled over the long run, both the nation-state system and the cold-war coalitions need to be fundamentally transformed. Given the ideological differences between the superpowers, however, a thoroughgoing construction of a new world order does not appear to be even remotely possible in the foreseeable future. Short of this, peacemakers should try at least to modify existing structures to counteract their most dangerous war-stimulating tendencies.

Accordingly, a strategy for peace that addresses both immediate requirements and long-term desiderata for avoiding an armed clash of the superpowers should include: (1) policies and the creation of institutions to engender greater international accountability and reliance on international dispute resolution processes; (2) institutional innovations that enable movements and communities other than states to effectively assert their values and protect their rights in the world arena; and (3) efforts to avoid and reduce unnecessary polarization of global and regional alignments along cold-war lines.[16]

Expansion of international accountability. The contemporary revolutions in communications, transportation, and industrial processes that link nation to nation economically and environmentally make it necessary for them to develop a better system of international accountability. The governing principle should be that those whose behavior substantially affects the well-being of others must be held accountable to them. Acknowledging that the crisis of the contemporary political order stems precisely from the lack of congruence between the primary jurisdictions of governance, the nation-states, and the actualities of interdependence among peoples, this principle expands the concept of consent of the governed to include consent of the affected.

A special responsibility falls on the superpowers and other economically and militarily well-endowed countries to take the lead in fostering a spirit of international accountability and in giving it political and legal reality.

The scaffolding is already there in some fields for elaborating and strengthening processes and institutions for accountability—for example, in international transportation and communications: The traditional might-makes-right mode of establishing rules of the road at sea and in airspace for the convenience of the powerful has begun to give way to institutionalized processes for assuring more equitable rules—negotiated and implemented through the Intergovernmental Maritime Consultative Organization (IMCO) for ocean navigation and the International Civil Aeronautics Organization (ICAO) for the use of airspace. Similarly, preemption of the best international telecommunications frequencies by the most powerful broadcasters is no longer regarded as legitimate, unless it is approved by the International Telecommunication Union (ITU). The ITU's mandate for allocating communciations frequencies is being extended to the allocation of preferred locations in outer space for communications satellites.

It is not altruism that has moved the big powers away from their previous commitment to regimes of open access and free use of ocean space, airspace, and outer space but rather the recognition, born of self-interest, that without at least a measure of mutual accountability small users and big users in their proliferating activities were producing chaotic and even dangerous situations in these environments.[17]

A serious retrogressive movement has occurred, however, with respect to the use of the world's oceans as a result of the U.S. government's refusal to sign the new Law of the Sea Treaty. The treaty, which most countries have signed, holds the signatory governments and the private firms they charter accountable to one another for how they use the ocean "commons," and also establishes the principle of mutual accountability for activities within national offshore "economic zones." Some international accountability applies even within territorial seas and straits traditionally under exclusive national jurisdiction. The signatories agree to subject themselves to a cooperative ocean regime of rules and dispute-resolution processes for actions, including fishing, waste disposal, and special navigation procedures, that can degrade ocean resources or significantly interfere with the normal oceanic activities of other countries.

The Reagan administration's excuse for reneging on the commitments of previous administrations to sign the Law of the Sea Treaty—after more than a decade of international negotiation in which the United States played a leading role—is that the treaty's provisions for an intergovernmental enterprise for managing the mining of minerals on the deep seabed constitute, in effect, "international socialism." The administration has said it will adhere only to those treaty provisions with which it wholly agrees, meaning most of the treaty apart from the deep-sea mining regime. But such selective adherence, if it were to be practiced also by other countries, would destroy both the regime of international accountability on the ocean and provisions for which the United States fought long and hard, such as unimpeded transit through straits and internationally standardized navigation rules for coastal waters.[18]

The failure of the United States to subscribe to the principle of international accountability in use of the seas not only undermines the chances for peaceful resolution of disputes in this field; it contributes as well to the alienation from the United States of many Third World countries that had been committed to the Law of the Sea negotiations, providing fresh opportunities for the Soviet Union to fish, literally and figuratively, in troubled waters. The result is an increase in the likelihood that indigenous Third World conflicts will catalyze super-power confrontation.

A spirit of mutual accountability and international mechanisms to give it effect are needed across the broad front of North-South economic relations. A continuous dialogue needs to be instituted between the advanced industrialized countries and the poor, debt-ridden developing countries with the objective of reducing the extreme vulnerability of the developing countries to the cruelly indifferent forces of the global economy.

This book is not the place to argue the pros and cons of the standard package of demands the developing countries make for a new international economic order (including indexing commodity prices to the price of industrial goods, preferential access to the markets of industrialized countries, loan-repayment extensions and forgiveness of interest, special claims on the reserve assets of the International Monetary Fund, and increased representation in international economic institutions). These demands can, however, be viewed as points of departure for sustained and regularized negotiations between the advantaged and the disadvantaged nations.

Again, the reasons for expanding North-South accountability networks are not primarily altruistic. Private lending institutions with huge outstanding loans to developing countries know this, as do many multinational corporations with major investments and manufacturing subsidiaries in the Third World. It is not just petrodollars that can be recycled into the industrialized world; economic collapse and extreme political instability flowing from high interest rates, tight credit, and reduced demand can be also. The well-being of workers in the industrialized world may be threatened less by exporting jobs to countries with lower wages than by the import and export of recession to and from the Third World. In the "global city," no less than in New York, London, and Rome, a severe depression in the populous lower classes can endanger the well-being and civic order of the whole community.

Legitimation of nonstate communities. Institutional innovation is also needed to handle the growing determination of ethnic, religious, and ideological minorities to mobilize themselves, often obtaining support from their "brothers" and "sisters" in other lands, to oppose majority or government policies offensive to them. President Carter's assertion in 1977 that "no member of the United Nations can claim that mistreatment of its citizens is solely its own business,'' along with his administration's serious but not very successful effort to make human rights a centerpiece of U.S. foreign policy, was one attempt to respond to this phenomenon.[19]

The growing capacity of aggrieved groups to organize transnational networks and movements to transform themselves from mere objects of diplomacy into major actors on the world stage is illustrated by the activities of the Shiite Muslims of the Middle East and by the Palestine Liberation Organization. Because such groups can topple governments and undermine the actions of established international organizations, they have the potential to play havoc with the prospects for peaceful intercourse among countries—unless adaptations are made in traditional structures of the nation-state system.

Finding ways of allowing underrepresented groups and movements to prosecute their demands in international forums, negotiating arenas, and adjudicatory bodies—giving them hope to obtain redress without having to resort to violence and terrorism—may well be as important a challenge to contemporary statesmanship as the direct mitigation of conflict between the superpowers. The danger now, certainly as great as in the past, is that the international turmoil stirred by groups that feel inadequately represented in the established order will draw the great powers into confrontations that precipitate the holocaust.

Any enduring legal-political order must reflect the distribution of power—which in the contemporary world means taking into account formally, even legitimizing, powerful nonstate groups. The only alternative to such political-legal accommodation is to attempt to smash them; but threats to destroy them only stimulate the vulnerable nonstate groups to form alliances with one another or with powerful states willing to come to their aid—hardly a prescription for durable peace.

Nothing, of course, can guarantee that policies and structural innovations to accommodate the stateless communities of the world in particular instances will be more conducive to peace than policies of confrontation and repression would be. Moreover, in many regions of the globe, workable sympathetic responses are likely to take decades to evolve, and fundamental institutional reforms may take even longer. In the meantime violent conflict generated by the unsatisfied grievances of nonstate communities is becoming an increasingly familiar feature of the international scene.

Accordingly, strategies for preventing stateless communities from precipitating international violence that could ignite global war must attempt to isolate and quarantine the violence when it does occur. The prevailing polarization of world politics, the structural element to which we now turn, is of crucial importance in avoiding global chain reactions from local political violence.

Depolarization. For the reasons adduced in Chapter 4, the persistence of the basic bipolar structure of world politics—the legacy of the cold war alliance-building of the 1950s and 1960s—is more likely to bring on World War III than to prevent it. Accordingly, policies for depolarizing international relations have become essential elements of a strategy for world peace.

The two extended cold-war alliances can no longer be relied upon to perform their principal functions effectively. Each was designed to deter the rival superpower from picking on relatively defenseless countries and to provide the allied superpower with bases outside its homeland from which to conduct military operations against the other in the eventuality of another world war. Now that these presumed security benefits to the superpowers have become highly problematic, the principal risk borne by all coalition members—the prospect of local wars turning into global holocaust—has become a terrible, insufficiently compensated liability to the protectors and the protected alike.

The ability of the superpowers to hold reliable protective military umbrellas over their allies and the value of allies for forward defense operations have been undermined by a set of basic developments:

1. The condition of mutual assured destruction (MAD) between the United States and the Soviet Union, assuring that whichever power might launch its strategic nuclear weapons at the other would be vulnerable to massive destruction in return, has almost totally eroded the credibility of pledges by either to protect its allies against attack from the rival superpower. The stark reality of mutual exposure to devastation is expressed in the macabre rhetorical question: "Will the United States, at the moment of truth, be willing to sacrifice New York, Chicago, Los Angeles—take your pick—to save Berlin or Paris?" The negative implications of this question and its inverse formulation for the Soviet Union have been clear for some time, not only for U.S. allies on every continent but also for past and present Soviet allies in Pankow, Peking, Pyongyang, Hanoi, and Havana. The

requirements of a creative response to these implications have not been so clear.

2. The decline in the strategic value of allies for the United States and the Soviet Union is also caused by developments in military technology. The capability of attacking all important enemy targets by using strategic weapons based at home or in the oceans—or in outer space, if current research and development programs continue—substantially reduces the need of the superpowers to use military bases in the territory of their allies. Similarly, the superpowers are becoming less and less dependent on ground stations based on allied territory to obtain early warning and military reconnaissance, as earth-circling satellites have assumed most of the essential warning and reconnaissance tasks.

3. Developments in international economics have been eroding the material-interest cement of coalition solidarity that in the earlier cold-war period buttressed the mutual security arrangements making up the coalition. Having recovered from the devastation of World War II, Japan and the principal European allies of the United States are now America's principal competitors and are inclined to pursue their own economic interests in relationships with members of the Soviet coalition. Indeed, U.S. allies are often suspicious that pleas from Washington for close coordination of commercial policies toward the Soviet Union and its allies are motivated less by political-security considerations than by American desires to keep others from getting ahead in the competitive arena of East-West trade. The Soviet Union keeps a tighter rein on the activities of its allies in international commerce; but many of its partners have been straining at the bit and attempting to negotiate independent economic deals with countries outside the Soviet orbit. Moscow has been compelled more and more often to give way to these centrifugal pressures to keep its commercial bloc from falling too far behind the capitalist world in industrial development. The diversification of international economic relationships within and between the superpower coalitions makes for a growing incongruence between security alignments and economic interdependencies, with the resulting crosscutting of adversarial and alliance relationships further weakening the collective security commitments among coalition members.

4. The military and economic pressures that weaken coalition solidarity reinforce, and are reinforced by, the ideological pluralism now evident in both camps, resulting in each superpower's loss of

ideological authority over its coalition. As coalition members find it in their material self-interest to pursue policies of peaceful engagement with members of the other coalition, it becomes difficult to sustain a picture of the other side as the embodiment of evil. And if, in an attempt to counter the centrifugal forces, the coalition leader tries to revive the good-guys-versus-bad-guys view of the world, as Ronald Reagan attempted early in his presidency, other members of the coalition will be confirmed in their growing skepticism regarding the leader's fitness to lead.

The observable disintegration of coalition unity and commitments in each camp is fraught with dangers. One is that it may stimulate aggressive probes at tempting targets of opportunity in the rival camp, on the assumption that the attacked country's allies are no longer sufficiently committed to its defense; yet in the event of aggression this may turn out to be a gross miscalculation. The result could be a major war between the coalitions.

A scenario can be envisioned in which the starting calculation of one superpower (say, the Soviet Union) that it could get away with a particular power play (say, a grab of the Norwegian island of Svalbard) might not be that wrong initially. But if U.S. leaders came to interpret the Kremlin's decision to take Svalbard as the product of a confident assessment that its aggressive move would not activate a military response by NATO, the Americans could easily conclude that if they now explicitly threatened a military response (even though not really planning to have to carry it out) the Soviet Union would back off. However, if the Soviet leaders sensed that the U.S. threat was a bluff, they might therefore persist in their aggressive move against Svalbard. Suddenly, the stakes would change dramatically: one superpower would be in danger of having its bluff called by the other, with a consequent severe drop in its prestige, credibility, and power—and perhaps even the total unraveling of its coalition. A changed definition of the situation by U.S. policymakers could compel them to transform their original bluff into an operational plan. Then if the Kremlin still believed that the U.S. threat of direct military action was a bluff, a war between the superpowers—a war of mutual miscalculation that neither wanted and neither thought would occur—would become extremely difficult to avoid.

Because such dangers are present in the fragmentation of the cold-war coalitions now taking place, some statesmen want to reverse the trend, to reintegrate and resolidify at least NATO and the Warsaw

Pact. But we have seen that the technological, economic, and ideological forces producing the fragmentation are of such a fundamental nature that it is an illusion to think they can be substantially reversed unless complete unity is forced by an actual war between NATO and the Warsaw Pact.

The time has come to pursue the opposite course: to try deliberately to transform the international order from the outmoded bipolar system of highly militarized superpower coalitions into a more complex pluralistic system consistent with the reality of multiple, often crosscutting, coalitions and adversary relationships.

A prime objective should be to overcome the East-West division of Europe, and the strategies and institutions that sustain the division.

Up to now the Soviet Union and its allies have been the source of proposals for a dissolution of NATO and the Warsaw Pact; these proposals have been summarily rejected by the United States and its allies as a transparent ruse to remove the United States from Europe, leaving the Soviet Union as the dominant European power. Similarly, the Soviets have been the source of radical troop withdrawal schemes envisioning the virtually complete removal of U.S. military deployments on the continent in exchange for the withdrawal of Soviet forces in Eastern Europe to behind the Soviet border. Understandably, proposals for wholesale military disengagement by the superpowers have also been rejected by Western governments as dangerously destabilizing to the balance of power in Europe. The Soviet forces would remain only 400 miles from Berlin while the U.S. forces would need to be transported 3,000 miles across the ocean to reach Western Europe. It is largely this asymmetry in deployment distances that has thus far frustrated agreement in the mutual and balanced force reduction (MBFR) negotiations to reduce superpower forces in Europe—either marginally or comprehensively.

The Soviets have known that in proposing the dissolution of the military blocs and/or a major disengagement of superpower military forces from central Europe they are making offers the West will reject out of hand, giving them the propaganda advantage of appearing to be more interested in peace than the Americans. The Kremlin has no expectation of needing to adapt to the profound changes that would be set in motion in its own sphere of control in Eastern Europe in the event that its proposals should be accepted.

Perhaps these proposals should not have been rejected so quickly by the West, even in the past.

We need to transcend the cold-war mentality, which regards any proposal made by the other side as obviously designed to hurt the recipient and benefit the proposer. It is time not only to look at new ideas, but to reconsider, in the new international context, proposals that may have been prematurely offered and rejected in the past.

The depolarization required to reduce the likelihood of World War III may well be served by restructuring alliances and arranging military disengagement in Europe—such arrangements could provide a net gain in the security of the United States and the Western European countries. Proposals for restructuring NATO and the Warsaw Pact and for mutually disengaging superpower military forces in Europe should be reassessed in light of the following considerations.

As matters now stand, the Soviet Union can augment and rearrange its forces in Eastern Europe under the cover of basic Warsaw Pact arrangements: it does not need to engage in major negotiations with each government. Moreover, it can increase its capabilities in Eastern Europe incrementally, and therefore somewhat ambiguously at each step, without their being generally recognized as dangerously destabilizing to the balance of power. Consequently, the Western democracies might not be able to react decisively to a gross change in the balance of power until well after the fact.

Following a formal dissolution of NATO and the Warsaw Pact and a mutual withdrawal of superpower armies from the heart of Europe, however, any reentry of Soviet forces into Eastern Europe would constitute the crossing of an unambiguous and internationally recognized threshold. The Soviets would be expected to negotiate any return of their forces with the affected countries—countries politically strengthened by the new continental nonalignment norms in objecting strongly to Soviet demands. A violation of these norms by the Soviet Union would in itself be a major political warning to others in the system that a new, perhaps stronger anti-Soviet coalition was required. In short, the political deterrence installed by a truly pluralistic all-European system against Soviet hegemonic drives might more than compensate for the tactical asymmetries that could result from the contemplated superpower withdrawals.[20]

Less radical variants of this model of alliance dissolution and military disengagement, of course, should also be considered. But the more radical model shows that even a fundamental restructuring of the status quo in Europe need not be disadvantageous to the United States and the European democracies; it might, indeed, provide them with considerably more security than the present polarized and militarized European system.

Recognizing, however, that political leaders in the United States and the other Western democracies are unlikely to run the domestic political risks of embracing a radical proposal, and recognizing also that the Soviet Union is far from ready to relinquish direct military control over its Eastern European satellites, it may be best to work first on a less dramatic depolarization of the European system. For example, in a more incremental strategy the United States could take the lead in transforming NATO—without waiting for a comparable Soviet alteration of the Warsaw Pact—into an umbrella organization for bilateral and special multilateral defense arrangements that vary in membership and mutual obligation according to the unique defense needs of the different sets of countries.

In such a modular restructing of NATO, there might be a special mutual security arrangment for countering possible Soviet threats in the Scandinavian region, involving as primary members West Germany, Denmark, Norway, and neutralist Sweden, with the United States pledging a strategic backup. Key arrangements for the conventional defense of the central front might be mainly between the United States and West Germany, if France, Britain, and Canada were reluctant to share the defense burden in sufficient measure. Alternatively, if France and Britain were to join West Germany as the core powers in a revived European defense community, the United States might be able to move more quickly than otherwise toward a more residual defense role.

In this modular variant, integration of forces throughout NATO should probably be kept to a bare minimum and restricted to narrowly defined tasks: the more extensive a multinational integration of forces is, the more politically cumbersome it is to employ the forces in support of alliance commitments. Even the present arrangements require more integration of command and control than is consistent with timely response and flexible military operations.

When it comes to involving members of NATO in contingencies outside the European theater, still looser arrangements are recommended. Surely, the United States should maintain flexibility in projecting its power into the Middle East through bilateral arrangements with cooperative governments around the Mediterranean, independent of formal NATO involvement.

Farther from the European core of the bipolar system, the strategy of depolarization involves much less of an alteration of existing patterns. Most countries in the Third World prefer to be nonaligned between the United States and the Soviet Union. They prefer a diversity of dependent relationships rather than to be dependent on one superpower for their security and economic well-being.

The United States, accordingly, should consider making the following Third World depolarization initiatives to the Soviet Union:

- First, the United States could invite the Soviet Union to join with it in a series of military disengagement/neutralization pacts (either explicit or tacit) for these areas, in which as a minimum neither would establish military bases and as a maximum both would refrain from sponsoring the military buildup of client states and political movements.
- Second, the superpower military disengagement would be reinforced by encouraging genuine nonalignment of countries in the relevant regions with either of the superpowers. The various countries would, of course, maintain flexibility to support, on grounds of their own interests, particular policies pursued by either the United States or the Soviet Union and to seek the support of either or both superpowers for their own projects and policies. But the United States and the Soviet Union would refrain from pressuring these countries to become full allies; they would not be castigated or threatened with material sanctions to prevent their benign cooperation with the rival superpower.
- Third, a special policy could be adopted by the United States: The U.S. government would make known its tolerance for ideologically diverse regimes. Washington would not insist, for example, that countries wishing to qualify for economic assistance renounce Marxist principles of political and economic organization and not be headed by Marxists or by coalitions including Marxists; nor would the United States actively sponsor anti-Marxist opposition groups within countries governed by Marxist or neo-Marxist regimes. Criteria for countries to qualify for substantial help from the United States might include that

the recipient governments not be involved in acts of international aggression, not grossly violate the human rights of their own people, not be financially corrupt, and so on, but these performance standards should be applied neutrally with respect to whether regimes were "leftist" or "rightist."

Such a depolarization strategy would rely primarily on the determination of indigenous communities themselves to resist outside domination. The United States and the Soviet Union would resist the temptation to match or preempt each and every intervention by the other with one's own intervention—conspiring with each other, as it were, to escalate every local political struggle into a high-stakes superpower competition for prestige and global influence.

In a depolarized world where most countries maintained cooperative relationships with both the United States and the Soviet Union while remaining politically independent of each—in short where nonalignment had become the basis of the legitimate world order—neither superpower would need be so compulsive about protecting the position of its ideological brothers and sisters wherever they might be threatened. Both superpowers (or either one, which in some cases would be sufficient to avoid an unnecessary confrontation) would be provided with acceptable justifications for refusing to become militarily involved in conflicts whose outcome, one way or another, would not really threaten their vital security interests.

Depolarization does, of course, cut across the grain of the two-worlds approach to international relations still prominent in the behavior of both the Soviet Union and the United States in the Third World. When the Soviets are in an assertive phase, they justify their sponsorship of political clients worldwide on the grounds of the responsibility the Soviet Union bears, as the world's leading socialist power, to give assistance to "progressive" forces struggling to throw off the yoke of capitalist imperialism. The United States at its most globally assertive claims to be waging the noble fight for freedom against totalitarianism. More often than not, however, each side justifies its global search for allies and clients on every continent as a defensive geopolitical reaction to the expansionary alliance-building of the other, which if allowed to proceed unopposed could presumably tip the global balance of power in favor of the enemy. A strategy of active depolarization could be of particular value in reducing the force of this latter geopolitical rationale.

Although we can state the conditions for a moderation of the Soviet-American global rivalry and for the avoidance of situations leading to high-stakes confrontations that could lead to war, and while we can attempt to move the Soviets toward a nonexploitative acceptance of such a new geopolitical regime, it would be illusory to expect that in fact we will succeed in avoiding all such war-threatening superpower conflicts in the years ahead. Some are bound to occur; and for these not to result in nuclear holocaust, we must enter into the uncomfortable realm of confrontation management, which includes not only the diplomacy of conflict control and arms control, but also strategies of conflict prosecution—some of them military.

DIPLOMACY

It is clear that changes in the structure of world society are needed to deal adequately with the conditions likely to cause severe international conflict. But since the appropriate structural reforms, such as those suggested above, are unlikely to be fully realized in the short term, avoiding war meanwhile requires countries to find ways of managing even their intense conflicts with one another nonviolently within the existing structure. Diplomatic bargaining between countries remains the primary means of international conflict-resolution or moderation in the nation-state system. Deft or clumsy practice of diplomacy often makes the difference between war and peace. Once war begins, diplomacy can also determine whether the warring countries stop fighting before they totally destroy one another or whether an ongoing local war expands to become a major regional or even world war.

The diplomat who hopes to protect or advance his or her country's interests without resorting to war needs a keen sense of what can be demanded of other countries, as well as of how to demand it without provoking a violent response. This requires knowledge of the interests and behavior patterns of other countries and a sensitivity to the meaning of their sometimes surprising reactions. Achieving a cease-fire or limiting the further escalation of a war requires an equally sophisticated awareness of the values and characteristic behavior of a country's enemies.[21]

The fact that, despite their global rivalry, the United States and the Soviet Union have not become embroiled in a war with each other should not lead to the conclusion that the two sides have learned the diplomatic arts well. In part because of their inept diplomacy in recent decades each of the superpowers has been drawn into or sponsored wars that cost it more than it gained: the Soviet-sponsored North Korean invasion of South Korea, the American provocation of Chinese entry into the Korean War, the Sino-Soviet border war, the U.S. military involvement in Vietnam, Soviet sponsorship of Arab attacks against Israel in 1967 and 1973, and the Soviet invasion of Afghanistan. And in a number of Soviet-American confrontations over Berlin and in the Cuban missile crisis, the two powers came perilously close to blows.

Indeed, the wrong lessons may have been learned from past American "successes"—particularly the Berlin crises of 1958–1959 and 1961 and the Cuban missile crisis. Any of these could have led to a direct Soviet-American clash; but in the face of tough and unequivocal demands by the United States, the Soviets prudently backed away from positions they had taken. These war-avoiding Soviet retreats, however, took place when the United States still held a decisive advantage in the global balance of power because of U.S. strategic nuclear superiority, and the cold-war polarization of world politics was then much less ambiguous than it has become.

It is doubtful that similar coercive diplomatic posturing by the United States in confrontations with the Soviet Union would produce comparable results under the changed "correlation of forces" (to use the Soviet term). Not only essential strategic parity, but also the constriction of the scope of external interests that each superpower considers truly vital, along with the corollary blurring of alliance commitments, may well induce the Soviets to expect as much prudence from the Americans in future confrontations as the Americans previously required of them.

In the past, for the Soviets to yield in a confrontation with the United States, especially one over an objective not absolutely essential to the security of the Soviet Union, could be justified as elementary Bolshevik realism. Under today's changed correlation of forces, the United States should be equally prepared to yield—at the same time that the Soviet leadership is more likely than before to regard backing down under pressure as un-Bolshevik.

This means that more than at any time in the history of the U.S.-Soviet relationship, conditions are now ripe for terrible games of chicken, with both sides so heavily and visibly committed to incompatible objectives that neither can back down without great humilation; consequently each becomes all the more determined to demonstrate an irrevocable commitment to persist toward its objective, hoping that the certainty of a head-on collision will convince the other side to swerve out of the way.[22]

How can diplomacy help avoid such catastrophic miscalculations?

In part what is needed is a reorientation of diplomacy and a reeducation of diplomats to de-emphasize the military chips in international bargaining, which have become the stock-in-trade of cold-war diplomacy, so that they can exploit instead the new economic and institutional chips becoming available as depolarization proceeds and webs of international accountability are woven.

A depolarizing world of diversified relationships offers far more opportunities and incentives to bargain with carrots than with sticks. Because adversaries on one issue may be partners on others, prudence dictates that, even when dealing with adversaries, diplomats should refrain from tactics that may engender long-standing hostility. A country like the United States, particularly, which has the assets needed to establish cooperative relationships around the globe, has enough cards to play without resorting to military coercion when the bargaining gets tough.

To pursue their interests in an increasingly interdependent world, the superpowers, like other countries, will need to garner votes in various international institutions. The institutional arena, in fact, will increasingly become the setting for their global rivalry for influence and prestige. But in some fields requiring international regulation— the control of nuclear materials, air and sea navigation, broadcasting frequency allocation, plant and human disease control, atmospheric and water pollution, meteorology and weather control—the superpowers are just as likely to find themselves natural coalition partners as adversaries. There should be increasing opportunities for them to practice a diplomacy of linkage (of both a positive and a negative sort) between some of these fields and the standard geopolitical fields in which they have had very few positive chips to introduce into what has been coercive bargaining.

In other words, a new diplomacy needs to develop from the realization that many negative and positive pressures, short of the threat and use of force, are now available to the superpowers and to other adversaries to utilize when their interests conflict.

It would be an illusion, of course, to expect that conciliation and cooperation will largely replace coercion and confrontation in international relations, or that the threat and use of force will no longer be prominent instruments of diplomacy. But the imperative of avoiding World War III puts a premium on the diplomatic art of keeping bargaining processes going during intense confrontations, as the United States and the Soviet Union did during the Cuban missile crisis. Technical and institutional devices to facilitate communication between adversaries in intense crises—hot lines, joint crisis control centers, advance working out of signaling codes—are crucial.[23]

Even more important than the technical and institutional devices, however, is cultivation of sensitivity among diplomats and national leaders to the likely behavior and psychology of their adversaries. Political-military games and crisis-simulation exercises are important in both training diplomats and keeping them alert to the way changes may be affecting an adversarial relationship. Such exercises also help detect distortions of reality on the part of a country's own responsible decision makers, whether resulting from misinformation or emotional factors.

Neutral, third-party adjudicatory and mediational processes need to be enhanced and then relied on by the superpowers as well as by smaller countries, as standard means of conflict resolution—not just in desperation when nothing else has worked. The more such procedures are given legitimacy and prestige, the more likely it is that adversaries will be willing to accept such procedures and their outcomes as substitutes for military combat.

Because the path to total holocaust would most likely lead from smaller, initially limited, wars that escalate out of control, the diplomatic arts and devices of conflict control need to be projected into potential and actual wartime environments—including nuclear war. A narrowly moralistic or head-in-the-sand refusal to recognize the importance of preparing in advance to continue political bargaining and other diplomatic interaction between adversaries during wartime could contribute to the materialization of the very events considered "unthinkable." If deterrence fails, the necessary pauses in combat, mutual restraints in escalation, and cease-fires will require intensive communication and negotiation between belligerents, all the way up the escalation ladder.

MILITARY CAPABILITY

Attention to the levels and characteristics of the military forces deployed or being developed by adversaries is clearly a necessary element in a strategy of war prevention and control. If a country perceives it can overpower or intimidate its adversary in a clash of arms it may be tempted to try to force the adversary to accept its demands, thus risking starting or provoking a war rather than trying to arrive at a mutually acceptable compromise of conflicting interests.

Accordingly, traditional statesmen try to prevent their international adversaries from making excessive demands on their country or its allies by providing themselves (and their allies) with at least as much military capability as their adversaries. On the other hand, some peace groups suspicious of their own government's inclinations to use force to press its demands on foreign adversaries will try to effect reductions in their country's military capabilities to levels at which government leaders could not hope to win a war.

Some statesmen and some peace groups feel most secure with essential military parity between their country and its adversaries. And traditional statesmen who aspire to be global peacemakers may try to assure that particular sets of adversaries are in essential military balance with each other (as Henry Kissinger did with Israel and her Arab opponents in the period of the 1973 war).

The destructive power of nuclear weapons, however, calls into question traditional notions about military balances. It has established vast asymmetries, between the nuclear and nonnuclear countries, that even alliances are unable to redress. And the volatility of the new technology injects precarious instability into whatever nuclear balances are temporarily achieved.

One response to the new dangers is to try to stop the spread of nuclear weapons to more countries than already have them. Another is to try to effectuate substantial nuclear disarmament of the superpowers. Still another is the effort to put limits on the size and characteristics of the arsenals of the nuclear countries. The various efforts to limit nuclear weapons, whether pursued individually or in combination, also require attention to regional and global levels of nonnuclear forces.

Preventing the spread of nuclear weapons. It has come to be generally accepted around the world that the United States and the

Soviet Union are in a class by themselves militarily and that other countries should not try to catch up with them, especially if this means acquiring nuclear weapons. But acquiescence in the super-power status of the United States and the Soviet Union is coupled with an insistence, frequently reiterated in UN resolutions, that they negotiate "significant reductions of, and qualitative limitations on strategic arms . . . in the direction of nuclear disarmament and, ultimately, of establishment of a world free of such weapons."[24]

The Treaty on the Non-proliferation of Nuclear Weapons (NPT) reflects and is an attempt to sustain the nuclear "class" system. In signing the NPT, 125 countries have agreed not to obtain their own nuclear weapons—thus perpetuating, for the time being at least, a three-tier ranking of military powers: (1) the two superpowers; (2) Britain, France, and China, each of which has a nuclear arsenal; and (3) all the other countries.[25]

However, by 1986 thirty-eight of the countries without nuclear weapons had refused to sign the NPT. China and France also refused to sign (the treaty obligates nuclear-weapons countries to refrain from transferring nuclear weapons or nuclear weapons materials or pro-duction facilities to countries without these weapons).

That there are thirty-eight nonnuclear holdouts from the NPT, despite considerable diplomatic pressure from the United States and the Soviet Union, and that France and China have refused to sign the treaty, may unfortunately be a stronger portent of things to come than the provisions of the treaty. It has become increasingly difficult to avert the further spread of nuclear weapons now that the technical capability for making the weapons is available to more and more countries. Since the superpowers continue to act as if the essence of power is military power, with the military trump card each country's nuclear arsenal—no matter that the balance of terror strongly inhibits the superpowers from going to war against each other—the consid-erations that prompted first France and then China to obtain their own nuclear forces are bound to lead some other countries to try to obtain their own nuclear arsenals. The leading candidates now are Israel, India, Pakistan, the Republic of South Africa, Argentina, Brazil, Iraq, and Libya.[26]

Some military strategists and academic theorists discount the consequences of the spread of nuclear weapons, predicting that the threat of nuclear devastation that has kept the United States and the Soviet Union from going to war against each other will produce similar responsible inhibitions on the part of other countries acquiring nuclear weapons. The theory is that even war-prone adversaries like India and Pakistan or Israel and her Arab neighbors would be injected with a healthy fear of the consequences of war, once they acquired the means to swiftly obliterate each other. And the superpowers presumably would be deterred from attempting to engage in "nuclear blackmail" against nuclear countries with which they were in confrontation, thus reducing one of the principal sources of dangerous miscalculation between the superpowers.[27]

The flaw in such sanguine appraisals—and it could be a fatal flaw, not only for the countries involved, but for the world—is that they fail to take into account the high likelihood that the arsenals acquired by less powerful countries would probably comprise, or appear to comprise, vulnerable, "use them or lose them," weapons. In an intense crisis, incentives would be high to fire such weapons preemptively to hobble the enemy's weapons before they could destroy one's own. Moreover, the argument that spreading such weapons around would reduce the chances of nuclear blackmail and miscalculation overlooks the great asymmetry sure to remain between superpower arsenals and those of countries with fledgling nuclear capabilities. There would be the very real possibility that a superpower in a confrontation with a country beginning to deploy nuclear weapons would be tempted to remove its small enemy's new arsenal with a "surgical strike" before the weapons could be fully deployed. Rather than produce a secure system of universal deterrence, a world in which virtually every country had its own nuclear weapons would most likely be a trigger-happy nuclear state of nature in which life would be nasty, brutish—and perhaps soon over for everyone.

Fortunately, most foreign-policy officials and strategists around the world still regard the acquiring of nuclear weapons by many countries as a potentially disastrous development that must be prevented (even though some officials of nonnuclear countries might wish the nuclear club could be opened to just one more country: theirs). They are realistic enough to understand that any new breach in the barrier to proliferation in any region of the world could open the floodgates. Therefore, there still is remarkably widespread support, even on the part of countries with the capability to develop an arsenal, such as Sweden and Japan, for the nonproliferation regime of strict restraints on the utilization and international transfer of weapons-grade nuclear materials and nuclear-energy equipment that could be used to produce weapons. (See Chapter 9 above for details on the existing nonproliferation regime.)

Though it is important to support these technical controls and safeguards, they cannot prevent countries from acquiring nuclear weapons if they are determined to have them. The heart of the problem is to find means to counteract the political and strategic incentives for countries to obtain independent nuclear arsenals; and this urgently requires coming to grips with the profound security dilemma of the nonnuclear countries.

Because most attention has been focused on the symptom of the problem—namely, the declining credibility of superpower pledges to protect allies or friendly neutrals from the other superpower—the standard prescription is to attempt to shore up alliance commitments and other security guarantees to nonnuclear countries. But the alliances and security guarantees have become flimsy precisely because it is now too scary for either superpower to initiate nuclear war against the other for any reason except to preempt an apparently inevitable attack against itself—or perhaps, short of that, to prevent or blunt an attack that could, if it succeeded, irreversibly make the other the dominant world power. The standard rhetoric, deployments, or alliance-reconsolidation measures simply fail to deal with this unprecedented situation.[28] They are, as it were, tilting at windmills.

Paradoxically, efforts by the superpowers to enhance security guarantees to the nonnuclear countries exacerbate the predicament they are supposed to deal with, since they increase attention to the importance of nuclear weapons in the present international system, emphasizing the nakedness of those who are not protected by them.

A nonproliferation regime with any real prospect of avoiding the otherwise inevitable spread of nuclear weapons would need to deemphasize the political and military value of nuclear weapons for the countries that already possess them. Tangible indications of such a deemphasis would be substantial reductions in existing nuclear deployments and arsenals and moratoria on the testing and development of new nuclear war-fighting capabilities.

Dismantling existing nuclear arsenals. More easily wished for than accomplished is a substantial reduction in nuclear arms. Some of the obstacles are technical. Some are strategic and political.

For arms reductions to be agreed to by both sides in an adversary relationship, the ability of each side to be satisfied that the other lives up to its side of the bargain is a major problem. Without intrusive inspection within the adversary's borders, it may be difficult to verify conclusively that weapons supposed to have been removed from its arsenal are not simply hidden away and capable of being redeployed quickly enough to establish an immediately exploitable edge in the military balance.

Technology has been a friend of progress on this issue, however, since the capabilities for remote reconnaissance have been developing faster than new means of concealment. Major weapons complexes could not now be rebuilt without early detection from earth-orbiting satellites.

Still, small numbers of strategic offensive or defensive weapons can be made ready behind thick walls or underground for sudden deployment. No matter how good the detection technology, suspicions of such clandestine violations of arms-reduction agreements probably can never be totally allayed between deeply antagonistic countries. This puts constraints on what can be accomplished through nuclear arms-reduction agreements, and those negotiating agreements will do better to admit the constraints than be seen as naive by denying them. Accordingly, realistic nuclear arms-reduction proposals for the foreseeable future must allow each side to retain a nuclear arsenal large enough to assure that, if one of them were to attempt to overturn the strategic balance by violating the reduction agreement, it would have to make such a dramatic augmentation in its forces as to be virtually certain of early detection. Given this allowance, significant nuclear arms-reduction agreements should be adequately verifiable by remote national means that do not require the physical presence of inspectors on the adversary's territory.

The obstacles to such reduction agreements would then reside in strategic doctrine or other political considerations, which will be discussed below in the section on military strategy.

Nuclear arms control. Regardless of the success or failure of negotiations to achieve nuclear-weapons reductions, it is imperative that the nuclear countries refrain from deploying new weapons that give the side that launches the first strategic nuclear blow a large advantage. The advanced technologies of detection help make such arms control feasible because they allow each side to monitor the other's weapons tests, which in most cases of strategic significance would need to be undertaken before deploying the new systems.

That there should be no advantage to a nuclear first strike was a premise of the SALT and START negotiations to limit strategic nuclear weapons: it is reflected most notably in the 1972 treaty restricting antiballistic missiles (ABMs). The theory behind the ABM treaty is that neither side should deploy weapons that could tempt it to initiate a strategic nuclear war under the assumption that it could keep damage to itself to tolerable levels.

If this basic arms-control philosophy still holds—it is now under strong doctrinal attack—the superpowers must refrain from deploying such defenses against strategic nuclear attack as those envisioned under Ronald Reagan's Strategic Defense Initiative ("Star Wars"), the main purpose of which is to protect the population at large from the enemy's strategic missiles.

Another reason for restricting if not eliminating the Star Wars program has less to do with the danger of its stimulating first-strike temptations when fully deployed than with its current effects on the arms race. Research and testing designed to attain a comprehensive missile defense stimulates accelerated offensive programs by the other side—designed to overcome the defenses that may be deployed. Each step can only lead to ever-larger outlays for offensive and defensive strategic weapons by both sides; and the fears and hostility that such an all-out, new arms race would engender would surely undermine an integrated strategy for the prevention and control of war.

A current and urgent objective of nuclear arms control, on the other hand, should be to modify provocative features of the existing nuclear arsenals and some of the weapon modernization programs about to come to fruition. The most provocative weapons are those that could be very effective in hobbling the enemy's military capability if they were used at the outset of hostilities or at the beginning of a particular phase of a war—but that are highly vulnerable to destruction by the enemy if not used at the outset.

The multiple-warhead, land-based ICBMs now deployed by each side have these dangerous use-them-or-lose-them characteristics. Their accuracy and destructive power pose a threat to enemy ICBMs, while their vulnerability to destruction prior to launch (and the damage they can inflict if launched) make them high-priority targets for attack. An arms-control agreement to phase such weapons out of the inventories of both sides would be highly desirable, and it could be sufficiently verifiable with national, nonintrusive means of inspection. In fact, neither side need wait for a negotiated agreement before starting to phase these provocative weapons out of its inventory: a unilateral move of this kind would enhance the security of the side that undertook it, particularly if the unilateral reduction of ICBMs were accompanied by a substitution of less vulnerable strategic weapons, such as those carried in submarines or new single-warhead and mobile land-based ICBMs.

Another high priority and crucial item on the arms-control agenda is dealing with the vulnerability to destruction of the command and control systems for strategic nuclear forces. Since the command and control systems must be intact for effective retaliation to take place, their vulnerability leads each side to adopt dangerous and highly provocative arrangements to launch prime strategic forces at the enemy before enemy weapons can land on its territory. This means, in effect, launching thousands of strategic nuclear weapons simply on the basis of a warning that an enemy attack is coming.

Again, much of what needs to be done to reduce the vulnerability of command and control can be accomplished unilaterally, through measures to disperse and protect the highest national command centers and their subordinate commands. In some fields, however, agreement between the superpowers would be important. For example, communications used in strategic command and control are highly dependent on communications satellites, and therefore a mutual ban on antisatellite weapons should be pursued.[29]

These restraints on new deployments and modifications of existing forces to reduce the incentives for both sides to launch their strategic nuclear weapons first, or preemptively, are unlikely to be adopted without major revisions in military strategy. The strategy requirements for reducing the likelihood and damage of wars will be discussed in a later section of this chapter.

Equalizing nonnuclear arms.   Imbalances of conventional military power between adversaries need to be rectified, not only because they tempt military aggression by the conventionally superior side but also because they compel the inferior side to rely on nuclear first-use strategies to negate the conventional imbalance. Such conventionally inferior countries constitute an international lobby, as it were, against nuclear arms-control policies and changes in strategic doctrine to reduce reliance on nuclear weapons.[30]

Conventional military imbalances can be rectified either by upgrading the conventional capabilities of the inferior side or by reducing the conventional forces of the superior side. Such equalizations are inherently difficult to achieve because the side with superior forces usually has convinced itself that its force levels are essential to its security; it will regard as threatening any adjustments in the balance that seem to amount to a relative increase in its opponents' military power. Countries typically regard increases in their opponents' conventional forces as evidence of aggressive intent; similarly, they consider their opponents' proposals for asymmetrical decreases in deployed forces to be either trickery or mere propaganda exercises. For more than a decade, such suspicions have frustrated East-West agreement in the mutual and balanced force reduction negotiations between NATO and Warsaw Pact countries.

If their actions are not to be counterproductive, force planners and arms controllers need to be sensitive to the understandable reactions of the other side to unilateral moves and negotiating proposals for rectifying a conventional imbalance. Imaginative combinations of increases and decreases in various components of the overall force balance—including nuclear forces—which may be nonsymmetrical in particular categories but contribute to an essential equalization of military power might help overcome suspicions. An example of a potentially successful negotiating package—which has been offered and refused but could be revived in a fresh negotiating context—might include a NATO proposal to reduce U.S. battlefield nuclear weapons deployed in West Germany in exchange for a Warsaw Pact reduction in Soviet battlefield tank deployments in East Germany and other Eastern European countries.[31]

Perceptions on the part of those with superior conventional capabilities that those trying to catch up really have aggressive intentions can also be countered if the inferior side concentrates its buildup in forces designed to defend territory against invading forces and forswears forces that would substantially augment its capability of invading the opponent's territory. For example, a buildup of air-defense capabilities could be concentrated in surface-to-air missiles rather than in sophisticated fighter aircraft, and the opponent's superiority in tanks could be countered by deploying precision-guided antitank weapons rather than by increasing tank forces.

However, a bedeviling ambiguity remains between the offensive and defensive functions of most modern weapons that complicates, and can be expected to frustrate, attempts to define force buildups as nonhostile measures for stabilizing dangerous military imbalances. Thus Syria's deployment of advanced surface-to-air missiles ostensibly to shoot down Israeli fighter aircraft if they should penetrate Syrian airspace is regarded by the Israelis as an aggressive move because Israel maintains air superiority over its Arab neighbors as an essential counter to the numerical superiority of the combined Arab armies: it relies on air striking power to respond to crossborder terrorist attacks as well as to provide a capability, in case of war, of interdicting the movement and supply of attacking Arab ground forces. For every buildup of Arab air-defense capabilities, the Israelis believe they require a compensatory increase in their own fighter aircraft. Yet both sides claim to be acting only to redress an imbalance.

Only an integrated approach to conventional arms control—embedded in a grand strategy for reducing hostility and resolving conflict among the armed adversaries—is likely to achieve genuine and durable equalizations of conventional balances. Indeed, such equalizations, if part and parcel of a larger set of improved relations, could even take the form of military disengagement from zones of confrontation and substantial mutual reductions in conventional forces.

Controlling military transfers.   For small powers to avoid the conventional arms races that are dangerous not only for them but for the big powers that may be drawn into the resulting wars requires attention to relationships of mutual dependency between the arms suppliers and their clients.

Once a supplier-client relationship develops, the supplying country can become dependent for export earnings on perpetuating it. The pernicious effects of this dependency work against the legitimate objectives of arms transfers, which are to stabilize local balances of power, deter aggressors from taking advantage of defenseless countries, and help governments maintain domestic public order.

The arms-transfer client may attempt to blackmail the supplier politically by threatening to seek more advantageous and less restrictive transfer arrangements with the supplier country's international rivals. But a supplier that for pecuniary reasons wants to sustain the client country's need for arms transfers can subtly transmute what began as an interest in helping the client avoid war into an interest in prolonging its insecurity. The client may then be tempted to play along by inflating its internal problems and external tensions into dire threats to its national existence—the audience being groups in the supplier country that might otherwise be reluctant to approve further arms transfers. This latter stratagem is often accompanied, in both the United States and the Soviet Union, with efforts to portray the arms transfers at issue as required by a regional, or even global, struggle for dominance between the superpowers. The recipient country's internal problems and external rivalries are made ideological and geopolitical until the hypotheses become self-confirming: the prospects then become real that the superpowers will be actively drawn in on opposite sides of a local conflict.

Alertness to the ease with which such symbiotic supplier-client relationships can materialize in the field of arms transfers, with understanding of their negative implications for world peace, is the first step toward devising controls on them. An important control is close oversight by the defense and arms-control agencies of government (in the United States, congressional as well as executive) to assure that commercial motives do not shape assumptions about security interests. Another control is to put the burden of proof on those who claim that a given transfer of military capability is necessary to the supplier's security interests and that the contemplated transfers will not inject the cold-war rivalry into a primarily indigenous conflict.

MILITARY STRATEGY

Some elements of the strategy of war prevention and control outlined above may not be in place in time to avoid war in particular situations, or to adequately control wars that do materialize. And even if they are in place, they may not work as hoped, for although presented as imperatives, they probably can serve only as constraints on the behavior of fallible human beings interacting in a world of enormous complexity.

Once wars start, efforts to control or stop them will be strongly affected by the prevailing strategies for conducting military operations. (Prevailing military strategies may, of course, also affect decisions to go to war in the first place.) And since nuclear holocaust, if it ever comes, is not likely to be a leap from political crisis into the cauldron of all-out war but rather to be an expansion in intensity and size of a war that was relatively limited at the outset, any serious strategy for its prevention must pay close attention to strategies for conducting and, most importantly, terminating, military operations short of nuclear holocaust.

To be sure, many objectives besides preventing nuclear holocaust will continue to shape the way countries fight wars and prepare to fight them. But we must insist—not only on moral grounds but for the practical reason that none of the other objectives, except perhaps destruction of the enemy, could be attained if there were a nuclear holocaust—that no other objectives should be pursued in ways that could bring on nuclear holocaust. Some military strategies that would be attractive on other grounds must be forsworn. And new strategies must be developed and given priority to serve the objectives of war control and termination.

The Concept of Firebreaks

The objective of controlling and terminating war short of nuclear holocaust requires the Soviet and American military establishments to construct and maintain "firebreaks" against the escalation of combat. A military firebreak strategy cannot by itself guarantee the control and termination of war. It is, however, essential for allowing slow enough escalation of combat to give political leaders the opportunity to limit the destruction of ongoing wars and to terminate them while there is something left of human life worth preserving. Particular strategies for using force in particular contingencies, and characteristics of the associated military deployments, must be specifically designed to reinforce firebreaks; and military commanders must understand that the objective of winning a particular engagement will rarely, if ever, justify the breach of a crucial firebreak.

The concept of a military firebreak is an analogy to the strips of plowed or cleared land used to arrest the spread of fires in prairies or forests. In the military realm such lines are as much definitional or psychological distinctions between levels of warfare as they are physical barriers or demilitarized zones—though the "location" of a firebreak has implications for the design and deployment of military weapons as well as for their use.

A number of firebreaks are vitally important to prevent escalation of combat to holocaust. These are the firebreaks between: (1) wars that do not involve the superpowers as combatants against each other, and a U.S.-Soviet war; (2) a U.S.-Soviet (or NATO-Warsaw Pact) conventional war, and a U.S.-Soviet (or NATO-Warsaw Pact) nuclear war; (3) a U.S.-Soviet war conducted outside both home-lands, and a U.S.-Soviet war in which the homeland of at least one of them is attacked; and (4) a U.S.-Soviet war involving highly con-strained nuclear attacks, and full-scale nuclear war.

Superpower nonengagement/superpower war. Direct military combat between the United States and the Soviet Union could let loose a conflagration that would overwhelm all existing firebreaks and rapidly engulf the world in the dreaded holocaust. Recognition of this awful prospect surely is one of the main reasons that the cold war has not, for over four decades, resulted in a hot Soviet-American war. But it would be foolhardy to assume that the inhibitions will continue to hold automatically. Both sides, in addition to pursuing the kind of diplomatic and institutional policies for nonviolent conflict manage-ment outlined above, need to refrain from military strategies and deployments that virtually guarantee a Soviet-American clash if their allies or clients are attacked. The superpowers must avoid declara-tory strategies and posturing that lead to games of chicken in which the superpower that does not enter combat on the side of its ally suffers tremendous loss of prestige. This is the most compelling reason for instituting "modular" alliance arrangements (described on pp. 235–236) as soon as possible. The superpowers must recognize their needs for flexibility in committing their forces, including the need to disengage and decommit their combat forces from particular zones of confrontation.

Conventional war/nuclear war. The firebreak between conven-tional war and nuclear war must be kept psychologically profound and resistant to weakening by weapons developments and strategies that blur the distinction between nuclear and nonnuclear warfare. Proposals for deploying controlled-blast nuclear weapons, like the neutron bomb or various "micro" nuclears, usually contemplate integrating these "clean" nuclear weapons into normal battlefield tactics. But the gain in firepower would be achieved at the price of eroding an enormously significant threshold of warfare, a firebreak that—even in the event of a U.S.-Soviet war—might still provide a salient demarcation and basis for leveling off and deescalating hostilities before everything blows up. In addition to not bringing new ambiguous or hybrid weapons into the inventory, already deployed nuclear weapons should be removed to positions far behind possible war zones to prevent their having to be detonated early in a military engagement to avoid being captured or disabled; and all nuclear weapons in any theaters of operation should be sufficiently invulnerable to a disarming first strike to avoid provoking an enemy nuclear attack or needing to be used preemptively. Weapons that cannot meet this invulnerability criterion should be removed.

Proposals for NATO's abandoning reliance on a nuclear first use strategy should not be dismissed as creating an overall imbalance favorable to the Soviets but welcomed for their contributing to strengthening the conventional/nuclear firebreak. The dialogue in NATO should be directed toward achieving conventional force modernizations and, perhaps, negotiated NATO-Warsaw Pact force reductions to assure that a no-first-use posture would not mean a relative decline in the West's overall power vis-à-vis the East. As McGeorge Bundy, George Kennan, Robert McNamara, and Gerard Smith argue, once the military leaders of the alliance learn to operate on the assumption that if a war has to be fought in Europe it must be kept at the conventional level, the NATO forces "will be better instruments for stability in crises and for general deterrence as well as for the maintenance of the nuclear firebreak so vital to us all."[32]

Superpowers as sanctuaries/superpowers under attack. Keeping the homelands of the United States and the Soviet Union as sanctuaries from each other's attack could provide the last and only hope for avoiding total holocaust once a U.S.-Soviet or Nato-Warsaw Pact war became nuclear. The prospect of superpower sanctuaries is understandably anathema to other members of these alliances, particularly the two Germanies, for whom the nuclear holocaust would have arrived already. Indeed, French President Charles De Gaulle's principal justification for France having its own nuclear deterrent was the prospect of such a superpower mutual sanctuary policy persisting during a Soviet incineration of Western Europe and a retaliatory U.S. incineration of Eastern Europe.

Surely it would be imprudent for either the United States or the Soviet Union to publicly endorse a strategic sanctuary policy. Any such public declaration could only work against efforts to achieve a modulated and stable depolarization of Europe and other regions, causing some countries to adopt a plague-on-both-your-houses neutralism and to attempt to acquire their own nuclear weapons.

It is neither necessary nor desirable for the superpowers to rule out in advance the possibility of their territories becoming prime strategic target areas in a Third World War. Yet elementary survival does require each superpower to retain the *option* of keeping its nuclear attacks away from the other's territory, and to maintain means of communicating this intention even in the midst of ongoing local nuclear wars. The fear that merely retaining the option will tempt one or the other superpower to start a major war in Europe or elsewhere is misplaced, for neither could have sufficient confidence before the event that its territory would indeed be spared from devastation in a big Soviet-American war.

Limited strategic attacks/nuclear holocaust.   Firebreaks even beyond the start of a Soviet-American strategic nuclear war are essential if we are to take seriously the wise admonition of the strategist Bernard Brodie that "the main war goal upon the beginning of a strategic nuclear exchange should surely be to terminate it as quickly as possible and with the least amount of damage possible on both sides."[33]

There would be at least two requirements for *attempting* to achieve termination of a strategic war short of nuclear holocaust. (I emphasize "attempting" because I do not believe there is a high probability of terminating a small U.S.-Soviet strategic war in time to avoid the holocaust. But as long as even a small chance of such termination exists, it is imperative to try.) The first requirement would be assured survival of responsible national command authorities on both sides. The second would be the retention of some capability to launch some highly selective retaliatory strikes after having suffered the first nuclear blow, while withholding the bulk of one's nuclear striking power. The second requirement is born of the political condition that no Soviet or American leader could be expected to approve a strategic posture that seemed to allow no capacity for credible retaliation against a nuclear aggressor.[34]

Without the survival of high national leadership on both sides— authorities who still retain command of the strategic nuclear forces— there would be no hope of terminating the war short of holocaust.

Unless a central authoritative agency could command restraint and the cessation of further attacks, the paroxysm of devastating lethal exchanges could continue until all major destructive capabilities had been expended. Certainly, there would be no way to negotiate a mutual standdown of forces, cease-fires, truces, and the end to hostilities unless authoritative leadership continued to exist to conduct negotiations credibly.

As indicated in the discussion on pp. 192–193, various physical and organizational improvements can be made in command and control systems to increase their chances of surviving a limited strategic attack: they should be developed and installed at once.

Of equal, if not greater, importance is the delegitimation of so-called decapitation strategies, named for their objective of destroying the national command centers of the enemy. Not only would decapitation attacks negate the chances of control and termination of war if they were successfully carried out, but the mere threat to engage in such attacks compels the adversaries to predelegate weapons-release authority to subordinate commands and to put their main forces on a preemptive launch-on-warning basis, in part to deter the other side from ever attempting a decapitation strike but also to assure actual retaliation in the event deterrence fails.

At a minimum, each superpower—either one could do this unilaterally, without putting itself at a disadvantage, if the other is not ready to act—should announce that it is expunging decapitation attacks from its inventory of strategic options.

Finally, each superpower—in addition to itself renouncing decapitation strategies and unilaterally improving the physical capacity of its command and control system to withstand any nuclear attacks that come—should institute a policy of no immediate second use of nuclear weapons. This policy should also be openly announced. It would eliminate the need to order strategic alerting procedures in crises that, to the enemy, look like preparations for preemptive attack; and it allows for greater attention in a nuclear crisis to be devoted to emergency dispersal and other command and control security measures that, if picked up by enemy intelligence, could reduce the incentives to preemptive attack. Moreover, a policy of no immediate nuclear retaliation would allow time in a preattack, or even immediate postattack, situation to bring to maximum readiness the various command and control arrangements that would be required to keep all military operations completely responsive to the top political leadership's requirements for controlling and terminating hostilities.[35]

ESTABLISHING PRIORITIES
AND MANAGING CONTRADICTIONS

Not all of the policies recommended can be pursued simultaneously and with equal emphasis. Situation by situation, some will have to be subordinated to others temporarily because of the immediacy of a threat to peace or the rapidity with which an ongoing conflict is escalating toward nuclear holocaust. Long-term projects may need to be put on hold while dangerous crises are being controlled. And terrible judgments will sometimes have to be made to sacrifice some values, even lives, in order to avoid more awful consequences.

It is not possible to prescribe in detail, before the unfolding of events, precisely which priorities should be established and exactly how the contradictions should be resolved. But this does not mean that policymakers and public interest groups should beg off completely from attempting to set priorities and formulate guidelines for the management of those crises that can be anticipated. Some priorities emerge from situations that we are already in; some basic judgments must be made today about what policies to set in motion now if we are to counter the most dangerous threats likely to confront the world in the near future.

The analysis in these pages has attempted to provide a basis for the needed integrated strategy of war prevention and control—a strategy that can be embraced, at least by the United States, as consistent with its basic security and well-being, and that is not inconsistent with the basic security and well-being of the Soviet Union and of most of the other countries in the world.

Let me underscore, then, the prescriptive conclusions of this book by recapitulating in abbreviated form the policy imperatives essential to an integrated strategy:

1. *Work to prevent all war*—by the mobilization of moral concern, by enhancing institutions and processes of conflict resolution, by geopolitical and diplomatic policies of depolarization—but

if war starts anywhere in the international system, work urgently to quarantine it against superpower involvement on opposite sides.

2. *Work to prevent any war between the United States and the Soviet Union*; but if war between them should start, give highest priority to controlling its escalation and stopping the fighting between them, even if this means allowing fighting among other belligerents to continue.

3. *Reinforce the firebreak between conventional and nuclear war.* Keep this barrier psychologically profound and technically difficult to cross; but in the event of its being breached, especially in a U.S.-Soviet war, then do everything possible to limit the combat geographically to ensure that the territories of the United States and the Soviet Union are not brought under attack.

4. *Localize and quarantine any nuclear combat to keep attacks away from the homelands of the superpowers*; but if a nuclear war does become "strategic," in the sense of involving direct attacks on the territory of the superpowers, then give immediate and overriding priority to totally terminating the nuclear attacks—and short of that to limiting nuclear strikes to purely military targets, minimizing collateral damage to people, and keeping leadership groups alive to negotiate the essential cease-fires and deescalations.

These policy imperatives raise dilemmas that could become stark in attempts to implement the integrated strategy. The dilemmas should not be glossed over. It is better to highlight them by singling out the five most bothersome questions, starting from the level of strategic nuclear war and working our way down:

1. How can we prepare for controlling and limiting strategic nuclear war without undermining the most important deterrent to the onset of such a war—the prospect that any strategic nuclear war will surely lead to the destruction of everything we and the enemy value, and that no strategic war therefore can ever be worth fighting for either side?

2. And how can we prepare to fight tactical or battlefield nuclear wars without undermining the crucial firebreak between conventional and nuclear wars, which is based on fears that any nuclear war, no matter how localized at the outset, will spread uncontrollably to become a strategic nuclear war?

3. And how can we shore up the firebreak between conventional and nuclear war without making a big conventional war less risky and therefore more likely to start—thereby increasing the prospect of a war between the superpowers, which could plunge the world into nuclear holocaust anyway?

4. How can we try to make any war between the United States and the Soviet Union totally impermissible without thereby undermining their respective alliance systems, or tempting each superpower to pick on smaller powers under the assumption (which may be a fatal miscalculation) that the other superpower will be inhibited from intervening on behalf of its friends?

5. And finally, if we try to transcend all these dilemmas by working to transform the world from its anarchic and war-prone condition—assuming that we do find some better way to structure world society—what should we do in the meantime, before the new world system is in place, to ensure that a world remains to transform tomorrow and the next day?

The "solutions" (the quotation marks indicate that there are no complete solutions, only approximations, to these terrible dilemmas) are partly suggested by the questions themselves: in large part they must be sought in, and created out of, the process of attempting to implement the integrated strategy. Surely there are risks; but the new risks need to be balanced against the risks involved in persisting with policies we have identified as clearly threatening to the continued survival of the human species.

The recommended strategy for war prevention and control is not a filled-in blueprint for survival. It contains some specific here-and-now policy imperatives, but it is also a set of desiderata for specific policies we have yet to invent:

- *We must search for and be inventive in designing the means of controlling and stopping any strategic war short of total holocaust, but in ways that do not increase the likelihood of one starting.*
- *We must search for and be inventive in designing means for controlling and quarantining local nuclear wars, but in ways that do not undermine the crucial conventional/nuclear firebreak.*
- *We must search for and be inventive in designing means of keeping conflicts, especially conflicts between the superpowers,*

*from becoming violent, without prematurely dismantling the
deterrent forces, including local balances of military power,
that constitute disincentives to waging war.*

- *We must take up the immense challenge of designing and
constructing a new world order without letting the process
undermine the features of the existing world society that we still
need to rely on to prevent and control war.*

NOTES

1. National Conference of Catholic Bishops on War and Peace, *The Challenge of Peace: God's Promise and Our Response* (Washington, D.C.: United States Catholic Conference, 1983).

2. For another approach to the need to give weight to moral considerations in national security decisions, see Joseph S. Nye, Jr., *Nuclear Ethics* (New York: Free Press, 1986). Nye's book is a useful primer on how to apply moral reasoning to matters of nuclear strategy and is less directed than is this chapter toward developing a consensus on certain basic imperatives.

3. National Research Council, *The Effects on the Atmosphere of a Major Nuclear Exchange* (Washington, D.C.: National Academy Press, 1985); Paul Ehrlich, Carl Sagan, Donald Kennedy, and Walter Orr Roberts, *The Cold and the Dark: The World After Nuclear War* (New York: Norton, 1984); A. B. Pittock, et al., *Environmental Consequences of Nuclear War, Volume I: Physical and Environmental Effects* (New York: Wiley, 1986); M. A. Harwell and T. C. Hutchinson, *Environmental Consequences of Nuclear War, Volume II: Ecological and Agricultural Effects* (New York: Wiley, 1985).

4. Carl Sagan, "Nuclear War and Climatic Catastrophe: Some Policy Implications," *Foreign Affairs* (Winter 1983/84), 3(62):257–292, quote from 292. See also the articles by Sagan and other scientists in *Science*, 222 (December 23, 1983), 1283–1300.

5. Starley L. Thompson and Stephen H. Schneider, "Nuclear Winter Reappraised," *Foreign Affairs* (Summer 1986), 64(5):981–1005. Sagan's reply is in the correspondence section of *Foreign Affairs* (Fall 1986), 65(1):163–168.

6. A view opposed to my philosophy for settling on relatively low thresholds at which to institute firm prohibitions on using weapons of mass destruction, especially nuclear weapons, is reflected in the argument by G. W. Rathjens and R. H. Siegel that such difficult policy decisions "should *not* be made on the basis of the possibility that nuclear winter cannot be excluded." (Rathjens and Siegel, "Nuclear Winter: Strategic Significance," *Issues in Science and Technology*, Winter 1985, p. 127.)

7. The Catholic bishops wrestled in their pastoral letter (*The Challenge of Peace*) with the issue of distinguishing clearly immoral uses of nuclear weapons from threats to use nuclear weapons in such ways for purposes of preventing the actuality of such uses. Unable to satisfactorily resolve the issue, they relied for the time being on the formulation by Pope John Paul II that "in current conditions 'deterrence' based on balance, certainly not as an end in itself but as a step on the way toward a progressive disarmament, may still be judged morally acceptable." For a hard-hitting critique of the bishops' position on this matter, see Albert Wohlstetter, "Bishops, Statesmen, and Other Strategists on the Bombing of Innocents," *Commentary* (June 1983), 75(6):15–44.

The United Methodist Council of Bishops, in a document largely modeled on the Catholic bishops' pastoral letter, have taken issue with the legitimation of conditional nuclear deterrence. The Methodist bishops argue that

the moral case for nuclear deterrence, even as an interim ethic, has been undermined by unrelenting arms escalation. Deterrence no longer serves, if it ever did, as a strategy that facilitates disarmament. . . .

Deterrence must no longer receive the churches' blessing, even as a temporary warrant for the maintenance of nuclear weapons. The interim possession of such weapons for a strictly limited time requires a different justification—*an ethic of reciprocity* as nuclear-weapons. states act together in agreed stages to reduce and ultimately to eliminate nuclear arms. (United Methodist Council of Bishops, *In Defense of Creation: The Nuclear Crisis and a Just Peace* [Nashville, Tenn: Graded Press, 1986], pp. 47–48)

Moved by these and other criticisms of the doctrine of conditional nuclear deterrence, the American Catholic bishops set up a special panel in 1986 to re-examine the morality of their 1983 position. The Rev. J. Bryan Hehir, one of the principal drafters of the 1983 pastoral letter, explained, "When you give conditional acceptance to deterrence, you have committed yourself to stay in the nuclear debate, because you obviously have to measure whether your conditions are being met." (Eric Pace, "Bishop's Panel to Re-evaluate Nuclear Deterrence," *New York Times*, May 4, 1986).

8. National Conference of Catholic Bishops, *The Challenge of Peace*, Sections 147 and 148.

9. See Susan Moller Okin, "Taking the Bishops Seriously," *World Politics* (July 1984), 36(4):527–554.

10. See Desmond Ball, "Can Nuclear War Be Controlled?" *Adelphi Papers*, No. 161 (London: International Institute for Strategic Studies, 1981).

11. These cases are, of course, often very difficult to judge (see the

discussion of "necessary" violence in Chapter 1). What, for example, is the moral content of the act of killing two thugs to prevent their killing a baby? Obviously, killing two in this situation (assuming no real alternatives are available) is not worse than allowing them to kill one. Indeed, many countries when they go to war, or contemplate going to war, conceive of their situations in analogous terms: the prevention of international thugs (aggressors) from attacking small and defenseless countries. The recognition of these complications is important, and the essence of statesmanship is to face them and deal with them as situations emerge; but all too often this "realistic" awareness of the complications is used as an excuse to throw away the moral rule book.

Granting these difficulties, the argument here is that these elementary moral premises remain essentially valid and should be part of an international consensus; and that the burden of justification should lie with those who would violate the moral premises. This posture is in fundamental opposition to the diplomacy of *realpolitik* and to the academic school of "realism" in international relations—both of which dismiss the function of moral considerations in international relations.

12. See the discussion in Chapter 9, pp. 197–204, on limiting the destructiveness of war.

13. Recent research shows that the top U.S. decision makers and their advisers were well aware, and in some cases bothered, by the realization that the use of the atomic bomb on Japanese cities was contrary to the traditional rules of proportional violence and the sparing of noncombatants. See Gar Alperovitz, *Atomic Diplomacy: Hiroshima and Potsdam* (New York: Penguin, 1985).

14. In late 1979 and 1980, the U.S. government regarded the Soviet invasion of Afghanistan as posing "a grave threat to the free movement of Middle Eastern oil," and consequently announced, in the so-called Carter Doctrine, that "any attempt by any outside force to gain control of the Persian Gulf region will be regarded as an assault on the vital interests of the United States. It will be repelled by use of any means necessary, including military force." President Jimmy Carter, State of the Union Address, January 23, 1980, *Weekly Compilation of Presidential Documents*, 16(4):194–203. In retrospect, however, the imputation to the Soviets of a serious intention to make a grab for control of Persian Gulf oil appears to have been unduly alarmist.

15. For a more extensive analysis of the essential characteristics of the nation-state system, its historical evolution, its inherent contradictions, and its prospects for change, see Seyom Brown, *New Forces, Old Forces, and the Transformation of World Politics* (Boston: Little, Brown, forthcoming).

16. Some of these ideas for structural reform were developed in Seyom

Brown, "New Forces Revisited: Lessons of a Turbulent Decade," *World Policy Journal*, Winter 1984, pp. 397–418.

17. Seyom Brown, Nina W. Cornell, Larry L. Fabian, and Edith Brown Weiss, *Regimes for the Ocean, Outer Space, and Weather* (Washington, D.C.: Brookings Institution, 1977).

18. Seyom Brown, "New Forces Revisited," p. 412.

19. Jimmy Carter, Address before the United Nations General Assembly, March 17, 1977.

20. Anticipating some of the contemporary challenges to the cold-war coalitions, I proposed in 1976—perhaps somewhat prematurely—in a Council on Foreign Relations study group, a transformation of alliances in Europe similar to the arrangement proposed here. The original proposal was published in my essay, "A World of Multiple Relationships," in the council book *Atlantis Lost: U.S.-European Relations After the Cold War*, edited by James Chace and Earl C. Ravenal (New York: New York University Press, 1976), pp. 103–118.

21. Useful insights into the dynamics of international bargaining during crises can be found in Richard Ned Lebow, *Between Peace and War* (Baltimore, Md.: Johns Hopkins University Press, 1981). On negotiating during war, see Paul R. Pillar, *Negotiating Peace: War Termination as a Bargaining Process* (Princeton, N.J.: Princeton University Press, 1983). For war termination specifically, see Fred Iklé, *Every War Must End* (New York: Columbia University Press, 1971); Nissan Oren, ed., *Termination of Wars: Processes, Procedures, and Aftermaths* (Jerusalem: Magnes Press, Hebrew University, 1982); and Clark C. Abt, *A Strategy for Terminating a Nuclear War* (Boulder, Colo.: Westview Press, 1985). On negotiations in general, see Howard Raiffa, *The Art and Science of Negotiation* (Cambridge, Mass.: Harvard University Press, 1982); and Roger Fisher and William Ury, *Getting to Yes: Negotiating Agreement Without Giving In* (Boston: Houghton Mifflin, 1981).

22. I have elaborated on the dangers of U.S.-Soviet games of chicken in my paper, "Confronting the Soviet Union: Why,Where, and How?" for the Eighth Annual National Security Affairs Conference (July 13–15, 1981) of the National Defense University, published by the National Defense University Press in 1981 in *The 1980s: Decade of Confrontation?* See also my essay, "Power and Prudence in Dealing with the USSR," in Richard A. Melanson, ed., *Neither Cold War Nor Detente? Soviet-American Relations in the 1980s* (Charlottesville: University Press of Virginia, 1982), pp. 215–236.

23. Imaginative and realistic suggestions for improving crisis communications between the superpowers are outlined in William Langer Ury and Richard Smoke, *Beyond the Hotline: Controlling a Nuclear Crisis* (Cambridge, Mass.: Nuclear Negotiation Project, Harvard Law School, 1984).

24. Final Document of the First United Nations Special Session Devoted to Disarmament, UN Document, A/RES/S-10/2, 13 July 1978, Section 52.

25. Treaty on the Non-Proliferation of Nuclear Weapons, in United States Arms Control and Disarmament Agency, *Arms Control and Disarmament Agreements* (Washington, D.C.: U.S. Government Printing Office, 1982), pp. 91–95.

26. For a worldwide assessment of capabilities to make nuclear weapons, see Leonard S. Spector's study for the Carnegie Endowment for International Peace, *Nuclear Proliferation Today* (New York: Vintage, 1984).

27. The argument that a spread of nuclear weapons to many countries would advance world peace was developed by the French strategist Pierre Gallois in his *Balance of Terror* (Boston: Houghton Mifflin, 1961). It has been most prominently supported in the United States by the international relations theorist Kenneth Waltz in his "What Will the Spread of Nuclear Weapons Do to the World?" in John Kerry King, ed., *International Political Effects of the Spread of Nuclear Weapons* (Washington, D.C.: U.S. Government Printing Office, 1979). Similar arguments from an Israeli point of view are presented by Shai Feldman, *Israeli Nuclear Deterrence: A Strategy for the 1980s* (New York: Columbia University Press, 1982).

28. The lack of sufficient fresh thinking on how to deal with the nuclear proliferation dilemma is revealed in the recommendation by Graham T. Allison, Albert Carnesale, and Joseph S. Nye, Jr.: "*Do maintain security guarantees.* While several factors push countries in the direction of nuclear weapons, concern for national security clearly leads the list. Accordingly, the United States should maintain and reinforce its guarantees of security wherever credible, as in Europe, Japan, and Korea." In *Hawks, Doves, and Owls: An Agenda for Avoiding Nuclear War* (New York: Norton, 1985), p. 239.

29. For measures to secure survivable command and control systems, see Bruce G. Blair, *Strategic Command and Control: Redefining the Nuclear Threat* (Washington, D.C.: Brookings Institution, 1985).

30. See, for example, the counterarguments raised by a group of West German strategists (typical of other European reaction) to the 1982 proposal by a group of American strategists that NATO adopt a policy of no first use of nuclear weapons simultaneously with a buildup of its conventional forces. The debate was initiated by McGeorge Bundy, George F. Kennan, Robert S. McNamara, and Gerard Smith in "Nuclear Weapons and the Atlantic Alliance," *Foreign Affairs* (Spring 1982), 60(4):753–768; the German counterarguments appeared in Karl Kaiser, George Leber, Alois Mertes, and Franz-Josef Schulze, "Nuclear Weapons and the Preservation of Peace," *Foreign Affairs* (Summer 1982), 60(5):1157–1170, followed by "The Authors Reply," in the same journal, pp. 1178–1180.

31. On the offer of nuclear weapons for tanks see William R. Bowman,

Limiting Conventional Forces in Europe (Washington, D.C.: National Defense University Press, 1985), pp. 16–19.

32. Bundy et al., *Foreign Affairs* (Spring 1982), 60(4):753–758.

33. Bernard Brodie, "The Development of Nuclear Strategy," *International Security*, Spring 1978, p. 79. See also the eloquent plea for a war-termination strategy by Leon Wieseltier in his "When Deterrence Fails," *Foreign Affairs* (Spring 1985), 63(4):827–847.

34. I endorse the arguments of Desmond Ball, Robert Jervis, and other strategic analysts that the low likelihood of being able to control the escalation of a nuclear exchange calls for rejection of strategic "war-winning" strategies. I disagree, however, with the conclusion that because of this high uncontrollability we should give up trying to build greater postattack control into the superpower strategic arsenals, gambling instead on assured destruction to deter any strategic war from starting in the first place. See Desmond Ball, "Can Nuclear War Be Controlled?" and Robert Jervis, *The Illogic of American Nuclear Deterrence* (Ithaca, N.Y.: Cornell University Press, 1984).

35. The rationale and essential features of the *no immediate second use of nuclear weapons* policy are presented in greater detail in Blair's *Strategic Command and Control*, pp. 289–295. There is much wisdom in his conclusion that "retaliation might not be swift, but it would be sure and would be better aligned with coherent national purposes. Such a prospect would surely not invite aggression; it would instead bolster deterrence" (p. 295).

Index

Growth, maturation, and body composition documents one of the most remarkable and significant long-term studies in the field of human biology. The Fels Longitudinal Study is the longest, largest and most productive serial study of human growth, maturation and body composition. This book shows how data collected from more than 1000 participants during the past 60 years have been analysed to test a wide range of hypotheses, and describes how the findings have led to the development of improved research methods. With more than 1000 specialized publications of Fels data to date, the present book provides a unique overview of this fascinating research program, which will be of interest to a wide range of researchers, including those in the fields of physical anthropology, nutrition science, pediatrics, gerontology, epidemiology, endocrinology, human genetics, as well as statistics.

Cambridge Studies in Biological Anthropology 9

Growth, maturation, and body composition
the Fels Longitudinal Study 1929–1991

Cambridge Studies in Biological Anthropology

Series Editors

G.W. Lasker
Department of Anatomy, Wayne State University,
Detroit, Michigan, USA

C.G.N. Mascie-Taylor
Department of Biological Anthropology,
University of Cambridge

D.F. Roberts
Department of Human Genetics,
University of Newcastle-upon-Tyne

R.A. Foley
Department of Biological Anthropology,
University of Cambridge

Also in the series

G.W. Lasker *Surnames and Genetic Structure*
C.G.N. Mascie-Taylor and G.W. Lasker (editors) *Biological Aspects of Human Migration*
Barry Bogin *Patterns of Human Growth*
Julius A. Kieser *Human Adult Odontometrics – The study of variation in adult tooth size*
J.E. Lindsay Carter and Barbara Honeyman Heath *Somatotyping – Development and applications*
Roy J. Shephard *Body Composition in Biological Anthropology*
Ashley H. Robins *Biological Perspectives on Human Pigmentation*
C.G.N. Mascie-Taylor and G.W. Lasker (editors) *Applications of Biological Anthropology to Human Affairs*

Growth, maturation, and body composition

the Fels Longitudinal Study
1929–1991

ALEX F. ROCHE

Professor of Community Health and Pediatrics, Wright State University,
Dayton, Ohio, USA

 **CAMBRIDGE**
UNIVERSITY PRESS

Published by the Press Syndicate of the University of Cambridge
The Pitt Building, Trumpington Street, Cambridge CB2 1RP
40 West 20th Street, New York, NY 10011–4211, USA
10 Stamford Road, Oakleigh, Victoria 3166, Australia

© Cambridge University Press 1992

First published 1992

Printed in Great Britain at the University Press, Cambridge

A catalogue record for this book is available from the British Library

Library of Congress cataloguing in publication data available

ISBN 0 521 37449 9 hardback

UP

To
Stanley Marion Garn

with respect and admiration for his unlimited energy and vision

Contents

Preface

I am fortunate to have been able to write this book. This good fortune began with my appointment to the Fels Staff 23 years ago. It has taken me all that time to understand the complexities of the Fels Longitudinal Study. Writing this book about the study has been a pleasure. I trust the reader will find it pleasant also. Quoting Daniel Defoe: 'If this work is not both pleasant and profitable to the reader ... the fault ... cannot be any deficiency in the subject.'

Many helped. Some added to the quality of the study, particularly the generous participants and their relatives, outstanding collaborators and consultants, efficient secretaries and dedicated research assistants. Particular thanks are due to Ruth Bean and Lois Croutwater who, during a joint span of more than 56 years of extraordinary effort, have organized the examinations and maintained contact with the participants. Doctors Lester Sontag and Frank Falkner, the past Directors, provided effective leadership from 1929 to 1979. The Fels Longitudinal Study, supported in its early years by the Samuel S. Fels Fund, continues as part of the Division of Human Biology of the Department of Community Health at Wright State University. This division receives enthusiastic support from the Departmental Chairman (Dr Robert Reece), the School of Medicine and the central administration of Wright State University. Continuation of this support is important because the story is not complete. The significance of the Fels Longitudinal Study increases as the data base enlarges, the serial records become longer, and new techniques are introduced. Additionally, the focus of the Study is shifting rapidly to more applied areas.

Many helped write this book, but they are not to blame for its defects. Jean Bolin prepared the illustrations, and Joan Hunter typed all the early drafts. The later drafts, typed by the helpful staff of the Word Processing Center in the School of Medicine, were read by Rick Baumgartner, Cameron Chumlea, Shumei Guo, Roger Siervogel, and my wife, Eileen. Nancy Kern of the Health Sciences Library and Cheryl Caddell were indefatigable in their search for sources and Jane Smith copy-edited the manuscript thoroughly and pleasantly. The Samuel S. Fels Fund provided encouragement and generous financial assistance. Last in this sequence,

but not least in importance, are Dr Alan Crowden and Dr Sara Trevitt of the Cambridge University Press who waited patiently for the delayed manuscript and guided it through all stages of the publication process in a charming and effective manner. To all these friends, I am most grateful.

Alex F. Roche

Abbreviations

BD = body density (g/cc)
DNA = deoxyribonucleic acid
LPCA = longitudinal principal component analysis
P = probability
PHV = age at peak height velocity (years)
PTC = phenylthiocarbamide
R = resistance (ohms)
SD = standard deviation
S = stature (cm)
W = weight (kg)
X_c = reactance (ohms)
Z = impedance (ohms)
Φ = phase angle (degrees)

1   *Introduction*

What has been accomplished is only an earnest of what shall be done in the future. Upon our heels a fresh perfection must tread, born of us, fated to excel us. We have but served and have but seen a beginning. Personally, I feel deeply grateful to have been permitted to join in this noble work and to have been united in it with men (and women) of such high and human ideas.

William Osler (1849–1919)

The above quotation from the writings of Sir William Osler is fully appropriate. It has been an honor for me to work in the Fels Longitudinal Study. Indeed, all the members of the Fels staff are fully conscious of their debt to those who laid the foundations for the studies that are summarized in this volume. Although much has been achieved, all realize that those who follow will greatly extend our present limited horizons.

This book describes the progress that has been made during the first 60 years of the Fels Longitudinal Study of Growth, Maturation and Body Composition. The remarkable nature of the study justifies this volume. Very few, if any, investigations of human beings are so longlived. Despite its longevity, the Fels Longitudinal Study continually becomes more vigorous and active. Few studies have been responsible for equally important research related to serial changes in physical growth and maturation and body composition in normal individuals.

The Fels Research Institute was founded in 1929 with a single complex research project that came to be called the Fels Longitudinal Study. As the name implies, this was a serial study and it was multidisciplinary. Between 1927 and 1932 several such studies were founded in the US, which in addition to the Fels Longitudinal Study, included the Bolton–Brush Study at Western Reserve University (Cleveland, Ohio), the Berkeley Growth Study, Guidance Study, and Oakland Growth Study at the Institute of Human Development of the University of California (Berkeley), the Child

Research Council Study at the University of Colorado (Denver), and the Harvard School of Public Health Growth Study (Boston, Massachusetts).

This sudden rush to begin serial multidisciplinary studies of child growth and development between 1927 and 1932 sprang, in part, from desires to shield children from the worst effects of the Great Depression. These same concerns led to the 1933 White House Conference on Child Health and Protection which recommended that such studies be undertaken. It was recognized that further knowledge was required to determine both the effects of the Great Depression and the possible influence of programs intended to mitigate these effects.

Serial data for individuals were recorded in each of these studies but, generally, the data were analyzed cross-sectionally. Each study had its area of concentration and outstanding expertise. The Bolton–Brush Study was responsible for major advances in methods for the study of craniofacial growth (Broadbent, 1931; Broadbent, Broadbent & Golden, 1975), and of maturation (Greulich & Pyle, 1959), and useful information was provided about growth changes in various anthropometric dimensions (Simmons, 1944). This study is scarcely active, although occasional use is made of the records which are intact but not in an electronic format.

The three studies at Berkeley (Berkeley Growth Study, Guidance Study, Oakland Growth Study) were responsible for important research contributions in child growth, psychology and sociology, including advances in methods for the analysis of serial data and the measurement of psychological development. The results of these studies have been summarized by Jones *et al.* (1971). The Berkeley group of studies is now inactive except for occasional sociological studies of participants in adulthood.

The Child Research Council Study contributed valuable information about diet, tissue growth, electrocardiography and basal metabolic rate, although few of the analyses were serial. Data collection in this study ceased in 1968. Many of the recorded data are stored electronically and were reported by McCammon (1970). The Harvard School of Public Health Growth Study was responsible for influential advances in methods for the radiographic measurement of subcutaneous adipose tissue and substantial findings relating to tissue growth and skeletal maturation.

The designs of the Fels Longitudinal Study and the Child Research Council Study were similar in many respects. Each was a study of individuals within families and, in each case, the examinations continued at intervals during adulthood. Physical growth and maturation dominated the Child Research Council program, but there was an approximate balance between research activities in physical areas and in psychological areas in the Fels Longitudinal Study. The balance altered in the Fels Study

in 1974 when the collection of psychological data ceased and analysis of the existing psychological data slowed considerably.

A little history

Until 1977, the Fels Longitudinal Study was conducted within the Fels Research Institute and it included concomitant studies of cognitive development, behavior, and family functioning. These studies have been excluded from the present account, which is restricted to physical growth, physical maturation and body composition. In 1977, the Fels Research Institute became part of the School of Medicine at Wright State University and the Fels Longitudinal Study was subsumed as the Division of Human Biology, at first within the Department of Pediatrics and later within the Department of Community Health. Many other investigations by scientists in the Fels Research Institute or in its successor have been omitted from the present account because they were not derived from the Fels Longitudinal Study, even if they relate to the themes of this book.

Many are puzzled by the location of the Fels Longitudinal Study and the Fels Research Institute in Yellow Springs, unaffected by the flow of resources and expertise to large well-known universities such as Harvard and Stanford. The answer concerns two close friends, Arthur E. Morgan and Samuel S. Fels, who were responsible for the foundation of the study and of the institute. In 1929, Arthur Morgan was the President of Antioch College in Yellow Springs. Therefore, it was natural that, from their conception to their maturity, the study and the institute that these men initiated were in Yellow Springs and associated with Antioch College.

Arthur Morgan posed a question that sounds simple: 'What makes people different?' This is one of many questions that sound simple but are extremely difficult to answer. Mr Morgan concluded that a longitudinal study from conception to adulthood was required. He discussed this with many biologists and social scientists but they were skeptical. Mr Morgan was not deterred; he approached Mr Fels, a Philadelphia businessman and philanthropist, about his plans and did not conceal the doubts of the scientists whom he had consulted. Mr Fels was not troubled by the opinion of the 'experts.' Although he realized the results of the study would be delayed, he gave it enthusiastic support and financial backing.

The parents of Samuel Simeon Fels had come from Bavaria to Philadelphia in 1848. They stayed there briefly before moving to Virginia where Samuel Fels was born in 1860. In 1873, his family returned to Philadelphia and achieved financial success in soap manufacturing. For Samuel Fels, financial success was not an end in itself but a means to do

good. He used his wealth to assist the establishment and the work of many local, national and international causes that were related to education, labor laws, crime prevention, local government, science, and Jewish charities.

The early support by Samuel Fels of the program suggested by Arthur Morgan was given structure in 1932 when a corporation was established in Ohio. The purpose clause stated: 'The principal initial problem to which the organization shall devote its energies is the furtherance of knowledge of the effect of physical, emotional, and nutritional environment during and shortly after the period of gestation upon the physical and mental constitution of the child.' This is remarkable because, at that time, there was widespread scientific belief that a fetus was shielded from environmental effects. Time has shown the wisdom of the stated purpose which matched the attitude expressed by Samuel Fels in his 1933 book 'This Changing World.' He wrote that long-term studies of large groups of children should be made and they 'should begin before the child is born and continue to maturity.' In 1935, the Ohio Corporation was replaced by the Samuel S. Fels Fund which was incorporated in Pennsylvania with much broader charter purposes that matched the wide-ranging interests of Samuel Fels.

The Fels Longitudinal Study began in 1929 with the appointment of Lester W. Sontag as the Director. At that time, Lester Sontag was the Physician at Antioch College in Yellow Springs, having recently received his MD degree from the University of Minnesota. Dr Sontag received further training at various major centers in the US while he planned the Fels Longitudinal Study. The examinations of participants began in 1930 when the institute had a staff of three and an annual budget of $5000. While the institute was small, Lester Sontag was deeply involved in all the research and also managed administrative matters. Until his retirement in 1970, he continued to be active in research concerning skeletal maturation, skeletal variations and developmental changes in intelligence. His major contribution, however, was the foundation and nurturing of the Fels Longitudinal Study which he directed during a long period of growth and increasing effectiveness, and from its initiation under the protective umbrella of Antioch College to the status of a free-standing institution in 1947.

The Fels Research Institute was owned and operated by the Fels Fund of Philadelphia, with considerable assistance from the US Government through grants and contracts. This arrangement continued until 1977 when, as a result of increasing financial strains, the Fels Fund donated the institute to the School of Medicine at Wright State University, with an

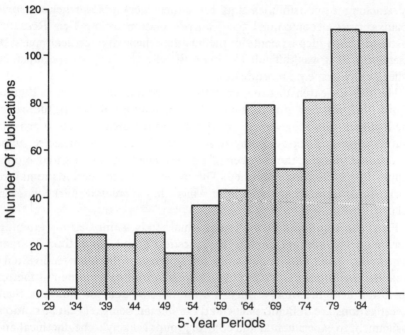

Fig. 1.1 The number of publications (articles, chapters, books, and monographs) dealing with physical growth and maturation from the Fels Longitudinal Study within 5-year periods. The numbers on the horizontal axis refer to calendar years at the beginning of these periods (e.g., '29 = 1929–1933).

agreement to fund the institute for a further 5 years. Wright State University is situated in Dayton, about 8 miles (13 km) from the institute. It was expected that the institute would be beneficial to the school of medicine that had just been established at the university by providing an immediate research base. This expectation was realized to some extent, but the institute was fragmented when part was moved to the main campus and it rapidly became weaker and smaller as scientists who resigned or retired were not replaced. Now, the institute is reduced to the Division of Developmental Psychology in the Department of Psychiatry and the Division of Human Biology in the Department of Community Health. Both these divisions are located in Yellow Springs near the building that housed the institute from 1947 through 1984.

On balance, the decision to locate the Fels Longitudinal Study and the Fels Research Institute in Yellow Springs was a good one. The local population is more stable in place of residence than is usual in the US; this stability is very important for a long-term serial study. Since the institute was not on a university campus, the professional staff were not burdened

by teaching responsibilities and committee work. Nevertheless, some disadvantages accompanied the relative isolation of the Fels Research Institute. Each department in the institute lacked a critical mass of scientists and it was difficult to obtain the effective help of specialists in other disciplines, e.g., biostatistics.

The Fels Research Institute grew from its commencement in 1929 until about 1968, whether growth is judged by the number of staff or the size of the building. The achievements of the staff in research related to growth, maturation, and body composition are difficult to measure. One inadequate guide is the number of articles, chapters, books and monographs that have been published. The totals for 5-year periods remained fairly stable until about 1954, after which they increased markedly (Fig. 1.1).

From the beginning of the longitudinal study, some serious attempts were made to address directly the question posed by Arthur Morgan concerning what was responsible for differences between individuals. Analyses were made to determine the influence of environmental factors operating near the time of birth on the development of children. Such investigations are difficult, particularly in human beings, because random assignment to experimental and control groups is likely to be unethical and unacceptable. These topics were studied at Fels in what are sometimes called 'natural experiments' without controlling the conditions. With this approach, the data must be adjusted statistically for the influences of intervening variables. Consequently, large samples are required and data must be collected for many variables that could influence the results. Even then, the findings from such studies commonly remain inferential. Any observed effects may be due to another variable or set of variables for which data were not collected.

Instead of beginning with the recognition and measurement of effects, the institute staff, quite properly, began by describing the status and patterns of change with age in variables related to growth, maturity and body composition. In this they followed the wise advice of William Harvey: 'I am of the opinion that our first duty is to inquire whether a thing be or not, before asking wherefore it is.' Throughout its history, the Fels Longitudinal Study has resulted in many hypotheses that have been tested by the analysis of facts.

Until about 1945, almost all the research activities of the Fels Research Institute concerned the longitudinal study. In those days, the longitudinal study *was* the institute. In subsequent years, many other projects were located in the institute; some of these did not have direct relationships to the hypotheses that could be tested using data from the longitudinal study.

Biographical sketches

Brief biographical sketches follow, ordered alphabetically, of some of the scientists who worked at the Fels Research Institute and were leaders in the analysis of data relating to growth, maturation, and body composition. The list does not include the many scientists who worked at the Fels Research Institute in areas such as biochemistry, endocrinology, psychology and physiology. Others who came to Fels for short periods to work in the areas of growth, maturation and body composition so that they could share their special skills or acquire new ones are not listed. Many of these visitors and fellows reported analyses of Fels data, as is clear from the author index which contains the names of many distinguished scientitsts. The years in parentheses after each name in the following sketches give the period during which the scientist worked at the institute.

Richard N. Baumgartner (1985–1990). Rick Baumgartner received a PhD in Public Health from the University of Texas at Houston in 1982. He has contributed greatly to the longitudinal study by supervising the measurement procedures and by analyzing serial changes in patterns of adipose tissue distribution (fat patterns) and their relationships to risk factors for cardiovascular disease and to diabetes. In addition, he investigated new methods for the measurement of body composition including electrical impedance, computed tomography, and magnetic resonance imaging.

Pamela Byard (1981–1982). Pam Byard obtained a PhD degree in Biological Anthropology from the University of Kansas in 1981. While at the Fels Research Institute, she worked partly in Roger Siervogel's study of blood pressures within large family groups. She has also analyzed data from the Fels Longitudinal Study both while at Fels and after she left. These analyses concerned familial associations for growth, body composition and craniofacial variables and secular changes in body composition variables.

Wm Cameron Chumlea (1978–). Cameron Chumlea obtained a PhD in Physical Anthropology from the University of Texas at Austin in 1978. He was responsible for all measurement procedures in the Fels Longitudinal Study until 1985 and plays an important part in the general design of the study. One of his major research interests is the assessment of nutritional status from body measurements, especially in the elderly. He is prominent in research related to adipocytes (fat cells), body composition,

bioelectric impedance, the measurement of total body water, and the assessment of skeletal maturity.

Christine E. Cronk (1980–1982). Chris Cronk was awarded a DSc degree by the Harvard School of Public Health in 1980. While she worked in the Division of Human Biology, her research addressed the application of recently developed statistical methods to analyses of serial body composition data. She also developed national reference data and reported studies of growth and body composition in children with Down syndrome.

Frank Falkner (1971–1979). Frank Falkner received his medical training in England where he graduated in 1945, becoming a Fellow of the Royal College of Physicians in 1972. He succeeded Lester Sontag as the Director and steered the institute through a period of financial and administrative difficulties. In addition, he established the Fels Division of Pediatric Research at the University of Cincinnati and began a multinational study of infant mortality. While at Fels, Dr Falkner's personal research related to the assessment of nutritional status, infant mortality, and the joint editorship, with James M. Tanner, of a three-volume treatise on human growth.

Stanley M. Garn (1952–1968). Stanley Garn obtained a PhD in Physical Anthropology from Harvard University in 1948. During a stay of exactly 16 years as Chairman of the Department of Growth and Genetics, he gave the institute national and international prominence by his many publications and his answers to novel questions. Dr Garn's major research contributions related to skeletal and dental maturation, age changes in subcutaneous adipose tissue, the gain and loss of bone substance, and the sizes and shapes of teeth.

Shumei Guo (1985–   ). Shumei Guo received her PhD in Biostatistics from the University of Pittsburgh in 1983. She is in charge of all statistical matters in the Division of Human Biology, including the management of our large and complex data bases. In addition to acting as a statistical consultant to other staff members, Dr Guo is particularly active in the development of new methods for the analysis of serial data, in the use of new procedures to construct equations that predict body composition variables from values that are relatively easy to obtain, and in the analysis of risk factors for cardiovascular disease.

John H. Himes (1976–1979). John Himes obtained a PhD in Physical

Anthropology from the University of Texas at Austin in 1975. While working in the Division of Human Biology, he supervised data collection for studies of body composition and hearing ability. His main research interests concerned bone lengths, the estimation of stature from bone lengths, the correct interpretation of observed statures, the hearing ability of children in relation to noise exposure, the assessment of nutritional status, body composition, and the provision of reference data for growth rates.

Harry Israel III (1964–1975). Harry Israel obtained his DDS degree from the University of Michigan in 1956 and a PhD degree from the University of Alabama in Birmingham in 1971. During the long period that he worked part-time at the Fels Research Institute, his research interests were related to growth and aging in the craniofacial part of the skeleton, variations in the bones of the fingers, aging of vertebrae, and the radiographic density of bones and teeth.

Arthur B. Lewis (1939–   ). Arthur Lewis obtained his DDS degree from Ohio State University in 1933 and was awarded an MS in Orthodontics by the University of Illinois in 1935. He has a remarkable half-century record of part-time voluntary work at the Fels Research Institute. His research publications describe the sizes and shapes of teeth, dental development including its genetic control, the occasional failure of teeth to develop, and craniofacial growth.

Debabrata Mukherjee (1980–1984). Debu Mukherjee received a PhD in Biostatistics from the University of Alabama in Birmingham in 1980. At the Fels Research Institute, he was responsible for statistical analyses and the management of data bases. His main publications concerned serial analyses related to body composition, hearing ability, craniofacial growth, the development of equations to predict body composition variables, infant growth patterns, and the measurement of skeletal mass.

Earle L. Reynolds (1943–1951). Soon after he obtained a PhD degree from the University of Wisconsin, Earle Reynolds came to the Fels Research Institute as Chairman of the Department of Growth and Genetics. While at Fels, he published landmark papers dealing with age changes in adipose and other tissues, the growth of the pelvis, and methods for grading the development of secondary sex characters.

Meinhard Robinow (1939–1943). Meinhard Robinow obtained his MD

degree from the University of Hamburg in 1934. While at the Fels Research Institute, he made very thorough physical examinations of the participants and recorded his findings in a script that was very easy to read. His research publications related to the maturation of bones and teeth, methods for grading the posture of children, and the provision of reference data for growth rates.

Alex F. Roche (1968–   ). The present author graduated in medicine from the University of Melbourne (MB, BS) in 1946 and subsequently received PhD, DSc and MD degrees from the same university before becoming a Fellow of the Royal Australasian College of Physicians. He came to the institute as Chairman of the Department of Growth and Genetics and was later Head of the Division of Human Biology and Director of the Fels Longitudinal Study. He is in charge of research relating to physical growth, maturation, and genetics. His research interests include growth of the whole body and of the craniofacial region, skeletal maturation, the prediction of adult stature, body composition, risk factors for cardiovascular disease, hearing ability in relation to noise exposure, and methods for the analysis of serial data.

Roger M. Siervogel (1974–   ). Roger Siervogel obtained a PhD in Human Genetics from the University of Oregon in 1971. He has led the Fels Division of Human Biology into the computer age and is active in research related to body composition, risk factors for cardiovascular disease especially blood pressure, dermatoglyphic patterns, hearing ability in children in relation to noise exposure, and genetic and familial factors that affect these traits.

Lester W. Sontag (1929–1970). Soon after graduating in medicine from the University of Minnesota in 1926, Lester Sontag became the resident physician at Antioch College, and in 1929 he was appointed as the Founding Director of the Fels Research Institute. His research work, in relation to the topics covered in this book, concerned prenatal growth, nutrition, genetics, the growth and maturation of bones, and basal metabolic rate. After 1945, Dr Sontag's interests became more behavioral and his administrative activities occupied more of his time.

The major US longitudinal studies

Sontag (1971)[281], in an illuminating review of the major longitudinal studies in the US, drew attention to the changes that had occurred in these studies since they began in the late 1920s and early 1930s. All of them

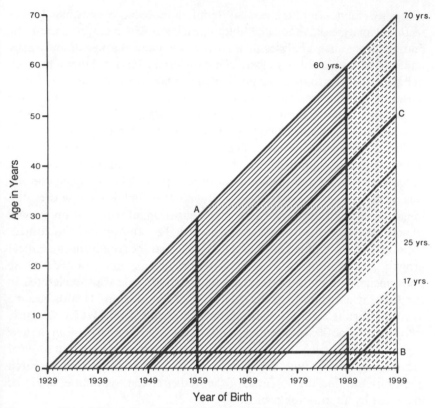

Fig. 1.2 The design of the Fels Longitudinal Study with lines drawn to illustrate subsets of the data that could be analyzed separately. An analysis of data crossed by line A could furnish information about the status of participants in 1959. The data crossed by line B could provide data about 2-year-old children, and those exemplified by line C could be informative about patterns of growth.

started with a global approach – the aim was to study the whole child until adulthood with an emphasis on the variations between children in their patterns of change. This serial multidisciplinary goal was a tall order for which the measurement and analytic procedures were grossly inadequate at that time.

As a result, masses of data were collected in the major US longitudinal studies. Many of the variables were of dubious value in the study of normal children although data of the same type were useful in clinical diagnosis. The studies began without hypotheses and this, in large part, explains the unselective accumulation of data. Almost all the early reports were cross-sectional and descriptive. The decision to publish cross-sectional reports was mandated by the nature of the data base early in the studies but it

continued long after analyses of serial data became possible. Cross-sectional analyses have considerable appeal because it is easy to present the findings from such analyses in ways that are clinically useful and easily understood, unlike findings from complex serial analyses. Due to the lack of balance between data collection and data analysis and the unimaginative nature of the analyses, the more productive scientists tended to leave the longitudinal studies during the 1930s and 1940s, while those who were satisfied with the accurate collection of data tended to stay.

This situation did not last. The studies were forced to change as the foundations that supported them became discouraged at the small number of research reports and the nature of these reports. The changing attitude was expressed rather vaguely by Reynolds (1949a) who wrote: '... longitudinal data appear to give much superior information on growth trends.' More precise attitudes were needed. The studies began to address hypotheses that centered around the concept that the conditions that affect growth, maturation or risk factors for disease may precede these phenomena by long intervals. This change in attitude was accelerated in the 1950s when support from the National Institutes of Health became available through a grant mechanism that included reviews by scientists who were hypothesis oriented. This did not necessarily mean a new beginning. Gradually, the scientists within the studies realized that some of the existing serial data could be used to answer important research questions and that the potential of the studies to test hypotheses could be increased by altering the protocols.

The Fels Longitudinal Study

The design of the Fels Longitudinal Study matched that of the Child Research Council Study that had started in Denver, Colorado, two years before the former began. Originally the Fels Study was to continue until the participants were 16 years old, then its termination was delayed to 18 years, and still later it was extended into adulthood without mention of a final age. These extensions have added to our ability to answer research questions of great health-related significance.

The design of the Fels Longitudinal Study is shown in Fig. 1.2. The horizontal axis shows the calendar years since 1929 when the study commenced and the vertical axis refers to the ages of the participants. The oblique lines trace the passage of each annual cohort as its members become older. The vertical line passing through 1989 represents the recent state of the study as it cuts across the lines for cohorts at ages from birth to 60 years. The interrupted oblique lines to the right of this vertical line represent the planned enrollment of additional cohorts and the changes

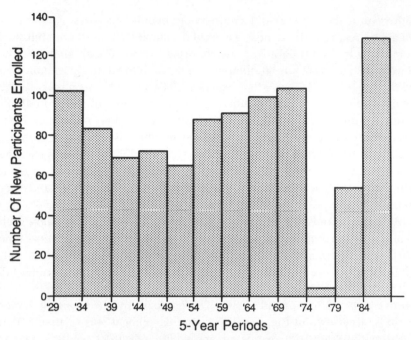

Fig. 1.3 The number of new participants enrolled by 5-year calendar periods;
the numbers on the horizontal axis refer to the calendar years at the beginning
of each period (e.g., ′29 = 1929–1933).

that will occur in the ages of all participants up to 1999. Figure 1.2 does not
indicate one important change with time in the protocol for the Fels
Longitudinal Study. Since it began there has been a marked increase in the
number of variables measured; the increase has been very rapid since 1974
and became possible at this time when the collection of psychological data
stopped. The present physical program, in terms of the number of
procedures and the time required for a set of examinations, would have
been too onerous for the participants if combined with the previous
psychological program.

This diagram of the Fels design in Fig. 1.2 represents not only the
pattern of enrollments and examinations but also the nature of the data
base; it can be used to illustrate some of the analytic possibilities. A vertical
slice through the data would allow, for example, the analysis of all the
measurements recorded in 1959 as indicated by the vertical line (A) in Fig.
1.2. The results could provide information about the status of individuals
between birth and 30 years of age. Alternatively, a horizontal slice (B)
could be made through the data as shown by the line drawn through the
figure at the 2-year level. The analysis of the data in this slice could provide

information about 2-year-old children born in different years; conclusions might be reached about possible secular changes and the possibility of combining (pooling) data from neighboring cohorts for an analysis. The third possibility is to cut an oblique slice through the data set as indicated by the line (C) in the figure that begins at 1949 on the horizontal axis. The analysis of the data in this oblique slice could provide information about changes within individuals. Such an analysis is not likely to be effective if restricted to those enrolled in one calendar year because the annual cohorts are small. If cohorts are combined, this type of analysis presents exciting possibilities that cannot be achieved without access to longitudinal data. This third analytic possibility directs attention to the exciting and very unusual nature of the Fels data base.

Between 12 and 20 participants were enrolled into the Fels study each year during the pregnancy of the mother, and the first measurements of the participants were made near the time of birth. At the time of enrollment, all the families lived in the southwestern part of Ohio within 30 miles (48 km) of the Fels Research Institute. Now, five of the active participants live abroad and 150 live outside Ohio. The numbers enrolled, during 5-year periods, are shown in Fig. 1.3. The rate of enrollment was relatively high early in the study but decreased gradually until 1949 to 1953. It has increased since then, except for the period 1974 to 1981 when enrollment was suspended due to lack of funds.

There are 1036 Fels participants, of whom 537 have been examined during the past 8 years. In addition, data have been recorded from many non-participant relatives who have been examined less frequently. Some participants were lost from the study due to early death (miscarriages, stillbirths, neonatal deaths), but most of the loss of participants from the study reflects unwillingness to continue and changes in places of residence to unknown locations. The loss (attrition) from the study has been random in regard to some variables, e.g., weight, at the most recent examinations.

All the participants are white except for 15 who are black. Blacks are underrepresented in the study by any measure; they form about 25% of the Yellow Springs population. Blacks were welcome in the study but few volunteered. Plans have been developed recently to enroll a large number of blacks. At enrollment, about 35% of the families lived in cities of medium size (population 30 000 to 60 000), about half in small towns (population 500 to 5000) and the remainder lived on farms. The families of the participants have a wide range of socioeconomic status (Sontag, Baker & Nelson, 1958[283]; Crandall, 1972 and unpublished) as shown by the distributions of scores on the Hollingshead Two Factor Index of Social Position (1957). The distributions of these scores for the Fels families are

similar to those in national US samples except for an underrepresentation of the lowest of the five Hollingshead groups for the families of participants born after 1939.

When the participants were 6 years old, about 23% of the fathers were major professionals, 16% were lesser professionals, executives or businessmen, 26% were minor professionals, executives or businessmen, 9% were clerical workers, technicians or salesmen, 16% were skilled manual employees, 6% were semi-skilled manual employees, and 2% were unskilled or unemployed. Bachelors degrees had been obtained by 39% of the fathers and 27% of the mothers. Masters or doctoral degrees had been obtained by 13% of the fathers and 3% of the mothers.

The Fels Longitudinal Study is based on a sample of convenience. Participants were enrolled at the request of pregnant women from local families considered to be 'stable.' While 'stable' was not defined clearly, it included judgments of geographic stability and of attitudes likely to be associated with a long-term commitment.

There are four sets of triplets and 14 sets of twins, including five sets of identical twins, amongst the Fels participants. In all analyses, only one random member of each identical pair has been included and triplets have been excluded from some analyses because they are overrepresented in the sample. The non-identical twins have been included in most analyses because their growth data do not differ significantly from those of the other participants. Gestational age is poorly established for many of the participants but birth weight is known. At birth, 6.6% weighed less than 2500 g, 2.1% weighed less than 2000 g and only 0.4% weighed less than 1500 g. These frequencies are in reasonable agreement with the US national distribution of birth weights.

Fourteen of the participants were abnormal at birth and 36 developed serious chronic illnesses postnatally. These participants have followed the study protocol but their data have been excluded from analyses if there was any possibility that the pathological condition could have influenced the variables being analyzed.

After the Fels Longitudinal Study had been conducted for a few years, some of the mothers became pregnant again and requested that their next children be enrolled. These requests were granted and siblings were enrolled. Totally, 344 offspring of participants (second generation), and 90 of their offspring (third generation) have been enrolled. Some terms used within the Fels study need clarification. 'First generation participants' are those who do not have a parent enrolled in the study since birth. Those with a parent who has participated in the study since birth are called 'second generation participants' and those with a grandparent and a

Table 1.1. *Tolerances* ($\pm$ *days*) *for ages at examinations in relation to scheduled ages*

Scheduled ages (years)	Tolerances	Scheduled ages (years)	Tolerances
6 months and younger	2	4.0	14
9 months	3	4.5	16
1	4	5.0	17
1.5	5	5.5	18
2.0	7	6.0	22
2.5	9	6.5	23
3.0	11	7.0	25
3.5	13	7.5 and older	30

parent who have participated in the study since birth are called 'third generation participants.' There is now one fourth-generation participant – a girl whose great-grandparent has been studied since birth.

The active participants can be grouped into about 200 kindreds, some of which contain several nuclear families. There are from one to seven participant siblings within each nuclear family. In addition, data have been obtained from unenrolled spouses when they were adult and from unenrolled siblings at 7, 11 and 17 years of age.

Advantages and disadvantages are associated with the familial relationships among the Fels participants. The advantages relate to the ability to analyze associations between family members for measured variables. This can be done in the Fels study using data collected at matching ages, for example, in pairs of mothers and daughters both measured at 12 years; this is not possible with any other existing data set. The disadvantages concern potential statistical bias if related individuals are included in some types of analyses. Only small problems are caused by this type of bias in the Fels study.

The examinations were scheduled at fixed chronological ages that were not related to the presence of illnesses (mothers were asked to bring their children for examination whether well or sick) or the achievement of developmental landmarks. Through 1973, the scheduled ages were 1, 3, 6, 9 and 12 months, then each half-year to 18 years in each sex. After 1973, the half-year examinations were omitted from 5 through 10 years and from 16 through 18 years in the boys and from 5 through 9 years and from 14 through 18 years in the girls. The age ranges for these omissions are periods when the rates of growth differ little with age. After 18 years, the examinations were scheduled at 20, 22 and 24 years. Examinations after 24

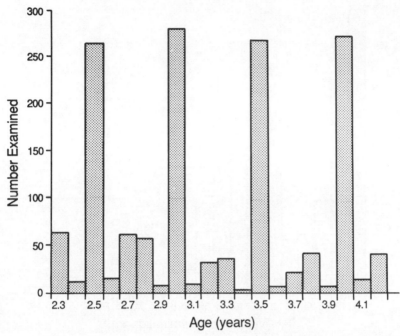

Fig. 1.4 The frequency of the actual ages at examinations for girls from 2.3 through 4.2 years; note the occurrence of some examinations at each 0.1 year interval despite the efforts to measure at the scheduled ages (2.5, 3.0, 3.5, 4.0 years).

years have been less regular. They have been dependent on extramural funding since 1976 when all examinations after 8 years were subsumed into the Body Composition Study which is described in Chapter 7.

Age tolerances were set for the examinations from the beginning of the Fels study (Table 1.1) because it was realized that variations in ages at examinations would influence the results. For example, the mean increase in stature from 4 to 5 years can be determined accurately as the difference between the mean at 4 years and the mean at 5 years, if all the participants were examined at exactly 4 years and 5 years. If, however, the ages at examinations vary, the difference between the pair of means labeled as '4 years' and '5 years' will only approximate the true mean increase from 4 years to 5 years.

Despite all efforts, many participants were measured at ages outside the tolerances. An example of the distribution of actual ages at examinations is shown in Fig. 1.4. This figure shows the number of examinations of girls at each 0.1 year interval from 2.3 to 4.2 years. Despite the large peaks at 2.5, 3.0, 3.5 and 4.0 years, a considerable number of examinations was

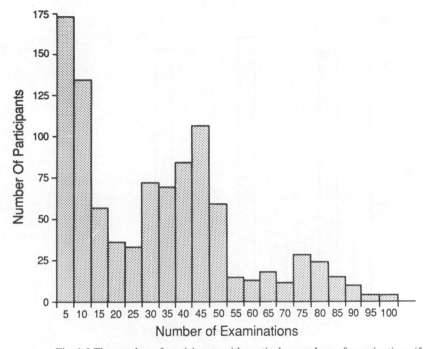

Fig. 1.5 The number of participants with particular numbers of examinations (5 = 0 to 5 examinations; 10 = 6 to 10 examinations, etc.). The large number with fewer than 10 examinations reflects continuing enrollment at birth.

made at intermediate ages. Until 1972, it was not common to use data recorded at examinations outside the age tolerances in analyses because it was considered they were not useful. Later, it was realized that estimated values for scheduled ages could be made from the serial data. A detailed description of these adjustments to the data is given in Chapter 2.

There are large variations among the participants in the number of times they have been examined (Fig. 1.5). These variations reflect the continuing enrollment into the study. Many of those with few examinations are still very young. A total of 720 participants has been examined more than 10 times and 440 have been examined more than 20 times. The total number of examinations for the group exceeds 24 000. The number of participants with records of particular lengths is shown in Fig. 1.6; about 370 have records extending more than 25 years.

The data recorded or measured in the Fels study may be grouped as follows.

Physical growth: total body size, body proportions, length and sizes of segments.

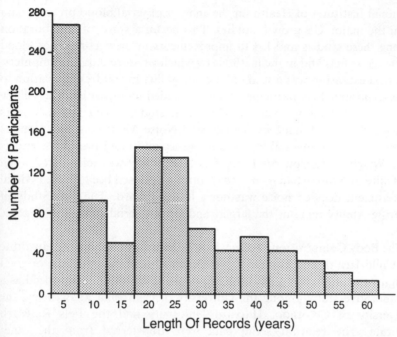

Fig. 1.6 The number of participants with records of particular lengths (5 = 0 to 5 years; 10 = 6 to 10 years, etc.).

Physical maturity: body photographs and ages at reaching developmental milestones, grades of secondary sex characters, menarche and menopause, skeletal and dental ages, and ages at peak height velocity and peak weight velocity.

Skeletal and dental data: sizes and shapes of bones and teeth, skeletal mass, skeletal variations.

Body composition: total body composition (total body fat, fat-free mass and percent body fat from underwater weighing, impedance and total body water, dual photon absorptiometry), regional body composition (thicknesses and areas of subcutaneous adipose tissue, muscle and bone), grip strength, and adipocyte size.

Other: risk factors for cardiovascular disease (blood pressures, lipids and lipoproteins), dietary intakes, genetic markers, data from physical examinations and medical histories, hearing ability, noise exposure, menstrual histories, and histories of physical activity.

There have been some extensions to the basic plan of the Fels study. The first major extension occurred in 1972 when a contract was awarded by the

National Institutes of Health for the analysis of serial blood pressure data from the major US growth studies. This began a spirit of collaboration among these studies and led to improvements in the recording of blood pressures at Fels and in the methods by which we store data in computers. The next extension was a study of hearing ability in children in relation to noise exposure. Fels participants were included along with some Yellow Springs High School students. This serial study, which lasted 8 years (1975–1982), was funded by the Office of Noise Abatement and Control within the Environmental Protection Agency and monitored by scientists from Wright-Patterson Air Force Base. The study was terminated when the Office of Noise Abatement and Control was closed because the Federal Government decided noise was not a health hazard. The Fels Study of Hearing Ability remains the largest and longest serial study in this topic area.

The Body Composition Study, which is funded by the National Institute for Child Health and Human Development, began in 1976. The original design was complex and its complexity has increased. It commenced as a collaborative study among the University of California at Berkeley, the University of Colorado, Harvard University and the Fels Research Institute. The relevant serial data were transferred from the other institutions to Fels, follow-up studies were made at the University of California and at Harvard University, and an intense program to record body composition variables began at Fels. The Fels Body Composition Study, which in its present cycle is funded through 1993, is the largest serial body composition study anywhere. Many of the data recorded in this study are relevant to the risk of cardiovascular disease in middle age, for example serial measurements of blood pressure and blood lipids. It is one of three major long-term US studies of serial changes in cardiovascular risk factors during childhood and adulthood.

The well-planned long-term longitudinal study
Few have the opportunity to work in longitudinal studies for as long as the present author, who began the University of Melbourne Growth Study in 1954. Therefore, it is appropriate to weave into this text some reflections on the design of such studies.

There are many reasons why it is difficult to plan a longitudinal study of human growth; the implementation of such a study may be even more difficult. The study must continue for a long period but not necessarily for the whole life span. To take a simple example, a longitudinal study of premature infants extending to 6 years could test many hypotheses. An adequate design for such a study could be based on a single cohort of all

premature infants born in a selected county during a specified interval. Some infants would be omitted, however, because their mothers chose not to participate and there would be attrition from the sample during the study. It is unlikely that the measurement procedures would become outmoded during the 6-year study, but the applicability of the findings will be reduced if there are major changes in the management of premature infants either during or after the study.

A series of such studies could be planned that, in combination, would cover all ages from birth to adulthood. Ages at enrollment would vary: perhaps birth for one cohort, 6 years for another, etc. This approach has considerable appeal because, in comparison with a single study based on one cohort, the work will be completed quickly with less attrition and less risk that the hypotheses will cease to be of interest. A group of such studies, conducted simultaneously, should be associated with greater investigator interest but will probably require a large staff and substantial funding.

There are problems in designing a serial study that may extend from birth to adulthood or continue throughout the whole life span. Such a study should be contemplated only if many important hypotheses are to be tested that require very long-term serial data. Such hypotheses could relate status or change during childhood to adult status. Some have claimed that human beings cannot conduct such studies because they will not live long enough (Falkner, 1973b), but such studies are possible with a succession of investigators (Roche *et al.*, 1981a[235]).

The study should be multidisciplinary only if the hypotheses require it and there is a convincing rationale. The multidisciplinary aspects must be included during the design phase (Roche, 1974b[179]). The mere existence of serial data for several disciplines within a single study does not lead to multidisciplinary analyses. These analyses require, as stated above, appropriate hypotheses and also real interest by investigators who work in different disciplines but have mutual respect.

The study design should include a plan to test sequential groups of hypotheses; some will require data from infants, others will require data from children or adults. It is unlikely that all the final hypotheses will be formulated before the study begins, but a comprehensive listing should be attempted and revised as the study proceeds. This list should be made as a template for progress, not just as a mechanism to obtain funds that will be forgotten as soon as possible.

As stated earlier, the design should be dependent on analytic consider-ations and, of course, these will depend on the hypotheses. It can be assumed that the serial nature of the data will be taken into account in the analyses, but the exact serial nature of the data, and thus the design, will be

determined by the specific hypotheses and the analytic approaches they require. Is this a follow-up study for which the analytic procedure may be logistic regression which requires data for a pair of ages? Is it a study of patterns of change within individuals requiring a substantial number of serial data points for each individual to which a mathematical function will be fitted? If the latter, there must be short intervals between examinations, particularly when growth is rapid or there are large changes in growth rates. If the hypotheses are similar in nature for the different measurements, the same set of intervals between examinations should be suitable for most body measurements, except those of the craniofacial region for which a relatively large proportion of growth occurs during infancy. A different set of intervals may be suitable for other variables such as blood lipids.

The specific hypotheses and the analytic procedures to be applied will affect the sample sizes that are required. The sample sizes needed are likely to differ among hypotheses. If some of the hypotheses relate to groups near the extremes of the distributions, large samples or specially selected samples should be enrolled. Those planning the study must decide the level beyond which a further increase in sample size to allow testing additional hypotheses is not justified.

The examinations must be scheduled at predetermined target ages that are independent of possible illness. Despite all efforts, many ages at examination will differ from the target ages (see Fig. 1.4). Until about 1970, most of those who analyzed serial data excluded data gathered outside the tolerances for target ages. It is now realized that all the recorded data are informative and that none should be disregarded.

A long-term study of human growth is very expensive and it is unrealistic to expect a funding commitment for a period longer than about 5 years. Therefore, the hypotheses and the design must facilitate the publication of research reports based on tests of hypotheses during the first few years of the study at a rate that will convince the funding agency to continue its support and will encourage the continued participation of key scientists. These considerations affect the enrollment plan. A choice could be made between one large cohort of newly born infants, or small annual cohorts. If one large cohort is enrolled, some analyses can be made early. This is not the case if small annual cohorts are enrolled.

Enrollment of a large cohort at birth is associated with logistic problems due to the need for closely spaced examinations during infancy. The work load may be overwhelming at a time when funding is restricted because the funding agency lacks confidence. In the early phase of a study, recording forms must be prepared, informed consent obtained, data entry procedures established, and computer programs written. At the same time, the staff

must be trained and monitored in data collection procedures. There is a risk that the single large cohort may be unrepresentative or that one or more important variables may be omitted at the beginning of the study. There is no practical way to remedy such defects. If all enrollments were at birth, the hypotheses could be tested in an order determined by the sample size required for this testing. If, however, the design includes the enrollment of annual cohorts, their representative natures can be compared and variables omitted from the initial design may be added for later cohorts. On the contrary, variables that prove unrewarding can be discontinued. In some situations, an intermediate design may be appropriate in which cohorts of medium size are enrolled at, say, 5-year intervals.

Another design that can be considered is the enrollment of a single cohort of families each of which includes a newly born infant. The older participants within these families will require less frequent examinations than the younger participants and hypotheses that require only short-term data can be tested early in the study for numerous age groups. In addition, associations within families can be analyzed. The introduction of bias is a disadvantage but this can be overcome by including only one randomly chosen participant of each sex from each family in a specific analysis, when the need for this is demonstrated. An additional disadvantage of this design is the delay that would occur before sufficient data were available to allow analyses relating to particular age groups.

There is no perfect solution; planning is never perfect. With any enrollment plan, it is unlikely that a random sample will be obtained for a longitudinal study. Therefore, generalizations to a total population may not be defensible. If the effects of specific environmental variables are to be estimated, in the absence of random assignment to experimental and control groups, many intervening variables must be recorded so that statistical adjustments can be made. The need for these adjustments increases the sample sizes required to test the hypotheses. Measuring a large number of variables is expensive and requires considerable staff time for data collection and data entry. It also increases the burden on the participants. Consequently, as the study proceeds, variables should be added only after careful attention has been given to the possible consequences. Finally, it is essential to protect the study participants, who will already be burdened by the planned examinations, from other scientists who may regard them as a ready pool of volunteers for additional projects.

Having enrolled the participants, great efforts must be made to ensure that they do not miss examinations, that they complete all the procedures scheduled for each examination, and, most importantly, that they do not withdraw from the study. Even if the examination procedures are painless

and non-invasive, these goals will not be fully achieved. Various rewards and study newsletters help but the most important element is a set of staff attitudes and behaviors that make an examination a pleasant experience. On balance, the enrollment of families rather than individuals probably increases long-term participation in a study.

All measurements must be made in a standardized fashion that provides valid reliable data, as stressed by Roche (1974b[179]). Therefore, one early goal of a long-term study may be the validation of some measures. The study may be an excellent milieu for testing new procedures but this testing should involve separate groups of subjects recruited for this purpose. Reliability of data is an on-going concern that will continue throughout the study. Additionally there is always the possibility that repeated examinations may alter the phenomena being measured leading to confounding of age effects and examination effects. It is possible to separate these effects for a procedure that is added to the protocol in a chosen calendar year and is applied to participants of all ages (Roche *et al.*, 1983a[255]).

When there are improvements in equipment or techniques, they should be incorporated cautiously into the study protocol, in accordance with the view of Alexander Pope:

> Be not the first by whom the new are tried,
> Nor yet the last to lay the old aside.

As a long-term study proceeds, it is likely that changes will be needed in the variables recorded and, perhaps, the ages at examinations. These changes will be justified if they assist the testing of the original hypotheses or other hypotheses that are closely related to them. Additional hypotheses are justified only if they relate to the original topics. New topics should be added to the study only if the data collected earlier are relevant to them. The general principle is that all additions should strengthen or extend the original study, the link between the original and the added parts must be more than a common sample of participants.

Secular trends may be important in the interpretation of findings from a long-term study. These trends, that usually reflect decades of slow change, are, in a strict sense, alterations in recorded values with calendar year within a fixed population that does not gain or lose members by migration or differential mortality. Commonly, however, the term 'secular trends' is applied, somewhat loosely, to a national population despite migration and differential mortality. Generally, secular trends reflect alterations in the environment that may involve nutrition, illness, health care, pollutants, or other factors. Cross-sectional studies are commonly confounded by secular

changes in the features measured and by selective mortality. In longitudinal studies, each participant acts as his or her own control and changes with time can be estimated more accurately. It may be desirable, however, to conduct parallel cross-sectional studies of larger groups so that secular trends in a more general population can be evaluated and used to interpret the findings from the longitudinal study.

Secular trends can be a nuisance to a data analyst because they make it necessary to analyze the data within subgroups based on birth years or the data may have to be adjusted for these trends prior to further analysis. The trends may, however, be of real interest and, if analyzed together with intervening variables, may direct attention to possible causes of the changes with year of birth in the variables studied. It is unlikely, however, that the cause of the changes will be established within a serial growth study; this requires a different design.

I wish to end this chapter with a note about collaboration. Long-term serial studies are rare and they are expensive. Therefore, it is important that the recorded data be utilized as fully as possible. Widespread realization of this is the basis for the cooperation that now exists among all the US longitudinal studies, and between them and the major cross-sectional studies in the same topic areas. Due to this spirit, and the availability of electronic data transfer, information from other studies is used commonly to replicate findings. This occurs frequently at Fels, and we are most grateful to our colleagues who make it possible.

2 The management and analysis of data

No human investigation can be termed true science if it is not capable of mathematical demonstration.

Leonardo da Vinci (1452–1519)

In the Fels Longitudinal Study, as should occur in any long-term serial study, great efforts were made to ensure that the data collected were reliable and that this reliability was retained during the transfer of the data to computers. High levels of data quality can be achieved in a prospective longitudinal study but not in a retrospective study. Additionally, the hypotheses posed and the analyses made in the Fels Longitudinal Study ensured, as far as possible, that the maximum information was derived from the serial nature of the data. Aspects of data management and analysis in the study will be described in the sequence: (i) the need for accurate data, (ii) quality control, (iii) data management, (iv) interpolation, (v) derivation of variables, (vi) transformation of variables, and (vii) statistical analyses.

The need for accurate data

In a cross-sectional study, errors in the measurement of some individuals have little effect on the results of analyses unless these errors are large and common. If it is concluded that outlying values denote abnormal individuals or that large errors occurred during data collection, these data points can be excluded from cross-sectional analyses. This exclusion should be documented, and based on objective rules.

Large errors may be detected by comparing observed data with the distribution of values for the same variable in other groups of children of the same sex and age. For example, a recorded stature of 90 cm for a 6-year-old boy can be recognized as an outlier by comparison with the 5th

26

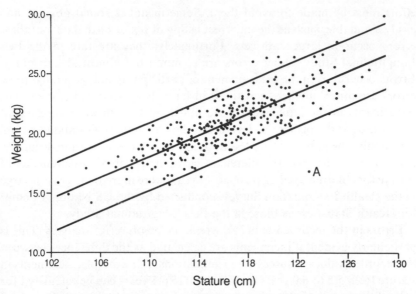

Fig. 2.1 A linear regression of weight on stature for 6-year-old boys in the Fels study. The upper and lower oblique lines (± 2 SD) indicate the limits of the normal range for this relationship. Point A indicates an unusual combination of values that may be associated with an error of measurement or an abnormality.

percentile level (108.5 cm). An alternative is to use a bivariate regression that shows the relationship between two variables. The second variable should be one that has a constant or proportional relationship to the first. If weight is regressed on stature for 6-year-old boys in the Fels study, the combination of a stature at about the 95th percentile level of national data with a weight at about the 5th percentile level will be apparent as an outlying pair of values although the stature-for-age and the weight-for-age are independently acceptable (point A in Fig. 2.1).

An abnormal bivariate relationship of weight to stature for an individual could be due to a truly unusual value for weight or stature or to a recording error that affected either the value for weight or that for stature. Other data may be available, such as sitting height which is highly correlated with stature. The normality of sitting height relative to the recorded stature for the individual can be determined using a bivariate regression. If the recorded sitting height is within the expected range for the recorded stature, this provides presumptive evidence that the recorded stature is accurate and that suspicion should be directed at the value for weight.

Errors of measurement or recording have much more serious effects in longitudinal studies than in cross-sectional studies. Consequently, every

effort must be made to avoid them. Some mistakes sound obvious and easily avoidable, such as the incorrect listing of sex or birth date, but these errors occur in large data sets. Fortunately, they are rare in the Fels Longitudinal Study. Other errors are common but almost all are minor. Errors occur during the measurement of participants but, generally, these errors are much smaller than those in large cross-sectional studies. The participants in the latter studies are not familiar with the measurement procedures or the personnel, less time is devoted to each examination and, commonly, the personnel are less aware of the need for care and accuracy. For example, the median differences between repeated measurements of stature for children aged 12 through 17 years were more than twice as large in the Health Examination Survey, conducted by the US National Center for Health Statistics, as those in the Fels Longitudinal Study.

Errors in the recorded data can wreak havoc on serial analyses. This is particularly evident if increments are calculated as the differences between the recorded values at successive examinations. For example, increments in stature from 5.5 to 6.0 years and from 6.0 to 6.5 years can be calculated for individuals by subtracting their statures at 5.5 years from their values at 6.0 years, and by subtracting their statures at 6.0 years from their values at 6.5 years. Any participants whose values at 6 years were recorded higher than reality will have erroneously high calculated increments for the interval 5.5 to 6.0 years and erroneously low calculated increments for the interval 6.0 to 6.5 years. Thus a single recording error leads to two errors in the calculated increments.

Reference data for increments are useful clinically partly because of their conceptual simplicity and because they treat growth as a dynamic process. Nevertheless, more complex mathematical approaches are needed to describe the patterns of growth of individuals. This need was recognized by Palmer and Reed as long ago as 1935. They wrote: 'If long series of observations are available it will be found advisable, probably, to derive individual growth curves and thus to make the final analysis of growth in terms of the parameters or mathematical characteristics of these curves.'

The description of growth data for an individual by a mathematical function (curve-fitting) is basic to the modern analysis of serial data. This procedure is very effective if an appropriate function is chosen, but there may be some individuals in the group for whom the function does not fit the data. This may occur because these individuals differ from the remainder of the group in their growth patterns. If this is the case, the divergence from the common growth pattern, shown as the difference between the recorded data and the fitted curve, will typically involve the data recorded at successive examinations and will involve more than one

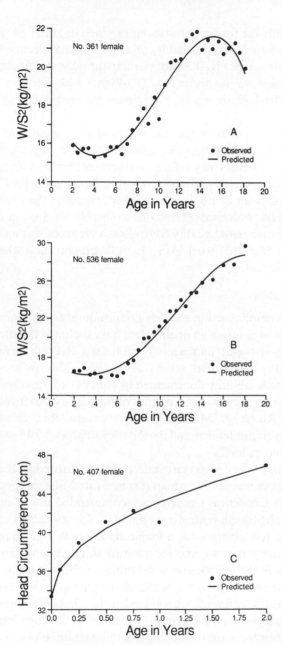

Fig. 2.2 Examples of serial data to illustrate how curve-fitting can identify variations in growth patterns (A, B) and erroneous points (the value at 1.0 years in C).

variable. The changes with age for weight/stature^2 (kg/m^2) in about 80% of Fels participants could be fitted by a family of functions that declined after about 14 years, as shown in Fig. 2.2A for participant number 361. In most of the remainder, there was no decrease after 14 years and, therefore, a different model was fitted, as shown for participant number 536 (Fig. 2.2B).

Curve-fitting is not only essential for the description of growth patterns, it directs attention to measurement errors. A large discrepancy between the recorded data and the fitted values may reflect measurement error. This is illustrated by the data for head circumference in participant number 407 (Fig. 2.2C). The recorded point at 1.0 years is markedly smaller than the value recorded at 0.75 years, which would lead one to suspect the accuracy of the points. With computer-based quality control such erroneous points would be recognized while the participant is still present and the measurement would be repeated.

Quality control

Quality control has been emphasized in the Fels Longitudinal Study since its inception. The actions to ensure high quality data have included the use of equipment that is state-of-the-art and carefully calibrated. Records have been kept of the monthly calibration results since 1969. The anthropometric procedures, which are fully documented in volumes of *Standard Operating Procedures*, match the recommendations of the Airlie Consensus Conference (Lohman, Roche & Martorell, 1988) except that chest circumference, mid-thigh circumference and the anterior thigh skinfold are measured at slightly different levels.

In the Fels Longitudinal Study, chest circumference is measured at the level of the nipple, except in women for whom it is measured just inferior to the breasts. The Airlie Consensus Conference recommended that it be measured at the level of the fourth costosternal junction. Identification of the latter level would be too invasive for a longitudinal study including women. The mid-thigh circumference and the anterior thigh skinfold are measured at the junction of the middle and distal thirds of a line from the anterior superior iliac spine to the proximal border of the patella in the Fels study. The Airlie Consensus Conference recommended that these measurements be made at the mid-point of a line from the center of the inguinal ligament to the superior border of the patella. Again, these landmarks were considered too invasive of privacy for a longitudinal study. These pairs of levels differ by less than 1.0 cm, and paired measurements at the two levels are almost identical. Measurements of gonial skinfold thickness, acromiale height and knee height are made in the Fels Longitudinal Study, although

these are not among the measurements for which recommendations were made at the Airlie Consensus Conference.

The standardization and documentation of procedures are important for collaborative studies and in training new personnel. Fortunately, the latter need is uncommon. The four staff members who have close contact with the participants have worked in the study for a total of 50 years. Despite their experience, they are monitored by Dr Cameron Chumlea who joins them in the measurement of one participant each week. Doctor Chumlea is also responsible for training new anthropometrists.

Since 1929, all anthropometric variables have been obtained by a pair of anthropometrists working independently, except during the measurement of recumbent length for which they worked as a team and repeated the measurement after exchanging roles. The only landmarks marked on the participant are the levels of the mid-arm, maximum calf, and mid-thigh circumferences, and acromiale. These locations are checked by another anthropometrist. Complete replication of measurements, as at Fels, may be unique. By comparison, Goldstein (1979) describes the quality control procedures in the cross-sectional Cuban National Growth Study as elaborate and implies they are a model to be followed, although only 0.9% of the participants in this study were re-measured (Jordan *et al.*, 1975).

Until 1970, means of paired measurements were recorded but the original measurements were not retained. Children were re-measured four times if the differences between paired measurements were large, but the decisions to re-measure were not based on operational rules. Since 1970, the measurements made by both anthropometrists have been entered into a computer within the anthropometric laboratory while each participant is present. A program identifies those variables for which the differences between the observers' measurements exceed the set tolerances (maximum acceptable values; Table 2.1) or for which the mean of the paired measurements is outside the 5th to the 95th percentile range for age and sex.

When the tolerance for an interobserver difference is exceeded, or the mean is outside the 'normal range,' a computer program prompts a 'warning sign,' and both observers measure the variable again without knowing whether the reason for the repetition is a large interobserver difference or an unusual mean. When a participant is re-measured, the mean of the third and fourth measurements is used in the data analyses unless these measurements differ by more than the set tolerance or the mean of the third and fourth measurements is outside the normal range. In one or both of these circumstances, the mean of all four measurements is used. The frequency with which this occurs for each variable and for each

Table 2.1. *Set tolerances for interobserver differences in anthropometric variables*

Weight: 100 g except before 3 years (40 g)
Stature, recumbent length, sitting height, acromiale height: 1.0 cm
Arm length: 0.5 cm
Circumferences: head, thigh, arm, calf, 0.2 cm; hip, abdomen, chest, 1.0 cm
Breadths: knee, 0.2 cm; elbow, 0.3 cm; biacromial and bicristal, 1.0 cm
Skinfolds: triceps, biceps, subscapular, anterior chest, gonial, 0.2 cm; suprailiac, midaxillary, lateral calf, 0.3 cm

---

Table 2.2. *Selected distribution statistics for interobserver differences in skinfold thickness measurements for children aged 12–18 years*

Site	Number of pairs	Technical error (mm)[a]	Coefficient of reliability (%)[b]
Triceps	738	0.76	97.94
Biceps	739	0.72	96.02
Subscapular	738	0.69	98.38
Midaxillary (vertical)	738	0.93	96.46
Midaxillary (horizontal)	266	0.86	97.15
Anterior chest	715	0.99	95.30
Suprailiac	738	1.29	96.81
Lateral calf	722	0.69	97.49
Gonial	185	0.58	92.42

[a] The technical error is a measure of the extent of agreement between two corresponding values recorded for the same individuals.

[b] The coefficient of reliability is a measure of the agreement between two corresponding values recorded for the same individuals, adjusted for the difference between individuals.

anthropometrist is reviewed at fixed intervals to determine whether further re-training is indicated. This set of procedures constrains the technical errors and increases the reliability.

The first computer program used in the Fels study to check the accuracy of the recorded data also calculated the increments from the previous examinations and identified those outside the range from the 5th to the 95th percentile for the group. Children whose measurements were deemed acceptable on the basis of interobserver errors and the levels of the means were re-measured if their increments were outside the normal range. This check of increments was discontinued for several reasons. Good incremental reference data were lacking for many of the variables being measured, and the program was slow because the observed increments had to be adjusted for variations in the lengths of the intervals between

examinations before they were compared with reference data. The most compelling reason for omitting this check was, however, the fact that the increments must be correct if the status values at the beginning and the end of the interval are correct, as assured by the other checks.

All the recorded data are retained in computer files except the first set of blood pressure measurements. This set is made to relax the participant and to compress the vessels prior to the measurements that will be recorded. The means of the second and third sets of blood pressure measurements are used in the analyses unless pairs of corresponding values differ by 10 mmHg or more. When this occurs, two more sets of measurements are obtained and the means of the fourth and fifth sets are used in the analyses unless, as occurs rarely, these also differ by 10 mmHg or more. On such occasions, the means of the second through the fifth measurements are used in the analyses.

Summary statistics of observer differences for all variables, are calculated within seven age groups, at 6-month intervals. These statistics relate to data recorded during the previous 6 months and also to all the data recorded since January 1976. Some of these results are presented in Table 2.2. It has been claimed that skinfold thicknesses cannot be measured reliably, but these coefficients of reliability show that, in children aged 12 to 18 years, the percentages of the total variance due to measurement errors range from only 1.62% to 7.58%. Methods for the measurement of body composition and risk factors for cardiovascular diseases are described in Chapter 7, together with the measures taken to assure that the recorded data are of high quality.

The important topic of radiation protection has received considerable attention at Fels. The radiographs have been used in studies of maturation of bones and teeth, and of body composition. In the early years of the Fels study, many radiographs were taken to assist studies of the growth of long bones and the craniofacial skeleton and to analyze the maturation of the skeleton. Therefore, great care was taken to minimize irradiation. As a result, the recorded skin doses in the gonadal region and elsewhere were too low to be meaningful (Garn, Silverman & Sontag, 1957b[168]; Garn, Silverman & Davis, 1963a[165], 1964d[166]; Garn et al., 1967a[90]). These low doses were achieved by the use of fast film, external filtration, gonadal shields and a collimator cone. Nevertheless, the radiation doses tended to increase with age and were larger for radiographs of the thorax than for the extremities. A set of radiographs, in 1964, resulted in a gonadal dose of 0.15–0.30 mrem, which should be considered relative to the irreducible background radiation from the environment of about 200 mrem/year. Currently, very few radiographs are taken.

Data management

Data management in the Fels Longitudinal Study is designed to eliminate ambiguities in the recorded data, to facilitate the entry of data to a computer and to check relentlessly for errors at various stages of the process. Despite this, some errors escape detection. The Fels data management system can be considered a computerized filing program that also ensures that the data are of high quality.

Each questionnaire is designed to be as unambiguous as possible. The completed questionnaires are reviewed while the participants are present so that further information can be obtained if any answers are unclear. The recording forms for measurements are designed to accept data in the sequence set in the protocol. Firm adherence to a set sequence reduces the number of errors in the recorded data because measured values are less likely to be assigned to the wrong variables, and anthropometrists become accustomed to the order of the measurements.

Figure 2.3 shows the major steps in data management. At the steps in double rectangles, checks are made for possible errors by comparing printed data (print-outs) with the original records. After any errors have been corrected, the accuracy of the changes is checked on a subsequent print-out before the next step. The first step is the entry of the measurement or questionnaire data through a keyboard to a microcomputer. The entered data are listed in print-outs and checked against the hand-written records. Any discrepancies are corrected and the accuracy of these corrections is checked by comparing corrected print-outs with the hand-written records.

The data are then outputted as a sequential file which is checked and corrected as necessary before being converted to PC/SAS data format. In the next step, descriptive statistics are obtained that may lead to the identification of outlying values which are checked against the original records. Again, any necessary corrections are made and these corrections are checked on a print-out before the data are added to the master data base. Copies of the master file are maintained in several locations.

Working files that are retrieved from the master data base are fully documented. In the construction of a working file, care is taken to include all the variables that will be needed, but exclude other variables. These working files are retained on tape for at least 1 year after the results of the analyses have been published.

While it is hoped that there would not be any loss of participants from a longitudinal study, this hope is not realistic. Because loss of participants (attrition) does occur, the Fels' data are examined at 4-year intervals to determine whether the attrition has been random. If withdrawals from the

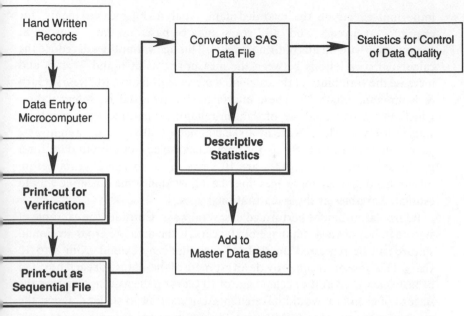

Fig. 2.3 A diagram of the steps in the management of data from their collection to their addition to the master data file.

study were more common among particular types of participants than others, the resulting bias would reduce the ability to generalize from the study findings to other groups. Participants who withdraw from the study may differ in some way from the remainder, but many of these differences, e.g., place of residence, may not affect the variables being analyzed. For the variables that have been examined, the last measurements of those who withdrew from the Fels Longitudinal Study did not differ significantly from the measurements of those who remained in the study. Therefore, the loss of participants appears to be random in regard to the measured variables and it can be concluded that the distributions of the data from the present participants are similar to those that would have been obtained had data been collected from all those enrolled.

Interpolation

For some analyses, it is necessary to adjust the recorded data for the differences between the ages at which the participants were measured and the scheduled ages for measurement. Many small differences between these ages occur because examinations are not scheduled on Sundays or public holidays; larger differences occur when participants are sick or away on vacations (see Fig. 1.4). These variations in ages at examinations may have

important effects on the recorded data. Analyses of measurements, for example, 'at 6 years' and 'at 7 years' may be based on data recorded at various ages with means of 6 and 7 years. This age variation will reduce the calculated correlations between the measurements at 6 and 7 years and increase the variability of the calculated increments from 6 to 7 years (Garn & Rohmann, 1964b[140]). These effects can be removed by interpolation which also assists analyses of data in relation to maturational events or stages: for example, stature at a skeletal age of 10 years, or weight at 2 years before menarche. Since it is impractical to collect growth data for a group when the skeletal ages are 10 years or at an age 2 years before menarche, data near these ages must be adjusted in some objective way to estimate variables at these maturational ages.

Interpolation can be performed in several ways. Consider the example of stature in boys at a skeletal age of 10 years. If the data are cross-sectional, stature can be regressed on skeletal ages that may extend from 8 to 12 years. This approach can provide an estimate of the stature of each boy had he been measured at the skeletal age of 10 years on the assumption that the stature of each boy would have changed in relation to skeletal age at the mean rate for the group. Although this assumption is incorrect for most boys, it is used commonly because it is the only way to interpolate from cross-sectional data.

Other interpolation methods are preferable when the data are serial. One simple method is linear interpolation between the values recorded at the last examination before and the first examination after the age for which the estimate is required. For example, if the stature of a boy were measured at skeletal ages of 9.4 and 10.2 years, his stature at a skeletal age of 10 years can be estimated by linear interpolation. This usually provides acceptable estimates if the pair of measurements are 1–2 years apart, but the estimates may be erroneous during periods when growth rates change rapidly. Nevertheless, this may be the best available method when a participant has only two data points.

When there are numerous serial data points for each participant, a mathematical function should be fitted to the data for the individual; the parameters of this function are used to estimate stature at a skeletal age of 10 years. In this context, a mathematical function is a set of transformed ages that are differentially weighted by coefficients and usually combined with a constant (intercept) to describe the change in the variable after the age of the intercept and to estimate the value of the variable at an age. This procedure works well if there is a close match between the fitted values and the observed data, and if there are sufficient serial data points near the age for which the estimate is required.

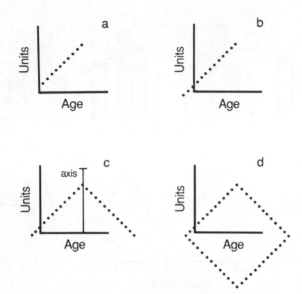

Fig. 2.4 Stages a–d in the transformation of serial data prior to fitting a Fourier function (see text for details).

Beginning in 1974, a Fourier function was used in the Fels Longitudinal Study to estimate values at target chronological ages and at selected maturational ages or events. This procedure involved transforming the data into two orthogonal components (Fig. 2.4). A set of hypothetical data is shown in Fig. 2.4a. In Fig. 2.4b, the first three points have been rotated to the left around a vertical axis passing through the first point and then rotated downwards around a horizontal axis through this point. This new data set was then rotated to the right around a vertical axis passing through the last point to obtain the data in Fig. 2.4c. Finally, the data were rotated downwards, around a horizontal axis passing through the first and last points, to obtain the enclosed area shown in Fig. 2.4d. A Fourier function was then applied to the margin of this area using a program that provided measures of the goodness of fit. This procedure was applied to all the variables that were analyzed commonly and separate files of observed and interpolated data were maintained. The routine application of this method was stopped in 1978 because it was expensive, time consuming, and the program had to be run whenever additional data points were recorded.

The Fourier method was replaced by mathematical functions which, if they fit well, can provide interpolated values based on all the serial data for an individual. Mathematical functions are now used at Fels to interpolate when there is a specific need. A mathematical function fitted to stature, for

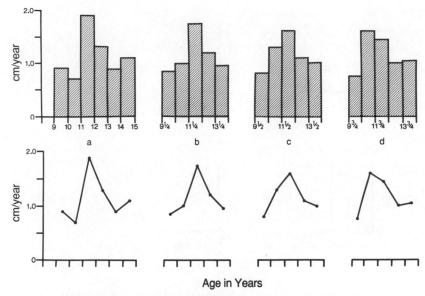

Fig. 2.5 Annual increments in bicristal diameter measured on radiographs of a female Fels participant (No. 170). The pairs of bar graphs and linear plots illustrate how variation in the ages at which annual intervals begin can alter the observations and selection of the age at the peak rate of growth. (Roche, A.F. 1974a. Differential timing of maximum length increments between bones within individuals. *Human Biology*, **46**, 145–7[178]. Redrawn with permission from *Human Biology*.)

example, will smooth the data and will assist determination of the age of occurrence of peak rate of growth (peak height velocity, PHV).

A simpler approach to the identification of the age at peak height velocity is to calculate annual increments in stature and record age at PHV as the midpoint of the annual interval with the largest increment. This approach can lead to large errors, as demonstrated by data for annual increments in bicristal (hip) diameter in one Fels girl (Fig. 2.5). The pairs of matching bar and linear graphs indicated by 'a' show annual increments (cm/year) for intervals beginning at birthdays. There would be marked differences in the increments if the annual examinations had been made 3, 6, or 9 months after each birthday (pairs b, c, and d, respectively) assuming that the growth rate was constant during each annual interval. Whereas the midpoint of the interval with the maximum increment is 11.5 years for a, it varies from 11.25 to 12.0 years among b, c, and d.

Derivation of variables

Within the Fels study, some statistical analyses are based on variables derived from the observed data. There are two groups of derived variables from the viewpoint of data management. Monthly calculations are made of those that are analyzed commonly and are easy to compute; the calculated values are added to the permanent computer file. Those that are analyzed less frequently and are more difficult to compute are calculated only when needed.

The derived variables that are regularly added to the permanent file include the following.

(i)   Weight/stature^2 (W/S^2). This is related to total body fat and to the percentage of the body weight that is fat (percent body fat; Roche *et al.*, 1981b[265]).

(ii)   Muscle and adipose tissue areas of the arm and calf. These areas are calculated from a circumference and a skinfold thickness at the same level, assuming the cross-sectional area of the arm or calf is circular. For example, arm muscle area (cm^2) = [arm circumference − 3.14 (triceps skinfold thickness)/10]^2/12.56. Additionally, the total area of the arm or calf is easily calculated from its circumference and the adipose tissue areas can be obtained as the differences between the total areas and the muscle areas. Although these calculated values are only indices of the true areas, they assist predictions of the total amounts of fat and fat-free mass in the body (Himes, Roche & Webb, 1980; Guo, Roche & Houtkooper, 1989a).

(iii)   Body density (BD). Body density is calculated from weight-in-air, weight-in-water, water temperature and residual volume. The last-mentioned is the amount of air remaining in the lungs at maximal expiration. The calculation of body composition variables, such as total body fat and fat-free mass, from body density is generally regarded as the best available procedure that is applicable to the living (Roche, 1984a[196], 1985a[199], 1987a[204]).

(iv)   Stature^2/resistance (S^2/R). The resistance of the body to the passage of a small alternating electric current can help predict the lean mass of the body (fat-free mass) and the total amount of water in the body (total body water; Kushner & Schoeller, 1986; Guo *et al.*, 1987a; Guo, Roche & Chumlea, 1989b). Resistance is useful for this purpose only when it is used in combination with an index of the length and volume of the conductor; stature^2 is effective as such an index. The accuracy of this approach is

increased further when resistance and stature^2 are combined with reactance (X_c). Reactance, which is measured with the same equipment as resistance, is the inverse of capacitance. Capacitance is the storage of voltage by a condenser for a brief moment in time.

(v)   Relative skeletal age. This is calculated as (skeletal age – chronological age) or as skeletal age/chronological age. These values are preferred to observed skeletal ages because they are less dependent on chronological ages.

Other derived variables added to recent working files include the following.

(i)   Phase angle (Φ). As part of bioelectric impedance studies, the phase angle (Φ) may be calculated from resistance (R) and reactance (X_c) as:

$$\Phi = atan\ (X_c/R)$$

and converted to degrees by multiplying by 57.297.

(ii) $W^{1.2}/S^{3.3}$. This is the weight–stature ratio that is maximally related to percent body fat in the Fels data (Abdel-Malek, Mukherjee & Roche, 1985; Roche, Abdel-Malek & Mukherjee, 1985[210]).

(iii)   Ages at peak height velocity estimated from mathematical functions fitted to the serial data for each participant.

(iv)   Parent-specific values for recumbent lengths and stature. Since tall parents tend to have tall children, and the reverse, it is desirable to adjust observed recumbent lengths and statures for the statures of the parents before performing some analyses. These procedures should be applied also in the clinical evaluation of children with unusual recumbent lengths or statures and in some comparisons between groups (Himes, Roche & Thissen, 1981; Himes *et al.*, 1985).

(v)   Weight-for-stature. Because weight and stature are correlated, weight should be adjusted for stature in some evaluations of children and in some statistical analyses. These adjustments can be made in several ways. One simple procedure, that is applicable on an age-independent basis before pubescence, is to compute percentile levels of weight-for-stature corresponding to the values observed in a large survey (Hamill *et al.*, 1977, 1979).

Transformation of variables

Some recorded variables should be transformed before they are analyzed statistically. These transformations may be mandated by the nature of the data and by the statistical test to be applied. Tests of the significance of

differences between groups for one variable (e.g. t-test) or for several groups simultaneously (analysis of variance) require that the data be normally distributed. This requirement was recognized early in the Fels study (Sontag & Wallace, 1935a[305]). Problems arising from the non-normality of the distributions may be circumvented by using a distribution-free test. The specific question being examined will determine whether a distribution-free test, or normalization of the distributions, is indicated.

For some variables, such as skinfold thicknesses and ages at onset of ossification, skewed distributions are common but not universal (Garn *et al.*, 1965g[71]). Such a distribution can be normalized using a Box–Cox transformation or logarithmic (log) transformation (Edwards *et al.*, 1955; Box & Cox, 1964; Patton, 1979). Log transformations may be appropriate also in the presence of multiplicative relationships in the data, as may occur between the independent variables in a predictive equation. In these circumstances, log transformations simplify the demonstration and analysis of the multiplicative relationships. Finally, log transforms of one or both variables commonly change a curvilinear bivariate relationship to a rectilinear one that is easier to interpret. This occurs for some ratios used to describe fat patterning. Some have suggested the use of Box–Cox (1964) transformations to develop reference percentile curves. This approach has been criticized by Roche and Guo (1988)[237].

Statistical analyses in the Fels Longitudinal Study

This section presents an overview of the methods that have been applied to analyze data in the Fels study. More detailed descriptions of any unusual methods will be given in the parts of this volume that present the substantive results of the analyses. Additionally, this section will direct attention to improvements in statistical methods for which Fels investigators, or colleagues working with Fels data, have been responsible. Generally, the statistical methods applied were appropriate for the questions to be answered or the hypotheses to be tested, but some exceptions occurred early in the study when statistical tests were applied to some samples that were too small to provide conclusive results.

Some statistical methods that were developed at Fels for specific purposes have had considerable influences. Examples are the excellent review of statistical methods by Garn (1958b[53]) that improved the statistical analyses of a whole generation of orthodontists and papers that have had a major impact on the statistical analyses made by pediatric nephrologists (Roche, 1978a[184], 1978b[185]; Potter *et al.*, 1978).

One common statistical procedure is the calculation of descriptive statistics such as the mean and standard deviation (SD). Commonly,

growth data, particularly those related to body fat and those for increments, are not normally distributed (Garn, Rohmann & Robinow, 1961c[152]; Garn & Rohmann, 1964b[140]). Therefore, skewness and kurtosis have been evaluated and, when indicated, percentiles have been used to describe the distributions, and the significance of differences between non-normal distributions for group means has been tested by the non-parametric Mann–Whitney test, or the distributions have been transformed.

When distributions were skewed, some consideration was given to possible causes for this skewness. Severe error bias is unlikely, but truncation and mixtures of normal distributions are possible. Truncation occurs, as pointed out by Garn and his co-workers (1961b[144]), in the distribution of stature increments after 17 years because some will have reached adult stature at 17 years. Other distributions may be non-normal because several normal distributions are combined in the data set. A family of distributions with location and scale factors was developed that can be fitted to a set of data (Mukherjee, 1982; Mukherjee & Siervogel, 1983; Mukherjee *et al.*, 1984). In addition, a set of multimodal distributions has been developed for use when a mixture of normal distributions is untenable (Mukherjee & Siervogel, 1983). These analyses of distributions can be valuable in genetic studies. In addition, Mukherjee and Hurst (1984) described procedures that facilitate descriptions of the distributions of discrete or continuous data. In other statistical work, a curve-fitting procedure was developed that provides a normal approximation to a binomial distribution (Lee & Guo, 1986). This facilitates the testing of hypotheses using data from large samples.

Hypotheses relating to differences between groups have been tested in many analyses made at Fels. Severe methodological problems are not present if the test is for one variable and it relates to the difference between the means for boys and girls. Caution is necessary, however, when testing the significance of differences between, for example, the means for head circumference in 4-year-old boys and 5-year-old boys. When the data come from a longitudinal study, they will be biased due to the inclusion of many of the same boys in both age groups. If only a few were measured at both ages, which is unusual in data from the Fels study, it might be preferable to exclude these and thereby make the data independent at the two ages. Sometimes, multiple measurements of individuals can be an advantage. For example, such data allowed a multivariate analysis of variance for repeated measures to estimate the examination effects in serial measures of hearing ability (Roche *et al.*, 1983a[255]).

During the analysis of Fels data, regressions have been calculated to

describe the relationship between a variable and age or between two or more variables at an age. The simplest type of regression is a linear model. As an example, a linear model can be used to describe the relationship of weight to stature in 6-year-old boys, as shown in Fig. 2.1. The regression equation (weight in kilograms $= 30.915 + [0.446 \times$ stature in centimeters]) summarizes this relationship and allows predictions of weight from stature. The 95% confidence limits of this regression, which are included in Fig. 2.1, allow the identification of outlying data points. In some analyses, one variable has been regressed on a logarithmic transformation of another variable.

Multiple regression has been used commonly at Fels in the development of predictive equations that estimate one variable from a combination of other variables. This is used in the Roche–Wainer–Thissen method for the prediction of adult stature from variables observed during childhood (Roche, Wainer & Thissen, 1974a[270], 1974b[271], 1975a[272], 1975b[273]).

Typically, predictive equations are derived by least squares regression in which the sum of the squares of the residuals is minimized. In this sense, 'residuals' are the differences between the fitted values and the observed points. This approach provides the best equation for the given data but, if the multiple predictor (independent) variables are significantly correlated (multicollinearity), the coefficients in the predictive equation are likely to be unstable. In the presence of this instability, predictive equations may perform poorly when applied to other samples. This is a major problem because such equations are, of course, developed so that they can be applied to samples other than those from which they were derived.

The severity of the problem can be determined by calculating the variance inflation factor for each independent variable included in a predictive equation. The variance inflation factor $(1/1 - R^2)$ reflects the extent to which each independent variable can be predicted from the other independent variables in combination; values greater than 10.0 are generally accepted as indicating potentially serious multicollinearity.

The solution to the problem is not to abandon the least squares approach but to modify the data from which the predictive equation is derived. Ridge regression should be considered for this purpose. In ridge regression, the interrelationships between the independent variables are reduced by adding a small constant to the diagonal elements of the variance–covariance matrix of the independent variables.

The constant employed is the smallest value beyond which further increases in the constant would have little effect on the coefficients in the predictive equation. Unfortunately, these possible values for the constant differ slightly from one independent variable to another, making it difficult

to select the optimal value for the constant in this way. Alternatively, the value can be determined precisely using a PRESS procedure in which one data point is omitted at a time, after which it is estimated from the remaining information. The differences between these estimates and the omitted data are the PRESS residuals; the sum of the squares of these residuals is called the PRESS statistic, and the value chosen for the constant is that at which the PRESS statistic is smallest.

The PRESS procedure also identifies data points with large residuals. These points, that were estimated poorly by the data remaining after the omission, one at a time, of values for independent variables, are called leveraged observations because they make large contributions to the instability of predictive equations. Their effects are reduced in robust estimations because leveraged observations are given smaller weights than other data points when predictive equations are being developed. The equations developed by robust estimation perform better than equations derived from the original data when both are applied to other samples (Roche, Guo & Houtkooper, 1989b[241]).

Piecewise regressions have been used at Fels to identify the ages at which changes occur in the patterns of growth (Roche & Davila, 1972[222]; Roche, Davila & Mellits, 1975c[227]). Using this procedure, the ages of cessation of growth in stature and the ages at which increases in weight change from being curvilinear to rectilinear have been estimated for individuals. For this purpose, a pair of mathematical functions was fitted to the serial data for each participant from the age at peak height velocity to 28 years, and the junction between the two curves was changed by one data point at a time. The goodness of fit for the total data set was determined for each junction, and the junction (age) at which the goodness of fit was maximal was selected as the age at which the pattern changed for the individual. Although the procedure worked well, particularly for stature, a single function would be fitted in a future analysis of this topic and the function would be integrated to estimate ages at critical points in the growth pattern.

Logistic regression has been used to predict a dichotomous outcome, for example the absence or presence of a value greater than a 'cut-off' level. In logistic regression, the probability (P) of the outcome is divided by $(1-P)$. This mathematical expression $(P/1-P)$ is called the odds ratio; the logarithm of this (log odds ratio) is used as the outcome variable. Logistic regression has been applied to Fels data when the outcome variable was the presence or absence of 'overweight' in adulthood, and the independent (predictor) variable was the corresponding measurement at various ages during childhood (Roche & Guo, 1987[236]; Roche, 1987c[206]; Siervogel, Guo

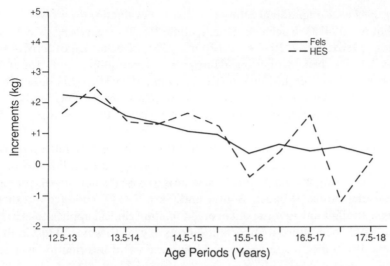

Fig. 2.6 Median values for 6-month increments in weight for girls from the Fels study and from the US Health Examination Survey (HES) conducted by the National Center for Health Statistics, at ages from 12.5 to 18.0 years. (Roche, A.F., Davila, G.H. & Mellits, E.D. (1975c). Late adolescent changes in weight. In *Biosocial Interrelations in Population Adaptation*, ed. E.S. Watts, F.E. Johnston & C.W. Lasker, pp. 309–18[227]. Redrawn with permission from Mouton Publishers.)

& Roche, 1991). Corresponding analyses have been made of serum lipid levels (Guo, Chumlea, Siervogel & Roche, 1991). Logistic regression has been used also to test hypotheses that specific genetic markers are linked to particular phenotypes (Falk *et al.*, 1982).

The central purpose of any longitudinal study is to describe change in individuals. The simplest mathematical description, both conceptually and computationally, is the calculation of increments between successive examinations. Each increment must be adjusted so that it matches the change during a fixed interval that is typically 6 months or 1 year. These adjustments are necessary because it is highly unlikely that participants in a longitudinal study will be examined at intervals of exactly 6 months or 1 year.

Increments describe growth rates during particular intervals but they provide little information about growth patterns and they can be affected markedly by measurement errors. Additionally, the ages at measurement will not coincide with critical points on the growth curves (Roche, 1980a[190]). Because increments require only two data points per individual, they can be readily applied by clinicians and others. Reference data for increments during 1-month and 6-month intervals have been published

from the Fels Longitudinal Study to assist the evaluation of growth rates (Robinow, 1942a; Roche & Himes, 1980[247]; Baumgartner, Roche & Himes, 1986a; Guo, Roche & Moore, 1988; Roche, Guo & Moore 1989a[242]). The benefit of using data from a longitudinal study for this purpose is illustrated in Fig. 2.6 (Roche *et al.*, 1975c[227]). This shows the median values for 6-month increments in weight from the Fels Study are more regular than corresponding data from a nationally representative US study.

The description of patterns of growth within individuals requires a more complex approach. Fundamentally, the problem is to draw a line through a set of data. Anyone can do this. The issue is to base the line on reasonable criteria that can be defended. Sontag and Garn (1954[285]) pointed out that fitting a straight line to serial data could facilitate clinical applications and that it would be justified if important aspects of growth were not lost in the process. It is almost certain, however, that important information will be lost.

Typically, the changes in a variable are analyzed in relation to age. These changes must be described by a mathematical function that summarizes the pattern of growth using a few numbers that are called the coefficients of the parameters in the fitted mathematical function. It is not easy to choose the best function because the patterns of change in individuals tend to be more complex than those in group data and they vary among individuals.

The most direct benefit of fitting a mathematical function to serial data for individuals is the description of change. To be useful, this description must be considerably more parsimonious than the observed data. Expressing this another way, the number of mathematical terms in the function must be considerably less than the number of data points. Ideally, each term in the model will be biologically interpretable, e.g., rate of growth, change in rate of growth, but commonly, such interpretations are uncertain due to correlations between the coefficients of the model. In this area, as in so many others, interrelationships are the rule, not the exception. As stated poetically by Francis Thompson: 'Thou cans't not stir a flower without troubling a star.'

Since the chosen model will have fewer parameters than the number of data points, some smoothing will result. This is desirable because many changes in observed serial data result from measurement errors or small fluctuations that are not biologically informative, e.g., fluctuations in weight due to variations in the sizes of previous meals. If there were many parameters in the function, there would be little smoothing and the estimates of the coefficients of the parameters may be unstable (large

confidence limits), thereby complicating biological interpretations and statistical inferences.

The function can have too few parameters. A very simple function will smooth excessively with the loss of important information. The choice of an equation that provides a parsimonious solution, retains critical information, fits well, smooths moderately, and can be readily integrated requires considerable judgment and experience on the part of a biostatistician. This approach is not recommended for clinical purposes. Mathematical functions are fitted to serial data to serve research purposes; many data points are required and the approach is retrospective in nature.

Early steps in the description of growth patterns are the selection of the features that are critical for testing particular hypotheses, e.g., age at peak height velocity, and the determination of the general nature of the serial changes by visual examination of plots for some individuals chosen at random. An experienced biostatistician can then derive a reasonable set of functions and test them for goodness of fit. The patterns of the residuals in relation to age may show that the functions need to be modified. Large correlations between successive residuals could show that the chosen model is not providing an accurate description of the growth patterns (Bock & Thissen, 1980).

Functions that describe growth patterns can assist comparisons between individuals and between variables, the prediction of adult status and evaluations of the effectiveness of therapy (Roche, 1971a[174]; Holm *et al.*, 1979). In the best of circumstances, the description provided by a function is an approximation because one cannot be sure that all the errors and only the errors have been removed by the smoothing process. One takes heart from the attitude of Tukey: 'An approximate answer to the right problem is worth a good deal more than an exact answer to an approximate problem.'

Some flexible functions have been fitted to serial data from the Fels Longitudinal Study but usually fixed functions have been used. Flexible functions do not have predetermined shapes and, therefore, they are suitable for variables, such as skinfold thicknesses, for which the growth patterns differ among individuals. Longitudinal principal components, splines and kernel estimation are examples of flexible functions. Fixed functions are appropriate when the growth patterns have the same shape for all individuals even though they differ in the timing and the amounts of change. Logistic functions are examples of fixed functions that fit well to variables such as stature and head circumference from birth to 6 years.

Longitudinal principal components analysis (LPCA) is one type of flexible model that has been used to describe growth patterns. This method

is a variant of principal component analysis which is usually applied to an intercorrelation matrix for multiple variables at one age while LPCA is applied to an intercorrelation matrix for one variable at multiple ages. This procedure yields a set of components that vary with age but are common to all individuals. Each participant has a specific positive or negative age-invariant coefficient for each component. To some extent, the components can be interpreted biologically and their coefficients can be analyzed statistically. This method has been used in the Fels Longitudinal Study to describe changes in recumbent length, weight/stature[2] and skinfold thicknesses, although it requires a complete data set for each individual (Roche, 1971a[174]; Cronk *et al.*, 1982a, 1982b, 1983a).

A new flexible function for the analysis of serial data, that is robust to missing values, has been developed (Guo *et al.*, 1987b) and is being applied in cancer research and drug trials. In this method, serial data for individuals are pooled between groups receiving different drugs or different dosages, and the data are ranked at each age. These ranks are summed for each group and the significance of the differences between the groups can be tested.

A cubic spline has been used to smooth empirical percentile values for weight, recumbent length and head circumference that were obtained by cross-sectional analyses of Fels data (Hamill *et al.*, 1977, 1979). On other occasions, low-term Fourier analysis has been used to smooth empirical percentiles and serial data for individuals (Roche & Himes, 1980[247]; Roche, 1980a[190]; Cronk & Roche, 1982).

More recently, kernel estimation has been used to smooth data for blood pressure and other variables (Guo *et al.*, 1988, 1989c). Kernel estimation is based on weighted averaging of the observed values within specified age intervals (Guo, 1990). The lengths chosen for these intervals determine the extent of smoothing and the goodness of fit; short intervals lead to less smoothing but the fits are better. The weights given to the values within each age interval vary in relation to the differences between the ages at examinations and the midpoints of the age intervals. The data points that are more divergent from the midpoints are given lower weights. A procedure for calculating the confidence limits of kernel estimates has been developed (Guo, Siervogel & Roche, 1990).

In a comparative study, kernel regression, the triple logistic model, and the Preece–Baines model were fitted to serial data for stature (Guo *et al.*, in press). The Preece–Baines model did not describe the mid-growth spurt, which occurs at about 6 years, and the parameters from this model showed an earlier onset and longer duration of the pubescent spurt with a less rapid increase in velocity than either kernel regression or the triple logistic

model. The kernel regression and triple logistic methods provided similar descriptions of the pubescent spurt, but the estimates from kernel regression showed an earlier onset and a more rapid increase in velocity for the mid-growth spurt than did the triple logistic model.

A need arose to smooth, across age, the coefficients in numerous age-specific multiple regression equations developed for the prediction of adult stature from childhood variables (Roche *et al.*, 1974a[270], 1974b[271], 1975a[272], 1975b[273]). After this smoothing, a function was fitted to the smoothed data and interpolations were made to intermediate ages. The new statistical method developed for this work took the interrelationships between the variables into account (Roche *et al.*, 1975a[272]; Wainer & Thissen, 1975).

This multivariate smoothing was accomplished after transforming the coefficients so that they became independent of each other (Björck, 1967). Initially, they were smoothed by the '53h' method of Tukey (1972) in which running medians are obtained of each successive five points and then of each successive three points. This provided two smoothed estimates for each age; the means of these pairs were subtracted from the observed values and the same procedure was applied to the residuals. These steps were repeated until further changes did not occur in the smoothed values. After this initial smoothing, a polynomial function was fitted to the smoothed values and these polynomial functions were transformed back to the original variables.

Time series has not been used often in the analysis of Fels data but it was applied to determine whether patterns of change in bioelectric impedance (resistance) were related to timing within the menstrual cycle, assuming a first-order autocorrelation (Roche, Chumlea & Guo, 1986a[217]).

A three-parameter polynomial function, that was used to describe serial changes in weight and recumbent length during infancy (Kouchi, Mukherjee & Roche, 1985a; Kouchi, Roche & Mukherjee, 1985b), included a constant term (intercept), a scale term (slope) and a power term (change in rate of growth). The function fitted well to the data, which is essential but, in many analyses, it is also important that the parameters of the model be biologically interpretable. Such interpretations are difficult, if the parameters are significantly intercorrelated. In these analyses by Kouchi and her colleagues, the total intercorrelation matrices of the parameters were adjusted for the within-individual correlations, using a procedure introduced by Bock *et al.* (1973) in an earlier analysis of Fels data. The new matrices obtained for the within-individual correlations provided more stable parameter estimates for individuals and facilitated comparisons between individuals.

A four-parameter polynomial function has been used to describe growth in head circumference from birth to 18 years (Roche *et al.*, 1987b[258]; Guo, Roche & Moore, 1988) and three-parameter polynomials have been applied to logarithms of weight/stature[2] and to weight and recumbent length during infancy (Siervogel, Mukherjee & Roche, 1984; Roche, Guo & Moore, 1989a[242]). Since the function fitted well to the data for infancy, and because observed data at 1-month intervals are scarce, the function was used to estimate values for status at 1-month intervals and for increments during 1-month intervals for weight and recumbent length from birth to 1 year.

Fixed functions have been developed to describe growth in skeletal dimensions (Bock *et al.*, 1973; Thissen *et al.*, 1976; Roche *et al.*, 1977a[251]). The general patterns of growth in these variables are similar among individuals despite differences in intercepts, rates of change, and the timing of critical events. A double logistic function was developed to describe growth in recumbent length from 1 to 18 years within individuals (Bock *et al.*, 1973). In this function, the first logistic component describes pre-pubertal growth and continues at a low level to 18 years. The second logistic component describes the adolescent growth spurt. Although the fit is generally good, the function tends to over-predict from 4 to 6 years and to under-predict slightly in early pubescence and late adolescence. Only three, or at most four, of the six parameters in the function are needed to describe individual differences. Publication of this function sparked a sudden increased interest in fitting functions to growth data.

Later, Bock & Thissen (1976, 1980) developed a triple logistic function to provide a better description of growth from 1 to 18 years, and used it to characterize the unusual patterns of growth in some Fels participants (Bock, 1986). This function fitted better than the double logistic function and it defined the mid-growth spurt clearly. Bock & Thissen also described elegant methods for adjusting the correlations between parameters. Different fixed models were used to describe individual patterns of growth in weight and recumbent length from 3 months to 6 years and changes in weight/stature[2] from 2 to 18 years (Siervogel *et al.*, in press; Byard, Guo and Roche, 1991).

Lestrel (Lestrel & Brown, 1976; Lestrel & Roche, 1984, 1986) extended mathematical modelling to the description of two-dimensional shapes using Fourier series analysis. Radii were drawn from a centroid to landmarks on the outline of the shape, after which a polynomial with Fourier terms was used to describe the lengths of the radii. This description of shape was made independent of size. The method has been applied to the silhouette of the cranial vault and paired ectocranial and endocranial

outlines to measure cranial thickness (Lestrel & Roche, 1977) and to outlines of nasal bones (Lestrel, Engstrom & Bodt, 1991).

Principal components analysis has been used to describe the patterns of adipose tissue distribution. The aim of these cross-sectional analyses was to identify primary dimensions of patterns in the anatomical distribution of adipose tissue that are independent of overall body fatness (Baumgartner *et al.*, 1986b). In addition, principal component analysis has been used, in the development of predictive equations, to investigate the intercorrelation matrices and assist the selection of independent variables from many candidates (Roche *et al.*, 1975a[272]). Cluster analysis of the variables has been used for the same purpose (Roche *et al.*, 1975a[272]; Baumgartner, Siervogel & Roche, 1989b).

In principal component analysis, a reduced set of linear combinations of variables is sought that provides essentially the same information as the original variables. If two or more variables within a principal component have closely similar loadings, then only one member of such a set need be retained for further analysis. Scores for individuals can be calculated from the loadings for each component creating new variables that are independent. These new variables retain all the crucial information and they can be used in multivariate analyses without fear of multicollinearity. In principal components analysis, the potential independent variables are grouped and, if there are high correlations between the group members, only one member of a group is retained for further analysis. Alternatively, the groups themselves may become the object of analysis.

Profile analysis has been used to analyze patterns of adipose tissue thicknesses and ages at onset of ossification in the Fels study using both absolute and relative values (Sontag & Reynolds, 1944[297]; Sontag & Lipford, 1943[288]; Garn, 1955a[44]). These profiles have been compared visually and they have been analyzed statistically in relation to genetic hypotheses using either correlations between corresponding values for pairs of related individuals or the standard deviations of the differences among values.

Robinow (1968) wrote an interesting paper relating to sample size determination and described simple statistical procedures that can be applied in the field. He suggested that data for weight and recumbent length could be combined for the two sexes during infancy, thus reducing the sample size required. It has been shown that this is not justified for recumbent length (Roche & Guo, unpublished data). Robinow noted that chi-square tests can be used in the field to determine whether groups differ in the percentage under the 5th percentile and he described a method by which data for weight from 1 month to 5 years can be adjusted to an

'equivalent' weight at a central age because there is little change in the shapes of the distributions during this age range. This approach could be helpful if differences in growth between shorter age intervals are not obscured.

The preceding discussion provides an overview of statistical applications in the Fels Longitudinal Study. The wide range of purposes and the consequent variety of analytic methods used, even within topic areas, will become more evident in the later chapters. The methods applied recently are more elegant and effective than those applied in the early years of the study, but we have not reached the end of these advances. Further improvements in data management and statistical methods must occur and they will lead to increased understanding of the phenomena being studied.

3 *Prenatal, familial and genetic studies*

'The growth of the fetus increases more and more, in equal time, till it escapes the womb.'

George LeClerc Buffon (1707–1788)

The original mission of the Fels Research Institute included the serial study of individuals before birth; this aspect of the mission has not been neglected. Particularly during the early years of the Fels Longitudinal Study, strenuous efforts were made to perform prenatal studies and successes were achieved although the available technology allowed only a narrow range of investigations. Better methods are now available that could assist prenatal studies of growth, maturation and body composition, but some involve radiation (computerized tomography), and others are expensive (ultrasonography, magnetic resonance imaging). Imaging procedures have not been applied serially in normal pregnancies although these studies have great potential.

Some investigations made within the Fels Longitudinal Study that relate to the fetal period are described with physical growth (Chapter 4) and skeletal and dental studies (Chapter 6). The prenatal investigations described in this Chapter have been grouped under the headings: prenatal studies, and familial and genetic studies.

Prenatal studies
Diet and nutrition
During the 1930s and early 1940s, the relationships between prenatal maternal diets and the size of the infant at birth were studied. This was a Herculean task. Daily dietary records were kept by 205 mothers for 4 to 7 months. These mothers were not given dietary advice; this was a 'natural experiment,' as is generally true for the observations made in the Fels

Table 3.1 *Coefficients of variation* (CV^a; *%) for creatinine and creatine in 24-hour urine samples measured daily during pregnancy (from Seegers & Potgieter, 1937)*

Participant	Number of days	Creatinine	Creatine
III	7[b]	6.9	31.8
VI	7[b]	0.7	33.5
X	8[b]	7.0	51.8
IX	7[c]	17.1	52.2
VIII	5[c]	11.9	52.3
XIII	26	33.6	184.7
XIV	21	29.5	130.4
XIV[d]	21	40.3	120.2

[a] CV is the coefficient of variation which equals standard deviation/mean.
[b] 28-day intervals.
[c] Successive days.
[d] Diet rigorously controlled.

Longitudinal Study. These, and other dietary data, provided some important information.

Interest in protein intake and metabolism during pregnancy was stimulated by findings from animal experiments at the Fels Research Institute (Seegers, 1937a). These studies showed that the offspring of pregnant albino rats fed a nitrogen-free diet had low nitrogen values per unit body weight during pregnancy and low birthweights. At the time this study was published, many considered that a low protein diet during pregnancy did not affect the fetus although contrary findings had been reported from the Harvard Growth Study. It was also shown that nitrogen retention in a young primipara was similar to that reported for older pregnant women (Seegers, 1937b).

In an extension of this work, Fels data for daily intakes of protein were averaged for individuals and used to place the mothers in one of five groups (Sontag & Wines, 1947[308]). After excluding data for pregnancies resulting in premature or multiple births and those in which pathological conditions occurred in either the mother or the infant, correlations between group membership and values for weight and recumbent length at birth were not significant. This implies that homeostatic mechanisms maintain the blood levels for protein and that these levels fall only when the dietary reductions are drastic, and interfere with the supply of nutrients to the fetus.

The difference between these results and those from the Harvard study may have been due to the generally lower protein intakes in the Harvard study and their failure to exclude toxemic mothers who were treated with

low protein diets. These and other findings were included in a critical review published by Sontag in 1941.

Earlier, Seegers and Potgieter (1937) reported the 24-hour excretion of creatinine and creatine in the urine of pregnant women during the third day of a uniform diet. These measurements did not change with gestational age, but they fluctuated irregularly even for the participant (Number XIV) whose diet was 'rigorously controlled' (Table 3.1). The correlations between the intake and the urinary excretion of nitrogen were also variable; the correlations within participants ranged from $r = -0.5$ to $+0.4$ for creatinine and from $r = -0.7$ to $+0.2$ for creatine.

Other studies concerned the intake of calcium and phosphorus during pregnancy. It was shown that, in Wistar rats, very low levels of vitamin D and calcium in the maternal diets led to low values for weight, and for the content of calcium and phosphorus in the offspring at birth, but the calcium:phosphorus ratio was high (Sontag, Munson & Huff, 1936[289]). These animal studies were conducted in concert with studies of calcium and phosphorus in Fels mothers. A significant correlation was reported between the serum calcium of mothers during pregnancy and that of their infants soon after birth, but many other correlations between maternal and infant variables were not significant (Sontag, Pyle & Cape, 1935[296]). Sontag and his associates concluded that maternal dietary reports were too unreliable for such investigations and that future studies should be based on weighed food portions. This decision was not implemented in the Longitudinal Study.

In partial response to this conclusion, however, Pyle and Huff (1936) described a procedure in which fixed intakes of calcium and phosphorus were maintained for 3 days. They considered this would stabilize conditions sufficiently to allow studies of calcium and phosphorus. The 3-day method was used at Fels for logistic reasons and also because it was argued that: 'One needs as short a balance period as possible if he is studying metabolism during pregnancy when the rates of change in both the fetal and maternal organism are not constant.' This is doubtful at best, particularly when the 3-day periods used in the Fels study were separated by 28-day intervals. To 'validate' the 3-day records, it was shown that the variability of calcium, protein, and nitrogen in the food, feces and urine from such records was similar to the variability reported from studies in which fixed intakes were maintained for longer periods (Pyle & Huff, 1936; Sontag & Potgieter, 1938[293]). Data from 3-day and longer periods on fixed intakes were not compared within individuals.

Applying their 3-day method to Fels mothers, Huff and Pyle (1937) identified periods of positive and negative nitrogen balance and for

calcium and phosphorus jointly. They showed differences in the fecal excretion of calcium and phosphorus between those in positive and those in negative balance but not in the ingestion or urinary excretion of these minerals. If such a study were conducted now, residence in a metabolic ward would be considered mandatory and the period of fixed intake would be substantially longer.

The Fels qualitative method of recording dietary intakes and calculating nutrient intakes was compared with a quantitative method in six women who kept dietary records for a combined period of 30 weeks (Sontag, Seegers & Hulstone, 1938[301]). In the qualitative method, food diaries were kept for a week. The number of servings for each food group was used in combination with the average serving size to calculate nutrient intakes from food composition tables. In comparison with estimates from a quantitative method, the qualitative estimates were low, but the paired estimates were correlated with coefficients ranging from r = 0.4 for fat to r = 0.8 for protein. The authors concluded that the qualitative method was suitable for group comparisons but 'obviously, the method is not applicable as a part of balance study technique.' The conclusion was justified.

In 1938, Pyle, Potgieter and Comstock studied nine pregnant women using 3-day balance periods (two to six periods per women). These mothers were told how to weigh their food and instructed to eat the same kinds and quantities for three successive days. On the third day, the food was sampled and 24-hour collections were made of urine and feces. On the fourth day, blood was obtained to measure serum calcium, and basal metabolic rate (oxygen consumption) was recorded. There were significant correlations between serum calcium and calcium balance (r = −0.4), serum calcium and fecal calcium (r = 0.8) and calcium balance and gestational age (r = 0.6). Many correlations were calculated but they were not adjusted for the effects of multiple comparisons. Consequently the significance levels may be lower than they appear. In this study, the calcium balance data were obtained for short periods without sufficient control of intake and losses. Furthermore, the unequal loading of the women, due to between-subject variations in the number of study periods, would have led to some confounding. Better studies could be made now, but they are likely to occur in departments of nutrition where it is hoped the efforts of the pioneers are remembered.

It was noted by Sontag (1944a[279]) that some obstetricians attempt to reduce birthweight, and thereby reduce the incidence of obsterical complication, by limiting the maternal caloric intake during pregnancy. Sontag considered that this reflected a lack of concern about the possible

effects of the maternal diet on the fetus. Furthermore, he postulated that the fetus may be affected by maternal emotions which can elevate the circulating levels of some chemicals that pass through the placenta. He noted that the infants of mothers with severe emotional stress during pregnancy tend to be hyperactive and irritable after birth.

Physiology

Despite limited equipment, judged by present standards, the early Fels staff made valiant efforts to study fetal physiology (Sontag, 1944a[279], b[280]). One set of these studies related to fetal heart rates. It was noted that these rates increased significantly with maternal smoking and it was concluded that this was probably due to the passage of toxins into the fetal circulation (Sontag & Wallace, 1935a[305]). In this impressive study, the reliability of counting the heart rates was established, partly by having two observers count simultaneously. In one investigation, the fetal heart rates were determined from 5 minutes before until 14 minutes after lighting a cigarette; this counting was done 81 times in five women. There was a mean increase in rate of seven beats/minute except in one participant who was a non-smoker and did not inhale. This was one of the very earliest studies that reported an effect of maternal smoking on the fetus. Later, Sontag and Richards (1938[300]) again observed effects of maternal smoking on the fetal heart rate but, because of the marked variability and the small sample, they were unable to demonstrate statistically significant changes.

In a series of studies, it was shown that the fetal heart rate increased by an average of 12 beats/minute when a vibrating frequency of 120 beats/minute was applied to the maternal abdomen or the mother was exposed to an air-conducted tone (Sontag & Wallace, 1934[304], 1936[307]; Bernard & Sontag, 1947). These increased rates occurred independently of fetal movements and were not noted until the last trimester of pregnancy. Sontag and his colleagues suggested that these effects were associated with the innervation of the heart by sympathetic fibers or with maturation of the fetal adrenal gland.

Sontag and Richards (1938[300]) published an excellent review of the maturation of the physiological mechanisms that might regulate fetal heart rates. They realized their studies of fetal heart rates were limited because 'our organism is not seen, nor scarcely felt nor heard.' Nevertheless, they persevered and used the best methods available without concealing their defects. As they wrote: 'No amount of calibration or recalibration will reduce certain sources of error inherent in the situation.' This perseverance was dictated by strict adherence to the original Fels mission. Their stated aims were: (1) 'to secure sufficiently reliable criteria of fetal activity and

reactivity so that these variables measured in the fetal period may be related to others measured in post-natal life' and (2) to clarify developmental sequences.

In a study of 30 pregnant women, observed repeatedly, Sontag and Richards (1938[300]) found marked variations in fetal heart rates within and between individuals. The mean rates tended to decrease slightly after the sixth month of pregnancy but rates exceeding 160 beats/minute occurred with a frequency of 6% in the last month of pregnancy indicating that caution should be exercised when rapid rates are used as an index of fetal distress. These findings were confirmed many years later by Welford *et al.* (1967). Sontag and Richards (1938[300]) also reported observations of 16 fetuses in a study that extended to 2 weeks after birth. The fetal and infant data for heart rates and for variability of heart rates in these Fels participants were not significantly correlated. These workers repeated the observations of Sontag and Wallace (1935b[306]) and showed that a vibrator placed on the maternal abdomen tended to increase the fetal heart rate, particularly late in pregnancy, but the effects they noted were not statistically significant. They reported that increases in fetal heart rates were associated with fetal movements but not with maternal heart rates, or maternal sleeping or eating.

Sontag and Newbery (1940[291], 1941[292]) reported the incidence and nature of fetal arrhythmias, which they considered were usually of sinus origin and influenced by external factors such as pressure and vibration. In group data, Sontag and Richards (1938[300]) found that increases in heart rate were accompanied by an increased number of extrasystoles.

This work on fetal heart rate was theoretically interesting and it provided some direction to future research, but it was limited by its restriction to brief time intervals.

Fetal movements

The first report from the Fels Research Institute described an apparatus for recording fetal movements (Sontag & Wallace, 1933[303]). Four air-filled rubber sacs held firmly against the maternal abdomen simultaneously recorded the movements of all parts of the abdomen. Pens mounted on these sacs produced records on moving paper. Fetal movements caused differential shifts of the pens, whereas maternal breathing caused similar shifts in all the pens. This apparatus was used for only a brief period because it was cumbersome and close correspondence was shown between the records of fetal movements from the apparatus and those from maternal reports (Sontag & Wallace, 1935b[306]).

Instances in which women stated that fetal movements were increased

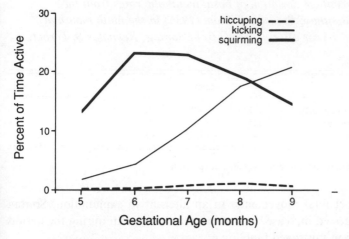

Fig. 3.1 The percentages of time spent hiccuping, kicking and squirming by fetuses at various gestational ages (data from Newbery, 1941).

with fear, anxiety, fatigue and auditory stimulation were reported (Sontag & Wallace, 1934[304]; Sontag, 1944a[279]). Richards, Newbery and Fallgatter (1938) considered that errors in the maternal reports of fetal movement may have obscured some real relationships. There was some consistency across time in the amounts of movement recorded for fetuses with month-to-month rank order correlations of about $+0.7$. There was not, however, any evidence of a diurnal rhythm or a relationship to maternal activity. Nevertheless, changes in the maternal basal metabolic rate during 2–6-month intervals were significantly correlated with the frequency of fetal movements, but not their intensity. After about 32 weeks of gestation, there was a marked increase in fetal movements and these movements increased in response to a sound stimulus. This response might be an index of neuromuscular maturation (Sontag & Wallace, 1935b[306]; Bernard & Sontag, 1947).

The possibility that the frequency of fetal movements could be associated with the fat content of the infant at birth was explored by Sontag (1940[277]). He found a significant negative correlation between the amount of fetal movement during the last 8 weeks of pregnancy and weight/recumbent length[3] which he used as an index of fat stores.

In another study of 12 women, it was shown that the frequency of fetal movements accounted for 30–70% of the variance in the performance of the infant on the Gesell scale at 6 months (Richards & Newbery, 1938; Richards & Nelson, 1938). The authors postulated that this could reflect bias in the maternal reports if more alert and intelligent mothers were more

Table 3.2 *Percentage deviation of basal metabolic rates from the standards of Boothby, Berkson & Dunn (1936) in the ninth month of pregnancy and 1 year after delivery (from Sontag, Reynolds & Torbet, 1944*[299]*)*

	N	Mean	SD
Ninth month of pregnancy	158	+5.89[a]	8.5
One year after delivery	115	−8.33[b]	9.7
Gain in pregnancy	142	+14.27	10.8

The difference between a and b is significant (p < 0.01).

likely to report fetal movements. In an alternative explanation, Sontag (1941[278]) suggested increased use of the nervous system during the period of myelinization improved function.

Newbery (1941) directed attention to possible differences in the types of fetal movements. She wrote: 'Some fetuses are constantly turning and squirming. Others keep the same general position but kick and thrust with hands and feet. Some fetuses have hiccups almost every day, others not at all.' The recognition of kicking and squirming appeared to be highly reliable with coefficients of 0.8 between measurements made 2 weeks apart. The percentages of time spent by the fetuses in these activities are shown in Fig. 3.1. Some trends were evident despite the marked variability. With advancing gestational age, there was an almost linear increase in the mean percentage of time spent kicking and there was a slight decrease in the percentage of time spent squirming after a gestational age of 6 months. Newbery suggested that these trends may be related to changes in the size of the fetus and the force it can exert or they may be responses of the fetus to slight anoxemia late in pregnancy.

In the Fels study, fetal hiccups were described by a mother as 'sudden, quick jerks or thumps, recurring at regular intervals every 2 to 4 minutes' (Norman, 1942). Fetal hiccups have a pronounced sound component and become less frequent minute by minute. Norman first noted them as being reported by mothers in the fifth month of pregnancy; they became more common as pregnancy advanced except for a decrease during the final 2 weeks. The hiccup scores were markedly variable, but did not differ with parity or obesity (Newbery, 1941). The incidence of fetal hiccups seemed to be related to changes in maternal position that may cause pressure on the fetus or the cord. The general conclusion was that the unreliability of the data did not justify further studies. Fetal hiccups are now recognized as a real phenomenon, but they are not known to be functionally significant.

Fels was unique among the US longitudinal studies in the emphasis placed on the prenatal period. The Fels scientists conducted many prenatal studies that required massive efforts and many resources; at least 15 000 hours of fetal movements were recorded. These studies tended to become institutionalized and, although subjected to some critical appraisal, this did not include consideration of their termination until 1970. Many recent changes have occurred in this scientific area resulting from the introduction of expensive equipment which almost mandates that studies be hospital-based (Cronk, 1983).

Basal metabolic rate

Basal metabolic rate was a major component of the early Fels observations, as it was in the Denver Growth Study. Measures of basal metabolic rate are useful guides to the active cell mass of the body and to caloric needs. The Fels reports emphasize that the recorded values tended to be lower than the 'standards' because the latter had been obtained in clinics from patients who were anxious and were not accustomed to the procedure. Also, the Fels data were obtained in duplicate and the lower of the paired values was used in the analyses. Some of the Fels interest in basal metabolic rates concerned their possible associations with maternal and fetal tissue changes during pregnancy. Sontag, Reynolds and Torbet (1944[299]) reported basal metabolic rates from 158 Fels mothers who were free of pathological conditions that might have altered their basal metabolism. Despite marked variability, the values at the ninth month of pregnancy were significantly higher than those 1 year after delivery; the increases during pregnancy were negatively correlated ($r = -0.6$) with the values 1 year post partum (Table 3.2).

A further analysis was made of relationships between basal metabolic rates and some other variables in five pregnant participants each of whom had multiple 3-day balance studies (Pyle, 1938). A rationale was not presented for the associations tested. There were significant positive correlations of gestational age with urinary creatine and basal metabolic rate, but the correlations between urinary nitrogen and hemoglobin were negative. When the stage of pregnancy was held constant, there was a negative correlation between basal metabolic rate and hemoglobin. The author realized that the sample size was too small for definitive conclusions. This exploratory work exemplifies the far-ranging interests of Fels scientists.

Familial and genetic studies

Many analyses within the Fels Longitudinal Study have been based on familial associations and, therefore, reflect the combined effects of genetic and environmental factors. An overview of these studies will be presented in this chapter; they are considered in other chapters in relation to the determinants of particular traits.

Between 1971 and 1977 two types of genetic data were collected from the Fels participants and their blood relatives: (i) 24 red cell markers, 17 blood proteins or enzymes and saliva factors that are completely genetically determined, and (ii) traits with a large genetic component that are also influenced by the environment. The traits in the second group include hand and foot dominance, tongue gymnastics, shapes of epicanthic folds and auricles, ear wax consistency, color vision, iris pigmentation, hair and skin color, phenylthiocarbamide (PTC) tasting ability, and dermatoglyphic patterns. Additionally, deoxyribonucleic acid (DNA) has been extracted from white blood cells and stored for future use.

In general, genetic data remain fixed for an individual throughout life. Consequently, it is hoped they will amplify the biological description of the Fels participants and that associations will be demonstrated between these variables and patterns of growth and maturation. A proposal to the National Institutes of Health to study possible linkages between variations in DNA and those in growth patterns has been funded recently. There is enthusiasm for this investigation which may greatly increase knowledge of the genetic control of growth patterns. It is only in the Fels Longitudinal Study that data exist that can provide this knowledge.

Familial studies

Many data collected from Fels participants who share family relationships have demonstrated the presence of genetic control over growth and maturation (Sontag & Garn, 1957[286]; Garn & Rohmann, 1966a[141]). In a series of studies related to dental maturation, it was shown that the degree of tooth calcification at an age and the timing of dental emergence were more highly correlated within monozygous twin pairs than within dizygous twin pairs, and that these maturational traits were significantly correlated between sibling pairs (Garn, Lewis & Polacheck, 1960c[123]; Garn, Lewis & Kerewsky, 1965a[107], 1965b[108], 1967c[113]). Additionally, evidence was presented that the order of dental calcification, tooth size, and the number and pattern of dental cusps were under genetic control (Garn *et al.*, 1965a[107], 1965b[108], 1965c[118]; Garn, Lewis & Shoemaker, 1956a[124]; Garn, Lewis & Kerewsky, 1967b[112], 1967c[113], 1967d[114]; Garn, 1966a[66]). Furthermore, the X chromosome may be important in some of these aspects of

dental development (Garn *et al.*, 1960a[74], 1965a[107], 1965b[108]). This evidence for genetic control over dental maturation is not surprising since dental maturation is affected little by levels of nutrition (Garn *et al.*, 1965b[108]). In related studies, the genetic control of Carabelli's polymorphism on the first maxillary molar was found to be independent of tooth size and cusp number (Garn *et al.*, 1966g[76]; Garn, 1966a[66]).

The skeleton is influenced by both nutritional and endocrine variations. Nevertheless, evidence has been reported from the Fels study of genetic involvement in rates of skeletal maturation, the sequence of onset of ossification within groups of bones and the rates of periosteal bone growth (Garn & Rohmann, 1960a[134], 1966b[142]; Sontag & Lipford, 1943[288]; Reynolds, 1943; Garn & Shamir, 1958[164]; Garn *et al.*, 1961b[144]). Furthermore, there were sibling concordances in the patterns of ossification, especially for missing ossification centers in the foot and for the presence of pseudoepiphyses in the hand (Garn, 1966a[66]; Garn & Rohmann, 1966a[141]). The presence of a bony spur crossing the vertebral artery, as it passes superior to the posterior arch of the atlas, was shown to be inherited in a fashion consistent with a Mendelian dominant trait (Selby, Garn & Kanareff, 1955). A spur was present in some children when it was absent in the parents, and spurs were more common in boys than girls.

Other aspects of genetic involvement with skeletal growth were shown by analyses of data for recumbent length and stature in which there appeared to be evidence of X-chromosome effects (Garn, 1966a[66]; Garn & Rohmann, 1962a[136], 1966b[142]), and by analyses of parent–child correlations for stature (Garn & Rohmann, 1966b[142]). Himes and colleagues (1981) explored this matter further. They calculated correlations between the average statures of the two parents (mid-parent stature) and the statures of sons and daughters at ages from 2 through 18 years. These coefficients were about 0.4 at ages up to 13 years for the offspring and then increased rapidly with age in boys but not girls.

Analyses based on sibling pairings led Reynolds (1951) to conclude there was considerable genetic involvement in the thickness of subcutaneous adipose tissue, but later analyses of Fels data failed to confirm this (Garn, 1961c[59]). Significant correlations were reported, however, between the chest breadths of parents and stature, mental test performance and the rates of skeletal maturation in the offspring (Garn *et al.*, 1960a[74]; Garn, 1962b[61]; Kagan & Garn, 1963). These familial correlations and those for age at menarche and Gesell test item achievement (Garn & Rohmann, 1966a[141]) could be due to genetic or environmental influences.

Dermatoglyphic records of the fingers and palms were obtained from

Fels participants older than 8 years, and from their relatives. Dermato-glyphic patterns form between the 7th and 24th weeks of fetal life; a critical period for their development occurs at about the 13th week. There is marked genetic control over the development of dermatoglyphic patterns but the mode of inheritance, while almost certainly polygenic, is not clearly established. The local factors involved in their development are poorly understood. Since, once formed, these patterns do not change, they reflect the genetic and local environmental factors operating early in development and, therefore, have great biological interest.

The distribution of dermatoglyphyic patterns on digits was described by Roche, Siervogel & Roche (1979a[268]). In the Fels population, arches were common on digits II and III, but rare on digit V. Radial loops and radial loop closures were more common on digit II than on the other digits and, on each digit except digit I, plain whorls were more common than double loop whorls.

Ridge counts on the radial and ulnar sides of the fingers for unrelated Fels participants were subjected to principal components analysis (Sier-vogel, Roche & Roche, 1978). Three components were obtained that were consistent across sex and hand and represented three regions: (i) digit I, (ii) digits II and III, and (iii) digits IV and V. These are probably distinct developmental fields that provide varying local environments which interact with specific gene sets that are involved in the formation of dermal ridges. Additionally, there were significant correlations between digits in radial and ulnar ridge counts and in the totals of these (Siervogel, Roche & Roche, 1979).

Siervogel and colleagues (1978, 1979) derived a radio–ulnar whorl ratio to measure the asymmetry of ridge counts for digits that have whorls. This index increased from digit II to digit V, indicating that asymmetry favored the radial ridge count in digit II and favored the ulnar side in digits IV and V. A developmental gradient between digital areas in combination with local environmental factors would account for these findings.

Data from a three-generation pedigree were reported in detail because an extremely rare variant, absence of triradius d, was noted in one Fels participant (Roche, Roche & Siervogel, 1979c[275]). Some relatives of this participant had other rare dermatoglyphic features, but not an absent triradius d. Therefore, a sporadic non-genetic cause could have been responsible. A continuum of variants at this location was described, with absence of the triradius as the extreme.

In an unusual and interesting study, Meier, Goodson & Roche (1987) analyzed dermatoglyphic data in relation to whether individuals pass through pubescence relatively early or relatively late. Groups of rapidly

and slowly maturing males differed significantly in ridge counts and digital pattern intensities while the corresponding groups of females differed only in palmar pattern types. Since dermatoglyphic patterns are established early in fetal life, the data suggested that the tempos of fetal development and of pubescent development are related. In each sex, those who were late to reach pubescence tended to have more complex dermatoglyphic patterns, although the affected areas differed between the sexes. This work provided suggestive evidence of a possible link between the rates of fetal and pubescent development. It is one of many exciting possibilities presented by the Fels data.

The failure of teeth to develop was used also as an index of variation in the intrauterine environment during the first trimester of pregnancy (Garn, Lewis & Kerewsky, 1963b[104]). The prevalence of missing teeth was established and it was demonstrated that absence of a third molar tooth tended to be associated with the absence of other teeth or reduction in their size. These studies by Meier and by Garn represent attempts to understand more about prenatal characteristics and their relationships to traits observed after birth.

In an investigation that exemplifies the widespread interests of Fels investigators, especially during the early years of the study, Sontag and Allen (1947[282]) reported that children with pulmonary calcification were more likely to be sensitive to histoplasmin than to tuberculin and the timing of the development of sensitivity, in relation to the development of calcification, was closer for histoplasmin than for tuberculin. Lung calcification tended to be familial, but there was no familial tendency for the histoplasmin skin reactions.

Genetic studies

There was an intentional over-enrollment of triplets into the Fels study because of interest in comparing individuals within these trios, especially when the trios included monozygous pairs. This interest led to a paper by Robinow (1943) concerning the diagnosis of zygosity based on con-cordance for traits inherited in a Mendelian fashion. His statistical approach was based on concordance–discordance ratios from studies of randomly selected twins. This approach led to estimates of the probability of monozygosity and of polyzygosity within sets of twins or triplets when genetic traits were concordant.

Some studies of triplets focused on phenotypic similarities. A set of identical triplets was the subject of three reports. Sontag and Nelson (1933[290]) described their physical and mental traits. Later, Sontag and Reynolds (1944[297]) described the onset of ossification which tended to be

the same in all the triplets, except for the metatarsals. Reynolds and Schoen (1947) described the growth and maturation of these triplets, including the distribution of subcutaneous adipose tissue and muscle thicknesses. Despite considerable similarity, many minor differences were noted in all the variables examined.

Linkage studies attempt to establish the presence of statistically significant associations between genes or genetic markers. Falk *et al.* (1982) and Spence *et al.* (1984), using Fels data in combination with data from other studies, demonstrated significant linkages between some pairs of genetic markers and the absence of linkage for some other pairs. Other analyses at Fels have utilized the records of traits that have a large genetic component. Contrary to some claims in the literature, it was shown that iris pigmentation, which is genetically determined, was not associated with hearing thresholds at various frequencies in children (Roche *et al.*, 1983b[256]).

Segregation analysis of pedigree data from 1152 individuals in 120 families, including many Fels participants, was used to examine alternative genetic models that could explain the patterns of inheritance of the ability to taste phenylthiocarbamide (PTC); some find this very bitter but others find it tasteless (Olson *et al.*, 1989). These models, unlike the usual ones, allowed for the occurrence of taster matings with non-taster offspring, as occurs in the Fels and some other studies. The best fit to the data was obtained with a two-loci model in which one locus controlled PTC tasting and the other controlled more general tasting ability.

Skin color is determined partly by genes and partly by environmental influences. Skin color is usually graded by its ability to reflect light. A series of interesting analyses concerned possible endocrine effects on skin reflectance measured at various body sites in the Fels participants (Garn, Selby & Crawford, 1956b[161], 1956c[162]; Garn & French, 1963[81]). The observations were made during the bright months, May through October, at sites exposed to a lot of solar radiation, those exposed to little radiation and those, such as the scrotum and the areola of the breast, where reflectance is markedly responsive to sex hormones. Despite the low coefficients of reliability for measurements 6 months apart, some clear differences and trends were established. In males, but not in females, reflectance decreased with age at the sites exposed to little solar radiation, but there were decreases at the areolar site in each sex with age, particularly after 50 years in the women. The marked decreases in areolar reflectance during pregnancy persisted through the first year after delivery and showed a significant tendency to accumulate with successive pregnancies.

The genetic studies made in the past at Fels, and those likely to be made

in the near future, concern isolated topics that are not easily grouped as a set of hypotheses that could be supported by external funding. In the past, the Fels Fund might have helped, but that is no longer possible. Given the absence of graduate students, many of these possibilities are likely to remain unexplored in the forseeable future. Exceptions are (i) the set of familial and genetic hypotheses that is being addressed as part of the body composition studies (Chapter 7), (ii) the investigation of the genetic control of growth patterns that has just started and (iii) the genetic control of changes in serum lipid levels. Plans are being developed for studies of the last-mentioned topic.

4 *Physical growth*

'Growth is the only evidence of life.'

John Henry Cardinal Newman (1801–1890)

This chapter could be disproportionately long because so much has been achieved at Fels in the area of physical growth. To reduce its length, the growth of bones and teeth and studies of body tissues are described in Chapters 6 and 7 respectively. The present chapter will describe research concerning (i) the development and standardization of anthropometric methods, (ii) age changes in anthropometric variables, (iii) methods of growth assessment, (iv) secular changes in anthropometric variables, (v) determinants of growth, (vi) the final phase of growth, (vii) the prediction of adult stature, (viii) associations between growth and behavioral variables, and (ix) future directions. Fels research related to these topics that extends beyond the period of adolescent growth will be included.

Development and standardization of anthropometric methods
The Fels Research Institute has long been recognized as a center of excellence in anthropometry. Few of the methods used at Fels are novel but they are described in considerable detail in the research protocol and they are applied with unusually high reliability. In discussing the assessment of nutritional status, Garn (1962c[62]) complained that anthropometry was often regarded as a set of crude procedures and little or no attention was given to the need for standardization and training. To meet the need for better standardization of anthropometric techniques between studies, a North American Consensus Conference was held in 1985 under the leadership of Tim Lohman. Fels staff members contributed significantly to the success of this conference, at which agreement was reached on the procedures for measuring 40 body dimensions (Lohman, Roche & Martorell, 1988).

68

Robinow (1968) considered the applicability of anthropometric procedures to field studies. He stated that crown–rump length was not useful during infancy although it can provide data about leg length as a percentage of total body length (relative leg length). This ratio could be important because its rate of increase is reduced by malnutrition during infancy. Despite this potential importance, crown–rump length was not reproducible in his data and was considered to be affected by the size and firmness of the buttocks. Robinow further recommended that choices be made between arm circumference and calf circumference and between biceps and triceps skinfolds because these measures were highly correlated.

Robinow (1968) considered the interpretation of head circumference in the context of nutritional assessment. He demonstrated positive associations between head circumference and body size (recumbent length and weight) in normal and in malnourished children.

Accuracy of measurement has long been recognized as important. As the Bible puts it: 'A false balance is an abomination to the Lord; but a just weight is his delight' (Proverbs 11:1). The potential introduction of automated equipment to increase accuracy was suggested several decades ago (Garn, 1962c[62]; Garn & Helmrich, 1967[89]). Automated equipment was described that can transfer anthropometric data directly to computers, thus eliminating errors during recording, transcribing and keyboard data entry, and that can be used to measure lengths and produce punch cards automatically.

A new inexpensive stadiometer, known as the Accustat® Ross Stadiometer, was tested by comparison with the expensive Holtain instrument and with Healthometer scales that have a vertical rod attached for the measurement of stature (Roche, Guo & Baumgartner, 1988b[239]). Repeated measurements of children with all three instruments showed the Accustat was the most reliable. Consequently, it was recommended for general use. A new sliding caliper (Mediform®) of moderate cost was shown to be slightly more accurate for the measurement of body lengths than much more expensive calipers that are in common use for research (Chumlea, 1985a[5]). The new caliper was recommended for the measurement of arm length, knee height, and similar body dimensions.

Comparisons were made among two expensive commercially available calipers and an inexpensive caliper developed by Ross Laboratories for the measurement of knee height (Cochram & Baumgartner, 1990). Intracaliper reliability was similar for all three instruments.

Many aspects of anthropometry, particularly the measurement of adipose tissue, knee height and somatotypes, were considered in recent

critical reviews (Roche, Baumgartner & Guo, 1991a[213]; Chumlea, in press[13]).

Age changes in anthropometric variables

It is commonly stated, as a truism, that human beings cannot be studied throughout their life spans because the investigator will not live long enough. This attitude ignores the possibility that a succession of investigators, using the same procedures, can conduct such studies. Figure 4.1 shows serial status-at-age values and annual increments for stature and recumbent length from 1 to 56 years in one Fels participant, reported by Roche *et al.* (1981a[235]). This paper was entitled 'The first seriatim study of human growth and middle aging' so that it would be a companion piece to Scammon's classic paper of 1927 entitled 'The first seriatim study of human growth.' The 1981 report contains what is believed to be the longest record of human growth ever made. In this case, five successive investigators were responsible for the data collection. The early part of Fig. 4.1 presents data for recumbent length and the later part presents data for stature. Both are measures of the total length of an individual. While these values are highly correlated, recumbent length is systematically greater than stature (Roche & Davila, 1974a[223]). The figure shows rapid, but decelerating, growth during infancy, a pubescent spurt at about 12 years, and only small increases in stature after 16 years that are followed by decreases after about 36 years. While this figure shows values for only one Fels participant, it illustrates the unusual duration of the Fels study. The Fels study is also unusual in its collection of growth data after 18 years. This has led to several interesting analyses that are described later in this chapter and were summarized by Roche (1975[182]).

Falkner (1971a) emphasized the changes in growth rates with age and the need to collect data that would allow the description of growth patterns. Later, summarizing for a WHO Expert Committee, Falkner (1977a) directed attention to the rapid changes in size during pubescence and the myriad other changes, such as alterations in mental and psychosocial development, that occur about this time. He pointed out that these changes have their origins long before puberty. Chumlea (1982[2]) also reviewed physical growth during adolescence. He directed attention to the hormonal control of the initiation of pubescence and described changes that occur during the maturation of secondary sex characters, including familial associations in their timing. Chumlea emphasized the variability in timing of sexual maturation and noted that this is more marked than the differences in the sequence of changes. Despite the variation in timing

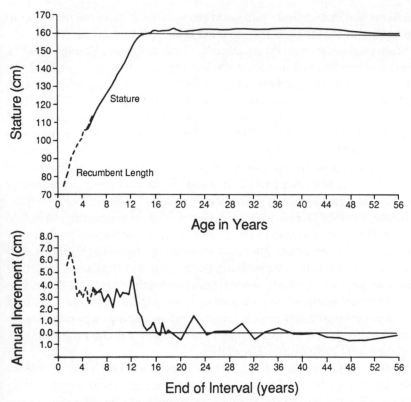

Fig. 4.1 Serial recumbent lengths and statures in one Fels participant from 1 to 56 years, with the annual increments. Note the pubescent spurt with its peak at 12 years and the decrease in stature after 36 years (data from Roche *et al.*, 1981a[235]).

between individuals, there are high correlations within individuals for the timing of grades and, consequently, the timing of later stages can be inferred from status at younger ages. He noted the similarity between the procedures for grading sexual maturity by direct visual examination and from photographs, and he criticized the theory that menarche occurs when a critical level of body weight or of total body fat is reached.

As Chumlea (1982[2]) noted, the skeletal changes during pubescence are generally larger in boys than in girls; this sex-associated difference is marked for shoulder breadth. Additionally, the later pubescent spurt in boys allows growth to continue about 2 years longer in boys than in girls. Viewed somewhat simplistically, this delay in boys is responsible for their greater adult stature and their longer legs and arms relative to stature. The timing of pubertal spurts tends to differ between bones with disto-proximal

gradients within each limb: pubescent changes occur earlier in the bones of the hand and foot than in the proximal bones of these limbs.

Scalp thicknesses were investigated by Garn, Selby and Young (1954[163]). These workers showed that scalp thicknesses on radiographs tended to be greater in males than females after 10 years but not at younger ages. In each sex, the means increased to about 20 years but changed little from then to 40 years. Later, Young (1959), using similar data, reported increases in these thicknesses from 1 to 9 months and then little change to 3 years, after which there was a steady increase. At young ages, the greatest thickness was near the root of the nose but after 10 years the scalp was thickest on the posterior part of the head. Scalp thicknesses were greater for men than for women at corresponding sites.

Roche (1985b[200]) reviewed continuities and discontinuities in child growth, directing attention to the greatly increased opportunities that now exist to answer important questions using computer-based methods. For example, serial data for a variable can be analyzed by fitting a mathematical model to the data. Analyses of serial data for multiple variables depend on the implementation of two successive steps: (i) fitting a mathematical model to the serial data for each variable and estimating its parameters for each individual, and (ii) using these parameters in a multivariate analysis as if they were cross-sectional variables.

In two major studies, Kouchi and her co-workers (1985a, 1985b) described the patterns of growth in weight and recumbent length during infancy. Weight and weight gain are important, particularly during infancy, because of their associations with disease and mortality. Recumbent length is important also because slow growth in length indicates the presence of an influence that is retarding this physiological process. Additionally, recumbent length values assist the interpretation of weight, particularly as part of the ratio weight/recumbent length^2.

The data were from 441 Fels participants, including 87 parent–offspring pairs and 282 sibling pairs, all of whom had been examined at ages from near birth through 24 months with few missing data. A flexible mathematical model with three parameters (intercept, intrinsic rate of growth and growth pattern) was fitted to the serial data for each participant. The three biologically meaningful parameters summarized the growth of each infant in three values (coefficients) for weight and three values for recumbent length. The model fitted very closely to the observed data, even for participants with extreme coefficient values: the mean square residuals were less than the measurement errors. The fits for weight tended to be better in the girls than in the boys, but the fits to the recumbent length data were equally good in each sex.

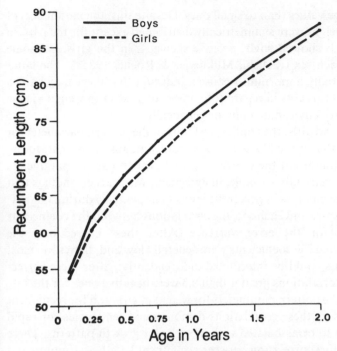

Fig. 4.2 Plots of recumbent length during infancy for boys and girls based on the means of parameters of mathematical models. (From Kouchi, M., Roche, A.F. & Mukherjee, D. (1985b). Growth in recumbent length during infancy with relationships to adult status and familial associations of the estimated parameters. *Human Biology*, **57**, 449–72. Redrawn with permission from *Human Biology*.)

For both weight and recumbent length, the intercepts were significantly larger for the boys than the girls, showing that the boys had larger birth weights and larger values for recumbent length at 1 month. Similarly, the boys had significantly more rapid intrinsic rates of growth in weight and in recumbent length. The third parameter (growth pattern) was significantly smaller for the boys than the girls, indicating that the growth patterns were more curved in the boys than in the girls for these variables. Figure 4.2 shows plots of recumbent length for boys and girls based on the sex-specific means of the parameters of the model. This figure presents the mean patterns of growth and not the means of values at a series of ages considered cross-sectionally. The latter would be misleading. Because the boys had a more curved growth pattern, the curves for the two sexes were closer to each other at each end of the age range than near the center of this range.

Weight-at-an-age tends to be positively skewed, with a more marked

tendency to large values than to small ones. Despite this, the parameters of the model for weight were symmetrically distributed except for the pattern parameter which showed slight positive skewness in the girls and some bimodality in each sex (Kouchi, Mukherjee & Roche, 1985a). The latter finding is potentially important because it indicates that there may be two distinct groups of infants in regard to patterns of growth in weight. These groups may differ environmentally or genetically.

In both boys and girls, the confidence limits of the pattern parameter for weight showed that growth was a square root function of weight during infancy. The estimates of the growth rate and growth pattern parameters for weight were markedly variable, in agreement with earlier findings that there are marked changes in percentile levels in individuals during infancy.

For each measure and each sex, the correlations between the coefficients were corrected for the error variance. After these corrections, the correlations among the coefficients were generally low and, therefore, most of the coefficients could be interpreted independently. After these corrections, the only correlations greater than 0.3 were negative ones for the rate of growth with the pattern parameters for weight in girls and for recumbent length in each sex; these correlations demonstrated tendencies for rapid intrinsic growth to be associated with more linear growth patterns. There was also a negative correlation between recumbent length at 1 month and the rate of growth in recumbent length during infancy, which showed that catch-up growth in recumbent length during infancy should not be assumed.

Correlations were calculated between the parameters of growth during infancy and measurements of the same individuals at 18 and 30 years (Kouchi *et al.*, 1985a, 1985b). Many of these correlations were significant but most were modest, ranging from 0.2 to 0.6 for weight and from 0.2 to 0.5 for recumbent length. The parameters for growth in infancy did not explain more than 30% of the variation in the adulthood measures of weight, stature, head circumference and calf adipose tissue thicknesses. These correlations showed little consistency between the sexes or between weight and recumbent length, but significant correlations were more common for the intercepts and the rates of growth than for growth patterns.

Birth weights (intercepts) were positively correlated with weight and weight/stature^2 at 18 and 30 years. Recumbent length at 1 month in females was significantly correlated with weight at 18 and 30 years. Additionally, recumbent length at 1 month and the rate of growth in recumbent length were significantly correlated with stature at 18 and 30 years in each sex. Head circumference at 18 and 30 years was significantly

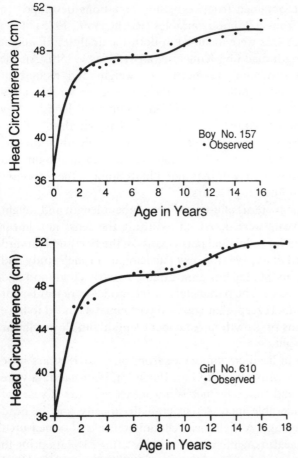

Fig. 4.3 The observed values for head circumference and the fitted models for a boy (No. 157) with a very low value for final head circumference, and for a girl (No. 610) with a very low value for initial size. (Roche, A.F., Mukherjee, D. & Guo, S. (1986b). Head circumference growth patterns: Birth to 18 years. *Human Biology*, **58**, 893–906[257]. Redrawn with permission from *Human Biology*.)

correlated with the rate of growth in weight during infancy. The low associations between growth rates for weight during infancy and adult status for adipose tissue thicknesses are consistent with other Fels findings obtained using different analytic procedures (Cronk *et al.*, 1982a; Roche *et al.*, 1982a[264]). They provide further evidence that fatness during infancy is not significantly associated with the level of fatness in adulthood.

It is particularly interesting that the correlations between the rates of growth in weight during infancy and adult stature were as high as those between stature at 2 years and adult stature. These findings are in general

agreement with those obtained from regression equations developed to predict adult stature from childhood variables (Roche *et al.*, 1975a[272]).

Many of the participants were included in both the analyses of weight and of recumbent length made by Kouchi *et al.* (1985a, 1985b). All the correlations between matching parameters for weight and recumbent length were positive and significant, but there was considerable independence between growth in weight and in recumbent length. Any parameter for weight accounted for no more than one-third of the variation in the corresponding parameter for recumbent length at an age. This indicates that different mechanisms underlie growth in weight and recumbent length during infancy or that individuals differ in the responses of these processes to influencing factors.

In another study, the patterns of growth in recumbent length and weight from 3 months to 6 years were described by fitting the Jenss non-linear model to the serial data for individual participants in the Fels and Harvard Growth studies (Byard *et al.*, 1991). A few participants in each study had average or low values in infancy but grew rapidly in early childhood and had high values at 18 years. The parameters of the model were similar for the Fels and Harvard data except that Harvard participants tended to have less curvilinear patterns of growth in recumbent length and slower linear rates of growth in weight.

Patterns of growth in head circumference from birth to 18 years have been described (Roche, Mukherjee & Guo, 1986b[257]). Unusual data were available; typically, head circumference is not measured after 2 years of age despite the considerable increases in cranial capacity and in head circumference after that age. At Fels, head circumference is now measured at all ages but these measurements were not made after 13 years prior to 1952 and they were not made after 2.5 years from 1952 to 1969. Head circumference is an important index of brain size, particularly during infancy when the cranium is thin. Although the changes in head circumference are small after 13 years, head circumference differs markedly between individuals and it is a potentially important predictor of fat-free mass (Chapter 7).

A mathematical model was fitted to serial data for each individual, using the non-linear least squares procedure (Roche *et al.*, 1986b[257]). This model had four parameters: (i) the estimated head circumference at 18 years, (ii) a dimensionless parameter that was a function of size at birth, age at peak growth rate during pubescence, and the velocity at peak growth rate, (iii) the rate of change in acceleration (cm/year^{-1}), and (iv) a critical age when both the slope (cm/year^{-1}) and the acceleration (cm/year^{-1}) were zero. This final parameter indicated the onset of the pubescent spurt. The model

fitted well and therefore the four parameters effectively summarized the serial data, even for participants with unusual values as illustrated in Fig. 4.3.

The means for head circumference in the boys were greater than those for the girls at birth and at 18 years, with differences of 0.5 and 1.5 cm respectively. Furthermore, the boys were about 9 months older than the girls at the onset of the pubescent spurt in head circumference and about 18 months older when the maximum rate of growth occurred. Growth in head circumference during pubescence was more rapid in the girls than in the boys, and pubescent growth was slower in each sex when pubescence was delayed.

Growth patterns in the Fels, Denver, and Harvard Growth studies and in the Guidance Study at Berkeley were compared (Thissen *et al.*, 1976). Because some of the studies included numerous familial relationships, the samples were limited to the oldest child of each sex within each family. The double logistic model fitted well, although it tended to overestimate the data in mid-childhood and after puberty and to underestimate the data in early adolescence. To overcome problems due to systematic differences between the studies in the timing of the scheduled examinations, a least squares fitting procedure was used in which each observation was weighted by the inverse of the number of observations during each year.

The variances of the parameter estimates were similar for all the studies but some subtle differences in the growth patterns were demonstrated by sex-study interactions. Additionally, there were significant study effects in the maximum velocities of the prepubertal and adolescent components of the model and in adult stature. The general conclusion from this comparison was one of similarities rather than differences between patterns of growth in these studies although, in each sex, mature stature was about 2 cm less in the Harvard study than in the other studies.

The mean differences between the growth patterns of girls in the Fels and Berkeley Guidance studies are shown in Fig. 4.4. These groups of girls had almost identical mean adult statures although the Fels girls had about 3 cm less prepubertal growth. These small differences in growth patterns between the four studies suggested there were only minor regional variations in growth for US white children and that results from studies of Fels participants were likely to be applicable to other groups of children. In passing, it should be noted that growth patterns for stature are more regular for girls than for boys in the Fels study (Roche *et al.*, 1975a[272]).

Fels data for weight and recumbent length have been used to provide reference data for body surface area from birth to 3 years (Roche, Guo & Moore, 1991[244]). Published equations were used to calculate empirical

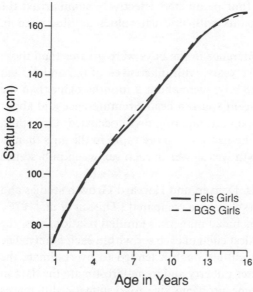

Fig. 4.4 Median patterns of growth in stature for females in the Fels and Berkeley Growth Studies. (Thissen, D., Bock, R.D., Wainer, H. & Roche, A.F. (1976). Individual growth in stature: Comparison of four U.S. growth studies. *Annals of Human Biology*, 3, 527–42. Redrawn with permission from *Annals of Human Biology*.)

values for selected percentiles and these were smoothed across age by non-parametric kernel regression. The percentiles increased rapidly from birth to about 6 months, after which the increases were slower. At all ages, the values for boys tended to be larger than those for girls. Sex-specific reference data are needed from 6 months to 2 years. These data can be used to judge the normality of body surface area which is important in the standardization of some physiological and metabolic variables such as renal function and caloric needs.

Methods of growth assessment

If measurements of growth-related variables are made at only one age, the values can be regarded as increments since conception. These values are useful in screening, and in the evaluation of infants and children. Repeated measurements can be plotted on status reference charts and their positions and changes in position can be judged subjectively, relative to the age changes in cross-sectional data that are displayed in the reference charts. This approach can show whether the increments between examinations are smaller or larger than average, but evaluations made in this way are likely

to be inaccurate soon after birth and during pubescence when growth rates change rapidly. Reference data for increments are needed to judge whether the variation from the central tendency is unusual. The importance of increments in growth assessment, particularly during infancy, was stressed by Garn (1962a[60]). If increments are evaluated, unusual rates of change will be recognized earlier than if judgments are based on serial data for status (Roche *et al.*, 1989a[242]; Guo *et al.*, 1988).

Reference data

Fundamentally, growth assessment depends on comparisons between recorded data and reference data. The information needed for comparisons in growth assessment should be referred to as 'reference data.' This term may not have originated at Fels but the Fels staff have certainly contributed to its widespread use (Hamill *et al.*, 1977, 1979). The distinction between reference data and 'standards' is important. The word 'standard' is appropriate in the physical sciences. For example, until 1960, the standard meter was the length of a particular metal rod kept in Paris. We do not have a standard child or a 'correct' (optimal) value for the weight of a 5-year-old boy. Healthy boys of this age can differ in weight by large amounts and without significantly increased risks of disease. We can, however, obtain percentiles for weight in 5-year-old boys by the study of large samples and judge the weights of other 5-year-old boys by reference to these percentiles.

In an approach that was innovative at the time, standard deviations were used to develop reference data arranged as T-scores and as standard deviation levels for several variables (Sontag & Reynolds, 1945[298]; Reynolds & Sontag, 1945). These 'composite sheets' allowed the simultaneous assessment of weight, stature, number of ossification centers and illness. These charts were used routinely to monitor the growth progress of Fels participants until 1970, and they were used by many outside the institute.

Garn (1965[65]) considered the applicability of growth reference data derived from North American children to children in developing countries. He postulated that a few well-known sets of reference data would be preferable to a large number of sets for use in world-wide nutrition surveys. This is similar to the current WHO view that a single set of reference data facilitates international comparisons. This WHO view is appropriate for the major body dimensions but not for some other characteristics, e.g., fat patterns. It is based, in part, on knowledge that the distributions of major growth-related variables would be similar in many countries if environmental differences were removed. Some differences would remain, however, particularly for populations that differ in body build (e.g., weight–

stature relationships, relative leg length). Garn (1965[65]) made the interesting suggestion that US reference data for the growth of children of short parents be used tentatively in countries where the populations have not been studied, and he suggested that privileged groups in a developing country, that are genetically the same as the general population, could indicate the expectations for growth under better environmental conditions.

Later, Garn (1966b[67]) cogently argued in favor of population-specific sets of growth reference data. In this publication, he suggested that these reference data be based on mid-parent stature but pointed out that this would require an immense study, even if restricted to a few categories of parental stature. The need for large samples of parents of different statures has been circumvented in analyses at Fels by treating the data in a continuous fashion, as will be described later (Himes *et al.*, 1981).

Falkner (1971a) addressed general aspects of growth assessment. He outlined the purposes of such assessments and stressed the 'whole child' and the recognition of retarding environmental influences. He claimed that 'norms' of size at an age, or a series of ages, were of little use to those wishing to screen children. In this context, he used 'norm' as synonymous with 'mean.' He stated that the normal ranges should be provided although these ranges are statistically based and do not lead to easy evaluation of an individual child as normal or abnormal.

Later, writing on behalf of a Committee of the International Union of Nutritional Sciences, Falkner (1972) recommended the establishment of sets of cross-sectional growth reference data for each country that should be derived from subgroups of national populations for which growth was not retarded by the environment or disease. As Falkner noted, in many countries, it is difficult to find large groups of children who meet this criterion. As he pointed out, national reference data must be constructed with careful attention to study design, sample size, and quality control. Futhermore, appropriate statistical procedures must be applied to obtain and smooth reference percentile values. Even then, limitations will remain due to the genetic diversity present within most countries. This diversity is important if the genetic differences cause growth variations, but a considerable literature indicates that genetic differences cause only a minor part of the growth variations between populations. This implies that a single set of reference data could be used internationally if it were obtained by excellent procedures from a population free of retarding influences.

Falkner (1978a) noted that the reference data from developed countries for growth during infancy are largely derived from formula-fed infants. This led him to conclude that breast-fed infants at the lower percentile

levels of these reference data may not need supplementation. In this paper, he directed attention to the need to group low-birth-weight infants on the basis of gestational age and he stressed the importance of increments in the assessment of growth, especially during infancy.

Roche and Falkner (1975[232]) critically reviewed the reference data available for US children and expressed concern about their applicability. Reluctantly, they recommended the Kaiser/Permanente charts for infants and the Iowa charts for older children. At about the same time, a conference report concluded that, despite recognized differences in growth among ethnic groups in the US, a single national set of reference data would be unlikely to cause serious errors (Roche & McKigney, 1975[253]). This recommendation, together with others, soon led to the publication of the first set of US national growth data. These data are displayed in the National Center for Health Statistics growth charts for weight, recumbent length, stature, weight-for-recumbent length, weight-for-stature, and head circumference (Hamill *et al.*, 1977, 1979). The data for ages from birth to 3 years came from the Fels Longitudinal Study, and those for ages 2 to 18 years came from US National Surveys. Originally it was expected that these reference data would be used widely in the US. It was not foreseen that they would be used in other countries and that WHO would recommend their world-wide use to assist international comparisons.

The measurement of total body length is necessarily made with the subjects recumbent during infancy, but standing erect when they are older. The Hamill reference data are for recumbent length to 3 years and for stature after 2 years. Roche and Davila (1974a[223]) showed these measures were almost exactly correlated, but recumbent length is the larger. The differences between these measures were the same for both sexes except from 11 to 14 years when they were significantly larger in girls. The mean difference was about 1.2 cm but this value differed between studies, presumably due to variations in methods of measurement.

Other sets of reference data are needed to assess the growth of special groups of children or for uncommon measurements. It may be difficult, however, to locate suitable data. Consequently, Roche and Malina (1983[252]) compiled a two-volume *Manual of Physical Status and Performance in Childhood* to meet the need for a convenient source of reference data. This manual contains tabular data for a wide range of variables relating to body size and proportions, maturity, performance, function, body composition, and hormonal, dietary, physiological, and biochemical status. To the best of their ability, the authors included data from all relevant studies in North America published between 1941 and 1981; many of these utilized Fels data.

Several reviews from Fels concern growth assessment in normal and abnormal children. Methods for the assessment of growth and maturity and for the study of determinants of growth and maturation were reviewed in a book resulting from a NATO Advanced Study Institute (Johnston, Roche & Susanne, 1980). Later, Chumlea (1986a[8], in press[13]) reviewed methods for the assessment of growth in children with developmental disabilities. He noted the scarcity of reference data for particular groups and the need to measure many of these children in unusual positions. When handicapped children are measured standing, their posture should be examined carefully to be sure the data will be valid. The use of arm span as an alternative to stature was discussed but emphasis was placed on the use of recumbent anthropometric procedures for children who are unable to assume the correct positioning for the measurement of stature.

Roche (1978a[184], 1978b[185]) described methods of growth assessment that were disseminated widely in a booklet entitled *Pediatric Anthropometry*, jointly authored by Moore (Moore & Roche, 1982, 1983, 1987). This material has had a major influence on clinical anthropometry in relation to children. It was stressed that growth data are sensitive indicators of health and development and that serial growth data, either plotted on status charts or used to calculate increments, can help monitor the progress of a child during nutritional intervention or the treatment of a disease. The recommended procedures for obtaining common growth measurements were described in detail. It was stressed that the data should be plotted and also recorded in tabular form; the latter allows checks as to whether the plotting was accurate and it is from the tabular data that increments must be calculated if there is concern about the growth of a child.

Increments can provide more sensitive information about the normality of growth progress than status at an age or at a series of ages. These increments should be calculated for 1-month intervals during the year after birth and for 6-month intervals at older ages. Tables of consecutively numbered days were provided to assist the calculation of increments when, as is common, the interval between measurements is not exactly 1 month or 6 months (Ross Laboratories, 1981).

Guidelines were given by Moore and Roche (1982, 1983, 1987) for the interpretation of growth data by comparison with reference values for status or increments. Since stature tends to be similar within families, observed statures should be adjusted for the average of the statures of the two parents (Roche, 1978a[184], 1978b[185]; Himes *et al.*, 1981). Both the observed and the adjusted statures should be plotted. This approach, which was made widely available by Ross Laboratories (1983), allows the statures of children to be compared with the usual reference data after

removing the effects of the parental stature on the stature of the child. This may greatly alter the interpretation of the child's stature and thereby influence clinical management. The work done at Fels that provided a full range of parent-specific adjustments for childhood statures is described later in this chapter.

The level of maturity is clearly important for the assessment of growth early in infancy when prematurity has a large effect on growth status and growth rates. The growth of premature infants can best be evaluated by comparison with reference data that are specific for premature infants. An alternative is to 'adjust' the chronological age of the premature infant by subtracting the number of weeks by which the infant is premature from the chronological age and thus obtain a 'conception-corrected' age, as noted by Falkner (1977b). This approach assumes that there are no systematic differences in growth between premature and full-term infants after this adjustment has been made and that the growth of a premature infant soon after birth is the same as if the pregnancy had continued to term. The need for age-adjustment due to prematurity decreases with age; this reduced need is met, at least to some extent, by the deceleration in the rate of growth after birth. This deceleration reduces the effect of the age-adjustment at older ages during infancy.

Maturity status is also important in relation to the timing of pubescence. Rapidly maturing children tend to be taller and heavier than the general population before pubescence and they have early pubescent spurts. After pubescence, their size moves closer to the mean as they experience an early deceleration of growth. Opposite trends occur in slowly maturing children. Knowledge of the maturity status of a child, either from skeletal age or the development of secondary sex characters, can allow better judgments of the normality of growth.

As stated by Moore and Roche (1982, 1983, 1987), serial values of weight and stature plotted in relation to age should be regular relative to reference percentile lines. Irregularity can be due to errors of measurement or of plotting, particularly if the irregularity is restricted to one variable. When the most recent point is 'out-of-line,' another examination should be scheduled if the irregularity is not removed by re-measurement and re-plotting. A real change in growth status, relative to percentile lines, should cause concern if the change is marked, or occurs near the extreme percentiles.

Parenthetically, it could be noted that: 'It is better to be short and good,' as stated by Mozart. Because growth measurements are distributed in a continuous fashion, some children must be near the ends of the distributions. These children, whether small or large, are not necessarily

abnormal. Nevertheless, there is reason for concern when growth, which is a physiological process, proceeds at an unusual rate. The many possible causes include diseases, abnormal dietary intakes, psychosocial deprivation, congenital syndromes and familial short stature. It should be stressed that growth can be normal in the presence of a disease and that growth can be abnormal in the absence of a disease (Moore & Roche, 1982, 1983, 1987).

The purposes of growth assessments in children with renal diseases have been reviewed (Potter *et al.*, 1978). Growth assessments of these children can assist better understanding of the course of these diseases and the effects of treatment. Furthermore, serial growth assessments may help identify the types of renal diseases that most affect growth. Recommendations have been made about the timing and frequency of serial growth assessments in relation to the timing of dialysis and of renal transplantation, and the additional data that should be recorded at the time of these assessments. The paper by Potter and his associates recommended methods by which growth records should be utilized and interpreted. These methods include adjustments to observed statures for parental stature, the calculation of increments and comparisons with reference data on the basis of both chronological age and skeletal age. The latter is particularly important in judging the likely effect of the disease on adult stature.

Multivariate statistical analyses of cross-sectional data are needed commonly to compare a study population with a reference population; often access to the raw data is needed for both groups. Other statistical methods are used to test particular types of hypotheses. For example, cluster analyses can determine whether a group can be divided into statistically separate subgroups, discriminant analyses can determine the importance of particular variables in distinguishing between subgroups of individuals, and multiple regression procedures can estimate the relative importance of particular variables in predicting a continuous outcome such as blood pressure.

The use of standard deviation scores for several variables, derived for each individual, was recommended for the analysis of group data in children with renal disease (Potter *et al.*, 1978). This approach was used more than 30 years earlier by Sontag and Reynolds (1945[298]) and by Reynolds and Sontag (1945). These scores can be treated statistically in the same way as any other set of numbers. They may be used to compare children with renal disease to normal children, to compare the growth of children with various types of renal disease, and to evaluate the effects of treatment. It was concluded that predictions of adult stature are unlikely to

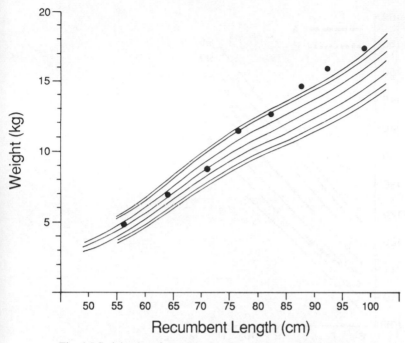

Fig. 4.5 Serial values for weight (kg) for one boy, plotted against recumbent length (cm) and related to national percentile levels (Hamill *et al.*, 1977).

be accurate in children with renal disease, except perhaps in those with uncomplicated renal tubular acidosis who, if treated adequately from a young age, may reach normal adult statures.

The assessment of growth in abnormal children was reviewed by Roche (1978a[184], 1978b[185]). He discussed the purposes of these assessments and directed specific attention to procedures for measuring recumbent length, stature, sitting height, weight, head circumference, upper arm circumference, and skinfold thicknesses, and for grading maturity. The necessary equipment was described and the sources from which it can be obtained were listed. The need for training and for documentation of reliability was emphasized, particularly for the assessment of skeletal age. References were provided to sets of recommended reference data.

In assessing the growth of abnormal children, as for normal children, it is important to interpret weight in relation to stature. Clearly, tall children tend to be heavier than short children. A convenient approach is to plot weight in relation to stature (weight-for-stature) on charts of reference data (Hamill *et al.*, 1977, 1979). Weight-for-recumbent length, of which an example from Fels is shown in Fig. 4.5, is nearly independent of age. The

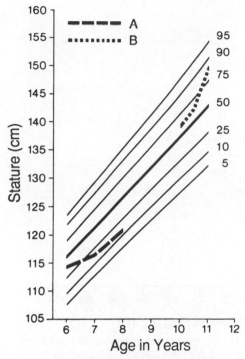

Fig. 4.6 Serial stature data for two boys plotted relative to reference percentile levels. See text for details.

interpretation of weight-for-recumbent length (weight-for-stature) depends on the relationship between trunk length and leg length. Children with relatively short legs are likely to have high values of weight-for-recumbent length. Usually these proportions are judged from the ratio of crown–rump length to recumbent length (sitting height to stature at older ages) because crown–rump length (sitting height) is a measure of trunk length. The growth of abnormal children can also be judged using model-fitting procedures (Holm *et al.*, 1979).

Roche (1978a[184], 1978b[185]) made suggestions regarding the interpretation of changes in 'channels.' In this context, 'channels' are the zones between adjacent selected percentile levels on growth charts. If serial statures are plotted against chronological age, a change of channel indicates a change in the rate of growth compared with the reference population. Thus Boy A in Fig. 4.6 had a slower rate of growth in stature than the reference population from 6 to 7 years and his stature percentile changed from the channel between the 25th and 50th percentiles to that

between the 10th and 25th percentiles. Boy B in Fig. 4.6 changed channels between 10 and 12 years from that between the 50th and the 75th percentiles to that between the 75th and 90th percentiles. This represents more rapid growth than is usual in the reference data. Many increases in percentile level near the age of pubescence, as for Boy B in Fig. 4.6, reflect rapid maturation and early pubescence, while many decreases at about this age reflect slow maturation and late pubescence.

When there are changes in the rate of growth in stature, relative to reference data, it is important to determine whether there is an associated change in the rate of skeletal maturation. When increments in stature are plotted against skeletal age, the mean and median stature increments should differ little from those relative to chronological age but the variance will differ in a way that is not documented. This procedure is likely to be restricted to research studies; skeletal age assessments are time-consuming and standardization is difficult.

Plotting serial values for an individual on growth charts for status-at-an-age commonly gives a false impression of steady growth because the vertical scale is small (Falkner, 1977b). For many clinical and research purposes, it is better to calculate increments in growth and compare them with corresponding reference data. Falkner (1971a) noted that environmental influences had larger effects on weight increments than on stature increments and he noted the value of increments in the recognition of catch-up growth, particularly in low-birth-weight infants. Later, Falkner (1978a) directed attention to the large increments in head circumference in low-birthweight infants after birth. These increments are larger in premature infants, who reach normal values by 2 to 3 years of age, than in infants who are small for gestational age.

The need for incremental reference data was recognized early by the Fels staff; Robinow (1942a) published one of the earliest sets of such data. Robinow provided means and standard deviations of increments for the intervals from birth to 1 month and from 1 to 3 months, and then each 3 months to 1 year, and each 6 months to 6 years, with annual increments from birth to 6 years. Robinow reported that the distributions of increments were near normal. Nevertheless, almost all sets of incremental data are skewed and the presentation of percentiles would have been more appropriate (Garn & Rohmann, 1964b[140]). Robinow (1942a) did not adjust the data for variations in the lengths of the intervals and he combined data from the two sexes without testing the significance of the differences between them. Despite its importance, this early work received little clinical attention.

Falkner (1973a, 1978b) stressed the importance of reference data for

increments and emphasized that they must be derived from accurate data (Sobel & Falkner, 1974; Falkner, 1978a). The attention given to detail during the recording of Fels data made them ideal for this purpose. Consequently, a set of reference data for increments during 6-month intervals was developed by Roche and Himes (1980[247]) who had a much larger data set than that available to Robinow. These reference data were originally presented in graphs but were later published in tabular form (Baumgartner *et al.*, 1986a). During the development of these reference data, adjustments were made for variations in the lengths of the intervals and it was shown that these increments did not demonstrate seasonal or familial effects. Earlier, however, Reynolds and Sontag (1944) reported slight seasonal trends in stature increments and larger ones in weight with peaks for stature increments in the summer and peaks for weight increments in the winter.

The reference data of Roche and Himes (1980[247]) were for recumbent length and head circumference (birth to 3 years), stature (2 to 18 years) and weight (birth to 18 years). For each of these variables, selected empirical percentile levels for each 6-month interval were smoothed across age using low-term Fourier transforms. Simple methods were provided by which users could adjust for variations in the intervals between measurements, together with guidelines to assist interpretation of the findings. In particular, it was stressed that serial percentile levels for increments within individuals were much less stable than corresponding values for status; the correlations between successive percentile levels for increments ranged from −0.4 to 0.7. Therefore, serial increments often showed changes in 'channel.' Reference data for increments allow earlier and more precise recognition of unusual growth than do reference data for status, but those presented by Roche and Himes (1980[247]) did not take into account the marked variations in the timing of the pubescent spurt. Therefore, while they were suitable for the assessment of groups of children unselected for age at pubescence, they were less satisfactory for the assessment of individual children as they pass through pubescence. This problem would be solved if there were an effective method of predicting the timing of pubescence from prepubertal data. In its absence, the charts that indicate the differences associated with rapid and slow maturation can only be applied retrospectively.

This work of Roche and Himes did not result in new insights but it provided graphs and tables, for use by clinicians and health-care providers, that were derived from data for a population similar in growth status to US national samples (Roche & Himes, 1980[247]; Baumgartner *et al.*, 1986a; Hamill *et al.*, 1977, 1979; Roche & Hamill, 1977[245], 1978[246]).

The growth of infants must be monitored at brief intervals. Therefore, reference data are needed for increments during 1-month intervals. In accordance with the accepted view, Falkner (1978a) claimed that measurements must be made at regular intervals to provide reference data for increments. Since there are few serial studies of large groups of infants in which measurements were made each month, an alternative approach was adopted to generate suitable reference data. Mathematical models fitted to sets of serial data for individuals allow interpolations to any ages within the range of the data. Of course, there must be a sufficient number of measured values spaced so that they can provide an adequate description of the growth changes, and the models must fit well.

Using Fels data recorded at seven ages from 1 through 24 months, a three-parameter mathematical model was fitted to serial values for weight, recumbent length and head circumference for each participant (Guo *et al.*, 1988; Roche et al., 1989a[242]). This model had the form:

$$f(t) = a + b\sqrt{t} + c \log t + e$$

where $f(t)$ is the measurement (cm, kg) at age t (years); a, b and c are estimated parameters, and e is an error term. Since the model fitted very well to the recorded data, interpolations were made to ages 1 month apart and 1-month increments were calculated. Empirical percentile levels were obtained for age intervals from 1 to 2 months through 11 to 12 months. In the publication containing these reference data, it was recommended that follow-up examinations be made of infants with values for weight, recumbent length, or head circumference outside the 5th to the 95th percentile range for status, and that their rates of growth be judged by comparing the observed increments with these reference data. These reference data for one-month increments demonstrated rapid decreases in the rate of growth during infancy (Guo *et al.*, 1988; Roche *et al.*, 1989a[242]). Estimates of 1-month increments could have been extended to older ages but the amounts of growth during 1-month intervals after 12 months were too small to allow the accurate categorization of children.

The use of reference data for 1-month increments in head circumference in the early recognition of abnormal growth is illustrated in Fig. 4.7a, which shows serial head circumferences for two theoretical girls each of whom had a head circumference at the 25th percentile at 1 month. It was assumed that Girl A grew slightly faster than the 95th percentile for 1-month increments and that Girl B grew slightly slower than the 5th percentile for these increments. When the data for these girls were plotted against the reference data for 1-month increments, the unusual growth of each girl was noted at 2 months (Fig. 4.7a). This would alert the clinician

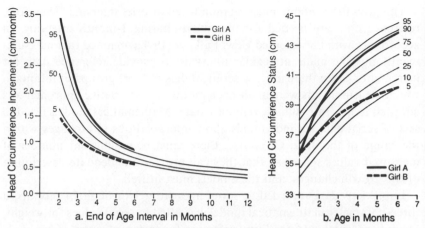

Fig. 4.7 Selected percentiles for 1-month increments and for status in head circumference for girls during infancy. In Fig. 4.7a, head circumference increments for two girls are plotted; the corresponding status values are plotted in Fig. 4.7b. See text for details.

who might re-examine these girls 1 month later or begin laboratory investigations immediately. In Fig. 4.7b, the serial data for these girls were plotted relative to the National Center for Health Statistics reference data for status that were derived from the Fels study. With this approach, there would be little clinical concern about Girl A but there might be concern about the declining growth status of Girl B by the age of 5 months.

These reference data for weight, recumbent length, and head circumference (Guo *et al.*, 1988; Roche *et al.*, 1989a[242]) are applicable to any 1-month interval from 1 to 12 months. For example, the interval could be 4 to 5 months or 4.2 to 5.2 months. Additionally, increments during intervals ranging from 3 to 5 weeks can be adjusted to approximate what would have been observed during a 1-month interval before they are compared with the reference data.

In an unusual but effective approach, growth data from treated phenylketonuric children were compared with Fels data (Holm *et al.*, 1979). Since all the data were serial, a mathematical model was fitted to the values for each child, after using a linear analysis of variance to estimate values at the scheduled ages. The model fitted well and showed remarkably close agreement between the groups in recumbent length, but the phenylketonuric children were lighter than Fels children from 2 to 3 years, and heavier at 4 years. The coefficients for head circumference did not differ between the Fels and phenylketonuric groups for boys, but in the girls the phenylketonuric group tended to have a higher value (intercept) at

birth and more rapid deceleration. This work was an impressive demonstration of one way in which the Fels data can assist the interpretation of data from other studies.

Secular changes in anthropometric variables

The term 'secular changes' refers to differences between individuals or groups that are correlated with year of birth but independent of age (Roche, 1979a[187]). For example, differences between the weights of 10-year-old girls born in 1900 and those born in 1970 would constitute secular changes if they were observed in the same population group. Secular changes in growth, by definition, reflect changes across time in environmental factors that influence growth. Therefore secular changes are relevant to studies of environmental effects on growth even if the specific aspects of the environment that are responsible remain unknown. Secular changes in growth have received considerable attention because of the striking acceleration of growth and maturation in Western Europe and North America during this century. One wonders whether Shakespeare had secular changes in mind when he wrote: 'Young boys and girls are level now with men.'

Secular changes in growth were the topic of a symposium organized by Roche (1979a[187]). In the introduction to this monograph, he stated: 'The study of secular trends is based, necessarily, on survey data from representative national populations or large well-defined groups within these populations: these groups must be measured or observed at several points in time, ideally separated by several decades or even longer.' Nevertheless, few studies of secular changes have been of defined groups that did not change due to migration. Much of the literature reviewed in this symposium was not based on Fels data, but knowledge of the extent of secular changes in the US, and in other countries, is important in relation to the general applicabililty of the findings derived from the Fels data. It is believed that secular increases in stature occurred in the US at least until 1965 but have now ceased or become much smaller. Chumlea (1982[2]) also reviewed this topic and concluded that the large increases in body size and rates of maturation may have ceased in some developed countries. In many other countries, secular changes have not occurred.

When only cross-sectional data are available and age is unknown, as occurs in excavated skeletal remains, it is difficult to estimate secular changes because age changes cannot be excluded. To assist the separation of secular changes from age changes, radiographic tibial lengths and statures were compared in a group of 288 adults that included many Fels participants (Hertzog, Garn & Hempy, 1969). Since the length of the tibia

Table 4.1. *The estimated and observed mean losses of stature (cm) due to aging (data from Hertzog et al., 1969)*

Age (years)	Men estimated	Women estimated	observed
35.0–44.9	0.95	−0.06	0.24
45.0–54.9	0.97	0.01	0.80
55.0–64.9	1.93	2.93	2.40
65.0–74.9	2.19	6.15	—
75.0–87.0	3.12	6.47	—

does not change with age during adulthood, differences in tibial length, relative to year of birth, must represent secular changes. Differences in stature adjusted for tibial length, within age groups, were then used to estimate the loss of stature in individuals with aging.

In each sex, the tibial lengths were greater for those born between 1900 and 1920 than for those born before or after this. Estimated decreases in stature due to aging showed a loss in men from early adulthood onwards but losses in women occurred only after 55 years when the decreases were much greater than in men (Table 4.1). The validity of these conclusions is dependent on the absence of a secular trend in the relationship of tibial length to stature. Hertzog indirectly documented such an absence by showing a close correspondence between his estimates of statural loss and the observed losses in 52 women. Additionally, Himes (1979), after a comprehensive review of the literature, concluded that there has not been a secular change in the ratio sitting height/stature. This secular constancy of body proportions may occur for tibial length/stature relationships also.

Secular changes for weight have been slight in the Fels study. For example, Garn and French (1967[82]) reported only slight tendencies for boys to become heavier and girls to become lighter as groups born in progressively later years were considered. Using data within age groups, Byard and Roche (1984) reported regressions of recumbent length and stature on dates of examination, which are directly related to dates of birth. There was evidence of a significant linear trend for girls during childhood and significant small increases in the early years of the Fels study that were reversed later. Additionally, head circumference spurts during pubescence now occur earlier than in the past and the maximum rate of growth during the spurt has increased (Roche *et al.*, 1986b[257]). Furthermore, there have been only small secular trends for weight/stature^2 in the Fels data (Siervogel *et al.*, 1989a).

The small secular changes in the Fels population are in contrast with some other reports. Bock and his colleagues, after the analysis of data for three generations of Fels families, reported that, within families, later-born children tend to be taller than others of the same sex (Bock, Sykes & Roche, 1985; Sykes, 1985; Bock & Sykes, 1989). Additionally, they showed that, when the Fels participants and their relatives were placed in one of three groups by date of birth, the mean adult statures within families increased in each sex from the first to the second group but not from the second to the third group. These intergenerational findings within families indicated that the secular increases at Fels ceased about 1950.

Other analyses of two-generation families showed differences between parents and offspring measured at corresponding ages during growth (Bock & Sykes, 1989). In the males, the mean parent–offspring difference was almost constant from 1 to 18 years. In the females, the differences at 1 year and at 18 years were similar but differences were absent or slight during pubescence. The increase of about 3–4 cm in stature between parents and adult offspring of the same sex was not influenced by decreases in parental statures due to aging. These parent–offspring differences remained about constant for offspring born between 1932 and 1968, indicating that the rate of secular increase within families did not decrease during this period (Fig. 4.8). The contrast between the continuing secular increase in stature within families and the lack of such an increase in the total Fels data set was largely due to the recruitment of new families after 1940 in which the adult statures were less than those for the families recruited earlier.

The analyses by Kouchi and her associates (1985a, 1985b) of patterns of change in weight and recumbent length during infancy included participants who were born between 1929 and 1970. Possible secular changes in infant growth were examined by placing the participants in four groups on the basis of year of birth. Each of these groups included about one decade of birth years and was identified by the mean birth year (1935, 1946, 1958 and 1969). The differences between the groups were small but some were significant. Birth weight and recumbent length at one month were smaller in the 1946 group than in the 1934 group in each sex, indicating a slight negative secular trend. These negative secular trends in the early years of the Fels study could reflect the early enrollment of many participants with parents who were members of the Faculty of Antioch College in Yellow Springs. Additionally, in the boys but not the girls, birth weight and recumbent length at 1 month increased significantly from 1946 to 1968 and the patterns of growth in weight became significantly more curvilinear from 1946 to 1958. The changes from one decade to another in birth weight

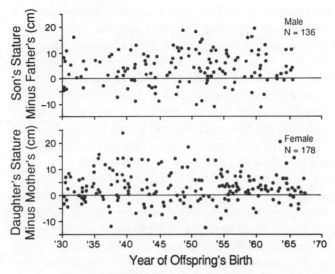

Fig. 4.8 Plots of the differences between the adult statures of parents and offspring of the same sex, plotted against the year of birth of the offspring. (Bock, R.D. & Sykes, R.C. (1989). Evidence for continuing secular increase in height within families in the United States. *American Journal of Human Biology*, **1**, 143–8, copyright 1989. Redrawn with permission from Wiley-Liss, Inc.)

and in recumbent length at 1 month for boys are shown in Fig. 4.9. While the changes were somewhat parallel between weight and recumbent length, they were larger for birth weight than for recumbent length.

In another approach to the analysis of possible secular changes, the parameters of the individual curves fitted to weight and recumbent length were regressed on year of birth and also on (year of birth)^2 to estimate linear and non-linear associations. These analyses showed significant linear associations with birth weight and the rate of growth in recumbent length, tendencies to more linear growth patterns in weight for each sex, and increases in the rate of growth in weight for girls. There were some significant negative correlations between (year of birth)^2 and the parameters of the model that showed the direction of the changes altered about 1952. Prior to that year, birth weight was decreasing, the patterns of growth in weight were becoming more curvilinear and the rate of growth in recumbent length was decreasing; these tendencies were reversed after 1952. There were many siblings in the sample, but birth order was not associated with these secular changes.

Roche *et al.* (1986b[257]) examined possible secular changes in the patterns of growth in head circumference. The participants were placed in three groups, on the basis of date of birth. The onset of the pubescent spurt in

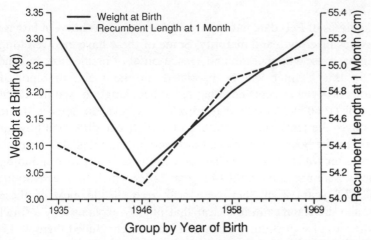

Fig. 4.9 Mean values for weight at birth and for recumbent length at 1 month, estimated from mathematical functions for boys grouped by year of birth. (Kouchi, M., Mukherjee, D. & Roche, A.F. (1985b). Curve fitting for growth in weight during infancy with relationships to adult status, and familial associations of the estimated parameters. *Human Biology*, **57**, 245–65, and Kouchi, M., Roche, A.F. & Mukherjee, D. (1985b). Growth in recumbent length during infancy with relationships to adult status and familial associations of the estimated parameters. *Human Biology*, **57**, 449–72. Redrawn with permission from *Human Biology*.)

head circumference occurred later during the early years of the Fels study compared with data recorded more recently. Additionally, the maximum rate of growth during the spurt was larger in those born recently. These secular changes in growth patterns were small and they were not associated with differences between birth groups in head circumference at birth or at 18 years.

Determinants of growth
Because the participants in the Fels study are, with few exceptions, healthy and well nourished, the Fels data are not ideal for the study of factors that affect growth. Nevertheless, some interesting observations have been made.

Type of infant feeding
In the Fels population, there were only small differences in growth between breast-fed and formula-fed infants from birth to 3 months, but at 6 months, a larger percentage of the breast-fed infants were below the fifth percentile in weight and recumbent length (Roche, Guo & Moore, 1989c[243]).

Fatness

Several analyses of Fels data have concerned associations between fatness and measures of growth and maturity. Some of these have involved long bone lengths, muscle thicknesses and ages at onset of ossification, but the account in this chapter will be restricted, in the main, to reported associations between fatness and either recumbent length or stature. Garn and Haskell (1960[88]) reported that correlations between adipose tissue thickness over the tenth rib and stature were higher in girls than boys at most ages. In the boys, these correlations were in the range 0.2–0.4 until 13.5 years, after which they were near zero. In the girls, the corresponding correlations were about 0.4 until 14.5 years, after which they were about 0.2 until 17.5 years when they were near zero. While most of these correlations were significant, it is clear that obesity explains only a small part of the variance in stature. Garn and Haskell concluded there was a linear relationship between stature and adipose tissue thickness over the tenth rib, within the limits of the study.

Garn (1962b[61]) reported correlations of about 0.3 between maternal weight in the first trimester of pregnancy or maternal weight gain during pregnancy, with birth weight. Although these correlations were significant, the maternal characteristics explained only a small part of the variance in birth weight. There were even lower correlations between maternal size and recumbent length at birth, which may have been due partly to the difficulties inherent in the measurement of recumbent length at this age. Sibling correlations in the Fels data for birth weight, recumbent length, and segment lengths at birth were about 0.3 (Garn, 1961c[59]).

Low correlations (about 0.2 to 0.3) between radiographic adipose tissue thicknesses and recumbent length in newly born and older infants were reported from early Fels studies (Garn, 1956a[46], 1958a[52]). At 1 month, infants above the median for fatness had larger recumbent lengths than those below the median. Nevertheless, the increments in recumbent length after 1 month were essentially the same in the two groups of infants and the differences were slight or non-existent after 6 months. Garn ascribed the marked differences at 1 month to variations in birth weight between the groups, but did not comment on possible group differences in recumbent length at birth. In another study, however, Garn (1962b[61]) did not find an association between fatness and recumbent length during infancy. He concluded that an asymptote had been reached beyond which the further accumulation of fat did not accelerate growth.

After analyzing data from children aged 7.5 and 11.5 years, Reynolds and Asakawa (1948) reported high correlations ($r = 0.7$ to 0.8) between weight and stature. More direct associations between fatness and stature

were presented by Reynolds (1951) in his landmark monograph. Reynolds reported correlations between radiographic adipose tissue thicknesses at six sites and stature at 7.5, 11.5 and 15.5 years (Table 4.2). The correlations tended to be highest for thicknesses at the calf and trochanteric sites. The correlations with stature were relatively high for boys aged 7.5 years and they decreased with age in each sex except from 7.5 to 11.5 years in the girls. Reynolds also reported partial correlations between the sums of adipose tissue thicknesses at these six sites and stature, with weight held constant. These coefficients were negative at each of the three ages in each sex and ranged from -0.3 to -0.7.

Garn and Haskell (1960[88]) concluded that there was a linear relationship between adipose tissue thickness at the tenth rib site and stature. They fitted a linear function to within-age plots of normalized adipose tissue thickness against stature and, of course, this did not reveal any within-age curvilinear relationship or asymptote. Almost all the correlations were significant to 12 years but later they decreased, particularly in the boys, and almost all were non-significant at older ages. The correlation coefficients tended to be higher for the girls than for the boys, but, even in the girls, fatness accounted for only a small part of the variance in stature.

It is interesting to note that the Fels data have been analyzed in relation to the same topic across a span of 26 years. Answers are never complete, but the data base gradually enlarges and better statistical methods become available. Himes and Roche (1986) returned to this topic when they analyzed the relationships of radiographic adipose tissue thicknesses at the medial calf and tenth rib sites to stature. Their findings were not in agreement with the earlier conclusions by Garn and Haskell (1960[88]) and by Garn (1962b[61]) that after infancy body size and maturational status can be increased almost indefinitely by stepping up the caloric surplus.

In the study by Himes and Roche, adipose tissue thicknesses were adjusted for radiographic enlargement and for the small differences between the scheduled and the actual ages at examinations. Linear and non-linear relationships (cubic polynomials) were evaluated. In the boys, the correlations for the calf increased from near zero in infancy until 11 years, after which they decreased. These correlations for the calf and for the tenth rib site in boys were significant at most ages from 5 to 15 years. In the girls, the correlations for the calf were significant at most ages from 3 through 12 years, and those for adipose tissue thicknesses at the tenth rib site were significant at all ages from 0.5 through 14 years.

In boys, the non-linear model had significantly larger coefficients than the linear model for the calf thicknesses at 9 and 11 years and the tenth rib thicknesses at 9 through 11 years. In the girls, the non-linear model had

Table 4.2. *Correlations between stature and radiographic adipose tissue thickness at six sites (data from Reynolds, 1951)*

Sites	Boys			Girls		
	7.5 years	11.5 years	15.5 years	7.5 years	11.5 years	15.5 years
Calf	0.52[a]	0.23	0.07	0.34[b]	0.32[b]	0.15
Trochanter	0.31[b]	0.20	−0.07	0.15	0.36[b]	−0.10
Waist	0.47[a]	0.14	−0.02	0.21	0.24	0.02
Chest	0.27	0.19	−0.02	0.20	0.20	−0.08
Forearm	0.27	0.16	−0.18	0.20	0.14	0.02
Deltoid	0.39[a]	0.21	−0.05	0.16	0.17	0.04

[a] $p < 0.01$.
[b] $0 < 0.05$.

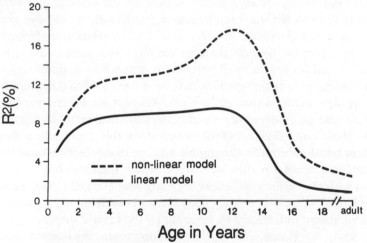

Fig. 4.10 Smoothed percentages of variance accounted for by linear and non-linear relationships among adipose tissue thickness at the 10th rib site and stature in girls. (Himes, J.H. & Roche, A.F. (1986). Subcutaneous fatness and stature: Relationships from infancy to adulthood. *Human Biology*, **58**, 737–50. Redrawn with permission from *Human Biology*.)

significantly larger correlations than the linear model for the calf thicknesses at 3, 11 and 12 years and for the tenth rib thicknesses at 9 through 14 years (Fig. 4.10). The non-linear correlations, but not the linear ones, increased markedly during pubescence. Plots of adipose tissue thicknesses against stature showed that increases in thickness beyond a 'threshold' level were not associated with further increases in stature (Fig. 4.11).

Familial studies

As noted earlier, there are significant correlations between the statures of parents and their children. These should be taken into account when childhood stature is evaluated. Garn (1961c[59]) categorized parents as tall, medium, or short and compared the statures of the children from various types of parental pairings, e.g., tall–tall, tall–medium. He concluded that 'height–weight tables that ignore parental size are unrealistic. They apply only to foundlings....' Later, they published means at various ages for stature relative to the average of the statures of both parents (mid-parent stature) (Garn, 1966b[67]; Garn & Rohmann, 1966a[141]). These tables did not distinguish between recumbent length and stature. To assist the application of these data, Garn and Rohmann (1967[143]) reported numerical estimates of mid-parent statures when the mother's stature was known but the father's was only categorized to tall, medium or short. Since the distributions of childhood statures within mid-parent stature groups were not provided, these data are not suitable for clinical application.

Garn (1958a[52]) reported a low correlation (r = 0.3) between the statures of fathers and the recumbent lengths of infants at birth. Later, in a slightly different approach, Garn (1962b[61]) showed marked differences between the statures of offspring from tall × tall matings and those from short × short matings. This led him to conclude that adult stature was not controlled by genes that were purely cumulative. Garn showed that serial statures and serial lengths of a hand bone (second metacarpal) were more alike for monozygotes than for dizygotes, but even the monozygotes showed some differences. He concluded that the controlling factors involved in these differences affected the whole organism.

In 1981, Himes and his co-workers published a detailed monograph dealing with parent–child similarities in stature and provided a method to adjust recorded childhood statures for mid-parent statures. Parent–child correlations for stature may be affected by a tendency for spouses to be similar in stature. There was some evidence of such mating in the Fels study where the husband–wife correlation for stature was 0.2, but this did not affect the adjustments calculated by Himes *et al.* (1981) because they were derived from mid-parent–child regressions. Parent–child correlations could be affected also by marked differences in the environments during growth for parents and children, but this possibility can be disregarded for the Fels data because secular changes have been small (Garn & French, 1967[82]; Roche *et al.*, 1975a[272]). The estimates made by Himes *et al.* (1981) could have been affected by the inclusion of several siblings of the same sex in some families, but it was shown that restriction of the data base to one child of each sex within each family did not alter the results.

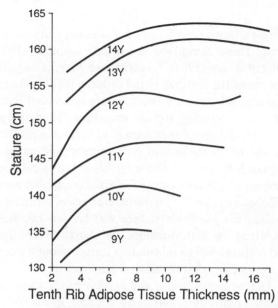

Fig. 4.11 Polynomial curves of stature against adipose tissue thickness at the 10th rib site in girls aged 9–14 years. (Himes, J.H. & Roche, A.F. (1986). Subcutaneous fatness and stature: Relationships from infancy to adulthood. *Human Biology*, **58**, 737–50, Redrawn with permission from *Human Biology*.)

Himes *et al.* (1981) analyzed data from 271 parents and 586 children. The data for children were adjusted to ages at scheduled examinations and the parental statures were those recorded closest to 30 years. They used a linear model of the form:

$$child\ stature = a + b\ (mid\text{-}parent\ stature) + error\ term.$$

The coefficients for the regressions between mid-parent statures and the statures of the offspring, which are the b terms in the equations, increased rapidly from birth to 2 years and then more slowly to 7 years (Himes *et al.*, 1981). After 7 years, the coefficients increased in a near linear fashion in each sex, with a considerably steeper slope for the boys than for the girls. These authors tested other models that allowed for non-linear relationships, differential effects of the statures of the mother and father, and interaction effects of the parental statures. These alternative models did not reduce the standard errors in either sex except for slight reductions with the interactive model at some ages in the boys but not in the girls (Himes, 1984a).

The regression coefficients and the standard errors were smoothed across age and were adjusted relative to the National Center for Health

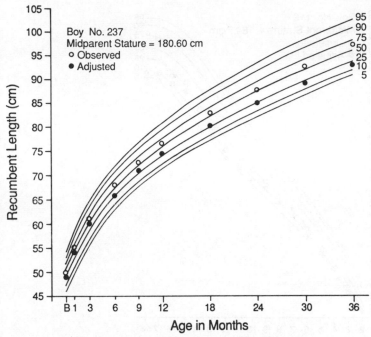

Fig. 4.12 Observed and adjusted recumbent lengths for mid-parent stature in a Fels boy with tall parents shown relative to NCHS percentiles.

Statistics reference data. The final parent-specific adjustments to observed childhood statures were presented for age- and sex-groups within categories of recumbent length and stature and distributed in a clinically useful format by Ross Laboratories.

These adjustments to the observed recumbent lengths and statures of children provide a powerful tool for distinguishing between children with 'normal' genetic causes of unusual stature and those with diseases that affect growth. For example, use of the adjustments will show whether a child with a stature less than the 5th percentile who has short parents is within the normal range, given the statures of the parents. These adjustments should be applied when the stature of a child is unusual and the parental statures are also unusual. Himes (1984b), after a thorough literature review, concluded that the parent-specific adjustments that had been derived from US whites were equally applicable to US blacks.

The measured and the adjusted values should be plotted on the National Center for Health Statistics growth charts (Hamill *et al.*, 1977, 1979). Figure 4.12 shows pairs of measured and adjusted recumbent lengths for an infant with tall parents. The measured values are near the median level

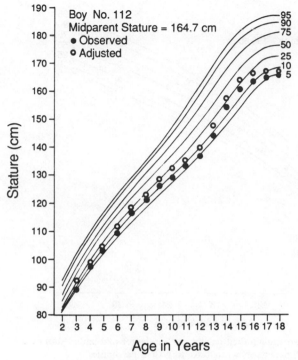

Fig. 4.13 Observed and adjusted statures for mid-parent stature in a Fels boy
with short parents.

but the adjusted values are near the 25th percentile. Figure 4.13 shows
corresponding data for an older boy with short parents. The observed
values are near the 10th percentile but most of the adjusted values are near
the 25th percentile. In these children, the adjustments led to considerable
changes in percentile levels.

These adjustments are important in the clinical assessment of children in
whom growth in stature is unusual. The adjustment makes important
differences if the average stature of the parents is unusual; in these
circumstances, it allows the child to be compared indirectly with the
'population' to which he or she belongs. This adjustment for inherited
factors makes it easier to evaluate the cause of an unusual stature and
choose the best management for it.

Familial correlations for recumbent length and stature were reported by
Byard, Siervogel and Roche (1983) using data for pairs of related
participants measured at corresponding ages. These correlations tended to
decrease during pubescence, but were mainly influenced by the degree of

relationship, age and sex. The sibling correlations were consistently higher than the parent–offspring correlations except after 15 years when both sets were similar. This method of analysis did not allow a separation of genetic, environmental and generational effects.

Later, Byard, Siervogel and Roche (1988) applied new path analysis techniques to annual measurements of recumbent length and stature to assess the transmissible and non-transmissible components of family resemblance for stature. The proportion that is transmitted reflects the joint influences of genes and culture, whereas the non-transmissible component is environmentally determined. The data they analyzed were for parents and their offspring all measured at corresponding ages. These workers calculated correlations using maximum likelihood procedures with adjustments for the variations among families in the number of children. Many of the sibling correlations exceeded 0.5, indicating that factors other than genes contributed to family resemblance. The importance of cultural inheritance from the parent was indicated by the finding that the sibling correlations were uniformly higher than the parent–offspring correlations. At about 4 years, the transmissible and non-transmissible components had their maximum coefficients. After this age, the coefficients for the non-transmissible components decreased rapidly, but those for the transmissible component were fairly constant.

Garn (1961c[59]) reported that parents with broad chests tended to have tall and heavy children with increased values for weight relative to stature. These effects were more marked in boys than girls and indicated a familial influence on this aspect of frame size.

Intrafamilial correlations were calculated for the three parameters of the model that was fitted to serial data for weight and recumbent length by Kouchi *et al.* (1985a, 1985b). All the correlations were positive but the parent–offspring correlations were not significant. The low parent–offspring correlations for birth weight were consistent with other evidence that birth weight is mainly determined by non-genetic maternal factors. All the sibling correlations were significant except those for some growth pattern parameters. The patterns of the correlations did not suggest sex-linked inheritance for changes in weight and recumbent length during infancy.

On average, parent–offspring and the sibling pairs have 50% of their genes in common. The lower correlations for parent–offspring pairs than for sibling pairs may have reflected differential environmental effects. Siblings share a common intra-uterine environment which is not the case for parent–offspring pairs. Also the postnatal environment is likely to be more similar for sibling pairs than for parent–offspring pairs. Much earlier,

Sontag and Garn (1957[286]) described four siblings in whom, from birth to 10 years, there were similar patterns of rapid growth in stature and weight, rapid maturation and slow motor development. Their findings indicated that these age-related changes may be genetically determined.

Correlations were calculated between values derived from the model fitted to serial data for head circumference by Roche *et al.* (1986b[257]) for parent–offspring pairs and for sibling pairs. These analyses took advantage of the unusual nature of the data set which contained measurements of these related participants at matching ages. All the sibling correlations, but none of the parent–offspring correlations, were significant. Even the sibling correlations were only low to moderate indicating that there was only slight genetic regulation of growth in head circumference. The differences in the correlations between parent–offspring and sibling pairs presumably reflected greater similarity of the environment (diet, illness) for siblings measured a few years apart than for parents and their offspring who were measured several decades apart. These findings matched those from other Fels studies of growth patterns in recumbent length, stature and weight (Byard *et al.*, 1983; Kouchi *et al.*, 1985a, 1985b).

Garn (1958a[52]) reported low correlations (~ 0.3) between siblings for birthweight. Additionally, Garn (1961c[59]) noted the occurrence of some sibships in which there was a clear pattern of decreases with age in standard scores for stature.

The final phase of growth

Fels scientists have conducted important analyses related to the final phase of growth in stature and the changes that occur in weight during the same period. The Fels data are ideal for such analyses. In contrast, many other growth studies have been based on school populations in which there has been considerable attrition at older ages and data collection has ceased at 18 years.

Garn *et al.* (1961b[144]) reported that the total increment in stature after the completion of epiphyseal fusion in the hand–wrist varied from zero to 4 cm, being larger in girls than boys. In a subsequent paper, Garn and Wagner (1969[170]) reported that slow-maturing children can grow as much as 7 cm after 17 years, although the mean total increases were 2.3 cm for males and 1.2 cm for females. Some of this variation could be due to differences in the rates of maturation between the long bones and the bones of the hand–wrist.

In later work, data from 194 Fels participants who had been examined to at least 28 years were used to determine the age at which adult stature was reached (Roche & Davila, 1972[222], 1975[225]; Roche, 1976[183]). Two

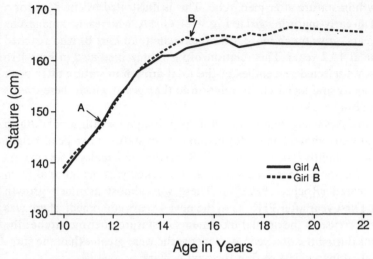

Fig. 4.14 Serial stature data for two Fels participants who differed markedly in age at menarche (see text for details).

mathematical models were fitted to the serial data recorded after the peak rate of growth in stature during pubescence (PHV). A polynomial (non-linear model) was fitted to the earlier data and a horizontal line was fitted to the later data. Piecewise regressions were calculated in which progressively more points were included in the 'earlier data.' The goodness of fit, measured by the differences between observed and predicted points for the two functions combined was calculated for each junction between the two models. The junction at which the goodness of fit was maximal was accepted as the age at which adult stature was reached. This method was effective in all the participants except a few in whom there were only small changes in the goodness of fit between successive junctions.

It was estimated that adult stature was reached at median ages of 21.2 years for males and 17.3 years for females. The amounts of growth after 16 years were considerably larger for males (2.4 cm) than for females (0.9 cm), and there were corresponding differences between the sexes in the amounts of growth after 18 years. Additionally, it was shown that stature increased about 1.5 cm in males and about 1.0 cm in females after the bones of the leg were completely mature (Roche & Davila, 1972[222], 1974b[224], 1975[225]). This growth must occur in the trunk.

In the females, growth in stature continued for almost 5 years after menarche with an increase in stature of 7.9 cm during this time. The increments in stature after menarche were negatively associated ($r = -0.5$) with the age of menarche, showing that late-maturing girls tended to have

less growth in stature after menarche. This is illustrated by the data for a late- and an early-maturing girl in Fig. 4.14. Girl A, who reached menarche at 11.6 years, grew much more after menarche than Girl B, who reached menarche at 15.2 years. This relationship is represented also in Fig. 4.15 which shows selected percentiles of the total growth in stature after peak height velocity and menarche in relation to the ages at which these events occurred (Roche, 1989a[207]).

Later analyses using data from 520 Fels participants with serial data to at least 20 years showed the total increments in stature after peak height velocity were slightly larger in males (17.8 cm) than in females (15.8 cm). As expected, the annual increments decreased markedly as the interval from PHV increased (Roche, 1989a[207]). There was almost as much growth during the first year after PHV as in the next 4 years combined. There was a similar decrease in the annual increments in stature after menarche: the increments during the first year after menarche were greater than the sums of the annual increments during the next 4 years.

Changes in weight after PHV were analyzed using data from 229 Fels participants with serial data extending to at least 22 years (Roche & Davila, 1974b[224]; Roche *et al.*, 1975c[227]). Piecewise regression was applied, as was done for stature, but in this case a polynomial was fitted to the earlier data and a linear function, that was not necessarily horizontal, was fitted to the later data. The junction at which the goodness of fit was maximal for the two functions combined was accepted as the age at which there was a change in the pattern of growth in weight. In some participants, more commonly than for stature, there were only slight differences in the goodness of fit between successive junctions and it was not possible to determine precisely the age at which the change in the pattern of growth occurred. The median ages for these junctions were 21.2 years in the males and 18.2 years in the females, with large ranges in each sex. For example, in males the 10th and 90th percentile ages were 16.9 and 25.1 years respectively. These ages were positively correlated with the weights at the junctions in the males (r = 0.4) but not in the females, and with age at PHV in each sex (males 0.4; females 0.3).

The total increments in weight were considerably larger in the males than in the females after particular ages and developmental events, such as PHV, and the completion of maturation of the bones of the leg. Furthermore, the functions fitted to the later data had much steeper slopes in the males than in the females, showing that the males gained weight more rapidly than the females after the change in the pattern of growth occurred. As was observed for stature, the increments in weight after menarche were negatively correlated (r = −0.4) with age at menarche.

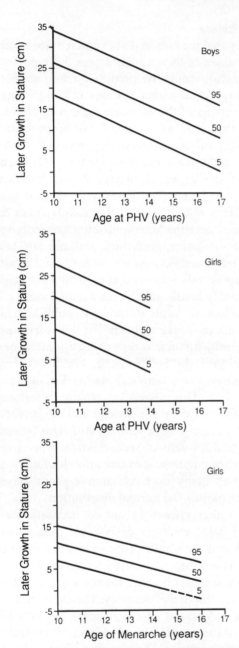

Fig. 4.15 Selected percentiles for the total growth in stature after peak height velocity and menarche in relation to the ages at which these events occurred. (Roche, A.F. (1989a). The final phase of growth in stature. *Growth, Genetics and Hormones*, **5**, 4–6[207]. Reproduced with permission from McGraw-Hill, Inc.)

The prediction of adult stature

In an early study, Garn (1966b[67]) used the notion that children of the same age have achieved similar percentages of their adult statures. He reported 'multipliers' by which adult stature could be predicted from present stature for children with 'average' mid-parent statures (167–175 cm). Neither the sample sizes nor the errors of the estimates were given, but it was claimed that, for children with skeletal ages within 0.5 sd of the mean, the accuracy was as good as that of more complex approaches. Garn recognized the importance of skeletal age and recommended that it be used in place of chronological age. In this paper, Garn argued that the knee skeletal age should, in principle, be better than hand–wrist skeletal age because regions of the body differ in maturity levels (Garn, Silverman & Rohmann, 1964e[167]) and the bones near the knee contribute markedly to stature attainment. In a review of stature prediction, Falkner (1971a) directed attention to the low correlations between size at birth and adult size and the rapid increase in these correlations soon after birth. He stated that adult stature became reasonably predictable by the age of 3 years.

A new method for the prediction of adult stature was published in monograph form by Roche and his co-workers (1975a[272]); this work was summarized and made more generally useful in other publications (Roche, Wainer & Thissen, 1974a[270], 1974b[271], 1975b[273]; Roche, 1980b[191]). This investigation was undertaken because many families have marked interest in the adult statures of their children. This interest can change to serious concern if the present statures of the children are unusual and the parents consider it likely that their adult statures will be unusual also. This family concern increases the psychological burdens of such children, who may have social difficulties. In this context, a physical examination leading to a diagnosis may be indicated, but many such children do not have pathological conditions; they are part of the normal distribution.

In children with diseases that alter growth in stature, accurate predictions of adult stature would help selection for possible therapy to increase the potential for growth and the results of such therapy could be monitored by serial predictions. This approach is better than assessing the elongation and maturation of the skeleton because the units of measurement and the distributions differ for length and maturity. This difference in units makes it difficult to judge differential effects on these two sets of variables. Predictions of adult stature could be used also to evaluate therapeutic effects for children with hormonal abnormalities or congenital heart disease and to assist the evaluation of 'catch-up growth' whether this follows medical, dietary or other types of intervention. Despite these claims for the utility of adult stature predictions, the predicted values are

not guarantees. They are only estimates for an individual and these estimates have errors that are often expressed as confidence limits.

A comprehensive review of the literature showed that predictions should be derived from a combination of variables that, almost certainly, would include the present age, stature or recumbent length, and maturity of the child and the statures of both parents (Roche *et al.*, 1975a[272]; Roche, 1980b[191]). It was clear also that the method should be sex specific. To be useful in a wide range of situations, the prediction method had to be applicable at many ages and when data from only one examination were available. The maturity measure had to be one that could be obtained at all childhood ages. Skeletal age is the only measure of maturity that meets this criterion.

Roche *et al.* (1975a[272]) used data from Fels participants who were at least 18 years old to develop their RWT stature prediction method. Data from examinations when skeletal maturation was complete or nearly complete were excluded because skeletal ages in years could not be assigned, and predictions made so late in relation to maturity would be of little practical value. Skeletal ages obtained by the atlas method were available for the hand–wrist, foot–ankle and knee, for individual bones and for combinations of these bones. These skeletal ages were a majority of the 80 independent (predictor) variables that were tested for inclusion in the final prediction equations. This set of possible predictor variables had to be considerably reduced. In the first steps principal components analysis and cluster analysis were used to exclude variables that could be represented by a linear combination of other variables. At the end of this process, it appeared that the same set of predictors could be used for all ages and both sexes. Fourteen variables were retained for further testing.

Recumbent length was chosen instead of stature because it can be measured at all ages. When only stature was available, it was adjusted to be approximately equivalent to recumbent length by adding 1.25 cm (Roche & Davila, 1974a[223]). The final selection of predictors was based, in part, on the view that variables should be easy to obtain and that radiation load and financial burdens should be minimized.

All possible subsets regression was used at each age: perhaps the first time this procedure was applied in a biological context. Area skeletal ages were shown to be more useful than bone-specific skeletal ages. Means and medians of groups of skeletal ages were about equally useful; medians were chosen because they are more resistant to effects of outlying values or adult levels of maturity in a few bones. The median skeletal age of the knee was slightly more useful than that of the hand–wrist, but hand–wrist skeletal age was chosen to reduce irradiation and to conform with common

Table 4.3. *Values for R^2 and selected percentiles for absolute differences (cm) between predicted and actual adult statures (data from Roche et al., 1975a[272])*

Age (years)	Boys Percentiles			Girls Percentiles		
	R^2	50th	90th	R^2	50th	90th
1	0.58	2.74	5.94	0.49	3.30	5.85
2	0.59	2.50	6.25	0.44	3.00	5.80
3	0.67	2.26	5.91	0.52	2.80	5.46
4	0.67	2.16	5.64	0.56	2.55	5.17
5	0.73	2.05	5.65	0.56	2.27	5.72
6	0.74	2.09	5.75	0.60	2.20	5.53
7	0.71	2.06	5.82	0.62	1.91	5.55
8	0.75	1.83	5.52	0.69	1.88	4.47
9	0.76	1.80	5.61	0.62	2.30	5.07
10	0.77	1.59	5.05	0.57	2.13	5.46
11	0.73	2.03	5.66	0.62	2.18	5.42
12	0.70	2.29	5.24	0.59	2.32	5.64
13	0.61	2.58	6.55	0.70	2.01	4.45
14	0.63	2.92	6.35	0.75	1.87	4.32
15	0.70	2.15	4.78	—	—	—
16	0.91	0.97	3.20	—	—	—

practice. Consequently, the final predictors were the present recumbent length, weight, and hand–wrist skeletal age of the child, and mid-parent stature, which is the average of the statures of the two parents. Some of these predictors were unnecessary at a few ages, but the complete set was retained for all ages to ensure consistency.

In the boys, the R^2 values from the age-specific regression equations showed that the predictions were only moderately accurate at ages younger than 2 years, but the average of the R^2 values was high (0.8) from 0.5 to 15.5 years. The accuracy of the predictions was assessed, in addition, from the differences between the actual and the predicted adult statures (residuals). The median residuals for the boys were about 2.0 cm to 5 years, slightly less from 6 through 11 years and markedly less at ages older than 15 years (Table 4.3). The R^2 values were slightly lower in the girls. The median residuals for the girls were slightly greater than 3.0 cm to 2 years, between 2.0 and 3.0 cm to 6 years, and close to 2.0 cm from 6 to 10 years. Later the residuals decreased rapidly. The 95th percentiles of these absolute differences were about 5.0 cm at most ages in each sex.

Skeletal age was a much more important predictor for the girls than for

the boys, particularly during pubescence, although the amounts of growth during pubescence are the same in each sex (Bock *et al.*, 1973). The sex difference in the importance of skeletal age as a predictor may be related to the greater growth after pubescence in boys than in girls (Roche, 1989a[207]). This may also be responsible for the greater decrease in the accuracy of predictions during pubescence for girls than for boys.

The weightings (coefficients) in the regression equations were smoothed across age. This allowed interpolations to ages between half-birthdays. This smoothing slightly reduced the accuracy of prediction in the Fels group but it was expected that it would increase the accuracy when the method was applied to other groups. It is difficult to smooth interrelated variables because the errors associated with smoothing are correlated unless precautions are taken.

To overcome this problem, the regression coefficients were transformed to unrelated (orthogonal) variables. After these transformed variables were smoothed, they were changed back to their original relationships. The smoothing was done with repeated running medians after which a polynomial was fitted. Figure 4.16 shows the progressive changes in the weightings for recumbent length in the girls from the unsmoothed state (a), to when they were smoothed by repeated running medians (b), to smoothing by a polynomial before (c), and (d) after they had been changed back to the original relationships.

These smoothed coefficients have biological interest in regard to the determinants of adult stature, but interpretation is difficult because of their interrelationships. The recumbent length weightings were positive and similar in the two sexes. They decreased from 3 to about 14 years, but increased at older ages. The weightings for body weight were negative at most ages, which is concordant with reports that obese children tend to become short adults. This is in agreement also with the finding that rapid increases in weight in some Fels participants were associated with reductions in their predicted adult statures (Roche & French, 1969[233]). The coefficients for weight were larger in the girls than in the boys, but, in each sex, they increased (larger negative values) to about 4 years and then decreased.

The coefficients for mid-parent stature were positive at all ages in each sex but were larger for the boys, which would be expected because of their greater adult statures. The coefficients for mid-parent stature decreased with age to about 8 years, after which there were marked increases in the boys but only slight increases in the girls. The skeletal age coefficients were near zero until 4 years in each sex. At older ages, they were generally negative and were larger in the girls than in the boys.

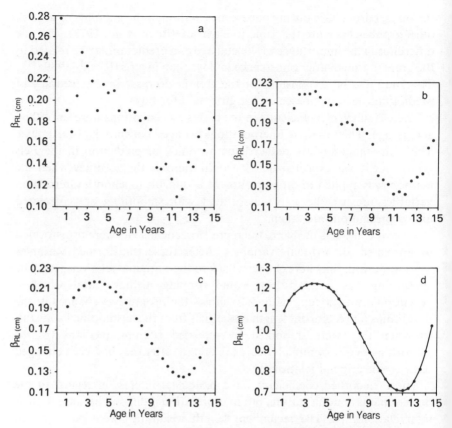

Fig. 4.16 Steps in the process by which the weightings (coefficients) for recumbent length in girls were smoothed during the elaboration of equations to predict adult stature. (Roche, A.F., Wainer, H. & Thissen, D. (1975a). Predicting adult stature for individuals. *Monographs in Pediatrics*, 3, 1–115[272]. Redrawn with permission from S. Karger AG, Basel.)

The final prediction equations were presented for 1-month age intervals from 1 through 16 years (Roche *et al.*, 1975a[272]). The guidelines for their application stated that a population mean can be used when the value for a predictor variable is missing. If stature is measured instead of recumbent length, the recorded value can be adjusted to approximate recumbent length (Roche & Davila, 1974a[223]). Commonly, the measured stature of the father will be unavailable. A reported stature can be used or even the mother's categorization of his stature to short, medium, or tall (Himes & Roche, 1982). Even if the father's stature is completely unknown, a population mean can be substituted with only small increases in the errors of prediction (Wainer, Roche & Bell, 1978).

With a few exceptions, other variables did not add to the accuracy of the predictions. The growth patterns of the children, as described by the double logistic model of Bock *et al.* (1973), did not assist except that the age at the maximum rate of growth in the adolescent component was significantly correlated with the residuals (errors of prediction) in each sex. In addition, the predicted statures tended to be lower than the observed statures in late-maturing children.

Differences in the timing of the adolescent spurt, that were not accounted for by hand–wrist skeletal ages, were responsible for about 16% of the errors. This finding cannot be applied in prediction because the children would be too old for useful predictions when this age becomes known. It was postulated, however, that better estimates of hand–wrist skeletal age than the Greulich–Pyle values could help. Subsequently, the FELS method for the assessment of the hand–wrist (Roche, Chumlea & Thissen, 1988a[221]) was applied to children aged 15 years by substituting FELS skeletal ages for Greulich–Pyle skeletal ages when applying the regression equations. The mean errors were reduced by about 0.5 cm in each sex. This indicated that, at least during pubescence, the RWT prediction equations could be improved if new analyses were made using FELS skeletal age as a predictor.

The errors of prediction with the RWT method were compared with those from the Bayley–Pinneau method both for the Fels participants and participants in the Denver Growth Study. These comparisons were restricted to ages older than 6 years because the Bayley–Pinneau method is not applicable at younger ages. The median errors were much smaller with the RWT method than with the Bayley–Pinneau method in each group (Fig. 4.17). The only exceptions occurred near 16 years for boys in the Denver group. The RWT method can be applied only when a median Greulich–Pyle skeletal age for the hand–wrist is available. In the Fels group, these skeletal ages were calculated only when less than half the bones of the hand–wrist were adult. The data from the Denver cross-validation sample included all boys up to 16 years of age. Consequently, the RWT method was applied to some older boys in the Denver study for whom it was not appropriate.

Roche and Chumlea (1980[215]) analyzed serial RWT predictions of adult stature. The mean differences between predictions made 1, 2 or 5 years apart were near zero, but the standard deviations of these differences were about 1.2 cm, 1.5 cm and 2.0 cm respectively in each sex (Fig. 4.18). These standard deviations were smaller for intervals beginning at 3 to 9 years than for earlier or later intervals. These data showed the age range during which significant differences in predicted adult statures are most likely to

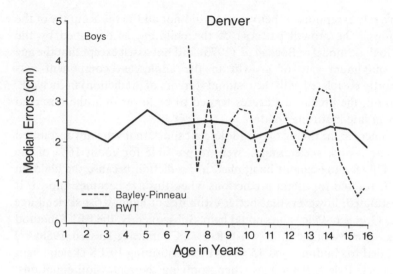

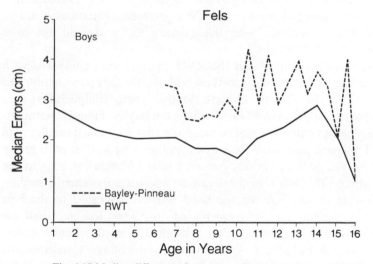

Fig. 4.17 Median differences between predicted and observed adult statures for boys in the Fels and Denver studies. (Roche, A.F., Wainer, H. & Thissen, D. (1975a). Predicting adult stature for individuals. *Monographs in Pediatrics*, **3**, 1–115[272]. Redrawn with permission from S. Karger AG, Basel.)

be detected in an intervention study. Additionally, these data can be used to analyze the significance of changes in predicted adult statures in association with therapy.

The prediction of adult stature has been reviewed in several publications in which attention was given to comparisons between methods (Roche,

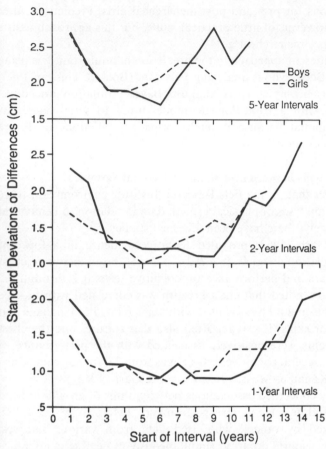

Fig. 4.18 Standard deviations of the differences between serial predictions of adult stature made 1, 2, and 5 years apart using the RWT method. (Roche, A.F. & Chumlea, W.C. (1980). Serial changes in predicted adult statures for individuals. *Human Biology*, **52**, 507–13[215]. Redrawn with permission from *Human Biology*.)

1980b[191], 1984b[197]). These comparisons were limited by the age ranges during which the methods are applicable. For example, only the RWT method can be used before the age of 4 years. The general conclusion from these comparisons, and those made by others, was that the RWT method is superior in regard to tendencies to under-predict or over-predict.

Random errors have been compared also. These were smaller and more consistent across age for the RWT than for the other methods. The only exception concerned older girls for whom the method of Tanner and colleagues has smaller random errors, presumably because it included

separate equations for pre- and post-menarcheal girls. Predictions after menarche are, however, of little practical value, but this approach assists predictions for pre-menarcheal girls.

An entirely different approach to the prediction of adult stature is being investigated by Bock, who is analyzing Fels data (Bock & Thissen, 1980; Bock, 1982). This incomplete work, that uses Bayes' estimation procedures in combination with a triple logistic model fitted to serial data, has tremendous potential because it might provide predictions of future growth patterns in addition to adult statures.

Associations between growth and behavioral variables

One might expect that, in the Fels Research Institute environment, there would be many analyses of physical growth data in relation to behavioral variables. Strangely, there have been few such studies.

Kagan and Garn (1963) provided tentative evidence of a low but significant correlation in girls (r = 0.2), but not boys, between chest breadth at 2 years and performance on cognitive tests at 2 through 3.5 years. The authors noted that chest breadth was correlated with fat-free mass and that this might be associated with items related to language and perceptual/motor skills. It was reported also that statures and the chest breadths of parents were positively associated with the performance of their children on several cognitive tests at ages from 2.0 to 3.5 years (Garn et al., 1960a[74]; Kagan & Moss, 1963; Kagan & Garn, 1963).

Another study concerned associations between rates of growth in head circumference and in mental test performance (McCall et al., 1983). Analyses reported by others, who used data from various samples, indicated that five spurts occurred simultaneously in head circumference and mental test performance between birth and 17 years. Furthermore, these earlier workers claimed that children were receptive to learning only during these spurts. Analyses of Fels data showed only one spurt for head circumference and three spurts in mental test performance between birth and 17 years. There were large differences between individuals in their patterns of change and between the patterns of growth in head circumference and those in mental test performance. It was concluded that there was no justification for changing school curricula because of supposed concurrent spurts in head circumference and mental test performance.

The literature concerning the growth of the brain, including that from the Fels study, has been reviewed critically (Roche, 1980c[192], 1981a[193]). The central topic addressed was the possible occurrence of 'catch-up growth' of the brain. The term catch-up growth refers to a period of rapid growth

in an individual who was growing slowly. During the period of catch-up, the individual grows more rapidly than usual and, if catch-up is complete, the individual's growth status becomes normal. Catch-up growth is well documented for many body dimensions and organs but uncertain for the brain. Since brain size is related to cognitive development, catch-up growth of the brain would be very important in children treated for malnutrition and social deficits.

Increase in brain size is dependent on increases in the number of brain cells and in the size of these cells. It had been suggested that reductions in cell number are permanent. This is true for reductions early in gestation due to irradiation, virus infections, or chromosomal abnormalities. It may not be true for reductions at older ages due mainly to malnutrition. In malnourished fetuses, there are proportional decreases in the number and size of brain cells, but infants with small heads *in utero*, measured by ultrasound, tend to catch up incompletely in head size during the first year after birth. In older malnourished children, the decrease in cell size is greater than that in cell number. The deficits in cell size and in synaptic and dendritic complexity can be reversed.

It is difficult to determine the ages during which catch-up growth of the brain can occur. Some important studies of infants with good socio-economic status, who had intrauterine growth retardation or diseases that cause malnutrition that can be treated, e.g., pyloric stenosis, show incomplete catch-up in head circumference.

The reduction in head circumference in malnourished children is not entirely due to decreases in brain size and alterations in brain cells. As noted by Robinow (1968), there are decreases in scalp thicknesses, and in cranial bone thickness, but increases in the amount of the subarachnoid fluid that surrounds the brain. These changes are reversible and they may obscure alterations in brain size, judged from head circumference, during the rehabilitation of malnourished children.

There can be extraordinarily rapid catch-up growth in head circumference when some malnourished children are treated. This is associated with increases in intracranial pressure that cause sutural separation if they occur before the sutures are interlocked at about the age of 5 years. These increases probably involve brain size but it is not known whether the changes are in cells, myelin, or fluid. Rapid increases in head circumference are not possible after 5 years, but dendritic complexity, and perhaps other aspects of brain development, can increase even in old age. No longer can one accept the view that nutritional intervention of malnourished children is ineffective in regard to the central nervous system after the first 2 years of life.

One unusual study used noise exposure as an indicator of behavior and related this to growth and maturation. Siervogel and his associates (1982a) found that 24-hour noise exposure, measured with dosimeters, was not correlated with body size and maturity in boys after age effects were removed. In girls, however, weight, weight/stature^2, and measures of maturity were correlated with noise exposure. Larger and more mature girls, matched for chronological age, tended to be exposed to more noise.

Finally, Goodson and Jamison (1987) used age at peak height velocity and the percent of adult stature achieved at this age as measures of maturity. These measures were used to show that rapidly maturing adolescents were more concerned with their peers, had higher expectations for their futures, and were less independent and less interested in intellectual activities. When adult, individuals who matured rapidly were more concerned with power and proving their competence.

Future directions

It is difficult to predict the long-term future of the Fels Longitudinal Study in regard to physical growth. As the Swedish proverb has it: 'The afternoon discovers what the morning never imagined.' Some short-term suggestions are possible, however, in keeping with the dictum of Winston Churchill: 'It is wise to look ahead but foolish to look further than you can see.'

Some possible future directions were included in a review by a National Institutes of Health panel chaired by Roche (1986a[201]). The following are some of the topics to which attention should be directed:

(i)   Reference data, including increments, are needed for the prenatal period. Incremental reference data would allow the early recognition of problems in prenatal growth that may indicate outcomes during the perinatal period and infancy. The extent and the timing of catch-up growth during infancy for fetuses with intrauterine growth retardation, across the range of severity and types of intrauterine growth retardation, are poorly known. Studies of change in fetal adipose tissue late in gestation are now possible due to improvements in ultrasonography.

(ii)   Reference data are needed for growth relative to maturity status during pubescence.

(iii)   There is a lack of studies of the associations of physical growth with mental and behavioral development although there are relevant data in longitudinal study archives. A fruitful field could

be the analysis of changes in mental test performance in relation to hormonal changes during pubescence.

(iv)   Methods are required for the prediction of adult stature in abnormal children but it is difficult to obtain sufficient serial data from homogeneous groups of such children.

While these are worthy goals, their achievement would involve major extensions to the Fels study.

5 *Physical maturation and development*

> Nature is comparatively careless of stature, permitting it to vary within relatively wide limits, but zealously keeps the program of maturation as nearly as possible to schedule.
>
> *T. Wingate Todd* (1885–1938)

Maturation is the process that leads to the achievement of adult maturity. Maturation is a part of development. Both relate to progressive increases in complexity, but maturation is restricted to those developmental changes that lead to the same end point in all individuals. For example, the percentage of adult stature achieved by a child is a measure of maturity: all reach 100% in adulthood. Levels of maturity that are intermediate between the absence of measurable indicators and the adult state indicate the extent to which a child, or a group of children, has proceeded toward the completion of maturation in a particular body system. Maturation occurs in all body systems, organs, and tissues. For example, 'skeletal maturation' refers to a set of radiographically visible changes that culminate in the achievement of adult skeletal status by the early 20s.

This broad subject has received considerable sustained attention from Fels scientists. For example, Roche (1974c[180]) published an introduction to a symposium on adolescent physiology in which variation in maturation was the dominant theme. Much of this variation is associated with differences in rates of maturation among individuals. Attention was also given to the hormonal control of adolescence and the factors that regulate the timing of menarche. Maturation has also been the subject of a review by Chumlea (in press[13]).

This chapter will deal with: (i) skeletal maturation, (ii) dental maturation, (iii) sexual maturation, (iv) other aspects of maturation, (v) the non-invasive assessment of maturity, (vi) the regulation of maturation and its associations, (vii) the timing and sequence of adolescent events, (viii) the

development of hearing ability, and (ix) developmental changes in skin reflectance.

Skeletal maturation

Assessments of skeletal maturity (skeletal ages) are associated with body size and shape, the percentage of adult stature achieved, body composition measures such as percent body fat, bone widths, the widths of the cortex of bones, the timing of pubescence, and the age at which adult stature is reached (Garn *et al.*, 1961b[144]; Chumlea *et al.*, 1981a[24], 1983[39]). These values can identify children who are maturing rapidly or slowly and thereby indicate a need for laboratory investigations. Furthermore, these assessments are used in studies that describe and compare groups of children, and studies that evaluate the effects of environmental deficits. Additionally, skeletal maturity assessments are applied to predict adult stature and craniofacial growth (Roche, Chumlea & Thissen 1988a[221]). In summary, these assessments help describe and categorize children for clinical and research purposes. The general topic of skeletal maturation assessment was the subject of a symposium organized by Roche (1971c[176]).

The histological and radiographic changes during skeletal maturation have been reviewed by Roche (1986b[202]). Sequential alterations occur as the embryonic precursors of a bone gradually change until adult levels of form are achieved. A few of these alterations are shown diagramatically in Fig. 5.1. In A, a centrally placed marrow cavity is present with cancellous bone at the ends of this cavity and cartilage at each end of the model. B shows a later stage when the cells within the cartilagenous ends of the model enlarge prior to the formation of a center of ossification (epiphysis) in the cartilage. Stage C shows a well-formed epiphysis that is separated from the shaft of the bone by a layer of cartilage called the epiphyseal zone, beyond which there is a thin layer of 'compact bone' called the terminal plate. The adult stage is shown in D, where the epiphyseal zone is replaced by bone and there is bony fusion between the epiphysis and the shaft. Terminology is important. Places where ossification begins should be called 'centers of ossification,' not 'growth centers,' because the latter term implies they control subsequent growth, which is not the case.

Only some of the changes visible in radiographs meet the criteria for useful indicators of maturity. Some of the changes in epiphyses are important indicators, particularly those that involve alterations in epiphyseal shape and increases in the ratios between the widths of the epiphyses and the widths of the ends of the shafts. There are changes also in the bones of the wrist (carpals) which, after they ossify, gradually occupy larger

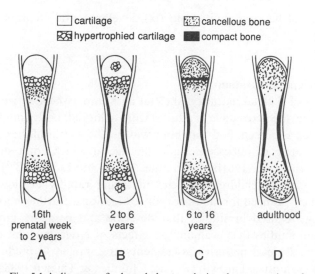

□ cartilage   ▨ cancellous bone
▨ hypertrophied cartilage   ■ compact bone

16th	2 to 6	6 to 16	adulthood
prenatal week	years	years	
to 2 years			
A	B	C	D

Fig. 5.1 A diagram of selected changes during the maturation of a long or short bone. Note the changes in the cartilage near the end of the bone that precede epiphyseal ossification (B), the formation of an almost fully ossified epiphysis (C), and the adult state (D).

proportions of the hand–wrist area as they change to become adult in shape. Epiphyses do not develop in the carpals but the changes in these bones are histologically and radiographically similar to those in the long and short bones. The long bones are those of the thigh, calf, upper arm, and forearm, whereas the short bones (metacarpals, metatarsals, phalanges) are in the palm, foot, fingers, and toes.

Onset of ossification

The recognition of the onset of ossification in the epiphyses of long and short bones and in the carpals was the first method developed for assessing skeletal maturity. Onset of ossification has advantages as an index of maturity because the recorded data are not influenced by even wide variations in radiographic positioning, little observer training is required, and the data are highly reliable.

Counting the number of ossified centers is the simplest method of grading skeletal maturity, but this method provided insufficient information when it was applied to the carpal bones or the hand–wrist (Garn, 1960a[54]). Consequently, Sontag, Snell & Anderson (1939[302]) applied this method to the left side of the whole skeleton and reported the number of ossification centers present between birth and 5 years. Their distribution statistics for (i) all bones, (ii) metacarpals, metatarsals and proximal

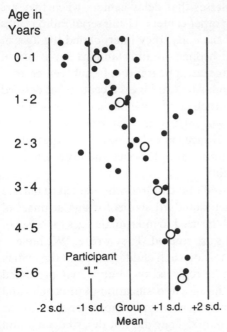

Fig. 5.2 Ages at onset of ossification of 38 centers plotted as z-scores (standard deviation levels). The open circles indicate means at annual intervals from 1 through 6 years for one Fels participant (data from Sontag & Lipford, 1943[288]). Note the tendency to more rapid maturation with advancing age in this participant.

phalanges, and (iii) the remainder showed a consistent advance of girls over boys that became marked at about 2 years of age.

Basing their views on earlier literature and on their own observations, Pyle and Sontag (1943) concluded that the timing of ossification in the hand–wrist may not be typical of that in the remainder of the skeleton. This topic received further attention at Fels during a long period, as will become evident later in this chapter. A further limitation was noted by Roche, Eyman and Davila (1971[230]) who showed that ages at onset of ossification were positively correlated with the later rates of skeletal maturation, which implied a negative correlation between the rates of maturation before and after the onset of ossification. Nevertheless, the number of centers ossified and atlas skeletal ages are highly correlated during infancy. This reflected the large contribution of onset of ossification to estimates of skeletal maturity with an atlas method in infancy (Pyle & Menino, 1939).

Sontag and Lipford (1943[288]) noted that variations in the sequence of onset of ossification were common and that some had considered these

variations were mainly due to illnesses that delay centers when they are about to ossify, while not affecting other centers. Using serial radiographs of the major joints on one side of the body, they interpolated the ages at which 38 centers ossified and published means and standard deviations of these ages. They converted the age at appearance of each center to a standard score and plotted the standard score for each center that ossified during selected annual intervals in each child. One of their plots is shown in Fig. 5.2 for participant 'L' who was slightly delayed in skeletal maturity at 1 year, but progressively more advanced at older ages. From these data, Sontag and Lipford identified the most variable bones and drew attention to individual differences in variability.

Pyle and Sontag (1943) also showed that children who tended to mature rapidly had little dispersion of their standard scores for age at onset of ossification. These authors stressed the need to interpolate ages for onset of ossification when serial radiographs are studied. They wrote: 'We have ... estimated from serial roentgenograms on each child, the *actual* time when each cartilaginous center began to be replaced by bone.' They presented means and standard deviations of the ages at ossification of 61 centers and noted that ages at onset of ossification tended to be more variable for the carpals and tarsals than for other bones. They did not describe a method of skeletal maturity assessment, but their basic data were included in the formulation of the Fels Composite Chart (Sontag & Reynolds, 1945[298]), that was described in Chapter 4. This work by Sontag and his associates was biologically important, but because half the body had to be radiographed for its application, it did not lead to the development of a clinically applicable method.

In an interesting study, Robinow (1942b) applied factor analysis to determine whether there were subgroups among 19 bones in regard to their associations for the timing of onset of ossification. These bones 'represented' the arm and leg, centers that ossify early and late, and irregular and long bones. Using data from 31 children, Robinow identified two groups of bones with high correlations within each group, but low correlations with data for other bones in regard to age at onset of ossification. These groups were: (i) carpals and tarsals, and (ii) epiphyses and the patella. The head of the femur was not closely related to either group, and the trapezium was related to both groups. A general factor explained 24% of the total variance in age at onset of ossification while 36% of the variance was explained by the round bone (carpals, tarsals) and epiphyseal factors. Robinow noted that centers in the arm, leg, and those that ossify early or late did not form groups. Robinow interpreted these findings as justification for assigning one skeletal age to a whole hand–wrist, but he

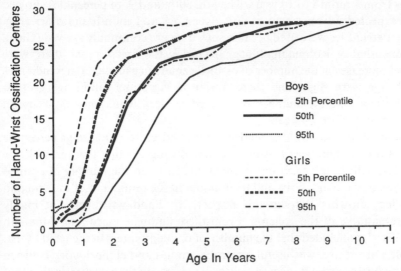

Fig. 5.3 Selected percentiles for the number of centers ossified in the hand–wrist at various ages in boys and girls (data from Garn & Rohmann, 1960b[135]).

warned that this age would be misleading in children with large differences in maturity levels between the carpals and the other bones of the hand–wrist. He recommended that, at least in these children, separate skeletal ages should be assigned to the carpal bones and to the other hand–wrist bones. An interesting aspect of this work is its sophisticated statistical nature, given that it was reported in 1942.

The lack of data relating to maturation during infancy was earnestly lamented by Falkner (1971b). Many such basic data have been provided, however, by Sontag and others (1939[302]), as noted earlier, and by Reynolds and Asakawa (1951) who presented tables of the number of centers ossified in the hand and foot from birth to 3 years. The Sontag group reported the distributions that Falkner sought, but Reynolds & Asakawa provided only ranges for children grouped according to five arbitrary rates of maturation. Reynolds and Asakawa (1951) provided data for ages at onset of ossification of selected centers near the hip, elbow, knee and shoulder, and they reported that the hand–wrist differed from the mean of the other areas by two categories in 1% of cases and by one category in 29% of cases. The foot–ankle was only slightly less representative of the total body than the hand–wrist. Their rapid method for the clinical assessment of the maturity level of the hand and foot was based on too few indicators to be precise.

Using a similar approach, Garn and Rohmann (1960b[135]) reported distributions of the number of hand–wrist centers ossified at particular

ages from 1 month to 10 years. The 5th, 50th, and 95th percentiles showed the expected advancement of girls over boys at 1 month and older (Fig. 5.3). Percentiles were used because such data are commonly skewed (Garn, Blumenthal & Rohmann, 1965g[71]). During the first 4 years, there were rapid increases in the number of ossified centers in each sex. Later increases with age were slight and there was little variation within age groups, indicating that the number of ossified centers would not be a useful discriminator after 4 years.

Serial data showed little tendency for children to retain their percentile levels for the number of ossified centers during the first few years of life. Additionally, there were low correlations between the number of ossified centers in the hand–wrist and the number in the remainder of the arm and the leg, showing that, in this respect, the hand–wrist was not highly representative of the skeleton. From these findings, Garn and Rohmann (1960a[134]) concluded that the number of ossified centers in the hand–wrist, while not precise, was useful for group studies and clinical work between birth and 4 years. This view was based, in part, on their earlier finding that the ages at ossification for the hand–wrist centers that ossify early were only slightly correlated with the ages at ossification of those that ossify later (Garn & Rohmann, 1959[133]).

The onset of ossification in 28 hand–wrist centers was analyzed by Garn and Rohmann (1959[133]). Having transformed the data to remove skewness, they calculated correlations between bones in their ages at onset of ossification and used the means of these correlations as communality indices for each bone. These indices were interpreted as measures of the extent to which timing in one bone was representative, or predictive, of timing in the group. This study ushered in an important new concept of the need to weight bones differentially when assessing skeletal maturity.

Garn and Rohmann (1959[133]) reported that girls tended to have higher communality indices than boys which they suggested might be due to redundancy of X-chromosomal material in girls. In each sex, the carpals, radius and ulna had relatively low communality indices in each sex, as did the first proximal phalanx in girls. Garn & Rohmann concluded that the carpals had less predictive power than the other bones of the hand–wrist in regard to the onset of ossification and, therefore, they were of little value in the assessment of skeletal maturity. Contrariwise, the proximal and distal phalanges and the metacarpals had high communalities for ages at onset of ossification of hand–wrist bones, and, therefore, indicated the general level of maturity in the hand–wrist.

A corresponding study of the foot was reported by Garn and Rohmann (1966b[142]). The proximal phalanges and metatarsals had relatively high

communality indices with other bones for ages at onset of ossification. As for the hand–wrist, communality indices in the foot tended to be higher for girls than boys; the values of these indices were similar for the hand and foot.

These analyses were extended when Garn *et al.* (1966a[146]) showed that communality indices were higher between joints within limbs than between either homologous (e.g., elbow, knee) or non-homologous (e.g., elbow, hip) joints in different limbs. These authors postulated that coordinated development within limbs may have favored evolutionary selection pressure. Garn and his colleagues also found a pattern of low communalities between bones that differed markedly in the timing of onset of ossification.

In another study, age at onset of ossification of the adductor sesamoid was shown to be highly variable, with median ages of about 13 years for boys and 11 years for girls (Garn & Rohmann, 1962b[137]). The adductor sesamoid is the name given to a bony nodule that forms in a tendon at the base of the thumb. The timing of adductor sesamoid ossification was not highly correlated with that of other bones that ossify at about the same age, but it was correlated with age at menarche and with age at epiphyseal fusion at the proximal end of the tibia ($r = 0.6$). Apparently, maturation of the adductor sesamoid is more closely allied to that of long bones than to maturation of the carpals. This is one of the few reports in which Garn and his colleagues considered external relationships of ages at onset of ossification. The need for such consideration was stated by Reed in a *Symposium on Assessment of Skeletal Maturation* (Roche, 1971b[175]). In discussing the assignment of numerical values to stages of skeletal maturation, he stated that these were commonly based on inter-relationships between bones and that stages with low internal relationships were excluded. Reed considered this approach was risky because the stages excluded may be closely related to important external characteristics such as illness.

Increments in the number of hand–wrist centers through 7.5 years were reported by Garn *et al.* (1961c[152]). Many of the distributions of these increments were markedly skewed and there was considerable variability to 3 years. Garn and his co-workers noted large differences between the trends for individuals and for the group which limited the practical value of these increments. These increments were not significantly correlated with increments in stature and weight.

A 'rational approach to the assessment of skeletal maturation' was described by Garn and his colleagues (Garn, Silverman & Rohmann, 1964e[167]; Garn *et al.*, 1966a[141]). They calculated an intercorrelation matrix

of the ages at onset of ossification in 52 centers in the hand–wrist and foot–ankle. Basing their judgments on communality indices (means of logs of correlation coefficients), they selected the 19 centers that were most informative about the ages at onset of ossification of other centers in the hand and foot. Later, they modified this approach when they identified the bones that were most informative about the remainder of the skeleton. Their results were unlikely to have been influenced by familial atypical ossification sequences because bones subject to these were excluded by their selection process. For example, one wrist bone, the triquetral, was excluded because it may ossify unusually early in some families without any relationship to ossification timing as a whole. Other centers, such as the middle phalanx, were excluded because commonly their epiphyses do not ossify.

Garn *et al.* (1966a[141]) stated that it was difficult to develop a method of skeletal age assessment because skeletal maturity levels varied between parts of the skeleton, particularly soon after birth and near the end of growth. They concluded that the bones of the hand–wrist, elbow, knee and foot–ankle had similar communality indices, but the hand–wrist may be more useful than the other areas because it contains many bones. This led Garn and his colleagues to recommend that skeletal maturity be assessed from radiographs of the hand–wrist, foot–ankle and knee for an overall appraisal, but that a particular area be assessed when there is specific interest in its maturity. This view is based on the assumption that communality indices for onset of ossification match those for later stages of maturation.

Garn, Rohmann and Silverman (1967e[154]), summarizing much of their earlier work, presented reference data for the timing of postnatal ossification. In this publication, they reported later timing for boys than girls and that the sex differences in timing varied by bone whether expressed in years or as ratios (male age/female age). Consequently, separate sets of reference data are needed for each sex and accurate estimates of skeletal maturity must be derived from bone-specific or indicator-specific data. They noted: 'Only now are we achieving an understanding of how to use the information from radiographs for the best possible appraisal of skeletal development.'

Garn and his colleagues (1967e[154]) selected the 20 centers with the highest communality indices for ages at onset of ossification in the major joint areas. This selection led them to modify their earlier recommendation; they suggested that both the hand–wrist and foot–ankle be radiographed to assess skeletal maturity. They claimed that their 20 centers provided a rational basis for the development of a 'point additive' system of skeletal

age assessment. They did not extend this approach to the development of a complete system for the stages of skeletal maturation that follow the onset of ossification.

The prevalence of missing ossification centers for the bones of the foot was documented by Garn, Rohmann and Silverman (1965e[153]). This is relevant to the assessment of maturity because an assessment method must be based on features that occur during the maturation of all normal individuals. Absence (agenesis) was more common in girls than boys. Siblings were alike in the number of missing centers, with closer concordance for sisters than brothers, which was consistent with X-linked dominant inheritance. In the foot, a center for the fifth middle phalanx was missing in about 98% of children and a center for the fourth middle phalanx was missing in 54% of boys and 70% of girls. The tendency to agenesis was a progressive phenomenon in which centers were eliminated medially and distally from an epicenter in the fifth toe. When a phalangeal center was missing, that toe tended to be short, with a narrowing of joint spaces or fusion between its segments.

Sequence of onset of ossification

The sequence of onset of ossification may be associated with rates of growth and maturation, and with illness experience, but variability in these sequences is masked when only mean ages at onset are reported. Serial data are needed to establish the sequences for individuals. Pyle and Sontag (1943) claimed that the sequence of onset of ossification was unusual for the carpals and tarsals when the rate of growth was either rapid or slow. This possible association has not received further attention. Unusual sequences of ossification in the hemiskeleton were said to be more common in slowly maturing children because they are more likely to be recognized in such children who have more radiographs than other children during a particular phase of maturation. Additionally, they are more likely to be observed when serial radiographs are closely spaced and when there are small differences between a pair of centers in their median ages of ossification. Nevertheless, unusual sequences of hand–wrist bones were not associated with the rate of skeletal maturation (Garn et al., 1966a[146]).

Unusual sequences were not associated with more frequent illnesses in girls, but there was a slight tendency to such an association in boys, even after the data for one boy with many illnesses and an unusual sequence were omitted (Garn et al., 1966a[146]). In a review article, Garn (1966c[68]) postulated that malnutrition may alter the order of appearance of ossification centers, but the prevalence of sequence variability in the hand–wrist was similar for moderately malnourished Guatemalan children

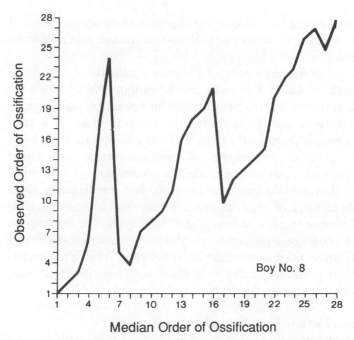

Fig. 5.4 An aberrant sequence of ossification in hand–wrist centers. The numbers on the horizontal axis indicate the median sequence; those on the vertical axis show the observed sequence in one Fels boy. (Garn, S.M. & Rohmann, C.G. (1960b). Variability in the order of ossification of the bony centers of the hand and wrist. *American Journal of Physical Anthropology*, **18**, 219–28[135]. Redrawn with permission from Wiley-Liss, Inc.)

and for Fels participants (Yarbrough *et al.*, 1973). The data of Garn *et al.* (1966b[142]) suggest, however, that malnutrition may cause small changes in the median sequence for boys, but there was no evidence of a similar effect for girls.

Garn and Rohmann (1960b[135]), using data from serial hand–wrist radiographs, analyzed variability in the sequence of ossification within individuals. An example of their data is shown in Fig. 5.4 in which the horizontal axis shows the median order of ossification for the group and the vertical axis shows the observed order for one boy. The centers that are ordered 8 and 17 in the group sequence ossified unusually early and the center that is ordered 6 for the group ossified unusually late. In this boy, an analysis of alternate sequences of ossification, such as: 'A' before 'B,' 'B' before 'A,' for 18 hand–wrist centers with similar median ages of ossification showed the number of associations between bones for alternate sequences greatly exceeded chance, particularly for metacarpal and phalangeal centers, although a single determinant did not explain all of

them (Garn, Rohmann & Wallace, 1961d[158]). These workers also noted that unusual sequences of onset of ossification tended to be familial (Garn & Shamir, 1958[164]; Garn & Rohmann, 1960b[165]; Garn et al., 1961c[152]).

The sequence of onset of ossification in the wrist was shown to be variable and it differed between the sexes (Garn et al., 1966b[145]). In girls, the triquetral tended to be later in the sequence, and it was less common for the trapezium to precede the trapezoid. Marked variations in sequence were common in the foot; the differences in sequence between the sexes were sufficient to require sex-specific reference data. Additionally, differences between the sexes in the sequence of ossification for the elbow, shoulder and knee necessitated the use of sex-specific reference data (Garn & Rohmann, 1960b[165]; Garn et al., 1966b[142], 1967e[154]).

The many studies of the sequence of onset of ossification and of associations between bones in ages at onset of ossification made by Garn and his colleagues could be expanded to maturity indicators that develop after the onset of ossification, but before epiphyseal fusion. This would be a huge task, and it may not serve a major need. The work done by Garn did not lead directly to a practical method for the assessment of skeletal maturity, but it provided much necessary basic information and important concepts. For example, Garn and his colleagues concluded that centers with marked common sequence variability should be omitted when skeletal maturity is assessed, although this diversity in sequence is part of the normal population variability (Garn et al., 1966b[145]).

Citing variability in timing and sequence, Garn and Rohmann (1960a[134]) expressed skepticism that a skeletal age assessment method could be based on the enumeration of centers. Yarbrough et al. (1973), however, described a method for pre-school children that was developed from Guatemalan data and validated using Fels data. It was shown by Yarbrough and his colleagues that the *number* of ossified centers in the hand–wrist allowed one to predict *which* centers were ossified with only small errors. Apparently, sequence variation is not of practical importance in the assessment of skeletal maturity. Furthermore, the number of centers ossified provided more accurate identification of the particular centers ossified than did the atlas method or the Tanner–Whitehouse method. The atlas and Tanner–Whitehouse methods utilize additional information but, at ages up to 6 years, they are strongly influenced by onset of ossification. This interesting approach was not developed further, mainly because it is not applicable at older ages.

Epiphyseal fusion

Fels scientists have given considerable attention to epiphyseal fusion which is the final stage in the maturation of a bone that has an epiphysis (Stage D in Fig. 5.1). Epiphyseal fusion is not detected as easily as the onset of ossification. Bones that are elongating rapidly may be wrongly supposed to be in an early stage of fusion due to the superimposition of the diaphyseal and epiphyseal outlines (Garn et al., 1967e[154]). Epiphyseal fusion is an important stage of maturation. It is part of growth dogma that elongation of a long or short bone does not occur after the epiphysis is fused to the shaft (diaphysis). Hertzog (1990), however, has presented evidence for slow elongation of epiphyseal bones in Fels adults; these changes presumably occurred at the non-epiphyseal ends of these bones (Roche, 1965[173]).

'Fields' of hand–wrist bones, in regard to the timing of epiphyseal fusion (Fig. 5.5), were described by Garn et al. (1961b[144]). These fields included groups of bones within which the timing of fusion was highly correlated. These fields were: (1) distal phalanges I–V; (2) middle phalanges II–IV and proximal phalanx I; (3) proximal phalanges I–V and metacarpal I, and (4) metacarpals II–V. They found that the timing of onset of ossification and of epiphyseal fusion were not associated, although the timing of both these events appeared to be partly gene related. Consequently, they concluded that skeletal maturation may not be a unitary phenomenon.

The timing of epiphyseal fusion in the hand–wrist is closely correlated ($r = 0.9$) with age at menarche and with age at fusion of the proximal epiphysis of the tibia (Garn et al., 1961b[144]). Garn and his colleagues made another very important observation: although the median ages of occurrence were similar for fusion at the proximal end of the tibia and the completion of fusion in the hand–wrist, the sequence of these events varied with differences in timing that may be as long as 2 years in each direction (Fig. 5.6). This illustrated the limitations of skeletal age assessments that were made for the whole skeleton from a radiograph of one area. Garn and his co-workers suggested that these variations in timing may explain why growth in stature continued in most children, but not all, after epiphyseal fusion in the hand–wrist was complete.

The atlas method of assessment

Several studies at Fels have utilized the atlas method of assessing skeletal maturity. This method is based on pictorial standards with which radiographs are compared. The best atlases were produced in Cleveland (Ohio) where many serial radiographs of normal children were available.

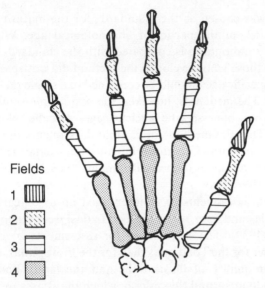

Fig. 5.5 Fields of hand–wrist bones in regard to the timing of epiphyseal fusion. (Data from Garn, Rohmann & Apfelbaum, 1961b[144].)

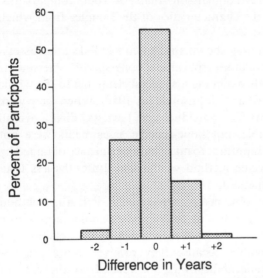

Fig. 5.6 The timing of the completion of fusion at the proximal end of the tibia relative to the completion of epiphyseal fusion in the hand; sexes combined. (Data from Garn, Rohmann & Apfelbaum, 1961b[144].)

Groups of radiographs for children the same age were ordered according to the maturity levels of one bone at a time. Subsequently, radiographs were selected that represented the central tendency of each bone and one of

these radiographs was chosen as the 'standard' for the maturity of the area, e.g., hand–wrist, at the particular chronological age. When this method is applied, a radiograph is compared with the standards for one bone at a time, but those who developed the method did not specify how the resulting bone-specific ages should be combined to a single skeletal age for the hand–wrist. The median is, however, the best simple summary of the information from bone-specific skeletal ages (Roche, Wainer & Thissen, 1975d[274]). The atlas method implied that the sequence of maturity indicators was fixed in normal children, but this was challenged by the findings of Garn and colleagues (Garn & Rohmann, 1960b[135]; Garn et al., 1961b[144], 1966b[142], 1967e[154]).

Paired hand–wrist assessments of children aged up to 5 years, made using the Florey atlas and later using the Todd atlas, were compared by Pyle and Menino (1939). The correlations for assessments by different observers were higher for the Todd atlas than for the Florey atlas, perhaps reflecting the better quality of illustrations and the larger number of standards in the Todd atlas, and the order in which the atlases were used. The Fels children tended to lag behind the standards in both these atlases, with larger deficits for Florey comparisons than for Todd comparisons. These differences reflected the characteristics of the samples from which the atlases were derived.

In other investigations it was shown that Greulich–Pyle atlas assessments of the hand–wrist were more replicable if bone-specific assessments were made instead of directly assigning a single skeletal age to the whole hand–wrist (Roche et al., 1970a[228]; Johnson et al., 1973). When there were wide ranges of maturity within individual hand–wrists, direct overall assessments were less reliable, but bone-specific assessments were not affected. Furthermore, it is important to note that skeletal ages obtained by the recommended bone-specific method were about 2 months less than those made by the overall method.

Bone-specific skeletal ages obtained by the Greulich–Pyle atlas method were more replicable at younger than at older ages. The differences within and between observers tended to be smaller for research workers than for pediatric radiologists, probably because they received more practice (Johnson et al., 1973). Replicability was not related to the rate of maturation, and changed only slightly when the carpal bones were excluded (Roche et al., 1970a[228], 1970b[263]). The carpals varied markedly in rates of maturation, which could be an advantage if they provided valuable discriminant data or information about environmental influences. Training was a major factor in replicability. Differences between observers were comparatively large when training was limited to reading the atlas, but

when it included assessing 30 radiographs, and discussing the assigned skeletal ages with an experienced person, reliability was similar to that for established assessors.

Later, Roche and Davila (1976[226]) analyzed the reliability of Greulich–Pyle atlas assessments in an unusual way. Repeated assessments were made of radiographs that were completely masked except for one bone. After this bone had been assessed in each radiograph, the masking was changed so that a different bone was visible. This approach provided independent skeletal ages for each bone that were compared with bone-specific assessments made when the whole of each radiograph was visible. Replicability was higher and the ranges of bone-specific skeletal ages within radiographs were much narrower for assessments made when the whole hand–wrist was visible, but replicability for bone-specific skeletal ages was lower, especially for the hamate and triquetral. It was concluded that when all the bones were visible the skeletal ages assigned to bones assessed late in the sequence were influenced by the ages assigned earlier.

Pairs of radiographs at different chronological ages were assessed by the Greulich–Pyle and Tanner–Whitehouse methods. Predictions of skeletal ages at older chronological ages, using skeletal ages at younger chronological ages as predictors, were more accurate with the Greulich–Pyle method than with the Tanner–Whitehouse method (Roche *et al.*, 1971[230]). The errors of prediction using linear trends fitted to serial data were greater than those from single measurements, unless many serial data points were available. These scientists described a simple method of prediction from a single value that was based on the assumption that the standard deviation score will be retained.

In another study, Himes (1977) reported that Greulich–Pyle and Tanner–Whitehouse skeletal ages were correlated more closely with ages at peak height velocity than with ages at menarche and that these correlations were consistently higher for Greulich–Pyle than for Tanner–Whitehouse skeletal ages.

The Roche–Wainer–Thissen (RWT) method for the knee and the FELS method for the hand–wrist

An early account of the statistical basis that led to the development of the RWT method for the knee and the FELS method for the hand–wrist (Roche *et al.*, 1975d[274], 1988a[221]) was published by Murray, Bock and Roche (1971). This was the first paper to suggest the use of maximum likelihood procedures and item response theory for the assessment of skeletal age. This major methodological advance is likely to replace the atlas method. In the RWT and FELS methods, a logical mathematical

process is used to combine the data from the various indicators to a single estimate of skeletal maturity for a child together with the standard error (confidence limit) of this estimate (Thissen, 1989).

The RWT method for the assessment of the knee was developed using almost 8000 radiographs (Roche *et al.*, 1975d[274]) and about 14000 radiographs were used to develop the FELS method for the hand–wrist. These radiographs were taken during several decades but there are no significant associations between the skeletal ages that were assigned and years of birth. Other analyses made by comparing skeletal ages of parents and their children of the same sex, when both were assessed at the same chronological age, showed only small irregular differences. Correspondingly, differences in age between mothers and daughters at menarche were near zero.

It is well known that boys mature more slowly than girls and, therefore, grades of brief duration are more likely to be observed in boys than in girls. This made it desirable to develop the new methods for boys and then apply them to girls. The work began with screening in which a few radiographs (primary test group) were used to determine which potential maturity indicators should be excluded because they were clearly not useful. The process included replicate grading by two independent assessors. Each radiograph was assessed without reference to earlier or later radiographs of the participant. An indicator was retained for further testing if it discriminated within chronological age groups, its most mature grade was universal at older ages, and it was reliable, valid, and complete.

Reliability was determined from differences in the grades assigned by different assessors and the differences when grading was repeated by the same assessor (inter- and intra-assessor differences). Validity, or the ability of the indicator to provide information about maturity, was judged from the frequency with which serial assigned grades changed illogically from more mature to less mature (reversals) with advancing chronological age. It was also determined whether each indicator had the quality of completeness, i.e., whether it could be assessed in all radiographs during the age range for which it was applicable.

After this primary testing, a group of serial radiographs of boys was used for further tests of the indicators that were retained. After this testing, the final indicators were chosen and graded on all the radiographs of the boys and the girls. The data from the assessments of all the radiographs were used to plot the changes in the prevalence of grades in relation to chronological age. Logistic functions fitted to these data, using maximum likelihood procedures, provided estimates of the age at which the prevalence of each indicator grade reached 50% (threshold), the rate of

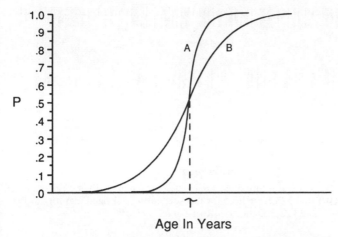

Fig. 5.7 Two theoretical indicators that have different slopes, but reach their thresholds (50% prevalence) at the same age. (Roche, A.F., Wainer, H. & Thissen, D. (1975d). *Skeletal Maturity: The Knee Joint as a Biological Indicator*. New York: Plenum Publishing Corporation[274]. Redrawn with permission from Plenum Publishing Corporation.)

change in prevalence with age (slope), and the regularity of the changes in prevalence.

Indicator grades may reach their thresholds at the same age but have different slopes (Fig. 5.7). The steeper the slope, the more rapid the change in prevalence with age, and the more informative the indicator. Some indicator grades had identical slopes but reached their thresholds at different ages. These indicators were equally informative, but they differed in the ages of greatest utility which are near the thresholds. Ideally, the ages of the thresholds would be evenly distributed across the age ranges during which the methods can be applied. This need was approximately met, but many of those for the hand–wrist occurred after 15 years and many of those for the knee occurred before 6 years (Fig. 5.8; Roche *et al.*, 1988a[221]).

The RWT and FELS methods were based on many maturity indicators, but at a specific chronological age only a few need be graded because each has a limited age range during which it is useful. The slopes and thresholds from each indicator are combined to a single index of maturity (estimated skeletal age) using techniques derived from item response theory, as developed for psychological measurement. This index was scaled in years with the means equivalent to the corresponding values for chronological age.

This Chapter began with a well-known extract from the writings of T. Wingate Todd who dominated this subject area during the 1920s and

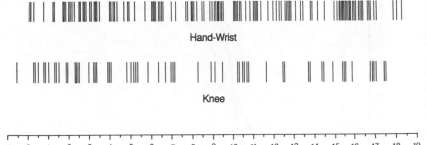

Fig. 5.8 Ages at which thresholds are crossed for the maturity indicators graded in the RWT and FELS methods for the assessment of skeletal maturity of the hand–wrist and knee. (Data from Roche *et al.*, 1975d[274], 1988a[221].)

1930s. This statement is expressed beautifully, but it is incorrect. These new methods for the assessment of skeletal maturity made it possible to adjust the observed variability in skeletal age for the errors of the estimates. Consequently, it could be shown that skeletal maturity was about twice as variable as stature.

The RWT and FELS methods provide the standard error of each estimate of skeletal age. The standard error of an individual estimate is small when many informative indicator grades are assessed with thresholds near the chronological age of the child, and it is large in the opposite circumstances. The errors were larger at some ages than others as shown by the total information curves for the knee and hand–wrist (Fig. 5.9). A relatively large amount of information was provided by a knee radiograph until 2 years, after which it decreased to 6 years and then remained approximately constant. The amount of information from the hand–wrist was similar to that from the knee until 3 years, but the hand–wrist was more informative than the knee after this age, despite decreases at ages after 14 years. The standard errors of the RWT and FELS methods were higher at ages older than 14 years because fewer maturity indicators can be assessed than at younger ages. There were only small sex differences in the amounts of information provided. The RWT and FELS methods allow for missing values, which is important if part of an area cannot be measured.

The RWT and FELS assessments were highly replicable (Table 5.1), with smaller assessor differences than those generally reported for other methods. There were, however, some large differences between the means for skeletal ages obtained with the atlas methods and those obtained with the RWT and FELS methods (Roche *et al.*, 1975d[274], 1988a[221]; Chumlea, Roche & Thissen, 1989a[37]). These reflected variations between the groups

Table 5.1. *Replicability of RWT and FELS assessments of skeletal ages in years (data from Roche et al., 1975d[274], 1988a[221])*

	Percentiles (years)		
	10	50	90
RWT (knee)			
Interobserver differences	0.02	0.26	0.80
Intraobserver differences (A)	0.0	0.18	0.71
Intraobserver differences (B)	0.0	0.08	0.59
	Mean	SD	
FELS (hand–wrist)			
Interobserver differences	0.20	0.21	
Intraobersver differences (A)	0.08	0.08	
Intraobserver differences (B)	0.17	0.13	

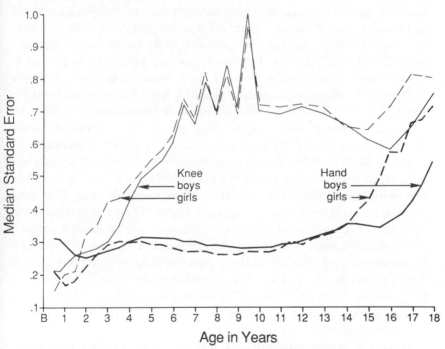

Fig. 5.9 The information available from the hand–wrist and knee at various ages as shown by the median standard errors. Small standard errors indicate relatively large amounts of information. (Roche, A.F., Chumlea, W.C. & Thissen, D. (1988a). *Assessing the Skeletal Maturity of the Hand–Wrist: FELS Method*, pp. viii + 339[221]. Redrawn, courtesy of Charles C Thomas, Springfield, Illinois.)

against which each method was scaled. Scaling for the RWT and FELS methods was appropriate for a method to be used in the US since the distributions of skeletal ages in the Fels Longitudinal Study are similar to those from US national surveys (Roche, Roberts & Hamill, 1974c[260], 1976a[261]).

Correlations between RWT skeletal ages and skeletal ages obtained by other methods ranged from 0.4 to 0.8, and the coefficients of reliability between FELS and other hand–wrist skeletal ages varied from 14% to 89%, which showed considerable independence (Roche *et al.*, 1975d[274], 1988a[221]).

Choice of a skeletal area for the assessment of maturity

The part of the skeleton chosen for the assessment of skeletal maturity should be one that is easy to position for radiography, and minimal radiation should be required. As few radiographic views as possible should be obtained, and all useful relevant information should be extracted from each radiograph. In general, the hand–wrist is the best area, but there are limitations to the accuracy with which one can generalize to the whole skeleton from assessments of the hand–wrist, as shown by analyses of ages at onset of ossification and skeletal maturity levels (Garn *et al.*, 1961b[144], 1964e[167], 1966b[145], 1967e[154], 1967f[147]; Roche & French, 1970[234]; Roche *et al.*, 1975d[274], 1988a[221]). Much earlier, Sontag *et al.* (1939[302]) warned against the assumption that 'as the hand grows, so grows the entire skeleton.'

Xi and Roche (1990) reported an analysis of paired skeletal ages for the hand–wrist (FELS method) and the knee (RWT method). They showed that, within age- and sex-specific groups, the mean absolute differences between paired skeletal ages were about 0.5 years. These differences tended to increase with age until an age of 9 years. It was concluded that the observed differences were too large to be entirely due to errors of measurement and that the skeletal ages of these two areas were not interchangeable. In at least 5% of children, the choice of an area for assessment would markedly influence an evaluation. Furthermore, descriptions of populations that are based on only one part of the skeleton may be misleading.

There has been considerable uncertainty as to whether the carpals should be included when the skeletal maturity of the hand–wrist is assessed. These bones are variable in their rates and patterns of maturation (Garn & Rohmann, 1959[133], 1960b[135]). This variability may make it more difficult to construct methods for their assessment, but their inclusion would be an advantage if it assisted meaningful discrimination between individuals. Their inclusion reduced the standard errors and, therefore, it

increased the stability of the estimates from 7 to 13 years in boys and 4 to 10 years in girls (Roche, 1989c[209]). Therefore, the carpals should be assessed during these age ranges.

Brother–sister correlations for FELS hand–wrist skeletal ages were generally lower than those for other types of sibling pairs, but they were similar to the brother–brother correlations after 11 years. After 12 years, the sister–sister correlations were considerably higher than the others, suggesting an X-chromosome influence at these ages (Xi, Roche & Guo, 1989b).

Dental maturation

Dental maturation has received considerable attention from Fels scientists who have based their analyses on the emergence of the crowns of teeth into the mouth and on maturational changes in teeth that can be observed in radiographs. Very useful reference data for ages at emergence of the deciduous teeth were provided by Robinow, Richards and Anderson (1942). After combining data from the two sides, these workers plotted frequency distributions for each sex that showed slight skewness to the right. There were significant tendencies for the lower incisors to emerge before the upper incisors and for emergence to occur earlier and be less variable in timing in girls than boys. After converting the values to standard scores, these workers calculated an intercorrelation matrix of ages at emergence, the ages of the children when their statures were equal to the median stature at 18 months in a reference group and their ages when the number of centers ossified in the extremities were equal to the median number ossified at 18 months in a reference group. Factors extracted from the matrix showed ages at emergence were highly correlated within but not between groups of anterior and posterior teeth and that ages at emergence were not closely related to the other indices of maturity that were studied. Correspondingly, there were only low correlations between the ages at which most dental maturity stages were reached and either stature, weight, number of hand–wrist centers ossified or Greulich–Pyle atlas skeletal ages (Lewis & Garn, 1960). Nevertheless, the correlations between the timing of late stages in the calcification and the emergence of the second mandibular molar tooth and the timing of either menarche or epiphyseal fusion at the proximal end of the tibia were higher (0.3 to 0.6).

In studies of fossils, dental emergence is commonly used as a taxonomic criterion, but the data for emergence differ from those in modern man (Koski & Garn, 1957; Garn, Koski & Lewis, 1957b[97]; Koski, Garn & Lewis, 1957; Garn & Lewis, 1958[99]) in whom 'emergence' refers to the appearance of part of a tooth through the gum. Some have established

fossil emergence sequences by extrapolation from the stages of maturity of unerupted teeth. Fels data show that the permanent teeth that succeeded the deciduous teeth emerged through the gum soon after the deciduous precursor was lost, but the permanent molar teeth did not emerge through the gum until they reached the occlusal level.

In significant papers, Garn *et al.*, (1956a[124]) and Garn, Lewis and Polacheck (1958b[120]) reported sequences of the onset of calcification in the cusps of the crowns of four permanent mandibular teeth (premolars, first and second molars). Calcification was first noted in the first molar; the second molar was usually the last of these teeth to calcify. The second premolar usually preceded the second molar in order of calcification, but there was considerable variability, and, in many children, priority of calcification within this pair of teeth could not be determined.

Sex differences in timing and variability of timing were smaller for dental maturation than for skeletal maturation, despite the fact that Garn and his colleagues documented considerably more variability in timing than had been reported previously (Garn *et al.*, 1958a[119], 1958b[120]; Garn, Lewis & Polacheck, 1959[121]; Garn, Lewis & Bonné, 1962a[103]; Lewis & Garn, 1960). Combining data from both sexes for five posterior mandibular teeth, Lewis and Garn (1960) showed that variability of timing increased with age (Table 5.2). Variability, adjusted for the period since conception, differed between stages of dental maturation, but this variability was less than that of skeletal age or dental emergence (Fig. 5.10). The median ages at which maturational stages were reached for the third mandibular molar tooth were no more variable than those for the other posterior mandibular teeth when corrected for the mean ages by calculating coefficients of variation (Table 5.2).

The rate of maturation of the third molar tooth showed marked constancy within individuals. If an early stage was advanced in timing, subsequent stages tended to be advanced also. The rate of maturation of this molar tooth was not correlated with age at menarche, but there were low correlations (0.1 to 0.4) with age at epiphyseal fusion at the proximal end of the tibia, and the age at completion of epiphyseal fusion in the hand–wrist (Garn *et al.*, 1962b[126]). These correlations were much lower than the corresponding correlations for the second mandibular molar tooth. In general, rates of dental maturation were only moderately associated with the timing of pubescence (Garn *et al.*, 1965b[108]). It was shown that dental maturation was less influenced by hormones than was skeletal maturation and that skeletal and dental maturity were essentially independent within chronological age groups (Garn *et al.*, 1965b[108]).

The timing of dental maturity stages were only moderately inter-

Table 5.2. *Variability (years) of timing of maturation for posterior mandibular teeth (sexes combined; data from Lewis & Garn, 1960)*

Stages	Percentiles	
	5	95
Beginning calcification		
First premolar	1.6	3.0
Second premolar	2.7	0.24
Second molar	2.8	4.8
Third molar	7.5	10.9
Crown completion		
First premolar	6.0	8.1
Second premolar	6.7	9.3
First molar	3.1	4.9
Second molar	7.3	10.2
Third molar	12.0	17.1
Apical closure		
First premolar	11.2	14.0
Second premolar	12.1	15.4
First molar	8.8	11.6
Second molar	12.8	17.6
Third molar	< 18.0	< 26.0

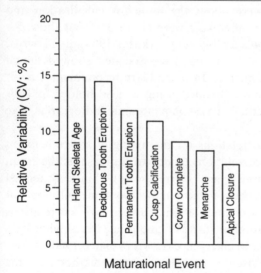

Fig. 5.10 A representation of the relative variability in the timing of selected aspects of skeletal, dental and sexual maturation. (Data from Lewis & Garn, 1960.)

correlated; reversals of sequence may occur during the maturation of pairs of teeth (Garn & Koski, 1957[96]). Garn *et al.* (1958b[120]) assigned one of five grades to each mandibular premolar and molar tooth and emphasized sequence variations between the second premolar and the second molar teeth. The proportion of children with a particular sequence varied from stage to stage of dental maturation. The order 'second premolar then first molar' was present for onset of calcification in 35% of the group, for the beginning of root formation in 58%, for apical closure in 7%, for alveolar emergence in 9%, and for reaching the occlusal plane in 9%. Almost all those with a 'second premolar then second molar' sequence of tooth formation had a corresponding sequence of emergence, but only half of those with a 'second molar then second premolar' sequence of tooth formation had the same sequence of emergence (Garn & Lewis, 1957[98]). The 'second molar then second premolar' sequence of tooth formation was associated with rapid maturation of the second molar.

Reference data for stages of dental maturation, based partly on work done at Fels, were reported by Garn *et al.* (1958a[119], 1959[121], 1960c[123], 1967f[147]). Fels data did not show secular trends in the rates of dental maturation, but girls tended to be advanced over boys by about 0.3 years (Garn *et al.*, 1958a[119]). The sex differences, expressed as percentages of the mean ages of occurrence, were about the same for calcification and emergence. These percentage differences were about 3%, but those for skeletal maturation were considerably larger (knee, 19%; hand–wrist, 12%). The data provided by Garn and his associates allowed dental maturity to be assessed from birth to 14 years. Garn recommended a 45° oblique radiograph of the jaw, obtained using a head-holder for this purpose. Since then, other methods based on panoramic radiographs have been developed.

It was reported that the correlations for the timing of stages between teeth were about 0.4; these correlations tended to decrease as the mean intervals between stages became longer. Correlations within teeth tended to be greater than correlations between teeth, indicating some autonomy of individual teeth in their rates of maturation. Furthermore, correlations that related stages of calcification or stages of emergence were higher than those that related calcification to emergence (Lewis & Garn, 1960). Later, Wolánski (1966a, 1967) devised a complex scoring method for the maturation and emergence of teeth that was based on the time a tooth remained in the same stage. With this method, the sum of the scores for all the teeth was used to assign a dental age.

Garn, Lewis & Bonné (1961a[102]) reported that the maturation of the mandibular premolar and molar teeth was delayed when the third molar

tooth failed to form (agenesis). Also, children with third molar teeth, in the same families as those in whom this tooth did not form, tended to be delayed in the maturation of the premolar and molar teeth. They concluded that absence of the third molar tooth expressed factors that delayed dental maturation between birth and 8 years.

In an extension from this work, Garn *et al.* (1961a[102]) compared the timing of dental maturation in three groups: (i) those with agenesis of the mandibular third molar, (ii) siblings of those in group (i) in whom the third molar was present, and (iii) unaffected siblings from unaffected sibships. Cusp calcification and emergence in the other posterior mandibular teeth tended to be delayed in those with third molar agenesis, and there were small delays in their siblings. The siblings may have had the same genotype as the affected individuals, but differed in its expression, or the siblings may have had only part of the genetic constitution that leads to third molar agenesis. Third molar agenesis may represent the extreme expression of a variable factor affecting the rate of dental maturation. Children with third molar agenesis tended to have rapid maturation of the second premolar, relative to the second molar.

Fels scientists, led by Garn, have shown clearly that there is genetic control over various stages of dental maturation and emergence and that sequences of maturation and emergence between pairs of teeth are, at least in part, genetically determined (Garn, 1961c[59]; Garn *et al.*, 1956a[124]; Sontag & Garn, 1957[286]; Lewis & Garn, 1960).

Sexual maturation

In two outstanding papers, Reynolds and Wines (1948, 1951) described the maturation of secondary sex characters in girls and boys and published 'standards' to assist grading, together with plots of the distributions of ages at which the grades were first noted. An example for girls is given in Fig. 5.11 which shows the cumulative percentages for the second grades of maturation of the breasts and of pubic hair.

Reynolds and Wines (1948) reported that the timing of early grades in the maturation of the breasts was more closely related to age at menarche (r = 0.9) than was the early development of pubic hair (r = 0.7). There were high correlations (r = 0.9) between the ages at which the early and later grades of sexual maturity were reached in girls, but breast size and breast shape were not related to the timing of breast maturation.

Genital maturation began before the appearance of pubic hair in 70% of boys, but growth in stature and weight accelerated when pubic hair was at grade 2 (Reynolds & Wines, 1951). The timing of the maturation of pubic hair was highly correlated between grades with coefficients ranging from

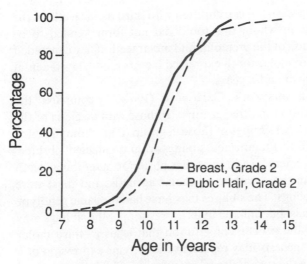

Fig. 5.11 Cumulative percentages for the prevalence of grade 2 of pubic hair and breast maturation. (Reynolds, E.L. & Wines, J.V. (1948). Individual differences in physical changes associated with adolescence in girls. *American Journal of Diseases of Children*, **75**, 329–50. Redrawn with permission from American Medical Association, copyright 1948.)

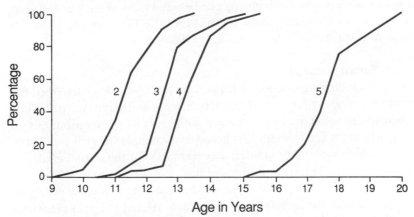

Fig. 5.12 Cumulative percentage prevalences for grades of maturation of the penis and scrotum. (Reynolds, E.L. & Wines, J.V. (1951). Physical changes associated with adolescence in boys. *American Journal of Diseases of Children*, **82**, 529–47. Redrawn with permission from American Medical Association, copyright 1951.)

0.5 to 0.9, despite marked variations in the duration of grades. For example, the mean duration was 0.6 years for grade 2, but 3.9 years for grade 4. Boys who were early in the attainment of grade 2 of pubic hair

maturation tended to have profuse body hair at 18 years (Reynolds & Wines, 1951). Additionally, boys who achieved grade 2 of pubic hair or scrotal maturity early tended to have long intervals from then until the attainment of grade 5 (Fig. 5.12). Additionally, Reynolds and Wines (1951) reported that ectomorphic boys tended to be advanced in sexual maturation. These boys had long and slender limbs and trunk.

Reynolds (1951) noted familial resemblances in the distribution of pubic hair and other body hair in boys and documented the distribution of particular types of pubic hair distribution in both men and women. In men, a 'masculine' pattern was more likely to be associated with thigh hair, but not with chest hair. Omitting cranial and facial hair, the sequence of development of hair was: pubic, axillary, leg, thigh, forearm, abdomen, buttocks, chest, lower back, arm and shoulder. The development of hair on the upper body of men was unusual at 20 years, but was present in about 30% at older ages. Also, hair on the abdomen became more common with age in males, increasing from 14% at 14 years to 75% at 18 years.

Weight at menarche
In an early study, Reynolds and Asakawa (1948) found that the first menstrual period (menarche) occurred earlier in girls with high values for either weight or weight/stature³ at 8 years. Later, Garn and Rohmann (1966a[141]) reported that age at menarche was associated with fatness. Subsequently, others suggested that menarche occurred when a critical level was reached for weight. An analysis of several sets of data, including some from Fels participants, showed that weight at menarche varied from 28 kg to 79 kg (Johnston *et al.*, 1975). Consequently, the concept of a critical weight at menarche is not applicable to individuals and should be discarded.

Other aspects of maturation
An investigation by Robinow, Johnson and Anderson (1943a) concerned angles measured on lateral radiographs of the foot during weight bearing. These angles were stable across age, with year-to-year correlations of 0.8. The major lateral antero-posterior angle changed little from 3 to 11 years despite large changes in footprints during this age range. Although this angle flattened with weight bearing, it did not flatten further when all the weight was carried on one foot. The antero-posterior angle was correlated between siblings (r = 0.4), but it was not significantly correlated with weight/stature, severity of knock-knees, or pronation of the foot. Values of this angle were distributed almost normally, indicating that low arches are part of the normal population variation.

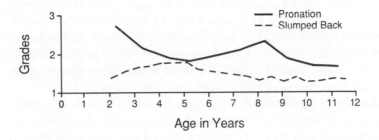

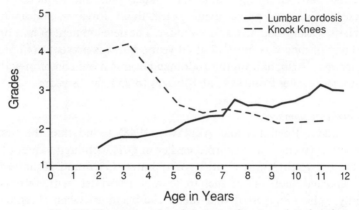

Fig. 5.13 The mean grades of elements of posture plotted against age (data from Robinow *et al.*, 1943b).

In a companion study, Robinow, Leonard and Anderson (1943b) reported a quantitative method for the analysis of posture in children. They prepared grades for body regions and provided photographs to assist the assignment of these grades. These photographs of front, back and lateral views were taken with the participants in a natural erect posture except that, for the lateral view, the participant was sometimes asked to move the arms slightly forward so that the curvature of the back could be observed. Robinow and his colleagues (1943b) considered these grades were applicable from 3 to 12 years and that they could be used directly without photographs. Correlations between raters were good for knock-knees and pronation, but not as good for the other aspects of posture.

Grades can be assigned easily for knock-knees using the rear view, if the feet are positioned with the medial borders parallel and the medial malleoli barely touching so that they do not support the ankles. This grading was based on the angulation of the Achilles tendon, tilting of the heel, and the

relative position of the medial and lateral malleoli. Hyperextended knees and lumbar lordosis were graded also. Finally, they rated 'slumped back,' which was mainly due to a relaxation of the upper trunk and was common in preschool children. This condition was associated with kyphosis of the thoracic spine; in some young children almost the whole back was involved. The age trends in these grades are shown in Fig. 5.13. The average child had considerable knock-knees at 3 years and lumbar lordosis was common at about 10 years. The grades given to knock-knees were correlated with weight/stature ($r = 0.6$) at 3 and 10 years, but these variables were not correlated at 6 years. The grades of pronation were correlated with knock-knee grades in various age groups ($r = 0.2$ to 0.6), but not with age or weight/stature. Robinow and his associates considered that inadequate muscle function was involved in most of these aspects of defective posture.

While not clearly an aspect of either maturation or development, Kingsley and Reynolds (1949) reported the relationship between illness patterns from birth to 5 years and birth order. First-born children had the highest mean incidence of gastro-intestinal upsets, feeding disorders, skin disorders, asthma and allergies, but second-born children led in respiratory and ear infections, tonsillitis, whooping cough, diarrhea, accidents and enuresis. These differences may have been related to the development of immune competence or to environmental variations.

The non-invasive assessment of maturity

It is not always practical to grade the maturity of secondary sex characters, such as the development of pubic hair, because this involves undressing and invasion of privacy. Furthermore, the grading of secondary sex characters is useful only during the age range when this discriminates among individuals. Similarly, the timing of peak height velocity or menarche is useful only during restricted age ranges. Assessments of skeletal maturity or dental maturity are based on radiographs and, consequently, there is some irradiation and high financial cost, in addition to which it is difficult to obtain assessments by trained individuals. To overcome these limitations, a method has been developed for the non-invasive estimation of maturity (Roche, Tyleshevski & Rogers, 1983c[269]).

To develop this non-invasive method, Fels data for stature, ages at peak height velocity and menarche, and skeletal age were analyzed (Roche *et al.*, 1983c[269]). The ratio (present stature/adult stature) is a measure of maturity because it has the same value (1.0) in all adults, and it increases monotonically with age during childhood. It had been assumed that this measure could only be obtained retrospectively when adult stature was

known, but Roche *et al.* (1983c[269]) described how this ratio could be applied prospectively without the use of invasive procedures. The key to this was the use of adult statures that were predicted without the use of skeletal age (Wainer *et al.*, 1978). The ratio (present stature/predicted adult stature) was moderately but significantly correlated with age at peak height velocity and skeletal age after about 4 years.

To apply this method, the stature and weight of the child and the stature of each parent must be known. Roche *et al.* (1983c[269]) provided reference data for this ratio; as expected, the means for girls tended to exceed those for boys by amounts that increased with age. The standard deviations also increased with age until pubescence, after which they decreased rapidly. This non-invasive method of assessing maturity is recommended for many situations, but it should not replace the assessment of skeletal maturity from radiographs and the grading of secondary sex characters when there is particular concern about individuals.

The regulation of maturation and its associations
Genetic regulation
Similarities within families in the sequence of ossification have provided evidence of genetic control over skeletal maturation (Reynolds, 1943; Sontag & Lipford, 1943[288]; Reynolds & Sontag, 1944; Garn & Shamir, 1958[164]; Garn, 1961c[59]; Garn & Rohmann, 1962c[138], 1966a[141], 1966b[142]; Garn *et al.*, 1961b[144]). Garn postulated that these familial tendencies could account for many of the differences in the relative lengths of body segments among adults.

In one study, parent–child correlations for the number of hand–wrist centers at an age were about 0.3 (Garn & Rohmann, 1962c[138]). The centers with the high parent–child correlations tended to be those with low communality indices which indicated that centers for which the timing was highly influenced by genetic factors were effective as predictors of timing for other centers. Garn, Rohmann and Davis (1963c[148]) showed that, as the average proportion of genes in common increased, there was a progressive similarity between pairs of related participants in the number of ossified hand–wrist centers at particular ages. Garn and his colleagues (Garn & Rohmann, 1962b[137]; Garn et al., 1967e[154]; Garn, Rohmann & Hertzog, 1969a[149]) also reported suggestive evidence of X-linked influence on the timing of ossification in the hand–wrist.

Genetic control over the rate of dental maturation was analyzed by Garn *et al.* (1961a[102]). The correlations for the rate of dental maturation were about 0.9 in monozygotic twins and about 0.3 between siblings. While teeth differed little in this regard, the pattern of correlations for various

types of sibling pairs led Garn and his colleagues to suggest there may be X-linked influences on the rate of dental maturation. This conclusion may be incorrect because the ascending order of correlations in their data was brother–brother, brother–sister, sister–sister, but with X-linked inherit-ance the brother–brother and brother–sister correlations would be equal.

The body build of parents was related to the rate of maturation of their offspring. Skeletal maturation in the pre-school period and at 11 years tended to be advanced in children of parents with wide chests (Garn *et al.*, 1960b[122]). The basis for this familial association is unclear.

Secular changes

Secular changes in the rates of maturation would imply a response to environmental alterations. The rate of maturation has accelerated in association with the well-documented secular increases in rates of growth and in adult size during the past century, particularly in Western Europe and North America (Roche & Davila, 1972[222]; Roche, 1979a[187]). The increases in adult stature imply that the secular increases in rates of maturation have been less than those in rates of growth.

More direct evidence was considered by Roche *et al.* (1974c[260], 1976a[261]) when they analyzed skeletal maturity data from US national surveys and compared the findings with reports from other studies including Fels. Convincing evidence of a secular trend was lacking, but data from high socioeconomic groups suggested maturation has become more rapid. In Fels data, evidence of secular changes in the timing of onset of ossification for the bones of the hand–wrist is lacking and there are only small differences in skeletal ages within parent–offspring pairs of the same sex when both were assessed at the same age (Garn & Rohmann, 1959[133], 1960b[135]; Roche *et al.*, 1975d[274]).

Seasonal influences

The appearance of ossification centers within 6-month intervals was related to seasons by Reynolds and Sontag (1944) who analyzed data from 1 through 5 years. In each sex, most centers appeared in the interval February to August and fewest in the interval August to February, but these seasonal variations were small.

Illness experience

Pyle and Sontag (1943) showed that children with more illnesses tended to mature rapidly, but illnesses were not associated with the sequence of ossification. Himes (1978a), in a review of the effects of nutrition on the rate of skeletal maturation, noted the possible confounding influences of

illnesses and emphasized the variability present in normal children as reported by Garn and his associates (Garn & Rohmann, 1960a[134]; Garn et al., 1961b[144], 1966b[142]).

Body composition and nutritional status

The possible associations between body composition and nutritional status with the rate of maturation have received the attention of Fels scientists over a long period. Sontag and Wines (1947[308]) did not find associations between the number of ossification centers at specific ages and the protein intakes of their mothers during pregnancy, but none of the mothers were suffering from a protein deficiency. There were, however, definite associations between rate of maturation and body composition in children.

Associations between radiographic measurements of calf tissues in girls and the timing of menarche and of the maturation of secondary sex characters were investigated by Reynolds (1946a). At ages 7 to 13 years, rapidly maturing girls had larger values than other girls for bone, adipose tissue and muscle widths and larger relative increases in these widths, especially muscle widths. The correlations between these tissue thicknesses and the timing of maturational events were about -0.5. Reynolds (1946a), in a novel approach, grouped girls with complete serial data who were matched for the total thickness of the calf at 7.5 years. He then chose contrast subgroups in which pubescent changes occurred either early or late. From 7.5 to 10.5 years, total calf thickness increased more in the rapidly maturing girls than in the slowly maturing girls, due to differences in muscle thickness. Additionally, Reynolds reported calf tissue thicknesses relative to the ages at which breast maturation reached grade 2. Rapidly and slowly maturing girls did not differ in bone widths at any age or in total calf width at 3 to 4 years before grade 2 of breast maturation was reached, but the total calf widths and muscle widths were larger in the rapidly maturing girls at older ages while the adipose tissue thicknesses were larger in the rapidly maturing girls at all ages.

Rapidly maturing children tended to have larger subcutaneous adipose tissue thicknesses and be taller and heavier, but the correlations between these variables and the timing of maturation were low, although they were slightly greater in girls than boys (Garn & Haskell, 1959a[86], 1960[88]; Garn, 1960b[55]). There were, however, close relationships between skeletal age and the percent of the body weight that was fat (%BF) in boys and the total weight of fat (TBF) in each sex (Chumlea et al., 1981a[24]).

The timing and sequence of adolescent events

Some analyses of Fels data have addressed variations in the timing and sequence of adolescent events (Roche, 1973[177], 1974a[178]). Most of these events can be defined only if serial data are available. For example, the age at peak height velocity can be determined only if data are available for about 3-year periods before and after this event. In the past, judgments of ages at peak height velocity were based commonly on annual increments beginning at birthdays, although rates of growth do not change at birthdays. This can cause misinterpretations as shown earlier (see Fig. 2.5).

There are differences in the sequences of maturational events during adolescence that include peak rates of bone elongation and of increase in bone breadths, peak height velocity, menarche and age at ossification of the ulnar sesamoid. Similar variations occur, as noted earlier, in the sequence of grades of skeletal and dental maturity.

The development of hearing ability

Beginning in 1975, a major study of hearing ability in relation to noise was commenced at Fels (Roche *et al.*, 1977b[266], 1978[267], 1983d[220], 1983e[259]). The aim was to provide knowledge that would assist public policy decisions concerning noise and help to explain why the sexes were similar in hearing ability before pubescence, but hearing ability was much better in girls than boys by 18 years. This work was supported financially by the Environmental Protection Agency and by the Aerospace Medical Research Laboratory at Wright–Patterson Air Force Base. It was terminated after 5 years because the Federal Government considered noise was not a problem. In this study, historical data were obtained for lifetime and recent exposure to noise, health histories were recorded, and otological inspections were made. The noise exposure data were used to obtain (i) a total 6-month quantitative score for each participant, and (ii) the number of individual events associated with noise exposure for each participant. One aim was to relate changes in hearing ability to growth and maturity.

Hearing ability (auditory thresholds) was measured in an audiometric booth located in a very quiet area. At each age, girls had better and less variable hearing ability than boys and, in each sex, hearing ability increased slightly with age (Roche *et al.*, 1978[267], 1979b[248]). Some of this age trend could have been due to greater concentration on the test by older children, better fit of the earphones to older children, and increasing familiarity with the procedure ('examination effect') as age and the number of examinations increased. 'Examination effects' were present in the data which lead to artefactual 'improvements' with repeated testing (Roche *et al.*, 1983a[255]). This may help explain why mean hearing ability in the Fels

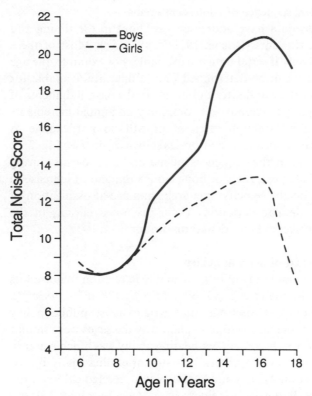

Fig. 5.14 Total noise scores for boys and girls at ages from 6 to 18 years (data from Roche *et al.*, 1982b[219]).

children was slightly better than the US national reference data at low frequencies, and markedly better than these reference data at high frequencies (Roche *et al.*, 1979b[248]; Roche, Chumlea & Siervogel, 1982b[219]).

Noise exposure from questionnaire data increased with age to 16 years, particularly in boys (Fig. 5.14). Noise exposure was not significantly correlated with body size or level of maturity in boys, but more mature girls at 13–15 years, who were also taller and heavier, were exposed to more noise. Despite this, the Fels data suggested that rapid maturation and tallness, especially in girls just before menarche, was associated with better hearing. Exposure to firearms, loud stereo music, loud TV, and farm machinery tended to be associated with reduced hearing ability, as were illnesses, abnormalities of the auditory meatus (ear canal), and of the color of the tympanum (ear drum, Roche *et al.*, 1982b[219]; Siervogel *et al.*, 1982d). Systolic and diastolic blood pressures and iris pigmentation were not

Table 5.3. *Descriptive statistics for* $L_{eq(t)}(dB)^a$ *in sound source categories with significant* ($p < 0.05$) *sex effects* (*data from Roche et al., 1982b*[219])

Categories		Mean	SD
Home, radio, TV	Boys	74.1	7.4
	Girls	70.8	7.7
Sleep	Boys	58.3	6.4
	Girls	55.1	8.3
School, normal class	Boys	74.5	5.7
	Girls	68.9	6.6
To and from school	Boys	79.1	6.2
	Girls	69.1	8.2
School year vs summer			
Sleep	School year	56.2	7.8
	Summer	61.2	2.2
Live music	School year	82.4	9.0
	Summer	90.7	6.0

^{a} $L_{eq(t)}$ is the equivalent sound exposure (dB) for the period t on a log scale.

associated with hearing ability (Roche *et al.*, 1978[267], 1979b[248], 1982b[219], 1983b[256]).

The final report from this study included an analysis of noise exposure using data from 24-hour measurements (Roche *et al.*, 1983d[220]). These data were obtained for 3-minute intervals within each day and they were combined with a detailed activity diary. The highest levels of noise came from lawn mowers, boats, live music, riding a school bus, and recesses or assemblies at school. Boys were exposed to significantly more noise than girls for many noise sources (Table 5.3). The amount of noise associated with specific activities decreased with age for conversation, outdoor activities, and school activities, but increased for live music. The duration of exposure also decreased with age except for music and noise associated with automobile use. The amounts of noise exposure during the school year and the summer did not differ significantly in the Fels group (Siervogel *et al.*, 1982a).

Developmental changes in skin reflectance
Studies of skin reflectance at ages 1 to 90 years were reported by Garn and his colleagues (Garn *et al.*, 1956c[162]; Garn & French, 1963[81]). Measurements were made on areas exposed to light, on protected areas and on the areola and scrotum where reflectance is markedly dependent on stimulation by sex hormones. Melanin is the major pigment involved in skin reflectance at the wave length used by Garn.

All skin sites reflected more light in infancy; this difference was marked for the areola and scrotum. Towards the end of pubescence, a large sex difference developed in the pigmentation of the chest and there was a reduction in reflectance from the areola, forehead and arm sites.

In men, the medial aspect of the upper arm and the chest reflected most light and the scrotum and areola reflected least. In men, reflectance tended to increase with age at the arm, chest and areolar sites, but decreased at the forehead site. In females, there was a marked decrease in areolar reflectance during pubescence, adulthood, and pregnancy, but pregnant women did not differ from controls in reflectance at the arm, breast or forehead sites (Garn & French, 1963[81]). Women who had delivered 3 to 11 months previously had less areolar reflectance than age-matched women of the same parity who had not been pregnant recently.

Work on the methodology of assessing maturity is, at least temporarily, in abeyance but analyses continue that relate established measures of maturity to the other recorded data.

6   *Bones and teeth*

'Can these bones live?'

Ezekiel 37:3 (*ca.* 630–570 *BC*)

Most of this chapter will be concerned with bones and teeth which share a
common embryological origin. The Fels studies of these organs will be
grouped as follows: (i) skeletal growth, (ii) growth of specific skeletal
regions, (iii) skeletal variations, (iv) skeletal mass, and (v) teeth.

Skeletal growth

Studies of skeletal growth at Fels have attempted to determine the
amounts of growth at specific locations and to examine changes in overall
dimensions such as length and width. In an early attempt to establish a
natural bone marker for use in studies of bone elongation, based on serial
radiographs, Pyle (1939) observed the nutrient foramen of the radius. She
found the groove leading to the foramen made it difficult to locate a fixed
radiographic point, although the foramen could be recognized in about
90% of radiographs of children. Some difficulties were associated with the
presence of multiple nutrient foramina in about 20% of radii and the
changing location of points at the external end of the obliquely aligned
nutrient canal as the cortex thickened. This interesting exploratory study
did not establish the nutrient foramen as a suitable fixed point from which
length measurements could be made.

Fels data have been analyzed to provide reference data derived for bone
lengths and widths measured in serial radiographs. Garn *et al.* (1972[93])
presented such data for the bones of the hand at annual intervals from 2
through 18 years. These workers defended the use of Fels data on the basis
that these data were derived from a well-nourished contemporary
population and, therefore, they should be applicable fairly generally to US
whites. All the length measurements included the epiphyses and, like the

157

widths, they were measured to the nearest 0.1 cm. These data, which showed a uniform tendency for the mean values to be larger for males than females until about 14 years but not at older ages, were used to make 'profile' plots of the standard deviation levels for the lengths of each hand bone in individuals (Poznanski *et al.*, 1972). These 'profile' plots are valuable in the recognition of abnormal patterns of hand-bone lengths and widths that may indicate the presence of a syndrome.

Garn and his colleagues (1972[93]) calculated the coefficient of variability (CV) for the lengths of each hand bone. These CV values were high in each sex for distal phalanges II and V and middle phalanx V, but variability was low for proximal phalanges II and IV in boys and for proximal phalanges III and V in girls. In general, bone lengths tended to be more variable in females than in males. Additionally, it was claimed that elongation tended to be proportional from infancy through adulthood with the addition of similar percentages to the lengths of all bones each year, despite the known changes in rates of growth at pubescence that had been established by others. In reviews, Roche (1978c[186], 1986b[202]) directed attention to these and other reference data from the Fels study and evaluated their utility.

Mean lengths of the tibia and the radius at ages from 1 month through 18 years were reported by Gindhart (1971, 1972, 1973). Until adolescence, there were only small sex differences in the length of the tibia but the radius was significantly longer in males than females at almost all ages. Additionally, Gindhart presented increments for four intervals during the first year, for 6-month intervals to 12 years, and then for annual intervals. These increments showed pubescent growth spurts at 12 to 15 years in males and 9 to 12 years in females for both the tibia and the radius. There were some significant differences between the sexes in tibial length increments but they varied in direction and timing and may have been due to chance, except for significantly larger increments in males from 12 to 17 years. There were few statistically significant sex differences in the increments in radial length before 10 years, but the increments were significantly larger in girls from 10.5 to 12 years and in boys from 13 to 18 years.

Gindhart analyzed 6-month increments in tibial and radial lengths from 1 to 9 years in relation to seasons and childhood disorders. After grouping the Fels participants by month of birth, she concluded that the tibia elongated most from October to December and least from April to June. In the male radius, the maximum rates of elongation occurred in October and November and the minimum rates occurred in April and May. The seasonal fluctuation was most marked in the male radius and least marked in the female tibia. The timing of maximum and minimum increments

differed more between bones within each sex than between sexes for the same bone which was difficult to interpret on any nutritional or hormonal basis. Presumably, these differences in timing were related to systematic variations in end organ responsiveness.

Three-month increments did not show seasonal trends in the rates of elongation of the tibia in males during infancy, but the maximum increments for the male radius occurred from June to August and the minimum increments from February to April (Gindhart, 1971). The corresponding findings for the female radius were less clear, but the minimum increments tended to occur from February to April. Gindhart (1971) commented on the findings of Reynolds and Sontag (1944) concerning seasonal influences on the rate of growth in stature from 1 to 5 years. The timing of the small seasonal effects found in this earlier study was the opposite of that found by Gindhart (1971). In both sets of data, there was marked variability during the first year, with the girls being more variable than the boys in elongation of the tibia, but there was little sex difference in the rates of growth in stature and in the length of the radius. Gindhart did not find significant relationships between childhood disorders and the rates of elongation of the tibia or the radius in either sex.

Using skeletal dimensions that were mostly bone lengths, Roche (1974a[178]) calculated annual increments and estimated the ages at the maximum rates of growth for individual participants in the Fels study and the Child Research Council (Denver) Study. The skeletal dimensions were measured with high reliability on standardized radiographs. There was remarkably good agreement between data from the Fels and Denver studies. The differences between dimensions in the mean ages of their maximum increments were small but the variances were large. Nevertheless, they were similar to the variance for age at peak height velocity with the exception of the cranial base lengths that had larger variances. The order of the mean ages at which these spurts occurred differed by sex, and there was marked sequence variability within individuals. The maximum increments in metatarsal V, metacarpal II and sella–nasion (a cranial base length) tended to occur relatively earlier in the sequence in girls than in boys. Associations between long bones in the timing of their maximum increments tended to be higher for girls than for boys and were markedly higher for bones in the upper extremity than for other groups of bones. It was concluded that, although the cells at the sites of elongation for various bones (the epiphyseal zones of long bones) respond to the same hormones, these cells must differ among individuals in the levels of hormones to which they are sensitive.

In another approach to the study of bone elongation, Falkner and

Roche (1987) reported high correlations between prenatal femoral lengths and measurements of recumbent length or crown–rump length soon after birth. Regression analyses showed that, soon after birth, recumbent length or crown–rump length could be estimated from femoral length with errors of 0.1–0.3 mm. These findings led to the conclusion that the continuum of prenatal and postnatal skeletal elongation could be evaluated using prenatal femoral lengths from ultrasonic examinations and postnatal data for recumbent length or crown–rump length.

In some Fels publications, comments have been made about the possible retarding effects of undernutrition on bone elongation (Robinow, 1968; Falkner, 1975). Contrariwise, Garn, Greaney and Young (1956d[84]) showed that tibial length was greater in fat infants (highest quartile of calf adipose tissue thickness at 1 month) than in lean infants (lowest quartile) but these groups did not differ significantly in tibial length after infancy. This could be related to the decreases in the differences in fatness between these groups after infancy. Similarly, at birth the lengths of long bones and crown–rump length were correlated ($r = 0.2$) with adipose tissue thickness over the 10th rib (Garn, 1958a[52]).

Reynolds (1944, 1946a) found marked increases in the total breadth of the tibia from birth to 6 months, after which there was a deceleration until the pubescent spurt. This spurt began at the time of peak height velocity in boys, but earlier than this in girls. In each sex, the spurt in width lasted about 2 years, being longer in boys than in girls. Calf bone widths, relative to the total width of the calf, were larger in males than females from birth to early adulthood (Reynolds, 1944, 1948; Reynolds & Grote, 1948).

Hertzog et al. (1969) reported correlations of 0.8 between tibial length and stature and that stature could be predicted from tibial length with an error of 3 cm. The systematic over-prediction in older individuals allowed estimations of the decrease in stature with aging. These decreases occur in the trunk, not the limbs. The estimated losses in stature with aging of about 3 cm for men and 6 cm for women were in agreement with those from serial data.

Growth of specific skeletal regions
Cranial vault

Using standardized lateral radiographs, a large amount of research has concerned the size and shape of the cranial vault. Cranial shape has been studied by physical anthropologists for more than a century because it reflects brain shape and because cranial shape was used to discriminate between racial groups. Using standardized lateral radiographs, Young (1956) investigated reported methods for the description of cranial shape.

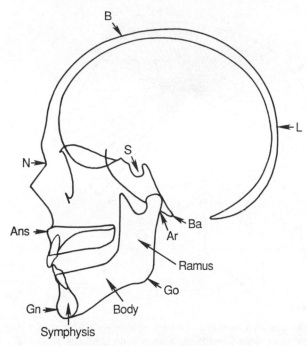

Fig. 6.1 A diagram to show some cranial points used in Fels studies. N = nasion; B = bregma; L = lambda; Ba = basion; S = sella; Ar = articulare; Go = gonion; Gn = gnathion; and Ans = anterior nasal spine.

Many descriptions have been subjective but others have been based on various craniometric procedures. Young's major aim was to compare the latter and determine which was the most useful. The measures compared were (i) the angle lambda–basion–nasion, (ii) the ratios chord length/arc length, height of arc from chord/chord length, and the radius of curvature for specific cranial bones, and (iii) for each bone, the lengths of nine equally spaced perpendiculars from each chord to the corresponding arc, adjusted for chord length (Fig. 6.1). All except the angle lambda–basion–nasion provide bone-specific data. Application of these methods consistently showed the frontal bone was more curved than the parietal bone and that frontal curvature was greater in females than in males. The inter-correlations between values from these methods exceeded 0.9, showing that they all yielded practically the same information.

Analyses of changes during growth in the size and shape of the frontal and parietal bones in males were made by Young (1957). He measured the ectocranial arcs and chords of these bones on lateral radiographs and showed that the patterns of change in size and shape were similar for these

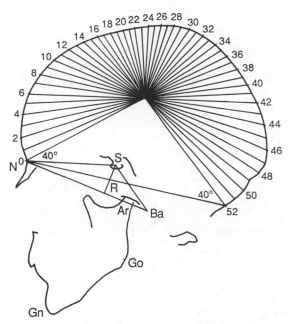

Fig. 6.2 The radii measured by Lestrel and Brown (1976) in their analyses of
cranial vault shape. R is the midpoint of a line from sella (S) drawn
perpendicular to nasion–basion (N–Ba). The line N–R was extended posteriorly
to the ectocranial margin. From this point and from N, lines were drawn at 40°
to N–R (extended) until they intersected. Fifty-two radii were drawn to the
ectocranial margin from the intersection of these lines (centroid). (Lestrel, P.E.
& Brown, H.D. (1976). Fourier analysis of adolescent growth of the cranial
vault: A longitudinal study. *Human Biology*, **48**:517–528. Redrawn with
permission from *Human Biology*.) For other abbreviations see Fig. 6.1.

two bones, with rapid decelerations to 4 years after which there was little
change. Indeed, from 4 to 16 years increases in size were not detectable in
50% of the boys. Growth appeared to be complete earlier in the parietal
than in the frontal. The arc lengths of these bones appeared to be
interrelated in a simple allometric fashion with low negative correlations
between the bones. The curvature increased to 2 years for the parietal and
to 3 years for the frontal, after which these bones progressively flattened.
Young measured cranial thickness at nine sites in each bone; the means of
these thicknesses increased to 16 years with some decelerations and with
correlations of about 0.5 between the frontal and parietal.

Using landmarks on the external (ectocranial) surface of the cranium,
Young (1957) measured the angles of the triangle lambda–bregma–nasion.
The angle at bregma increased gradually to 16 years, while the angle at
nasion decreased and there was little or no change in the angle at lambda.

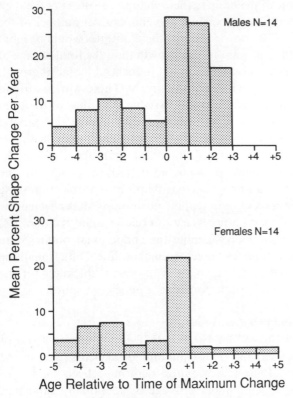

Fig. 6.3 Mean annual absolute percentage changes in cranial base shape plotted against years in relation to the maximum change in shape. (Lestrel, P.E. & Brown, H.D. (1976). Fourier analysis of adolescent growth of the cranial vault: A longitudinal study. Human Biology, **48**: 517–528. Redrawn with permission from *Human Biology*.)

These findings indicated more anteroposterior growth of the frontal bone than of the parietal.

After a lapse of about 20 years, Lestrel and Brown (1976) returned to this topic area. They obtained much more accurate descriptions of the size and shape of the ectocranial margin by applying Fourier analysis to the lengths of 52 radii drawn from a centroid (Fig. 6.2). Data from serial radiographs for the age range from 4 to 18 years showed marked changes in size at about the age of peak height velocity that were larger in males than in females (Fig. 6.3). The data in this figure are for only the first four Fourier terms; these accounted for about 96% of the variance. These workers also found a small tentative 'mid-growth spurt' at 10 to 11 years in males and at 8 to 9 years in females.

To help define the role of the brain in these changes, a subset of the data were used to analyze both the ectocranial and endocranial outlines of the parietal bone. Lestrel and Brown considered these outlines would be more likely than others to reflect effects of brain growth than the total outline of the vault because the parietal outlines are not influenced by facial growth anteriorly or by muscular attachments posteriorly. These workers found that the curvature of the parietal was less variable than that of the total cranial outline and that most of the changes with age in the parietal curvature were due to increases in size rather than alterations in shape. Pubescent spurts were more marked in males than females for the ectocranial margin and appeared to be restricted to males for the endocranial margin. These authors directed attention to problems in these data due to slight variations in radiographic positioning that affected the endocranial outline and made it necessary to exclude some radiographs. Consequently, the conclusions concerning the endocranial outline were less well established than those for the ectocranial outline. Data from these paired outlines were used to derive an index of cranial thickness for the parietal bone; this index did not demonstrate a pubescent spurt.

Cranial base and facial skeleton

Israel (1967a, 1968a, 1970, 1973a, 1973b, 1977), in a complex series of studies of adults, described the 'redistribution' of skeletal mass in the craniofacial area. Part of the redistribution may have been specific to tooth-bearing bone for which the loss with age is functionally important when it is due to periodontal disease and leads to reduced support for teeth and their ultimate loss. A second type of bone loss affected the remainder of the craniofacial skeleton where the changes resembled the remodelling and redistribution that occurs in the second metacarpal (Garn *et al.*, 1967e[154], 1967g[155]).

Israel (1967b) restricted his Fels sample to those with teeth in the area of interest and with pairs of lateral head radiographs taken at least 13 years apart. In this group, the loss of tooth-bearing bone was similar in each sex but the amount was small, presumably because there was no loss of teeth. 'Basal' bone, in the mandible, increased with age due to continued tooth migration towards the occlusal plane and possible apposition on the inferior border of the mandible where cortical thickness increased. There was little association between these mandibular changes and corresponding changes in the remainder of the craniofacial skeleton or the second metacarpal. The cortical thickness of the mandible was not correlated with that of the second metacarpal and there were only low correlations between cranial thickness and the width of the second metacarpal. In these

adults, there were increases in cranial thickness, total ectocranial length, upper face height and cranial base length, indicating that, unlike most parts of the skeleton, apposition exceeded resorption in these areas during middle age.

Israel (1971, 1973a, 1973b, 1977) found a generalized expansion of about 5% in the craniofacial skeleton after middle age, including ectocranial and endocranial dimensions. There were considerably larger increases in the thickness of the frontal bone, and the size of the paranasal sinuses and the sella turcica. In women, the increase in cranial thickness differed by area; it was about 1% at lambda but about 11% at bregma which is placed more anteriorly. These points are shown in Fig. 6.1. The increases in cranial thickness during intervals of 13 to 28 years in women were significantly different from zero at points anterior to bregma but not at points posterior to this craniometric landmark. In women, the external dimensions of the cranium increased until about 70 years due to apposition and there was concomitant resorption at the endocranial surface; after 70 years, resorption predominated at both the ectocranial and endocranial surfaces. Most mandibular dimensions increased about 4% in women during the same intervals but the height of the ramus increased only 1% and the change in the gonial angle was not significant. The gonial angle (Ar–Go–Gn) describes the relationship between the body and the ramus of the mandible. Similarly a change did not occur in the saddle angle (basion–sella–nasion). The saddle angle is often used in descriptions of the cranial base; sella is a constructed point in the middle of the pituitary fossa. Cranial base lengths (Ba–N, S–N, Ba–S; see Fig. 6.2) and upper face height (nasion–anterior nasal spine) also increased during adulthood by about 4%, and there was an increase in the anteroposterior thickness of the symphysis of the mandible of about 6% (Israel, 1971, 1973a, 1973b). The anterior nasal spine is on the anterior margin of the maxilla at the margin of the nasal aperture. The symphysis of the mandible is where the two halves of this bone join anteriorly. This extensive work by Israel is of particular importance because there are so few studies of changes in the craniofacial skeleton during adulthood.

Reference data for nine cranial base lengths and three angles from birth to 18 years, adjusted for radiographic enlargement, were reported by Ohtsuki *et al.* (1982a). Almost all these dimensions increased rapidly to 2 years, after which there were decelerations followed by pubescent spurts. The lengths were similar for the two sexes to 9 years, after which the values for the boys tended to be the larger. Cranial height and cranial length, both measured to the ectocranial margin, did not increase significantly after 7 years. A factor analysis of these data for 3-year age ranges showed the

Table 6.1. *Mean annual increments (mm/year) near the time of pubertal spurts (data from Roche & Lewis, 1976[250])*

Length	Boys			Girls		
	Before	During	After	Before	During	After
S–N	0.2	1.5	0.9	0.2	1.2	0.4
Ba–N	0.5	2.5	1.5	0.6	2.0	0.8
Ba–S	0.3	1.8	0.6	0.3	1.4	0.4

segments of the cranial vault and base were represented in different factors for these age groups which suggested that the cranial vault and base had their own growth patterns (Ohtsuki *et al.*, 1982b). The changes with age in factor structure were consistent with the ages at which changes occurred in the growth rates of individual segments (Ohtsuki *et al.*, 1982b). Only two factors were extracted for the 0–3-year group that may be labelled (i) cranial vault size and cranial base length, and (ii) posterior cranial base length. This indicated a uniformity of growth rates for these groups of dimensions during infancy. Four factors were extracted for the older age groups of boys that were labelled (i) cranial vault size, (ii) posterior cranial base length, (iii) basisphenoid length, and (iv) presphenoid length. The patterns were generally similar for the girls except at 13–15 years when the differences noted may have reflected the earlier fusion of the spheno-occipital synchondrosis in the girls than in the boys.

The common occurrence of pubertal spurts in the cranial base and the mandible has been documented in a series of papers (Lewis & Roche, 1974; Roche & Lewis, 1974[249], 1976[250]; Lewis, Roche & Wagner, 1982, 1985). These studies were based on lateral head radiographs, taken at annual intervals, in which three cranial base lengths and three mandibular lengths were measured. All the measurements were shown to be highly reliable and they were corrected for the known enlargement that occurs with radiography. Spurts in cranial base lengths were recorded for a participant when an annual increment exceeded the immediately preceding increment by at least 0.75 mm in the boys and 0.5 mm in the girls. These sex-specific criteria were employed because the prepubertal growth rates were more rapid in boys than girls. The ages at the spurts were recorded as the mid-points of the annual intervals for which they were first observed. These spurts tended to occur later in boys than girls and they tended to be larger in boys (Table 6.1). These spurts were commonly asynchronous within individuals although synchrony would seem to be functionally desirable.

Relationships between the growth of the cranial base and mandible with stature were investigated by comparing groups of tall and short children. The total increments in the cranial base and mandible after peak height velocity were larger for short boys than for tall boys in all dimensions except Go–Gn. This measurement from the angle of the mandible to its most anterior point represents the length of the body of the mandible. In tall boys, the spurts tended to be large for S–N and small for Ba–S. These distances are lengths of the cranial base from sella (S; the midpoint of the pituitary fossa) to nasion (N; the anterior end of the cranial base) and basion (Ba; the posterior end of the cranial base). The specialist will recognize the limitations of the definitions given in this chapter to these and other craniometric points; the articles referenced provide precise definitions. Tall girls tended to exceed short girls in the size of their cranial base spurts. The sizes of the pubertal spurts were also analyzed in relation to rates of maturation. In rapidly maturing boys, spurts in the cranial base tended to be smaller for Ba–N, which is a measure of the overall length of the cranial base and they tended to be larger for S–N. In rapidly maturing girls, the spurts tended to be larger in Ba–N and Ba–S but not S–N.

In the boys, spurts were most common for Ba–N and for two mandibular lengths (Go–Gn and Ar–Gn). The latter is a measure of the overall length of the mandible. The highest prevalences in the girls were for cranial base lengths, particularly Ba–N. While the prevalence of cranial base spurts was similar in the two sexes, spurts in the mandible were much more common and larger in boys than in girls. In each sex, spurts were least common for Ba–S. Within individuals, there were usually decreases in the rates of growth before the spurts and only slow growth after the spurts. Corresponding patterns were more evident at the upper centiles than the lower ones and when the data were related to maturational events, particularly age at menarche in girls.

In girls, cranial base spurts tended to occur at chronological and skeletal ages near 11.5 years, with similar variability of timing in relation to both these ages. In boys, their timing was less variable relative to age at peak height velocity. For girls, the variability of timing in relation to menarche and ulnar sesamoid ossification was slightly less than that in relation to peak height velocity.

Spurts in the cranial base occurred about 1.6 years earlier in girls than in boys but their timing in relation to maturational events was similar in the two sexes. They occurred about 1 year after the onset of ulnar sesamoid ossification, but preceded peak height velocity by about 0.5 years and preceded menarche by about 1.5 years. In the boys, percentiles of increments for cranial base lengths decreased from 2–6 years before the

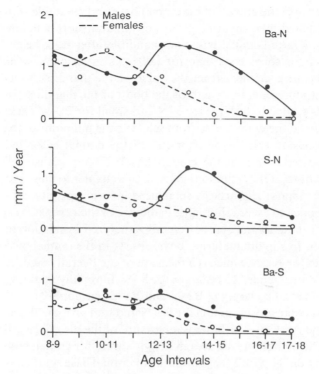

Fig. 6.4 Median rates of elongation of three cranial base lengths (Roche & Lewis, 1974[249]).

onset of ulnar sesamoid ossification. These decelerations were followed by accelerations from 2 years before to 2 years after the onset of ulnar sesamoid ossification for Ba–N and S–N. The acceleration in Ba–S ended, however, at about the time ossification began in the ulnar sesamoid.

Ages at spurts in pairs of lengths were consistently more highly correlated in girls (0.6) than in boys (0.4) but most of the correlations were significant in each sex. The median rates of elongation for cranial base lengths are shown in Fig. 6.4. In boys, Ba–N decelerated to 11.5 years and then accelerated to 13 years after which it again decelerated (Roche & Lewis, 1974[249]). Ba–N had a similar pattern of change in girls but the spurt occurred about 2 years earlier and was less marked. There were similar changes in S–N and Ba–S with more marked spurts for S–N in the boys but only small sex differences for Ba–S. The 90th percentiles for annual increments after 14 years were considerably higher in boys than girls for each cranial base length but there were only small sex differences at the 10th percentile level.

Table 6.2. *The mean total increments (mm) in cranial base lengths after selected ages and peak height velocity until 17.5 years (data from Roche & Lewis, 1976*[250]*)*

	After chronological ages (years)		After peak height velocity
	10	16	
Boys			
Ba–N	10.7	3.3	6.7
S–N	6.6	2.3	4.7
Ba–S	5.6	1.5	3.0
Girls			
Ba N	7.4	2.4	5.4
S–N	4.7	1.9	3.7
Ba–S	3.2	0.4	2.1

Comparisons were made between Ba–N and Ar–Gn because of the similar lengths and orientations of these measurements that relate to the total cranial base and length of the body of the mandible respectively. There were smaller decelerations in Ba–N before the pubescent spurts and less gradual decelerations after them. Growth was slower in Ba–N than in Ar–Gn before, during, and after the spurts. Comparisons were also made between S–N and Go–Gn because of their similar orientations. S–N is a measurement of anterior cranial base length and Ar–Gn is a measurement of the length of the body of the mandible. The spurts were smaller in S–N and the decelerations after the spurts were also smaller. A similar comparison was made between Ba–S (posterior cranial base length) and Ar–Go (mandibular ramus height). There were smaller decelerations in Ba–S than in Ar–Go before the spurts and the spurts were smaller.

The total increments in cranial base lengths after peak height velocity and selected chronological ages tended to be larger in boys than in girls (Table 6.2). There was considerable elongation after 16 years except for Ba–S in girls (Roche & Lewis, 1974[249]; Lewis & Roche, 1988). Since the posterior part of the cranial base elongates until at least 17.5 years in boys and 16.5 years in girls, the brainstem probably elongates to corresponding ages. This elongation demonstrated that the distance from the foramen magnum to the pituitary fossa increased and, presumably, the length of the brainstem increased correspondingly. This is not surprising since cross-sectional data show increases in the weights and cholesterol content of the brainstem during pubescence.

To describe more fully these late changes in the growth of the cranial

base, a double logistic model (sum of two logistic functions) was fitted to the serial data for individuals (Bock *et al.*, 1973; Roche *et al.*, 1977a[251]). This indicated that the pubescent phase of growth in the cranial base began at about 8 years in boys and 6 years in girls and that 95% of the adult lengths of cranial base dimensions was reached at about 15 years in boys and at 11.8 to 13.5 years in girls.

Sibling correlations for radiographic measurements of the cranium have been calculated using data for pairs of measurements made at the same ages (Byard *et al.*, 1984). These correlations were lowest during the first year of life and increased as adulthood approached. The patterns of change in these correlations varied during the intervening years. Most of the correlations were significant and many exceeded 0.5, which is the value expected for a completely heritable polygenic trait. This suggested that common sibling environment contributed to sibling resemblance for craniofacial dimensions.

Other studies of the cranial base have concerned the pituitary fossa and the sphenoid sinus. Analyses have been made of changes in the size of the pituitary fossa during childhood and adulthood. These studies are important because pituitary fossa size is related to the size of the pituitary gland. The Fels data were obtained from lateral cephalometric radiographs on which the outline of the fossa can be seen clearly. Silverman (1957) showed that measurements of the length and depth of the fossa were highly reliable in children and that they could be used to calculate its area. He presented selected percentiles of the area in relation to age and to stature. These areas showed a pubescent spurt in females but not males, that was particularly evident in the data for annual increments (Fig. 6.5). The relationship between the area of the pituitary fossa and stature was more nearly linear than the relationship with age. Relative to stature, the mean areas were greater in males than in females for the range of statures from 70 cm to 160 cm (which approximates the age range 1–13 years). At larger statures, the sexes did not differ in mean areas.

Other analyses showed that the pituitary fossa continued to enlarge during adulthood. This reflected bone loss, although aging in the craniofacial skeleton involves both remodelling and redistribution of bone (Israel, 1967a, 1968a, 1970). Israel (1970) measured radiographs of individuals aged more than 24 years and utilized serial data for some of these. Both the cross-sectional and the serial data showed an increase of about 10% in the area of the fossa during 14 years.

Attention has been directed to changes with age in radiographic measurements including the sphenoid sinus during childhood (Hinck & Hopkins, 1965). The interest in these studies is related to the light they shed

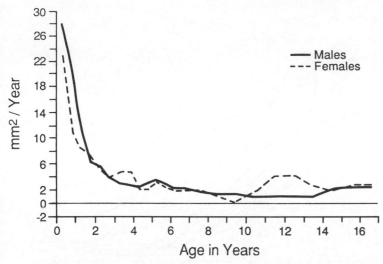

Fig. 6.5 Mean annual increments (mm²/year) in the area of the lateral outline of the pituitary fossa. (Silverman, F.N. (1957). Roentgen standards for size of the pituitary fossa from infancy through adolescence. *American Journal of Roentgenology, Radium Therapy and Nuclear Medicine*, **78**, 451–60. Redrawn with permission from Williams & Wilkins, Baltimore, MD.)

on the growth of the cranial base. The distance from the clivus (which is the part of the cranial base posterior to the pituitary fossa) to the sphenoid sinus showed near linear decreases in the Fels participants prior to pubescence (Fig. 6.6). These findings could, in part, have reflected changes on the dorsal surface of the clivus which, as will be described later, shifted anteriorly after the age of 9 years, but did not shift sufficiently to explain all the decreases noted by Hinck and Hopkins. The rate of decrease tended to be more rapid for boys than girls and it was not related to initial size. This distance was consistently larger in boys than girls to 13 years but not at older ages. There were only slight changes after pubescence.

Cranial base shape

Serial studies have used Fels data to describe age changes in the shape of the cranial base. This topic is important biologically and in orthodontia and facial surgery but shape, in general, is difficult to describe and it is even more difficult to understand. This was expressed succinctly by Sherrington a few decades ago when he wrote: 'To record shape has been far easier than to understand it.' Leaving understanding to one side, it is extremely difficult to describe the shape of the cranial base in an accurate metric fashion.

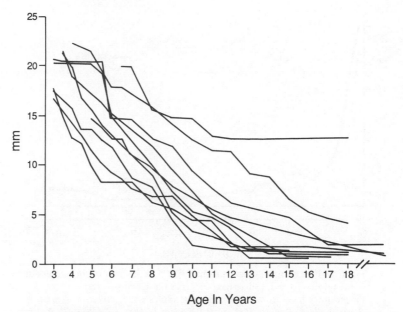

Fig. 6.6 Distances (mm) from the dorsal surface of the clivus to the sphenoid sinus in 10 girls. (Hinck, V.C. & Hopkins, C.E. (1965). Concerning growth of the sphenoid sinus. *Archives of Otolaryngology*, **82**, 62–6. Redrawn with permission from American Medical Association, copyright 1965.)

Changes in the relationships from 0.5 to 17 years between three cranial base planes defined by the foramen magnum, clivus, and planum sphenoidale and the plane of the palate were described by Koski (1961). In cross-sectional data, there were large changes in these relationships to 3 years but later changes were slight. There were, however, marked irregular changes in serial data for individuals in the angles between these planes during all the age ranges studied. Consequently, Koski rejected the concept of a fixed growth pattern for the craniofacial skeleton and the use of rigid norms for diagnosis, prognosis and classification.

The angle Ba–S–N, which is commonly called the saddle angle, is used as an inexact but useful index of the shape of the lateral silhouette of the cranial base. There has been considerable debate as to whether the saddle angle changes during growth. Cross-sectional data analyzed by Lewis and Roche (1977) and by Ohtsuki *et al.* (1982a) showed a significant linear decrease from 0 to 3 years, after which the changes were not significant to 40 years except for a decrease in males from 7 to 18 years. There were small consistent tendencies for the saddle angle to be larger in boys than in girls but there was a small sex difference in the opposite direction in adults.

Generalizing, the mean values were 139° at birth, 132° from 2 to 12 years, 131° from 12 to 24 years and 130° from then to 40 years.

Lewis and Roche (1977) reported that, after 2 years, the median increments in the angle Ba–S–N were negative for six age ranges that collectively extended from 2 to 30 years but the changes after 16 years were small. The high correlations between values 6 to 24 years apart attested to the reliability and stability of this measurement. Contrariwise, the correlations between successive increments within individuals were low, which reflected the small size of the changes. The saddle angle was correlated with Ba–N (r = 0.3) but the correlations with cranial vault length and stature were near zero. There were only minor differences in the saddle angle between groups with normal occlusion and those with malocclusion.

Age changes in the shape of the cranial base have also been described using Fourier analysis (Lestrel & Roche, 1984, 1986). Such an approach is needed because the irregular shape of the cranial base cannot be described effectively by a simple measurement such as the saddle angle. Additionally, Ba is the only conventional landmark on the endocranial surface of the base; S is a constructed point and N is ectocranial. The basic data for the Fourier analyses were the lengths of 61 radii measured on serial radiographs from a centroid that was chosen to reduce the effects of abrupt changes in curvature, especially near the posterior border of the pituitary fossa, Ba and the anterior part of the cranial base. This approach represented the endocranial outline accurately and allowed the irregular shapes to be measured while minimizing size differences. The dorsal aspect of the clivus and the anterior cranial base changed least with age while the pituitary fossa changed most. These data suggested that the cranial base was remodelled continually during growth.

The size of the cranial base was separated from its shape without ambiguity by making the area bounded by the Fourier construct equal between individuals. After adjustment for size, the mean shapes were similar for the two sexes in all age groups and these shapes changed with age within each sex. The data for females showed considerable changes between the shapes in infancy, pre-puberty and adolescence (Fig. 6.7). In each sex, the floor of the pituitary fossa tended to move superiorly from about 3 to 9 years and there was a marked antero-superior movement of the region near the tuberculum sellae, and anterior movement of the anterior wall of the pituitary fossa and the clivus near the dorsum sellae from 9 to 15 years. The shape of the cranial base did not change from adolescence to adulthood.

It was found that the region near the pituitary fossa was placed more

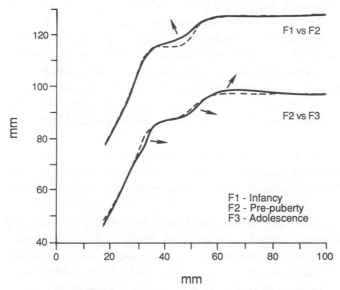

Fig. 6.7 Mean coordinates of the shape of the cranial base in girls during infancy (F1), before puberty (F2), and in adolescence (F3). In each comparison, the interrupted line represents the earlier shape. (Lestrel, P.E. & Roche, A.F. (1986). Cranial base shape variation with age: A longitudinal study of shape using Fourier analysis. *Human Biology*, **58**: 527–540. Redrawn with permission from *Human Biology*.)

superior in females than in males during infancy. From then until pubescence, the region near the dorsum sellae was more posterior in females and the posterior part of the pituitary fossa was more inferior. In females during adolescence and adulthood, the tuberculum sellae, and the posterior part of the floor of the pituitary fossa were more inferior and the clivus near the dorsum sellae was more posterior. With a different superimposition, these changes could have been interpreted differently but, regardless of the superimposition used, it was shown that the cranial base changed in shape during growth and that there were sex differences in shape at an age.

This work by Lestrel provided important findings but it is more significant for the method that he introduced to measure the shapes of parts of the skeleton. Lestrel *et al.* (1991) illustrated the further application of this method in a study of nasal bone growth from birth to 1 year. Sex differences in shape remained after standardizing for size. These differences, which were mainly related to greater length and reduced thickness in females, were present from birth and became significant at 1 year.

Garn (1961a[57]) reviewed research opportunities and limitations related

to malocclusion. He criticized conventional caliper measurements for the study of growth because they had been designed to compare races and not to describe 'the way the skull, the face, and the jaws actually grow.' Many caliper measurements are difficult to interpret because growth at several sites is included in a single dimension. With the mandible as an example, Garn noted that various parts of this bone must be considered separately because their growth is only moderately intercorrelated. Garn commented further on the independence of tooth formation from general somatic development and caloric intake.

Few studies have been made at Fels of the growth of the facial skeleton, other than the mandible, but Ohtsuki *et al.* (1982a) reported that the angle S–N–A, which is an indicator of maxillary position relative to the cranial base, decreased significantly in each sex until about 10 years; later it tended to increase. Low values for this angle indicate a more posterior position of the central part of the face.

There have been, however, several studies of the growth and development of the mandible. This concentration on the mandible partly reflects the presence of better landmarks for this bone than for the remainder of the face. In agreement with the views of Garn (1961a[57]), these studies of the mandible were related to specific regions of the bone. Israel (1969, 1978) analyzed the height of the body, cortical thickness near the premolar teeth and the distance from the apex of the second premolar to the superior and inferior margins of the body. His cross-sectional data for ages from 6 to 25 years showed that body height, in which there was a pubescent spurt, and cortical thickness were similar in the two sexes to 10 years but they were significantly larger in boys at older ages (Fig. 6.8). Men exceeded women by about 20% in cortical thickness and 13% in body height. This latter difference was associated with a larger distance from the apex of the premolar tooth to the inferior margin of the mandible, but the distance from the apex of this tooth to the superior margin of the mandible did not differ between the sexes.

A study of the height and anteroposterior depth of the mandibular symphysis was reported by Garn, Lewis and Vicinus (1963d[127]) who related their findings to the mesiodistal diameters of the central incisor and first molar teeth, and to adult values for stature and bony chest breadth. The symphyseal dimensions were effectively independent of the other recorded variables in adulthood except for low correlations between the height and depth of the symphysis and between both these measurements and tooth size. These workers separated adults into groups depending on whether symphyseal height or symphyseal depth was greater or less than the median. There were no significant tendencies to assortative mating for

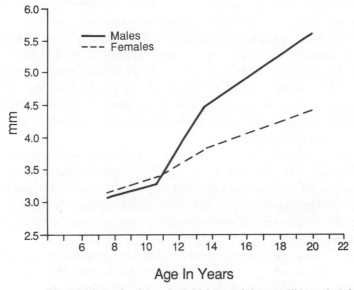

Fig. 6.8 Means for the cortical thickness of the mandible at the inferior margin of the body near the premolar teeth. (Israel, H. (1969). Pubertal influence upon the growth and sexual differentiation of the human mandible. *Archives of Oral Biology*, **14**, 583–90. Redrawn with permission from Pergamon Press, plc, copyright 1969.)

symphyseal size. The offspring of low × low and high × high matings differed in symphyseal height by about 2 mm which corresponded to about 40 percentile points. There was a similar difference in symphyseal depth between the offspring of thick × thick and thin × thin matings. Furthermore, the offspring of thick × thin and thin × thin matings were similar in symphyseal depth which suggested a form of inheritance in which thin is dominant over thick.

Heiber (1975) related the growth of the mandible in boys to the onset of ossification in the ulnar sesamoid and pubescent spurts in stature. He found a statistically significant increase in the rate of growth in S–Gn, which is a measure of chin position relative to the cranial base, that tended to parallel the pubescent spurt in stature. The overall length of the mandible (Ar–Gn) and Ba–Gn had pubescent spurts about 1 year after the onset of ossification in the ulnar sesamoid. These spurts tended to be later than those in S–Gn.

The growth of the mandible during pubescence was described in more detail by Lewis and co-workers (1982). In their data, there were spurts in three major dimensions of the mandible (Ar–Go, ramus height; Go–Gn, body length; and Ar–Gn overall length) in most children but they were

less common in girls than boys and less common in ramus height than in the other dimensions. The spurts tended to occur about 1.5 to 2.0 years later in boys than in girls and were about 33% larger in boys. The mean increments in mandibular dimensions decreased before the spurts occurred. The spurts tended to occur several months before peak height velocity and about 1 year after ossification of the ulnar sesamoid, but before menarche. Girls with early menarche tended to have larger mandibular spurts than those with late menarche, but the relationships between the prevalence of spurts and the rate of maturation were not consistent. The timing of spurts was more variable relative to ulnar sesamoid ossification than in relation to peak height velocity.

Boys with large spurts in all three mandibular dimensions tended to be late in ulnar sesamoid ossification but there was an opposite tendency in girls. Boys who passed rapidly through pubescence had small spurts in ramus length and body length but not in overall length, but girls who passed rapidly through pubescence tended to have larger spurts in all three dimensions. There were low correlations in the size of the spurts in the three dimensions considered.

Changes with age in the angle of the mandible (Ar–Go–Gn) in women aged 26 to 90 years were analyzed by Israel (1973a, 1973c). Each participant had a radiograph when aged at least 25 years and another after an interval of 14 years or longer. The difference in the mandibular angle between those who were edentulous and those with enough teeth to allow occlusion was not significant. Serial data did not demonstrate changes of more than 2.5°, nor did they reveal the marked changes in mandibular shape with aging that are commonly illustrated in textbooks.

Third cervical vertebra

Israel (1973d) using cross-sectional and serial data described increases with age in the width but not the height of the body of the third cervical vertebra in women aged 26–90 years. Israel considered this was part of a widespread remodelling of the skeleton during adulthood that includes increases in the breadth of the shafts of long bones and redistribution of bone in the craniofacial area.

Pelvis

Several major studies of the growth of the pelvis have been made at Fels. Indeed, one could claim that these are the only comprehensive studies of pelvic growth that have been reported. Reynolds (1945, 1946b) described pelvic growth from early infancy to 9 years. Many of the distances and angles measured may be unfamiliar. Those mentioned in this text are

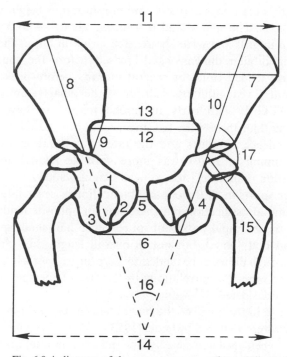

Fig. 6.9 A diagram of the measurements made on radiographs of the pelvis by Reynolds (1945, 1947): 1 = superior pubic ramus length, 2 = inferior pubic ramus length, 3 = inferior ischial ramus length, 4 = height of body of ischium, 5 = interpubic breadth, 6 = interischial breadth, 7 = ilial breadth, 8 = iliac length, 9 = breadth of greater sciatic notch, 10 = pelvic height, 11 = pelvic breadth, 12 = pelvic inlet breadth, 13 = interiliac breadth, 14 = bitrochanteric breadth, 15 = length of femoral neck, 16 = pelvic angle, and 17 = femoro–pelvic angle.

illustrated in Fig. 6.9. Reynolds reported that radiographic and anthropometric data showed matching age trends, although the latter were consistently larger. At birth, the superior pubic ramus, the inferior ischial ramus and much of the body of the ischium were ossified and there were some centers of ossification in the sacrum.

Reynolds divided his measurements into those that are parallel to the radiographic film and, therefore, only slightly distorted, and radiographic abstractions such as 'ischial length.' Various pelvic dimensions were highly intercorrelated at birth except for interpubic breadth, interischial breadth and iliac breadth. Later, during infancy, the intercorrelations between measurements were generally about 0.4 and tended to be higher in boys than in girls (Reynolds, 1945).

There were wide ranges of values at birth and rapid growth to 3 months

that was succeeded by progressive deceleration. There were only small sex differences in pelvic measurements during infancy, but there were some changes in shape during infancy. The iliac index (breadth/length) increased markedly to 1 month and then decreased slowly to 9 months, after which it increased until it reached about the same value as at birth. The greater sciatic notch widened to 1 month and narrowed from then to 3 months, after which it widened slowly to 1 year.

There was considerable tracking of growth during the first year: values at birth and 1 year were correlated about 0.6, except for the iliac breadth and the breadth of the greater sciatic notch for which the correlations were near zero. The iliac index and the height and breadth of the pelvis tended to be greater in boys than girls, but girls were larger in inlet breadth, interpubic breadth, interischial breadth, the greater sciatic notch, and pubic length. This led to the conclusion that boys tended to have large outer pelvic structures, while girls tended to have larger inner pelvic structures.

At birth, pelvic breadth was correlated with body weight and recumbent length in each sex and with weight/recumbent length^3 in girls but not boys. The inlet index of the pelvis (breadth/depth) and the cephalic index (cranial length/cranial breadth) were not significantly correlated, but inlet breadth and head circumference at birth were correlated ($r = 0.5$). In boys, but not girls, pelvic height was correlated with a skeletal maturity index derived from the number of ossified centers and with the age at emergence of the first tooth, but not with age at first walking. There were significant correlations between mothers and infants for the breadth, but not the depth, of the pelvis. Despite this, the correlations between siblings for pelvic size were not significantly larger than those between non-siblings.

Reynolds (1946b) described the growth of the pelvis from 1 to 9 years. He found few significant lateral differences, and based his report on the means for the two sides. An intercorrelation matrix at 34 months showed very close relationships within a group of measurements that included many breadths, ischial and pubic lengths, and the length of the neck of the femur. Another group of significantly interrelated variables included the breadth and depth of the pelvic inlet, the breadth and height of the pelvis, and iliac length. Unfortunately, these groupings were based on subjective judgments without the benefit of factor analysis, although this had been employed earlier at Fels by Robinow (1942b). Additionally, the breadth of the greater sciatic notch was related to the depth of the pelvic inlet and iliac length. In general, the intercorrelations at 34 months were slightly higher than those during early infancy and they tended to be larger in girls than in boys (Reynolds, 1945).

Generally, the growth rate decelerated from 1 to 9 years for most pelvic dimensions, but the pelvic angle was almost constant during this age interval. Boys tended to have significantly larger values than girls for pelvis height and breadth, iliac length, interiliac breadth, bitrochanteric breadth, length of the femoral neck and pelvic angle. The girls tended to have higher values for the inlet index, interpubic and interischial breadths, pubic length, breadth of the sciatic notch and the femoro-pelvic angle. As in infancy, boys had larger outer pelvic structures and girls had larger inner structures, but the sex differences tended to decrease with age. Reynolds (1946b) reported that those with large pelvises from 3 to 9 years tended to have greater trunk and limb circumferences and more subcutaneous adipose tissues. Also, there was evidence of relationships between pelvic size and maturity; those with large pelvises tended to be advanced in ossification of the proximal femoral epiphysis and the completion of the obturator foramen.

The age range of Reynolds' studies was extended by Coleman (1969), who analyzed data from 9 to 18 years. His main interest was in the apparent mechanisms by which the pelvis reaches its adult form, which involves marked sex differences. On tracings of radiographs, he drew vertical and horizontal reference planes aligned on the maximum bi-iliac breadth and the midpoint of the pubic symphysis. He used X and Y coordinates to locate landmarks that reproduced the pelvic outline, and fitted orthogonal polynomials to the serial coordinates after serial outlines for individuals were superimposed at their common mean points and rotated to minimize the differences within sets of serial data.

Distance curves were plotted for each point as a function of time. Almost all of the point locations had pubescent growth spurts. Coleman showed that the sex differences in the growth of the pelvis were due to variations in rates and directions of growth at local areas, particularly the greater growth of the internal acetabular and pubic regions in females. The middle part of the iliac crest tended to curve less laterally in females than in males at young ages. During growth, the iliac crest moved superiorly and laterally in each sex, but during the growth of this and the acetabulum, the lateral direction predominated in females. There was general remodelling and relocation over the ischial tuberosity in each sex, but this tended to be more laterally directed in females. There was more growth at the superior and medial borders of the pubis in females. With growth, the point at the greatest breadth of the pelvic inlet moved laterally and inferiorly in females, but in males it moved laterally and superiorly (Coleman, 1969).

This study by Coleman contributed to knowledge of sexual differentiation of the pelvis, particularly the pelvic inlet. For example, the inlet

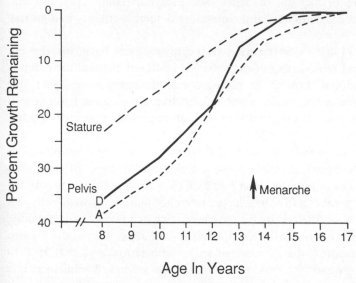

Fig. 6.10 The percentage of growth remaining for stature and pelvic breadths in girls at ages 8 to 17 years (A = inlet breadth; D = interischial breadth). Data from Moerman (1982).

breadth was about 1 cm greater in females than males at 18 years, due to more lateral growth of the acetabulum and pubis. The greatest breadth of the female inlet moved inferiorly because of the lateral growth of the ischia, but in males the upper half was the broader part.

Another study of the growth of the pelvis in females aged 8 to 18 years was made by Moerman (1981, 1982). She found that pelvic breadths increased more slowly than stature, but the growth of the pelvis continued to at least 18 years (Fig. 6.10). Much smaller percentages of size at 18 years were reached by pelvic breadths than by stature at ages 8 to 10 years, but the difference was reduced during the next few years due to large pubescent spurts in the pelvis.

In the Fels data, pelvic breadths 3 years after menarche did not differ significantly from those at 18 years (Moerman, 1982). Rapidly maturing girls, compared with slowly maturing girls of the same gynecological age, were smaller in general body dimensions and in pelvic size at menarche, but there were only minor differences between these groups at 18 years. From these findings, Moerman concluded that some risks of teenage pregnancy may be associated with early menarche and incomplete pelvic growth. In a later analysis of her data, Moerman (Lavelle, 1991) found decreases with age in the correlations between the width of the pelvic birth canal and

either stature or bicristal diameter. She concluded that hip width and stature might be useful indicators of maternal–fetal morbidity in high-risk populations.

Chumlea (1983[3], 1984[4]) reviewed the histological basis for the enlargement and remodelling of the pelvis. He pointed out that the pelvis is three-dimensional, but all its radiographic dimensions are linear. He noted that the pelvic angle is not informative about growth because it changes little after 2 years, but it may be an important indicator of adult shape.

In summary, the valuable work of Reynolds was purely descriptive, but Coleman attempted to explain the developmental basis of adult sex differences. The differences described by Coleman were for changes in the locations of points relative to selected reference planes. Consequently, his conclusions were affected by his choice of reference planes. Additionally, Coleman's procedure, while descriptively informative, did not distinguish between relocation due to resorption or apposition and that due to movement of bone segments. Moerman, in her studies, documented late growth changes that could have important obstetric effects. At the time of her work, its obstetrical applications were recognized, but its application to the design of automobile restraint devices was not recognized until much later (Chumlea, 1984[4]). This is a most important topic area because automobile injuries are a major cause of death during childhood.

Skeletal variations
A review of skeletal variations based largely on Fels data has been published by Garn (1966a[66]) who dealt with their genetic control. He pointed out that genetic variability may be maintained by differing directions of selection within a population. One genotype may be adaptive in childhood and another may be preferable at older ages, and in addition, some mechanisms may favor heterozygotes. Garn considered that descriptions of variations should be followed by attempts to apportion their causation to groups of genetic and environmental influences. In other reviews of skeletal variations, Roche (1978c[186], 1986b[202]) emphasized their importance in relation to the clinical applications of reference data.

Variations in ossification
In an early Fels study, attention was directed to a common variation in the pattern of calcification of the distal femoral epiphysis (Sontag & Pyle, 1941a[294]). In many children, the margin of this epiphysis was irregular, especially on its medial aspect, and calcified areas extended beyond this part of the margin without changes from normal in the density of the

epiphysis. This condition, which appears to be associated with a broad calcified zone, is known as disseminated calcification. It was very common at 1 to 3 years when the distal femoral epiphysis was enlarging rapidly, but it is not useful as a maturity indicator because it does not occur in all children. It usually appeared earlier in girls than in boys and in those who matured rapidly or were young when they first walked. This condition was of shorter duration in those who were growing rapidly. The condition generally lasted 1 to 6 years, but most of the irregularity was present for less than 2 years. Corresponding less severe changes occurred in the proximal epiphysis of the tibia and in the tarsal bones.

Missing secondary ossification centers (epiphyses) were shown to be common in the foot (Garn *et al.*, 1965e[153]). Individuals varied widely in this respect, but there was considerable sibling concordance that was partly explicable in terms of X-linked inheritance. Garn pointed out that when centers were missing, the nearby bones tended to fuse, with a consequent decrease in flexibility and, perhaps, in fine movements.

When pseudoepiphyses were present, the ossified epiphysis was joined to the shaft by bone long before the usual age for epiphyseal fusion. Consequently, elongation at the epiphyseal zone stopped at a very early age. Pseudoepiphyses were relatively common at the non-epiphyseal ends of the short bones of the hand and foot and they tended to be concentrated within families (Garn & Rohmann, 1966b[142]).

Notches near the non-epiphyseal ends of the metacarpals are a mild form of pseudoepiphyses (Lee & Garn, 1967). These notches have special interest because of their potential for use as natural bone markers from which elongation can be measured (Lee, 1967). In a survey of Fels participants, Lee, Garn and Rohmann (1968) found that notches occurred at multiple sites in normal children. They were common at the radial side of the base of the second metacarpal (30%) and the ulnar side of the base of the fifth metacarpal (88%). Each notch was graded as slight, moderate or marked, and a score was assigned to each metacarpal that was the total for its radial and ulnar sides. Because the scores tended to change with age, the maximum for each individual was used in subsequent analyses that showed notching of the second metacarpal tended to be associated with stature, but in ways that differed between the sexes. In males, there was a negative correlation that was significant at 3 years only, while in females there was a positive association that was significant in adults only. The degree of notching was not related to the rate of maturation, except that males with marked notching of the second metacarpal tended to have earlier fusion of the distal phalanges.

In a minority of children, some epiphyses of the bones of the hand and

foot were conical, with the apex of the cone directed towards the end of the shaft where there was a corresponding indentation. Conical epiphyses were more common in females than males (Hertzog, Garn & Church, 1968). In the hand, they were most common on the fifth middle phalanx and the first distal phalanx. They occurred at both these sites in some children; this combination was more common than would be expected due to chance, especially in females. It was shown by Hertzog that the shaft of the fifth middle phalanx is absolutely and relatively short prior to the development of a conical epiphysis. The ages at ossification and of fusion of conical epiphyses varied considerably, but fusion did not tend to occur early. This marked variability in timing indicates that this trait could affect the lengths of bones in which it occurs.

Brachymesophalangia
It has been noted that the fifth middle phalanx of the hand is commonly short and broad (brachymesophalangia). This condition is often associated with radial angulation of the fifth finger (clinodactyly). Brachymeso-phalangia was present in 0.6% of the Fels participants, in whom it appeared to be inherited in a dominant fashion (Garn, Fels & Israel, 1967h[79]; Hertzog, 1967; Garn et al., 1972[93]; Poznanski et al., 1972).

Variations of joints
Selby and colleagues (1955) described the prevalence and the familial nature of a bony bridge on the first cervical vertebra (atlas). This bridge crossed the groove for the first cervical nerve, the vertebral artery and its accompanying veins on the superior surface of the posterior arch of the atlas. There was a complete or incomplete bridge in 27% of the Fels participants who were aged more than 14 years; about half of these bridges were complete. Sex differences in prevalence were small. The mean age of appearance was 9 years. Familial tendencies were evident, although pedigree analysis showed that bridging may not be expressed in the next generation, and it may occur in children although it was absent in their parents. Selby considered this bony bridge might be inherited in a Mendelian dominant fashion.

Poznanski et al. (1985) reported reference data for some measurements of the knee joint spaces because these are reduced in juvenile arthritis. The apparent joint space was best measured in the midline in children up to 5 years, but on the medial side in older children. When used in combination with joint widths, these measurements assisted the detection of early stages of juvenile arthritis.

Fusion of the fifth lumbar vertebra to the first sacral vertebra was

present in about 16% of the Fels participants (Garn & Shamir, 1958[164]). It showed high concordance within sibling pairs and parent–offspring pairs.

Cysts

Benign asymptomatic cyst-like areas near the distal end of the shaft of the femur were described by Sontag and Pyle (1941b[295]). These areas rarely extended into the epiphyseal zone but maintained a constant distance from it. They were usually round or oval and some were sacculated. They were up to 3 cm in diameter with sharply defined borders, and were positioned just beneath the cortex posteriorly. The average age of appearance was 46 months and they soon reached their maximum size. On average, they were present for 29 months, being more common in boys (53%) than in girls (22%). Sontag and Pyle did not find evidence of trauma. They speculated that these cysts might be due to the presence of small cartilaginous nests in rapidly growing areas.

These cysts were investigated later by Selby (1961). He reported that the first sign of their development was a thickening of trabeculae, but sometimes they appeared at a site separated from the area of thickening. In Selby's data, the cysts remained for 1 to 11 years, which was much longer than the duration reported by Sontag and Pyle (1941b[295]). Additionally, while the prevalence in girls (29%) was slightly greater, the prevalence in boys (27%) was much less than that reported by Sontag and Pyle. Selby noted some evidence of a familial tendency.

Growth arrest lines

Growth arrest lines occur near the epiphyseal zones of long and short bones in some children. They reflect alterations in the architecture of the cancellous bone that may be associated with disease and slowing of growth. In an interesting paper, Sontag (1938[276]) was the first to describe opaque bands near the centers of ossification of some tarsal bones. These bands were similar radiographically to growth arrest lines. They were 1–2 mm wide and occurred about where the margin would have been in the neonatal period. Sontag considered that these bands may reflect a slowing of growth soon after birth. They were not due to infections, but they were common in the infants of malnourished mothers (Sontag, 1938[276]; Sontag & Harris, 1938[287]).

Growth arrest lines near the distal end of the tibia are very common in Fels participants (Garn, Hempy & Schwager, 1968b[92]). Since these lines may persist into the ninth decade, particularly in females, they form natural bone markers from which the contributions of the proximal and distal epiphyseal zones to the total length of the bone can be determined

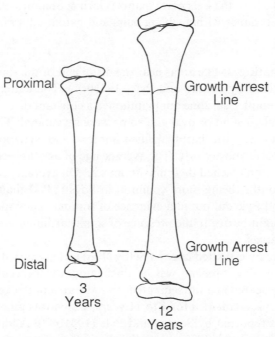

Fig. 6.11 A diagram to illustrate the use of growth arrest lines near the proximal and distal ends of the tibia at 3 and 12 years in the measurement of elongation at the proximal and distal epiphyseal zones. Since the lines are fixed, the distances from them to the ends of the bone increase due to elongation at the epiphyseal zones.

(Garn & Schwager, 1967[160]; Gindhart, 1969). Serial radiographs showed that some lines were resorbed, but others formed before this resorption occurred. Consequently, long series of measurements could be constructed from groups of lines overlapping in duration.

This method of using growth arrest lines is shown in Fig. 6.11 where the outlines of the tibial shaft for an individual at 3 and at 12 years are aligned on growth arrest lines near each end of the shaft. The positions of the proximal and distal growth arrest lines at 3 years can be projected onto the outline of the shaft at 12 years. As a result, measurements can be made of the elongation during the interval from 3 to 12 years at the proximal end and, separately, at the distal end. Garn and his co-workers concluded that slightly less than half the total elongation of the tibia occurred at its distal end and that this proportion increased slightly from 2 to 10 years. Additionally, growth arrest lines can be used to show the relative rates of apposition and resorption on the medial and lateral aspects of the shaft of the tibia.

Gindhart (1969) reported that almost all the Fels participants developed growth arrest lines at the distal end of the tibia before 13 years, but none appeared after this age. The development of new lines was most common from 1.5 to 3.0 years. There were low, but significant, associations between the formation of lines and the occurrence of infectious diseases, but not with tonsillectomies. The correlations between the number of arrest lines and adult stature were not significant. Arrest lines in the tibia were present in 14% of men and 30% of women aged 25 to 50 years and in 8% of men and 14% of women aged 51 to 86 years (Garn & Schwager, 1967[160]). The decrease with age was due to cortical remodelling at the endosteal and periosteal surfaces. Consequently, those in whom the lines were resorbed tended to have wider marrow cavities.

Growth arrest lines in a set of monozygous triplets were described by Sontag and Comstock (1938[284]). They estimated the ages at which the lines formed from the distances between the lines and the ends of the tibia, fibula, femur and radius. They could not identify a single factor that was associated with all the lines and they concluded that the differences between these monozygous triplets in their growth arrest lines demonstrated the involvement of environmental mechanisms.

Skeletal mass

A large amount of work at Fels has been related to skeletal mass. The early work was based on measurements of the cortical thickness of the second metacarpal. This bone was chosen because many hand–wrist radiographs were available, and the central part of the shaft is nearly circular in cross-section. The latter quality simplifies the derivation of areas from measurements of cortical thickness (Garn, 1963a[63], 1963b[64]). The cortical thickness of this bone is only an approximate index of skeletal mass despite the positive correlations between these values. Realization of the limitations of cortical thickness measurements led to the development of radiographic densitometry. In this technique, the amount of bone mineral in a transverse slice of a bone is estimated from light transmitted through a radiograph. This procedure was used extensively at Fels and numerous technical improvements were developed.

Both these methods provided local indices of skeletal mass, which is important in relation to osteoporosis. Somewhat surprisingly, Garn (1963a[63]) concluded that 'accurate estimates of bone weight are superfluous in obesity studies, where the loss of obesity tissue may exceed the total weight of the skeleton.' This is true for studies of changes in body weight, but for studies of fat-free mass or total body fat calculated from body density the influence of changes in skeletal mass is critical.

Cortical thickness

Cortical thicknesses were measured at Fels using fine-pointed dial calipers that were read to the nearest 0.1 mm. All these measurements were highly replicable, although replicability was higher for the total breadth of the bone (periosteal breadth) than for the breadth of the marrow cavity (Garn, 1970[70]). With the introduction of electronic digitizers, it became important to compare replicability between measurements made with this new equipment and those made with calipers. Both sets of data showed high replicability, but the intra-observer errors with a digitizer were much smaller than those with calipers. The systematic differences between these sets of measurements were very small (Chumlea, Mukherjee & Roche, 1984a[25]).

The advantages and limitations of cortical thickness measurements have been considered in several reviews. Few procedures other than the measurement of cortical thickness can provide information about long term serial changes (Roche, 1987b[205]). The changes in cortical thickness and, by inference, in skeletal mass, during childhood and pubescence are important because they are major determinants of skeletal mass in young adulthood. In turn, values in young adulthood play a major role in determining values for skeletal mass in middle and old age.

Roche (1978c[186], 1986b[202]) provided sources of reference data and described histological mechanisms that affected the total bone breadth and the breadth of the marrow cavity and, consequently, cortical thickness. Apposition on the external (subperiosteal) surface of a bone is due to the actions of osteoblasts in the deep layer of the periosteum. At the same time, bone is resorbed from the endosteal surface and, therefore, the marrow cavity widens. The balance between these changes determines the cortical thickness which may increase more in some parts of a bone than in others. Additionally, the cortex may drift medially or laterally due to remodelling. This can be demonstrated histologically or by changes in growth arrest lines (Garn, Davila & Rohmann, 1968f[78]). Reference data for the cortical thickness of the second metacarpal, and values derived from it, have been published by Garn et al. (1970[156]). Falkner (1975) stressed the need to take ethnic differences into account when applying these reference data.

In early Fels work, it was shown that the total bone width, relative to the total width of the calf, was greater in males than females at all ages from birth to young adulthood (Reynolds, 1948; Reynolds & Grote, 1948). In the tibia, cortical thickness tended to be greater in boys than in girls except during pubescence when some reversals occurred due to marked endosteal apposition in girls. The cortical thicknesses of the tibia were correlated with those of the humerus, but neither of these measurements necessarily

reflects skeletal mass. With aging, cortical thickness seemed to decrease proportionately less in the tibia than in the second metacarpal (Garn, Rohmann & Nolan, 1963e[150]; Garn *et al.*, 1964c[151], 1967g[155]; Spencer, Sagel & Garn, 1968). Cortical thickness of the second metacarpal increased during childhood because subperiosteal apposition exceeded endosteal resorption (Garn et al., 1963e[150]; Frisancho, Garn & Ascoli, 1970; Garn & Wagner, 1969[170]; Fig. 6.12). Endosteal resorption, as shown by increases in the breadth of the marrow cavity, continued until about 12 years in girls and 16 years in boys. Later, there was marked endosteal apposition in girls which reduced the breadth of the marrow cavity of the second metacarpal (Garn *et al.*, 1968h[171]; Garn, 1970[70]).

As a result of these changes, cortical thickness of the second metacarpal increased to about 25 years and then remained constant until about 45 years (Garn *et al.*, 1969b[157], 1970[156]). In both sexes decreases occurred after this age, so that by the late sixties the mean values were less than those during adolescence (Fig. 6.13). During adulthood, cortical thickness of the second metacarpal tended to be greater in men than women at all ages and it decreased more slowly in men than in women after 45 years. This decrease was due to resorption at the endosteal surface that began at about 40 years. It continued at a steady rate in women but the rate of loss decreased in men (Spencer & Coulombe, 1966; Spencer, Garn & Coulombe, 1966; Garn *et al.*, 1964c[151], 1967g[155]). Despite these common changes, the loss was small in some individuals, many of them tall, because increased periosteal apposition compensated for endosteal resorption.

From comparisons between Fels participants and poorly nourished children and adults from Central America, and from the analyses of pedigree data available at Fels, it was concluded that cortical thickness was determined more by genetic influences than dietary ones (Garn & Rohmann, 1964a[139], 1966a[141]; Garn, 1961c[59], 1966c[68], 1970[70]; Wolánski, 1966b; Falkner, 1975). For example, the correlations between cortical thickness and calcium intake were not significant (Garn, 1962a[60], 1967[69]; Garn, Pao & Rohmann, 1965d[132]). The low, but significant correlations for total bone width and cortical thickness within parent–offspring pairs and sibling pairs have a pattern consistent with a hypothesis of X-linked inheritance (Garn *et al.*, 1967g[155]).

Spencer *et al.* (1966) fitted a model to the mean cortical thicknesses at each age. This model, that fitted well, postulated that the value at an age was a balance between apposition and resorption.

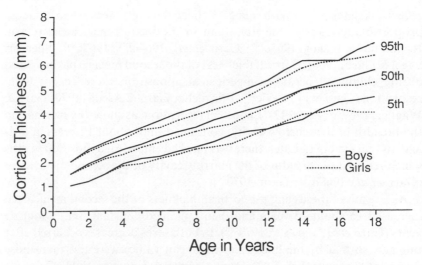

Fig. 6.12 Selected percentiles for the cortical thickness (mm) of the second metacarpal (data from Garn *et al.*, 1967e[154]).

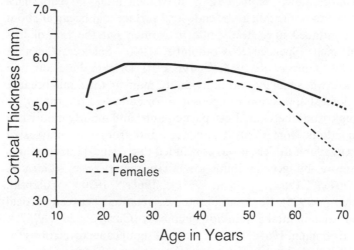

Fig. 6.13 Mean cortical thickness of the second metacarpal from 12 to 70 years. (Garn, S.M., Rohmann, C.G. & Nolan, P., Jr. (1964c). The developmental nature of bone changes during aging. In *Relations of Development and Aging*, ed. J.E. Birren, pp. 44–61[151]. Redrawn, courtesy of Charles C Thomas, Springfield, Illinois.)

Cortical area

If it is assumed that the cross-section is circular, the total breadth and the cortical thickness of the second metacarpal can be used to calculate cortical area. In Fels data, these areas were larger in boys than girls at all ages and

they showed spurts, from 12 to 14 years in boys and 10 to 12 in girls, that were considerably larger in boys than girls. About 23% of the increase in cortical area during pubescence was due to endosteal apposition in males compared with 36% in females. Cortical area, expressed as a percentage of the total cross-sectional area, was similar in the two sexes until 12 years, after which it was slightly larger in females than males (Frisancho *et al.*, 1970). The cross-sectional cortical area of the second metacarpal increased rapidly until about 20 years in males and 11 years in females. From 40 to 90 years, the total loss in this area was about 15% in men and 39% in women (Garn *et al.*, 1964c[151]). This loss was due to endosteal resorption; there was an increase in the total cross-sectional area of the second metacarpal (Rohmann *et al.*, 1967; Garn *et al.*, 1968h[171]). The proportion of the total cross-sectional area occupied by cortical bone was greater in women than in men, at least to 60 years. These findings from cross-sectional data were supported from data obtained after a 15-year interval during adulthood. These follow-up data also showed the loss of cortical thickness was correlated with the initial value (0.4).

Garn (1970[70]) reported an index of skeletal mass derived from the cross-sectional cortical area of the second metacarpal or tibia, and the length of the corresponding bone. By relating this index in adults to known population values for skeletal mass, he derived a proportionality constant (coefficient) to allow direct estimates of skeletal mass. This method has not been applied widely because of justifiable concerns about the limited representativeness of either the second metacarpal or the tibia. Garn, however, applied this method and published reference estimates. In turn, these estimates were used to calculate differences between annual means of skeletal mass from which Garn derived increases in the body stores of bone mineral (mg/day). This led to estimates of calcium retention/day that were about 100 mg/day, except during adolescence when there was a retention of about 300 mg/day by boys and about 200 mg/day by girls. Applying this approach, Garn and Wagner (1969[170]) claimed that skeletal mass increased by about 2% after 18 years. While much of this work remains interesting and relevant, better methods are now available for the measurement of skeletal mass.

Medullary cavity width

Garn *et al.* (1968f[78]) directed attention to 'normal' medullary stenosis in which the breadth of the marrow cavity of the second metacarpal is less than 1.0 mm. This condition occurs in some healthy individuals in whom it is probably inherited as a simple Mendelian dominant trait. At Fels, the men with the narrowest marrow cavities had low values at birth that

decreased through childhood and early adulthood due to endosteal apposition. The women with the narrowest marrow cavities had marked endosteal apposition during adolescence. In those with medullary stenosis, the second metacarpal was unusually narrow, but cortical thickness values were high.

Rapidly maturing boys and girls had wider bones but the differences from children maturing at average rates were more marked in girls than boys (Reynolds, 1946a, 1948; Reynolds & Grote, 1948). In young adulthood, tall individuals tended to have slightly more periosteal apposition, less endosteal resorption and increased cortical thickness. At ages older than 45 years, the total breadth of the second metacarpal tended to be greater and the decrease in breadth tended to be smaller in those who were tall (Garn & Hull, 1966[94]).

Radiographic densitometry

Radiographic densitometry is the measurement of the ability of a radiograph to prevent the transmission of light. The parts of a radiograph that transmit large amounts of light are those that were shielded from x-rays by dense objects, especially bones. The major application of radiographic densitometry concerns the estimation of skeletal mass. Garn et al. (1966c[80]) compared cortical thickness measurements and densitometry for the measurement of bone loss. Cortical thickness measurements were more suitable for tubular bones than for those that were mainly cancellous. Variations in radiographic techniques were much less critical for cortical thickness than for densitometry for which non-screen film and highly standardized processing are mandatory. There is also some 'hardening' of the x-ray beam as it passes through tissues. Garn and his associates considered that caliper measurements slightly overestimated the total breadth and underestimated the breadth of the marrow cavity. Colbert et al. (1980) reported correlations of about 0.6 between cortical area obtained using a densitometer, estimates of the total bone mineral of the second metacarpal, and bone mineral expressed per centimeter of the length of this bone (bone mineral content). It was shown that measurements of cortical area were insensitive to bone loss due to the poor precision of the measurements.

Densitometry can be used to compute bone mineral content if the cross-sectional area of the bone is known; subsequently the ratio of bone mineral to the volume of bone tissue can be used as an index of mineralization (Colbert, 1968, 1974; Colbert & Garrett, 1969). This mineralization index can help monitor change in an individual, but not to calculate absolute bone mineral concentration or to compare individuals. A simple theoretical

model for determining the absorption coefficient of bone specimens of regular or irregular shape *in vitro* was proposed by Colbert, Spruit and Davila (1967). This allowed the derivation of important parameters that were independent of the wave length of the x-rays. The results obtained with this model were in substantial agreement with observed data. Bone mineral content from densitometry was highly correlated (0.9) with ash weight and elemental calcium; the latter can be predicted with errors of about 6%. Data from densitometry were also highly correlated with those from single photon absorptiometry (Colbert, Schmidt & Mazess, 1969; Colbert, Spruit & Davila, 1970a; Colbert, Mazess & Schmidt, 1970b).

Much of the work done at Fels by the Colbert group was performed on the fifth middle phalanx. This is a convenient bone to scan, but it may have been a poor choice for biological reasons. Since abnormalities and variations of this bone are common, it is unlikely to be representative of the skeleton (Garn *et al.*, 1967h[79]). Colbert, Van Hulst and Spruit (1970c) provided graphs of reference values for bone areas measured directly on radiographs, estimated bone weights and estimated bone densities of the first distal phalanx and middle phalanges II–V of the hand.

Colbert (1968) applied his approach to bones of irregular shape. He showed that the measured areas were not closely related to the estimated bone weights until after 5 years and that the areas were not closely related to density until after 20 years. The measured bone sizes increased rapidly to 15 years and then slowly, whereas the estimated bone weights increased rapidly to 17 years. Bone density increased rapidly to 13 years; this was followed by a pubescent spurt to 17 years and a continuing slow increase to 35 years.

Israel (1968b) demonstrated that densitometry could provide an index of skeletal mass in a precise area, despite problems due to non-linear relationships between radiographic density and radiographic exposure, and variations in film type and processing. Other errors are produced by the polychromatic nature of the radiographic beam and by its scattering. Despite these limitations, a densitometric trace across a bone demonstrates its fine structure (Israel, 1967b; Israel, Garn & Colbert, 1967). Using this technique, Israel documented a 14-year persistence of trabeculae near the roots of incisor teeth and used these to document the loss of alveolar bone. He used the same approach to study changes in the calcaneum where trace patterns could be matched over time, if one allowed for stretching and compression of the image due to variations in positioning. The possible application of densitometry to dental enamel and dentine and to studies of craniofacial remodelling was noted (Colbert, Israel & Garn, 1966; Israel, 1967b).

Plasma alkaline phosphatase

Plasma alkaline phosphatase was studied by Clark and his associates (Clark & Beck, 1950; Clark, Beck & Shock, 1951a; Clark, Beck & Thompson, 1951b) because of its known relationship to osteoblastic activity and, therefore, the rate of bone growth and remodelling. In children and young adults, there was a marked consistency of measurements from year–to–year (r = 0.6–0.8), but marked variation in these measurements from hour to hour and from day to day. The plasma alkaline phosphatase values were high in infancy, but decreased near the end of the first year. Sex differences and age changes were slight until marked abrupt decreases occurred at 12 years in girls and 14 years in boys. The levels of this enzyme tended to parallel the rate of growth in stature. During pregnancy, women with male fetuses tended to have higher values than those with female fetuses, and there was a two- or three-fold increase during the last trimester of pregnancy that was not affected by lactation. In adults, the values were lower in males than females but they increased in old age, particularly in males, perhaps due to prostatic enlargement (Clark *et al.*, 1951b).

Teeth

An enormous body of work on the size and shape of the permanent teeth was performed by Fels scientists led by Garn and Lewis. Their careful measurements of dental models provided important descriptive information and many insights into relationships within the dentition and between the dentition and the remainder of the body. As a result of this work, our understanding of the determinants of tooth size and shape is greatly enhanced.

Tooth size

Reference data, including maximum confidence values, for the mesiodistal dimensions of the permanent teeth were published (Garn, Lewis & Walenga, 1968a[128]). Some of the these measurements were made using a transducer caliper (Garn, Helmrich & Lewis, 1967i[91]). In these data, lateral differences were small and inconsistent, both within individuals and on a group basis. The sex difference in mesiodistal diameter was about 4% for most teeth, but was larger for the canines and the teeth near them. Garn and his colleagues considered these variations in the sex differences constituted evidence of a canine 'field' for size difference between the sexes (Garn, Swindler & Kerewsky, 1966d[169]). The largest absolute sex difference was for the mandibular first and second molars followed by the canines; it was smallest for the incisors. The sex difference in tooth size was larger,

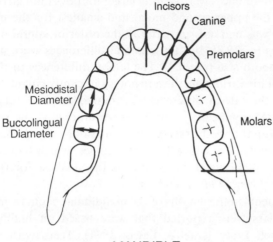

MANDIBLE

Fig. 6.14 A diagram to show the occlusal aspect of the groups of mandibular teeth and examples of their mesiodistal and buccolingual diameters.

about 6%, for the buccolingual diameter than for the mesiodistal diameter (Garn, Lewis & Kerewsky, 1964b[106], 1967b[112]). These diameters are illustrated in Fig. 6.14.

Garn *et al.* (1965c[118]) and Garn, Lewis and Kerewsky (1965f[109]) reported that communality indices for the mesiodistal diameter tended to be lower for the distal teeth in each morphological class than for the other teeth within these classes. The distal teeth also had lower size interrelationships with each other than did the more mesial teeth. This finding was not due to greater size variability of the more distal teeth. The lack of negative associations between adjacent teeth in mesiodistal diameters indicated that size variation was not dependent upon variations between teeth in their shares of the anlage (Garn *et al.*, 1966d[169]). Later, Garn *et al.* (1967j[115]) reported that the correlations for mesiodistal diameters between pairs of corresponding teeth in the upper and lower jaws were about 0.6. Correlations between teeth within a jaw for mesiodistal diameters showed the presence of canine and third molar fields and a field that included the more distal teeth of all classes (Garn *et al.*, 1963b[104], 1966d[169]). These findings indicated that the controlling factors could operate on part of the dentition.

The buccolingual diameter did not show systematic lateral differences, but, nevertheless, the differences tended to be larger for the more distal tooth in each morphological class (Garn, Lewis & Kerewsky, 1966e[110],

1967d[114]). These differences were slightly larger for boys than girls and they were largest for the upper second molar and smallest for the upper first premolar. There was marked similarity in the order of lateral differences for the two sexes (r = 0.8), but these lateral differences were not highly correlated with tooth size (r = 0.4). The lateral differences in the bucco-lingual diameters for various teeth were not significantly correlated within individuals and the lateral differences in mesiodistal and buccolingual diameters were not significantly correlated. Additionally, the rank order correlation between the sex differences in the mesiodistal and buccolingual diameters was low (0.2), due largely to the canines, which had the largest difference for the mesiodistal diameter, but the smallest for the bucco-lingual diameter (Garn *et al.*, 1966d[169]).

Annual increments in the lengths of the mandibular canines, premolars, and second molars were reported that were based on highly reliable procedures (Israel, 1966; Israel & Lewis, 1971). Teeth with extremely curved roots were excluded and the mean root lengths were used for teeth with multiple roots. The plots of annual increments in length against age showed a wide scatter and slopes that differed by tooth within sex. The slope for the canine differed from those for the other teeth in males, but the slopes for the canines and premolars were similar in females. The slopes were similar for the two sexes, although the mandibular teeth were shorter in women than men because apical closure occurred earlier. In each sex, the premolar was shorter than the second molar from 6 to 8 years, but not at older ages.

Garn *et al.* (1966e[110]) found that the mesiodistal diameters of teeth did not tend to be larger on a particular side of the jaw, either in the total sample or in those with congenital absence of some teeth. Such findings may be of concern to orthodontists. The lateral differences in mesiodistal diameters had significant relationships with tooth size, and those for the maxillary teeth tended to be larger than those for the mandibular teeth. Furthermore, the more distal tooth of each morphological class (incisors, premolars, molars) tended to show more lateral asymmetry than other members of the class (Garn *et al.*, 1966e[110]), and the positive correlations for lateral differences within individuals were larger for morphological classes of teeth than for the total dentition.

Tooth shape

There is an interaction between the sizes of molar teeth and the number of cusps in different populations. To determine the nature of this association within the Fels population, Garn, Dahlberg and Kerewsky (1966f[75]) used the mesiodistal diameters of the first and second molars as an index of their

size. The differences in size between these teeth were shown to be related to differences between them in the number of cusps (r = 0.4). Garn also defined tooth shape by the ratio buccolingual/mesiodistal diameter. There was a slight shape communality throughout the dentition (r = 0.2; Garn, Lewis & Kerewsky, 1967j[115]), with higher intercorrelations for adjacent teeth, especially those within the same morphological class. Furthermore, the ratio buccolingual/mesiodistal diameter was significantly larger in males, thus documenting sex differences in tooth shape (Garn *et al.*, 1967b[112]). These dimensions of teeth were moderately correlated (r = 0.5–0.6; Garn, Lewis & Kerewsky, 1968g[117]).

Garn *et al.* (1966f[75], 1966g[76], 1966h[77], 1966i[111]) also reported findings relevant to variations in the cusps and grooves on the crowns of molar teeth. Since they found greater similarity between brothers than sisters, and high concordance in monozygotic twins, they concluded that their findings were in reasonable agreement with genetic control by autosomal transmission. Furthermore, lateral differences were uncommon.

Congenital absence of teeth

Congenital absence (agenesis) of the third molar teeth was shown to be related to the prevalence of absence of other teeth, and the timing of dental maturation and eruption (Garn & Lewis, 1962[100]; Garn, Lewis & Vicinus, 1963d[127]). Children with congenital absence of a third molar had a marked tendency to congenital absences of other teeth except for the first molar, and a reduction in the mesiodistal diameters of the other teeth, but children with a third molar did not exhibit congenital absence of any other tooth except the lateral incisors and second premolars (Garn *et al.*, 1962a[103], 1963b[104]).

When the third molar was congenitally absent, lateral differences in mesiodistal diameters of the other teeth were slightly larger than usual (Garn & Lewis, 1962[100], 1970[101]; Garn *et al.*, 1962a[103]; Garn, Lewis & Kerewsky, 1964a[105], 1966e[110]). This size reduction was more marked in the anterior than the posterior teeth. Additionally, when the distal tooth of one morphological class was absent, the corresponding teeth of other classes were likely to be absent (Garn & Lewis, 1962[100]; Garn *et al.*, 1963b[104]).

Determinants of tooth size and shape

Genetic control over several aspects of dental size and shape has been documented at Fels by investigations based on correlations within families and the examination of pedigrees. There were significant correlations for mesiodistal diameters within sibling pairs that were larger for sister–sister pairs (0.6) than for brother–brother (0.4) or brother–sister pairs (0.2; Garn

et al., 1965a[107]). These genetic influences seemed to be more important than intrauterine pressure and other environmental influences. Additionally, profile patterns for mesiodistal diameters throughout the dentition were similar between siblings and parent–child pairs, and there was suggestive evidence of X-chromosomal involvement (Garn, Lewis & Walenga, 1968e[130]). The sex difference in mesiodistal diameters tended to be consistent within families. Some brother–sister pairs showed larger sex differences in mesiodistal diameters than did others; these sex differences were correlated about 0.5 between such pairs within families (Garn *et al.*, 1967k[125]). Additionally, data from siblings and twins showed that cusp number and cusp patterns were under genetic control (Garn *et al.*, 1966g[76]; Garn, Kerewsky & Lewis, 1966j[95]).

While definitive proof of a secular increase in tooth size was lacking, mesiodistal diameters tended to be larger in offspring than in their parents of the same sex (Garn, Lewis & Walenga, 1968c[129]). The increase was greater for males than females which would be expected because males are less influenced by genes on the X chromosome. This secular increase provided indirect evidence of environmental effects.

There were low (0.2) correlations between adult stature and the mesiodistal and buccolingual diameters of the permanent teeth (Garn & Lewis, 1958[99]; Garn, Lewis & Kerewsky, 1968d[116]). These low correlations led Garn and Lewis (1958[99]) to conclude that large fragmentary fossil teeth were not evidence that the prehistoric remains were those of giants. The sex differences in tooth size were correlated ($r = 0.3$) with the sex differences in stature within brother–sister pairs (Garn *et al.*, 1967c[113]).

7   Body composition and risk factors for cardiovascular disease

'It is not growing like a tree in bulk, doth make men better be.'

Samuel Johnson (1709–1784)

Interest in body composition at Fels is reflected in the data collection protocol from the first years of the study. This early interest was related to the amounts of adipose tissue, muscle and bone at local sites. The possible practical application of this work was soon realized. Garn (1962c[62]) wrote: 'Body composition attracts interest from clinical and preclinical disciplines,' but later (1963a[63]) he noted that, despite the established relationship of total body fatness to the probability of death (longevity) and of the amount of bone mineral to osteoporosis, little had been done to associate variations in regional body composition with the risk of disease or the probability of death. Garn (1963a[63]) also claimed that an excess of muscle mass predisposed to coronary atherosclerosis but tended to protect against osteoporosis.

The Fels Longitudinal Study was transformed in 1976 by placing an increased emphasis on serial changes in total and regional body composition in relation to risk factors for cardiovascular disease. The initial plan for the body composition aspect of the study was complex and further complicated by the irregularity of federal funding. As an overview, data are now collected annually from participants aged from 8 to 18 years who live within 80 km (50 miles) of Yellow Springs and then at 3-year intervals until 40 years, after which the examinations are at 2-year intervals. The intervals between examinations are longer for those who live further from Yellow Springs. The data collected at these examinations relate to the size, proportions, composition, maturity and density of the body, bioelectric impedance, blood lipids, selected hormones, and blood pressure. As a result, there are serial data for many important measures and near-unlimited analytic possibilities.

199

This chapter will consider work done within the Fels Longitudinal Study relating to: (i) methodological aspects, (ii) total body composition, (iii) bioelectric impedance, (iv) predictive equations, (v) regional body composition, (vi) adipocytes, (vii) the assessment of nutritional status, (viii) nutritional assessment in the elderly, (ix) influences on body composition, and (x) risk factors for cardiovascular disease.

Methodological aspects

These methodological considerations will be restricted to work done to improve measurements of body composition. Research related to the interpretation, relationships, and applications of findings will be considered later in this chapter.

Total body composition

The term 'total body composition' refers to the amounts of fat, fat-free mass, muscle, protein, bone mineral and water in the body. These amounts can be expressed using metric units or they can be expressed as percentages of body weight. Studies of bone mineral and skeletal mass are described in Chapter 6.

Many methods can provide body composition measures. Until recently, the most common laboratory procedure for the measurement of body composition was underwater weighing from which body density was obtained. Body density was then used to calculate the percentages of fat and fat-free mass in the body with the two-component model which assumed the densities of fat and fat-free mass were the same in all individuals.

The present method of choice is also based on the measurement of body density but the calculations of body composition are made using a multi-component model that takes account of variations in the composition of fat-free mass that affect its density (Garn, 1963a[63]; Roche, 1985a[199], 1987a[204]). From 7 to 25 years, age- and sex-specific group estimates for the density of fat-free mass can be applied; at older ages, total body bone mineral, total body water and body density must be measured to apply a multi-component model. There were large differences between values for body composition variables calculated from body density when the two-component model with a fixed value for the density of fat-free mass was used and those obtained from the current multi-component model (Lohman, 1986; Guo *et al.*, 1989a). These differences were larger in females than in males and they were larger at ages younger than 12 years when application of a fixed density for fat-free mass of 1.1 g/cc resulted in an underestimation of fat-free mass by about 2 kg.

The procedures now applied at Fels include the measurement of (i) total body bone mineral from photon absorptiometry using a dual-energy x-ray source, (ii) total body water from the dilution of deuterium oxide, and (iii) body density. This set of procedures allows the multi-component model to be applied on an individual basis, and thus provides excellent estimates for those old enough and fit enough to be weighed underwater. Furthermore, these data could lead to the development of improved multi-component models. Because these laboratory procedures require expensive fixed equipment, there is a need for effective field methods. These methods must be based on procedures that are easy to apply both to gather data and to use the data in predictive equations that provide accurate estimates of body composition values. The methods used to develop such predictive equations are described in Chapter 2; the efficacy of these equations will be described later in this chapter.

Garn and Nolan (1963[131]) described a tank for the measurement of body volume which, in combination with body weight, could be used to calculate body density. These workers chose a narrow tank to increase the accuracy of measurements of change in the water level when a participant was immersed. This level was read with an external vernier gauge to within 100 ml. The estimated combined errors of measurement of weight in air, residual volume, and body volume were considered to be more than 5%. Some of this error was due to the dimensional instability of the clear plastic tank.

In reviewing the progress of research concerning body composition, Roche (1984a[196]) referred to improvements in methods for developing predictive equations and the need either to discard the concept of frame size as a correlate of body composition or to develop an improved index of frame size. The present frame size measures explain little of the variance in percent body fat or fat-free mass that is not accounted for by weight or stature. The useful measures of frame size may be widths, such as knee width that is measured between bony landmarks over which there is little subcutaneous adipose tissue. Additionally, improved measurements of residual volume are required for the calculation of body density and, ideally, air in the gut would be measured. The variation introduced by the latter is reduced if the subjects are measured fasting (Roche, 1986c[203]). Later, Roche (1987a[204]) noted that load cells should be used to measure underwater weight; these measurements should be repeated ten times and the mean of the last three used in the calculations if these final measurements are representative of the total set. An alternative procedure is to use the mean of the three highest weights. Either of these means is a satisfactory choice but, of course, the choice must be fixed within a study

and for comparisons between studies. The inherent limitations of the models are more important sources of error in body composition determinations than the errors of measurement which are small in good studies.

Regional body composition

Attention to methods of measuring regional body composition at Fels have mainly been directed at subcutaneous adipose tissue. This is an important component of body composition, partly as an index of energy stores in the assessment of nutritional status (Himes, 1980a). Fat in adipose tissue is a highly labile energy store that accumulates due to a positive caloric balance. The amount of adipose tissue, however, is not a specific measure of caloric balance because it is affected by genetic influences, illness, malabsorption, parasitic infection, and habitual physical activity. The major rationale for the measurement of skinfold thicknesses is their close relationships to total body fatness.

Sites for the radiographic measurement of subcutaneous adipose tissue thickness must be chosen where the adipose tissue is sharply defined, standardized radiographic positioning is easy, and measurement errors are small (Reynolds, 1951). Slight variations in site location can have large effects on the recorded values. The best sites, such as the trochanteric, iliac crest and tenth rib, have underlying bony landmarks that allow accurate site location (Garn, 1957a[78]; Garn & Gorman, 1956[83]). Reliability was excellent for these sites and for the calf (Garn, 1961b[58]); measurements at them were highly correlated with weight and with corresponding thicknesses at other sites (Garn, 1954a[42], 1957b[49]). Measurement errors were large for sites that require oblique views such as the breasts and buttocks and for measurements over the abdomen where landmarks were lacking. Of course, if there is interest in a particular site, that is the one that should be measured. This interest may spring from known relationships between measures at the site and either total body fatness or risk factors for disease. At each site, the adipose tissue thickness is measured perpendicular to the skin surface and radiographic positioning must be such that pressure on the measurement site is avoided.

Subcutaneous adipose tissue thickness is also measured using calipers that exert the same pressure at all jaw openings. These measurements are limited to sites where the subcutaneous adipose tissue is loosely attached to the deep fascia and a double layer of skin and subcutaneous tissue (skinfold) can be elevated from the underlying muscle (Roche, 1979b[188]). It is commonly difficult to measure skinfold thicknesses over the abdomen, especially in the obese, because only mounds of tissue with non-parallel

sides can be elevated. Harrison *et al.* (1988), describing methods for the measurement of skinfold thicknesses, emphasized the need to standardize the directions of the folds.

Himes, Roche and Siervogel (1979) compared caliper measurements of skinfold thicknesses compressed by calipers with radiographic measurements of uncompressed single adipose tissue thicknesses after correcting the latter for radiographic enlargement. These data for the analysis of the compressibility of skinfolds were obtained from participants aged from 8 to 19 years for seven sites, most of which were on the trunk. The median differences between half the skinfold values and the radiographic values would be zero in the absence of compression. This was almost the case for the calf and ulnar forearm sites but compressibility was present and varied markedly among the other sites. There were low (r = 0.3) correlations between sites for compressibility. In agreement with the findings of Garn (1956b[47]) for measurements over the tenth rib, compressibility in the data of Himes *et al.* (1979) did not change significantly with adipose tissue thickness. The sex differences in compressibility were not significant but there were significant differences in compressibility among sites, and significant interindividual variations for males but not for females. The differences in compressibility among sites and individuals may have been related to adipocyte size or the proportion of adipose tissue that was not fat (Roche, 1979b[188]). While it is important to recognize variations in skinfold compressibility, adjustments for this compressibility did not improve predictions of body fatness (Himes, 1980b).

In another study, Townsend (1978) compared the well-known Lange calipers with small plastic calipers (Adipometer℠) developed and distributed by Ross Laboratories (Columbus, Ohio). With these plastic calipers, the pressure is exerted by the anthropometrist, not by a spring. Repeated bilateral measurements at the triceps and subscapular sites showed similar consistency for both types of calipers. The four plastic calipers were interchangeable for each site and measurements with them did not differ significantly from those with the Lange calipers. Nevertheless, as thicker skinfolds were considered, the differences between paired measurements (plastic–Lange) tended to change from positive to negative values and these differences were significant at both extremes of the distributions.

An alternative approach to the measurement of subcutaneous adipose tissue thickness employs ultrasonic waves. These waves do not compress the adipose tissue and, in theory, the method is applicable at sites where skinfolds cannot be measured. The ultrasonic waves are transmitted at right angles to the skin; in A-mode ultrasound the time required for their reflection from the surface of the underlying muscle to the skin is used to

estimate the thickness of subcutaneous adipose tissue. Consequently, these measurements should be made at sites where the external surface of the underlying muscle is parallel to the skin (Roche *et al,.* 1985a[199]). Ultrasound can be used to measure the thickness of breast adipose tissue but site location is difficult, especially in the elderly. Despite the theoretical appeal of the method, data from A-mode ultrasound were shown to be inaccurate, in part because it was difficult to position the probe (transducer) so that its face was parallel to both the skin and the underlying muscle surface. Additionally, incorrect data were obtained when fibrous layers in the adipose tissue reflected the ultrasonic waves (Roche, 1979b[188]; Chumlea & Roche, 1986[27]; Roche *et al.*, 1986a[217]).

In B-mode ultrasound, an image is obtained that can be stored as a permanent record on which tissue interfaces can be recognized. Therefore, the data are much more accurate than those from A-mode ultrasound. It is expected that B-mode ultrasound will be used more widely in the future despite its expense. B-mode measurements have recently been added to the examinations of Fels participants. Preliminary analyses of data from B-mode ultrasound show high reliability and close relationships to data obtained using calipers (Roche, Baumgartner & Siervogel, 1991b[214]). Considerable methodological work is in progress to evaluate this technique, with particular reference to deep abdominal adipose tissue.

Total body composition

The investigations of total body composition at Fels will be considered in relation to weight and weight/stature², which are indices of total body composition, and to percent body fat, total body fat, and fat-free mass, which are basic components of body composition but are difficult to measure directly.

Weight and weight/stature²

Body weight is highly relevant to body composition and it can be measured very accurately. It is important that measured values be used in the evaluation of either individuals or groups because reported data are inaccurate (Himes & Roche, 1982). Changes in adulthood have been documented. There were considerable increases in weight from 18 to about 30 years in men but the corresponding changes in women were small (Roche *et al.*, 1975c[227]). In men and women, weight increased slightly from 19 to 70 years despite some decreases after 50 years that were more marked in men (Reynolds & Asakawa, 1950; Chumlea, Falls & Webb, 1982a[21]).

Although weight is the non-specific sum of the weights of all body components, it is useful because of its significant correlations (r = 0.8) with

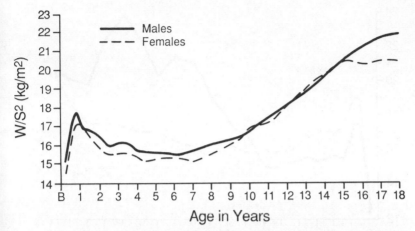

Fig. 7.1 Median values for weight/stature² plotted against age. (Cronk, C.E., Roche, A.F., Chumlea, W.C., Kent, R. & Berkey, C. (1982a). Longitudinal trends of weight/stature² in childhood in relation to adulthood body fat measures. *Human Biology*, **54**, 751–64, Redrawn with permission from *Human Biology*.)

total body fat and with the percentage of body weight that is fat (Roche *et al.*, 1981b[265]). Weight was also correlated with subcutaneous adipose tissue thicknesses at many sites; these correlations changed differently with age in boys and girls (Reynolds, 1951; Garn, 1961b[58]). In boys, the correlations increased from 7 to 11 years but decreased from 11 to 15 years. In girls, however, the corresponding correlations changed little from 7 to 11 years but increased from 11 to 15 years. In both sexes, there was considerable continuity of weight from one age to another after the age of 7 years, with correlations of 0.5 to 0.9 between values 5 to 6 years apart at ages ranging from 7 to 16 years (Reynolds, 1951).

Relative weight can be obtained by adjusting the observed weight to a median stature. This approach is not recommended, partly because comparisons between studies are difficult when the choice of reference data varies. Commonly, the weight of adults during middle age and old age is evaluated by comparison with data for weight at the same stature in young adults based on the assumption that increases in weight after young adulthood are due to increases in body fat and, therefore, undesirable. This view may be incorrect, especially for men in whom fat-free mass increases considerably after young adulthood (Roche, 1984c[198]).

The correlations between weight and body fatness were increased substantially when weight was divided by stature² to obtain the 'body mass index' (Roche *et al.*, 1981b[265], 1985[210]; Abdel-Malek, Mukherjee & Roche,

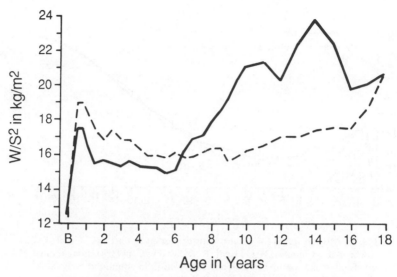

Fig. 7.2 Serial data for weight/stature² in two boys with markedly different scores for Principal Component 3 from 4 to 18 years. (Roche, A.F., Rogers, E. & Cronk, C.E. (1984) Serial analyses of fat-related variables. In *Human Growth and Development*, eds. J. Borms, R. Hauspie, A. Sand, C. Susanne & M. Hebbelinck, pp. 597–601[262], New York: Plenum Press. Redrawn with permission from Plenum Press, New York.)

1985). These correlations indicated that weight/stature² (W/S²) may be useful in screening, but the standard errors of the predictions were about 3 kg for total body fat and 4% for percent body fat. Therefore, W/S² is not a useful predictor of body fatness.

Abdel-Malek *et al.* (1985) devised a weight–stature index with fractional powers, i.e., W^m/S^k that were chosen to maximize the relationship between the index and percent body fat. These authors reported constants (coefficients) that, in combination with the new index, provided direct estimates of percent body fat with standard errors of 4–5%. The best index for Fels data was weight$^{1.2}$/ stature$^{3.3}$; the constants differed between the sexes but not with age. This index can be obtained easily from a published nomogram. This novel and logical approach to the development of an index of obesity was somewhat disappointing in that the chosen index was not significantly better than W/S² when judged by correlations with percent body fat. This work did, however, establish procedures that should be applied in the development of a weight–stature obesity index for non-whites or groups of abnormal individuals.

Serial changes in W/S² from 3 months to 18 years were described by Cronk *et al.* (1982a, 1982b). The medians increased rapidly to 1 year, then

decreased to 6 years and subsequently increased until 18 years in males and 15 years in females (Fig. 7.1). Variations of W/S^2 within individuals were more marked during infancy and adolescence than in childhood, and there was less continuity from infancy to childhood than from childhood to adolescence and less continuity in females than in males. Additionally, it was shown that the mean percentile level for W/S^2 during an age range was the best single predictor of the value for W/S^2 at an older age. Age-to-age correlations were low to moderate until about 18 years in boys and 13 years in girls (Roche et al., 1984[262]).

Using longitudinal principal component analysis of serial data for W/S^2 (Chapter 2), Cronk and her colleagues (1982b) assigned a coefficient to each component for every participant. Component 1 represented the average percentile level of the individual during the age range considered, while Component 2 represented the degree of directional change in percentile position (slope). Those with positive coefficients for Component 2 shifted upward with age relative to group percentiles. Components 3 through 6 represented smaller but increasingly more complex changes with age in W/S^2. These components described real aspects of individual variation in growth patterns as demonstrated by the data for two boys who differed markedly in their principal component coefficients from 4 to 18 years (Fig. 7.2).

There were strong relationships between the patterns of change in W/S^2 during growth and W/S^2 at 30 years (Cronk et al., 1982a). For these analyses, data were analyzed for infancy (3 months to 3 years), childhood (4 to 18 years), pubescence (10 to 17 years), and young adulthood (18 to 30 years). In males, about half the variance in W/S^2 at 30 years was explained by the coefficients for Components 1, 2, and 6 for the age range 4 to 18 years; a similar fraction of the variance in females was explained by the coefficient for Components 1 and 2 for the age range 10 to 17 years. The components for changes during infancy explained little of the variance. Changes in weight from 18 to 30 years were correlated with the coefficients for Component 2 (3 to 9 years) and those for Components 1 and 5 (4 to 18 years) in males, and with the coefficients for Component 2 (3 months to 3 years) and those for Component 5 (4 to 18 years) in females. Adipocyte number in adulthood was related to the level of W/S^2 and the changes in W/S^2 during later childhood and adolescence but not the levels or changes during infancy (Cronk et al., 1982a). The longitudinal principal components method described inflections but it did not provide clear descriptions of the variation in their timing, which is important (Siervogel et al., 1989a). Mathematical functions have been fitted to serial data for W/S^2 from 2 to 18 years (Guo et al., 1989c; Siervogel et al., 1989a) that

allow analyses of variation in the timing of inflections which is sometimes called the 'tempo' of growth. Since the fit was good, these models effectively described the patterns of change and allowed the calculation of the following for W/S^2: age at minimum value, the minimum value, age at maximum value, the maximum value, and maximum velocity. The maximum velocity and the maximum value occurred at younger ages in girls than in boys. Each of these estimated values, except age at maximum velocity, was related to the value of W/S^2 at 18 years, and early occurrence of the minimum value was related to high values for W/S^2 at 18 years.

There have been several analyses of the risk of having a weight of greater than the 75th percentile at 18 or 30 years, based on weight during childhood (Guo, 1988; Roche, 1987c[206]; Siervogel *et al.*, in press) or of a high value for weight/stature^2 based on the percentile level of this variable in childhood. The probability of being overweight at 18 years was estimated from a logistic function that fitted the data well except for those below the tenth percentile. The risk differed little between percentile groups until 3 years and older. This demonstrated that excess weight in early childhood was not related to the risk of overweight in adulthood but there was a significant risk when excess weight occurred later in childhood. This risk increased with age and with the percentile level for weight or weight/stature^2 at the younger age. For corresponding weight groups, the risk of overweight in adulthood tended to be greater for females than males except after 14 years.

Percent body fat and total body fat

In males, percent body fat calculated from the two-component model increased slightly early in adolescence but decreased by an average of 1.1% per year from 10 to 18 years; there was little change in females during the same age range and the age-to-age correlations were higher in females (Chumlea *et al.*, 1981a[24], 1982b[38], 1983[39]). These conclusions may need revision when better multi-component models are available. Mukherjee and Roche (1984) fitted a quadratic function to serial predicted values for percent body fat during adolescence in each sex and showed marked variations in level but considerably less variation in the patterns of change. In men and women, percent body fat increased with age and the values tended to be higher in women at all ages (Chumlea *et al.*, 1981b[33], 1982a[21]).

Total body fat calculated from body density did not change in boys during adolescence, but there was an average increase of 1.1 kg per year in girls (Chumlea *et al.*, 1981a[24], 1982b[38], 1983[39]; Chumlea & Knittle, 1980[23]). The relationships between total body fat and maturity as measured by skeletal age were not significant in either sex (Chumlea, 1981[1]). Total body

fat was greater in women than men from 20 to 24 years but, at older ages, the sex difference was not significant (Chumlea *et al.*, 1981b[33], 1982a[21]).

In early work at Fels, total body fat was predicted from trochanteric adipose tissue thickness (Garn & Harper, 1955[85]; Garn, 1957a[48], 1957d[51]). This approach yielded fat-free mass values that did not alter with changes in body weight, which is in conflict with many studies that show weight gains are associated with increases in both fat and lean tissues and that the reverse occurs when weight is lost. In fairness, Garn recognized that his approach was not applicable during periods of rapid weight change. This method may, however, be of value in screening but more data than a single skinfold thickness or radiographic adipose tissue thickness are needed for the accurate prediction of total body fatness.

Fat-free mass
Little attention has been given at Fels to changes in fat-free mass with age, but Chumlea *et al.* (1983[39]) reported an average increase of 4.4 kg per year in boys from 10 to 18 years, with only slight changes in girls. Work related to fat-free mass has mainly concerned its prediction and its relationships to blood pressure, as will be described later in this chapter.

Muscle mass is an important part of fat-free mass but the measurement of muscle mass requires complex procedures based on measures of total body nitrogen and total body potassium. These methods were not applied in the Fels study but analyses were made of various indices of muscle mass. Muscle thicknesses were measured at selected sites on radiographs (Reynolds, 1951; Garn, 1961b[58], 1962b[61]), but these thicknesses are unlikely to be representative of total muscle mass, partly because the size of local muscle groups can be influenced by exercise. This view was supported by the near zero correlations between radiographic muscle thicknesses and visual ratings of 'muscle mass' (Garn, 1961b[58]). It was concluded, however, from local muscle thicknesses, that muscle mass increased by 5% from 17 to 35 years when the maximum was reached (Garn & Wagner, 1969[170]). Measurements of muscle thickness can be used to calculate muscle volumes for body segments, as has been done for the thigh muscle mass which is approximately cylindrical (Garn & Gorman, 1956[83]).

An index of muscle mass is provided by the amount of creatinine excreted daily in the urine. The mean values for creatinine excretion were similar in boys and girls until about 12 years when there were rapid increases in boys but not girls (Reynolds & Clark, 1947). Creatinine excretion had high day-to-day stability and its rate did not change during pregnancy (Seegers & Potgieter, 1937; Garn & Clark, 1955[72]). Despite the

many sources of error in this index, Garn (1963b[64]) concluded that it was valuable from its correlation of about 0.7 with 17-keto-steroid excretion, stature, and calf muscle thickness.

Creatinine excretion corrected for body weight was proposed as an index of obesity because low values for the index reflected low values for muscle mass and fat-free mass relative to body weight (Garn & Clark, 1955[72]). The means for this index were larger in men than women and they were negatively correlated with adipose tissue thickness at the trochanteric site (r = −0.4). Nevertheless, this index was shown to be of limited value in men because of low sensitivity.

Bioelectric impedance

Since the 1960s, it has been known that measures of the resistance of the body to the passage of a very small alternating electric current are influenced by the amount of body water. Water is a major constituent of the human body. Indeed, it has been remarked by Tom Robbins in *Another Roadside Attraction* that 'human beings were invented by water as a device for transporting itself from one place to another.' In a more serious vein, Saint-Exupéry described water as: 'Not necessary to life but rather life itself.' An estimate of total body water, in combination with selected anthropometric data, could assist the prediction of fat-free mass because all the body water is in the fat-free mass. This approach received a substantial boost in the early 1980s with the introduction of reliable electronic circuits and stable power sources. At the same time, considerable research was initiated to determine the extent to which this technique was useful, its underlying mechanisms, and its potential for surveys of nutritional status or body composition. The current commonly used is 800 μA with a frequency of 50 kHz. Pairs of source and receiving electrodes are applied to a hand–wrist and a foot–ankle.

The general topic of bioelectric impedance has been the subject of a critical review (Baumgartner, Chumlea & Roche, 1990). Resistance and reactance can be measured. Resistance is the opposition of the body to the flow of an alternating current. Capacitance, which is the reciprocal of reactance, causes the current to lag behind the voltage producing a phase shift that is quantified geometrically as the phase angle. At very low frequencies, the capacitance of the human body is effectively an open circuit (Fig. 7.3). Consequently, the reactance is zero and the measured impedance is purely resistive. With increasing frequency, reactance increases more rapidly than resistance and the phase angle enlarges until the critical frequency is reached. At frequencies higher than the critical level, reactance decreases relative to resistance until impedance is again

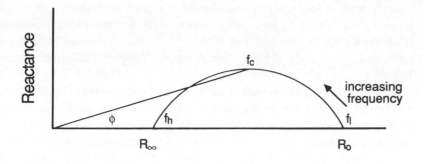

Resistance

Fig. 7.3 An impedance plot that shows the relationship between resistance, reactance, and phase angle (ϕ). The phase angle for a biological conductor is maximal at a critical frequency (fc). Very high frequencies are represented by fh where the capacitative component is essentially short circuited so that the measured impedance is purely resistive (R∞). At low frequencies (fl) the capacitative component is effectively an open circuit: the reactance is equal to zero and the measured impedance is purely resistive. (Baumgartner, R.N., Chumlea, W.C. & Roche, A.F. (1988a). Bioelectric impedance phase angle and body composition. *American Journal of Clinical Nutrition*, **48**, 16–23. Copyright 1988. Redrawn with permission from *American Journal of Clinical Nutrition*.)

completely resistive at very high frequencies (Baumgartner *et al.*, 1990). In Fels data, the phase angle did not differ significantly between age and sex groups and it was not significantly correlated with fat-free mass in females, but there were low positive correlations in males (Baumgartner, Chumlea & Roche, 1988a).

Whole body impedance

The application of bioelectric impedance to the measurement of body composition is based on the better conduction of electricity by fat-free mass than by fat, due to the high water content of fat-free mass. If the geometry of the human body were simple, few anthropometric data would be needed in combination with impedance to allow accurate predictions of body composition. Since the human body geometry is complex, whether one considers the whole body or its major conducting portion (water or fat-free mass), several anthropometric variables must be measured to assist the prediction of fat-free mass from resistance (Guo *et al.*, 1987a).

Measures of resistance were highly reliable and were not significantly related to the time of measurement within the range from 9 a.m. to 5 p.m., timing within the menstrual cycle, the use of oral contraceptives, or the interval from the previous meal or drink. Resistance was not associated

with the level of habitual physical activity in adults, but women with a high level of physical activity had higher values for fat-free mass when estimated from resistance in combination with anthropometric values than when estimated from body density (Roche et al., 1986a[217]; Chumlea et al., 1987a[29]).

In work that was an important guide in the development of equations to predict fat-free mass from impedance and anthropometric values, it was shown that resistance was not correlated significantly with stature but had significant negative correlations with weight, circumferences, 'bone plus muscle' cross-sectional areas of the limbs, and skinfold thicknesses on the trunk (Baumgartner, Chumlea & Roche, 1987a). In combination, these anthropometric variables explained about 70% of the variance in resistance. Stature^2/resistance markedly improved the prediction of body composition in the absence of skinfold thicknesses but its contribution was markedly reduced when these thicknesses were included in the predictive model (Guo, 1986; Roche, Chumlea & Guo, 1987c[218]).

Segmental impedance

Segmental impedance, which refers to the measurement of the resistance and reactance of body segments, is potentially important in the estimation of regional body composition, and in the estimation of total body composition for those in whom it is difficult or impossible to obtain impedance or anthropometric data for the whole body (Baumgartner et al., 1990).

Resistance and reactance can be measured for large body segments, such as the trunk and limbs. Investigations of the possible usefulness of segmental impedance in the bedfast, in the prediction of total or segmental body composition, and in explaining underlying mechanisms are areas of active research in which Fels scientists are taking a leading part (Chumlea & Baumgartner, 1990[15]). These analyses showed that resistance and reactance were larger in women than men for the limbs, but the sex differences were not significant for the trunk. The same pattern of sex differences occurred in children except that the reactance of the trunk was larger in boys than girls (Baumgartner et al., 1988).

For a uniform conductor, resistance is proportional to its length and inversely proportional to its cross-sectional area, i.e., $R = pL/A$ where L is the length of the conductor and A is its cross-sectional area. The coefficient, p, in this equation (specific resistivity) depends on the composition of the conductor. The resistivities for major parts of the body were higher for males than females and increased with age to 18 years after which there was little change (Baumgartner, Chumlea & Roche, 1989a;

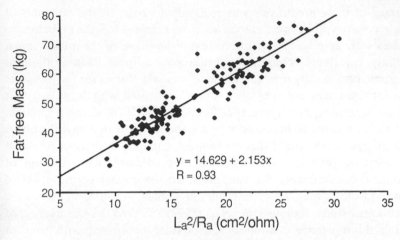

Fig. 7.4 The regression of fat-free mass (kg) on La^2/Ra for the sexes combined. La = arm length, Ra = resistance of the arm. (Baumgartner, R.N., Chumlea, W.C. & Roche, A.F. (1989a). Estimation of body composition from bioelectric impedance of body segments. *American Journal of Clinical Nutrition*, **50**, 221–6. Copyright 1989. Redrawn with permission from *American Journal of Clinical Nutrition*.)

Chumlea, Baumgartner & Roche, 1988a[18]). The resistivity of the trunk was about three times as great as that of the extremities in adults. This difference may be related to the direction of muscle fibers relative to the path of current flow. In general, the muscle fibers are parallel to the current in the extremities but not in the trunk, where resistivity may be influenced also by spaces that contain fluid or air.

Using this segmental approach, the sum of the predicted values for the fat-free mass in the arm, leg and trunk exceeded the whole body fat-free mass by a mean of 2 kg, but the values were highly correlated ($r = 0.9$; Chumlea, Baumgartner & Roche, 1986[16], 1987b[17]). These results would be assisted by better estimates of segmental volumes than those currently available from anthropometric data. Studies are planned in which segmental volumes will be measured from water displacement. Estimates of total body fat-free mass from the arm or trunk alone were reasonably accurate (Fig. 7.4). This major finding shows the possibility of using segmental impedance and anthropometry to predict body composition in those unable to stand (Baumgartner *et al.*, 1989b; Chumlea & Baumgartner, 1990[15]). This is important because few procedures are applicable to such individuals.

Chumlea *et al.* (1988a[18]) used the specific resistivity of muscle and estimates of muscle volume in the limbs to predict fat-free mass. The

accuracy of these predictions was reduced by errors in the estimates of muscle volumes which were calculated from segment lengths and circumferences with simplistic assumptions about the shape of the muscle mass. Similarly, calculated volumes of subcutaneous adipose tissue in the arm and trunk, obtained by subtracting the segmental volumes for fat-free mass from total segment volumes were highly correlated with total body fat (r = 0.8; Chumlea, Baumgartner & Roche, 1988b[19]). With this approach, total body fat could be predicted with a standard error of 3 kg if the phase angle of the trunk and either abdominal circumference (men) or calf circumference (women) were included as predictors. The inclusion of abdominal circumference for men indicated the greater contribution of trunk fat to total body fat in men than in women.

In another study, Baumgartner *et al.* (1990) analyzed the effectiveness of total body resistance combined with stature compared with that of segmental resistances, combined with segmental lengths, in the prediction of fat-free mass in children. In the boys, data from the arm were the most effective but in the girls they were less effective than data from the whole body.

Investigations of impedance continue. Validation studies are in progress related to the prediction of total body water and the potential of impedance measures at multiple frequencies to estimate intracellular and extracellular water.

Predictive equations

Fels scientists have been responsible for considerable progress in the development of predictive equations during the past 30 years. The most accurate methods for the measurement of body composition in living individuals require the use of sophisticated expensive equipment that is not portable and some require considerable cooperation from the subjects. These methods cannot be applied in field studies, or to large samples, or to individuals who are handicapped. Furthermore, methods that involve exposure to considerable amounts of radiation cannot be applied in serial studies due to the risks associated with cumulative effects. Therefore, simple procedures are needed that can provide data similar to what would be obtained by the complex laboratory methods. These simple procedures can be applied through predictive equations in which the independent variables are relatively easy to measure and the dependent variable is a body composition measure obtained with a complex laboratory method. The need for improved predictive equations was emphasized by Roche[203] (1986c) who noted that these equations should take account of variations in body water, skeletal mass, and, ideally, the sizes of some organs,

especially the brain during infancy, and the intra-abdominal mass in adulthood.

Some predictive equations are considered indirect because they predict variables that can be used to calculate body composition measures. For example, Roche and Mukherjee (1982[254]) developed equations to predict body density from which body composition values can be calculated. These authors noted marked correlations among the predictor variables (multicollinearity) which would lead to instability of the regression coefficients in the predictive equations and poor performance when the equations are applied to other groups ('population-specificity'). To overcome this problem, they applied ridge regression in which a small constant (shrinkage parameter) was added to the diagonals of the intercorrelation matrix to reduce the interrelationships among the predictor variables and thus stabilize the regression coefficients.

In another analysis, Mukherjee and Roche (1984) used the maximum R^2 method to develop equations that predict percent body fat. This may be the first time this procedure was applied to body composition data. The maximum R^2 method was preferred to stepwise regression partly because the latter implies an order of importance for the predictors. In the maximum R^2 method, all the predictors selected early are retained and the best possible additions are made to the set of predictors. In these data, multicollinearity was not a major problem. The final equations explained about 75% of the variance, with a standard error of 4.0% in each sex. The predictor variables were age, abdominal circumference, triceps, and midaxillary skinfolds in each sex, in addition to age^2 and stature in men and biacromial width and lateral calf skinfold thickness in women. In replication groups, the errors were about 30% larger than those for the validation groups. The general levels and trends of serial values were similar for predicted and observed values of percent body fat (Fig. 7.5).

Other equations were developed to predict fat-free mass at ages from 7 to 25 years (Roche *et al.*, 1989b[241]; Guo *et al.*, 1989a). The outcome variable was calculated from body density by applying age- and sex-specific values for the density of fat-free mass. Fat-free mass was chosen as the outcome variable because the potential predictors included resistance from bioelectric impedance. As stated earlier, resistance is an index of total body water and all the body water is in the fat-free mass.

The statistical procedures used by Roche and Guo had been applied rarely, if at all, in a biological context. Descriptions of these procedures are provided by Guo *et al.* (1989a); here, only brief mentions will be made. All possible subsets regression was used to obtain the best sets of predictor (independent) variables for the present data. The best size set for the data

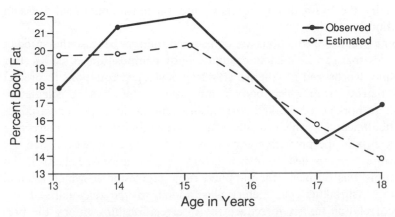

Fig. 7.5 A comparison between corresponding serial values for percent body fat estimated from an equation and calculated from body density ('observed') in one girl. (Mukherjee, D. & Roche, A.F. (1984). The estimation of percent body fat, body density and total body fat by maximum R^2 regression equations. *Human Biology*, **56**, 79–109, Redrawn with permission from *Human Biology*.)

was determined from R^2 and Cp values. Because the predictor variables might be highly intercorrelated, variance inflation factors were calculated. These variance inflation factors showed multicollinearity was a problem and, therefore, these correlations were reduced by ridge regression in combination with the PRESS procedure. Finally, to reduce the effects of individual values that have large effects on the regression coefficients, robust regression was used. As a result of these procedures in combination, it was considered that the best equation was selected and that its coefficients were modified to make it more likely to work well when applied to other groups.

The best equations for males and females had R^2 values of 0.98 and standard errors of 2.3 kg. The retained predictor variables were weight, lateral calf and midaxillary skinfold thicknesses, stature²/resistance, and arm muscle circumference for males. The last-mentioned measurement is calculated from arm circumference and triceps skinfold thickness. For females, the retained predictor variables were weight, lateral calf, triceps and subscapular skinfolds and stature²/resistance. Figure 7.6 shows the close correspondence between the predicted and observed values even at the extremes of the distribution.

Roche, Guo and Chumlea (1989d[240]) also developed equations that predict fat-free mass and percent body fat in adults. Resistance and reactance were 'forced in' as predictors and the selection of other predictor variables was determined by all possible subsets regression in combination

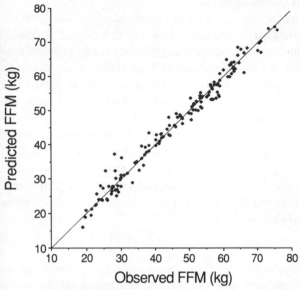

Fig. 7.6 The regression of values of fat-free mass (FFM) predicted from
bioelectric impedance and anthropometry on 'observed' values from body
density in males aged 7 to 25 years. (Guo, S., Roche, A.F. & Houtkooper, L.
(1989a). Fat-free mass in children and young adults from bioelectric impedance
and anthropometric variables. *American Journal of Clinical Nutrition*, **50**,
435–43. Copyright 1989. Redrawn with permission from *American Journal of
Clinical Nutrition*.)

with the R^2 and Mallow's Cp procedures. The standard errors were about
2.5 kg for fat-free mass and 3.8% for percent body fat in each sex, which
is extremely good since the errors in the outcome variables are probably
about 1.8 kg for fat-free mass and 2.5% for percent body fat. Internal
replication using a jackknife procedure yields closely similar results.

In another analysis, Roche and Guo (1990[238]) developed equations to
predict fat-free mass in adults using all possible subsets regression with
ordinary least squares to estimate the regression coefficients. The predictors
were stature^2/resistance, reactance, reactance/resistance in each sex, with
arm muscle area in men and calf muscle area in women.

The work done at Fels to develop equations that predict body
composition variables from simple measures is far from complete. The
data base enlarges week by week, new variables are being collected, and
new statistical procedures applied. The most important of the latter is total
body bone mineral which is now measured by dual photon absorptiometry
which involves a very small amount of radiation and is, therefore,
appropriate for serial studies.

Regional body composition

There is considerable interest in regional body composition which concerns the distribution of tissues within the body. Much of this interest is related to well-established relationships between large amounts of adipose tissue over the trunk (truncal or central obesity) and the risk of some diseases, particularly non-insulin-dependent diabetes mellitus. Truncal obesity is a characteristic of men rather than women and may explain, in part, the greater risk of men for non-insulin-dependent diabetes mellitus and heart disease. As stated by Benjamin Franklin with a characteristically direct choice of words: 'Men run to belly and women to bum.' Garn (1963b[64]) lamented that 'human biologists interested in taxonomically important characters ignored fat because it is so obviously linked with the nutritional state.' This characteristic of adipose tissue makes it important for reasons not associated with taxonomy.

Adipose tissue

As stated earlier in this chapter, local thicknesses of adipose tissue can be measured on radiographs, or by skinfold calipers, or ultrasound. From the early 1930s, following the lead of the Harvard Growth Study and the Child Research Council (Denver), radiographs were taken of Fels participants to allow the measurement of tissue thicknesses at standardized sites. The radiographic approach requires considerable attention to detail; even then, the error of measurement is about 4%. The recorded data should be corrected for radiographic enlargement, but commonly this was not done. While the radiographic method has many advantages, the associated irradiation is a serious problem, although the skin dose can be very low and the gonadal dose can be near zero (Garn, 1961b[58]).

Garn (1957d[51]) reported that in young men, the correlations between radiographic adipose tissue thicknesses at various sites were generally highest for the deltoid, tenth rib, iliac crest and trochanteric sites. Due to these findings, and because the thicknesses at these sites were most highly correlated with weight, Garn selected them as the most useful for the assessment of nutritional status (Garn, 1954a[42], 1957a[48], 1957b[49], 1957c[50], 1957d[51]; Garn & Clark, 1955[72]). Later, Roche (1979b[188], 1979c[189]; Roche *et al.*, 1985[210]), mainly on the basis of practicality and relationships to percent body fat reported by Siervogel *et al.* (1982b), recommended the triceps, anterior chest and subscapular skinfold sites for children. Roche further recommended that measurements at the anterior chest and triceps skinfold sites be included for the assessment of nutritional status in young men and women, that the midaxillary and paraumbilical sites be included for men, and the subscapular and supra-iliac sites for women. For older

men, he recommended the subscapular site and for older women the anterior chest, paraumbilical, subscapular and chin sites.

Age changes in adipose tissue thicknesses

A large effort has been expended at Fels to describe changes with age in thicknesses of adipose tissue. It was shown that during pubescence, adipose tissue thicknesses decreased in males but increased in females. These thicknesses tended to be larger and more variable for girls than for boys and they were about twice as large in women as in men (Reynolds, 1948, 1951; Reynolds & Grote, 1948). Reynolds (1946a) reported that rapidly maturing girls had larger calf adipose tissue thicknesses and larger relative gains than slowly maturing girls but less variability. Rapidly and slowly maturing boys differed in a similar way but to a lesser extent. Garn and Haskell (1959b[87]) showed that adipose tissue thicknesses over the tenth rib increased from 6 to 18 years in an almost linear fashion in girls but there were only small changes in boys during the same period.

Garn (1954a[42], 1957b[49]) reported that adipose tissue thicknesses tended to be greater in women than men except at the iliac crest and deltoid sites where the thicknesses for men were slightly greater. Additionally, Garn (1960c[56]) reported large increases from 20 to 40 years in males at the iliac crest and in females at the trochanteric site.

Reynolds (1949b) constructed a ratio of adipose tissue/total bone thicknesses for the calf which he proposed as a sex-differentiating character. This index had an error of about 30% in sex determination at 7 to 13 years, but the error was about 6% during adolescence and was 4% for men and 16% for women. Adipose tissue thicknesses relative to the total width of the calf were also greater in females than males at all ages (Reynolds, 1948; Reynolds & Grote, 1948).

In an extraordinarily complete monograph, Reynolds (1951) reported radiographic thicknesses of adipose tissue at various sites from 6 to 17 years and he analyzed data for infants and adults including some unusual sites. On the medial aspect of the thigh, measurements were made at the level of the crotch, and where the adipose tissue thickness is maximal just proximal to the knee. Both these adipose tissue thicknesses were larger in girls than boys. Thicknesses on the lateral aspect of the thigh at the level of the crotch were considerably larger in girls than boys from 6 to 10 years although the increases were larger in boys than girls during this age range. Reynolds also reported that adipose tissue at the base of the neck tended to be larger in girls than in boys but changed only slightly from 6 to 10 years.

The median thicknesses decreased before pubescence in boys, especially

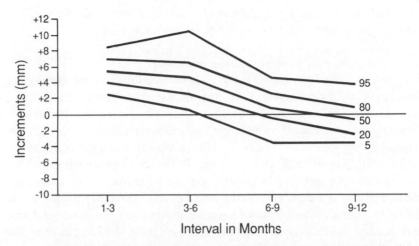

Fig. 7.7 Percentiles for increments in the sums of medial and lateral calf adipose tissue thicknesses in girls during infancy. (Garn, S.M., Greaney, G. & Young, R. (1956d[84]). Fat thickness and growth progress during infancy. *Human Biology*, **28**, 232–50. Redrawn with permission from *Human Biology*.)

at the waist; this decrease ceased earlier at the tenth rib site than at other sites. When expressed relative to the sum of the adipose tissue thicknesses for the six sites measured, the relative thickness of the calf adipose tissue decreased linearly with age in each sex from 8 to 16 years (Reynolds, 1951). In girls, there was a linear relative increase at the trochanteric site to 18 years, but the increase in boys stopped at 12.5 years and was followed by a decrease. The relative thickness at the tenth rib site increased linearly but at a slow rate in each sex, while that at the forearm site decreased linearly in each sex. In both boys and girls, there were slow linear decreases in relative adipose tissue thickness at the deltoid site after 8 years. At the waist site, the relative thickness increased linearly in boys to 18 years but the increase stopped at 13 years in girls (Reynolds, 1951). This was in agreement with other data showing the early development of truncal fat distribution in males (Roche & Baumgartner, 1988[211]).

There were only small sex differences in the medians but wider distributions in females than males for the sum of medial and lateral calf adipose tissue thicknesses in infants (Garn, 1956b[47]). In each sex, the sums increased rapidly to 6 months, then slowly to 9 months and decreased slightly from then to 12 months. While the group data indicated only slight changes after 6 months, there were large increments in many infants but they differed in direction. This phenomenon is illustrated in Fig. 7.7, which shows negative increments were increasingly common after 3 months.

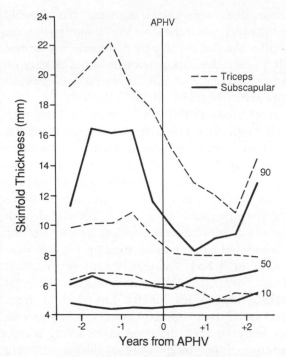

Fig. 7.8 Percentiles for triceps and subscapular adipose tissue thicknesses (mm) in relation to age at peak height velocity (APHV) in boys. (Cronk, C.E., Mukherjee, D. & Roche, A.F. (1983b). Changes in triceps and subscapular skinfold thickness during adolescence. *Human Biology*, **55**, 707–21, Redrawn with permission from *Human Biology*.)

Cronk, Mukherjee and Roche (1983b) calculated selected percentiles for skinfold thicknesses grouped at ages relative to the timing of peak height velocity (age at peak height velocity, APHV). In boys, triceps skinfold thicknesses increased prior to PHV but decreased near the time of PHV. The corresponding values for girls increased prior to PHV, declined near this event except at the 90th percentile level, and increased later. The percentiles for subscapular skinfold thicknesses in boys and girls showed only slight changes at about the time of PHV, except at the 90th percentile level where there was an increase followed by a decrease (Fig. 7.8).

Adipose tissue areas

The calculation of adipose tissue areas in cross-sections of the limbs has received the attention of Fels scientists for many years. Garn (1961b[59]) and Roche (1979b[188], 1979c[189], 1986c[203]) recognized the limited validity of cross-sectional tissue areas but accepted their conceptual appeal and

potential usefulness. These areas were calculated from the skinfold thickness at a site and the circumference at the same level assuming that the total cross-section was circular and that the adipose tissue within it formed an annulus of fixed width. In fact, the adipose tissue thicknesses vary on different aspects of a limb at the same level and the correlations between these thicknesses were only about 0.6 (Garn, 1954a[42], 1957c[50]).

These adipose tissue areas could distinguish between children with equivalent circumferences but different skinfold thicknesses and, therefore, different areas of adipose tissue. Indeed, calf adipose tissue area was more highly correlated with weight than was calf adipose tissue thickness; the correlations were even higher between weight and estimates of calf adipose tissue volume (Garn, 1961b[58]). Garn also showed that adipose tissue thicknesses and areas of the arm were more highly correlated with measures of total body fatness than were corresponding measures of the calf. Himes *et al.* (1980) found that adipose tissue areas for the arm were more highly correlated with total body fat than the triceps skinfold thicknesses but the correlations of areas and thicknesses with total body fat were about equal. Adipose tissue areas for the arm derived from circumferences and biceps skinfold thicknesses had lower correlations with total body fat or percent body fat than those calculated using triceps skinfold thicknesses. Correspondingly, biceps skinfold thicknesses were less closely correlated with total body fat or percent body fat than were triceps skinfold thicknesses.

Distribution of adipose tissue
The potential importance of the distribution of adipose tissue was recognized early at Fels. Garn and Harper (1955[85]) wrote: 'It is not unlikely that the location of the fat, as well as the gross amount, may elucidate the differential mortality rates of different weight groups.' The topic of adipose tissue distribution was, however, bedeviled by uncertainty about definitions and methods of measurement (Roche, 1986c[203]) despite the significant methodological contributions made by Garn (1955b[45]) and by Baumgartner *et al.* (1986b). The usual approach was to contrast measures of adipose tissue on the upper and lower parts of the body or measures on the trunk with those on the extremities (Reynolds, 1951; Garn, 1954a[42], 1955b[45]). The measures of adipose tissue may be radiographic thicknesses, skinfold thicknesses, or circumferences. Indices based on circumferences, such as the waist–hip ratio, are not specific to subcutaneous adipose tissue because they are affected by muscle, bone and deep adipose tissue. Nevertheless, they are commonly regarded as indices of adipose tissue distribution. Logarithms may be utilized and measure-

ments may be combined as an index or one value may be regressed against another. When there are measurements at three or more sites, principal components analysis has been used to define indices of adipose tissue distribution.

Garn (1955a[44], 1955b[45]) converted adipose tissue thicknesses at nine sites to standard scores and used these to describe profiles for adults. The standard deviations of the standard scores for individuals were regarded as measures of variability. In men, variability was not related to age or the mean adipose tissue thickness but it increased when the adipose tissue was relatively thick at the trochanteric site. This could indicate that the thickness at this site was relatively independent of the thicknesses at the other sites, but the trochanteric site had the highest mean correlation coefficient (communality index) for men and the iliac crest had the highest for women.

Garn (1954a[42]) reported an association between the distribution of adipose tissue and body weight. In men weighing less than 74 kg, the largest mean adipose tissue thickness was at the deltoid site, but in heavier men the trochanteric thickness was the largest. Later, Garn (1955b[45]), in agreement with Reynolds (1951), considered that the pattern of adipose tissue distribution was independent of body fatness.

A large literature relates the ratio between hip and waist circumferences to the risk and presence of some chronic metabolic diseases. These interesting publications have led to conjecture about which of the tissues included in these circumferences are responsible for the relationships that have been noted. There is little relevant information but, Reynolds (1951) reported correlations of about 0.7 between radiographic trochanteric adipose tissue thickness and bi-trochanteric width measured without pressure. The corresponding correlations between this adipose tissue thickness and bi-iliac width, which is essentially a skeletal measure recorded with pressure, was only 0.4. Furthermore, Reynolds (1951) reported only moderate correlations ($r = 0.5$) between pairs of adipose tissue thicknesses and circumferences at the same level for the calf, upper arm, and waist.

These findings indicate that a circumference measurement is influenced by tissues (adipose tissue, muscle, and bone) that are not highly correlated. Therefore, ratios between circumferences may lack specificity regarding adipose tissue distribution. This has been demonstrated using hospital records from computed tomography (Baumgartner *et al.*, 1988b). It was shown that the ratio of abdominal to hip cross-sectional areas was correlated strongly with intra-abdominal fat but also with muscle and bone areas. After adjustments for body fatness, the ratio between waist and hip circumferences was only 0.3 to 0.4.

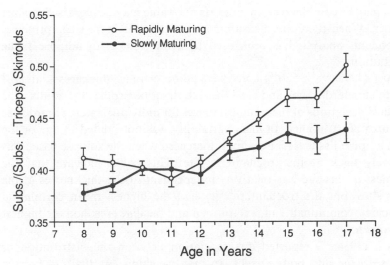

Fig. 7.9 Changes with chronological age in the ratio (subscapular/ subscapular + triceps skinfold thickness) for rapidly and slowly maturing boys. (Xi, H., Roche, A.F. & Baumgartner, R.N. (1989a). Association of adipose tissue distribution with relative skeletal age in boys: The Fels Longitudinal Study. *American Journal of Human Biology*, 1, 589–96, Copyright 1989. Redrawn with permission from Wiley – Liss.)

Investigating a novel aspect of body composition, Garn *et al.* (1954[163]) showed that baldness was not associated with scalp thickness. Scalp thicknesses, which are largely determined by adipose tissue, measured on lateral radiographs, increased rapidly from 4 to 15 years in each sex and then increased slowly to 30 years.

Patterns of change in adipose tissue distribution

The distribution of adipose tissue in childhood is of interest because of the possible tracking of patterns from childhood to adulthood. Garn documented the concurrent gain of adipose tissue thickness at some sites and loss at others for adults (Garn & Young, 1956[172]; Garn, 1956a[46]) but little information is available about the tracking of adipose tissue distribution because few serial studies have included measurements of adipose tissue thickness at multiple sites. Some tentative conclusions are possible from Fels reports.

Reynolds (1951) reported serial data for a few individuals. In a boy, the changes at the forearm site differed from those at the other sites but there was considerable parallelism (tracking) between sites in the girl whose data were displayed in his monograph. Correlations between ratios of skinfold thicknesses across 5-year intervals, beginning at 7 to 13 years, were about

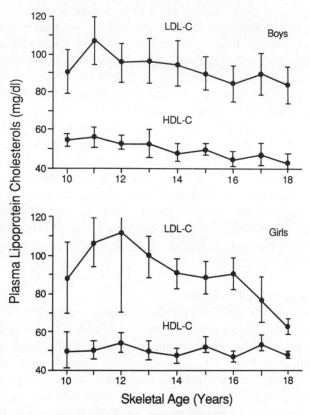

Fig. 7.10 Means for low-density lipoprotein-cholesterol (LDL-C) and high-density lipoprotein-cholesterol (HDL-C) plotted in relation to skeletal age. (Siervogel, R.M., Baumgartner, R.N., Roche, A.F., Chumlea, W.C. & Glueck, C.J. (1989b). Maturity and its relationship to plasma lipid and lipoprotein levels in adolescents. The Fels Longitudinal Study. *American Journal of Human Biology*, **1**, 217–26. Copyright 1989. Redrawn with permission from Wiley–Liss.)

0.7. The correlations tended to be higher for boys than girls and increased significantly with age in the boys but not the girls (Roche & Baumgartner, 1988[211]). From 11 to 18 years, particularly in boys, changes in indices of adipose tissue distribution reflected an increasing relative concentration of adipose tissue on the trunk (Baumgartner *et al.*, 1986b).

Xi, Roche and Baumgartner (1989a) analyzed the relationship between the distribution of adipose tissue and relative skeletal age (skeletal age less chronological age) in boys. This was prompted by the possibility that pubescent changes in adipose tissue distribution might occur earlier in rapidly maturing boys than in slowly maturing boys. These workers

showed that after 13 years, rapid maturation was associated with a more truncal pattern (Fig. 7.9) but the rate of maturation from 7 to 14 years did not predict the adipose tissue distribution at 17 years, when adjustments were made for baseline values. Relationships between skeletal age and plasma lipids have been analyzed (Siervogel *et al.*, 1986b; Fig. 7.10). These analyses showed that low-density lipoprotein-cholesterol (LDL-C) changed little with increasing skeletal age in boys but decreased markedly in girls. The values for high-density lipoprotein-cholesterol (HDL-C) changed only slightly with increasing skeletal age in each sex.

Despite more than 50 years of effort, much remains unknown in relation to regional body composition. To some extent, this is due to the limitations of the methods. Particular areas of interest include tracking, the measurement of superficial adipose tissue with B-mode ultrasound and of deep adipose tissue with magnetic resonance imaging or ultrasound, and the measurement of segmental body composition by dual photon absorptiometry and bioelectric impedance.

Tracking of fat-related variables

In addition to studying the differences between means or medians of adipose tissue thicknesses at successive ages, there is considerable interest in 'tracking.' Tracking refers to the maintenance of rank order within a group of individuals over time. This can lead to the identification of childhood antecedents of adult obesity and thus assist the planning of effective preventive strategies. The simplest measure of tracking is an age-to-age correlation. Tracking can be judged also from the degree to which well-fitted curves for individuals are parallel within a specific time period. Some consider 'tracking' can also refer to 'canalization' which is the tendency of a trait to proceed to a predictable endpoint. Canalization is best judged by fitting a mathematical model to the serial data for an individual; the extent of canalization can be judged by the goodness of fit of the model.

In an early Fels study, it was shown that adipose tissue thickness at the tenth rib site at birth was correlated (r = 0.5) with calf adipose tissue thickness at 1 month (Garn, 1958a[52]). There was also a low negative correlation (r = −0.3) between the adipose tissue thickness at the tenth rib site and positive correlations in weight gain from birth to 3 months and both weight (r = 0.3) and recumbent length (r = 0.2) at 3 months. These studies did not directly concern tracking since the variables were different at the two ages but they demonstrated slight continuity of growth.

Garn (1956a[46], 1962b[61]) separated infants into quartiles for total calf adipose tissue thickness at 1 month. The initially 'fat' infants were larger

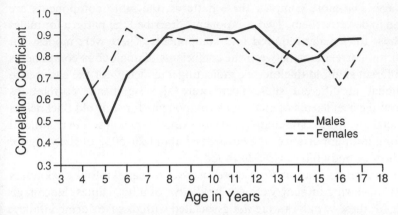

Fig. 7.11 Age-to-age correlations across 1-year intervals for triceps skinfold thicknesses. (Roche, A.F., Siervogel, R.M., Chumlea, W.C., Reed, R.B., Valadian, I., Eichorn, D. & McCammon, R.W. (1982a). Serial changes in subcutaneous fat thicknesses of children and adults. *Monographs in Paediatrics*, **17**. Karger, Basel[264]. Redrawn with permission from Karger, A.G., Basel.)

and had larger calf muscle thicknesses than those in the lowest quartile at 1 month but these differences were not significant at 6 months. Reynolds (1951) reported moderate correlations (r = 0.7) between adipose tissue thicknesses 5 years apart for various sites and for girls and boys, except from 8 to 13 years when the correlations for boys tended to be lower. Additionally, Reynolds reported close relationships between the sums of adipose tissue thicknesses at 8 years and at menarche in girls and for values at corresponding ages in boys. In an earlier study, Reynolds (1944) reported that children typically retained their patterns of tissue components in the calf from 7 to 10 years.

Age-to-age correlations for skinfold thicknesses and W/S^2 increased markedly to 6 years for most sites on the arm and trunk but not on the calf (Roche *et al.*, 1982a[264]; Roche, Rogers & Cronk, 1984[262]). Data for the triceps skinfold thickness are shown in Fig. 7.11. These age-to-age correlations decreased during pubescence for only a few sites. Correlations between values at younger ages and those at 16 years or in adulthood increased rapidly to 6 years for most sites. The levels of the correlations were similar in both sexes and were generally similar on the trunk and the extremities. The correlations for radiographic data were consistently higher than those for skinfold thicknesses. This may have reflected the smaller errors of measurement.

Cronk *et al.* (1983a) analyzed serial skinfold thicknesses using longitudinal principal components to summarize significant patterns of change

with age. The more complex these patterns, the more components are needed to describe them. Two components described the pattern for males but those for females required four components. There were modest but significant correlations between the coefficients of analogous components for different skinfold thicknesses, indicating a tendency for the changes to be similar at different sites. There were also significant correlations between the coefficients of analogous components for skinfold thicknesses and weight/stature^2. The components for skinfold thicknesses in childhood had long-term importance; they explained about 20–50% of the variance in indices of body fatness in adulthood.

The general conclusion from these analyses is that skinfold thicknesses and W/S^2 during infancy were not predictive of adult values. Since high values for these variables were not associated with disease during infancy, obesity during the first few years after birth is not a medical problem (Roche, 1979b[188]). The proverbial wisdom of Sei Shonagon can be accepted: 'Small children and babies ought to be plump.' Nevertheless, there was significant tracking to adult values after 4 years, despite which, childhood skinfold thicknesses were not closely related to the changes in the same variables from 18 to 30 years.

Muscle

Muscle thicknesses in the calf, measured on radiographs, changed similarly with age in each sex from birth until pubescence, when there were much more rapid increases in males than in females, particularly in rapidly maturing children (Reynolds, 1944, 1948; Reynolds & Grote, 1948). Muscle thicknesses continued to be greater in males than females throughout adulthood (Garn & Saalberg, 1953[159]). Cross-sectional areas of adipose tissue and 'muscle plus bone' in the arm and calf decreased with aging, which indicated decreases in the fat-free mass and fat of the extremities (Chumlea, Roche & Mukherjee, 1986[31]). At ages from birth to 6 years, there were only low correlations between the thicknesses of muscle and adipose tissue in the calf and both of these thicknesses had only low correlations with total bone width (Reynolds, 1944, 1951; Reynolds & Asakawa, 1950; Garn, 1956a[46]).

Reynolds and Asakawa (1950) found associations between unusual tissue distributions in the calf and unusual body shapes in adults. Using terms derived from somatotype studies, they defined endomorphs as individuals with rounded contours and large circumferences, especially of the abdomen, while mesomorphs were defined as individuals with a large frame and well-developed muscles. Ectomorphs were recognized by their slender build. In the Fels group, endomorphs had wider calves with

relatively more adipose tissue, while mesomorphs had calves of inter-mediate width with large thicknesses of bone and muscle. Each of these tissues had low values in ectomorphs. Some behavioral associations were reported by Garn (1962b[61], 1963b[64]) who found that muscle thickness in the calf at 6 months was predictive of the age at which an infant will first stand, crawl and walk.

Adipocytes

The cells in adipose tissue that store fat, mostly triglycerides, are known as adipocytes. There is considerable interest in these cells because the amount of body fat must approximate the product of the number of adipocytes and the mean weight of these cells. In addition, there are small amounts of fat in body fluids, cell membranes and neurological cells. When simple procedures became available to measure the weight of adipocytes using osmium tetroxide, there was a marked increase in research relating to them. Some of this research was done at Fels although estimates of the weight and number of adipocytes are limited in accuracy (Roche, 1979b[188]). Adipocyte weight can be measured reliably but in small samples that are not representative (Chumlea et al., 1981a[24], 1981b[33]). The small samples lead to errors when adipocyte number is calculated by dividing total body fat by mean adipocyte weight. This subject is further confounded by the presence of cells (pre-adipocytes) that lack fat and, therefore, are not measured, but can mature into adipocytes that store fat.

In critical reviews, Roche (1979b[188], 1981b[194]) evaluated the hypothesis that obesity during infancy is associated with an increased number of adipocytes that persists throughout life and provides a mechanism for the development and persistence of obesity. The near zero correlations between measures of body fatness in infancy and adulthood are not in agreement with the view that adult obesity is determined by the number of adipocytes present in infancy (Roche et al., 1982a[264]). In addition, the estimated number of adipocytes can change in adults, and rapid increases in total body fat during infancy may reflect increases in adipocyte weight, number, or both.

Chumlea and his colleagues (1981a[24]) reported that, from 10 to 18 years, girls had larger gluteal adipocytes than boys and larger estimates of total adipocyte number. During this age range, adipocyte weight decreased significantly with age in boys ($r = -0.4$) but not girls and adiopocyte number increased in both sexes. These findings were not in agreement with the hypothesis that adipocyte number is fixed early in life. But during childhood, age-to-age correlations across annual intervals were significant for adipocyte number but not for adipocyte weight. Adipocyte number

increased slightly with age in men and women and, as expected, gluteal adipocytes were heavier in women than in men (Chumlea & Knittle, 1980[23]; Chumlea *et al.*, 1981b[33]).

These findings for gluteal adipocytes can be generalized to some extent because there are high correlations among adipocyte weights at various sites in children. In addition, gluteal adipocyte weight is more highly correlated with total body fat than is adipocyte weight at other sites. Nevertheless, the use of a single site and the inability of the osmium tetroxide method to detect adipocytes containing little or no fat lead to the need for caution in any generalization from these results (Chumlea *et al.*, 1982b[38]).

After adjusting for age, there was a small but significant ($r = 0.3$) correlation between blood pressure and adipocyte number in each sex, but the correlations with adipocyte weight were not significant. Furthermore, total body fat was not correlated with gluteal adipocyte weight, so differences in total body fat appeared to be associated with gluteal adipocyte number (Siervogel *et al.*, 1982c).

Further analyses of data for adipocyte weight are in progress that relate to values at an age, patterns of change, tracking, and associations with risk factors.

Assessment of nutritional status

Nutritional status can be assessed for an individual or a group and it has both static and dynamic connotations. Nutritional status can be determined completely only by measuring the circulating levels and body stores of all nutrients. A complete set of direct measurements would require many organ biopsies and fluid samples and a multitude of chemical analyses. Such an assessment is clearly impractical and its effectiveness would be limited by the inaccuracy of many laboratory methods and the rapid changes that occur in some of these measures. Work at Fels concerning the assessment of nutritional status has been limited to body stores of fat and bone mineral and to the measurement of bone, adipose and muscle tissues, and fat-free mass. The scope of this work has been wide in that procedures have been developed to predict and interpret these values in field studies of large samples and reference data have been provided (Malina & Roche, 1983). This account relates to the application of indices of nutritional status and of equations that predict body composition variables from data that are easy to obtain without invasive procedures.

The need for such methods was stressed in a Wenner–Gren Conference on the Measurement of Nutritional Status (Roche & Falkner, 1974[231]). It

was recommended that field measures should be simple, cheap, and applicable by observers who need only a moderate amount of training. The instruments should be light and the measurements must be acceptable to the population to be studied. Anthropometric variables are almost always included in a list of measurements for the assessment of nutritional status in a field study. These measurements, in common with all others, must be made accurately and be capable of interpretation. For example, a deficit in head circumference at 2 years may indicate malnutrition during infancy; such inferences regarding the timing of malnutrition may be improved by the concurrent evaluation of weight, recumbent length, and weight-for-length. These inferences should be made cautiously, especially for individuals, since genetic influences may be involved.

The findings of Roche *et al.* (1981b[265]) are relevant if the assessment of nutritional status is oriented towards body fat. These authors considered the grading of body fatness when only limited anthropometric data were available. This work was undertaken because the associations between common measurements and body fatness were not well-established and, therefore, the interpretation of these measurements was uncertain. Using data from 6 to 49 years, they compared the relationships between several measured and derived variables and percent body fat and total body fat. They concluded that the triceps skinfold was the best single index of percent body fat in children and women, and the best index for men was W/S^2. These authors suggested that these measures be compared with national reference data in screening for body fatness. To facilitate this, a nomogram was published that provided W/S^2 from the measured variables.

In the assessment of nutritional status, observed anthropometric values may be adjusted, such as the adjustment of weight for stature, or they can be used in predictive equations to estimate body composition variables (Roche, Baumgartner & Guo, 1987a[212]; Roche & Chumlea, in press[216]). The latter procedure should be applied only after the equations have been satisfactorily replicated on a subset of the study population or one closely similar to it. Additionally, as explained in Chapter 2, it may be desirable to transform observed variables to remove skewness or to calculate areas, ratios or other indices from them.

Roche (1974d[181], 1982[195], 1989b[208]) and Roche *et al.* (1985[210]) warned against the ready acceptance of the sensitivity of W/S^2 because its relationship with body fatness could differ markedly among populations. Indices of body fatness derived from weight and stature need not be independent of stature as has been claimed by some. Indeed, this characteristic would make an index undesirable during childhood, when

fatness is related to stature (Himes & Roche, 1986). The best basis on which to judge such indices is the proportion of the variance in body fatness for which they account.

Attention was directed to the importance of the ratio head circumference/chest circumference which changes with age due to the different rates of growth of these body parts. This ratio is a guide to long-term malnutrition during the pre-school years. Additionally, weight-for-length, weight-for-stature and arm circumference are useful in rapid screening, particularly in developing countries. Due to their essential independence from age in early childhood, age need not be known to interpret the values. Robinow (1968) suggested that low values for arm circumference were due to decreases in 'muscle plus bone' rather than adipose tissue and, therefore, they are guides to protein reserves.

Reynolds and Asakawa (1948) presented a tentative set of screening procedures relating to body fatness using bivariate relationships between weight, stature, and calf adipose tissue thickness. This interesting approach was not developed to the stage at which it could be applied. Later, Garn (1962c[62]) suggested the use of weight adjusted for radiographic chest breadth because weight was highly correlated with chest breadth.

Following Roche (1984c[198]), Chumlea (1985b[6], 1985c[7], 1986a[8], 1986b[9]) pointed out that total body fat and percent body fat differ in their social acceptability during childhood and in their associations with disease in adulthood. Consequently, the assessment of nutritional status should take into account both total body fat and percent body fat.

These authors reviewed the anthropometric approach to the assessment of nutritional status, including total body fat and percent body fat, in children with developmental disabilities. Excessive curvature of the vertebral column may interfere with the measurement of stature and complicate its interpretation. In such children, arm span can replace stature, with an adjustment for the expected differences between these measures, but in many disabled children arm span cannot be measured accurately. Some disabled children must be measured in unusual body positions and there is a lack of disease-specific reference data with which values can be compared. This lack is difficult to overcome because data are needed from large groups of children with the same disease and the same treatment. In those unable to stand, whether children or adults, a chair scale can be used to record weight, and recumbent anthropometric techniques can be applied (Chumlea, Roche & Mukherjee, 1984b[30], 1986[31]; Chumlea *et al.*, 1985b[36]; Chumlea, 1988[10]; Chumlea & Roche, 1984[26], 1988[28]). These techniques are preferable to a system of measurements made when such individuals are sitting in wheelchairs because the latter

measurements have larger errors and many measurements must be omitted. As for anthropometry in other children, but even more so, measurements of disabled children should be repeated until the differences between pairs of values are less than set tolerances. This is particularly important in such children because the differences between paired measurements tend to be large.

Nutritional assessment in the elderly

Much innovative work done at Fels on the nutritional assessment of the elderly has been summarized previously (Chumlea *et al.* 1985b[36]; 1990[41]; Chumlea & Roche, 1988[28]; Chumlea, Roche & Steinbaugh, 1989b[35]; Chumlea, 1991a[11], 1991b[12]). Although the data were not obtained from Fels participants, the concepts and procedures that were developed are linked closely to those used to study Fels participants. Chumlea and Baumgartner (1989[14]) reviewed published anthropometric and body composition data for the elderly and concluded that many standing and recumbent measurements could be combined in a study because the differences between them were not significant. The interobserver errors for recumbent anthropometric data in the elderly were larger than those for corresponding standing measurements of younger individuals so that recumbent measurements should be repeated to obtain equivalent levels of reliablility (Chumlea, Roche & Rogers, 1984c[32]; Chumlea, Roche & Steinbaugh, 1985a[34]). As stated by Chumlea and Baumgartner, relative weight and weight/stature^2 should be based on the measured present stature of an elderly person, not the stature assumed for young adulthood. To assist the assessment of nutritional status in elderly individuals who are unable to stand, Chumlea and his colleagues presented equations to predict stature from knee height, and to predict weight from a combination of anthropometric values (Chumlea *et al.*, 1985a[34]; Chumlea *et al.*, 1985c[40], 1986[31], 1988c[22]; Chumlea, 1991a[11]). Furthermore, they presented ways in which segmental impedance could be developed for this purpose (Chumlea, 1991b[12]; Chumlea, Baumgartner & Vellas, 1991[20]).

The relationships of total body fat to skinfold thicknesses seemed to be less close in the elderly than in young adults, but the relationships between abdominal circumference and total body fat appeared to be closer (Roche *et al.*, 1981b[265]). These differences between younger and older adults are important in the interpretation of anthropometric values. The increased difficulty of measuring skinfolds in the elderly is due to poor separation between the subcutaneous adipose tissue and the deep fascia and the greater compressibility of skinfolds which may underlie these differences. Skinfold thicknesses or W/S^2 used alone are not effective predictors of

body fat in all age groups. Furthermore, W/S^2 may lack specificity because it is related to both body fat and fat-free mass in some age groups, for example adolescent boys.

Much work is needed to improve the assessment of nutritional status. Too often choices of procedures are made from those existing – some new procedures should be developed for use in surveys. These procedures include B-mode ultrasound and segmental impedance. Emphasis should be on validation, which has been difficult in the disabled because they cannot be weighed underwater. Data from dual photon x-ray absorptiometry should prove valuable in this regard.

Influences on body composition
Familial and genetic influences
Work done at Fels relating to familial influences on body composition has been reviewed in detail by Siervogel (1983). Himes, Roche and Garn participated in a meeting of The Committee on Nutrition of the Mother and Pre-school Child in 1978 at which Garn, drawing on his Fels experience, provided heritability estimates for fatness based on intrafamilial correlations. Typically, these estimates neglect environmental–genetic interactions and describe only the proportion of the variance explained by the additive component of genetic variance. Garn found low but significant correlations between mothers and infants at birth for weight and weight-for-stature and for estimates of fat-free mass from chest breadth. Interestingly, these findings were partly dependent on the length of gestation, which was slightly correlated with maternal fat-free mass ($r = 0.2$), but the fat-free mass of the father was not correlated with that of the infant at birth (Garn, 1961c[59], 1962b[61]; Garn et al., 1960a[74]; Kagan & Garn, 1963). Since, in these studies, fat-free mass was estimated from chest breadth, the correlations reflected associations for chest breadth; those for fat-free mass were inferential. There were also significant sibling and spouse correlations for chest breadth (Garn, 1962a[60]).

Reynolds (1951) and Garn (1962a[60]) did not find a tendency for higher correlations between adipose tissue thicknesses at various sites in pairs of related individuals than in unrelated individuals, indicating an absence of significant genetic control over patterns of adipose distribution. Nevertheless, Reynolds (1951) showed that differences between sites in standard scores for adipose tissue thicknesses were progressively smaller as pairs of relatives sharing larger percentages of genes were considered. This topic requires more attention.

Siervogel et al. (1984) described serial values of W/S^2 and concluded that most of the family resemblance was due to shared environments

because the parent–offspring correlations were near zero but the sibling correlations were significant for W/S^2 at birth and 8 years, and for ages at minimum and maximum velocity of W/S^2. Quite correctly, however, Garn (1962a[60]) pointed out that familial analyses of W/S^2 are difficult to interpret because weight and stature may be independently subject to many genetic and environmental influences.

Byard and colleagues (1983, 1989) reported familial correlations that suggested sex linkage for W/S^2 and calf circumference but not for stature. Byard *et al.* (1988) reported age trends in the transmission of W/S^2 based on correlations calculated by maximum likelihood methods at annual intervals from 1 to 18 years for parent–offspring, sibling, and cousin pairs. A model in which the transmission is greater to the opposite sex than to the same sex gave the best fit before puberty. This pattern, which is consistent with X-linked inheritance, was supported by other findings that suggested the presence of a gene for greater values of W/S^2 that had a frequency of about 3%. This gene would affect the phenotype in 3% of boys but only 0.9% of girls. Correspondingly, there was a bimodal distribution of W/S^2 in boys but not girls before puberty. After puberty, an autosomic polygenic model fitted well regardless of sex, with hereditability estimates of about 40% at ages older than 10 years.

Maternal influences

Maternal weight at 3 months of gestation and the maternal weight gain during pregnancy were not significantly correlated with the thickness of subcutaneous adipose tissue in the infant, but there were low significant correlations between these maternal influences and birth weight (Garn, 1958a[52]).

Dietary influences

Mathematical models were used to describe the patterns of change in weight during infancy. The parameters of these models did not differ significantly between breast-fed and formula-fed infants (Himes, 1978b). This work was done in combination with a study of milk intakes and feeding patterns of breast-fed infants (Pao, Himes & Roche, 1980). It should be noted also that Garn (1967[69]) found that the caloric intakes of adults in the Fels study were about 15% lower than the US Recommended Daily Allowances. This is not surprising since these allowances are set at levels considered adequate for a large majority of the population. The lower intakes at Fels were not due to differences between the mean weight of the Fels sample and the reference weights used to develop the allowances. In

Garn's data, the caloric intakes decreased by about 5% per decade of age and were lower in women with an artificial menopause than in age-matched pre-menopausal or post-menopausal women. His data indicated that occupation was a more important influence on caloric intake than either stature or weight.

Basal metabolic rate

It was shown that basal metabolic rate was slightly higher in males than females to 7 years, but the differences were large enough at older ages to require sex-specific reference data (Garn, Clark & Harper, 1953[73]). These sex differences were reduced after the data had been corrected for body size or surface area but differences remained that were probably due to variations in body composition. Fat-free mass, indexed by the thickness of muscle in the calf, was a major determinant of basal metabolic rate ($r = 0.8$). Nevertheless, basal metabolic rate per kilogram of body weight was higher in boys than girls matched for calf muscle thickness. These sex differences were associated with differences in the urinary excretion of ketosteroids (Clark & Garn, 1954). Basal metabolic rate was also related to skin temperature which can be measured accurately by a thermistor placed in close contact with the skin (Clark & Trolander, 1954; Garn, 1954b[43]). Furthermore, it was shown that gains in basal metabolic rates during pregnancy were related to pre-pregnancy rates; the gains were larger in those who had low pre-pregnancy rates (Sontag *et al.*, 1944[299]).

The general topic of factors that influence body composition is likely to receive much more attention at Fels in the future than in the past. Areas of special concentration are likely to include genetic influences and habitual physical activity.

Risk factors for cardiovascular disease

Particularly since 1976, there has been considerable interest in risk factors for cardiovascular disease within the Fels Longitudinal Study. The factors that will be considered here are blood pressure and levels of plasma 'lipids.'

Blood pressure

Familial and genetic studies related to hypertension were reviewed critically by Siervogel (1984). Roche *et al.* (1980[229]) investigated long-term changes in blood pressure using data from the major US growth studies. Systolic blood pressure became higher in boys than in girls at about 3 months, but there was an opposite sex difference from 2 to 7 years. The median values for systolic blood pressure increased considerably in boys

but not girls from 14 to 18 years and there were gradual increases in both men and women. The medians for men were higher than those for women by about 12 mmHg.

Diastolic blood pressures, like systolic blood pressures, increased during infancy and childhood with the values for boys exceeding those for girls after 6 months (Roche *et al.*, 1980[229]). The sex differences in diastolic pressure were small until about 14 years, when the means became considerably larger for boys than girls; this difference persisted into adulthood. As for systolic blood pressure, the medians for girls were essentially stable after 15 years. There was significant skewness and kurtosis in systolic and diastolic blood pressures after 10 years. This was equally marked in each sex for systolic blood pressures but was more marked for females in diastolic blood pressures. During infancy, median pulse pressures (systolic pressure less diastolic pressure) changed little with age and the sex differences were inconsistent. Pulse pressures became larger for boys than girls at about 15 years and this difference continued into adulthood (Roche *et al.*, 1980[229]).

The between-subject variability of systolic and diastolic blood pressures, as measured by the standard deviations, decreased to 6 months and then slowly increased until 14 years, with little sex difference. At about 14 years, the standard deviations became larger in boys than in girls, particularly for diastolic pressure. In men, the standard deviations for systolic pressure decreased with age but those for diastolic pressure did not change, while in women, the standard deviations increased with age for both systolic and diastolic pressures.

There were low correlations between blood pressure and stature within age groups (Roche *et al.*, 1980[229]; Siervogel *et al.*, 1982c). For systolic pressure, these correlations changed from $r = -0.4$ at 2 years to $r = 0.3$ at 7 years and then remained stable in each sex until 15 years (Roche *et al.*, 1980[229]). The correlations then decreased to about $r = -0.3$ at 26 years after which they were stable. There were low positive correlations between diastolic pressure and stature at all ages except for men, in whom there were low negative correlations. The correlations between systolic and diastolic pressures with weight and subcutaneous adipose tissue thicknesses were low in each sex at all ages (Roche *et al.*, 1980[229]).

There were low positive correlations between systolic or diastolic blood pressure and relative skeletal age (skeletal age less chronological age) (Roche *et al.*, 1980[229]). Additionally, age at menarche and age at peak height velocity had low negative correlations with blood pressure, especially from 8 to 14 years. These findings indicated that rapidly maturing children had a slight tendency to higher blood pressures during

pubescence that was more marked for systolic than for diastolic blood pressure.

There were low parent–offspring and sibling correlations for either systolic or diastolic blood pressure, measured at the same age; some of this association may be due to common effects of body size and rates of maturation, but the sibling correlations for rates of change from 9 to 18 years were not significant (Roche *et al.*, 1980[229]; Woynarowska *et al.*, 1985).

The possible tracking of blood pressure is important because of its relevance to the early institution of programs to prevent adult hypertension in those at risk. Age-to-age correlations for values 1 year apart were similar for systolic and diastolic blood pressure. These correlations increased from about 0.2 in infancy to 0.5 at 10 years but changed little after this. More importantly, correlations between childhood values and blood pressure at 18 or 30 years increased rapidly with the age of the earlier measurement until the first measurement was at the age of 4 years after which the increases were small. These correlations were higher for systolic pressure than for diastolic pressure. Finally, multiple regressions of childhood stature and weight on adult blood pressures had low R^2 values with negative coefficients for stature but positive coefficients for weight (Roche *et al.*, 1980[229]). This indicated a slight tendency for short heavy children to have higher blood pressures in adulthood.

The tracking of Fels blood pressure values was addressed again by Smith *et al.* (1990; in press), who fitted a model to the serial values during childhood. This work showed tracking correlations of about 0.4 for 4-year intervals and 0.2 for 20-year intervals. The relative risk of hypertension at the age of 35 years was estimated at 1.9 for 15-year-old males and 2.6 for 15-year-old females with a true diastolic pressure of 80 mmHg, in comparison with this risk of hypertension in those with a diastolic pressure of 60 mmHg.

Relationships of blood pressure to body composition

Siervogel *et al.* (1982c) reported associations of systolic and diastolic blood pressures with body composition in children and adults. The correlations with fat-free mass and adipocyte volume were significant in children but not in adults. Furthermore, the correlations between diastolic pressure and total body fat, percent body fat or adipocyte number were not significant in adults. Baumgartner *et al.* (1987b), however, reported significant but low correlations of systolic and diastolic blood pressures with percent body fat in adults. After adjustments for age and sex, fatness appeared to be related to blood pressure, but the correlations were low.

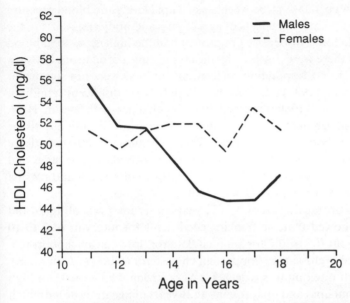

Fig. 7.12 Mean values of high density lipoprotein (HDL) cholesterol for boys and girls. (Baumgartner, R.N., Siervogel, R.M., Chumlea, W.C. & Roche, A.F. (1989c). Associations between plasma lipoprotein cholesterols, adiposity and adipose tissue distribution during adolescence. *International Journal of Obesity*, **13**, 31–41. Redrawn with permission from MacMillan Press Ltd.)

The sensitivity and specificity of the various methods used to describe adiposity and adipose tissue distributions in the context of hypertension have not been evaluated. Therefore, as noted by Siervogel and Baumgartner (1988), the reported studies may not have used the best descriptors to elucidate relationships between adiposity, adipose tissue distribution and blood pressure. Baumgartner *et al.* (1987b) used the logarithm of the ratio subscapular/lateral calf skinfold thicknesses which was correlated highly with a more complex index based on a principal components analysis of multiple skinfold thicknesses. They found that, after controlling for age, age^2 and percent body fat, and plasma lipids, a centripetal (truncal) pattern has low positive correlations with systolic and diastolic blood pressures in women.

Levels of plasma 'lipids'
The means for plasma levels of high-density lipoprotein (HDL) cholesterol tended to be slightly higher in boys than girls from 11 to 13 years but not from 13 to 18 years (Baumgartner *et al.*, 1989b, 1989c). These sex differences were statistically significant only at 17 and 18 years (Fig. 7.12).

There were low correlations between plasma lipid levels and blood pressure in children after removing effects of age, fatness and body size. Girls in the lowest quartile for high-density lipoprotein had the highest systolic blood pressures and there were low but significant negative correlations between these values. The corresponding correlations for boys were not significant (Siervogel *et al.*, 1981). In another study of adolescent children, Baumgartner *et al.* (1989c) showed that the changes with age in HDL cholesterol had significant associations with changes in adipose tissue distribution in boys but not girls. These changes in adipose tissue distribution were independent of changes in total body fat. In men and women there were associations between the degree of obesity and plasma cholesterol levels (Thomas & Garn, 1960).

An analysis of tracking from 9 to 21 years in serum levels of lipids and lipoproteins showed that the tracking coefficients for intervals of 2 to 10 years were about 0.5 to 0.7 for total cholesterol, low-density lipoprotein cholesterol and high-density lipoprotein cholesterol (Guo *et al.*, in press). This significant tracking was reflected in very strong relative risks of high values for serum lipid and lipoproteins at 21 years of age in those with high values at 9 years.

During adolescence there are changes in body composition and in the levels of circulating hormones, such as testosterone and estrogen, that directly influence the rate of maturation. Therefore, associations between lipid levels and maturity status would be expected. Nevertheless, the correlations between maturity levels and plasma lipids during adolescence were not significant within chronological age groups in either sex, but changes in lipid and lipoprotein levels were more apparent between skeletal age groups than between chronological age groups (Siervogel *et al.*, 1989b).

Fels research into body composition has been intense for the past 14 years, yet, in some ways, it is just beginning. Many data await analysis and numerous possibilities exist for the exploration of novel subject areas using new techniques, old skills, and clear thoughts.

Epilogue

The future of the Fels Longitudinal Study is uncertain. One can look ahead with great expectations but it is 'foolish to look further than you can see,' as stated by Winston Churchill. The study is more exciting than ever: more data, more brilliant young investigators, more health-related and socially significant questions to be addressed. Consequently, the near future is viewed with optimism that is based, in part, on the knowledge that what we have done in the last few decades has contributed to knowledge, met with the approval of review groups and has received support from the Federal Government and others.

It is impossible, however, to predict how long this happy state of affairs will last. The National Institutes of Health, which provide most of the funding for the Fels study, have support cycles that do not extend longer than 5 years and funding is highly competitive. Therefore, there is some apprehension. Our view of the Fels study is biased and scientific progress becomes more difficult when all the low apples have been picked. Anything may occur. As a Swedish proverb states: 'The afternoon knows what the morning never suspected.' Despite uncertainties, we will continue as long as possible. An observational longitudinal study becomes more valuable as its duration increases and more complete descriptions of natural changes become possible, leading to more complete understanding of human development.

I wish to conclude with three quotations that are apposite. Venerable Bede wrote: 'It is better never to begin a good work than, having begun it, to stop.' A similar thought was expressed by Sir Francis Drake: 'It is not the beginning of the task, but the continuing of the same until it be well and truly finished wherein lies the true glory.' These are bold words. We do not seek glory. Rather we are mindful of our modest role and would echo the words of Isaac Newton: 'We do not know how we appear to the world, but to ourselves we seem to have been only like children playing on the seashore, and diverting ourselves in now and then finding a pebble or a prettier shell than ordinary, whilst the great ocean of truth lay all undiscovered before us.'

References

References for the following authors have been numbered below, and have corresponding superscript numbers in the text, to enable the reader to identify them more easily: Chumlea (1–41), Garn (42–172), Roche (173–275), Sontag (276–308).
*Not based on data from the Fels Longitudinal Study.

Abdel-Malek, A. K., Mukherjee, D. & Roche, A. F. (1985). A method of constructing an index of obesity. *Human Biology*, **57**, 415–30.

Baumgartner, R. N. (1988). Associations between plasma lipoprotein cholesterols, adiposity, and adipose tissue distribution during adolescence. *American Journal of Physical Anthropology*, **75**, 184.

Baumgartner, R. N., Chumlea, W. C., Guo, S. & Roche, A. F. (1990). Prediction of growth in fat-free mass from bioelectric resistance and anthropometry in children. *American Journal of Human Biology*, **2**, 195.

Baumgartner, R. N., Chumlea, W. C. & Roche, A. F. (1987a). Associations between bioelectric impedance and anthropometric variables. *Human Biology*, **59**, 235–44.

Baumgartner, R. N., Chumlea, W. C. & Roche, A. F. (1988a). Bioelectric impedance phase angle and body composition. *American Journal of Clinical Nutrition*, **48**, 16–23.

Baumgartner, R. N., Chumlea, W. C. & Roche, A. F. (1989a). Estimation of body composition from bioelectric impedance of body segments. *American Journal of Clinical Nutrition*, **50**, 221–6.

Baumgartner, R. N., Chumlea, W. C. & Roche, A. F. (1990). Bioelectric impedance for body composition. *Exercise and Sport Sciences Reviews*, **18**, 193–224.

Baumgartner, R. N., Heymsfield, S. B., Roche, A. F. & Bernardino, M. (1988b). Abdominal composition quantified by computed tomography. *American Journal of Clinical Nutrition*, **48**, 936–45.

Baumgartner, R. N., Roche, A. F., Chumlea, W. C., Siervogel, R. M. & Glueck, C. J. (1987b). Fatness and fat patterns: Associations with plasma lipids and blood pressures in adults, 18 to 57 years of age. *American Journal of Epidemiology*, **126**, 614–28.

Baumgartner, R. N., Roche, A. F., Guo, S., Lohman, T., Boileau, R. A. & Slaughter, M. H. (1986b). Adipose tissue distribution: The stability of principal components by sex, ethnicity and maturation stage. *Human Biology*, **58**, 719–35.

Baumgartner, R. N., Roche, A. F. & Himes, J. H. (1986a). Incremental growth tables. *American Journal of Clinical Nutrition*, **43**, 711–22.

Baumgartner, R. N., Siervogel, R. M., Chumlea, W. C. & Roche, A. F. (1989c).

Associations between plasma lipoprotein cholesterols, adiposity and adipose tissue distribution during adolescence. *International Journal of Obesity*, **13**, 31–41.

Baumgartner, R. N., Siervogel, R. M. & Roche, A. F. (1989b). Clustering of cardiovascular risk factors in association with indices of adiposity and adipose tissue distribution in adults. *American Journal of Human Biology*, **1**, 43–62.

Bernard, J. & Sontag, L. W. (1947). Fetal reactivity to tonal stimulation: A preliminary report. *Journal of Genetic Psychology*, **70**, 205–10.

*Björck, A. (1967). Solving linear least squares problems by Gran–Schmidt orthogonalization. *Nordisk Tijdschrift Informationsbehandlung*, **7**, 1–21.

Bock, R. D. (1982). Predicting the mature stature of preadolescent children. In *Genetic and Environmental Factors During the Growth Period*, ed. C. Susanne, pp. 3–19. New York: Plenum Press.

Bock, R. D. (1986). Unusual growth patterns in the Fels data. In *Human Growth: A Multidisciplinary Review*, ed. A. Demirjian, pp. 69–84. London: Taylor & Francis.

Bock, R. D. & Sykes, R. C. (1989). Evidence for continuing secular increase in height within families in the United States. *American Journal of Human Biology*, **1**, 143–8.

Bock, R. D., Sykes, R. C. & Roche, A. F. (1985). *The Fels Three-generation data: evidence for continuing secular increase in height*. Abstract No. 11.22, p. 63, IVth International Congress of Auxology, Montreal, Quebec, Canada, June 16–20.

*Bock, R. D. & Thissen, D. (1976). Fitting multi-component models for growth in stature. *Proceedings of the 9th International Biometric Conference*, **1**, 432–42.

Bock, R. D. & Thissen, D. (1980). Statistical problems of fitting individual growth curves. In *Human Physical Growth and Maturation: Methodologies and Factors*, ed. F. E. Johnston, A. F. Roche & C. Susanne, pp. 268–90. New York: Plenum Press.

Bock, R. D., Wainer, H. C., Peterson, A., Thissen, D., Murray, J. & Roche, A. F. (1973). A parametrization for individual human growth curves. *Human Biology*, **45**, 63–80.

Boothby, W. M., Berkson, J. & Dunn, H. L. (1936). Studies of the energy of metabolism of normal individuals; a standard for basal metabolism, with a nomogram for clinical application. *American Journal of Physiology*, **116**, 468–84.

*Box, G. E. P. & Cox, D. R. (1964). An analysis of transformations. *Journal of the Royal Statistical Society*, Series B 26, 211–52.

*Broadbent, B. H., Sr. (1931). A new X-ray technique and its application to orthodontia. *Angle Orthodontist*, **1**, 45–66.

*Broadbent, B. H., Sr., Broadbent, B. H., Jr. & Golden, W. H. (1975). *Bolton Standards of Dentofacial Developmental Growth*. St Louis, Missouri: C. V. Mosby.

Byard, P. J., Guo, S. & Roche, A. F. (1991). Model fitting to early childhood length and weight data from the Fels Longitudinal Study of Growth. *American Journal of Human Biology*, **3**, 33–40.

Byard, P. J., Ohtsuki, F., Siervogel, R. M. & Roche, A. F. (1984). Sibling

correlations for serial cranial measurements from radiographs. *Journal of Craniofacial Genetics and Developmental Biology*, **4**, 265–9.

Byard, P. J. & Roche, A. F. (1984). Secular trend for recumbent length and stature in the Fels Longitudinal Growth Study. In *Human Growth and Development*, ed. J. Borms, R. Hauspie, A. Sand, C. Susanne & M. Hebbelinck, pp. 209–14. New York: Plenum Press.

Byard, P. J., Siervogel, R. M. & Roche, A. F. (1983). Familial correlations for serial measurements of recumbent length and stature. *Annals of Human Biology*, **10**, 281–93.

Byard, P. J., Siervogel, R. M. & Roche, A. F. (1988). Age trends in transmissible and nontransmissible components of family resemblance for stature. *Annals of Human Biology*, **15**, 111–18.

Byard, P. J., Siervogel, R. M. & Roche, A. F. (1989). X-linked pattern of inheritance of serial measures of weight/stature[2]. *American Journal of Human Biology*, **1**, 443–49.

1. Chumlea, W. C. (1981). Associations between changes in adipose cellularity and total body fatness in adolescence. *American Journal of Physical Anthropology*, **54**, 208–9.

2. Chumlea, W. C. (1982). Physical growth in adolescence. In *Handbook of Developmental Psychology*, ed. B. B. Wolman, G. Stricker, S. J. Ellman, P. Keith-Spiegel & D. S. Palermo, pp. 471–85. Englewood Cliffs, New Jersey: Prentice Hall.

3. Chumlea, W. C. (1983). *Development of pelvic bone shape and tissue in children*. DTNH22-83-P-07365. US Department of Transportation, Washington, DC: US Government Printing Office.

4. Chumlea, W. C. (1984). Growth of the pelvis in children. *Transactions of the Society of Automotive Engineers*, **4**, 649–59.

5. Chumlea, W. C. (1985a). Accuracy and reliability of a new sliding caliper. *American Journal of Physical Anthropology*, **68**, 425–7.

6. Chumlea, W. C. (1985b). Assessment of body composition in nonambulatory persons. In *Body Composition Assessments in Youth and Adults*, Report of the Sixth Ross Conference on Medical Research, ed. A. F. Roche, pp. 86–90. Columbus, Ohio: Ross Laboratories.

7. Chumlea, W. C. (1985c). New methods of nutritional assessment of the elderly. *Consultant Dietician Newsletter*, **10**, 19–22.

8. Chumlea, W. C. (1986a). Assessing growth and nutritional status in children with developmental disabilities. *Consultant Dietician Newsletter*, **11**, 23–5.

9. Chumlea, W. C. (1986b). Clinical methods of assessing obesity in children. *Perspectives in Lipid Disorders*, **3**, 14–19.

10. Chumlea, W. C. (1988). Methods of nutritional anthropometric assessment for special groups. In *Anthropometric Standardization Reference Manual*, ed. T. Lohman, A. F. Roche & R. Martorell, pp. 93–5. Champaign, Illinois: Human Kinetic Books.

11. Chumlea, W. C. (1991a). Anthropometric assessment of nutritional status in the elderly. In *Anthropometric Assessment of Nutritional Status*, ed. J. Himes, pp. 399–418. New York: Wiley-Liss.

12. Chumlea, W. C. (1991b). Bioelectric impedance in the elderly. Possibilities and pitfalls. *Age and Nutrition*, **2**, 4–6.

13. Chumlea, W. C. (in press). Growth and development. In *Pediatric Nutrition: A Reference Manual*, ed. C. E. Lang & P. Queen. New York: Aspen Publishers.

14. Chumlea, W. C. & Baumgartner, R. N. (1989). Status of anthropometry and body composition data in elderly subjects. *American Journal of Clinical Nutrition*, **50**, 1158–66.

15. Chumlea, W. C. & Baumgartner, R. N. (1990). Bioelectric impedance methods for the estimation of body composition. *Canadian Journal of Sports Science*, **15**, 172–9.

16. Chumlea, W. C., Baumgartner, R. M. & Roche, A. F. (1986). Segmental bioelectric impedance measures of body composition. Poster, International Conference on 'In Vivo Body Composition Studies,' Brookhaven, New York.

17. Chumlea, W. C., Baumgartner, R. N. & Roche, A. F. (1987b). Segmental bioelectric impedance measures of body composition. In *In Vivo Body Composition Studies*, ed. K. J. Ellis, S. Yasumura & W. D. Morgan, pp. 103–107. Proceedings of an International Symposium held at Brookhaven National Laboratory, New York. *Institute of Physicists in Science and Medicine*, **47**, 35.

18. Chumlea, W. C., Baumgartner, R. N. & Roche, A. F. (1988a). Specific resistivity used to estimate fat-free mass from segmental body measures of bioelectric impedance. *American Journal of Clinical Nutrition*, **48**, 7–15.

19. Chumlea, W. C., Baumgartner, R. N. & Roche, A. F. (1988b). Fat volumes and total body fat from impedance. *Medicine and Science in Sports and Exercise*, **20**, S82.

20. Chumlea, W. C., Baumgartner, R. N. & Vellas, B. P. (1991). Anthropometry and body composition in the perspective of nutritional status in the elderly. *Nutrition*, **7**, 57–60.

21. Chumlea, W. C.. Falls, R. A. & Webb, P. (1982a). Body composition in adults after 60 years of age. *American Journal of Physical Anthropology*, **57**, 176–7.

22. Chumlea, W. C., Guo, S., Roche, A. F. & Steinbaugh, M. L. (1988c). Prediction of body weight for the nonambulatory elderly from anthropometry. *Journal of the American Dietetic Association*, **88**, 564–8.

23. Chumlea, W. C. & Knittle, J. L. (1980). Associations between fat cellularity and total body fatness in adolescents and adults. *American Journal of Physical Anthropology*, **52**, 213.

24. Chumlea, W. C., Knittle, J. L., Roche, A. F., Siervogel, R. M. & Webb, P. (1981a). Size and number of adipocytes and measures of body fat in boys and girls 10 to 18 years of age. *American Journal of Clinical Nutrition*, **34**, 1791–7.

25. Chumlea, W. C., Mukherjee, D. & Roche, A. F. (1984a). A comparison of methods for measuring cortical bone thickness. *American Journal of Physical Anthropology*, **65**, 83–6.

26. Chumlea, W. C. & Roche, A. F. (1984). Nutritional anthropometric assessment of non-ambulatory persons using recumbent techniques. *American Journal of Physical Anthropology*, **63**, 146.

27. Chumlea, W. C. & Roche, A. F. (1986). Ultrasonic and skinfold caliper measures of subcutaneous adipose tissue thickness in elderly men and women. *American Journal of Physical Anthropology*, **71**, 351–7.

28. Chumlea, W. C. & Roche, A. F. (1988). Assessment of the nutritional status of

healthy and handicapped adults. In *Anthopometric Standardization Reference Manual*, ed. T. Lohman, A. F. Roche & R. Martorell, pp. 115–19. Champaign, Illinois: Human Kinetics Books.

29. Chumlea, W. C., Roche, A. F., Guo, S. & Woynarowska, B. (1987a). The influence of physiological variables and oral contraceptives on bioelectric impedance. *Human Biology*, **59**, 257–69.
30. Chumlea, W. C., Roche, A. F. & Mukherjee, D. (1984b). *Nutritional Assessment of the Elderly through Anthropometry*. Columbus, Ohio: Ross Laboratories.
31. Chumlea, W. C., Roche, A. F. & Mukherjee, D. (1986). Some anthropometric indices of body composition for elderly adults. *Journal of Gerontology*, **41**, 36–9.
32. Chumlea, W. C., Roche, A. F. & Rogers, E. (1984c). Replicability for anthropometry in the elderly. *Human Biology*, **56**, 329–37.
33. Chumlea, W. C., Roche, A. F., Siervogel, R. M., Knittle, J. L. & Webb, P. (1981b). Adipocytes and adiposity in adults. *American Journal of Clinical Nutrition*, **34**, 1798–803.
34. Chumlea, W. C., Roche, A. F. & Steinbaugh, M. L. (1985a). Estimating stature from knee height for persons 60 to 90 years of age. *Journal of the American Geriatric Society*, **33**, 116–20.
35. Chumlea, W. C., Roche, A. F. & Steinbaugh, M. L. (1989b). Anthropometric approaches to the nutritional assessment of the elderly. In *Human Nutrition and Aging*, ed. H. N. Munro, pp. 335–61. New York: Plenum Press.
36. Chumlea, W. C., Roche, A. F., Steinbaugh, M. L. & Gopalaswamy, N. (1985b). Nutritional assessment of the elderly by recumbent anthropometric methods. In *Nutrition, Immunity and Illness in the Elderly*, ed. R. K. Chandra, pp. 53–61. New York: Pergamon Press.
37. Chumlea, W. C., Roche, A. F. & Thissen, D. (1989a). The FELS method of assessing the skeletal maturity of the hand–wrist. *American Journal of Human Biology*, **1**, 175–83.
38. Chumlea, W. C., Siervogel, R. M., Roche, A. F., Mukherjee, D. & Webb, P. (1982b). Changes in adipocyte cellularity in children ten to 18 years of age. *International Journal of Obesity*, **6**, 383–9.
39. Chumlea, W. C., Siervogel, R. M., Roche, A. F., Webb, P. & Rogers, E. (1983). Increments across age in body composition of children 10 to 18 years of age. *Human Biology*, **55**, 845–52.
40. Chumlea, W. C., Steinbaugh, M. L., Roche, A. F., Mukherjee, D. & Gopalaswamy, N. (1985c). Nutritional anthropometric assessment in elderly persons 65 to 90 years of age. *Journal of Nutrition in the Elderly*, **4**, 39–51.
41. Chumlea, W. C., Vellas, B. J., Roche, A. F., Guo, S. & Steinbaugh, M. (1990). Paticularités et intéret des measures anthropométriques du status nutritionnel des personnes agées. *Age and Nutrition*, **1**, 7–12.

Clark, L. C., Jr. & Beck, E. (1950). Plasma 'alkaline' phosphatase activity. I. Normative data for growing children. *Journal of Pediatrics*, **36**, 335–41.
Clark, L. C., Jr., Beck, E. I. & Shock, N. W. (1951a). Serum alkaline phosphatase in middle and old age. *Journal of Gerontology*, **6**, 7–12.
Clark, L. C., Jr., Beck, E. & Thompson, H. (1951b). The excretion of acid

phosphatase as a measure of prostatic development during pubescence. *Journal of Clinical Endocrinology*, **11**, 84–90.

Clark, L. C., Jr. & Garn, S. M. (1954). Relationship between ketosteroid excretion and basal oxygen consumption in children. *Journal of Applied Physiology*, **6**, 546–50.

Clark, L. C., Jr. & Trolander, H. (1954). Thermometer for measuring body temperature in hypothermia. *Journal of the American Medical Association*, **155**, 251–2.

Cochram, D. B. & Baumgartner, R. N. (1990). Evaluation of accuracy and reliability of calipers for measuring recumbent knee height in elderly people. *American Journal of Clinical Nutrition*, **52**, 397–400.

Colbert, C. (1968). *Bone Mineral Measurements from X-ray Images*, NIH Conference on Progress in Methods of Bone Mineral Measurements, ed. G. D. Whedon, pp. 80–95, Bethesda, Maryland.

Colbert, C. (1974). Radiographic absorptiometry. PhD Thesis, University Without Walls, Antioch College, Yellow Springs, Ohio.

Colbert, C., Bachtell, R. S., Bailey, J., Spencer, R. & Himes, J. H. (1980). Comparison of radiogrammetry with 'Radiographic Absorptiometry' (photo-densitometry). In *Proceedings of the Fourth International Conference on Bone Measurement, pp. 439–40. Washington, DC: US Department of Health and Human Services, US Government Printing Office.*

Colbert, C. & Garrett, C. (1969). Photodensiometry of bone roentgenograms with an on-line computer. *Journal of Clinical Orthopedics*, **65**, 39–45.

Colbert, C., Israel, H. & Garn, S. M. (1966). Absolute radiographic densities of dentin and enamel. *Journal of Dental Research*, **45**, 1826.

Colbert, C., Mazess, R. B. & Schmidt, P. B. (1970b). Bone mineral determination in vitro by radiographic photodensitometry and direct photon absorptiometry. *Investigative Radiology*, **5**, 336–40.

Colbert, C., Schmidt, P. B. & Mazess, R. B. (1969). Bone mineral determination: A comparison of radiographic photodensitometry and direct photon absorptiometry. *American Association of Physicists in Medicine, Quarterly Bulletin*, **3**, 25.

Colbert, C., Spruit, J. J. & Davila, L. R. (1967). Biophysical properties of bone; determining mineral concentrations from the X-ray image. *New York Academy of Science, Transactions*, **30**, 271–90.

Colbert, C., Spruit, J. J. & Davila, L. R. (1970a). Fels microdensitometer/computer for bone mineral determination from roentgenograms. *Critical Reviews in Radiological Sciences*, **1**, 459–71.

Colbert, C., Van Hulst, H. & Spruit, J. J. (1970c). A phalangeal atlas: An application of radiographic photodensiometry. In *Proceedings of the Bone Mineral Conference*, ed. J. R. Cameron, pp. 224–35. Madison, Wisconsin: University of Wisconsin.

Coleman, W. H. (1969). Sex differences in the growth of the human bony pelvis. *American Journal of Physical Anthropology*, **31**, 125–52.

Crandall, V. C. (1972). The Fels Study: Some contributions to personality development and achievement in childhood and adulthood. *Seminars in Psychiatry*, **4**, 383–97.

Cronk, C. E. (1983). Fetal growth as measured by ultrasound. *Yearbook of Physical Anthropology*, **26**, 65–90.

Cronk, C. E., Mukherjee, D. & Roche, A. F. (1983b). Changes in triceps and subscapular skinfold thickness during adolescence. *Human Biology*, **55**, 707–21.

Cronk, C. E. & Roche, A. F. (1982). Race- and sex-specific reference data for triceps and subscapular skinfolds and weight/stature^2. *American Journal of Clinical Nutrition*, **35**, 347–54.

Cronk, C. E., Roche, A. F., Chumlea, W. C., Kent, R. & Berkey, C. (1982a). Longitudinal trends of weight/stature^2 in childhood in relation to adulthood body fat measures. *Human Biology*, **54**, 751–64.

Cronk, C. E., Roche, A. F., Kent, R., Berkey, C., Reed, R. B., Valadian, I., Eichorn, D. & McCammon, R. (1982b). Longitudinal trends and continuity in weight/stature^2 from 3 months to 18 years. *Human Biology*, **54**, 729–49.

Cronk, C. E., Roche, A. F., Kent, R., Jr., Eichorn, D. & McCammon, R. M. (1983a). Longitudinal trends in subcutaneous fat thickness during adolescence. *American Journal of Physical Anthropology*, **61**, 197–204.

*Edwards, D. A. W., Hammond, W. H., Healy, M. J. R., Tanner, J. M. & Whitehouse, R. H. (1955). Design and accuracy of calipers for measuring subcutaneous tissue thickness. *British Journal of Nutrition*, **9**, 133–43.

Falk, C., Rubinstein, P., Roche, A. F., Siervogel, R. M., Molthan, L., Fotino, M., Martin, M. & Allen, F. H. (1982). Lod scores for linkage analysis of 28 genetic markers: a survey report on 600 families. *Cytogenetics and Cell Genetics*, **32**, 272.

Falkner, F. (1971a). Skeletal maturity indicators in infancy. *American Journal of Physical Anthropology*, **35**, 393–4.

Falkner, F. (1971b). Physical growth of the child. *Carnets de l'enfance, Assignment Children, United Nations Children's Fund*, **15**, 15–22.

Falkner, F. (1972). The creation of growth standards: A committee report. *American Journal of Clinical Nutrition*, **25**, 218–20.

Falkner, F. (1973a). Velocity growth. *Pediatrics*, **51**, 746–7.

Falkner, F. (1973b). Long term developmental studies: A critique. *Early Development*, **51**, 412–21.

Falkner, F. (1975). Nutrition and bone development. *Modern Problems in Paediatrics*, **14**, 185–8.

Falkner, F. (1977a). Health Needs of Adolescents. *World Health Organization Technical Report Series*, **609**, 1–12.

Falkner, F. (1977b). Normal growth and development: Current concepts. *Postgraduate Medicine*, **62**, 58–63.

Falkner, F. (1978a). Early postnatal growth evaluation in full-term, pre-term, and small-for-dates infants. In *Auxology–Human Growth in Health and Disorder*, eds. L. Gedda & P. Parisi, pp. 79–86. New York: Academic Press.

Falkner, F. (1978b). Postnatal growth. In *Perinatal Physiology*, ed. U. Stave, pp. 37–45. New York: Plenum Press.

Falkner, F. & Roche, A. F. (1987). Relationship of femoral length to recumbent length and stature in fetal, neonatal and early childhood growth. *Human Biology*, **59**, 769–73.

Fels, S. S. (1933). *This Changing World – As I See Its Change and Purpose.* Boston: Houghton Mifflin.

Frisancho, A. R., Garn, S. M. & Ascoli, W. (1970). Subperiosteal and endosteal bone apposition during adolscence. *Human Biology*, **42**, 639–64.

42. Garn, S. M. (1954a). Fat patterning and fat intercorrelations in the adult male. *Human Biology*, **26**, 59–69.
43. Garn, S. M. (1954b). The measurement of skin temperature. *American Journal of Physical Anthropology*, **12**, 127–30.
44. Garn, S. M. (1955a). Applications of pattern analysis to anthropometric data. *New York Academy of Science Annals*, **63**, 537–52.
45. Garn, S. M. (1955b). Relative fat patterning: An individual characteristic. *Human Biology*, **27**, 75–89.
46. Garn, S. M. (1956a). Comparison of pinch-caliper and X-ray measurements of skin plus subcutaneous fat. *Science*, **124**, 178–9.
47. Garn, S. M. (1956b). Fat thickness and growth progress during infancy. *Human Biology*, **28**, 232–50.
48. Garn, S. M. (1957a). Selection of body sites for fat measurement. *Science*, **125**, 550–1.
49. Garn, S. M. (1957b). An improved method of estimating body fat content by the use of teleoroentgenograms. ASTIA Document No. AD 115 085.
50. Garn, S. M. (1957c). Fat weight and fat placement in the female. *Science*, **125**, 1091–2.
51. Garn, S. M. (1957d). Roentgenogrammetric determinations of body composition. *Human Biology*, **29**, 337–53.
52. Garn, S. M. (1958a). Fat, body size and growth in the newborn. *Human Biology*, **30**, 265–80.
53. Garn, S. M. (1958b). Statistics: A review. *Angle Orthodontist*, **28**, 149–65.
54. Garn, S. M. (1960a). The number of hand–wrist centers. *American Journal of Physical Anthropology*, **18**, 293–9.
55. Garn, S. M. (1960b). Growth and development. *50th Anniversary White House Conference on Children and Youth*, Vol. 2: *Development and Education of the Nation's Children*, ed. E. Ginzberg, pp. 24–42. New York: Columbia University Press.
56. Garn, S. M. (1960c). Fat accumulation and aging in males and females. In *The Biology of Aging*, ed. B. L. Strehler, pp. 170–80. Symposium No. 6, Gatlinburg, Tennessee, May 1–3, 1957. Washington , DC: American Institute of Biological Sciences.
57. Garn, S. M. (1961a). Research and malocclusion. *American Journal of Orthodontics*, **47**, 661–73.
58. Garn, S. M. (1961b). Radiographic analysis of body composition. In *Techniques for Measuring Body Composition*, ed. J. Brozek & A. Henschel, pp. 36–58. Washington, DC: National Academy of Sciences.
59. Garn, S. M. (1961c). The genetics of normal human growth. In *De Genetica Medica*, ed. L. Gedda, pp. 413–32. Instituto Gregorio Mendel: Rome, Italy. Reprinted in *Physical Anthropology 1953–1961*, ed. G. W. Lasker, pp. 291–310. Mexico City: Instituto de Investigaciones Historicas, Universidad Nacional Autonoma de Mexcio and Instituto Nacional e Anthropologia e Historia.

60. Garn, S. M. (1962a). Anthropometry in clinical appraisal of nutritional status. *American Journal of Clinical Nutrition*, **11**, 418–32.
61. Garn, S. M. (1962b). Determinants of size and growth during the first three years. *Modern Problems in Paediatrics*, **7**, 50–4.
62. Garn, S. M. (1962c). Automation in anthropometry. *American Journal of Physical Anthropology*, **20**, 387–8.
63. Garn, S. M. (1963a). Some pitfalls in the quantification of body composition. *New York Academy of Science Annals*, **110**, 171–4.
64. Garn, S. M. (1963b). Human biology and research in body composition. *New York Academy of Science Annals*, **110**, 429–46.
65. Garn, S. M. (1965). The applicability of North American growth standards in developing countries. *Canadian Medical Association Journal*, **93**, 914–19.
66. Garn, S. M. (1966a). The evolutionary and genetic control of variability in man. *Annals of the New York Academy of Sciences*, **134**, 602–15.
67. Garn, S. M. (1966b). Malnutrition and skeletal development in the pre-school child. In *Pre-School Malnutrition*, pp. 43–62. Washington, DC: National Academy of Sciences – National Research Council.
68. Garn, S. M. (1966c). Body size and its implications. *Review of Child Development Research*, **2**, 529–61.
69. Garn, S. M. (1967). Food intakes of older people: Recommended vs. observed. National Academy of Science – National Research Council. *Proceedings, Food and Nutrition Board*, **27**, 9–11.
70. Garn, S. M. (1970). The earlier gain and the latter loss of cortical bone. In *Nutritional Perspective*, p. 146. Springfield, Illinois: Charles C. Thomas.
71. Garn, S. M., Blumenthal, T. & Rohmann, C. G. (1965g). On skewness in the ossification centers of the elbow. *American Journal of Physical Anthropology*, **23**, 303–4.
72. Garn, S. M. & Clark, L. C., Jr. (1955). Creatinine–weight coefficient as a measurement of obesity. *Journal of Applied Physiology*, **8**, 135–8.
73. Garn, S. M., Clark, L. C., Jr. & Harper, R. V. (1953). The sex difference in the basal metabolic rate. *Child Development*, **24**, 215–24.
74. Garn, S. M., Clark, A., Landkof, L. & Newell, L. (1960a). Parental body build and developmental progress in the offspring. *Science*, **132**, 1555–6.
75. Garn, S. M., Dahlberg, A. A. & Kerewsky, R. S. (1966f). Groove pattern, cusp number and tooth size. *Journal of Dental Research*, **45**, 970.
76. Garn, S. M., Lewis, A. B., Kerewsky, R. S. & Dahlberg, A. A. (1966g). Genetic independence of Carabelli's trait from tooth size or crown morphology. *Archives of Oral Biology*, **11**, 745–7.
77. Garn, S. M., Dahlberg, A. A., Lewis, A. B. & Kerewsky, R. S. (1966h). Cusp number, occlusal groove pattern and human taxonomy. *Nature*, **210**, 224–5.
78. Garn, S. M., Davila, G. H. & Rohmann, C. G. (1968f). Population frequencies and altered remodeling mechanisms in normal medullary stenosis. *American Journal of Physical Anthropology*, **29**, 425–8.
79. Garn, S. M., Fels, S. L. & Israel, H. (1967h). Brachymesophalangia of digit five in ten populations. *American Journal of Physical Anthropology*, **27**, 205–10.
80. Garn, S. M., Feutz, E., Colbert, C. & Wagner, B. (1966c). Comparison of cortical thickness and radiographic microdensitometry in the measurement of

bone loss. In *Progress in Development of Methods in Bone Densitometry*, pp. 65–77, NASA SP-64. Washington, DC: National Aeronautics and Space Administration.

81. Garn, S. M. & French, N. Y. (1963). Postpartum and age changes in areolar pigmentation. *American Journal of Obstetrics and Gynecology*, **85**, 873–5.
82. Garn, S. M. & French, N. Y. (1967). Magnitude of secular trend in the Fels population: stature and weight. Private printing.
83. Garn, S. M. & Gorman, E. L. (1956). Comparison of pinch-caliper and teleroentgenogrammetric measurements of subcutaneous fat. *Human Biology*, **28**, 407–13.
84. Garn, S. M., Greaney, G. & Young, R. (1956d). Fat thickness and growth progress during infancy. *Human Biology*, **28**, 232–50.
85. Garn, S. M. & Harper, R. V. (1955). Fat accumulation and weight gain in the adult male. *Human Biology*, **27**, 39–49.
86. Garn, S. M. & Haskell, J. A. (1959a). Fat and growth during childhood. *Science*, **130**, 1711.
87. Garn, S. M. & Haskell, J. A. (1959b). Fat changes during adolescence. *Science*, **129**, 1615–16.
88. Garn, S. M. & Haskell, J. A. (1960). Fat thickness and developmental status in childhood and adolescence. *American Journal of Diseases of Children*, **99**, 746–51.
89. Garn, S. M. & Helmrich, R. H. (1967). Next step in automated anthropometry. *American Journal of Physical Anthropology*, **26**, 97–100.
90. Garn, S. M., Helmrich, R. H., Flaherty, K. M. & Silverman, R. N. (1967a). Skin dosages in radiation-sparing techniques for the laboratory and field. *American Journal of Physical Anthropology*, **26**, 101–6.
91. Garn, S. M., Helmrich, R. H. & Lewis, A. B. (1967i). Transducer caliper with readout capability for odontometry. *Journal of Dental Research*, **46**, 306.
92. Garn, S. M., Hempy, H. O., III & Schwager, P. M. (1968b). Measurement of localized bone growth employing natural markers. *American Journal of Physical Anthropology*, **28**, 105–8.
93. Garn, S. M., Hertzog, K. P., Poznanski, A. K. & Nagy, J. M. (1972). Metacarpophalangeal length in the evaluation of skeletal malformations. *Radiology*, **105**, 375–81.
94. Garn, S. M. & Hull, E. I. (1966). Taller individuals lose less bone as they grow older. *Investigative Radiology*, **1**, 255–6.
95. Garn, S. M., Kerewsky, R. S. & Lewis, A. B. (1966j). Extent of sex influence on Carabelli's polymorphism. *Journal of Dental Research*, **45**, 1823.
96. Garn, S. M. & Koski, K. (1957). Tooth eruption sequence in fossil and recent man. *Nature*, **180**, 442–3.
97. Garn, S. M., Koski, K. & Lewis, A. B. (1957a). Problems in determining the tooth eruption sequence in fossil and modern man. *American Journal of Physical Anthropology*, **15**, 313–31.
98. Garn, S. M. & Lewis, A. B. (1957). Relationship between the sequence of calcification and the sequence of eruption of the mandibular molar and premolar teeth. *Journal of Dental Research*, **36**, 992–5.
99. Garn, S. M. & Lewis, A. B. (1958). Tooth-size, body-size and 'giant' fossil. *American Anthropologist*, **60**, 874–80.

100. Garn, S. M. & Lewis, A. B. (1962). The relationship between third molar agenesis and reduction in tooth number. *Angle Orthodontist*, **32**, 14–18.
101. Garn, S. M. & Lewis, A. B. (1970). The gradient and the pattern of crown-size reduction in simple hypodontia. *Angle Orthodontist*, **40**, 51–8.
102. Garn, S. M., Lewis, A. B. & Bonné, B. (1961a). Third molar polymorphism and the timing of tooth formation. *Nature*, **192**, 989.
103. Garn, S. M., Lewis, A. B. & Bonné, B. (1962a). Third molar formation and its developmental course. *Angle Orthodontist*, **32**, 270–9.
104. Garn, S. M., Lewis, A. B. & Kerewsky, R. S. (1963b). Third molar agenesis and size reduction of the remaining teeth. *Nature*, **200**, 488–9.
105. Garn, S. M., Lewis, A. B. & Kerewsky, R. S. (1964a). Third molar agenesis and variation in size of the remaining teeth. *Nature*, **201**, 839.
106. Garn, S. M., Lewis, A. B. & Kerewsky, R. S. (1964b). Sex difference in tooth size. *Journal of Dental Research*, **43**, 1039.
107. Garn, S. M., Lewis, A. B. & Kerewsky, R. S. (1965a). X-linked inheritance of tooth size. *Journal of Dental Research*, **44**, 439–41.
108. Garn, S. M., Lewis, A. B. & Kerewsky, R. S. (1965b). Genetic, nutritional, and maturational correlates of dental development. *Journal of Dental Research*, **44**, 228–42.
109. Garn, S. M., Lewis, A. B. & Kerewsky, R. S. (1965f). Size interrelationships of the mesial and distal teeth. *Journal of Dental Research*, **44**, 350–54.
110. Garn, S. M., Lewis, A. B. & Kerewsky, R. S. (1966e). The meaning of bilateral asymmetry in the permanent dentition. *Angle Orthodontist*, **36**, 55–62.
111. Garn, S. M., Lewis, A. B. & Kerewsky, R. S. (1966i). Bilateral asymmetry and concordance in cusp number and crown morphology of the mandibular first molar. *Journal of Dental Research*, **45**, 1820.
112. Garn, S. M., Lewis, A. B. & Kerewsky, R. S. (1967b). Sex difference in tooth shape. *Journal of Dental Research*, **46**, 1470.
113. Garn, S. M., Lewis, A. B. & Kerewsky, R. S. (1967c). The relationship between sexual dimorphism in tooth size and body size as studied within families. *Archives of Oral Biology*, **12**, 299–302.
114. Garn, S. M., Lewis, A. B. & Kerewsky, R. S. (1967d). Buccolingual size asymmetry and its developmental meaning. *Angle Orthodontist*, **37**, 186–93.
115. Garn, S. M., Lewis, A. B. & Kerewsky, R. S. (1967j). Shape similarities throughout the dentition. *Journal of Dental Research*, **46**, 1481.
116. Garn, S. M., Lewis, A. B. & Kerewsky, R. S. (1968d). The magnitude and implications of the relationship between tooth size and body size. *Archives of Oral Biology*, **13**, 129–31.
117. Garn, S. M., Lewis, A. B. & Kerewsky, R. S. (1968g). Relationship between the buccolingual and mesiodistal tooth diameters. *Journal of Dental Research*, **47**, 495.
118. Garn, S. M., Lewis, A. B., Kerewsky, R. S. & Jegart, K. (1965c). Sex differences in intraindividual tooth size commualities. *Journal of Dental Research*, **44**, 476–9.
119. Garn, S. M., Lewis, A. B., Koski, K. & Polacheck, D. L. (1958a). The sex difference in tooth calcification. *Journal of Dental Research*, **37**, 561–7.

120. Garn, S. M., Lewis, A. B. & Polacheck, D. L. (1958b). Variability of tooth formation in man. *Science*, **128**, 1510.
121. Garn, S. M., Lewis, A. B. & Polacheck, D. L. (1959). Variability of tooth formation. *Journal of Dental Research*, **38**, 135–48.
122. Garn, S. M., Lewis, A. B. & Polacheck, D. L. (1960b). Interrelations in dental development. I. Interrelationships within the dentition. *Journal of Dental Research*, **39**, 1049–55.
123. Garn, S. M., Lewis, A. B. & Polacheck, D. L. (1960c). Sibling similarities in dental development. *Journal of Dental Research*, **39**, 170–5.
124. Garn, S. M., Lewis, A. B. & Shoemaker, D. W. (1956a). The sequence of calcification of the mandibular molar and premolar teeth. *Journal of Dental Research*, **35**, 555–61.
125. Garn, S. M., Lewis, A. B., Swindler, D. R. & Kerewsky, R. S. (1967k). Genetic control of sexual dimorphism in tooth size. *Journal of Dental Research*, **46**, 963–72.
126. Garn, S. M., Lewis, A. B. & Vicinus, J. H. (1962b). Third molar agenesis and reduction in the number of other teeth. *Journal of Dental Research*, **41**, 717.
127. Garn, S. M., Lewis, A. B. & Vicinus, J. H. (1963d). Third molar polymorphism and its significance to dental genetics. *Journal of Dental Research*, **42**, 1344–63.
128. Garn, S. M., Lewis, A. B. & Walenga, A. J. (1968a). Maximum-confidence values for the human mesiodistal crown dimension of human teeth. *Archives of Oral Biology*, **13**, 841–4.
129. Garn, S. M., Lewis, A. B. & Walenga, A. J. (1968c). Evidence for a secular trend in tooth size over two generations. *Journal of Dental Research*, **47**, 503.
130. Garn, S. M., Lewis, A. B. & Walenga, A. J. (1968e). The genetic basis of the crown-size profile pattern. *Journal of Dental Research*, **47**, 1190.
131. Garn, S. M. & Nolan, P., Jr. (1963). A tank to measure body volume by water displacement (BoVoTa). *New York Academy of Science Annals*, **110**, 91–5.
132. Garn, S. M., Pao, E. M. & Rohmann, C. G. (1965d). Calcium intake and compact bone loss in adult subjects. *Federation Proceedings*, **24**, 567.
133. Garn, S. M. & Rohmann, C. G. (1959). Communalities of the ossification centers of the hand and wrist. *American Journal of Physical Anthropology*, **17**, 319–23.
134. Garn, S. M. & Rohmann, C. G. (1960a). The number of hand–wrist centers. *American Journal of Physical Anthropology*, **18**, 293–9.
135. Garn, S. M. & Rohmann, C. G. (1960b). Variability in the order of ossification of the bony centers of the hand and wrist. *American Journal of Physical Anthropology*, **18**, 219–28.
136. Garn, S. M. & Rohmann, C. G. (1962a). The adductor sesamoid of the thumb. *American Journal of Physical Anthropology*, **20**, 297–302.
137. Garn, S. M. & Rohmann, C. G. (1962b). X-linked inheritance of developmental timing in man. *Nature*, **196**, 695–6.
138. Garn, S. M. & Rohmann, C. G. (1962c). Parent–child similarities in hand–wrist ossification. *American Journal of Disease of Children*, **103**, 603–7.
139. Garn, S. M. & Rohmann, C. G. (1964a). Compact bone deficiency in protein–calorie malnutrition. *Science*, **145**, 1444–5.

140. Garn, S. M. & Rohmann, C. G. (1964b). On the prevalence of skewness in incremental data. *American Journal of Physical Anthropology*, **21**, 235–6.

141. Garn, S. M. & Rohmann, C. G. (1966a). 'Communalities' in the ossification timing of the growing foot. *American Journal of Physical Anthropology*, **24**, 45–50.

142. Garn, S. M. & Rohmann, C. G. (1966b). Interaction of nutrition and genetics in the timing of growth and development. *Pediatric Clinics of North America*, **13**, 353–79.

143. Garn, S. M. & Rohmann, C. G. (1967). 'Midparent' values for use with parent-specific, age–size tables when paternal stature is estimated or unknown. *Pediatric Clinics of North America*, **14**, 283.

144. Garn, S. M., Rohmann, C. G. & Apfelbaum, B. (1961b). Complete epiphyseal union of the hand. *American Journal of Physical Anthropology*, **19**, 365–72.

145. Garn, S. M., Rohmann, C. G. & Blumenthal, T. (1966b). Ossification sequence polymorphism and sexual dimorphism in skeletal development. *American Journal of Physical Anthropology*, **24**, 101–15.

146. Garn, S. M., Rohmann, C. G., Blumenthal, T. & Kaplan, C. S. (1966a). Developmental communalities of homologous and non-homologous body joints. *American Journal of Physical Anthropology*, **25**, 147–51.

147. Garn, S. M., Rohmann, C. G., Blumenthal, T. & Silverman, F. N. (1967f). Ossification communalities of the hand and other body parts: Their implications to skeletal assessment. *American Journal of Physical Anthropology*, **27**, 75–82.

148. Garn, S. M., Rohmann, C. G. & Davis, A. A. (1963c). Genetics of hand–wrist ossification. *American Journal of Physical Anthropology*, **21**, 33–40.

149. Garn, S. M., Rohmann, C. G. & Hertzog, K. P. (1969a). Apparent influence of the X chromosome on timing of 73 ossification centers. *American Journal of Physical Anthropology*, **30**, 123–8.

150. Garn, S. M., Rohmann, C. G. & Nolan, P. H., Jr. (1963e). Aging and bone loss in a normal human population. *Excerpta Medica Foundation*, **57**, 90.

151. Garn, S. M., Rohmann, C. G. & Nolan, P., Jr. (1964c). The development and nature of bone changes during aging. In *Relations of Development and Aging*, ed. J. E. Birren, pp. 44–61. Springfield, Illinois: Charles C Thomas.

152. Garn, S. M., Rohmann, C. G. & Robinow, M. (1961c). Increments in hand–wrist ossification. *American Journal of Physical Anthropology*, **19**, 45–53.

153. Garn, S. M., Rohmann, C. G. & Silverman, F. N. (1965e). Missing ossification centers of the foot – inheritance and developmental meaning. *Annales de Radiologie*, **8**, 629–44.

154. Garn, S. M., Rohmann, C. G. & Silverman, F. N. (1967e). Radiographic standards for postnatal ossification and tooth calcification. *Medical Radiography and Photography*, **43**, 45–66.

155. Garn, S. M., Rohmann, C. G., Wagner, B. & Ascoli, W. (1967g). Continuing bone growth throughout life: A general phenomenon. *American Journal of Physical Anthropology*, **26**, 313–18.

156. Garn, S. M., Rohmann, C. G., Wagner, B. & Davila, G. H. (1970). Dynamics of change at the endosteal surface of tubular bones. In *Progress in Methods of*

Bone Mineral Measurement, ed. G. D. Whedon & J. R. Cameron, pp. 430–79. Washington, DC: US Government Printing Office.

157. Garn, S. M., Rohmann, C. G., Wagner, B., Davila, G. H. & Ascoli, W. (1969b). Population similarities in the onset and rate of adult endosteal bone loss. *Clinical Orthopaedics*, **65**, 51–60.

158. Garn, S. M., Rohmann, C. G. & Wallace, D. K. (1961d). Association between alternate sequences of hand–wrist ossification. *American Journal of Physical Anthropology*, **19**, 361–4.

159. Garn, S. M. & Saalberg, J. H. (1953). Sex and age differences in the composition of the adult leg. *Human Biology*, **25**, 144–53.

160. Garn, S. M. & Schwager, P. M. (1967). Age dynamics of persistent transverse lines in the tibia. *American Journal of Physical Anthropology*, **27**, 357–8.

161. Garn, S. M., Selby, S. & Crawford, M. R. (1956b). Skin reflectance studies in children and adults. *American Journal of Anthropology*, **14**, 101–17.

162. Garn, S. M., Selby, S. & Crawford, M. R. (1956c). Skin reflectance during pregnancy. *American Journal of Obstetrics and Gynecology*, **72**, 974–6.

163. Garn, S. M., Selby, S. & Young, R. (1954). Scalp thickness and the fat loss theory of balding. *Archives of Dermatology and Syphilology*, **70**, 601–8.

164. Garn, S. M. & Shamir, Z. (1958). *Methods for Research in Human Growth*. Springfield, Illinois: Charles C Thomas.

165. Garn, S. M., Silverman, F. N. & Davis, A. A. (1963a). Skin and gonadal dosages during investigative radiography. *American Journal of Physical Anthropology*, **21**, 561–8.

166. Garn, S. M., Silverman, F. N. & Davis, A. A. (1964d). Gonadal dosages in investigative radiography. *Science*, **143**, 1039.

167. Garn, S. M., Silverman, F. N. & Rohmann, C. G. (1964e). A rational approach to the assessment of skeletal maturation. *Annales de Radiologie*, **7**, 297–307.

168. Garn, S. M., Silverman, F. & Sontag, L. W. (1957b). X-ray protection in studies of growth and development. *American Journal of Physical Anthropology*, **15**, 452.

169. Garn, S. M., Swindler, D. R. & Kerewsky, R. S. (1966d). A canine 'field' in sexual dimorphism in tooth size. *Nature*, **212**, 1501–2.

170. Garn, S. M. & Wagner, B. (1969). The adolescent growth of the skeletal mass and its implications to mineral requirements. In *Adolescent Nutrition and Growth*, ed. F. P. Heald, pp. 139–61. New York: Appleton-Century-Crofts.

171. Garn, S. M., Wagner, B., Rohmann, C. G. & Ascoli, W. (1968h). Further evidence for continuing bone expansion. *American Journal of Physical Anthropology*, **28**, 219–21.

172. Garn, S. M. & Young, R. W. (1956). Concurrent fat loss and fat gain. *American Journal of Physical Anthropology*, **14**, 497–504.

Gindhart, P. S. (1969). The frequency of appearance of transverse lines in the tibia in relation to childhood illness. *American Journal of Physical Anthropology*, **31**, 17–22.

Gindhart, P. S. (1971). Growth of the tibia and radius studied longitudinally in normal children in relation to childhood disorders. PhD Thesis, University of Texas at Austin.

Gindhart, P. S. (1972). The effect of seasonal variation on long bone growth. *Human Biology*, **44**, 335–50.

Gindhart, P. S. (1973). Growth standards for the tibia and radius in children aged one month through eighteen years. *American Journal of Physical Anthropology*, **39**, 41–8.

*Goldstein, H. (1979). *The Design and Analysis of Longitudinal Studies*. London: Academic Press.

Goodson, C. S. & Jamison, P. (1987). Relative rate of maturation: A reaffirmation of its significant psychological effect. *Journal of Biosocial Science*, **19**, 73–88.

*Greulich, W. & Pyle, S. I. (1959). *Radiographic Atlas of Skeletal Development of the Hand and Wrist*, 2nd edn. Stanford: Stanford University Press.

Guo, S. (1986). The use of impedance in the estimation of body composition. *American Journal of Physical Anthropology*, **69**, 209.

Guo, S. (1988). An application of logistic regression to study tracking of overweight. *American Journal of Physical Anthropology*, **75**, 218.

Guo, S. (1990). A computer program for smoothing using Kernel estimation. *American Statistical Association*, Proceedings, 306–308.

Guo, S., Chumlea, W. C., Siervogel, R. M. & Roche, A. F. (in press). Longitudinal analysis of plasma lipid levels in children and young adults. *Proceedings of the Fifth Conference for Federally Supported Human Nutrition Research Units and Centers*, Washington, DC.

Guo, S., Roche, A. F. & Chumlea, W. C. (1989b). Predicting fat-free mass (FFM) and percent body fat (%BF) from anthropometry, resistance and reactance. *American Journal of Human Biology*, **1**, 135.

Guo, S., Roche, A. F., Chumlea, W. C., Miles, D. S. & Pohlman, R. A. (1987a). Body composition predictions from bioelectric impedance. *Human Biology*, **59**, 221–33.

Guo, S., Roche, A. F. & Houtkooper, L. (1989a). Fat-free mass in children and young adults from bioelectric impedance and anthropometric variables. *American Journal of Clinical Nutrition*, **50**, 435–43.

Guo, S., Roche, A. F. & Moore, W. M. (1988). Reference data for head circumference status and 1-month increments from 1 to 12 months of age. *Journal of Pediatrics*, **113**, 490 4.

Guo, S., Siervogel, R. M. & Roche, A. F. (1989c). Tracking in body mass index from 2 to 18 years: The FELS Longitudinal Study. *Clinical Research*, **37**, 963A.

Guo, S., Siervogel, R. M. & Roche, A. F. (1990). Confidence limits for least-squares Kernel estimates. *Annual Meeting of the American Statistical Association*, pp. 119.

Guo, S., Siervogel, R. M., Roche, A. F. & Chumlea, W. C. (in press). Mathematical modelling of human growth: A comparative study. *American Journal of Human Biology*.

Guo, S., Simon, R., Talmadge, J. E. & Klabansky, R. L. (1987b). An interactive computer program for the analysis of growth curves. *Computers and Biomedical Research*, **20**, 37–48.

Hamill, P. V. V., Drizd, T. A., Johnson, C. L., Reed, R. B. & Roche, A. F. (1977). NCHS growth curves for children. Birth–18 years, United States. *Vital and*

Health Statistics, National Center for Health Statistics, Series 11, No. 165. Washington, DC: US Government Printing Office.

Hamill, P. V. V., Drizd, T. A., Johnson, C. L., Reed, R. B., Roche, A. F. & Moore, W. M. (1979). Physical growth: National Center for Health Statistics Percentiles. *American Journal of Clinical Nutrition*, **32**, 607–29.

Harrison, G. G., Buskirk, E. R., Carter, J. E. L., Johnston, F. E., Lohman, T. G., Pollock, M. L., Roche, A. F. & Wilmore, J. (1988). Skinfold thicknesses and measurement technique. In *Anthropometric Standardization Reference Manual*, ed. T. Lohman, A. F. Roche & R. Martorell, pp. 55–70. Champaign, Illinois: Human Kinetics Books.

Heiber, R. G. (1975). *The relationship of the ulnar sesamoid bone in males to circumpuberal growth rates of the mandible and body height and weight*. MSc Thesis, Ohio State University.

Hertzog, K. P. (1967). Shortened fifth middle phalanges. *American Journal of Physical Anthropology*, **27**, 113–18.

Hertzog, K. P. (1990). Evidence for continuing bone elongation in adults based on longitudinal hand radiographs. *Acta medica Auxologica*, **22**, 57–60.

Hertzog, K. P., Garn, S. M. & Church, S. F. (1968). Cone-shaped epiphyses in the hand. *Investigative Radiology*, **3**, 433–41.

Hertzog, K. P., Garn, S. M. & Hempy, H. O., III. (1969). Partitioning the effects of secular trend and aging on adult stature. *American Journal of Physical Anthropology*, **31**, 111–15.

Himes, J. H. (1977). Gruelich–Pyle and Tanner–Whitehouse skeletal age: Associations with pubertal events. *American Journal of Physical Anthropology*, **47**, 136–7.

Himes, J. H. (1978a). Bone growth and development in protein–calorie malnutrition. *World Review of Nutrition and Dietetics*, **28**, 143–87.

Himes, J. H. (1978b). Infant feeding patterns and subsequent obesity. *American Journal of Physical Anthropology*, **48**, 405–6.

Himes, J. H. (1979). Secular trends in body proportions and composition. In *Secular Trends in Child Growth, Maturation and Development*, ed. A. F. Roche, pp. 28–59, Monographs of the Society for Research in Child Development, **44**.

Himes, J. H. (1980a). Subcutaneous fat thickness as an indicator of nutritional status. In *Social and Biological Predictors of Nutritional Status, Physical Growth and Neurological Development*, ed. L. S. Greene & F. E. Johnston, pp. 3–26. New York: Academic Press.

Himes, J. H. (1980b). Skinfold compression and the estimation of total body fat. *American Journal of Physical Anthropology*, **52**, 237–8.

Himes, J. H. (1984a). Appropriateness of parent-specific stature adjustment for US black children. *Journal of the National Medical Association*, **76**, 55–7.

Himes, J. H. (1984b). Appropriateness of the linear midparent model for parent–child stature studies. *American Journal of Physical Anthropology*, **63**, 170.

Himes, J. H. & Roche, A. F. (1982). Reported versus measured adult statures. *American Journal of Physical Anthropology*, **58**, 335–42.

Himes, J. H. & Roche, A. F. (1986). Subcutaneous fatness and stature: Relationships from infancy to adulthood. *Human Biology*, **58**, 737–50.

Himes, J. H., Roche, A. F. & Siervogel, R. M. (1979). Compressibility of skinfolds and the measurement of subcutaneous fatness. *American Journal of Clinical Nutrition*, **32**, 1734–40.

Himes, J. H., Roche, A. F. & Thissen, D. (1981). Parent-specific adjustments for assessment of recumbent length and stature. *Monographs in Pediatrics*, **13**, 1–88.

Himes, J. H., Roche, A. F., Thissen, D. & Moore, W. M. (1985). Parent-specific adjustments for evaluation of recumbent length and stature. *Pediatrics*, **75**, 304–13.

Himes, J. H., Roche, A. F. & Webb, P. (1980). Fat areas as estimates of total body fat. *American Journal of Clinical Nutrition*, **33**, 2093–100.

Hinck, V. C. & Hopkins, C. E. (1965). Concerning growth of the sphenoid sinus. *Archives of Otolaryngology*, **82**, 62–6.

*Hollingshead, A. (1957). *The Two Factor Index of Social Position*. Atlanta, Georgia: Emory University.

Holm, V. A., Kronmall, R. A., Williamson, M. & Roche, A. F. (1979). Physical growth in phenylketonuria: II. Growth of children in the PKU collaborative study from birth to four years of age. *Pediatrics*, **63**, 700–7.

Huff, C. E. & Pyle, S. I. (1937). Differences in the utilization of calcium and phosphorus in negative and positive balances during pregnancy. *Human Biology*, **9**, 29–42.

Israel, H. (1966). Radiogrammetric replicability and direct validity of small mandibular measurements in the 45-degree projection. *Journal of Dental Research*, **45**, 1570.

Israel, H. (1967a). Loss of bone and remodeling–redistribution in the craniofacial skeleton with age. *Federation Proceedings*, **26**, 1723–8.

Israel, H. (1967b). Microdensitometric analysis for the study of cranio-facial growth in the living subject. *American Journal of Physical Anthropology*, **27**, 236.

Israel, H. (1968a). Continuing growth in the human cranial skeletal. *Archives of Oral Biology*, **13**, 133–8.

Israel, H. (1968b). *In vivo* assessment of skeletal morphology by radiographic densitometry. *Journal of Periodontology*, **38**, 667–76.

Israel, H. (1969). Pubertal influence upon the growth and sexual differentiation of the human mandible. *Archives of Oral Biology*, **14**, 583–90.

Israel, H. (1970). Continuing growth in sella turcia with age. *American Journal of Roentgenology*, **108**, 516–27.

Israel, H. (1971). The impact of aging upon the adult craniofacial skeleton. PhD Dissertation, University of Alabama at Birmingham.

Israel, H. (1973a). Age factor and the pattern of change in craniofacial structures. *American Journal of Physical Anthropology*, **39**, 111–28.

Israel, H. (1973b). Progressive enlargement of the vertebral body as part of the process of human skeletal aging. *Age and Aging*, **2**, 71–9.

Israel, H. (1973c). Recent knowledge concerning craniofacial aging. *Angle Orthodontist*, **43**, 176–84.

Israel, H. (1973d). The failure of aging or loss of teeth to drastically alter mandibular angle morphology. *Journal of Dental Research*, **52**, 83–90.

Israel, H. (1977). The dichotomous pattern of craniofacial expansion during aging. *American Journal of Physical Anthropology*, **47**, 47–52.

Israel, H. (1978). The fundamentals of cranial and facial growth. In *Human Growth*, vol. 2, ed. F. Falkner & J. M. Tanner, pp. 357–80. New York: Plenum Press.

Israel, H., Garn, S. M. & Colbert, C. (1967). The recording microdensitometer as a research tool in the study of oral–facial development. *Journal of Dental Research*, **46**, 164.

Israel, H. & Lewis, A. B. (1971). Radiographically determined linear permanent tooth growth from age 6 years. *Journal of Dental Research*, **50**, 334–42.

Johnson, G. F., Dorst, J. P., Kuhn, J. P., Roche, A. F. & Davila, G. H. (1973). Reliability of skeletal age assessments. *American Journal of Roentgenology*, **158**, 320–7.

Johnston, F. E., Roche, A. F., Schell, L. M. & Wettenhall, H. N. B. (1975). Critical weight at menarche. Critique of an hypothesis. *American Journal of Diseases of Children*, **129**, 19–23.

Johnston, F. E., Roche, A. F. & Susanne, C. (1980). *Human Physical Growth and Maturation: Methodologies and Factors.* New York: Plenum Press.

*Jones, M. C., Bayley, N., Macfarlane, J. W. & Honzik, M. P. (1971). *The Course of Human Development.* Waltham, Massachusetts: Xerox College Publishing Co.

*Jordan, J., Ruben, M., Hernandez, J., Bebelagua, A., Tanner, J. M. & Goldstein, H. (1975). The 1972 Cuban National Growth Study as an example of population health monitoring: design and methods. *Annals of Human Biology*, **2**, 153–71.

Kagan, J. & Garn, S. M. (1963). A constitutional correlate of early intellective functioning. *Journal of Genetic Psychology*, **102**, 83–9.

Kagan, J. & Moss, H. A. (1963). *Birth to Maturity: A Study in Psychological Development.* New York: Wiley.

Kingsley, A. & Reynolds, E. L. (1949). The relation of illness patterns in children to ordinal position in the family. *Journal of Pediatrics*, **35**, 17–23.

Koski, K. (1961). Growth changes in the relationships between some basicranial planes and palatal plane. *Suomen Hammaslaakariseuran Toimituksia*, **57**, 15–26.

Koski, K. & Garn, S. M. (1957). Tooth eruption sequence in fossil and modern man. *American Journal of Physical Anthropology*, **15**, 469–88.

Koski, K., Garn, S. M. & Lewis, A. B. (1957). Tooth eruption sequence in fossil and modern man. *American Journal of Physical Anthropology*, **15**, 451–2.

Kouchi, M., Mukherjee, D. & Roche, A. F. (1985a). Curve fitting for growth in weight during infancy with relationships to adult status, and familial associations of the estimated parameters. *Human Biology*, **57**, 245–65.

Kouchi, M., Roche, A. F. & Mukherjee, D. (1985b). Growth in recumbent length during infancy with relationships to adult status and familial associations of the estimated parameters. *Human Biology*, **57**, 449–72.

*Kushner, R. F. & Schoeller, D. A. (1986). Estimation of total body water by bioelectrical impedance analysis. *American Journal of Clinical Nutrition*, **44**, 417–24.

Lavelle, M. (1991). Predictors of small size of the human birth canal. *American Journal of Physical Anthropology*, **12**, 112.

Lee, M. M. C. (1967). Natural markers in bone growth. *American Journal of Physical Anthropology*, **27**, 237.

Lee, M. M. C. & Garn, S. M. (1967). Pseudoepiphyses or notches in the non-epiphyseal end of metacarpal bones in healthy children. *Anatomical Record*, **159**, 263–72.

Lee, M. M. C., Garn, S. M. & Rohmann, C. G. (1968). Relation of metacarpal notching to stature and maturational status of normal children. *Investigative Radiology*, **3**, 96–102.

Lee, P. S. T. & Guo, S. (1986). A curve fitting analysis of the normal approximation to binomial distribution. In *Program and Abstracts*, p. 170, Chicago: Joint Statistical Meetings. American Statistical Association; Biometric Society, Institute of Mathematical Statistics.

Lestrel, P. E. & Brown, H. D. (1976). Fourier analysis of adolescent growth of the cranial vault: A longitudinal study. *Human Biology*, **48**, 517–28.

Lestrel, P. E., Engstrom, C. & Bodt, A. (1991). Quantitative analysis of nasal bone growth: The first year of life. *American Journal of Physical Anthropology*, **112**, 114–15.

*Lestrel, P. E. & Roche, A. F. (1977). A comparative study of cranial thickness in Down's syndrome: Fourier analysis. *Acta Medica Auxologica*, **9**, 27.

Lestrel, P. E. & Roche, A. F. (1984). Variability in cranial base shape with age: Fourier analysis. *American Journal of Physical Anthropology*, **63**, 184.

Lestrel, P. E. & Roche, A. F. (1986). Cranial base shape variation with age: A longitudinal study of shape using Fourier analysis. *Human Biology*, **58**, 527–40.

Lewis, A. B. & Garn, S. M. (1960). The relationship between tooth formation and other maturation factors. *Angle Orthodontist*, **30**, 70–7.

Lewis, A. B. & Roche, A. F. (1974). Cranial base elongation in boys during pubescence. *Angle Orthodontist*, **44**, 83–93.

Lewis, A. B. & Roche, A. F. (1977). The saddle angle: Constancy or change? *Angle Orthodontist*, **47**, 46–54.

Lewis, A. B. & Roche, A. F. (1988). Late growth changes in the craniofacial skeleton. *Angle Orthodontist*, **58**, 127–35.

Lewis, A. B., Roche, A. F. & Wagner, B. (1982). The growth of the mandible during pubescence. *Angle Orthodontist*, **52**, 325–42.

Lewis, A. B., Roche, A. F. & Wagner, B. (1985). Pubertal spurts in cranial base and mandible: Comparisons within individuals. *Angle Orthodontist*, **55**, 17–30.

*Lohman, T. G. (1986). Applicability of body composition techniques and constants for children and youths. *Exercise and Sport Science Reviews*, **14**, 325–57.

Lohman, T. G., Roche, A. F. & Martorell, R. (1988). *Anthropometric Standardization Reference Manual*. Champaign, Illinois: Human Kinetics Books.

Malina, R. M. & Roche, A. F. (1983). *Manual of Physical Status and Performance in Childhood*. Vol. II, *Physical Performance*. New York: Plenum Press.

McCall, R. B., Meyers, E. D., Jr., Hartman, J. & Roche, A. F. (1983). Development changes in head-circumference and mental-performance growth

rates: A test of Epstein's prenoblysis hypothesis. *Developmental Psycho-biology*, **16**, 457–68.

*McCammon, R. W. (1970). *Human Growth and Development*. Springfield, Illinois: Charles C Thomas.

Meier, R. J., Goodson, C. S. & Roche, E. (1987). Dermatoglyphic development and timing of maturation. *Human Biology*, **59**, 357–73.

Moerman, M. L. (1981). A longitudinal study of growth in relation to body size and sexual dimorphism in the human pelvis. PhD Thesis, University of Michigan: Ann Arbor, Michigan.

Moerman, M. L. (1982). Growth of the birth canal in adolescent girls. *American Journal of Obstetrics and Gynecology*, **143**, 528–32.

Moore, W. M. & Roche, A. F. (1982). *Pediatric Anthropometry*. Columbus, Ohio: Ross Laboratories.

Moore, W. M. & Roche, A. F. (1983). *Pediatric Anthropometry*, 2nd edn. Columbus, Ohio: Ross Laboratories.

Moore, W. M. & Roche, A. F. (1987). *Pediatric Anthropometry*, 3rd edn. Columbus, Ohio: Ross Laboratories.

Mukherjee, D. (1982). Fitting distributions to non-normal data. *American Journal of Physical Anthropology*, **57**, 212.

Mukherjee, D. & Hurst, D. C. (1984). Maximum entropy revisited. *Statistica Neerlandica*, **38**, 1–13.

Mukherjee, D., Neiswanger, K., Siervogel, R. M., Roche, A. F. & Roche, E. (1984). Genetic analyses of discrete or continuous traits upon fitting a finite mixture of flexible maximum entrophy distributions. *American Journal of Human Genetics*, **36**, 176S.

Mukherjee, D. & Roche, A. F. (1984). The estimation of percent body fat, body density and total body fat by maximum R^2 regression equations. *Human Biology*, **56**, 79–109.

Mukherjee, D. & Siervogel, R. M. (1983). An alternative to the mixture of normal distributions. *American Journal of Human Genetics*, **35**, 202A.

Murray, J. R., Bock, R. D. & Roche, A. F. (1971). The measurement of skeletal maturity. *American Journal of Physical Anthropology*, **35**, 327–30.

Newbery, H. (1941). Studies in fetal behavior. IV. The measurement of three types of fetal activity. *Journal of Comparative Psychology*, **32**, 521–30.

Norman, H. N. (1942). Fetal hiccups. *Journal of Comparative Psychology*, **34**, 65–73.

Ohtsuki, F., Mukherjee, D., Lewis, A. B. & Roche, A. F. (1982a). A factor analysis of cranial base and vault dimensions in children. *American Journal of Physical Anthropology*, **58**, 271–9.

Ohtsuki, F., Mukherjee, D., Lewis, A. B. & Roche, A. F. (1982b). Growth of cranial base and vault dimensions in children. *Journal Anthropological Society of Nippon*, **90**, 239–58.

Olson, J. M., Boehnke, M., Neiswanger, K., Roche, A. F. & Siervogel, R. M. (1989). Alternative genetic models for the inheritance of the phenylthio-carbamide taste deficiency. *Genetic Epidemiology*, **6**, 423–34.

*Palmer, C. E. & Reed, L. J. (1935). Anthropometric studies of individual growth. I. Age, height and growth in height; elementary school children. *Human Biology*, **7**, 319–24.

Pao, E. M., Himes, J. H. & Roche, A. F. (1980). Milk intake and feeding patterns of breast-fed infants. *Journal of American Dietetic Association,* **77**, 540–5.

Patton, J. L. (1979). A study of distributional normality of skinfold measurements. Master's Thesis. Seattle, Washington: University of Washington.

Potter, D. E., Broyer, M., Chantler, C., Gruskin, A., Holliday, M. A., Roche, A. F., Scharer, K. & Thissen, D. (1978). The measurement of growth in children with renal insufficiency. *Kidney International,* **14**, 378–82.

Poznanski, A. K., Garn, S. M., Nagy, J. M. & Gall, J. C., Jr. (1972). Metacarpophalangeal pattern profiles in the evaluation of skeletal malformation. *Radiology,* **104**, 1–11.

Poznanski, A. K., Roche, A. F., Mukherjee, D., Pachman, L. M. & Brewer, E. J., Jr. (1985). Norms of the apparent width of the knee joint: Useful measures in the evaluation of children with juvenile arthritis. *American Journal of Roentgenology, Radium Therapy and Nuclear Medicine,* **145**, 870.

Pyle, S. I. (1938). Interrelations of hemoglobin, basal metabolism, and creatine, creatinine and magnesium excretion during human pregnancy. *Human Biology,* **10**, 528–36.

Pyle, S. I. (1939). Observations on the size and position of the nutrient foramen in the radius. *Human Biology,* **2**, 369–78.

Pyle, S. I. & Huff, C. E. (1936). The use of 3-day periods in the human metabolism studies. Calcium and phosphorus. *Journal of Nutrition,* **11**, 495–509.

Pyle, S. I. & Menino, C. (1939). Observations on estimating skeletal age from the Todd and Flory bone atlases. *Child Development,* **10**, 27–34.

Pyle, S. I., Potgieter, M. & Comstock, G. (1938). On certain relationships of calcium in the blood serum to calcium balance and basal metabolism during pregnancy. *American Journal of Obstetrics and Gynecology,* **35**, 283–9.

Pyle, S. I. & Sontag, L. W. (1943). Variability in onset of ossification in epiphyses and short bones of the extremities. *American Journal of Roentgenology and Radium Therapy,* **49**, 795–8.

Reynolds, E. L. (1943). Degree of kinship and pattern of ossification. *American Journal of Physical Anthropology,* **1**, 405–16.

Reynolds, E. L. (1944). Differential tissue growth in the leg during childhood. *Child Development,* **15**, 181–205.

Reynolds, E. L. (1945). Bony pelvic girdle in early infancy. *American Journal of Physical Anthropology,* **3**, 321–54.

Reynolds, E. L. (1946a). Sexual maturation and the growth of fat, muscle and bone in girls. *Child Development,* **17**, 121–44.

Reynolds, E. L. (1946b). The bony pelvis in prepubertal childhood. *American Journal of Physical Anthropology,* **5**, 165–200.

Reynolds, E. L. (1948). Distribution of tissue components in the female leg from birth to maturity. *Anatomical Record,* **100**, 621–30.

Reynolds, E. L. (1949a). Anthropology and human growth. *Ohio Journal of Science,* **49**, 89–91.

Reynolds, E. L. (1949b). The fat/bone index as a sex-differentiating character in man. *Human Biology,* **21**, 199–204.

Reynolds, E. L. (1951). The distribution of subcutaneous fat in childhood and adolescence. *Monographs of the Society for Research in Child Development,* No. 50.

Reynolds, E. L. & Asakawa, T. (1948). Measurement of obesity in childhood. *American Journal of Physical Anthropology*, **6**, 475–87.

Reynolds, E. L. & Asakawa, T. (1950). A comparison of certain aspects of body structure and body shape in 200 adults. *American Journal of Physical Anthropology*, **8**, 343–65.

Reynolds, E. L. & Asakawa, T. (1951). Skeletal development in infancy. *American Journal of Roentgenology and Radium Therapy*, **65**, 403–10.

Reynolds, E. L. & Clark, L. C., Jr. (1947). Creatinine excretion, growth progress and body structure in normal children. *Child Development*, **18**, 155–68.

Reynolds, E. L. & Grote, P. (1948). Sex differences in the distribution of tissue components in the human leg from birth to maturity. *Anatomical Record*, **102**, 45–53.

Reynolds, E. L. & Schoen, G. (1947). Growth patterns of identical triplets from 8 through 18 years. *Child Development*, **18**, 130–51.

Reynolds, E. L. & Sontag, L. W. (1944). Seasonal variations in weight, height and appearance of ossification centers. *Journal of Pediatrics*, **24**, 524–35.

Reynolds, E. L. & Sontag, L. W. (1945). Variations in growth patterns in health and disease. *Journal of Pediatrics*, **26**, 336–52.

Reynolds, E. L. & Wines, J. (1948). Individual differences in physical changes associated with adolescence in girls. *American Journal of Diseases of Children*, **75**, 329–50.

Reynolds, E. L. & Wines, J. V. (1951). Physical changes associated with adolescence in boys. *American Journal of Diseases of Children*, **82**, 529–47.

Richards, T. W. & Nelson, V. L. (1938). Studies in mental development: II. Analysis of abilities tested at the age of six months by the Gesell schedule. *Journal of Genetic Psychology*, **52**, 327–31.

Richards, T. W. & Newbery, H. (1938). Studies in fetal behavior: III. Can performance on test items at six months postnatally be predicted on the basis of fetal activity? *Child Development*, **9**, 79–86.

Richards, T. W., Newbery, H. & Fallgatter, R. (1938). Studies in fetal behavior: II. Activity of the human fetus in utero and its relation to other prenatal conditions, particularly the mother's basal metabolic rate. *Child Development*, **9**, 69–78.

Robinow, M. (1942a). The variability of weight and height increments from birth to six years. *Child Development*, **13**, 159–64.

Robinow, M. (1942b). Appearance of ossification centers. Groupings obtained from factor analysis. *American Journal of Diseases of Children*, **64**, 229–36.

Robinow, M. (1943). The statistical diagnosis of zygosity in multiple human births. *Human Biology*, **15**, 221–35..

Robinow, M. (1968). Field measurement of growth and development. In *Malnutrition, Learning and Behavior*, ed. N. S. Scrimshaw & J. E. Gordon, pp. 409–25. Cambridge, Massachusetts: Massachusetts Institute of Technology Press.

Robinow, M., Johnson, M. & Anderson, M. (1943a). Feet of normal children. *Journal of Pediatrics*, **23**, 141–9.

Robinow, M., Leonard, V. L. & Anderson, M. (1943b). A new approach to the analysis of children's posture. *Journal of Pediatrics*, **22**, 655–63.

Robinow, M., Richards, T. W. & Anderson, M. (1942). The eruption of deciduous teeth. *Growth*, **6**, 127–33.

173. *Roche, A. F. (1965). The sites of elongation of human metacarpals and metatarsals. *Acta Anatomica (Basel)*, **61**, 193–202.

174. Roche, A. F. (1971a). New statistical technique that assist the interpretation of serial growth data. In *Growth and Development*, pp. 9–11. Proceedings XIII International Congress of Pediatrics, Vienna.

175. Roche, A. F. (1971b). Summary of discussion. *American Journal of Physical Anthropology*, **35**, 467–70.

176. Roche, A. F. (1971c). Symposium on Assessment of Skeletal Maturity. *American Journal of Physical Anthropology*, **35**, 315–469.

177. Roche, A. F. (1973). The timing and sequence of some adolescent events. In *Report on Workshop on Trauma in Adolescents in Sports and Recreation*, pp. 1–40. Committee on Prosthetics Research and Development. Washington, DC: National Academy of Science.

178. Roche, A. F. (1974a). Differential timing of maximum length increments between bones within individuals. *Human Biology*, **46**, 145–57.

179. Roche, A. F. (1974b). The design of studies for measuring growth. *Proceedings of XIV International Congress of Pediatrics*, **58**, 320–31.

180. Roche, A. F. (1974c). Introduction to symposium: Some aspects of adolescent physiology. *Human Biology*, **46**, 115–16.

181. Roche, A. F. (1974d). Anthropometric indices as nutritional indicators. *Proceedings of XIV International Congress of Pediatrics*, **5**, 1–12.

182. Roche, A. F. (1975). Some aspects of adolescent growth and maturation. In *Nutrient Requirements in Adolescence*, ed. H. N. Munroe & J. I. McKigney, pp. 33–56. Cambridge, Massachusetts: Massachusetts Institute of Technology Press.

183. Roche, A. F. (1976). Growth after puberty. In *Youth in a Changing World: Cross-cultural Perspectives on Adolescence*, ed. E. E. Fuchs, pp. 17–53. The Hague: Mouton Publishers.

184. Roche, A. F. (1978a). Growth assessment in abnormal children. *Kidney International*, **14**, 369–77.

185. Roche, A. F. (1978b). Parametros de crecimiento. *Archivos Argentinos de Pediatria*, **76**, 8–13 + 52.

186. Roche, A. F. (1978c). Bone growth and maturation. In *Human Growth*, ed. F. Falkner & J. M. Tanner, pp. 318–55. New York: Plenum Publishing Corporation.

187. Roche, A. F., ed. (1979a). *Secular Trends in Human Growth, Maturation and Development*. Monographs of the Society for Research in Child Development, **44**.

188. Roche, A. F. (1979b). Postnatal growth of adipose tissue in man. *Studies in Physical Anthropology*, **5**, 53–73.

189. Roche, A. F. (1979c). Growth assessment of handicapped children. *Dietetic Currents*, **6**, 25–30.

190. Roche, A. F. (1980a). The analysis of serial data. *Studies in Physical Anthropology*, **6**, 71–88.

191. Roche, A. F. (1980b). Prediction. In *Human Physical Growth and Maturation: Methodologies and Factors*, ed. F. E. Johnston, A. F. Roche & C. Susanne,

pp. 177–91. NATO Advanced Study Institute, Sogesta, Italy. New York: Plenum Publishing Corporation.

192. Roche, A. F. (1980c). Possible catch-up growth of the brain. *Acta Medica Auxologica*, **12**, 165–79.

193. Roche, A. F. (1981a). Recent advances in child growth and development. Eleventh International Congress of Anatomy. In *Glial and Neuronal Cell Biology*, ed. S. Fedoroff, pp. 321–9. New York: Alan R. Liss.

194. Roche, A. F. (1981b). The adipocyte number hypothesis. *Child Development*, **52**, 31–43.

195. Roche, A. F. (1982). Anthropometric variables: Effectiveness and limitations. In *Assessing the Nutritional Status of the Elderly – State of the Art*, ed. C. W. Calloway & G. Harrison, pp. 22–8. Report of the Third Ross Roundtable on Medical Issues. Columbus, Ohio: Ross Laboratories.

196. Roche, A. F. (1984a). Research progress in the field of body composition. *Medicine and Science in Sports and Exercise*, **16**, 579–83.

197. Roche, A. F. (1984b). Adult stature prediction: A critical review. *Acta Medica Auxologica*, **16**, 5–28.

198. Roche, A. F. (1984c). Anthropometric methods: New and old, what they tell us. *International Journal of Obesity*, **8**, 509–23.

199. Roche, A. F. (1985a). Concluding remarks. In *Body Composition Assessments in Youth and Adults*, ed. A. F. Roche, pp. 107–8. Proceedings of Sixth Ross Conference on Medical Research, Williamsburg, Virginia, December 1984. Columbus, Ohio: Ross Laboratories.

200. Roche, A. F. (1985b). Continuities and discontinuities in postnatal growth. *Book of Abstracts*, p. 601. XII International Anatomical Congress 1985, London, Barbican Centre.

201. Roche, A. F. (1986a). Physical growth. In *An Evaluation and Assessment of the State of the Science. Report of the Study Group on Developmental Endocrinology and Physical Growth*, ed. S. L. Kaplan & G. D. Grave, pp. 43–73. Washington, DC: US Department of Health and Human Services.

202. Roche, A. F. (1986b). Bone growth and maturation. In *Human Growth. A Comprehensive Treatise*, 2nd edn., vol. 2, *Postnatal Growth, Neurobiology*, ed. F. Falkner & J. M. Tanner, pp. 25–60. New York: Plenum Press.

203. Roche, A. F. (1986c). The need for improvements in the measurements of body composition: Some critical issues. *American Journal of Physical Anthropology*, **69**, 256.

204. Roche, A. F. (1987a). Some aspects of the criterion methods for the measurement of body composition. *Human Biology*, **59**, 209–20.

205. Roche, A. F. (1987b). Skeletal status in normal children. Report of the Seventh Ross Conference on Medical Research. *Osteoporosis: Current Concepts*, ed. A. F. Roche, pp. 8–11. Columbus, Ohio: Ross Laboratories.

206. Roche, A. F. (1987c). Risk of overweight at 18 years dependent on weight and weight/stature^2 during childhood. *Clinical Research*, **35**, 907a.

207. Roche, A. F. (1989a). The final phase of growth in stature. *Growth, Genetics and Hormones*, **5**, 4–6.

208. Roche, A. F. (1989b). Infants, children, and adolescents. In *Nutritional Status Assessments of the Individual*, ed. G. E. Livingston, pp. 179–87. Trumbull, Connecticut: Food and Nutrition Press.

209. Roche, A. F. (1989c). Relative utility of carpal skeletal ages. *American Journal of Human Biology*, **1**, 479–82.
210. Roche, A. F., Abdel-Malek, A. D. & Mukherjee, D. (1985). New approaches to clinical assessment of adipose tissue. In *Body Composition Assessments in Youth and Adults*, ed. A. F. Roche, pp. 14–19. Proceedings of Sixth Ross Conference on Medical Research, Williamsburg, Virginia, December 1984. Columbus, Ohio, Ross Laboratories.
211. Roche, A. F. & Baumgartner, R. N. (1988). Tracking in fat distribution during growth. In *Fat Distribution During Growth and Later Health Outcomes*, ed. C. Bouchard & F. E. Johnston, pp. 147–62. New York: Alan R. Liss.
212. Roche, A. F., Baumgartner, R. N. & Guo, S. (1987a). Population methods: Anthropometry or estimations. In *Human Body Composition and Fat Distribution*, ed. N. G. Norgan. *Euronut Report*, **8**, 31–48.
213. Roche, A. F., Baumgartner, R. N. & Guo, S. (1991a). Anthropometry: Classical and modern approaches. In *New Techniques in Nutritional Research*, ed. R. G. Whitehead & A. Prentice, pp. 241–59. San Diego, CA: Academic Press.
214. Roche, A. F., Baumgartner, R. N. & Siervogel, R. M. (1991b). B-mode ultrasound measurement of subcutaneous adipose tissue. *American Journal of Clinical Nutrition*, **53**, 27.
215. Roche, A. F. & Chumlea, W. C. (1980). Serial changes in predicted adult statures for individuals. *Human Biology*, **52**, 507–13.
216. Roche, A. F. & Chumlea, W. C. (in press). New approaches to clinical assessment of adipose tissue. In *Obesity*, ed. B. N. Brodoff & P. Bjorntorp. New York: J. B. Lippincott.
217. Roche, A. F., Chumlea, W. C. & Guo, S. (1986a). *Identification and Validation of New Anthropometric Techniques for Quantifying Body Composition*. Technical Report Natick/TR-86/058. Natick, Massachusetts: United States Army Natick Research, Development and Engineering Center.
218. Roche, A. F., Chumlea, W. C. & Guo, S. (1987c). Estimation of body composition from impedance. *Medicine and Science in Sports and Exercise*, **19**, S40.
219. Roche, A. F., Chumlea, W. C. & Siervogel, R. M. (1982b). *Longitudinal Study of Human Hearing: Its Relationship to noise and other factors. III. Results from the first five years*, AMRL-TR-82-68, pp. 216. Wright-Patterson Air Force Base, Ohio: Aerospace Medical Research Laboratory.
220. Roche, A. F., Chumlea, W. C., Siervogel, R. M. & Mukherjee, D. (1983d). *Lonitudinal Study of Human Hearing: Its relationship to noise and other factors. IV. Data from 1976 to 1982. Final Report*, AMRL-TR-83-057, pp. 62. Wright-Patterson Air Force Base, Ohio: Aerospace Medical Research Laboratory.
221. Roche, A. F., Chumlea, W. C. & Thissen, D. (1988a). *Assessing the Skeletal Maturity of the Hand–Wrist: FELS Method*, pp. viii + 339. Springfield, Illinois: Charles C Thomas.
222. Roche, A. F. & Davila, G. H. (1972). Late adolescent growth in stature. *Pediatrics*, **50**, 874–80.
223. Roche, A. F. & Davila, G. H. (1974a). Differences between recumbent length and stature within individuals. *Growth*, **38**, 313–20.

224. Roche, A. F. & Davila, G. H. (1974b). Growth after puberty. *Proceedings, XIV International Congress of Pediatrics, Buenos Aires*, **5**, 138–52.
225. Roche, A. F. & Davila, G. H. (1975). Prepubertal and postpubertal growth period. In *Fetal and Postnatal Growth – Hormones and Nutrition*, ed. D. B. Cheek, pp. 409–14. New York: John Wiley.
226. Roche, A. F. & Davila, G. H. (1976). The reliability of assessments of the maturity of individual hand–wrist bones. *Human Biology*, **48**, 585–97.
227. Roche, A. F., Davila, G. H. & Mellits, E. D. (1975c). Late adolescent changes in weight. In *Biosocial Interrelations in Population Adaptation*, ed. E. S. Watts, F. E. Johnston & C. W. Lasker, pp. 309–18. The Hague: Mouton Publishers.
228. Roche, A. F., Davila, G. H., Pasternack, B. A. & Walton, M. J. (1970a). Some factors influencing the replicability of assessments of skeletal maturity (Greulich–Pyle). *American Journal of Roentgenology*, **109**, 299–306.
229. Roche, A. F., Eichorn, D., McCammon, R. W., Reed, R. B., Valadian, I., Himes, J. H., Kent, R. L., Jr. & Siervogel, R. M. (1980). *The Natural History of Blood Pressure*. Report on Contract N01-HV-42985, 1400 pp.
230. Roche, A. F., Eyman, S. L. & Davila, G. H. (1971). Skeletal age prediction. *Journal of Pediatrics*, **78**, 997–1003.
231. Roche, A. F. & Falkner, F., eds. (1974). *Nutrition and Malnutrition: Identification and Measurement*. New York: Plenum Press.
232. Roche, A. F. & Falkner, F. (1975). Physical growth charts. In *Pediatric Screening Tests*, ed. W. K. Frankenburg & B. W. Camp, pp. 63–73. Springfield, Illinois: Charles C Thomas.
233. Roche, A. F. & French, N. Y. (1969). Rapid changes in weight and growth potential during childhood. *American Journal of Physical Anthropology*, **31**, 231–33.
234. Roche, A. F. & French, N. Y. (1970). Differences in skeletal maturity levels between the knee and hand. *American Journal of Roentgenology*, **109**, 307–12.
235. Roche, A. F., Garn, S. M., Reynolds, E. L., Robinow, M. & Sontag, L. W. (1981a). The first seriatim study of human growth and middle aging. *American Journal of Physical Anthropology*, **54**, 23–24.
236. Roche, A. F. & Guo, S. (1987). Tracking of weight (W) and weight/stature^2 (W/S^2) from one month to 30 years. *International Journal of Obesity*, **11**, 436A.
237. Roche, A. F. & Guo, S. (1988). Review of the paper by Cole, T. J.: Fitting smoothed centile curves to reference data. *Journal of the Royal Statistical Society*, **151**, 414.
238. Roche, A. F. & Guo, S. (1990). Prediction of fat-free mass (FFM) from bioelectric impedance and anthropometry. *Clinical Research*, **38**, 756A.
239. Roche, A. F., Guo, S. & Baumgartner, R. N. (1988b). The measurement of stature. *American Journal of Clinical Nutrition*, **47**, 922.
240. Roche, A. F., Guo, S. & Chumlea, W. C. (1989d). *Equations to Predict Fat-free Mass in Adults*. Report to RJL Systems, Inc. Detroit, Michigan.
241. Roche, A. F., Guo, S. & Houtkooper, L. (1989b). Biased estimation of fat-free mass. American Statistical Association. *Proceedings of the Biopharmaceutical Section*, pp. 188–91. 51st Annual Meeting, New Orleans, Louisiana.
242. Roche, A. F., Guo, S. & Moore, W. M. (1989a). Weight and recumbent

length from 1 to 12 months of age: Reference data for 1-month increments. *American Journal of Clinical Nutrition*, **49**, 599–607.

243. Roche, A. F., Guo, S. & Moore, W. M. (1989c). Infant growth and breast-feeding. *American Journal of Clinical Nutrition*, **50**, 1117–18.

244. Roche, A. F., Guo, S. & Moore, W. M. (1991). Body surface area of infants: reference data. *American Journal of Physical Anthropology*, **12**, 152.

245. Roche, A. F. & Hamill, P. V. V. (1977). United States Growth Charts. In *Proceedings of the First International Congress of Auxology, Rome*, pp. 143–8.

246. Roche, A. F. & Hamill, P. V. V. (1978). United States Growth Charts. In *Auxology: Human Growth in Health and Disorder*, ed. L. Gedda & P. Parisi, pp. 133–8. London, England: Academic Press.

247. Roche, A. F. & Himes, J. H. (1980). Incremental growth charts. *American Journal of Clinical Nutrition*, **33**, 2041–52.

248. Roche, A. F., Himes, J. H., Siervogel, R. M. & Johnson, D. L. (1979b). *Longitudinal Study of Human Hearing: Its Relationship to Noise and Other Factors. II. Results from the first three years*, AMRL-TR-79-102, pp. 221. Wright-Patterson Air Force Base, Ohio: Aerospace Medical Research Laboratory.

249. Roche, A. F. & Lewis, A. B. (1974). Sex differences in the elongation of the cranial base during pubescence. *Angle Orthodontist*, **44**, 279–94.

250. Roche, A. F. & Lewis, A. B. (1976). Late growth changes in the cranial base. In *Symposium on Development of the Basicranium*, ed. J. Bosma, pp. 221–36. Department of Health, Education and Welfare, Publication No. NIH 76-989, Bethesda, MD: US Government Printing Office.

251. Roche, A. F., Lewis, A. B., Wainer, H. & McCartin, R. (1977a). Late elongation of the cranial base. *Journal of Dental Research*, **56**, 802–7.

252. Roche, A. F. & Malina, R. M. (1983). *Manual of Physical Status and Performance, in Childhood, Vol. I. Physical Status*. New York: Plenum Press.

253. Roche, A. F. & McKigney, J. (1975). Physical growth of ethnic groups compromising the United States population. *American Journal of Clinical Nutrition*, **28**, 1071–4.

254. Roche, A. F. & Mukherjee, D. (1982). Ridge regressions to estimate body density and their serial errors. *American Journal of Physical Anthropology*, **57**, 221.

255. Roche, A. F., Mukherjee, D., Chumlea, W. C. & Champney, T. F. (1983a). Examination effects in audiometric testing of children. *Scandinavian Audiology*, **12**, 251–6.

256. Roche, A. F., Mukherjee, D., Chumlea, W. C. & Siervogel, R. M. (1983b). Iris pigmentation and AC thresholds. *Journal of Speech and Hearing Research*, **26**, 151–4.

257. Roche, A. F., Mukherjee, D. & Guo, S. (1986b). Head circumference growth patterns: birth to 18 years. *Human Biology*, **58**, 893–906.

258. Roche, A. F., Mukherjee, D., Guo, S. & Moore, W. M. (1987b). Head circumference reference data: birth to 18 years. *Pediatrics*, **79**, 706–12.

259. Roche, A. F., Mukherjee, D., Siervogel, R. M. & Chumlea, W. C. (1983e). Serial changes in auditory thresholds from 8 to 18 years in relation to environmental noise exposure. In *Noise as a Public Health Problem*, ed. G. Rossi, pp. 285–96. Milano, Italy: Centro Richerche e Studi Amplifon.

260. *Roche, A. F., Roberts, J. & Hamill, P. V. V. (1974c). Skeletal Maturity of Children 6–11 Years: United States.* Vital and Health Statistics, Series 11, No. 140, Washington, DC: National Center for Health Statistics, Government Printing Office.

261. *Roche, A. F., Roberts, J. & Hamill, P. V. V. (1976a). Skeletal Maturity of Youths 12–17 Years: United States.* Vital and Health Statistics, Series 11, No. 160, Washington, DC: National Center for Health Statistics, Government Printing Office.

262. Roche, A. F., Rogers, E. & Cronk, C. E. (1984). Serial analyses of fat-related variables. In *Human Growth and Development*, ed. J. Borms, R. Hauspie, A. Sand, C. Susanne & M. Hebbelinck, pp. 597–601. New York: Plenum Press.

263. Roche, A. F., Rohmann, C. G., French, N. Y. & Davila, G. H. (1970b). Effect of training on replicability of assessments of skeletal maturity (Greulich–Pyle). *American Journal of Roentgenology, Radium Therapy and Nuclear Medicine*, **108**, 511–15.

264. Roche, A. F., Siervogel, R. M., Chumlca, W. C., Reed, R. B., Valadian, I., Eichorn, D. & McCammon, R. W. (1982a). Serial changes in subcutaneous fat thicknesses of children and adults. *Monographs in Paediatrics*, **17**. Karger, Basel.

265. Roche, A. F., Siervogel, R. M., Chumlea, W. C. & Webb, P. (1981b). Grading body fatness from limited anthropometric data. *American Journal of Clinical Nutrition*, **34**, 2831–8.

266. Roche, A. F., Siervogel, R. M., Himes, J. H. & Johnson, D. L. (1977b). *Longitudinal Study of Human Hearing: Its Relationship to Noise and Other Factors. I. Design of Five Year Study; Data from First Year.* AMRL-TR-76-110, pp. 158. Wright-Patterson Air Force Base, Ohio: Aerospace Medical Research Laboratory.

267. Roche, A. F., Siervogel, R. M., Himes, J. H. & Johnson, D. L. (1978). Longitudinal study of hearing in children: Baseline data concerning auditory thresholds, noise exposure and biological factors. *Journal of the Acoustical Society of America*, **64**, 1593–601.

268. Roche, A. F., Siervogel, R. M. & Roche, E. M. (1979a). Digital dermatoglyphics in a white population from Southwestern Ohio. *Birth Defects: Original Article Series*, **15**, 389–409.

269. Roche, A. F., Tyleshevski, F. & Rogers, E. (1983c). Non-invasive measurement of physical maturity in children. *Research Quarterly for Sport and Exercise*, **54**, 364–71.

270. Roche, A. F., Wainer, H. & Thissen, D. (1974a). The RWT method for predicting adult stature. *Compte Rendu de La XIIe Reunion des Equipes Chargees des Etudes sur la Croissance et le Developpement de l'enfant Normal*, pp. 50–62. Paris, France: Centre Internationale D'Enfance.

271. Roche, A. F., Wainer, H. & Thissen, D. (1974b). The prediction of growth in individual children. *Proceedings XIV International Congress in Pediatrics*, Buenos Aires, Argentina. No. 5005, pp. 1–11.

272. Roche, A. F., Wainer, H. & Thissen, D. (1975a). Predicting adult stature for individuals. *Monographs in Pediatrics*, **3**, 1–115.

273. Roche, A. F., Wainer, H. & Thissen, D. (1975b). The RWT method for the prediction of adult stature. *Pediatrics*, **56**, 1026–33.

274. Roche, A. F., Wainer, H. & Thissen, D. (1975d). *Skeletal Maturity: The Knee Joint as a Biological Indicator*. New York: Plenum Press.

275. Roche, E. M., Roche, A. F. & Siervogel, R. M. (1979c). Absence of triradius d in a three-generation pedigree and other variations of main-line d. *American Journal of Physical Anthropology*, **51**, 389–92.

Rohmann, C. G., Garn, S. M., Israel, H. & Ascoli, W. (1967). Continuing bone 'expansion' as a general phenomenon. *American Journal of Physical Anthropology*, **27**, 247.

Ross Laboratories. (1981). *Incremental Growth Charts*. Columbus, Ohio: Ross Laboratories.

Ross Laboratories. (1983). *Parent-specific Adjustments for Evaluation of Length and Stature*. Columbus, Ohio: Ross Laboratories.

*Scammon, R. E. (1927). The first seriatim study of human growth. *American Journal of Physical Anthropology*, **10**, 329–36.

Seegers, W. H. (1937a). The nitrogen balance of a young primipara. *American Journal of Obstetrics and Gynecology*, **34**, 1019–22.

Seegers, W. H. (1937b). The effect of protein deficiency on the course of pregnancy. *American Journal of Physiology*, **119**, 474–9.

Seegers, W. H. & Potgieter, M. (1937). The quantity of creatine and creatinine excreted in normal human pregnancy. *Human Biology*, **9**, 404–9.

Selby, S. (1961). Metaphyseal cortical defects in the tubular bones of growing children. *Journal of Bone and Joint Surgery*, **43-A**, 395–400.

Selby, S., Garn, S. M. & Kanareff, V. (1955). The incidence and familial nature of a bony bridge on the first cervical vertebra. *American Journal of Physical Anthropology*, **13**, 129–41.

Siervogel, R. M. (1983). Genetic and familial factors in essential hypertension and related traits. *Yearbook of Physical Anthropology*, **26**, 37–64.

Siervogel, R. M. (1984). Heredity of hypertension. In *National Heart, Lung and Blood Institute Workshop on Juvenile Hypertension*, ed. J. M. H. Loggie, M. J. Horan, A. B. Gruskin, A. R. Horn, J. B. Dunbar & R. F. Havlik, pp. 111–24. New York: Biomedical Information Corporation.

Siervogel, R. M. & Baumgartner, R. N. (1988). Fat distribution and blood pressures. In *Fat Distribution During Growth and Later Health Outcomes*, ed. C. Bouchard & F. E. Johnston, pp. 243–61. New York: Alan R. Liss.

Siervogel, R. M., Baumgartner, R. N., Roche, A. F., Chumlea, W. C. & Glueck, C. J. (1989b). Maturity and its relationship to plasma lipid and lipoprotein levels in adolescents. The Fels Longitudinal Study. *American Journal of Human Biology*, **1**, 217–26.

Siervogel, R. M., Guo, S. & Roche, A. F. (in press). Risk of adult overweight predicted from childhood values of body mass index. *Proceedings of the Fifth Conference for Federally Supported Human Nutrition Research Units and Centers*, Washington, DC.

Siervogel, R. M., Mukherjee, D. & Roche, A. F. (1984). Familial resemblance for patterns of change in weight/stature^2 (W/S^2) from 2 to 18 years. *American Journal of Human Genetics*, **36**, 180S.

Siervogel, R. M., Roche, A. F. & Chumlea, W. C. (1982a). Environmental sound exposure in children: its major sources and its effects on hearing and growth.

Proceedings of the III International Congress of Auxology, Brussels, Belgium, p. 129.

Siervogel, R. M., Roche, A. F., Chumlea, W. C., Morris, J. G., Webb, P. & Knittle, J. L. (1982c). Blood pressure, body composition, and fat tissue cellularity in adults. *Hypertension*, 4, 382–6.

Siervogel, R. M., Roche, A. F., Guo, S., Mukherjee, D. & Chumlea, W. C. (1989a). Patterns of change in adiposity during childhood and their relation to adiposity at 18 years. *American Journal of Human Biology*, 1, 136.

Siervogel, R. M., Roche, A. F., Guo, S., Mukherjee, D. & Chumlea, W. C. (in press). Patterns of change in weight/stature² from 2 to 18 years: Findings from long-term serial data for children in the Fels Longitudinal Growth Study. *International Journal of Obesity*.

Siervogel, R. M., Roche, A. F., Himes, J. H., Chumlea, W. C. & McCammon, R. (1982b). Subcutaneous fat distribution in males and females from 1 to 39 years of age. *American Journal of Clinical Nutrition*, 36, 162–71.

Siervogel, R. M., Roche, A. F., Johnson, D. L. & Fairman, T. (1982d). Longitudinal study of hearing in children. II. Cross-sectional studies of noise exposure as measured by dosimetry. *Journal of the Acoustical Society of America*, 71, 372–7.

Siervogel, R. M., Roche, A. F., Morris, J. G. & Glueck, C. J. (1981). Blood pressure and its relationship to plasma lipids and lipoproteins in children: Cross-sectional data from the Fels Longitudinal Study. *Preventive Medicine*, 10, 555–63.

Siervogel, R. M., Roche, A. F. & Roche, E. M. (1978). Development fields for digital dermatoglyphic traits as revealed by multivariate analysis. *Human Biology*, 50, 541–56.

Siervogel, R. M., Roche, A. F. & Roche, E. M. (1979). The identification of developmental fields using digital distributions of fingerprint patterns and ridge counts. *Birth Defects: Original Article Series*, 15, 135–47.

Silverman, F. N. (1957). Roentgen standards for size of the pituitary fossa from infancy through adolescence. *American Journal of Roentgenology, Radium Therapy and Nuclear Medicine*, 78, 451–60.

*Simmons, K. (1944). *The Brush Foundation Study of Child Growth and Development. II. Physical growth and development. Monographs of the Society for Research in Child Development*, 9.

Smith, L., Rosner, B., Roche, A. & Guo, S. (1990). Modelling the correlation structure of blood pressure in the Fels data. *Annual Meeting of the American Statistical Association*, p. 137.

Smith, L. A., Rosner, B., Roche, A. F. & Guo, S. (in press). Serial changes in blood pressures from adolescence into adulthood. *American Journal of Epidemiology*.

Sobel, E. & Falkner, F. (1974). Normal and abnormal growth patterns of the newlyborn and the preadolescent. In *Endocrine and Genetic Disorders of Childhood and Adolescence*, 2nd edn, ed. L. I. Gardner, pp. 6–18. Philadelphia: W. B. Saunders.

276. Sontag, L. W. (1938). Evidences of disturbed prenatal and neonatal growth in bones of infants aged one month. *American Journal of Diseases of Children*, 55, 1248–56.

277. Sontag, L. W. (1940). Effect of fetal activity on the nutritional state of the infant at birth. *American Journal of Diseases of Children*, **60**, 621–30.
278. Sontag, L. W. (1941). The significance of fetal environmental differences. *American Journal of Obstetrics and Gynecology*, **42**, 996–1003.
279. Sontag, L. W. (1944a). War and the fetal maternal relationship. *Marriage and Family Living*, **6**, 3–5.
280. Sontag, L. W. (1944b). Differences in modifiability of fetal behavior and physiology. *Psychosomatic Medicine*, **6**, 151–4.
281. Sontag, L. W. (1971). The history of longitudinal research: Implications for the future. *Child Development*, **42**, 987–1004.
282. Sontag, L. W. & Allen, J. E. (1947). Lung calcifications and histoplasmin–tuberculin skin sensitivity. *Journal of Pediatrics*, **30**, 657–67.
283. Sontag, L. W., Baker, C. T. & Nelson, V. L. (1958). *Mental growth and personality development: A longitudinal study. Monographs for the Society of Research in Child Development*, **23**.
284. Sontag, L. W. & Comstock, G. (1938). Striae in the bones of a set of monozygotic triplets. *American Journal of Diseases of Children*, **56**, 301–8.
285. Sontag, L. W. & Garn, S. M. (1954). Growth. *Annual Review of Physiology*, **16**, 37–50.
286. Sontag, L. W. & Garn, S. M. (1957). Human heredity studies of the Fels Research Institute. *Acta Genetica et Statistica Medica*, **61**, 494–502.
287. Sontag, L. W. & Harris, L. M. (1938). Evidences of disturbed prenatal and neonatal growth in bones of infants aged one month: II. Contributing factors. *American Journal of Diseases of Children*, **56**, 1248–55.
288. Sontag, L. W. & Lipford, J. (1943). The effects of illness and other factors on the appearance pattern of skeletal epiphyses. *Journal of Pediatrics*, **23**, 391–409.
289. Sontag, L. W., Munson, P. & Huff, E. (1936). Effects on the fetus of hypervitaminosis D and calcium and phosphorus deficiency during pregnancy. *American Journal of Diseases of Children*, **51**, 302–10.
290. Sontag, L. W. & Nelson, V. L. (1933). A study of identical triplets. Part I. Comparison of the physical and mental traits of a set of monozygotic dichorionic triplets. *Journal of Heredity*, **24**, 473–80.
291. Sontag, L. W. & Newbery, H. (1940). Normal variations of fetal heart rate during pregnancy. *American Journal of Obstetrics and Gynecology*, **40**, 449–52.
292. Sontag, L. W. & Newbery, H. (1941). Incidence and nature of fetal arrhythmias. *American Journal of Diseases of Children*, **62**, 991–9.
293. Sontag, L. W. & Potgieter, M. (1938). The variability of nitrogen excretion in twenty-four hour periods as compared with that in longer periods. *Human Biology*, **10**, 400–8.
294. Sontag, L. W. & Pyle, S. I. (1941a). Variations in the calcification pattern in epiphyses. *American Journal of Roentgenology, Radium Therapy, and Nuclear Medicine*, **45**, 50–4.
295. Sontag, L. W. & Pyle, S. I. (1941b). The appearance and nature of cyst-like areas in the distal femoral metaphyses of children. *American Journal of Roentgenology, Radium Therapy, and Nuclear Medicine*, **46**, 185–8.
296. Sontag, L. W., Pyle, S. I. & Cape, J. (1935). Prenatal conditions and the status of infants at birth. *American Journal of Diseases of Children*, **50**, 337–42.

297. Sontag, L. W. & Reynolds, E. L. (1944). Ossification sequences in identical triplets. A longitudinal study of resemblances and differences in the ossification patterns of a set of monozygotic triplets. *Journal of Heredity*, **35**, 57–64.

298. Sontag, L. W. & Reynolds, E. L. (1945). The Fels Composite Sheet. I: A practical method for analyzing growth progress. *Journal of Pediatrics*, **26**, 327–35.

299. Sontag, L. W., Reynolds, E. L. & Torbet, V. (1944). The relations of basal metabolic gain during pregnancy to non-pregnant basal metabolism. *American Journal of Obstetrics and Gynecology*, **48**, 315–20.

300. Sontag, L. W. & Richards, T. W. (1938). *Studies in fetal behavior: I. Fetal heart rate as a behavioral indicator. Monograph of Society for Research in Child Development* **3**.

301. Sontag, L. W., Seegers, W. H. & Hulstone, L. (1938). Dietary habits during pregnancy (with special reference to the value of qualitative food records). *American Journal of Obstetrics and Gynecology*, **35**, 614–21.

302. Sontag, L. W., Snell, D. & Anderson, M. (1939). Rate of appearance of ossification centers from birth to the age of five years. *American Journal of Diseases of Children*, **58**, 949–56.

303. Sontag, L. W. & Wallace, R. F. (1933). An apparatus for recording fetal movement. *American Journal of Psychology*, **55**, 517–19.

304. Sontag, L. W. & Wallace, R. F. (1934). Preliminary report of the Fels Fund. Study of fetal activity. *American Journal of Diseases of Children*, **48**, 1050–7.

305. Sontag, L. W. & Wallace, R. F. (1935a). The effect of cigarette smoking during pregnancy upon the fetal heart rate. *American Journal of Obstetrics and Gynecology*, **29**, 77–82.

306. Sontag, L. W. & Wallace, R. F. (1935b). The movement response of the human fetus to sound stimuli. *Child Development*, **6**, 253–8.

307. Sontag, L. W. & Wallace, R. F. (1936). Changes in the rate of the human fetal heart in response to vibratory stimuli. *American Journal of Diseases of Children*, **51**, 583–9.

308. Sontag, L. W. & Wines, J. (1947). Relation of mothers' diets to status of their infants at birth and in infancy. *American Journal of Obstetrics and Gynecology*, **54**, 994–1003.

Spence, M. A., Falk, C. T., Neiswanger, K., Field, L. L., Marazita, M. L., Allen, F. H., Jr., Siervogel, R. M., Roche, A. F., Crandal, B. F. & Sparks, R. S. (1984). Estimating the recombination frequency for the PTC–Kell linkage. *Human Genetics*, **67**, 183–6.

Spencer, R. P. & Coulombe, M. J. (1966). Quantification of the radiographically determined age dependence of bone thickness. *Investigative Radiology*, **1**, 144–7.

Spencer, R. P., Garn, S. M. & Coulombe, M. J. (1966). Age-dependent changes in metacarpal cortical thickness in two populations. *Investigative Radiology*, **1**, 394–7.

Spencer, R. P., Sagel, S. S. & Garn, S. M. (1968). Age changes in five parameters of metacarpal growth. *Investigative Radiology*, **3**, 27–34.

Sykes, R. C. (1985). Secular Change in Highly Heritable Traits: IQ and Stature. Doctoral Dissertation, Department of Behavioral Science, Chicago, Illinois: The University of Chicago.

Thissen, D. (1989). Statistical estimation of skeletal maturity. *American Journal of Human Biology*, **1**, 185–92.

Thissen, D., Bock, R. D., Wainer, H. & Roche, A. F. (1976). Individual growth in stature: Comparison of four U.S. growth studies. *Annals of Human Biology*, **3**, 527–42.

Thomas, C. B. & Garn, S. M. (1960). Degree of obesity and serum cholesterol level. *Science*, **131**, 42.

Townsend, E. (1978). Comparison of a new skinfold caliper to Lange and Harpenden calipers. *American Journal of Physical Anthropology*, **48**, 443.

*Tukey, J. W. (1972). *Exploratory Data Analysis*, 2nd preliminary edn. Reading: Addison-Wesley.

Wainer, H., Roche, A. F. & Bell, S. (1978). Predicting adult stature without skeletal age and without paternal data. *Pediatrics*, **61**, 569–72.

Wainer, H. & Thissen, D. (1975). Multivariate semi-metric smoothing in multiple prediction. *Journal of the American Statistical Association*, **70**, 568–73.

Welford, N., Sontag, L. W., Phillips, W. & Phillips, D. (1967). Individual differences in heart rate variability in the human fetus. *American Journal of Obstetrics and Gynecology*, **98**, 56–61.

*White House Conference on Child Health and Protection, Section I. (1933). *Growth and Development of the Child*. Part II. *Anatomy and Physiology*, pp. 1–629. New York: Century.

Wolański, N. (1966a). A new method for the evaluation of tooth formation. *Acta Genetica*, **16**, 186–97.

Wolański, N. (1966b). The interrelationship between bone density and cortical thickness in the second metacarpal as a function of age. In *Progress in Development of Methods in Bone Densitometry*, pp. 65–77. NASA SP-64. Washington, DC: National Aeronautics and Space Administration.

Wolański, N. (1967). New method for the evaluation of tooth formation. *Journal of Dental Research*, **46**, 875.

Woynarowska, B., Mukherjee, D., Roche, A. F. & Siervogel, R. M. (1985). Blood pressure changes during adolescence and subsequent adult blood pressure level. *Hypertension*, **7**, 695–701.

Xi, H. & Roche, A. F. (1990). Differences between the hand–wrist and the knee in assigned skeletal ages. *American Journal of Physical Anthropology*, **83**, 95–102.

Xi, H., Roche, A. F. & Baumgartner, R. N. (1989a). Association of adipose tissue distribution with relative skeletal age in boys: The Fels Longitudinal Study. *American Journal of Human Biology*, **1**, 589–96.

Xi, H., Roche, A. F. & Guo, S. (1989b). Sibling correlations for skeletal age assessments by the FELS method. *American Journal of Human Biology*, **1**, 613–19.

Yarbrough, C., Habicht, J. P., Klein, R. E. & Roche, A. F. (1973). Determining the biological age of the preschool child from a hand–wrist radiograph. *Investigative Radiology*, **8**, 233–43.

Young, R. W. (1956). The measurement of cranial shape. *American Journal of Physical Anthropology*, **14**, 59–71.

Young, R. W. (1957). Postnatal growth of the frontal and parietal bones in white males. *American Journal of Physical Anthropology*, **15**, 367–86.

Young, R. W. (1959). Age changes in the thickness of the scalp in white males. *Human Biology*, **31**, 74–9.

Index

A

M